THE CAMBRIDGE COMPANION TO
AMERICAN PROTESTANTISM

American Protestantism has been the dominant form of Christianity in United States since the colonial era and has had a profound impact on American society. Understanding this religious tradition is, thus, crucial to understanding American culture. This Companion offers a comprehensive overview of American Protestantism. It considers all its major streams – Anglican, Reformed, Lutheran, Anabaptist, Baptist, Stone-Campbell, Methodist, Holiness, and Pentecostal. Written from various disciplinary perspectives, including history, theology, liturgics, and religious studies, it explores the beliefs and practices around which American Protestant life has revolved. The volume also provides a chronological overview of the tradition's entire history, addresses its prominent theological and sociological features, and explores its numerous intersections with American culture.

Aimed at undergraduate and graduate students, as well as an interested general audience, this Companion will be useful both for insiders and outsiders to the American Protestant tradition.

Jason E. Vickers is Professor of Theology at Asbury Theological Seminary, Wilmore, KY. He is a past president of the Wesleyan Theological Society, editor of the *Wesleyan Theological Journal*, and author or editor of a dozen books, including *The Cambridge Companion to American Methodism* (2013) and *Methodist Christology: From the Wesleys to the Twenty-First Century* (2020).

Jennifer Woodruff Tait is the editor of *Christian History* magazine, the leading magazine about church history for a popular audience. She is the author of *The Poisoned Chalice: Eucharistic Grape Juice and Common-Sense Realism in Victorian Methodism* (2011) and *Christian History in Seven Sentences* (2021).

CAMBRIDGE COMPANIONS TO RELIGION
This is a series of companions to major topics and key figures in theology and religious studies. Each volume contains specially commissioned chapters by international scholars, which provide an accessible and stimulating introduction to the subject for new readers and nonspecialists.

Other Titles in the Series

(Continued after index)

THE CAMBRIDGE COMPANION TO

AMERICAN PROTESTANTISM

Edited by

Jason E. Vickers
Asbury Theological Seminary, Kentucky

Jennifer Woodruff Tait
Christian History Magazine

CAMBRIDGE
UNIVERSITY PRESS

CAMBRIDGE
UNIVERSITY PRESS

University Printing House, Cambridge CB2 8BS, United Kingdom

One Liberty Plaza, 20th Floor, New York, NY 10006, USA

477 Williamstown Road, Port Melbourne, VIC 3207, Australia

314–321, 3rd Floor, Plot 3, Splendor Forum, Jasola District Centre,
New Delhi – 110025, India

103 Penang Road, #05–06/07, Visioncrest Commercial, Singapore 238467

Cambridge University Press is part of the University of Cambridge.

It furthers the University's mission by disseminating knowledge in the pursuit of
education, learning, and research at the highest international levels of excellence.

www.cambridge.org
Information on this title: www.cambridge.org/9781108485326
DOI: 10.1017/9781108756297

First published 2022

A catalogue record for this publication is available from the British Library.

Library of Congress Cataloging-in-Publication Data
Names: Vickers, Jason E., editor. | Tait, Jennifer L. Woodruff, editor.
Title: The Cambridge companion to American Protestantism / edited by Jason E.
Vickers, Jennifer Woodruff Tait.
Description: Cambridge ; New York, NY : Cambridge University Press, 2022. | Series:
Cambridge companions to religion | Includes bibliographical references and index.
Identifiers: LCCN 2021062739 (print) | LCCN 2021062740 (ebook) | ISBN
9781108485326 (hardback) | ISBN 9781108756297 (ebook)
Subjects: LCSH: United States – Church history. | Protestantism – United – States –
History. | Protestant churches – United States – History. | BISAC: RELIGION / History
Classification: LCC BR515 .C275 2022 (print) | LCC BR515 (ebook) |
DDC 280/.40973–dc23/eng/20220310
LC record available at https://lccn.loc.gov/2021062739
LC ebook record available at https://lccn.loc.gov/2021062740

ISBN 978-1-108-48532-6 Hardback
ISBN 978-1-108-70683-4 Paperback

For all the saints,
who pray without ceasing for those in need

This time, finally, for
Edwin Robert
Catherine Elanor
Elizabeth Beatrice
"Yea, there is strength in striking root, and good in growing old."
(G. K. Chesterton)

Contents

Contributors

Candy Gunther Brown is Professor in the Department of Religious Studies, Indiana University. She is the author of *Testing Prayer: Science and Healing* (2012) and *The Healing Gods: Complementary and Alternative Medicine in Christian America* (2013).

Elesha J. Coffman is Associate Professor of History, Baylor University. She is the author of *The Christian Century and the Rise of the Protestant Mainline* (2013) and *Margaret Mead: A Twentieth-Century Faith* (2021).

Dennis C. Dickerson is Reverend James M. Lawson Chair in History, Vanderbilt University. He is the author of *African American Preachers and Politics: The Careys of Chicago* (2010) and *The African American Episcopal Church: A History* (2020).

Maura Jane Farrelly is Associate Professor and Chair of American Studies, Brandeis University. She is the author of *Papist Patriots: The Making of an American Catholic Identity* (2012) and *Anti-Catholicism in America, 1620–1860* (2017).

Elizabeth H. Flowers is Associate Professor of Religion, Baylor University. She is the author of *Into the Pulpit: Southern Baptist Women and Power since World War II* (2012).

Mark Granquist is Professor and Lloyd and Annelotte Svendsbye Chair in Church History, Luther Seminary. He is the author of *Lutherans in America: A New History* (2015).

Chris E. W. Green is Professor of Public Theology, Southeastern University. He is the author of *Foretasting the Kingdom: Toward a Pentecostal Theology of the Lord's Supper* (2012) and *Pentecostal Ecclesiology: A Reader* (2016).

Jonathan Den Hartog is Chair and Professor, Howard College of Arts and Sciences, Samford University. He is the author of *Patriotism and Piety: Federalist Papers and Religious Struggle in the New American Nation* (2015).

Steven Hoskins is Associate Professor of Religion, Trevecca Nazarene University. He is co-editor of *Justified in Jesus Christ: Evangelicals and Catholics in Dialogue* (2017).

William Kostlevy is Director of the Brethren Historical Library and Archives (ret.). He is the author of *Holy Jumpers: Evangelicals and Radicals in Progressive Era America* (2010).

Melody Maxwell is Associate Professor of Church History and Director of Acadia Centre for Baptist and Anabaptist Studies, Acadia Divinity College. She is author of *The Woman I Am: Southern Baptist Women's Writings 1906–2006* (2014) and *Doing the Word: Southern Baptists' Carver School of Church Social Work and Its Predecessors, 1907–1997* (2019).

Mark E. Powell is Dean and Professor of Theology, Harding Graduate School. He is the author of *Papal Infallibility: A Protestant Evaluation of an Ecumenical Issue* (2009) and *Centered in God: The Trinity and Christian Spirituality* (2014).

Jonathan A. Powers is Assistant Professor of Worship Studies, Asbury Theological Seminary.

Robert W. Prichard is the Arthur Lee Kinsolving Professor of Christianity in America, emeritus, Virginia Theological Seminary. He is the author of *A History of the Episcopal Church* (2014).

Nicholas T. Pruitt is Assistant Professor of History, Eastern Nazarene College. He is the author of *Open Hearts, Closed Doors: Immigration Reform and the Waning of Mainline Protestantism* (2021).

Skylar Ray is a Ph.D. student in American Religious History, Baylor University.

Karen K. Seat is Director, School of International Languages, Literatures, and Cultures, and Head of the Department of Religious Studies and Classics, University of Arizona. She is the author of *"Providence Has Freed Our Hands": Women's Missions and the American Encounter with Japan* (2008).

Douglas M. Strong is Paul T. Walls Professor of Wesleyan Studies and Professor of the History of Christianity, Seattle Pacific University. He is the author of *They Walked in the Spirit: Personal Faith and Social Action in America* (1997) and *Perfectionist Politics: Abolitionism and the Religious Tensions of American Democracy* (1999).

Joshua R. Sweeden is Dean of the Faculty and Professor of Church and Society, Nazarene Theological Seminary. He is the author of *The Church and Work: The Ecclesiological Grounding of Good Work* (2014).

Edwin Woodruff Tait is contributing editor at *Christian History* magazine.

Jennifer Woodruff Tait is the editor of *Christian History* magazine. She is the author of *The Poisoned Chalice: Eucharist Grape Juice and Common-Sense Realism in Victorian Methodism* (2011) and *Christian History in Seven Sentences* (2021).

Andrea L. Turpin is Associate Professor of History and Graduate Program Director, Baylor University. She is the author of *A New Moral Vision: Gender, Religion, and the Changing Purposes of American Higher Education, 1837–1917* (2016).

Heather Hartung Vacek is Dean and Vice President, Moravian Theological Seminary and Lancaster Theological Seminary. She is the author of *Madness: American Protestant Responses to Mental Illness* (2015).

Jason E. Vickers is Professor of Theology, Asbury Theological Seminary. He is the author of *Invocation and Assent: The Making and Remaking of Trinitarian Theology* (2008) and *Minding the Good Ground: A Theology for Church Renewal* (2012).

Jeffrey B. Webb is Professor of American History, Huntington University. He is the author of *The Complete Idiot's Guide to Christianity* (2004) and *The Complete Idiot's Guide to Exploring God* (2005).

Daniel K. Williams is Professor of History, University of West Georgia. He is the author of *Defenders of the Unborn: The Pro-Life Movement before Roe v. Wade* (2015) and *The Politics of the Cross: A Christian Alternative to Partisanship* (2021).

Acknowledgments

Jason E. Vickers would like to thank Jennifer Woodruff Tait for her many contributions to the conception and production of this volume; Graham Hoppstock-Mattson for proofreading; Dr. James Thobaben and colleagues in the School of Theology and Formation at Asbury Theological Seminary for support and theological friendship; St. Andrew's Anglican Church in Versailles, KY, for welcoming and supporting my family; my family, Lacey, Garrett, McKenna, and Henley, for their constant support.

Jennifer Woodruff Tait would like to thank Jason Vickers, for inviting me along on this adventure; Beatrice Rehl of Cambridge University Press, for waiting through an entire pandemic; Grant Wacker, for building the foundation on which I could contribute to this endeavor and building a network of students-turned-colleagues that provided so many contributors to the volume; St. Mark's (Hazard, KY) and St. John's (Corbin, KY), the two Episcopal churches I have been privileged to serve as a priest during this time, for their support; and First United Methodist Church of Richmond, KY – not only have they been a source of strength, renewal, and intellectual stimulation, but I first got the invitation from Jason to collaborate on this project while attending an Emmaus Gathering in their basement. My family has been extraordinarily patient (and, in the case of my husband Edwin, contributed in material as well as immaterial ways to the comprehensiveness and success of this book): thank you, Trudy, Barry, Melissa, Jonathan, Will, Edwin, Catherine, Elizabeth, and Aunt Jane. Finally, I remember with gratitude Frank and Mardelle Stanger, Eugene and Esther Woodruff, Bill Woodruff, Frank B. Stanger, Jr., and Marilyn and John Woodruff. May their memory be for a blessing, and may light perpetual shine upon them.

Introduction

JASON E. VICKERS AND JENNIFER WOODRUFF TAIT

Over the last three decades, there has been an explosion of scholarship related to American Protestantism. Hundreds, if not thousands, of monographs and journal articles have appeared on this broad topic across the fields of history, theology, ethics, politics, sociology, and literary studies. Numerous scholarly societies – including the American Academy of Religion, the American Historical Association, the American Society for Church History, and the Southern Historical Association, to name just a few – have taken the breadth and diversity of American Protestantism as a subject for extensive discussions.

Taken collectively, this recent torrent of scholarly activity has dramatically altered and enriched our understanding of American Protestantism. First and foremost, by shifting the focus away from narrow denominational histories and the stories of elite theologians and institutions, recent scholarship has yielded a much more dynamic understanding of the relationship between Protestantism and American culture. On this front, several early works (relative to the period under consideration) were especially influential: Nathan Hatch's *The Democratization of American Christianity* (1989), Randall Balmer's *Mine Eyes Have Seen the Glory* (1989), David Hall's *Worlds of Wonder, Days of Judgement* (1990), Jon Butler's *Awash in a Sea of Faith* (1990), and Roger Finke and Rodney Stark's landmark work, *The Churching of America* (1992).[1]

All of these helped permanently shift historical focus away from the traditional focus on New England Puritanism and further challenged and complicated our understanding of the relationship between church and American culture. Instead of telling the story of American Protestantism through the lens of denomination-building or through the lives and thought of significant theological figures, these works focus our attention on the dialectical relationship between American culture and Protestant religion. They broaden the categories of which religious movements are considered acceptable and interesting to explore historically, and they also identify larger Protestant groups or movements that cross denominational boundaries in ways that both reflect and ultimately shape American cultural and political sensibilities.

In the thirty or so years following the publication of these landmark works, the scholarly study of American Protestantism has continued to focus on the relationship between Protestant religion and American culture, and the dynamic (and often deeply contested) identities of larger subgroups within American Protestantism. With respect to the first category, scholars have examined Protestant attitudes toward and involvement in numerous aspects of American culture and politics, including (but not limited to) war and violence, mental illness, the penitentiary system, slavery and race, gender, sex and sexuality, education, consumer culture, religious pluralism, populism, and popular culture.[2] A second major area of recent scholarship consists of works that examine the dynamic and often contested identities of major subgroups within American Protestantism, most notably evangelicalism, liberal or "mainline" Protestantism, and Pentecostalism.[3]

How to make sense of such a broad, diverse, and deeply rooted tradition? This survey volume treats American Protestantism in all of its forms. It is interdisciplinary in scope and covers a wide range of topics. The list of contributors includes scholars who are personally affiliated with a branch of American Protestantism as well as scholars who have no such affiliation.[4] Together, the chapters serve to trace the way in which Protestantism and America have reacted on and reacted against each other.

The first part of this *Companion* provides readers with an historical overview of American Protestantism, beginning with the early colonial period and concluding with the present day. Chapters 1–4 give readers a wide-ranging narrative backdrop against which they can more readily understand the more specialized topics that follow. Chapter 1 surveys major events, figures, and developments in early American Protestantism against the backdrop of Reformation roots, while Chapter 2 examines American Protestantism from the time of the Revolutionary War through the Civil War, especially the role of Protestantism in the building of the new republic. Chapter 3 turns to major developments in American Protestantism during the Industrial Age, including the emergence of the Social Gospel and progressive movements, the growth and influence of Protestant liberalism, fundamentalist-modernist debates, and Protestant involvement in and reaction to the world wars. Finally, Chapter 4 explores the shifting landscape of both American Protestantism and American culture from the 1960s to the present day, including the growth and influence of evangelicalism, the impact of mass media, the numerical decline of mainline denominations, and responses to political and social turmoil.

The second part of the volume deals with a diverse list of topics and themes essential to understanding the religious culture of American Protestantism. We begin with Protestants in church, seminary, and Bible study: Chapter 5 explores the ways in which American Protestants have understood and used Scripture as well as the intimate connection between Scripture, doctrine, and theology, and Chapter 6 explores worship and preaching in the Protestant tradition, especially the prominence of the revivalistic tradition to trends in liturgy, music, architecture, and sacramental approaches.

We then move outwards to consider Protestants in school, workplace, and civil society. Chapter 7 discusses the deep commitment to education in American Protestantism as well as the tensions that have arisen; Chapter 8 focuses on views of work and vocation, locating them within the larger horizon of American Protestant understandings of providence and divine call; Chapter 9 provides an overview of attitudes toward and involvement in American politics and government; and Chapter 10 discusses American Protestantism's perhaps most characteristic reform, the temperance movement.

We next turn to a set of significant issues that have often divided American Protestants: gender and sexuality (Chapter 11), race (Chapter 12), divine healing (Chapter 13) and a companion essay on mental illness (Chapter 14), and relationships with Roman Catholics (Chapter 15). Finally, in Chapter 16, we look at the strong missionary impulse that has always motivated the American Protestant tradition.

The third part introduces readers to major theological traditions within American Protestantism: Anglicanism (Chapter 17), Reformed (Chapter 18), Lutheran (Chapter 19), Mennonite and Brethren (Chapter 20), Baptist (Chapter 21), Wesleyan and holiness (Chapter 22), Stone-Campbell (Chapter 23), and Pentecostal (Chapter 24). These chapters provide a brief historical and demographical overview, a description of theological and liturgical characteristics, and an analysis of the respective tradition's disposition toward American culture. This part will assist readers to apprehend and appreciate the diversity and complexity of American Protestantism in a way that moves beyond binary categories of evangelical and liberal.

The dominance and influence of Protestantism in American history, culture, and politics is difficult to understate. Yet at the same time, that influence is not monolithic, and that dominance has surged and ebbed. This volume reveals it to be a multifaceted, living tradition.

NOTES

1 Nathan O. Hatch, *The Democratization of American Christianity* (New Haven, CT: Yale University Press, 1989); Randall Balmer, *Mine Eyes Have Seen the Glory: Evangelical Subculture in America* (New York: Oxford University Press, 1989); David Hall, *Worlds of Wonder, Days of Judgment: Popular Religious Belief in Early New England* (Cambridge, MA: Harvard University Press, 1990); Jon Butler, *Awash in a Sea of Faith: Christianizing the American People* (Cambridge, MA: Harvard University Press, 1990); Roger Finke and Rodney Stark, *The Churching of America, 1776–1990: Winners and Losers in Our Religious Economy* (New Brunswick, NJ: Rutgers University Press, 1992), rev. ed. *The Churching of America, 1776–2005* (New Brunswick, NJ: Rutgers University Press, 2005).

2 On violence, see Harry Stout, *Upon the Altar of the Nation* (New York: Penguin Random House, 2005); Mark Noll, *The Civil War as a Theological Crisis* (Chapel Hill: University of North Carolina Press, 2006); Jeffrey Williams, *Religion and Violence in Early American Methodism: Taking the Kingdom by Force* (Bloomington: Indiana University Press, 2010); and George Bogaski, *American Protestants and the Debate over the Vietnam War* (Lanham, MD: Lexington Books, 2014). On mental illness, see Heather Vacek, *Madness: American Protestant Responses to Mental Illness* (Waco, TX: Baylor University Press, 2015). On the penitentiary system, see Jennifer Graber, *The Furnace of Affliction* (Chapel Hill: University of North Carolina Press, 2014). On slavery and race, see Michael Emerson and Christian Smith, *Divided by Faith: Evangelical Religion and the Problem of Race in America* (Oxford: Oxford University Press, 2000); Mark Noll, *America's God: From Jonathan Edwards to Abraham Lincoln* (Oxford: Oxford University Press, 2005); and Katharine Gerbner, *Christian Slavery: Conversion and Race in the Protestant Atlantic World* (Philadelphia: University of Pennsylvania Press, 2019). On gender, see Susan Juster, *Disorderly Women, Sexual Politics and Evangelicalism in Revolutionary New England* (Ithaca, NY: Cornell University Press, 1996) and Clifford Putney, *Muscular Christianity: Manhood and Sports in Protestant America* (Cambridge, MA: Harvard University Press, 2003). On sex and sexuality, see Amy DeRogatis, *Saving Sex: Sexuality and Salvation in American Evangelicalism* (New York: Oxford University Press, 2014) and R. Marie Griffith, *Moral Combat: How Sex Divided American Christians and Fractured American Politics* (New York: Basic Books, 2017). On education, see George Marsden, *The Soul of the American University: From Protestant Establishment to Established Nonbelief* (New York: Oxford University Press, 1994) and *The Soul of the American University Revisited: From Protestant to Postsecular* (New York: Oxford University Press, 2021). On consumer culture, see

Kathryn Lofton, *Consuming Religion* (Chicago: University of Chicago Press, 2017). On religious pluralism, see Thomas Kidd, *American Christians and Islam: Evangelical Culture and Muslims from the Colonial Period to the Age of Terrorism* (Princeton, NJ: Princeton University Press, 2013). On populism, see John Wigger, *Taking Heaven by Storm: Methodism and the Rise of Popular Christianity in America, 1770–1820* (Champaign: University of Illinois Press, 1998) and John Fea, *Believe Me: The Evangelical Road to Donald Trump* (Grand Rapids, MI: Eerdmans, 2020). Finally, on popular culture, see William D. Romanowski, *Reforming Hollywood: How American Protestants Fought for Freedom at the Movies* (New York: Oxford University Press, 2012).

3 Recent significant works on evangelicalism (and its relationship to funda-mentalism) include Joel Carpenter, *Revive Us Again: The Reawakening of American Fundamentalism* (New York: Oxford University Press, 1997); George Marsden, *Fundamentalism and American Culture*, 2nd ed. (New York: Oxford University Press, 2006); Darren Dochuck, *From Bible Belt to Sunbelt: Plain-Folk Religion, Grassroots Politics, and the Rise of Evangelical Conservatism* (New York: W. W. Norton, 2011); Grant Wacker, *America's Pastor: Billy Graham and the Shaping of a Nation* (Cambridge, MA: Harvard University Press, 2014); Molly Worthen, *Apostles of Reason: The Crisis of Authority in American Evangelicalism* (New York: Oxford University Press, 2016); Frances FitzGerald, *The Evangelicals: The Struggle to Shape America* (New York: Simon and Schuster, 2017); John Wigger, *PTL: The Rise and Fall of Jim and Tammy Faye Bakker's Evangelical Empire* (New York: Oxford University Press, 2017); Matthew Sutton, *American Apocalypse: A History of Modern Evangelicalism* (Cambridge, MA: Belknap Press, 2017); and Kristin Kobes Du Mez, *Jesus and John Wayne: How White Evangelicals Corrupted a Faith and Fractured a Nation* (New York: Liveright, 2020). Recent significant works on mainline Protestantism include Gary Dorrien's monumental three-volume work, *The Making of American Liberal Theology* (Louisville, KY: Westminster John Knox, 2001–2006); Steven Tipton, *Public Pulpits: Methodists and Mainline Churches in the Moral Argument of Public Life* (Chicago: University of Chicago Press, 2007); Elesha Coffman, *The Christian Century and the Rise of the Protestant Mainline* (New York: Oxford University Press, 2013); *Margaret Mead: A Twentieth-Century Faith* (New York: Oxford University Press, 2021); Seth Dowland, *Family Values and the Rise of the Christian Right* (Philadelphia: University of Pennsylvania Press, 2015); and Christopher Evans, *The Social Gospel in American History* (New York: New York University Press, 2017). Significant recent works on Pentecostalism include David Martin's *Pentecostalism: The World Their Parish* (Malden, MA: Blackwell Publishers, 2002); Grant Wacker, *Heaven Below: Early Pentecostals and American Culture* (Cambridge, MA: Harvard University Press, 2003); and Estrelda Alexander, *Black Fire: One Hundred*

Years of African American Pentecostalism (Downers Grove, IL: InterVarsity Press, 2011).

4 Contributors include scholars affiliated with Anglican, Wesleyan, Baptist, Reformed, Lutheran, Stone-Campbell, Brethren, and Pentecostal traditions, as well as Roman Catholic contributors and those with no religious affiliation.

Part I
Historical Overview

1 Early America

JONATHAN DEN HARTOG

INTRODUCTION

Although the extended story of Protestantism in early America begins with England's first permanent settlements, those Protestants were not the first in North America. Those came earlier, with the French Huguenots who attempted to settle on the coast at Fort Caroline before being slaughtered by the Spanish in 1565, and the Anglicans who launched the Roanoke Colony in 1585, only to disappear into the American wilderness.[1] More permanent Protestant settlements came with the first successful English endeavors in North America – colonies at Jamestown (1607), Plymouth (1620), and Boston (1630). These Protestants brought their expressions of Christianity from England, just as later settlers would bring other Protestant expressions from the European continent. Early America could be seen as a period of tension as believers on one hand tried to continue and root their traditions in the New World, while on the other their practice was constrained, shaped, and transformed by the setting: small colonies on the far side of the Atlantic from England.[2] American Protestantism in early America developed from many significant dynamics: planting European Protestantism in the New World, encountering Native American religion, reckoning with slavery, experiencing the Great Awakening and the rise of evangelicalism, defining roles for women, engaging American enlightenments, and interacting with politics. In the process, American Protestantism took on many characteristics that would long influence its course and identity.

PLANTING AND DEVELOPING EUROPEAN TRADITIONS

Understanding American Protestantism in the colonial period requires comprehending its European origins. Colonists saw themselves as carrying on European traditions and working to root them in the "wilderness" of North America. The Protestants who settled on the Atlantic seaboard felt themselves to be inheritors of the great movement of the Protestant Reformation – the religious upheaval that had launched many colonists into the world.[3]

The Spanish had already begun exploring the New World in 1517, the year that an Augustinian monk named Martin Luther posted ninety-five theses for debate in Wittenberg, Germany. Luther initially directly challenged the practice of selling indulgences, but as he escalated his claims, he ended up questioning much medieval Catholic doctrine. Through debates over the next years and then in a series of books, Luther articulated key Protestant ideas. Luther found himself existentially driven to consider how an individual could know he or she was saved, and he concluded this came through faith alone, apart from the practice of works which the medieval church had insisted were inseparable from faith. In pursuing this conviction, Luther had to settle the issue of authority: what is to be followed? Here, in contrast to the medieval Catholic insistence that the Scripture be interpreted by the institutional church (guided by its own tradition), he asserted that Scripture alone was to guide the church, even as he and other reformers insisted that scriptural authority was to be comprehended not individually but within the churches and interpreted by trusted authorities.

From Luther's teaching grew a number of implications. Despite emphasizing salvation by faith alone, Luther promoted an active faith, where good works flowed from genuine faith. Luther also gave more prominence to the laity, insisting on the "priesthood of all believers," and emphasizing their involvement in the church over against priests. In worship, he elevated corporate worship, congregational singing, and engagement with preaching from the Bible.[4]

Luther's ideas spread in multiple directions from Germany. They produced quick acceptance by a Swiss priest by the name of Ulrich Zwingli, who led Zurich to reform its church life before his death defending the city and its reform. Zwingli thus laid the groundwork for a Swiss version of the Reformation.[5] In France, the ideas converted a university student named John Calvin. Forced to flee France, he wandered from Geneva to Strasbourg and back to Geneva, while composing *The Institutes of the Christian Religion* (1536 and revised throughout his life), which formed a systematic theology for the Reformed wing of the new movement. Calvin defended Luther's basic beliefs, while heightening his emphasis on the sovereignty of God – divine oversight of all things, including the election of those who would be saved. Calvin provided pastoral leadership in Geneva for decades and built it into the central hub for what became known as the Reformed version of Protestantism. Calvin's coherent doctrine would prove compelling for many in the Protestant movement, and Reformed Protestantism would spread into France and the Low Countries, where it inspired Dutch independence from Spain.[6] John Knox (who had trained in Geneva) helped turn Scotland Protestant and then pioneer a new form of church government: Presbyterianism.

Reformation ideas also made a few inroads in England under Henry VIII, influencing scholars such as Thomas Cranmer and William Tyndale. Tyndale, inspired by Luther's example, would take on the task of translating the Bible into English, until he was arrested and executed. Henry opposed the Lutheran Reformation, even publishing a pro-Catholic polemic, but he soon developed political reasons for breaking away from the Roman Catholic Church as he searched for a divorce from his wife Catherine, in order to marry a second wife (of an eventual six) in pursuit of a male heir. Henry endorsed a break with Rome and an Act of Supremacy making the king the head of the Church of England. The Anglican church was thus inauspiciously born. However, Henry named Cranmer his Archbishop of Canterbury; Cranmer guided the church in a doctrinally Protestant direction, a trajectory that continued with Henry's heir Edward VI. The Protestant cause received a setback under Edward's sister "Bloody" Mary, who, desiring to return England to the Catholic fold, embarked on a program of persecution. Mary's rule was short-lived, and when her sister Elizabeth came to the throne, the new queen again directed the Anglican church in a Protestant direction. Some Protestants who had fled England during the Marian persecutions had gone to Calvin's Geneva, where they had not only produced their own Bible translation (the Geneva Bible) but developed a vision to purify the Anglican church of its "Romish" traditions. This "hotter sort" of Puritan would clash with Elizabeth, who desired a moderate, comprehensive church. The clash forced the movement underground, but it would reemerge in the seventeenth century, with sights set on colonization.[7]

Although most of these leading Protestant groups would be classified as "magisterial" Protestants (so called because they cooperated with the magistrates), another strand of Protestantism had also developed – the radicals. Radicals rejected all state alliances in favor of a pure church. Confessing believers' baptism, they were labeled "Anabaptists" and persecuted widely. Some Anabaptists would make their way to America, and others would contribute to the earliest Baptist churches in London.

All of these groups worked to plant themselves in the New World. The Anglican endeavors came first, with the first permanent settlement at Jamestown, Virginia, in 1607; the chaplain for the expedition was Robert Hunt, even though he perished in 1608. Subsequent attempts to reinvigorate Jamestown included regulations mandating religious observance (called Dale's Code).[8] Through sustained colonization from England, Anglicanism gained strongholds in Virginia, the broader Chesapeake region, South Carolina, and New York (where it was centered on Trinity Church in Manhattan). In the Chesapeake, Anglicanism was strongly tied to the social order, and Anglican services became great centers for sociability. The church worked to nurture an Anglican piety, emphasizing the reception of Scripture informed by reason and tradition.[9]

Despite state support in New York and the South, Anglicanism continued to struggle with the challenges of the new world. Their parishes were much larger than in England, so ministering to parishioners was more difficult. The quality of clergy varied; some were serious and devoted, while others were the dregs of the English clergy who had sailed to the colonies after failing in England. Further, with no American bishop, all Anglican priests had to go to England to get ordained, which often led to candidates being lost at sea or tempted to remain in England. In the eighteenth century, Anglican leaders would petition for a resident American bishop, an appointment viewed as threatening by many other colonial Protestants. Meanwhile, the conscientious labored on, including James Blair, who served as the administrator of the Virginia church for over fifty years and was instrumental in the founding of the College of William and Mary.[10]

The next significant group to colonize were the Reformed, those most influenced by Calvin's Geneva. In light of the Anglican church's failure to move in a stricter Protestant direction, they had a choice between two alternatives. The less popular option was to separate altogether from the Anglican church, even if it meant persecution. This was the route traveled by a congregation in Scrooby, England. Their path took them in 1608 to Leiden, in the Netherlands, in search of greater religious toleration. They found religious liberty, but other components of their new setting were not so congenial: labor was very hard, and they disliked Dutch social mores and feared their children were drifting away. This prompted them to seek a haven in the New World, journeying to America in 1620 aboard the *Mayflower*. These Pilgrims (as they are remembered) aimed to land in Virginia but were blown northward, settling at Plymouth, Massachusetts. There, under the leadership of Elder

William Brewster and Governor William Bradford (who chronicled their experience in *Of Plymouth Plantation*), they demonstrated what an independent congregation could look like. Part of their practice was the regular implementation of fast days and thanksgiving days, even if their "first" thanksgiving was much simpler than the popular commemoration of it.[11]

More common in response was to remain within the Anglican church but seek to "purify" it – a strategy lending its name to the Puritan movement. Puritans grew increasingly uncomfortable within the Anglican church during the 1620s, as Archbishop of Canterbury William Laud, for political and theological reasons, removed some Puritans from church appointments. This opposition provided a motivation to emigrate, and in 1630 English Puritans launched a "Great Migration" that over the next decade brought thousands of them to settle in New England – first around Boston and then spreading into Massachusetts, Connecticut, and New Hampshire. John Winthrop provided political leadership for the colony, while significant ministerial voices included John Cotton and Richard Mather.[12] A movement that had sought to purify the church in England now found itself without an established church to purify. Instead, the Puritans had the freedom to innovate and shape their churches as they believed most in line with Scripture. The end result was a significant Congregationalist movement. Each congregation would be independently governed, while the churches would be tied together through ministerial networks and voluntary agreements such as the Cambridge Platform of 1648.[13]

New England Puritanism has received much scholarly attention, and this is understandable, given the number of words the movement produced and preserved in books and sermons. Further, the movement was complex enough to reward examination from multiple angles. As a religious phenomenon, its internal religious experience can be appreciated on multiple levels, including the preaching and sermonic culture and the experience of conversion as reported by church members.[14] The Puritans believed in a supernatural world, which had room for the working of divine Providence and the danger of demons and witchcraft.[15] The intellectual coherence of the movement has made it attractive to intellectual historians, who see in it both comprehensible claims and thought patterns that would endure in American history.[16] Puritan intellectual life was nurtured with the establishment of Harvard College as a place to train both ministers and other colonial elites. The Puritans struggled with political questions but established political structures that would last down to the American Revolution.[17] They also produced a society that encouraged hard work and following divinely appointed vocations; those efforts often produced wealth as the colony succeeded.[18] Finally, they reflected deeply on family life, with some of the most moving Puritan poetry produced by Anne Bradstreet.[19] Through these intense endeavors, New England Puritanism laid deep patterns for American Protestantism.

If the Anglican and Puritan expressions were the most pronounced in colonial America, they were not the only churches. Indeed, the colonial experience demonstrated growing pluralism in its expressions of Protestant Christianity. Specifically, Baptists dissented from both Anglican and Puritan dominance. Baptist ideas showed up in America as early as the 1640s, having been imported from English Baptist debates; English Baptist leaders like Thomas Helwys had themselves been influenced by European Anabaptists. In the early decades, these Baptists were largely offshoots of other Reformed groups, as illustrated by Henry Dunster, the President of Harvard who turned Baptist.[20] Baptists, whether more Calvinist or Arminian, asserted that baptism should not be for infants but for those who could give expression of personal faith.[21] Baptists remained small and marginal in New England, although they made inroads through efforts by such effective leaders as Isaac Backus. The Baptists moved into the Southern colonies after 1700, and their numbers grew significantly with the Great Awakening. In Virginia, they presented a strong challenge to Anglican society, and they were persecuted as dissenters.[22] Socially marginal, early Baptists proved relatively more egalitarian on questions of both race and gender.[23]

Several other groups drew on English origins to flourish in the New World. Colonial Presbyterians drew inspiration from Scots Presbyterians but even more so from theological debates during the English Civil War and Protectorate when the Westminster Assembly gathered clergy to provide a Reformed church order for England. The Assembly created both the Westminster Confession and the Westminster Catechism, and it attempted to replace the Anglican episcopal hierarchy with a national Presbyterian church. That endeavor failed in England with the Restoration of Charles II to the throne in 1660, but it inspired Presbyterian work in the colonies, where it was organized by Francis Makemie. Presbyterians especially flourished in the Mid-Atlantic colonies, and their denominational college became the College of New Jersey (Princeton). Doctrinally, Presbyterians concurred with New England Congregationalists, differing only on the form of church governance.[24]

Also growing out of the English Civil War and flourishing in the colonies were the Quakers, who had originated with a preacher named George Fox. Fox, who preached extensively in England, Wales, and even America, emphasized the significance of the Inner Light. Since the Holy Spirit illuminated each person, many of the normal arrangements of church life could be set aside. Culturally, early Quakers challenged social structures. Their meetings allowed anyone to testify – including women. Their pacifism undermined calls for imperial or colonial defense. Their emphasis on equality challenged those who claimed elite power. Their refusal to swear oaths challenged the legal system. These challenges led to persecution both in England and in New England, where the Puritans executed several Quakers in 1660. It was thus an extremely counter-cultural act when nobleman William Penn joined the Quakers in the 1660s, soon being imprisoned himself. However, because King Charles II owed his father a great debt, Penn became the owner of a huge tract of land in America. Penn set it up as a refuge for Quakers, and he founded Philadelphia in 1682. Quakerism would become a significant expression throughout the Mid-Atlantic colonies.[25]

Finally, several other Continental European Protestant groups made their way to the colonies. Lutherans became established in early America as small groups of Germans immigrated; their key organizing figure was Henry Melchior Muhlenberg.[26] Some Mennonites also migrated. These were Anabaptists who followed Menno Simons. Finally, several Moravian settlements developed. Moravians grew out of the Reformation in Central Europe, and they had expanded under the protection and leadership of Count Nicholas von Zinzendorf. Because they were strongly missionary-minded, they sent missions into both the Caribbean and the North American colonies.[27] One cadre of Moravians famously inspired John Wesley, the future founder of Methodism. Others worked among the Natives in the Pennsylvania backcountry.[28]

ENCOUNTERING NATIVE AMERICAN RELIGION

Protestant colonists had to confront the strong presence of Native Americans in the New World. Natives were an existential threat to colonists' lives. Their religious beliefs also threatened the certainty of Protestant colonists' religious claims. Native beliefs connected spiritual power to the natural world, and they used ceremonies to connect with the realm of spirits to help their daily tasks (such as hunting or agriculture). Native religion could be syncretistic, and it was certainly non-dogmatic: natives were willing to politely tolerate missionaries without fundamentally agreeing. Still, in colonizing, many Protestants hoped to convert the natives to Protestant beliefs. The Massachusetts Bay Company's seal even illustrated this with a native saying (in words from Acts 16:9) "Come over here and help us."

In their endeavors, British Protestants adopted a different approach from the Jesuit missionaries in New France. There, Jesuits sought an enculturation strategy involving deep engagement with native languages and culture and a willingness to translate Catholic beliefs into familiar idioms. Over time, Jesuit missionaries contributed to stable Catholic Native populations and even a Catholic saint.[29]

By contrast, English Protestant endeavors – where they existed – tended to be more focused on literacy and doctrine. Thus, in Puritan Massachusetts, John Eliot worked to translate the Bible and other Puritan works into the Native American languages. He also organized Indian converts into "praying towns."[30] Similarly, in the 1740s, David Brainerd preached to the Native American tribes in Delaware and Pennsylvania.[31] Even Jonathan Edwards sought to bring Indians to conversion through somewhat simplified sermons.[32] Other Protestant groups showed more success through cultural interaction. Moravian missions to the Natives (as in Pennsylvania) led to stable churches and communities. Cultural exchange around supernatural manifestations occurred during the Great Awakening. So, for example, the Native emphasis on dreams and visions became more important to Anglo settlers during the Awakening. Influence could also move in the other direction, as Natives selectively adopted some Protestant beliefs for their own uses.[33]

Unfortunately, these Protestant attempts to evangelize were more often disrupted than furthered by colonial endeavors. In New England, a major disruption occurred with King Philip's War (1675–1676). Led by Chief Metacom, this massive Native American uprising threatened the colony and brought down heavy retribution from the English. Once the tribes were defeated, those not killed were sold into slavery.[34] Along other frontiers, English settlement advanced through conflicts with native tribes – such as the Yamasee War in South Carolina. On the frontier between English and French settlement, tribes were recruited as allies to advance imperial goals. These conflicts produced ongoing low-level tensions, raids, skirmishes, and recurring conflicts, culminating in the French and Indian War.[35] Only in William Penn's Pennsylvania was the attempt to create a "Peaceable Kingdom" moderately successful – and even that noble experiment broke down in the decades before the American Revolution.

RECKONING WITH SLAVERY

Another cultural development that American Protestants had to reckon with was the establishment and growth of race-based African slavery. Over the course of the seventeenth century, under the influence of British imperial policy and the example of the Caribbean sugar plantations, slavery became established as a social system throughout the colonies.[36] Many Protestants not only accepted this development but actively encouraged it. Considering the public nature of Anglo-American Protestantism, most of those involved in the institution of slavery would have identified as Protestant. Protestants owned slaves throughout the colonies, and this included such luminaries as Jonathan Edwards and George Whitefield.[37] More than just participating, Protestants actively built justifications for slavery. They argued that race trumped faith and that conversion did not cancel out the status of enslavement.[38] Scholars have especially observed such a transformation in Virginia, where Christian language and practice drew lines of racial identity and exclusion.[39] From the establishment of racial identity, it was then an easy step to develop a pro-slavery version of Christianity.[40]

In the face of this large-scale social change, Protestants responded in various ways. In the seventeenth century in the Southern colonies, little concern was shown for the souls of enslaved persons, despite the fact that the Middle Passage had largely alienated the enslaved from their African religions.[41] Minimal outreach existed until the Great Awakening. In the 1740s Presbyterian Samuel Davies in Virginia made a concerted effort to evangelize enslaved persons.[42] This outreach bore fruit over time, as enslaved people were converted to Protestant denominations. These converts would worship in white churches, but even in this period, segregated seating was recognized, with the enslaved banished to galleries.

Also in the colonial period, though, resistance to slavery began to grow in some religious quarters. Quakers were on the forefront of opposing slavery, and they were urged on by committed, courageous voices from figures such as John Woolman and Benjamin Lay. The Society of Friends eventually expelled from Quaker meetings those who continued as slaveholders.[43] At the same time, some more evangelical voices also came to oppose slavery. Here, the most prominent was Samuel Hopkins. Hopkins had trained for the ministry with Jonathan Edwards, but in his own pastorate in Newport, Rhode Island he had grown even more direct in his attacks on the institution.[44] Therefore, even though there was no strong organization opposed to slavery, there were already arguments and religious motivations that had been articulated in the colonial period – voices that could, and did, grow during and after the American Revolution.

EXPERIENCING THE GREAT AWAKENING AND THE RISE OF EVANGELICALISM

Given long-standing trends in colonial Protestantism, the Great Awakening arrived as a shock and altered dynamics of church life and practice. Although some historians have questioned the existence of a movement that could be denominated a "Great Awakening," strong evidence appears that something significant and transformative did happen, beginning in the 1730s and lasting into the 1750s or longer, in some areas.[45] The Awakening took part in a transatlantic movement that emphasized conversion, individual faith, and internal piety.[46] Elements of the Awakening developed from within New England Puritanism, as ministers like Solomon Stoddard encouraged "revival seasons."[47] The phenomenon also adopted elements from European Pietism (as nurtured at the Lutheran Pietist center of Halle), Scottish awakenings, the Wesleyan revivals in England, and the aforementioned Moravians.

The two figures most associated with the Great Awakening in America are George Whitefield and Jonathan Edwards. Whitefield served as the trans-colonial symbol of the awakening, and his dramatic preaching throughout the colonies touched many souls. By using the techniques of theater, deploying his booming voice, and presenting a simple message of individual conversion, Whitefield communicated broadly, addressing thousands of people at once. His first tour of the colonies started in 1740, and it caused a sensation. The immediate effect of Whitefield's preaching is well illustrated by an account of a Connecticut farmer, Nathan Cole, who described dropping his tools in the field and rushing with his wife to hear Whitefield.[48] Similarly, Benjamin Franklin, in his *Autobiography*, attested to Whitefield's sway as the evangelist addressed thousands of Philadelphians and even convinced the thrifty Franklin to empty his pockets for the offering – although Franklin reported that Whitefield never convinced him to convert.[49] Still, Whitefield and Franklin found another association, as Franklin published Whitefield's sermons and thereby helped spread his ideas throughout the colonies. Whitefield made multiple tours through the colonies before his death in 1770.[50]

The other towering figure of the Awakening was its most adept theologian, Jonathan Edwards. Edwards grew up in Puritan Connecticut and attended the fledgling Yale College. Becoming a minister, he entered the work under his grandfather, Solomon Stoddard in Northampton, Massachusetts. When Stoddard died, Edwards took over Stoddard's church, one of the largest in the colony. Edwards led the church in a significant awakening in 1734–1735, and his report of the events, "A Faithful Narrative of a Surprising Work of God," generated both excitement and expectation for further awakenings on both sides of the Atlantic. Thus, Edwards was delighted when Whitefield's preaching – from Edwards's pulpit – brought further awakening throughout New England. Yet, divisions in his church later pushed Edwards out and sent him to a missionary post in Stockbridge, Massachusetts. In the last year of his life (1758) he took up the presidency of the College of New Jersey before a smallpox inoculation killed him. Through his writings, Edwards became the preeminent theologian of the Awakening. His *Religious Affections* attempted to define spiritual experience. Other significant works such as *Original Sin, The Freedom of the Will*, and *The Nature of True Virtue* defended traditional Protestant doctrines from the attacks of the rationalist Enlightenment. Edwards's works shaped Protestant theology significantly into the nineteenth century, and the last several decades have seen a flowering of scholarship into Edwards's life and thought.[51]

The Awakening had broader effects, as it mobilized individuals and groups. In New Jersey, through the preaching of Gilbert Tennent, many Presbyterians sided with the Awakening. The Awakening also impacted the South. Although population centers were smaller in the South, the movement spread through the region, albeit at a slower pace. These awakenings also produced the expansion of non-Anglican churches in the South. Samuel Davies provided strong leadership to Virginia Presbyterians. The Awakening also generated the explosion of Baptists in the South.[52] Without a doubt, the Awakening made the evangelical mode a powerful component of American Protestantism.

At the same time, the Awakening produced unintended consequences that also damaged Protestantism. It emphasized itinerant (traveling) preachers, which cut against the previous arrangement of prioritizing settled ministers who could provide leadership in their communities. Itinerancy challenged religious elites.[53] Because of the lack of oversight of these itinerants, some grew increasingly radical, best illustrated by James Davenport, who first questioned established ministers and then held several "bonfires of the vanities" to burn both books and expensive clothing. The Awakenings also caused church schisms, as churches and presbyteries divided between New Light (pro-Awakening) and Old Light (anti-Awakening) groups – divides that took years to heal, if at all. More generally, the Awakening caused a great deal of social disruption, and the end result of the Awakening was to prioritize emotion and individualism over against community solidarity.[54] Thus, although the Awakening did not directly cause the American Revolution, in its attack on authorities and rhetorical modes it laid the groundwork for that challenge to political authority one generation later.

DEFINING THE ROLES OF WOMEN

Recent scholarship on Early America has directed much attention to the place of women in Protestantism in this period. Thus, every component of this chapter can be connected back to their presence. Their significance for ordinary church life was particularly pronounced, as they were disproportionately over-represented in regular religious participation. In the Chesapeake, for example, women helped support Anglican churches and were the strongest proponents of the moderate piety the church encouraged.[55] In Puritan New England, women held – even within the strictures of Puritan doctrine – multiple opportunities for public involvement. The historian Laurel Thatcher Ulrich denominated eight roles a Puritan woman could take on – a housewife (minding the "internal economy"), a deputy husband (taking on masculine roles on behalf of her husband), a consort (providing companionship to her husband), a mother (taking care of children), a mistress (overseeing servants and dependents), a neighbor (participating in local community life), a heroine (if called upon by extreme circumstances), and finally a Christian (with strong standing in the local church).[56] Mary Rowlandson, taken captive in an Indian raid, later returned to give a Puritan meditation on her suffering in *The Sovereignty and Goodness of God*.[57] By contrast, Eunice Williams, taken in a raid on Deerfield, Massachusetts, never returned to the Puritan community, though she had the opportunity.[58]

Women were active in the Great Awakening; the Edwards family demonstrates this. Sarah Pierpont Edwards served as a model of godly piety, so much so that Jonathan Edwards reported her spiritual experiences in print. She also managed the large Edwards household, allowing for Jonathan to pursue his ministerial duties. Their daughters grew up around the Awakening and likewise supported it. Jerusha Edwards was engaged to Indian missionary David Brainerd, before both of their untimely deaths. Esther Edwards paid close attention to conversations around the Awakening, which she reported to close friends. She married Aaron Burr, Sr., the president of Princeton College (her son, Aaron Burr, Jr., would become vice president and then be disgraced for murdering Alexander Hamilton in a duel).[59] Another prominent woman of the Awakening was Sarah Osborn of Newport, Rhode Island. Osborn was influenced by Whitefield's preaching and recorded her own spiritual awakening in a published memoir. She went on to become a prominent advocate for the Awakening and to convert others herself.[60] Women were actively involved in Protestant life and helped shape its development throughout the colonial period.

ENGAGING AMERICAN ENLIGHTENMENTS

Colonial American Protestantism also engaged with the ideas of Enlightenment in America. Just as in the European context, Enlightenment could mean multiple ideas or movements.[61] Benjamin Franklin contributed to it with electrical experiments; David Rittenhouse added astronomical observations. Cotton Mather participated with natural history essays and became a Fellow of the Royal Society, while Jonathan Edwards hoped for the same as he investigated spiders.[62] Philip Vickers Fithian sought to embody it even in rural New Jersey.[63]

The most helpful traditional description of the Enlightenment in America has come from Henry May, who listed four different varieties of enlightenment. The Moderate Enlightenment drew on British sources and emphasized balance and harmony. The Skeptical Enlightenment was inspired by thinkers such as David Hume and French skeptics like Voltaire, but received little purchase in the colonies, especially before the American Revolution. The Revolutionary Enlightenment provided a means of thinking about politics in a rational way. The Didactic Enlightenment brought in the ideas of Scottish thinkers such as Adam Smith and Thomas Reid and promulgated Scottish "Common Sense" Philosophy in America.[64] However, additional descriptions of the American experience have added to May's portrayal. Ned Landsman has emphasized how Enlightenment culture was a way for the colonists to participate in larger imperial cultural discussions.[65] Meanwhile, Caroline Winterer has described the search for happiness in this world via enlightened discussions.[66]

Such a cultural movement would, of necessity, impact American Protestantism in myriad ways. American Protestants participated in the expanding economies of the eighteenth century, and they contemplated how to live faithfully in such a setting.[67] Protestant attempts to explain or order religious life participated in the spirit of the Enlightenment.

However, Enlightenment thought also questioned elements of orthodox Protestant Christianity, and so it produced both more strenuous apologetics and some willingness to question or modify Christian teaching. In the latter camp, Boston pastor Charles Chauncy demonstrated how Enlightenment categories could shape opinions. During the Great Awakening, Chauncy questioned its practices, arguing that they were not rational and hence not genuine, thereby aligning expectations of Christianity with human rationality. Later, at the end of his life, he questioned eternal damnation of sinners, opting instead for an urbane universalism.[68] Such challenges met with their own responses, but some of these apologetic defenses (of the Scriptures or of particular doctrines) were themselves shaped by the rationalist, enlightened grounds on which the questions were fought.[69] Many of Edwards's works can be read as extended responses to the enlightened discourses with which he was conversant. The engagement of Protestantism with versions of enlightened thought would endure well into the twentieth century.[70]

INTERACTING WITH POLITICS

Finally, Protestants in the colonial period engaged in political reflection and activity, and those experiences also shaped Protestant practice.[71] Considering the highest level of politics, Protestants largely supported the British monarchy.[72] They were further committed to the British empire as it promised to spread Protestantism in its wake.[73] At the county and local level, however, many Protestants welcomed a more representative government. Thus, the seeds of a Protestant republicanism were present from very early on.[74]

At the colony level, Protestants also wrestled with the presence of state churches.[75] Here, colonies represented a range of opinions. The most common choice was to replicate the European style of established churches. These churches received financial support, most often through taxes, and maintained a regulatory presence for religion in the state (even if other denominations were tolerated). In the Southern colonies of Virginia, Maryland (after 1689), South Carolina, North Carolina, and Georgia, the Church of England was established, as well as in the counties of New York around New York City. In New England (Massachusetts, Connecticut, New Hampshire), Puritan Congregationalism was the established church. Believers in other colonies may have desired an establishment but found their church too small to gain the majority for establishment.

Two other colonies, however, modeled alternative arrangements for church and state. Rhode Island celebrated its religious diversity and rejection of New England's establishment model. It built upon the beliefs of Roger Williams, who had sparred with Puritan leaders about how best to encourage a pure church within society.[76] By contrast, Pennsylvania also did not establish a church, but that choice came from William Penn's commitment to religious liberty.[77] Even though the state–church ideal may have been dominant, other models were present, and much of the population lived with a large degree of religious liberty. When the American Revolution made other options possible, American Protestants were able to embrace disestablishment and religious liberty.[78]

CONCLUSION

Thus, the experience of American Protestants in early America turned out to be different from what colonists anticipated. If they had originally hoped to plant simple extensions or purer varieties of English and Continental Protestantism, the colonial experience had disrupted those goals. As Protestants in the New World sought to organize their lives, they had to confront developing notions of gender and of race in the case of both Native Americans and enslaved Africans. Other cultural dynamics developed in conversation with Protestantism, such as the growing market economy and the intellectual movement of American enlightenments. Protestants also thought through the implications about beliefs about government and worked to instantiate them in their colonies. Within these frameworks, the Great Awakening of the mid-eighteenth century proved to be the most significant development for the period. It disrupted old patterns and set new trajectories for Protestants who responded to the Awakening in different ways, from full embrace to skeptical rejection. Although it is not right to say that by the end of the colonial period Protestantism was fully Americanized, it was well on its way, and many trends that would develop into the early nineteenth century were already apparent. They only awaited another great disruption, the American Revolution, to force them to full flower.

NOTES

1 Thomas S. Kidd, *American Colonial History: Clashing Cultures and Faiths* (New Haven, CT: Yale University Press, 2016), 31–32, 65–66.
2 This is a major theme in Mark Noll, *The Old Religion in a New World: The History of North American Christianity* (Grand Rapids, MI: Eerdmans, 2002).

3 Diarmaid MacCulloch, *The Reformation: A History* (New York: Viking, 2004) provides a useful synthetic survey.

4 Alistair McGrath, *Reformation Thought*, 4th ed. (Malden, MA: Wiley-Blackwell, 2012).

5 W. P. Stephens, *Zwingli: An Introduction to His Thought* (Oxford: Clarendon Press of Oxford University Press, 1992).

6 Bruce Gordon, *Calvin* (New Haven, CT: Yale University Press, 2009).

7 A. G. Dickens, *The English Reformation* (State College: Pennsylvania State University Press, 2005); Patrick Collinson, *The Elizabethan Puritan Movement* (New York: Oxford University Press, 1967, 1990).

8 For a brief summary, see John Fea, *Was America Founded as a Christian Nation? A Historical Introduction*, 2nd ed. (Louisville, KY: Westminster John Knox Press, 2016), 80–85; Edward Bond, "Source of Knowledge, Source of Power: The Supernatural World of English Virginia, 1607–1627," *Virginia Magazine of History and Biography* vol. 108, no. 2 (2000), 105–138.

9 Lauren Winner, *A Cheerful and Comfortable Faith: Anglican Religious Practice in the Elite Households of Eighteenth-Century Virginia* (New Haven, CT: Yale University Press, 2010).

10 Mark Noll, *A History of Christianity in the United States and Canada*, 2nd ed. (Grand Rapids, MI: Eerdmans, 2019), 56.

11 Michael P. Winship, *Godly Republicanism: Puritans, Pilgrims, and a City on a Hill* (Cambridge, MA: Harvard University Press, 2012); John G. Turner, *They Knew They Were Pilgrims: Plymouth Colony and the Contest for American Liberty* (New Haven, CT: Yale University Press, 2020).

12 Francis J. Bremer, *John Winthrop: America's Forgotten Founding Father* (New York: Oxford University Press, 2003).

13 The literature on Puritanism is vast. For very recent studies, see David D. Hall, *A Reforming People: Puritanism and the Transformation of Public Life in New England* (New York: Knopf, 2011) and *The Puritans: A Transatlantic History* (Princeton, NJ: Princeton University Press, 2019); Michael P. Winship, *Hot Protestants: A History of Puritanism in England and America* (New Haven, CT: Yale University Press, 2019).

14 Harry S. Stout, *The New England Soul: Preaching and Religious Culture in Colonial New England* (New York: Oxford University Press, 1986); Charles L. Cohen, *God's Caress: The Psychology of Puritan Religious Experience* (New York: Oxford University Press, 1989).

15 Michael P. Winship, *Seers of God: Puritan Providentialism in the Restoration and Early Enlightenment* (Baltimore: Johns Hopkins University Press, 1996); John Putnam Demos, *Entertaining Satan: Witchcraft and the Culture of Early New England* (New York: Oxford University Press, 1982); Mary Beth Norton, *In the Devil's Snare: The Salem Witchcraft Crisis of 1692* (New York: Knopf, 2002); Rick Kennedy, *The First American Evangelical: A Short Life of Cotton Mather* (Grand Rapids, MI: Eerdmans, 2015), 30–46, 63–71.

16 The great intellectual investigation of the Puritans was kicked off with Perry Miller's writings. See Perry Miller, *The Puritan Mind: The Seventeenth Century* (Cambridge, MA: The Belknap Press of Harvard University Press, 1939, 1982); and *The New England Mind: From Colony to Province* (Cambridge, MA: The Belknap Press of Harvard University Press, 1953, 1981).

17 Stephen Foster, *The Long Argument: English Puritanism and the Shaping of New England Culture, 1570–1700* (Chapel Hill: University of North Carolina Press for the Institute of Early American History and Culture, 1991); Winship, *Godly Republicanism*, 1–13, 233–250.

18 Mark Peterson, *The Price of Redemption: The Spiritual Economy of Puritan New England* (Palo Alto, CA: Stanford University Press, 1997).

19 Charles E. Hambrick-Stowe, ed., *Early New England Meditative Poetry: Anne Bradstreet and Edward Taylor* (New York: Paulist Press, 1988).

20 Jonathan Den Hartog, "'National and Provinciall Churches are nullityes': Henry Dunster's Puritan Argument against the Puritan Established Church," *Journal of Church and State* vol. 56 (Autumn 2014), 691–710; William G. McLoughlin, *New England Dissent, 1630–1833: The Baptists and the Separation of Church and State* (Cambridge, MA: Harvard University Press, 1971).

21 David Bebbington, *Baptists through the Centuries: A History of a Global People* (Waco, TX: Baylor University Press, 2010), 25–82.

22 Rhys Isaac, *The Transformation of Virginia, 1740–1790* (Chapel Hill: University of North Carolina Press for the Omohundro Institute of Early American History and Culture, 1982, 1999).

23 Susan Juster, *Disorderly Women: Sexual Politics and Evangelicalism in Revolutionary New England* (Ithaca, NY: Cornell University Press, 1994).

24 Noll, *A History of Christianity*, 59–60.

25 Andrew R. Murphy, *William Penn: A Life* (New York: Oxford University Press, 2018).

26 Noll, *A History of Christianity*, 62.

27 Jon F. Sensbach, *Rebecca's Revival: Creating Black Christianity in the Atlantic World* (Cambridge, MA: Harvard University Press, 2005).

28 Craig D. Atwood, *Community of the Cross: Moravian Piety in Colonial Bethlehem* (State College: Pennsylvania State University Press, 2004).

29 Allan Greer, *Mohawk Saint: Catherine Tekakwitha and the Jesuits* (New York: Oxford University Press, 2004); Bronwen McShea, *Apostles of Empire: The Jesuits and New France* (Lincoln: University of Nebraska Press, 2019).

30 Richard Cogley, *John's Eliot's Mission to the Indians before King Philip's War* (Cambridge, MA: Harvard University Press, 1999).

31 John Grigg, *The Lives of David Brainerd: The Making of an American Evangelical Icon* (New York: Oxford University Press, 2009).

32 George Marsden, *Jonathan Edwards: A Life* (New Haven, CT: Yale University Press, 2003), 375–413.

33 Richard Pointer, *Encounters of the Spirit: Native Americans and European Colonial Religion* (Bloomington: Indiana University Press, 2007); Linford Fisher, *The Indian Great Awakening: Religion and the Shaping of Native Cultures in Early America* (New York: Oxford University Press, 2012).

34 Jill Lepore, *The Name of War: King Philip's War and the Origins of American Identity* (New York: Knopf, 1998).

35 See, for example, the account of the raid on Deerfield, Massachusetts in John Demos, *The Unredeemed Captive: A Family Story from Early America* (New York: Knopf, 1994), 11–25.

36 Anthony S. Parent, *Foul Means: The Formation of a Slave Society in Virginia, 1660–1740* (Chapel Hill: University of North Carolina Press for the Omohundro Institute of Early American History and Culture, 2003); Philip D. Morgan, *Slave Counterpoint: Black Culture in the Eighteenth-Century Chesapeake & Lowcountry* (Chapel Hill: University of North Carolina Press for the Omohundro Institute of Early American History and Culture, 1998).

37 Marsden, *Jonathan Edwards*, 255–258; Peter Y. Choi, *George Whitefield: Evangelist for God and Empire* (Grand Rapids, MI: Eerdmans, 2018).

38 Catherine Gerbner, *Christian Slavery: Conversion and Race in the Protestant Atlantic World* (Philadelphia: University of Pennsylvania Press, 2018).

39 Rebecca Goetz, *The Baptism of Early Virginia: How Christianity Created Race* (Baltimore: Johns Hopkins University Press, 2012).

40 Charles F. Irons, *The Origins of Proslavery Christianity: White and Black Evangelicals in Colonial and Antebellum Virginia* (Chapel Hill: University of North Carolina Press, 2008), 1–54.

41 Jon Butler, *Awash in a Sea of Faith: Christianizing the American People* (Cambridge, MA: Harvard University Press, 1990), 129–163.

42 Noll, *A History of Christianity*, 97–98.

43 Thomas P. Slaughter, *The Beautiful Soul of John Woolman, Apostle of Abolition* (New York: Hill & Wang, 2008); Marcus Rediker, *The Fearless Benjamin Lay: The Quaker Dwarf Who Became the First Revolutionary Abolition* (Boston: Beacon Press, 2017).

44 Joseph A. Conforti, *Samuel Hopkins and the New Divinity Movement: Calvinism and Reform in New England between the Great Awakenings*, repr. ed. (Eugene, OR: Wipf & Stock, 1981, 2007).

45 Frank Lambert, *Inventing the "Great Awakening"* (Princeton, NJ: Princeton University Press, 1999); Jon Butler, "Enthusiasm Described and Decried: The Great Awakening as Interpretive Fiction," *The Journal of American History* vol. 69, no. 2 (September 1982), 305–325. For the most recent overview of the Awakening, see Thomas S. Kidd, *The Great Awakening: The Birth of Evangelical Christianity in Colonial America* (New Haven, CT: Yale University Press, 2007).

46 On the movement, see W. R. Ward, *Early Evangelicalism: A Global Intellectual History, 1670–1789* (New York: Cambridge University Press,

2006); Bruce Hindmarsh, *The Spirit of Early Evangelicalism: True Religion in a Modern World* (New York: Oxford University Press, 2018). In defining evangelicalism, a long-standing description has come from David Bebbington, who identified four markers: conversionism, activism, Biblicism, and crucicentrism; see Bebbington, *Evangelicalism in Modern Britain: A History from the 1730s to the 1980s* (Grand Rapids, MI: Baker Book House, 1989, 1992).

47 Indeed, Rick Kennedy has argued that Cotton Mather's ministry and style earn him the title "the first American evangelical." See Kennedy, *The First American Evangelical*, 78–97.

48 Michael J. Crawford, "The Spiritual Travels of Nathan Cole," *William and Mary Quarterly*, 3rd ser., vol. 33, no. 1 (January 1976), 89–126.

49 Benjamin Franklin, *The Autobiography and Other Writings*, ed. Kenneth Silverman (New York: Penguin Press, 1986), 116–121.

50 For Whitefield biographies, see Harry S. Stout, *The Divine Dramatist: George Whitefield and the Rise of Modern Evangelicalism* (Grand Rapids, MI: Eerdmans, 1991); Thomas S. Kidd, *George Whitefield: America's Spiritual Founding Father* (New Haven, CT: Yale University Press, 2014); and Choi, *George Whitefield*.

51 Examples include Allen Guelzo, *Edwards on the Will: A Century of American Theological Debate* (Middletown, CT: Wesleyan University Press, 1989); Gerald R. McDermott, *One Holy and Happy Society: The Public Theology of Jonathan Edwards* (State College: Pennsylvania State University Press, 2006); Oliver D. Crisp, *Jonathan Edwards among the Theologians* (Grand Rapids, MI: Eerdmans, 2015); Douglas A. Sweeney, *Edwards the Exegete: Biblical Interpretation and Anglo-Protestant Culture on the Edge of the Enlightenment* (New York: Oxford University Press, 2015).

52 Noll, *A History of Christianity*, 92–95.

53 Timothy D. Hall, *Contested Boundaries: Itinerancy and the Reshaping of the Colonial American Religious World* (Durham, NC: Duke University Press, 1994).

54 Douglas Winiarski, *Darkness Falls on the Land of Light: Experiencing Religious Awakenings in Eighteenth-Century New England* (Chapel Hill: University of North Carolina Press for the Omohundro Institute of Early American History and Culture, 2017).

55 This is an important theme for Winner in *A Cheerful and Comfortable Faith*.

56 Laurel Thatcher Ulrich, *Goodwives: Image and Reality in the Lives of Women in Northern New England, 1650–1750* (New York: Vintage Books, 1991), 9–10.

57 Mary Rowlandson, *The Sovereignty and Goodness of God, with Related Documents*, ed. Neil Salisbury (Boston: Bedford/St. Martins, 1997).

58 Demos, *The Unredeemed Captive*, 107–109, 146, 191–196, 227–229.

59 The lives of the Edwards women wind throughout Marsden's *Jonathan Edwards*. For Esther, see Carol F. Karlsen and Laurie Crumpacker, eds., *The

Journal of Esther Edwards Burr, 1754–1757 (New Haven, CT: Yale University Pres, 1984).

60 Catherine A. Brekus, *Sarah Osborn's World: The Rise of Evangelical Christianity in Early America* (New Haven, CT: Yale University Press, 2013).

61 Roy Porter and Mikuláš Teich, *The Enlightenment in National Context* (New York: Cambridge University Press, 1981).

62 Kennedy, *The First American Evangelical*, 106–122; Marsden, *Jonathan Edwards*, 64–66.

63 John Fea, *The Way of Improvement Leads Home: Philip Vickers Fithian and the Rural Enlightenment in Early America* (Philadelphia: University of Pennsylvania Press, 2008).

64 Henry F. May, *The Enlightenment in America* (New York: Oxford University Press, 1976).

65 Ned Landsman, *From Colonials to Provincials: American Thought and Culture, 1680–1760* (Ithaca, NY: Cornell University Press, 1997, 2000).

66 Caroline Winterer, *American Enlightenments: Pursuing Happiness in the Age of Reason* (New Haven, CT: Yale University Press, 2016).

67 Jon Butler, *Becoming America: The Revolution before 1776* (Cambridge, MA: Harvard University Press, 2000), 50–88; Mark Valeri, *Heavenly Merchandize: How Religion Shaped Commerce in Puritan America* (Princeton, NJ: Princeton University Press, 2010).

68 Edward M. Griffin, *Old Brick: Charles Chauncy of Boston, 1705–1787* (Minneapolis: University of Minnesota Press, 1980).

69 Michael J. Lee, *The Erosion of Biblical Certainty: Battles over Authority and Interpretation in America* (New York: Palgrave Macmillan, 2013).

70 This is a significant theme throughout Mark Noll, *America's God: From Jonathan Edwards to Abraham Lincoln* (New York: Oxford University Press, 2002).

71 For an extended reflection on religion and politics, see Jonathan Den Hartog, "Politics: Colonial Era," in *The Encyclopedia of Religion in America* (Washington, DC: CQ Press, 2010), vol. III, 1674–1682.

72 Benjamin Lewis Price, *Nursing Fathers: American Colonists' Conception of English Protestant Kingship, 1688–1776* (Lanham, MD: Lexington Books, 1999).

73 Carla Gardina Pestana, *Protestant Empire: Religion and the Making of the British Atlantic World* (Philadelphia: University of Pennsylvania Press, 2009).

74 Winship, *Godly Republicanism*; Glenn Moots, *Politics Reformed: The Anglo-American Legacy of Covenant Theology* (Columbia: University of Missouri Press, 2010); Patrick Mullins, *Father of Liberty: Jonathan Mayhew and the Principles of the American Revolution* (Lawrence: University Press of Kansas, 2017).

75 For specific experiences of the states, see Carl H. Esbeck and Jonathan J. Den Hartog, *Disestablishment and Religious Dissent: Church–State*

Relations in the New American States (Columbia: University of Missouri Press, 2019).

76 Edwin S. Gaustad, *Liberty of Conscience: Roger Williams in America* (Grand Rapids, MI: Eerdmans, 1991).

77 See Murphy, *William Penn*.

78 See Esbeck and Den Hartog, *Disestablishment and Religious Dissent*, 3–23.

2 From the Revolution to the Civil War

JEFFREY B. WEBB

In the ninety-year period between the start of the American Revolution and the end of the US Civil War, American Protestantism underwent a profound transformation. Protestant churches and ministers engaged on both sides of the revolutionary struggle between patriots and loyalists, and they argued over the relationship between church and state in the constitutional deliberations of the era. Religious liberty emerged as an article of faith amid the democratizing tendencies of American society and politics in the aftermath of the revolution. This encouraged the development of religious populism and the proliferation of new Protestant churches and denominations, which were reinforced by the dynamics of western expansion along the unfolding American frontier. The new nation also grew with the market revolution and industrialization, which in turn contributed to the shape and contours of Protestantism.

In the antebellum period, immigration, home missions, and the growth of the Black church added to the diversity and richness of Protestant Christianity, as did the explosion of reform movements and the religious fervor of the Second Great Awakening. These conditions encouraged doctrinal innovation as well as institutional change, all while abolitionism and the sectional crisis of the 1840s and 1850s further segmented religious organizations into Northern and Southern divisions. In the US Civil War, Protestant theology and piety coursed through both Union and Confederate societies as political leaders justified their actions in discourse brimming with evangelical Protestant language. The conflict provided the occasion for Protestantism to attain new heights of ascendancy in the life of the nation, both in the Civil War era and thereafter.

THE REVOLUTIONARY ERA

Colonists throughout British North America soured on their imperial relationship with Great Britain following new Parliamentary taxation and customs enforcement measures like the Sugar Act (1764), Stamp Act (1765), and the Townshend Acts (1767–1768). Their resistance to these measures was partly inspired by the writings and sermons of leading Congregationalist minister Jonathan Mayhew of Boston's West Church. Throughout his career Mayhew departed from Calvinist orthodoxy in important ways, and historians consider him a forerunner of Bostonian Unitarianism.[1] When the Church of England attempted to suppress the revivals of the Great Awakening, Mayhew developed arguments for religious liberty and resistance to tyranny based in some measure on the principles of natural rights and British constitutionalism.[2] He argued in 1748, "Nor has any man whatever, whether of a civil or sacred character, any authority to control us, unless it be by the gentle methods of argument and persuasion."[3]

Later, when colonial Anglicans petitioned to have a bishop for the colonies in the 1760s, Protestant denominations mobilized in opposition and deployed these same religious liberty arguments. They also added the prospect of a colonial Church of England episcopate to their growing list of complaints about British rule in America. Clearly, Mayhew's work profoundly influenced Bostonians James Otis and John Adams, and thus formed part of the intellectual architecture of the rapidly developing colonial resistance movement. Other Protestant clergy and leading laymen made vital contributions; historian Patricia Bonomi argues that "by turning colonial resistance into a righteous cause, and by crying the message to all ranks in all parts of the colonies, ministers did the work of secular radicalism and did it better."[4]

None of the Protestant clergy more neatly exemplified this pattern than Presbyterian minister Abraham Keteltas from Long Island. He studied theology at Yale and filled Dutch Reformed and Huguenot pulpits in New Jersey and New York. In 1774 he chaired the Jamaica, New York Committee of Correspondence and offered other support for the colonial resistance movement, so much so that when the British occupied Long Island, Keteltas fled and his home was looted.[5] Keteltas's pamphlet from 1777, *God Arising and Pleading His People's Cause; Or the American War . . . Shewn To Be the Cause of God* defined the war of independence in strongly religious terms: "the cause of truth, against error and falsehood . . . the cause of pure and undefiled religion, against bigotry, superstition, and human invention . . . in short, it is the cause of heaven against hell – of the kind Parent of the Universe against the prince of darkness, and the destroyer of the human race."[6] Ministers like Keteltas seized on the prevailing critique of the British's government's pattern of corruption, abuse of power, and tyranny, and linked this critique to the cosmic struggle of good and evil. Independence, they believed, providentially highlighted Americans' vulnerability to sinful corruption and set the stage for the further work of redemption. According to historian Gordon Wood, "the American clergy were already deep in the process of working out – in an elaborate manner congenial to their covenant theology – the concept of the Revolution as an antidote to moral decay."[7] Scholars refer to this innovative political and religious movement as Christian republicanism.[8]

American patriots, in the words of Samuel Adams, believed themselves to be "humble instruments and means in the great providential dispensation" to advance the moral regeneration of humankind.[9] But the revolution and war of independence moved other clergy and congregations to support the king and imperial rule in the colonies. Clergy of the Church of England took oaths of loyalty to the Crown as part of their consecration to the priesthood, and so most remained loyal to Britain. As relations between Britain and the colonies deteriorated, Anglican minister Samuel Seabury criticized the Continental Congress as unlawful and warned against possible tyranny by revolutionary associations and assemblies. He served time in a patriot prison in Connecticut after the war began before moving to New York City to become chaplain of the King's American Regiment. After the war, Seabury became the first American to be consecrated a bishop; he served in the Protestant Episcopal Church, successor to the Church of England in America.

Northern Anglicans suffered at the hands of patriots and many emigrated; Southern Anglican churches were better situated because they enjoyed the support of powerful local vestries, especially among the wealthy plantation gentry of the tidewater region. Meanwhile, the war proved to be a challenge for historic peace churches such as the Society of Friends (Quakers) and German Anabaptist sects. Their unwillingness to pledge support for the patriot cause brought suspicion and hostility from revolutionary state governments, but in doing so they reinforced the importance of religious liberty and freedom of conscience in the new republic. Protestant sects in colonies with established churches had fought for religious liberty before the revolution, but independence and the reorganization of colonies into states with new constitutions provided new opportunities to press the issue.

In Virginia, for example, Presbyterians, Baptists, and other dissenting groups had campaigned for an end to discriminatory policies (ministerial licenses, approval of meetinghouses, taxation) as far back at the Great Awakening, but the new emphasis on natural rights and constitutional liberties in the 1760s and 1770s served as a catalyst for the Virginia

Declaration of Rights in 1776.[10] Section 16 declared "all men are equally entitled to the free exercise of religion, according to the dictates of conscience."[11] Ten years later, the state of Virginia enacted Thomas Jefferson's Statute for Religious Freedom, which disestablished Anglicanism and formally separated church and state. Important in this connection is James Madison, an Anglican in Virginia who was educated at New Jersey's Princeton University, a Presbyterian college.

While in the Middle colonies, Madison observed the beneficial effects of religious freedom and diversity. He also came under the influence of Princeton's president, John Witherspoon, a Presbyterian minister and vocal critic of religious establishments due to their dependence on government support. Madison penned *Memorial and Remonstrance against Religious Assessments* (1784) to influence the debate over the Virginia Statue for Religious Freedom in the direction of further liberalization, and later wrote the Bill of Rights with its First Amendment religion clauses: "Congress shall make no law respecting an establishment of religion, or prohibiting the free exercise thereof."[12] Thus, a movement originally created by dissenting Protestants in the colonies inspired a national constitutional order that restricted the federal government's power to support particular religious institutions, and protected the individual's right to freedom of conscience in matters of religious belief.

RELIGION IN THE NEW REPUBLIC

This republican constitutional order offered a permissive environment for the growth of new religious institutions and movements. Nathan Hatch contends that "democratization is central to understanding the development of American Christianity" and "the years of the early republic are the most crucial in revealing that process."[13] The revolution encouraged Americans to question officials, challenge institutional authority, exercise freedom of choice, and self-organize in pursuit of common goals.

Within Protestantism, Hatch notes, a "populist" strain developed featuring itinerant preachers who thought themselves capable of understanding the plain meaning of Scripture without formal education. They believed the chief qualification for ministry was the presence of the Holy Spirit – not licensing by a consociation, synod, or episcopate.

Working both within and outside institutional walls, the religious populists built a wide following. Congregationalist minister Jedidiah Morse's *The American Geography* from 1792 counted Presbyterians in

Virginia as the most numerous, and Episcopalians the least, but the real object of his fascination were two other denominations most impacted by religious populism: "The Baptists and Methodists are generally supplied by itinerant preachers, who have large and promiscuous audiences, and preach almost every day, and often several times a day."[14] He went on to say that "the bulk of these religious sects are of the poorer sort of people, and many of them are very ignorant (as is indeed the case with the other denominations), but they are generally a moral, well-meaning set of people. They exhibit much zeal in their worship, which appears to be composed of the mingled effusions of piety, enthusiasm, and superstition."[15]

Morse's judgment on the Baptists and Methodists reflected the opinion of ministerial elites who bristled over criticism directed their way by firebrand preachers like Baptist John Leland and Methodist Lorenzo Dow. Regardless of Morse's disapproval, much of the institutional and numerical growth of Protestantism in the early nineteenth century came from this segment. Important events like Kentucky's Red River Revival (1800) and Cane Ridge Revival (1801) featured interdenominational meetings that proclaimed a simple message: repent and surrender one's life to God. Cane Ridge stands as "the most important religious gathering in all of American history" because of its lasting influence, according to historian Paul Conkin.[16] The revivals and their successor events impacted the mind of Methodist Francis Asbury, who had been in America since the 1770s and served as leader of the Methodist Episcopal Church since its founding in 1784. This camp meeting model impressed Jeffersonian-era Methodist leaders, Asbury biographer John Wigger notes, because the meetings "took the familiar Wesleyan message of repentance, conversion, and sanctification and presented it in a new, more culturally accommodating setting."[17] Cane Ridge also inspired the Stone-Campbell Movement to attempt to restore primitive Christianity; this gave rise to the Disciples of Christ and similar groups seeking to restore the apostolic faith. Cycles of revivals and camp meetings facilitated the Second Great Awakening of the antebellum period, which did more than anything else to crystallize the evangelical expression of Protestant faith and spirituality.

Democratization, coupled with the market revolution of the early republic, produced certain countervailing tendencies within Protestant evangelicalism. On one hand, these forces produced "new, up-and-coming northern entrepreneurial classes" who rejected the "gloomy Calvinist determinism of their parent's generation" and believed "every human being was a moral free agent and that individuals could overcome inherited human selfishness and be saved through repentance and prayer."[18] In these middle-class households, Protestant piety encouraged family prayer and attendance at class meetings. Fathers "willingly delegated day-to-day authority over child-rearing and other household affairs to their wives," who "taught their children (and very often their husbands) how to pray, how to develop an instinctive knowledge of right and wrong, and how to nurture the moral discipline that would prepare them for conversion and lifelong Christian service." Middle-class evangelical Protestant women participated in – and in many cases led – local and state religious societies and associations that combatted drunkenness, juvenile delinquency, poverty, and other ills while promoting distribution of the Bible, home missions, education, and many other social improvements.[19] In the words of historians Paul E. Johnson and Sean Wilentz, middle-class evangelical households "became models for what would eventually emerge as American Victorian domesticity."[20] On the other hand, democratization and the market revolution drove many less-educated, working-class evangelical Protestants to reaffirm traditional patriarchal views of marriage and family and hierarchical conceptions of the social order. The plain sense of Scripture led them to assert patriarchal values and even defend slavery as a biblical practice. Research by Christine Leigh Heyrman and Amanda Porterfield complicates the view that populist evangelical religion was an egalitarian movement with leveling tendencies.[21]

This was particularly true for the Southern region where affirmations of the traditional social order intersected with conceptions of masculine chivalry and white racial supremacy. Heyrman describes the antebellum Southern Protestant ideal as follows:

> Now a rising generation of preachers, often in league with their remaining elders, aimed at showing the godly brethren how admirably they upheld the customary ideals of southern manhood. That entailed not only endorsing the authority of masters over their dependents, white and black, but also affirming the importance of men commanding respect in the company of their peers. ... early-nineteenth-century clergymen would strive, by force of their own imitation, to impress upon the laity: that men of God were men of honor, initiates into the mysteries of competition, combat, and mastery.[22]

The enslaving tobacco and cotton planters of the South reasoned that God placed people in different stations of life, slavery being one of them, and expected performance of their duties within those stations.

In his well-known sermon "Rights and Duties of Masters," the Presbyterian minister and eventual president of South Carolina College James Henley Thornwell argued that the peculiar institution fit within the fabric of social relationships, and enslaved people had a moral duty to respect and honor their masters, just as masters had a duty to supervise and care for the enslaved and all other dependents in their households. Slavery, to Thornwell, was "not repugnant to the spirit of the Gospel, in its present relations to our race. It is one of the conditions in which God is conducting the moral probation of man – a condition not incompatible with the highest moral freedom, the true glory of the race, and therefore, not unfit for the moral and spiritual discipline which Christianity has instituted."[23]

On the other side of this debate, anti-slavery activists drew from a variety of sources to make the case for abolition, including the Bible and historic Christian teachings. The anti-slavery movement appeared in the middle of the colonial era, featuring pamphlets like Samuel Sewell's *The Selling of Joseph: A Memorial* (1700) which quoted liberally from Scripture. The Philadelphia Yearly Meeting of the Society of Friends began issuing advices against slavery in the eighteenth century, which became more forceful due to the work of Quaker anti-slavery activists Anthony Benezet and John Woolman. However, Quaker reformers in the eighteenth century were also involved with other causes, including poor relief, treatment of Native Americans, victims of war, and so on. Protestant activists in the early nineteenth century, both clergy and laity, picked up this mantle and began to address a variety of ills in response to what they considered a breakdown in the social order. They believed the market revolution and industrialization threw traditional economic and social relationships out of sync and spawned crime, alcoholism, and mental illness.

Instead of resigning themselves to these ills as the inevitable consequences of sin, reformers drew inspiration from the institution-building of the founding era, the growth of public civic participation, and a new emphasis on the perfectibility of society. According to David J. Rothman, "the changes in Protestant thinking from the eighteenth to the nineteenth century had certainly increased the clergy's concern and attention to social reform, and because of their insistence that men were to do good by improving the common weal, many Americans participated in benevolent activities."[24] Protestants – men and women alike – organized leagues and associations to address these problems, but they also wove these concerns into their ministries, revivals, and camp meetings.[25]

Lane Seminary offers a way to understand how reform and revival converged in this era of dramatic social and economic change. The founder, Rev. Lyman Beecher, began his career as a Presbyterian and Congregationalist minister in New York and Connecticut. An early reformer, he preached against dueling after Alexander Hamilton's death, and then took on drunkenness in the 1820s. He co-founded the American Temperance Society in 1826, which encouraged voluntary abstinence; within ten years one in ten Americans belonged to the organization.[26]

Beecher looked favorably on Charles Finney's Rochester, New York revival of 1831 – part of a series of evangelical revivals centered on the new communities that stretched along the Erie Canal. Beecher considered it "the greatest revival of religion that the world had ever seen."[27] On New Year's Eve the First Presbyterian Church held a temperance meeting where Methodist, Baptist, and Presbyterian ministers called for pledges of abstinence and asked merchants to stop selling liquor. One of the ministers, Finney's understudy Theodore Dwight Weld, "turned to the crowd and demanded that they not only abstain from drinking and encourage the reform of others but that they unite to stamp it out."[28] For historians of these revivals, there was no boundary between moral reform and evangelical Protestant expressions of faith: "temperance reformers urged their listeners to cast Demon Rum out of their lives just as evangelical ministers exhorted them to cast the Devil out of their hearts."[29]

The year after the Rochester revival of 1831, Weld convinced Beecher to serve as president of the newly formed Lane Seminary in Weld's hometown of Cincinnati, which was organized on the basis of manual labor for fees to ensure poor men the opportunity to receive a theological education for ministry in the West. Beecher's *Plea for the West* (1835) reflected contemporary ministerial concerns about the moral and spiritual condition of the working poor in America's frontier communities, but also expressed fears that Catholicism, not Protestantism, would carry the day in the West and threaten both the Christian faith and republican virtue. He claimed that "the conflict which is to decide the destiny of the West, will be a conflict of institutions for the education of her sons, for purposes of superstition, or evangelical light; of despotism, or liberty," thereby associating Catholicism with monarchism, tyranny, and moral apathy.[30]

During Beecher's tenure at Lane Seminary, student anti-slavery activism and benevolent work among the poor Black population in Cincinnati signaled an increasing tendency of abolition to overwhelm the other concerns of antebellum Protestant reformers, such as temperance, prison reform, reformation of the poor, women's rights, and so on.[31] The seminary sponsored a debate over abolition and colonization of African Americans, which ultimately resulted in the withdrawal of the Lane Rebels, including Theodore Weld himself, and publication of their views supporting immediate abolition in William Lloyd Garrison's new abolitionist newspaper, *The Liberator.* Garrison helped to steer the anti-slavery movement from moderate ideas like gradual, compensated emancipation and exile of freedmen to other countries toward radical demands for immediate, uncompensated abolition and integration of freedmen into American social, economic, and political life.[32]

Abolitionism even severed Protestant denominations like the Baptists and Methodists into separate Northern and Southern organizations. This trend from moderate pragmatism to divisive radicalism can be seen within Lyman Beecher's own family. He favored colonization, but his daughter Harriet Beecher Stowe went on to write *Uncle Tom's Cabin* (1852) – the anti-slavery novel that helped to deepen the sectional crisis of the 1850s – and his son Henry Ward Beecher, Lane Seminary graduate and an influential evangelical Protestant minister in New York, became a leading figure in the abolitionist movement. Henry Ward Beecher preached sermons and wrote essays against slavery and raised money to buy enslaved individuals out of captivity. He even helped raise funds to buy Sharps rifles for anti-slavery forces in Bleeding Kansas; a newspaper claimed that Henry Ward Beecher believed "there was more moral power in one of those instruments, so far as the slaveholders of Kansas were concerned, than in a hundred Bibles."[33]

This uncompromising view, together with the crusader spirit in which the view was expressed and lived, can be thought of as the logical extension of the sanctification and perfection movements of antebellum Protestantism, which reached fever pitch in the revivalist culture of the Second Great Awakening. Historian Vinson Synan observes that "by 1840 perfectionism was becoming one of the central themes of American social, intellectual, and religious life. And from the ground of perfectionist teaching sprang the many reform movements intended to perfect American social life – women's rights, the abolition of slavery, anti-masonry, and the various temperance campaigns."[34]

RISE OF REVIVALS

Under Francis Asbury and his successors the Methodist denomination grew exponentially in the first half of the nineteenth century, and the

Methodist General Conferences of 1824 and 1832 asserted the import-ance of John Wesley's doctrine of entire sanctification. In 1835, sisters Sarah Lankford and Phoebe Palmer from New York City's middle-class Methodist community formed the Tuesday Meetings for the Promotion of Holiness, designed to study and practice sanctification. Soon, these Tuesday Meetings spread throughout New England and the mid-Atlantic states with local groups seeking spiritual growth through surrender to Christ and the work of the Holy Spirit, which they believed were path-ways to victory over sin, entire sanctification, and the experience of the "fullness of the love of Christ." Holiness advocates preached at camp meetings and revivals during the height of the Second Great Awakening and their sermons and testimonials were printed in the popular magazine *The Guide to Christian Perfection*, which attained a circulation of 30,000 copies at its peak.

In 1843, anti-slavery Methodists energized by holiness teachings withdrew from the Methodist Episcopal Church, which they believed had made sinful compromises with the institution of slavery, and formed the Wesleyan Methodist Connection, later known as the Wesleyan Methodist Church. Wesleyan Methodists went on to mobil-ize against slavery, as well as for temperance, women's rights, and other social and political causes. As a way of understanding how to live out one's Christian convictions, both in the life of the believer and in the social and political life of the nation, the holiness idea appealed to Protestants across the denominational spectrum. In 1858, Presbyterian minister William E. Boardman published the highly popu-lar and widely read book *The Higher Christian Life* to explain the doctrine of holiness to Protestants who had not been reared in Methodist churches.

America's permissive culture for religious expression encouraged prophets of all shapes and sizes to issue their own unique revelations. In the 1820s, Baptist William Miller read Scripture and worked out Bible prophecy to predict the second coming of Jesus in 1843. When Jesus failed to return, Miller and his followers pushed the date back another year, but then after 1844 came and went without the second Advent, Millerites reformulated their eschatology and organized the Seventh-day Adventist Church, a new Protestant denomination. Joseph Smith's translation of the Book of Mormon (1830) and Doctrines and Covenants (1835) foretold a more elaborate scenario for the return of Jesus.[35] He believed Jesus would return to America when Christians formed the true Church in Zion, which Smith located near Independence, Missouri. The Mormon War pushed Smith's followers out of Independence, and further violence confronted them in Nauvoo, Illinois. After Smith's murder in Nauvoo in 1845, his successor Brigham Young led Mormon pioneers beyond the boundary of the United States into the Great Salt Lake region of present-day Utah. There, the Church of Jesus Christ of Latter-day Saints would await the millennial return of Jesus. These kinds of movements, both within and outside the mainstream denominations, reflect the growing importance of the millenarian impulse within American Protestantism.

Revivalism stressed the importance of individual moral autonomy and freedom of choice, which came to be featured in new Protestant thinking about sin and salvation. Early in the nineteenth century, the democratic spirit of the republic and the success of the revivals in converting new believers inspired minister and Yale professor Nathaniel William Taylor to depart from strict Calvinist orthodoxy and to develop the influential New Haven Theology, or Taylorism. Taylor rejected the conservative Reformed view of inherited moral depravity: "[W]hat is this moral depravity for which man deserves the wrath of God? I answer – it is man's own act consisting of a free choice of some object rather than God, as his chief good; – or a free preference of the world and of worldly good, to the will and glory of God." Taylor went on to say that the choice lay in the hands of the sinner: "Let us make him see and feel that he can go to hell only as a self-destroyer – that it is this fact, that will give those chains their strength to hold him, and those fired the anguish of their burning."[36]

Taylor's theology influenced Charles Finney, the self-taught revivalist who left the legal profession and persuaded New York's Saint Lawrence Presbytery to ordain him for service in the Burned-Over District in the 1820s and 1830s. Finney was "a crucial figure in American religious history" because he and his soul-winning campaigns "introduced democratic modifications into respectable institutions" like vernacular preaching, an emphasis on the conversion experience, prayer groups, and the camp-meeting chorus.[37] In one of his sermons, Finney described the new Protestant model of conversion this way: "There is a sense in which conversion is the work of God. There is a sense in which it is the effect of truth. There is a sense in which the preacher does it. And it is also the appropriate work of the sinner himself. The fact is, that the actual turning, or change, is the sinner's own act."[38] He likened this to a man about to walk off Niagara Falls when another man (akin to the preacher) calls to him to stop. The man turns away from the falls and then says the other man's call saved his life, but Finney points out that the man did his own turning. The key difference in this analogy is that in the matter of salvation, "the Spirit of God forces the truth home upon him with such tremendous power as to induce him to turn."

Taylor and Finney fitted out a new theology for the young United States that served the purpose of churching the vast American interior and elsewhere as the revivals moved east and south. It divided Presbyterianism into Old School (orthodox Calvinist) and New School (pro-revivalist Arminian) factions, generally associated with Princeton and Yale seminaries respectively; but it nevertheless pulled many of the different denominations of Protestantism closer in alignment and facilitated a distinctively American Protestant culture. In the 1830s, Alexis de Tocqueville observed that "the Americans combine the notions of Christianity and of liberty so intimately in their minds, that it is impossible to make them conceive the one without the other," and this was the key ingredient of Christianity's success in the antebellum period. He concluded: "[T]here is no country in the whole world in which the Christian religion retains a greater influence over the souls of men than in America; and there can be no greater proof of its utility, and of its conformity to human nature, than that its influence is most powerfully felt over the most enlightened and free nation of the earth."[39] This extended up and down the ranks of society and across all geographical regions of the country, including free Black communities in the Northern region and among enslaved people on Southern cotton plantations.

AFRICAN-AMERICAN FAITH, ABOLITIONISM, AND CIVIL WAR

Within the African-American population, Protestant Christianity became an increasingly important means of building community and identity in a context of racism, discrimination, and oppression. Figures like Richard Allen and Absalom Jones, Black ministers in Philadelphia, formed free Black Methodist congregations in the 1790s; but refusal by the white Methodist leadership to give Allen and Jones equal treatment and further attempts to control their churches from denominational offices led them to exit the church and form the African Methodist Episcopal Church denomination in 1816. Over the next few decades, free Blacks withdrew from mixed-race urban congregations, and new all-Black churches formed with their own homiletic approaches, their own liturgical styles, and their own doctrinal inflections. Nathan Hatch puts it this way: "Independent black churches, nurtured by biblical stories of consolation and hope, by visions of a promised land, by captivating songs of joy and sorrow, and by the warm embrace of brothers and sisters, forged a folk Christianity that constituted the core of an African-American identity."[40] The growth of this vernacular African-American Protestantism joined with growing demands for slave emancipation and justice for free Black Americans. Historian Eddie S. Glaude Jr. describes this as a kind of "Exodus politics," meaning "a form of common complaint against oppression, a 'hope against hope' for deliverance, a sense of obligation to and solidarity with those similarly situated, and the knowledge that the true test of American democracy rested with the nation's darker sons and daughters."[41]

In the communities of enslaved people, the Black church emerged as a vital institution that "gave the slaves the one thing they absolutely had to have if they were to resist being transformed" into abjectly docile people who could be exploited by their slaveholders. The faith practiced in the slave quarters – Christianity mixed with elements of African folk religion – "fired them with a sense of their own worth before God and man" and "enabled them to prove to themselves and to a world that never ceased to need reminding, that no man's will can become that of another unless he himself wills it," and that "the ideal of slavery cannot be realized, no matter how badly the body is broken and the spirit tormented."[42] Contemporary observers and later scholars commented extensively on the importance of the Black preacher, who "early became an important figure on the plantation and found his function as the interpreter of the supernatural, the comforter of the sorrowing, and as the one who expressed, rudely, but picturesquely, the longing and disappointment and resentment of a stolen people."[43] The church functioned as a means of conveying hope and a longing for freedom in the midst of repeated cycles of white repression, especially following the revolts of enslaved people like the German Coast Uprising (1811) and Nat Turner's Rebellion (1831).

In the late antebellum period, abolitionism and western expansion sparked a sectional crisis, which eventually led to the US Civil War. In the case of western expansion, Protestant churches concerned themselves with home missions throughout the colonial, revolutionary, and early national periods, in terms of both churching white settlers and converting Native Americans. When the War of Texas Independence (1835) dominated the American press, concerns about Catholic Mexico surfaced and mingled with American anxieties over Irish and German Catholic immigration. The nativist anti-Catholic movement, including the rise of Know-Nothing immigration restriction political organizations, derived from Protestant quarters; in this context, vocal Protestant clergy and lay leaders laid claim to the idea that the United States was not just a Christian nation, but specifically a Protestant Christian nation.[44]

Research on the subject of western expansion details how the idea of Manifest Destiny arose from historical Protestant visions of America as "God's new Israel," but also contemporary trepidation about Catholics in the American interior.[45] According to John Pinheiro, white Protestants believed Mexican Catholics were held in thrall to Romish superstition, as well as racially unfit for republican liberty. In their minds, this justified both the annexation of Texas and the 1848 war of conquest in México's northern regions of Alta California, Apachería, and Nuevo México. Through military victory, American Protestants reasoned, God's providence had caused these regions to come under the influence of true Christianity, democracy, and republican institutions.[46]

The Mexican-American War reopened the debate about the expansion of slavery into the western territories, debates that proceeded against a backdrop of evangelical Protestant revivalism and feverish abolitionism. These and other catalysts drove Northern and Southern regions of the nation closer toward civil war, but none of these catalysts was more important than John Brown's Raid in 1859. Brown believed slavery corrupted the nation and its laws, and acknowledged a higher power that called Americans to fight against slavery. For twenty years, he told James Blunt, "he had been possessed of an earnest and firm conviction that his mission here on earth was to be the instrument, in the hands of a divine Providence" for the liberation of America's enslaved people.[47]

When the Civil War began in April, 1861 leaders on both sides were careful to define war aims in secular terms, as preserving the Union or defending states' rights, but soon religious leaders, Southern and Northern women on the home front, newspaper editors, and even soldiers themselves searched for the conflict's deeper religious meanings. It became "a fiery gospel writ in burnished rows of steel," in the words of Julia Ward Howe's "Battle Hymn of the Republic," written in late 1861 and published in *The Atlantic Monthly* in February 1862. In a deeply Protestant culture on both sides of the Mason-Dixon Line, the war inevitably raised questions about God's providential design. Each battle and campaign triggered reflection from the home to the pulpit to magazines and newspapers of the era – in both the Union and the Confederacy – about the message God appeared to be sending to the faithful. In many ways, as historian Mark Noll has written, the Civil War was a "theological crisis" for American Protestants as they struggled to understand the pattern of God's blessings (battlefield victories) and chastisements (battlefield defeats) in relation to their spiritual condition.[48]

During the war, advancements in military technology combined with mindless offensive assaults and tactical failures resulted in casualties on an unprecedented scale. Suffering and death became commonplace as Christians mobilized new relief associations to deal with the crisis and ministers and priests struggled in their homilies and sermons to interpret the appalling loss of life. According to Drew Gilpin Faust: "Southerners and northerners alike elaborated narratives of patriotic sacrifice that imbued war deaths with transcendent meaning. Soldiers suffered and died so that a nation – be it the Union or the Confederacy – might live; Christian and nationalist imperatives merged in a redemptive vision of political immortality."[49]

After the Emancipation Proclamation, Abraham Lincoln explained at the dedication of the Gettysburg battlefield cemetery that all the bloodshed was necessary to ensure a "new birth of freedom" for Americans, both Black and white. In the Second Inaugural Address, Lincoln's use of Protestant language to explain the war and begin the process of national reconciliation was even more profound. He noted that both sides "read the same Bible and pray to the same God" for victory, but both discovered "the Almighty has his own purposes." God had sent the war as a mighty scourge on the nation because of the sin of slavery, with heavy loss of property and loss of life on all sides. In the end, Lincoln concluded with a note of resignation, "it must be said, 'the judgements of the Lord are true and righteous altogether.'"[50] Lincoln freely appropriated Protestant theology and language because he was deeply familiar with it, but also because he knew it would have broad appeal across the nation.

As historian Hugh Heclo explains, "[D]uring the nineteenth century, a majority of Americans came to embrace a messianic, anti-hierarchical, Jesus-centered faith," thus making the era a "Protestant Century."[51] The rise of religious populism, early revivalism, the formation of new Protestant denominations, and the spread of the Protestant faith into the west contributed to the vitality of Protestantism. It offered Americans a way to interpret and respond to the market revolution and industrialization, and to express their belief in progress through campaigns of social reform. While Protestantism offered slaveholders, imperialists, and nativists moral sanction for their regressive attitudes and manifold injustices, it also provided succor and cohesion to oppressed African Americans, drove the effort to abolish slavery, and strengthened the movement for women's rights. When the National

Reform Association of representatives from eleven denominations proposed to amend the US Constitution in 1864 in order "to acknowledge God, submit to the authority of his Son, embrace Christianity, and secure universal liberty," they spoke for many, if not most, who came to see congruence between the Protestant faith in America and the national life of its citizens.[52]

NOTES

1 John S. Oakes, *Conservative Revolutionaries: Transformation and Tradition in the Religious and Political Thought of Charles Chauncey and Jonathan Mayhew* (Cambridge: James Clarke & Co., 2017), 58–60.

2 J. Patrick Mullins, *Father of Liberty: Jonathan Mayhew and the Principles of the American Revolution* (Lawrence: University Press of Kansas, 2017).

3 Jonathan Mayhew, *Seven sermons upon the following subjects; viz. The difference betwixt truth and falshood, right and wrong. The natural abilities of men for discerning these differences. The right and duty of private judgement. Objections considered. The love of God. The love of our neighbour. The first and great commandment, & c.* (Boston: Rogers and Fowle, 1749).

4 Patricia Bonomi, *Under the Cope of Heaven: Society, and Politics in Colonial America*, updated ed. (New York: Oxford University Press, 2003), 216.

5 Thomas S. Kidd, *God of Liberty: A Religious History of the American Revolution* (New York: Basic Books, 2010), 108.

6 Abraham Keteltas, *God Arising and Pleading His People's Cause; Or the American War . . . Shewn To Be the Cause Of God* (Newbury-Port, MA: John Mycall for Edmund Sawyer, 1777), 30.

7 Gordon Wood, *The Creation of the American Republic, 1776–1787* (New York: W. W. Norton & Company, 1972), 114. See James P. Byrd, *Sacred Scripture, Sacred War: The Bible and the American Revolution* (Oxford: Oxford University Press, 2013) for an analysis of how revolutionaries brought biblical passages to bear on their arguments for armed resistance to authority.

8 Mark Noll, "The American Revolution and Protestant Evangelicalism," *The Journal of Interdisciplinary History* vol. 23, no. 3 (1993), 631.

9 Samuel Adams, August 1, 1776; in William V. Wells, *The Life and Public Services of Samuel Adams*, 3 vols. (Boston: Little, Brown, and Co., 1865), vol. III, 413.

10 Nicholas P. Miller, *The Religious Roots of the First Amendment: Dissenting Protestants and the Separation of Church and State* (New York: Oxford University Press, 2013).

11 The struggle of Presbyterians and Baptists against the powerful Anglican gentry in the local vestries and the House of Burgesses is detailed in Rhys Isaac, *The Transformation of Virginia, 1740–1790* (Chapel Hill: University of North Carolina Press, 1982); The Virginia Declaration of Rights

(1776), National Constitution Center, https://constitutioncenter.org/learn/e
ducational-resources/historical-documents/the-virginia-declaration-of-
rights.

12 Miller, *Religious Roots*, 145.

13 Nathan Hatch, *The Democratization of American Christianity* (New Haven,
CT: Yale University Press, 1989), 3.

14 Jedidiah Morse, *The American Geography: or, a View of the Present Situation
of the United States of America*, 2nd ed. (London: John Stockdale, 1792), 387.

15 Morse, *The American Geography*, 387.

16 Paul Conkin, *Cane Ridge: America's Pentecost*, The Curti Lectures
(Madison: University of Wisconsin Press, 1990), 3.

17 John Wigger, *American Saint: Francis Asbury and the Methodists* (New York:
Oxford University Press, 2009), 319. See also Jeffrey Williams, *Religion and
Violence in Early American Methodism: Taking the Kingdom by Force*
(Bloomington: Indiana University Press, 2011) for a study of the Methodist
notions of spiritual warfare and victory over sin.

18 Paul E. Johnson and Sean Wilentz, *The Kingdom of Matthias: A Story of Sex
and Salvation in 19th-Century America*, updated ed. (New York: Oxford
University Press, 2012), 7.

19 John Fea, *The Bible Cause: A History of the American Bible Society*
(New York: Oxford University Press, 2016), 57.

20 Johnson and Wilentz, *Kingdom of Matthias*, 8–9.

21 Christine Leigh Heyrman, *Southern Cross: The Beginnings of the Bible Belt*
(Chapel Hill:University of North Carolina Press, 1997) and
Amanda Porterfield, *Conceived in Doubt: Religion and Politics in the New
American Nation* (Chicago: University of Chicago Press, 2012).

22 Heyrman, *Southern Cross*, 207.

23 James Henley Thornwell, *The Rights and Duties of Masters, A Sermon
Preached at the Dedication of a Church, Erected in Charleston, S.C., for
the Benefit and Instruction of the Coloured Population* (Charleston, SC:
Walker & James, 1850), 43–44. The essential study of the use of the Bible
and Christian doctrine in defense of slavery is Charles F. Irons, *The Origins
of Proslavery Christianity: White and Black Evangelicals in Colonial and
Antebellum Virginia* (Chapel Hill: University of North Carolina Press,
2008).

24 David J. Rothman, *The Discovery of the Asylum: Social Order and Disorder
in the New Republic* (Boston: Little, Brown, and Co., 1971), 75. For a fuller
discussion of changing Protestant ideas about mental health, see
Heather Vacek, *Madness: American Protestant Responses to Mental Illness*
(Waco, TX: Baylor University Press, 2015).

25 Bruce Dorsey, *Reforming Men and Women: Gender in the Antebellum City*
(Ithaca, NY: Cornell University Press, 2002). See also Robert H. Abzug,
Cosmos Crumbling: American Reform and the Religious Imagination
(New York: Oxford University Press, 1994).

26 James Morone, *Hellfire Nation: The Politics of Sin in American History* (New Haven, CT: Yale University Press, 2004), 284.

27 Paul E. Johnson, *A Shopkeeper's Millennium: Society and Revivals in Rochester, New York, 1815–1837* (New York: Hill & Wang, 1978), 109.

28 Johnson, *A Shopkeeper's Millennium*, 113.

29 Judith N. McArthur, "Demon Rum on the Boards: Temperance Melodrama and the Tradition of Antebellum Reform," *Journal of the Early Republic* vol. 9, no. 4 (1989), 528.

30 Lyman Beecher, *A Plea for the West* (Cincinnati: Truman and Smith, 1835), 12.

31 On Protestantism and prison reform, see Jennifer Graber, *The Furnace of Affliction: Prisons and Religion in Antebellum America* (Chapel Hill: University of North Carolina Press, 2011).

32 The transformation of the anti-slavery movement from gradual emancipation to immediate abolition, particularly due to the efforts of William Lloyd Garrison, is described in Paul J. Polgar, *Standard-Bearers of Equality: America's First Abolition Movement* (Chapel Hill: University of North Carolina Press, 2019).

33 *New York Tribune*, February 8, 1856; see also Debby Applegate, *The Most Famous Man in America: The Biography of Henry Ward Beecher* (New York: Three Leaves Press/Doubleday, 2006).

34 Vinson Synan, *The Holiness-Pentecostal Tradition: Charismatic Movements in the Twentieth Century*, 2nd ed. (Grand Rapids, MI: Eerdmans, 1997), 17; see also Timothy L. Smith, *Revivalism and Social Reform in Mid-Nineteenth Century America* (Nashville: Abingdon Press, 1957).

35 Richard Lyman Bushman, *Joseph Smith: Rough Stone Rolling: A Cultural Biography of Mormonism's Founder* (New York: Alfred A. Knopf, 2005). For a fuller account of millenarianism in American history, see Paul Boyer, *When Time Shall Be No More: Prophecy Belief in Modern American Culture* (Cambridge, MA: Harvard University Press, 1992).

36 Nathaniel William Taylor, *Concio Ad Clerum. A Sermon Delivered in the Chapel of Yale College, September 10, 1828* (New Haven, CT: Hezekiah Howe, 1828).

37 Hatch, *Democratization of American Christianity*, 199–200. See also James Craig Holte, *The Conversion Experience in America: A Sourcebook on Religious Conversion Autobiography* (New York: Greenwood Press, 1992).

38 Charles G. Finney, *Sinners Bound to Change Their Own Hearts* (S. W. Benedict & Co., 1834), in *Issues in American Protestantism: A Documentary History from the Puritans to the Present*, ed. Robert L. Ferm (Gloucester, MA: Peter Smith, 1983), 164–165.

39 Alexis de Tocqueville, *Democracy in America*, trans. Henry Reeve, 4th ed. (New York: Henry Langley, 1845), vol. I, 332.

40 Hatch, *Democratization of American Christianity*, 112–113.

41 Eddie S. Glaude, Jr., *Exodus!: Religion, Race, and Nation in Early Nineteenth-Century Black America* (Chicago: University of Chicago Press, 2000), 111. See also Dennis C. Dickerson, *The African Methodist Episcopal Church: A History* (Cambridge: Cambridge University Press, 2020).

42 Eugene D. Genovese, *Roll Jordan Roll: The World the Slaves Made* (New York: Vintage Books, 1976), 210, 283.

43 W. E. B. DuBois, ed., *The Negro Church: Report of a Social Study Made under the Direction of Atlanta University; Together with the Proceedings of the Eighth Conference for the Study of the Negro Problems, Held at Atlanta University, May 26th, 1903* (Walnut Creek, CA: Altamira Press, 2003), 5.

44 Richard Carwardine, "The Know-Nothing Party, The Protestant Evangelical Community and American National Identity," *Studies in Church History*, vol. 18 (1982), 449–463. See also Elizabeth Fenton, "Birth of a Protestant Nation: Catholic Canadians, Religious Pluralism, and National Unity in the Early US Republic," *Early American Literature* vol. 41, no 1 (2006), 29–57.

45 Conrad Cherry, ed., *God's New Israel: Religious Interpretations of American Destiny* (Chapel Hill: University of North Carolina Press, 1998).

46 John C. Pinheiro, *Missionaries of Republicanism: A Religious History of the Mexican-American War* (New York: Oxford University Press, 2014).

47 Louis A. DeCaro, Jr., *Fire from the Midst of You: A Religious Life of John Brown* (New York: New York University Press, 2002), 239–240.

48 Mark A. Noll, *The Civil War as a Theological Crisis* (Chapel Hill: University of North Carolina Press, 2006), 78–79.

49 Drew Gilpin Faust, *This Republic of Suffering: Death and the American Civil War* (New York: Vintage Books, 2009), 189.

50 See Harry S. Stout, *Upon the Altar of the Nation: A Moral History of the Civil War* (New York: Viking, 2006).

51 Hugh Heclo, *Christianity and American Democracy* (Cambridge, MA: Harvard University Press, 2007), 170.

52 Thomas Sproull, ed., *Reformed Presbyterian and Covenanter*, vol. 25 (Pittsburgh: W. S. Haven, 1861), 353. On the National Reform Association, see Randall M. Miller, Harry S. Stout, and Charles Reagan Wilson, eds., *Religion and the American Civil War* (New York: Oxford University Press, 1998).

3 The Industrial Age: 1865–1945

ANDREA L. TURPIN

American Protestantism has never been monolithic. Lutherans, Episcopalians, Baptists, Methodists, Presbyterians, Quakers, Disciples of Christ, and other denominations have all worshipped in their own ways. Nevertheless, a broad evangelical consensus dominated American Protestantism in the first half of the 1800s. These Protestants advocated a relatively straightforward interpretation of the Bible; they believed that Christian conversion was necessary for an individual's salvation, and that the United States could only survive as a republic if a significant proportion of its population remained Protestant – because they believed their faith to be the wellspring of civic virtue.[1]

The social and intellectual changes of the decades after the American Civil War began to fracture this consensus, even as they shaped the United States into the nation we recognize today. More precisely, they created debate over how to achieve the still agreed-upon goal of Protestantizing the nation. Social shifts included industrialization, urbanization, and immigration from non-Protestant areas of the globe such as Eastern and Southern Europe and East Asia. Meanwhile, women's educational and professional opportunities expanded while the civil rights of African Americans contracted. Intellectual shifts included the popularization of Darwinian evolution and a new "higher critical" approach to interpreting the Bible that questioned its status as a direct revelation from God. The Civil War had also raised hermeneutical questions: Northern and Southern white Protestants had reached polar-opposite conclusions on the morality of slavery. Bullets, not scholars or pastors, adjudicated their differences. Yet even though subsequent economic, social, and political crises like the world wars and the Great Depression would further strain Protestant unity, American Protestants largely retained their cultural dominance throughout this era.

SOCIAL CHANGES

Prior to the Civil War, Black and white Protestants in the South often worshipped together in the same churches – with Black congregants relegated to the back or balcony. When the Southern Baptist Convention formed in 1845, it contained more Black than white members. After emancipation, however, African-American Protestants increasingly established their own denominations to escape white paternalism – and white congregants were only too happy to see them leave. Southern Black Protestants thereby followed the pattern of the African Methodist Episcopal Church (AME) and the African Methodist Episcopal Zion Church (AMEZ), which split off from the Methodist Episcopal Church in 1816 and 1824 respectively over dissatisfaction with that church's unwillingness to grant leadership positions to Black members. Thus began the contemporary truism that Sunday morning is the most segregated time slot in the United States.[2]

The largest Black denomination became the National Baptist Convention (NBC), founded in 1895, which, unlike its white counterparts, was truly national: the Southern Baptist and Northern (later American) Baptist Conventions never managed to reunite after their acrimonious antebellum split over slavery. The vast majority of Black Protestants were either Baptist or Methodist. Black Baptists and Black Methodists both numbered about three-quarters of a million in 1880; by 1940, the United States hosted 4 million Black Baptists and 1.5 million Black Methodists. These were also the top two white denominational traditions during this era.[3]

Women of both races formed Protestant subcultures during this era as well, but often within denominations. Antebellum Protestant women had founded benevolent associations to extend to American society at large the values associated with the home. Antebellum Americans believed women were more naturally moral and pious than men – and hence should be sheltered at home rather than sullied by the marketplace. But women turned this ideology on its head and argued that their superior morality and piety made them natural agents for social reform if done by volunteering rather than voting. The focus of female voluntary associations ranged from uncontroversial poor relief to controversial temperance, anti-prostitution, and abolitionist activism. Women's organizations tended to cut across denominations and involved cooperation with like-minded men.[4]

In the mid-1800s, American Protestant missionaries in India and China began calling for more single women missionaries to work among sequestered high-class women whom male missionaries could not visit. (Missionary wives' time was dominated by family responsibilities.) After the Civil War, newly founded American women's missions organizations answered this call by recruiting female missionaries and then praying for and financially supporting them. These women wanted to organize in the non-denominational style to which they were accustomed, but male denominational leaders pushed back because most American missionaries at the time were sponsored by a specific denomination. The compromise was semi-autonomous denominational women's auxiliaries dedicated to supporting female missionaries. These auxiliaries were so successful that by 1890, 60 percent of American missionaries were women. The popularity of these organizations also meant that through the end of World War I, American Protestant women maintained a separate subculture within their churches.[5]

In 1900, Black female Protestants founded an even more independent women's denominational auxiliary. That year Nannie Helen Burroughs addressed the meeting of the National Baptist Convention, the largest Black Protestant denomination, on "How the Sisters are Hindered from Helping," arguing that "a righteous discontent" led Black Baptist women to seek participation in the full range of the church's ministries. The convention's women responded by forming the Woman's Convention of the NBC, which dedicated itself not only to missions but also to education and racial uplift.[6]

Not only did race and gender relations shift within American Protestantism during this time, but class relations altered as well. The discovery of how to generate steam power from coal in an economical manner led to a rapid expansion of factories, in both size and numbers. Small businesses where owners knew and worked alongside employees – who might one day own a business themselves – gradually gave way to corporate behemoths where owners hired middle-managers and foremen to oversee masses of both immigrant and native-born workers, all of whom found it nearly impossible to rise through the ranks. These new factories were located in cities, so prospective employees flooded there from Europe, Asia, and the American countryside. The combination of city infrastructure and low wages meant workers often lived in crowded tenements, as documented by Jacob Riis's famous 1890 photojournalistic essay *How the Other Half Lives*.[7]

Poverty, crowding, and pluralism on this scale were new to the American experience. Prompted by both workers and middle-class reformers, Protestant theologians – professional and lay – pioneered a new theology known as the "Social Gospel" to bring the tradition to bear on the needs of the moment. Social Gospel theologians, prominently including Baptist Walter Rauschenbusch and Congregationalist Washington Gladden, looked to the teachings of Jesus to develop a vision for what a truly Christian society should look like, particularly in terms of class relations. Inaugurating such a society would constitute a natural outworking of the gospel, a social form of salvation. Some Social Gospelers concerned themselves both with individual and corporate salvation, while others rejected conversionist theology for a belief that fixing the social environment would automatically make better people. Charles Sheldon's bestselling 1896 novel *In His Steps* popularized the Social Gospel by encouraging Christians to ask "What Would Jesus Do?" in response to poverty and inequality in the cities. This theology fueled the growth of "institutional churches" that provided social services during the week, such as day care, medical care, and job training. Additionally, the Protestant deaconess movement attracted the energy of young unmarried women who lived in community and provided social services particularly to the urban poor – much like Catholic nuns.[8]

INTELLECTUAL CHANGES

At the same time American Protestants navigated these social challenges, they also encountered intellectual ones. Englishman Charles Darwin published his theory of biological evolution, *On the Origin of Species*, in 1859. He made explicit the inclusion of humans in this chain of evolutionary descent in *The Descent of Man* in 1871. American Protestants split in their response. Some evangelical Protestant intellectuals – like Scottish-American philosopher James McCosh at Princeton or botanist Asa Gray at Harvard – saw no fundamental threat to Christianity in the new theory. They believed it simply explained *how* God had created all living beings, and hence did not threaten the biblical Genesis account, whose point was *that* God had created all living beings. Other evangelical Protestants rejected the theory as in contradiction either to a literal reading of creation in six twenty-four hour days or to a common-sense reading of deliberate separate creation by God of different species "after their kind" (Gen. 1:21, KJV). Many liberal Protestants not as concerned with the exact veracity of every passage of Scripture adopted the theory, and some Protestants became liberal because of it.[9]

The historical critical approach to biblical scholarship originating in Germany proved even more divisive. Antebellum American evangelical Protestants largely believed that the Holy Spirit had supernaturally inspired biblical authors to write accurately about God and the world. Scripture therefore constituted a direct revelation from God. Historical criticism, also known as higher criticism, instead examined the Bible with the same tools used in the nineteenth century to approach other ancient texts. The conclusion was twofold: the text of its individual books had changed over time, and later books revealed a more developed ethical and theological outlook than earlier books. The Scriptures documented the progression of humanity gradually growing to understand God better. Most theologians who embraced historical criticism saw in this belief grounds for a different understanding of how humans came to know God. Rather than recording a flawless revelation of God to humans, the Bible provided a guide for the process of encountering God, whose Spirit would continue to guide people into greater understanding of the divine nature and its corresponding ethical mandate.[10]

How to derive personal and social ethics from the Bible grew hotly debated after the Civil War and the subsequent rise of industrialization, urbanization, and immigration. The inability of a common-sense reading of Scripture to adjudicate the question of slavery had called the traditional hermeneutic into question. Although many white Protestants were subsequently happy to turn a blind eye to the disfranchisement and social segregation of Jim Crow that arose in the 1890s, more of them were sensitive to the poverty and inequality growing in American cities. These social concerns added fuel to the fire of seeking a new approach to the Scriptures that would help Protestants navigate what they understood to be the new demands of the modern era.[11]

MISSIONS AND IMPERIALISM

Simultaneous with these social and intellectual changes on the domestic front came increasing interest in international missions. The international missions movement had taken flight in the first half of the 1800s and it continued to gain speed even after the added weight of four years of brutal civil war. As noted earlier, women's missions auxiliaries were a major engine. Young people were another. College students at a Christian men's summer conference hosted by popular revivalist Dwight L. Moody in Northfield, MA formed the Student Volunteer Movement (SVM) in 1886. Soon coeducational, its slogan was "The Evangelization of the World in This Generation." The SVM attracted conservatives focused on individual evangelism, liberals seeking to Christianize cultures through social service, and moderates pursuing both. From 1890 to 1930, the movement recruited over 15,000 students to serve as foreign missionaries.[12]

The American missions movement had a complicated relationship with American imperialism. In the decades just before and after 1900, the American people acquired an empire in the spirit of those compiled earlier by European nations such as Great Britain, France, and Germany. Motivated by a similar desire for materials and markets, the United States took control of the Philippines, Hawaii, Puerto Rico, and Guam, among others, against the wishes of their native populations.[13]

Protestants split on their attitude toward empire. Many, such as Congregationalist minister Josiah Strong and Methodist Senator Albert Beveridge, articulated a theology that tightly interwove their identity as Protestants with their identity as "Anglo-Saxons." These white, English-speaking Protestants believed that Anglo-Saxons like them had a natural inclination toward freedom, which led to both right doctrine and right government – which is to say Protestantism (as opposed to Catholicism or "heathenism") and democracy. This God-given superiority entailed a God-given responsibility to spread right doctrine and right government to more benighted races. Indeed, President William McKinley (1897–1901), a pious Methodist, finally concluded that Americans should occupy rather than liberate the Philippines after the Spanish-American War because the United States had a duty to "educate the Filipinos, and uplift and civilize and Christianize them." Of course, having been occupied by the Spanish for nearly 400 years, most Filipinos were Catholic.[14]

McKinley's opponent in the election of 1896, pious Presbyterian William Jennings Bryan, vehemently disagreed with this approach. Bryan, running as both the Populist and the Democratic candidate, interpreted the Christian duty to serve the weak differently – not as paternalism, but as liberation for the poor at home and abroad. Bryan won the Democratic nomination with his famous "Cross of Gold" speech that blamed rich merchants and bankers who wanted the gold standard for the problems of poor farmers who would be helped by the silver standard. He thundered, "You shall not press down upon the brow of labor this crown of thorns; you shall not crucify mankind upon a cross of gold." Alongside other less traditional Protestants such as Jane Addams, W. E. B. Du Bois, and Mark Twain, evangelical Bryan supported the Anti-Imperialist League, which argued that imperialism violated the American ideals articulated in the Declaration of Independence – namely the right of self-governance. Bryan, who supported foreign missions, additionally argued that true Christianity could not be spread by force and that imperialism violated Jesus's command, "Thou shalt love thy neighbor as thyself."[15]

Pro-imperialists were far more common among American Protestants than anti-imperialists, but missionaries on the field were often ambivalent. American imperialism opened foreign doors to missionaries, but it also exported aspects of American culture – particularly exploitative business practices – that missionaries critiqued. Missionaries wary of imperialism argued that missions were not inherently imperialistic and instead remained particularly necessary in the wake of imperialism: missionaries could correct via evangelism and social services the ills introduced by less scrupulous Americans. Meanwhile, some African-American missionaries combatted paternalism by arguing that Black Americans should be the ones to bring the gospel to Africa.[16]

Protestants also dedicated themselves to "home missions," a combination of evangelism and social service to underreached or underserved populations within the United States, often those not of western European ancestry. Many of these efforts targeted Native Americans. Shortly after the Civil War, President Ulysses S. Grant pursued a more peaceful approach toward Native tribes by coordinating with Protestant groups such as Methodists or Quakers in establishing policy and providing services. Native responses ran the gamut from retaining traditional religious commitments to conversion to Protestantism to a creative fusion of the two, such as the Ghost Dance of the late 1800s. This movement encouraged Native Americans to connect with their ancestors and purify themselves ritually and morally – in preparation for when Christ would free them from the white man.[17]

ECUMENISM

In the decades following the Civil War, American Protestants displayed a tendency to band together into various organizations. Several factors fed into this zeitgeist of consolidation and ecumenism. For one, American Protestants across denominations experienced the same large-scale challenges. Both evangelizing the world and solving the problems caused by industrialization, immigration, and urbanization called for coordinated action. For another, even as theological fissures began to appear, most Protestants continued to share the optimistic postmillennial outlook of their antebellum predecessors. Postmillennialism taught that the Holy Spirit was at work in the world bringing about a golden age of peace and righteousness (the millennium), after which Christ would return to earth to reign. While some liberals dropped the second half, they continued to embrace the first. Such a grand project undertaken in light of such a grand divine promise necessitated planning and cooperation. Furthermore, after the Civil War it was easier to think nationally and even internationally than when tensions had been brewing between the North and the South. Meanwhile, a more pessimistic premillennial theology that taught that things would just get worse until Christ returned to make them better would become popular among conservative Protestants in the early twentieth century.[18]

While missions organizations tended to remain organized along denominational lines, many other postbellum Protestant organizations dedicated to some combination of evangelism and social service were ecumenical. The Young Men's Christian Association (YMCA) and Young Women's Christian Association (YWCA) took as their goals to evangelize and provide wholesome activities and living arrangements for young unmarried men and women who moved to the cities in search of work. Soon they extended their work to college students as well. By the early 1900s, 20 percent of male students at state universities and a whopping 50 percent of female students there belonged to the "Ys." At private colleges and universities, the numbers were often higher. Increasingly, these organizations also involved students in social service, and in the cities advocated for laws friendlier to the workers they served. Meanwhile, the Women's Christian Temperance Union (WCTU) fought to end the sale and consumption of alcohol in the name of protecting the women and children whose livelihoods were diverted to the saloon by alcoholic husbands and fathers – who could also turn violent upon their drunken return. Pious Methodist Frances Willard, WCTU's most famous president (1879–1898), famously urged members to "Do Everything," namely all types of women's activism oriented toward creating a more Christian society – prominently including woman's suffrage advocacy. All these organizations were also international and involved in missions.[19]

In 1908, the major American Protestant denominations jointly formed the Federal Council of Churches (FCC). This umbrella organization coordinated action across denominations to disseminate the Christian message and accomplish the social reforms members believed would result in a more Christian society. One of its first acts was endorsing the "Social Creed of the Churches," which advocated measures designed to help the working class, such as arbitration in worker-management disputes, abolition of child labor, reduction of work hours, and payment of a living minimum wage. The FCC included some African-American and Eastern Orthodox churches but was dominated by "mainline" white-majority Protestant denominations: a standard list included "the Episcopal Church, the Presbyterian Church (USA), northern Baptist churches, the Congregational Church (now part of the United Church of Christ), [the denominations that would later combine into] the United Methodist Church [and] the Evangelical Lutheran Church, and the Disciples of Christ." These denominations believed they represented middle-of-the-road Protestantism and possessed a custodial sense for the direction of the nation.[20]

WORLD WAR I AND THE FUNDAMENTALIST– MODERNIST CONTROVERSY

This spirit of unified activism would not last. In the Great War (later called World War I), optimistic Protestant activism flew too close to the sun. President Woodrow Wilson, a modernist Presbyterian layman, famously argued the war would "make the world safe for democracy." He hoped it would pave the way for Progressive reforms, which he believed to be bringing about the Kingdom of God in America, to do likewise throughout the world. But he could not even get his fellow Americans to agree to join his brainchild the League of Nations, designed to mediate international disputes without armed conflict. Americans, Protestants in the pews included, just wanted a return to "normalcy."[21]

The war challenged not only Protestant sensibilities, but also Protestant theology. The missions movement had been built on the assumption that Protestantism produced not only saved individuals but an entire Christian civilization. Missions therefore exported not only the gospel, but also the western way of life. Then the most robustly Protestant nations on the globe began killing each other in the most brutal war the world had ever known. Humility followed. Some Protestants questioned postmillennialism: maybe the world would not get better until Christ personally returned to govern it. Others questioned Christian exceptionalism: perhaps Christianity was only one way of knowing God. Many American missionaries began to emphasize international friendship and cooperation where both parties learned from each other. Some continued to believe Christianity had the fullest understanding of God; others did not.[22]

Simultaneously, American Protestantism began to fracture. The social and intellectual fissures that split open after the Civil War widened into a deep valley. During the 1920s, the "fundamentalist– modernist controversy" shook most mainline denominations. Liberals, called "modernists" or "liberal evangelicals" depending on their exact stances, responded to Darwinian evolution and historical criticism by viewing the Bible as a human guide to encountering God rather than an infallible revelation from the deity. "Fundamentalists" retained belief in the Bible's accuracy. Most embraced the "inerrancy" of Scripture wherein it was not only free of theological errors, but also of even minor scientific or historical ones.[23]

The term "fundamentalist," first used in 1920, derived from the pamphlet series *The Fundamentals*, written 1910–1915 by a variety of theologians, and mailed free of charge to American ministers thanks to Presbyterian oil tycoon Lyman Stuart. The series argued which historic Christian beliefs a person needed to hold to merit the title "Christian." These prominently included the deity of Christ, his virgin birth, his substitutionary atonement for sins, his physical resurrection and future physical return to earth, the reality of other biblical miracles, and the inerrancy of Scripture.[24]

Modernists thought fundamentalists were raising unnecessary stumbling blocks to Christian commitment among contemporary Americans living in a new intellectual world. Harry Emerson Fosdick famously argued this point in his 1922 sermon "Shall the Fundamentalists Win?", mailed free of charge to many American ministers thanks to Baptist oil tycoon John D. Rockefeller. Fundamentalists thought modernists had abandoned historic Christianity and were now preaching an entirely different religion. Presbyterian theologian J. Gresham Machen famously argued this point in his 1923 book *Christianity and Liberalism*. The title contained the argument: modernists were not really Christians.[25]

Disagreements between liberals and conservatives reflected disparate understandings of what it meant to be Christian. Both agreed Christianity sought to repair both an individual's relationship with others and with God. Liberals focused on transforming relationships between people, which in turn transformed each individual's relationship with a God who was primarily concerned with our treatment of one another. Conservatives focused on transforming the individual's relationship with God, which in turn produced a new heart of love for others. Requiring difficult beliefs about God therefore made no sense to liberals: it hindered some people from embracing Christian teaching that would improve their relationships. Many liberals thus saw themselves as fundamentally concerned with evangelism, hence "liberal evangelicals." But if a certain understanding of Christ was necessary for placing the sort of trust in Him needed to reconcile a person with God, then – the fundamentalists argued – abandoning those doctrines threatened both an individual's salvation and the ability to love others.[26]

The Social Gospel got enmeshed in this debate as well. In the nineteenth and early twentieth centuries, the broad evangelical consensus had embraced both evangelism and social reform. After World War I, individuals continued to join the two, as did certain Protestant groups like the Salvation Army. But it grew harder to hold them together. By emphasizing interpersonal and social ethics, liberals deemphasized individual conversion – and deemphasized it further so as not to be associated with fundamentalists. In mirror image, by emphasizing individual conversion, fundamentalists deemphasized a more holistic message of the Christian life that included social reform for the common good – and, again, deemphasized this further so as not to be associated with modernists.[27]

Two main groups of Protestants avoided this dichotomy: African Americans and denominational women's auxiliaries. Although some Black Protestants like W. E. B. Du Bois embraced modernism, African-American denominations tended to hold more traditional theological beliefs, going so far as to declare modernism "white heresy." But Black American Protestants did not have the luxury of ignoring social reform. By the 1920s, Jim Crow had confined them for thirty years and they understood viscerally how the system failed to "love your neighbor as yourself." Some also accused white fundamentalists of heresy for separating the first great commandment – to love God – from the second to love your neighbor.[28]

Meanwhile, denominational women's auxiliaries had formed in the context of supporting female missionaries to oppressed women abroad – although they sometimes overlooked the political oppression of American women, not guaranteed suffrage until 1920. Foreign missionaries saw women in India forced into *sati* (widow immolation). They saw upper-class women in China forced into foot-binding (a painful process prohibiting full foot growth, making walking difficult, and serving as a status symbol of not needing to work). They saw women in both countries forced into seclusion and denied a robust education. Identification with these women as sisters led missionaries to redress what they believed to be both these women's spiritual darkness and their social oppression. Female missionaries – and their supporters back home – believed Christ brought women new life holistically; hence, they committed both to evangelism and to reform.[29]

Leaders of mainline Protestant denominations did not listen well to either group as they argued among themselves about the essence of Christianity. White Protestants by and large viewed African-American denominations paternalistically rather than believing Black Protestants might have a unique vantage point that could benefit the debate. Simultaneously, in the name of efficiency, male denominational leaders during the 1920s and 1930s sought to bring women's organizations under tighter control – rather than engaging with them as people with a separate and complementary perspective. Hence white male Protestant leaders muffled rather than amplified voices that might have helped mitigate the controversy.[30]

This behavior is particularly ironic because the majority of denominational leaders sought compromise. They believed that both spreading the gospel and Christianizing society were better accomplished through the coordination made possible by large denominations. Whether they personally leaned modernist or fundamentalist, these moderates believed the differences between camps were not insurmountable, or at least were both tolerable under the same roof for the accomplishment of a greater good.[31]

Denominations that weathered the storm without splitting leaned solidly conservative in their dominant theology: not only African-American denominations, but also Southern Baptists and the Methodist Episcopal Church, South. Here fundamentalists did not have much to rebel against. But denominations with larger modernist contingents – the Presbyterian Church USA and the Northern Baptist Convention (later American Baptists) – saw waves of resignations as fundamentalists jumped ship to found separate churches when they could not redirect the boat toward doctrinal purity. While Baptists and Presbyterians fractured, the Methodist Episcopal Church held together both camps reasonably well, and the fourth most populous American Protestant group – Lutherans – remained relatively unscathed by these debates because they were having other ones on the particulars of Lutheran theology.[32]

Starting in the 1920s, fundamentalist come-outers began to fashion a subculture of "militantly anti-modernist" churches, parachurch organizations, schools, and colleges. Fundamentalists lost the battle for cultural control of the American mainstream but built up a sizable encampment from which to wage future war. Although they understood themselves to be preserving the historic faith, fundamentalists embraced innovation to do so, eagerly latching on to new media such as radio to disperse their message.[33]

Among the movement's intellectual leaders, that message centered on the nature of Scripture, Christ, and salvation. The pews – and the press – more often focused on Darwinism, especially after the media disaster of the 1925 Scopes "Monkey" trial. Technically a victory for fundamentalists, the trial upheld the charge that John Scopes had violated a Tennessee law prohibiting teaching evolution. National news, however, focused on how defense attorney Clarence Darrow placed famous fundamentalist prosecuting attorney William Jennings Bryan on the stand as an expert witness on the Bible. Bryan was not, in fact, an expert on the Bible, and negative coverage of his testimony tainted perceptions of fundamentalists on one side and caused entrenchment on the other.[34]

An additional theological controversy rocked early twentieth-century American Protestantism: the charismatic movement. In 1901, Agnes Ozman, a student at Bethel Bible College in Topeka, Kansas, began speaking in tongues at a prayer meeting. In response, Bethel founder Charles Fox Parnham began itinerant preaching that tongues constituted evidence of baptism by the Holy Spirit that would enable Christians to lead lives of true holiness. African-American waiter William J. Seymour embraced this teaching and began hosting Pentecostal meetings in Los Angeles. The subsequent "Azuza Street revival" amplified the popularity of Pentecostalism, which proved attractive across racial lines as it drew converts from among white, Black, and Hispanic Americans.[35]

Like other Protestant denominations that placed strong emphasis on the Holy Spirit – such as Quakers and holiness Methodists – Pentecostals embraced more gender and racial diversity in their leadership. They understood talent for preaching or pastoring as a gift of the Spirit, and therefore interpreted Scripture in a more egalitarian manner. Apart from their theology of the Spirit, Pentecostals shared much in common with fundamentalists. The latter, however, more frequently disowned Pentecostals than cooperated with them. Nevertheless, the public associated some Pentecostal preachers, like the colorful and controversial (twice-divorced) Aimee Semple McPherson, with the fundamentalist cause.[36]

PROTESTANT RESPONSE TO THE GREAT DEPRESSION AND WORLD WAR II

Despite theological fractures within Protestantism, mainline leaders fought to retain cultural dominance. While fundamentalists feared mainstream colleges and universities had been overrun by liberal Protestants, liberal Protestants feared losing control of these culture-making institutions to secularists. The rise of the research university in the decades around 1900 had gradually sidelined religion from the curriculum into voluntary student organizations. Starting in the 1920s, mainline denominations sponsored university chaplains to maintain some influence among the educated of the next generation. Liberal Protestant leaders' embrace of a paternalistic form of pluralism with respect to other religions allowed them to maintain cultural dominance for the time being within both education and wider American society.[37]

While these national leaders modeled tolerance – within limits – some Protestants on the ground grew uneasy with the perceived threat of losing their privileged place within society. The most extreme manifestation of these fears was the rebirth in strength of the Ku Klux Klan (KKK), not only in the South, over the decade starting in 1915. The Klan advocated "100% Americanism," meaning white Anglo-Saxon Protestantism, and they terrorized not only African Americans, but also Catholics and Jews.[38]

Continuing functional Protestant authority could be clearly seen in the presidential election of 1928, when the first Catholic nominee from a major party, Democrat Al Smith, was soundly defeated by Quaker Herbert Hoover on the grounds of "prohibition, prejudice, and prosperity." True, the nation was thriving economically, so many voters saw little cause to switch away from a Republican in the White House. But Protestants also retained fear that a Catholic president would be the tool of a foreign pope. Plus, Smith advocated ending Prohibition, always less popular with urban Catholic immigrants. Established Protestants, both conservative and liberal, still saw the Eighteenth Amendment of 1919 – which outlawed the production, transport, and sale of alcohol – as a triumph in the battle to Christianize the nation and, through it, the world.[39]

The Great Depression of the 1930s raised further questions about the relationship of Protestantism to American government. Many fundamentalists feared the growing power of national government as President Franklin Delano Roosevelt sought to combat the economic depression through new means. Habituated to premillennial thinking, they believed a strong central government portended the one world state, warned of in the Book of Revelation, that would set itself up against God. By contrast, after an initial resistance to sharing power, mainline Protestant leaders generally saw government efforts as a continuation of the Protestant reform project. Mainliners in the pews consistently landed to the right of their ministers both theologically and socially, but many American Protestants, whatever their theology, appreciated government attempts to alleviate the effects of the economic crisis.[40]

Meanwhile, neo-orthodoxy chastened the liberalism of some mainline leaders. Karl Barth pioneered this theology in Europe in response to World War I, and Reinhold Niebuhr championed it in the United States.

It replaced an unbounded optimism in human and social perfectibility with greater grappling with the depth of sin lodged within both individuals and society. Understandably, its appeal grew during the Great Depression and buildup to World War II. In the 1920s and 1930s, many mainline leaders, such as *Christian Century* editor Charles Clayton Morrison, embraced pacifism alongside peace traditions like the Mennonites, but Niebuhr and other neo-orthodox theologians moved toward a more pragmatic theory of war even before the Japanese bombed Pearl Harbor.[41]

During this period, the Protestant church continued to debate not only the role of government, but also the role of women and African Americans. When mainline leaders took control of women's auxiliaries, they gave women some seats on denominational governing boards – but almost always fewer than 50 percent. Simultaneously, they began to consider women's ordination. By the late 1800s, Unitarians, Universalists, and some Methodists and other holiness denominations like the Salvation Army had already ordained women ministers. Some Baptists and Presbyterians followed in the early twentieth century, but more uniform female ordination in the major Protestant denominations would wait until after World War II.[42]

Meanwhile, fundamentalists were building infrastructure from scratch, which actually translated into more roles for women than in mainline denominations. Fundamentalist women taught at schools and Bible institutes, served as traveling evangelists, wrote books and spoke at conferences, and more often served as missionaries than did mainline women, whose denominations were changing priorities. Simultaneously, however, fundamentalists cracked down on women serving as pastors specifically, a shibboleth for their commitment to a literal biblical hermeneutic.[43]

Segregation remained the norm within Southern white Protestantism. As the Depression dragged into the late 1930s, many denominational leaders walked back their support for expanded government powers for fear the government might coerce racial integration. Integration also remained controversial in the North. The YWCA was working toward full desegregation, achieved in 1946, but they were on the vanguard. The Methodist Episcopal Church is perhaps a more representative example. Some bishops wanted full integration but others wanted an entirely separate Black Methodist church. In the end, desire to unify the northern-based Methodist Episcopal Church (MEC) and the Methodist Episcopal Church, South (MECS) overrode the desire for racial justice: the white-majority church voted in 1939 to establish multiple white regional jurisdictions and a separate Black one.[44]

World War II and its aftermath further challenged the Protestant status quo. The horrors of the Holocaust motivated many Protestants to incorporate Jewish Americans more fully into mainstream political and cultural life. Then the dawn of the Cold War led Protestants to join in common cause with both Jews and Catholics as "tri-faith America" against the godless Soviet threat. Simultaneously, Protestants hoped to retain dominant cultural influence over American life. A partial healing of the breach between liberal and conservative Protestants aided this quest. While neo-orthodoxy moved some liberal Protestants toward the center, the rise of neo-evangelicalism did the same for some fundamentalists. The National Association of Evangelicals, founded in 1942, consisted of fundamentalists who renounced separatism in favor of engaging with secular cultural institutions in hope of redeeming them. Accordingly, they reverted to the nineteenth-century name for socially active conservative Protestants: evangelicals. The uneasy cultural dominance of American Protestants would continue until being thoroughly shaken by the rights revolutions of the 1960s.[45]

NOTES

1 Mark A. Noll, *America's God: From Jonathan Edwards to Abraham Lincoln* (New York: Oxford University Press, 2002).
2 Thomas S. Kidd and Barry Hankins, *Baptists in America: A History* (New York: Oxford, 2015), 149–152; Russell E. Richey, Kenneth E. Rowe, Jean Miller Schmidt, *American Methodism: A Compact History* (Nashville: Abingdon Press, 2010), 65–67.
3 Kidd and Hankins, *Baptists in America*, 152–153, 164, 167; Edwin Scott Gaustad, *Historical Atlas of Religion in America*, rev. ed. (New York: Harper & Row, 1976), 58, 79, 43–44, 54.
4 Anne M. Boylan, *The Origins of Women's Activism: New York and Boston, 1797–1840* (Chapel Hill: University of North Carolina Press, 2002).
5 Dana Robert, *American Women in Mission: A Social History of Their Thought and Practice* (Macon, GA: Mercer University Press, 1997), 125–188, 130.
6 Evelyn Brooks Higginbotham, *Righteous Discontent: The Women's Movement in the Black Baptist Church, 1880–1920* (Cambridge, MA: Harvard University Press, 1993), 150, 150–184.
7 T. J. Jackson Lears, *Rebirth of a Nation: The Making of Modern America, 1877–1920* (New York: HarperCollins, 2009); Jacob A. Riis, *How the Other Half Lives: Studies among the Tenements of New York* (New York: Charles Scribner's Sons, 1890).

8 Heath W. Carter, *Union Made: The Rise of Social Christianity in Chicago* (New York: Oxford University Press, 2015); Gary Scott Smith, *The Search for Social Salvation: Social Christianity and America, 1880–1925* (New York: Lexington Books, 2000); Charles M. Sheldon, *In His Steps: "What Would Jesus Do?"* (Chicago: Advance Publishing, 1897); Jenny Wiley Legath, *Sanctified Sisters: A History of Protestant Deaconesses* (New York: New York University Press, 2019).

9 Jon H. Roberts, *Darwinism and the Divine in America: Protestant Intellectuals and Organic Evolution, 1859–1900* (Madison: University of Wisconsin Press, 1988).

10 Matthew Bowman, *The Urban Pulpit: New York City and the Fate of Liberal Evangelicalism* (New York: Oxford, 2014).

11 Bowman, *Urban Pulpit*, 1–17; Mark Noll, *The Civil War as a Theological Crisis* (Chapel Hill: University of North Carolina Press, 2006); Lears, *Rebirth of a Nation*, 1–11.

12 Michael Parker, *The Kingdom of Character: The Student Volunteer Movement for Foreign Missions, 1886–1926* (Lanham, MD: University Press of America, 1998).

13 Paul Kramer, *Blood of Government: Race, Empire, the United States, and the Philippines* (Chapel Hill: University of North Carolina Press, 2006).

14 Kramer, *Blood of Government*, 28; Albert J. Beveridge, "In Support of an American Empire," *Record*, 56 Cong., I Sess., pp. 704–712; Josiah Strong, *Our Country: Its Possible Future and Its Present Crisis* (New York: The Baker & Taylor Company for the American Home Missionary Society, 1885); General James Rusling, "Interview with President William McKinley," *The Christian Advocate*, January 22, 1903, 17.

15 Michael Kazin, *A Godly Hero: The Life of William Jennings Bryan* (New York: Knopf, 2006); *Official Proceedings of the Democratic National Convention Held in Chicago, Illinois, July 7, 8, 9, 10, and 11, 1896* (Logansport, IN, 1896), 226–234, repr. in *1895–1904: Populism, Imperialism, and Reform*, vol. XII of *The Annals of America* (Chicago: Encyclopedia Britannica, Inc., 1968), 100–105; Richard Seymour, *American Insurgents: A Brief History of American Anti-Imperialism* (Chicago: Haymarket Books, 2012); William Jennings Bryan, "William Jennings Bryan: Our Opponents Conscious of the Weakness of Their Cause, Seek to Confuse Imperialism with Expansion," *Boston Globe*, August 9, 1900, 4–5.

16 Robert, *American Women in Mission*, 265–267; Kidd and Hankins, *Baptists in America*, 152–153.

17 Louis S. Warren, *God's Red Son: The Ghost Dance Religion and the Making of Modern America* (New York: Basic Books, 2017).

18 George M. Marsden, *Fundamentalism and American Culture*, 2nd ed. (New York: Oxford University Press, 2006), 48–61.

19 Ian Tyrrell, *Reforming the World: The Creation of America's Moral Empire* (Princeton, NJ: Princeton University Press, 2010); David Setran, *The College*

"Y": Student Religion in the Era of Secularization, 1858–1934 (New York: Palgrave Macmillan, 2007), 80–81.

20 Robert A. Schneider, "Voice of Many Waters: Church Federation in the Twentieth Century," in *Between the Times: The Travail of the Protestant Establishment in America, 1900–1960*, ed. William R. Hutchison (New York: Cambridge University Press, 1989), 95–121; "Social Creed of the Churches," Adopted by the Federal Council of Churches on December 4, 1908, https://nationalcouncilofchurches.us/common-witness/1908/social-creed.php; Elesha J. Coffman, *The Christian Century and the Rise of the Protestant Mainline* (New York: Oxford University Press, 2013), 4.

21 Michael McGerr, *A Fierce Discontent: The Rise and Fall of the Progressive Movement in America, 1870–1920* (New York: Free Press, 2003), 279–320.

22 Robert, *American Women in Mission*, 255–316.

23 Marsden, *Fundamentalism and American Culture*, 3–10; Bowman, *Urban Pulpit*, 1–17.

24 Timothy E. W. Gloege, *Guaranteed Pure: The Moody Bible Institute, Business, and the Making of Modern Evangelicalism* (Chapel Hill: University of North Carolina Press, 2015).

25 Bowman, *Urban Pulpit*, 259–263; Robert Moats Miller, *Harry Emerson Fosdick: Preacher, Pastor, Prophet* (New York: Oxford University Press, 1985), 115–117; J. Gresham Machen, *Christianity and Liberalism* (New York: Macmillan, 1923).

26 Andrea L. Turpin, *A New Moral Vision: Gender, Religion, and the Changing Purposes of American Higher Education, 1837–1917* (Ithaca, NY: Cornell University Press, 2016), 15–19; Bowman, *Urban Pulpit*, 1–17.

27 Thomas S. Kidd, *America's Religious History: Faith, Politics, and the Shaping of a Nation* (Grand Rapids, MI: Zondervan, 2019), 180–185.

28 Mary Beth Swetnam Mathews, *Doctrine and Race: African American Evangelicals and Fundamentalism between the Wars* (Tuscaloosa: University of Alabama Press, 2017), 155.

29 Robert, *American Women in Mission*, 125–188.

30 Mathews, *Doctrine and Race*, 11–40; Robert, *American Women in Mission*, 255–316.

31 Bradley J. Longfield, *The Presbyterian Controversy: Fundamentalists, Modernists, and Moderates* (New York: Oxford University Press, 1991).

32 Norman F. Furniss, *The Fundamentalist Controversy, 1918–1931* (New Haven, CT: Yale University Press, 1954); Mark Granquist, *Lutherans in America: A New History* (Minneapolis: Fortress Press, 2015).

33 Marsden, *Fundamentalism and American Culture*, 4; Matthew Avery Sutton, *American Apocalypse: A History of Modern Evangelicalism* (Cambridge, MA: Belknap Press, 2014).

34 Marsden, *Fundamentalism and American Culture*, 184–190.

35 Grant Wacker, *Heaven Below: Early Pentecostals and American Culture* (Cambridge, MA: Harvard University Press, 2001) 5–6, 60.

36 Marsden, *Fundamentalism and American Culture*, 93–96; Matthew Avery Sutton, *Aimee Semple McPherson and the Resurrection of Christian America* (Cambridge, MA: Harvard University Press).

37 George M. Marsden, *Soul of the American University: From Protestant Establishment to Established Nonbelief* (New York: Oxford University Press, 1994).

38 Nancy K. MacLean, *Behind the Mask of Chivalry: The Making of the Second Ku Klux Klan* (New York: Oxford University Press, 1994).

39 Ahmet T. Kuru, "Assertive and Passive Secularism: State Neutrality, Religious Demography, and the Muslim Minority in the United States," in *The Future of Religious Freedom: Global Challenges*, ed. Allen D. Hertzke (New York: Oxford University Press), 242.

40 Sutton, *American Apocalypse*, 232–262; Alison Collis Greene, *No Depression in Heaven: The Great Depression, the New Deal, and the Transformation of Religion in the Delta* (New York: Oxford University Press, 2015); Coffman, *Christian Century and the Rise of the Protestant Mainline*, 3–11.

41 Coffman, *Christian Century and the Rise of the Protestant Mainline*, 111–144.

42 Michael S. Hamilton, "Women, Public Ministry, and American Fundamentalism, 1920–1950," *Religion and American Culture: A Journal of Interpretation* vol. 3, no. 2 (1993), 180–184; Nicholas Miller, "The Ordination of Women in the American Church," *Faculty Publications*, Paper 150 (2013), http://digitalcommons.andrews.edu/church-history-pubs/150.

43 Hamilton, "Women, Public Ministry, and American Fundamentalism," 171–196.

44 Greene, *No Depression in Heaven*, 163–193; Nancy Robertson, *Christian Sisterhood, Race Relations, and the YWCA, 1906–46* (Champaign: University of Illinois Press, 2007); Richey et al., *American* Methodism, 164–169, 176–179.

45 Kevin M. Schultz, *Tri-Faith America: How Catholics and Jews Held Postwar America to Its Protestant Promise* (New York: Oxford University Press, 2011); Molly Worthen, *Apostles of Reason: The Crisis of Authority in American Evangelicalism* (New York: Oxford University Press, 2013), 25–35; Coffman, *Christian Century and the Rise of the Protestant Mainline*, 145–223.

4 Protestantism and American Culture
From the Vietnam War to 9/11

SKYLAR RAY AND ELESHA J. COFFMAN

INTRODUCTION

Even in a century of tumult, the 1960s stood out as a period of particularly intense social ferment. A special retrospective issue of *Life* magazine called it, "The decade when everything changed." It was, newsman Tom Brokaw wrote in the magazine, "a time when all that had gone before was suddenly questioned, from war to panty hose, from separate but equal to gays in the closet, from male dominance to institutional authority, from virgin brides to nuclear families, from polite speech to religious faith, from music to other art forms." Everything on Brokaw's list directly affected American Protestantism. This chapter will explore the shifting landscape of American Protestantism and its relationship to American culture from the 1960s to the early twenty-first century, focusing on such major themes as membership decline in mainline denominations, the growth and influence of evangelicalism, the use and impact of television and other forms of mass media, responses to political and social turmoil, debates over marriage and sexuality, and the rise of non-denominational evangelicalism and megachurches.[1]

AMERICAN [DIS]ESTABLISHMENT

While there exists no establishment of religion in the United States, many historians regard mainline Protestantism as constituting a de facto religious establishment in the United States from the late nineteenth century to the middle decades of the twentieth.[2] Traditionally, observers of American religion have seen the 1960s as something of a watershed moment, after which time a hegemonic mainline Protestantism entered a period of precipitous decline even as evangelical Protestantism surged in popularity. Histories of the origins and nature of mainline Protestantism in America, however, have helped reframe and complicate this declension narrative. William Hutchison has shown that mainline Protestantism always had a preferential status in the United States, despite the nation's official separation of church and state.[3] He points out that, by the late nineteenth century, liberal Protestants made up only a minority of American religious adherents, and, far from constituting a majority, enjoyed a "cultural hegemony significantly out of proportion to Protestant or mainline strength in the American population." Elesha Coffman has examined the manner in which mainline Protestants cast themselves as a Christian intelligentsia. She argues that it was the quest for respectability that consolidated the mainline. In the absence of a central governing body, the mainline publication *The Christian Century* became the space where the doctrines and ethos of the mainline crystallized.[4] Coffman argues that mainline Protestants exercised an outsized role in American society by amassing "cultural capital," or those literary sensibilities and aesthetic tastes that amplify and signal social status.

Ever-present in twentieth-century mainline Protestantism was a sharp divide between the theological and cultural sensibilities of the clergy and laity. Trained at the nation's most prestigious seminaries, mainline clergy were, on average, more theologically and culturally liberal than their congregants, some of whom came to church less for spiritual nourishment than for reasons of family tradition or social respectability. The events of the 1960s, however, stressed the preexisting fissures within mainline Protestantism and American culture writ large. Clergy tended to take a more outspoken stance against racial discrimination and the war in Vietnam, and they often advocated for a more progressive politics of gender. Jill Gill has shown that the heavily mainline National Council of Churches (NCC) voiced opposition to the war in Vietnam and kept open communication with both North and South Vietnamese forces in an attempt to negotiate a settlement. In doing so, the NCC ultimately lost both access to realms of political power and the support of its constituent denominations, as government leaders and mainline congregants saw the organization as unpatriotic and radical.[5]

Furthermore, the NCC and like-minded mainline Protestants supported Palestinian independence from Israel, endorsed the resumption of American diplomatic relations with Cuba, put money and legal resources behind the United Farm Workers Union, rallied to the support of the American Indian Movement during the siege at Wounded Knee, and sided with Soviet-backed African insurgents against European colonial regimes. Liberal Protestant leaders and congregants who shared a concern for social reform made common cause with liberals of other faiths. The increasingly vocal support among mainline leadership for the civil rights movement, expansion of the welfare state, anti-war efforts, and, later, women's liberation and reproductive rights caused some adherents to worry that the church was advancing radical politics at the expense of spiritual formation.

While the civil rights movement and issues of race rocked mainline congregations during the 1960s, issues of sex and gender came to the fore during the 1970s. Liberal Protestant engagement with these issues determined the relative position of mainline Protestantism vis-à-vis an ascendant – and more conservative – evangelicalism. Before the 1970s, mainline Protestants had, historically, reflected the sexual norms of broader culture – showing more of an openness than their evangelical counterparts on sexual questions such as obscenity laws, birth control, and sex education. Indeed, R. Marie Griffith has argued that the culture wars of the 1970s and beyond have their roots in twentieth-century disputes over sexuality as the older Protestant consensus on matters of sexuality fractured.[6] Mainline Protestants also proved more supportive of the women's rights movement and the resulting Equal Rights Amendment than did evangelicals. Liberal clergy, such as those with the Clergy Consultation Service who helped connect women to abortion providers, adopted a more supportive position regarding abortion. Daniel K. Williams has demonstrated that before the *Roe* decision, opposition to abortion was led not by conservative Protestants, but rather Catholics and some mainline Protestants.[7] According to Griffith, the fight over abortion reinforced the perceived dichotomy between secular feminist forces and a more traditional, conservative Christianity.

Mainline Protestants also proved more sympathetic to the emerging Gay Liberation Movement. Heather White has argued that the increasingly prominent notion of homosexuality as a condition (as opposed to an act) had a dual effect on American Christians.[8] One the one hand, it drew mainline Protestants into greater engagement with homosexuals, and in turn resulted in outright support among liberal Protestants, especially clergy, for the cause of gay liberation and civil rights. On the other hand, the notion of homosexuality as a disease to be cured subsequently made its way into evangelical circles, where it reinforced the need to address homosexuality as a condition to be healed rather than supported.

MAINLINE RENEWAL MOVEMENTS AND SPLITS

Issues of sexuality and gender exacerbated existing tensions within mainline Protestantism and would soon contribute to several denominational splits, as denominational leaders began to assume more liberal stances on doctrinal and theological issues such as women's ordination, revision of liturgy, biblical criticism, the doctrine of salvation, feminist theology, and human sexuality. In addition to these doctrinal and theological matters, many moderates and conservatives cited a decreased emphasis on biblical literacy, evangelism, and catechesis as contributing to their sense of unease. Some saw the precipitous decline in mainline attendance after the 1960s as the result of theological deficiencies within the broader liberal Protestant establishment. This perceived leftward drift of denominational leadership led laity – and a number of clergy as well – to launch an attempt to restore their denominations to what they considered historic Christian belief and traditional denominational doctrine. Initially, the loci of these renewal impulses were found in various lay groups in the 1960s and 1970s. Other renewal impulses produced increased emphasis on Bible study, evangelism, discipleship, prayer, and ministry to the poor. Initially, these groups were intent upon reforming their churches from within – although one prominent exception to this desire to remain is the Presbyterian Church in America (PCA), which separated from the Presbyterian Church-USA (PCUSA) in 1973 in order to preserve more conservative Reformed doctrine and take a stance against women's ordination.

Renewal impulses gained momentum following controversial flashpoints in mainline denominations in the latter decades of the twentieth century. One such flashpoint was the 1993 Re-Imagining Conference, an ecumenical, majority-mainline feminist theology gathering where attendees invoked the Goddess Sophia, prompting accusations of heresy from across the denominational spectrum. The conference was especially polarizing in PCUSA, which had supplied a substantial amount of funding and personnel to host the conference. Still another flashpoint occurred when in 2004 the Episcopal Church (TEC) ordained Gene Robinson, the denomination's first openly gay noncelibate bishop. Although TEC had already taken a more liberal stance on questions of clerical homosexuality in the decades preceding, Robinson's election constituted a breaking point for many who had sought to draw the church toward a more historic interpretation of church doctrine. In 2009, those espousing a more conservative episcopal tradition withdrew from TEC and eventually formed the Anglican Church in North America (ACNA). Similarly, members of the PCUSA who grew dissatisfied with the denomination's shift away from historic Reformed theology broke away in 2012 to form A Covenant Order of Evangelical Presbyterians. These movements serve as a reminder of the complexity and diversity present within the American Protestant tradition – challenging views of the mainline and other traditions as monolithic and unchanging.

When mainline churches began to decline in membership after the 1960s even as evangelical denominations continued to grow, many posited that this lay/clergy divide in liberal Protestant circles drove mainline adherents to desert their liberal denominations for more conservative congregations. Scholars such as David Hollinger, however, have shown that this mainline "decline" had more to do with demographic shifts than a mass exodus from liberal Protestant churches; he argues that mainline birth rates lagged far behind those of evangelicals. Hollinger points out that mainline Protestants did not relegate women's roles to homemaking and approved of sex for purposes other than procreation: "These steps away from tradition resulted in a substantial loss of reproductive power relative to evangelicals, whose leadership was much slower to move in these directions."[9] As subsequent scholars would show, mainline Protestants did not (and do not) share with evangelicals the fear that their children may become unmoored from their faith and thus place little emphasis on keeping them within the fold. Even as mainline young people agreed with denominational leadership's abandonment of ideas increasingly seen as racist, sexist, imperialist, homophobic, unscientific, and excessively nationalistic, many did not affiliate with their ancestral church or with any other church. Often these young people found secular vehicles for the liberal values they had learned from their elders.

Historians charting the numerical decline of mainline Protestants also point to the rising number of non-Protestant immigrants and a growing trend among Americans to regard religion as chosen rather than inherited. This sociological explanation for membership trends is bolstered by data showing that Americans no longer feel the need to switch from conservative to mainline denominations in order to achieve upward social mobility. Given that mainline denominations relied upon inherited religious identity to greater extent than did more conservative traditions, mainline denominations suffered from cultural shifts in ways that evangelicalism did not. Sociologists perceive that mainline churches, with a membership largely composed of white, affluent, suburban individuals, are struggling – and will likely continue to struggle – to attract and retain younger members.[10] David Hollinger contends, though, that liberal Protestants in the 1960s and subsequent decades lost the churches but won the culture. Mainline Protestants "put their energies into an imposing collection of secular agencies, including the human rights organizations that flourished during the 1970s and after," he writes.[11] Thus, the influence of the mainline still pervades modern American life, albeit in realms outside of religious institutions.

EVANGELICAL ASCENDANCY

While mainline denominations began to decline in membership, evangelicalism emerged as culturally ascendant. This trend was visible by the late 1960s, when the Southern Baptist Convention (SBC) overtook the United Methodist Church (UMC) as the largest Protestant denomination in the United States. Twenty years later, the SBC was continuing to grow, even as UMC membership continued to dwindle. This shift coincided with what sociologist Robert Wuthnow has identified as a "decline in denominationalism," which "cleared the deck" for new religious groups – particularly special interest groups – to emerge.[12] The social and political nature of many evangelical special interest groups, he argues, resulted in a fracturing of American Protestantism along lines of social attitudes and education, rather than denomination.

Among the most notable religious shifts has been not simply the rise of evangelicalism, but a change in popular forms of evangelical worship and church life. Whereas the fundamentalism of yesteryear existed largely in small, independent congregations, the new evangelicalism in the latter decades of the twentieth century incorporated worship styles that had circulated through the charismatic renewal movement that swept through mainline denominations in the 1960s and saw the rise of charismatic-Pentecostal forms of spirituality throughout evangelical circles.

By the 1970s, many evangelicals had for decades worked to distance themselves from their fundamentalist forebears. Efforts of neo-evangelicals and the popularity of preachers such as Billy Graham went far in mainstreaming what was once a marginalized religious tradition. And then, during the 1970s, the evangelical movement enjoyed unprecedented mainstream success. Illustrating this ascendancy, presidential candidate Jimmy Carter's identification as a "born-again" Christian on national television in 1976 made headlines across the country, prompting *Newsweek* magazine to declare 1976 the "Year of the Evangelical." As journalists scrambled to understand a Protestant subset that had supposedly disappeared after the 1925 Scopes Trial, Carter's faith thrust evangelicalism once again into the public eye. This newfound focus prompted a surge in scholarship on the roots of evangelicalism and its role in American religious and cultural history. In the last several decades, historians have probed the origins of the movement with an eye toward the connections between fundamentalist and evangelical Protestantism and the rise of the Christian Right in the 1970s.

Initially, many historians assumed that fundamentalists retreated from the public sphere after the culture wars of the 1920s only to return in the late 1970s. As recent historians have shown, however, this seeming reemergence of evangelicalism actually constituted a continuance of evangelical involvement in politics. The ascendancy of evangelicalism did not emerge as a reaction against the counterculture and general tumult of the 1960s, but rather surfaced thanks to a confluence of complex historical factors. At mid-century, the efforts of neo-evangelicals such as Billy Graham, eager to shed their fundamentalist stigma, had gone far in mainstreaming conservative Protestantism. However, during the 1970s evangelicals not only became more visible but emerged as an identifiable political force and voting bloc in the form of what many historians refer to as the Religious Right.

Historian Darren Dochuk sees the origins of the Religious Right in the migration of "plain folk" fundamentalists from the Sunbelt – states like Oklahoma and Arkansas – to Southern California in the 1930s and 1940s, drawn by the promise of employment during the Great Depression and, later, by jobs created by the burgeoning defense industry.[13] In doing so, these migrants escaped their status as cultural outsiders and acquired a position of influence in society – first locally, then regionally and nationally. Holding to fundamentalist beliefs such as "primacy of individual conversion, the inerrancy and infallibility of the Bible, and the scriptural injunction to witness for Christ," they built religious networks of churches and educational institutions where conservative religion, politics, and economics comingled and became the foundation for a political ascendancy in the 1970s and 1980s.[14] Auto supply magnate George Pepperdine founded Pepperdine University, which promoted Christian libertarian thought among Southern California evangelicals, while candy manufacturer Bill Bright's organization Campus Crusade for Christ used educational and evangelistic outreach to draw in youth. Historian Kevin Kruse has also traced this connection between corporate interests and the emerging Religious Right, arguing that conservative businessmen and interest groups made common cause with conservative Christians to promote a Christian libertarianism at the heart of the conservative political movement.[15]

The scholarly "business turn" exemplified by Dochuk and Kruse is not the only thesis advanced to explain evangelical ascendance. Historian Matthew Avery Sutton has highlighted eschatology as the unifying and defining factor of the fundamentalism that would animate the evangelical politics of the 1970s and 1980s. He argues that this focus on the end of the world led would-be evangelicals to engage with the culture – especially the political culture – around them as they "occupied" politics while awaiting Christ's return.[16] Many evangelicals in the 1960s and 1970s saw atheistic communism in the expansion of government power and the growing civil rights movement; they argued that issues of race were best approached through the targeting of individual hearts and minds. Sutton shows that, for these evangelicals, Vietnam was the crucial, apocalyptic battle against communism.[17] Such works as Hal Lindsay's *The Late Great Planet Earth* (1970) and the film *A Thief in the Night* (1972) evidenced this preoccupation with eschatology. These apocalyptic concerns led evangelicals to identify closely with the new nation of Israel and to interpret such geopolitical events as the Six Days War as events foretold in the Book of Revelation. Anticipating God's judgment in the Last Days, evangelicals mobilized in the political arena to ensure that the United States was deemed righteous on the day of judgment.[18]

Historian Daniel K. Williams agrees that "conservative Christians had been politically active since the early twentieth century, and they never retreated from the public square."[19] The friendship that Billy Graham and Richard Nixon forged over anticommunism in the 1950s and 1960s illustrated the growing compatibility between evangelicals and the Republican party that would come to fruition in the 1970s. Williams notes that the "end of the civil rights movement facilitated the formation of a new Christian political coalition, because it enabled fundamentalists and evangelicals who had disagreed over racial integration to come together."[20] This political coalition found a ready partner in Ronald Reagan. Williams writes, "Evangelicals gained prominence during Ronald Reagan's campaign not because they were speaking out on political issues – they had been doing that for decades – but because they were taking over the Republican Party."[21]

Issues of gender, sexuality, and the family emerged as central to the evangelical coalescence in the latter decades of the twentieth century, and conservative Protestants united around such social issues as opposition to abortion, feminism, homosexuality, and pornography. Thanks to the work of such Christian thought leaders as Francis Schaeffer and such political organizers as Moral Majority founder Jerry Falwell, many evangelicals mobilized to combat and transform a culture that they became convinced was hostile to Christian belief. Some of this engagement was intellectual, as Schaeffer encouraged young evangelicals, especially, to develop and defend a "Christian worldview" against encroaching "secular humanism."[22] For many evangelicals, this transformation of culture entailed a defense of Christian morality and "family values" through the vehicle of Republican politics. As Daniel K. Williams has shown, opposition to abortion remained, until the 1970s, a primarily Catholic position connected to other "life" issues such as contraception, euthanasia, and the death penalty.[23] Schaeffer, Falwell, and other evangelical leaders reframed the abortion issue as a rights-based defense of fetal life, linking it instead with radical feminism and sexual immorality. Opposition to feminism and an embrace of militant masculinity became hallmarks of white evangelicalism, as shown by Kristin Kobes Du Mez.[24]

Historian Seth Dowland argues that many evangelicals considered themselves "custodians of morality" and believed that the family unit was central to a functioning society. Prominent conservative evangelicals crafted a "family-values" agenda that emphasized opposition to gay rights, feminism, and abortion, while supporting the proliferation of private Christian schools, homeschooling, and the military. It was this agenda that created the strong bond between evangelicalism and political conservatism, and as a result the Republican Party incorporated family-values language into its platforms.[25] This evangelical emphasis on the family extended beyond the realm of politics. In 1977, Christian psychologist James Dobson founded Focus on the Family, an organization that would ultimately provide advice literature, support, and family-friendly entertainment to millions of families. As historian Hilde Løvdal Stephens has demonstrated, Dobson and others argued that families – and society as a whole – thrived when husbands and wives "adhered to godly ordained roles, children respected parental authority, and when sex was limited to a monogamous heterosexual and lifelong marriage."[26] Such emphasis on godly ordained gender roles could be seen in evangelical denominational life, as in the SBC's 1998 adoption of a statement declaring that a woman should "submit herself graciously" to her husband. Scholars such as Barry Hankins argue that such articulations of divinely ordained gender roles were central to the conservative evangelical critique of American culture.[27]

The last quarter of the twentieth century saw the rise of groups that did not easily fit within the older categories of mainline or fundamentalist/evangelical. Historians such as David Swartz and Brantley Gassaway have examined the history of progressive evangelicals who, from the early 1970s, sought to transcend the extremes of both the 1960s social left and the more passive, politically conservative evangelicalism to the right. Those who constituted this "evangelical left" spoke out against the Vietnam War, nuclear armament, US intervention in Latin America, poverty, and continuing racial discrimination.[28] Leaders including Ron Sider and Jim Wallis gave voice to the evangelical left through print publications such as the magazine *Sojourners*. These progressive evangelicals often pursued a "third way" in American politics; they promoted feminism while opposing abortion and often privately supported a traditional scriptural interpretation of human sexuality while supporting gay rights and gender equality. Thus, while these Protestants more frequently associated themselves with the Democratic Party, their unique blend of theological conservatism and political progressivism won them few supporters among America's two major political parties. While a strain of progressive evangelicalism survived into the twentieth century, the fate of the evangelical left demonstrated that, on the American political stage, this middle ground could not hold.

NEWCOMERS

The late twentieth century also saw the emergence of new religious trends that would shape American Protestantism into the next millennium. These included the rise of charismatic and Pentecostal forms of spirituality, a decline in denominationalism, the growth of parachurch organizations, and the spread of the so-called "prosperity gospel."

For much of the twentieth century, Pentecostalism's ecstatic worship style, otherworldly emphasis, and appeal to social and racial minorities kept the tradition on the margins of American Protestantism. Beginning in the 1960s, however, the charismatic renewal movement in mainline denominations brought charismatic worship styles to socially respectable denominations. This charismatic Christianity was hardly the otherworldly Pentecostalism of yesteryear. Biographer Amy Artman has shown how charismatic leaders such as Kathryn Kuhlman leveraged decades of ministry experience into an evangelical stardom that included bestselling books, mass meetings, a national radio program, and syndicated television shows, essentially gentrifying charismatic Christianity.[29] Initially, this charismatic movement circulated within historic denominations, as participants hoped to renew these denominations through an emphasis on the work of the Holy Spirit, emotive worship, and prayer. Eventually, however, this charismatic impulse would spill over into broader swaths of American evangelicalism, as decidedly non-charismatic strands of Protestantism nevertheless abandoned more traditional practices – such as hymn-singing – for more contemporary styles of worship.

Other charismatic and Pentecostal leaders and organizations grew in size and popularity during the 1980s and 1990s, often employing the same openness to new media technology that had proved so effective to their evangelical forebears. The Southern California-based Trinity Broadcasting Network became the nation's first 24-hour Christian station. Television preachers – or "televangelists," as they came to be known – harnessed the power and popularity of television to gain millions of followers nationwide, often from the pulpits of megachurches. Historian John Wigger has examined the rise and fall of the ministry of Jim and Tammy Faye Bakker, whose ministry culminated in the PTL (Praise The Lord) television network and a 2,300-acre amusement park, Heritage USA, before the ministry's collapse in the wake of sexual and financial scandals.[30]

Many of the most successful television preachers have been those touting what many refer to as the "prosperity gospel." In recent years, scholars have explored the rise of this ideology, which teaches that faith is a causal agent in bringing about blessing, often in the form of health or wealth. In her study of the prosperity gospel, Kate Bowler shows that while the prosperity gospel has overlapped with evangelicalism, fundamentalism, and historically black Protestantism, the specific origins of prosperity faith can be traced through three intersecting strands: Pentecostalism, New Thought, and a confluence of uniquely American ideals including individualism, pragmatism, and upward mobility.[31] By the early years of the twenty-first century, the prosperity gospel was visible in the preaching of such figures as Joel Osteen, T. D. Jakes, and Benny Hinn.

The decline in denominationalism that accompanied the upsurge in evangelical, charismatic, and megachurch Christianity also allowed for the growth of parachurch organizations. R. Marie Griffith points out that the Women's Aglow fellowship, the women's arm of the Full Gospel Men's Business Fellowship, was by the 1990s the largest international Christian women's fellowship.[32] This charismatic parachurch organization became an independent, interdenominational women's network that was organized at the local, regional, and national levels, promoting both evangelism and spiritual gifts such as speaking in tongues and healing. As in other corners of American Protestantism, the Aglow organization evidenced a growing emphasis on therapeutic culture, as evangelical notions of guilt became linked to the concept of shame and the doctrine of repentance mingled with ideas about emotional healing. In her recent study of evangelical women celebrities, Bowler has shown how these popular speakers use personal experiences of brokenness,

repentance, and emotional healing – rather than educational achievements or professional certification – as their credentials for functioning
as lay counselors to their audiences.[33]

BLACK PROTESTANTS AND ISSUES OF RACE

While the last quarter of the twentieth century saw an uptick in scholarship on evangelicalism, little of this scholarship has constituted religious history of racial minorities within evangelicalism. Such a dearth
is telling. While a majority of Black Americans profess religious faith,
and a majority of those espouse a theologically conservative evangelicalism, they remained culturally distinct from white evangelicals. When
Martin Luther King, Jr., quipped that 11:00 a.m. on a Sunday was the
most segregated hour in America, he identified a crucial and persistent
division in American Protestantism, one that would endure into the
twenty-first century.

Paul Harvey has narrated the multivalent nature of Black
Protestantism in the United States through the early twenty-first
century.[34] As Harvey and countless others have illustrated, Black
churches at the time of the civil rights movement had for over
a century served as sites where Black Americans could exercise autonomy in worship and build religious community. While professing
a theology similar to that of white evangelicals and political inclinations
akin to those of mainline adherents, Black Protestants have occupied
a distinct cultural space in American religious history.

The religious tradition that Black Protestants nurtured would
become visible as the backbone of the civil rights movement during the
1960s. As Harvey writes, "A fundamentally Protestant imagery of
Exodus, redemption, and salvation inspired the revivalistic fervor of
the movement. Black Protestant thinkers and activists also deftly combined the social gospel and black church traditions infused with notions
of active resistance to social evil." As the movement evolved, however, it
became clear that nonviolent resistance and the legal right to access
public spaces could not alone correct centuries of economic inequality.
Radical leaders questioned the efficacy of Martin Luther King, Jr.'s brand
of Christian moral suasion that relied on appeals to what they considered
a white man's religion. These voices pointed to the evident complicity of
white Christianity in racism through the nation's history, especially as it
emerged in white backlash against the civil rights movement.

Carolyn Renée Dupont has probed these links between theology and
white supremacy, attacking the "cultural captivity" theory which held

that Southern religion was largely held captive by a racist Southern culture and rendered powerless to provide a prophetic witness. Dupont instead has argued that religion actively created and maintained segregation and racism. She sets out to demonstrate that the individualistic ethos of Southern evangelicalism not only discouraged collective action on behalf of the racially oppressed but also painted the plight of minorities as a problem among African- American individuals, rather than a societal fault. In this way, she argues, whites turned a blind eye to the economic and social conditions perpetuated by segregation. Dupont shows how a uniquely Southern Segregationist Folk Theology, which stressed the importance of the created order, undergirded the racial views of these Mississippi evangelicals, fueled by the threat of both communism and racial amalgamation in the minds of Southern whites.[35]

Increasingly, Black theologians and thinkers grew impatient with demands for what they considered to be nonviolent passivity in the face of ongoing injustice and a surrounding Christianity steeped in white supremacy. Leaders such as James Forman expressed the frustration of many when at the historic liberal Protestant Riverside Church he delivered the "Black Manifesto," in which he called for $500 million in reparations for Black people. Forman turned calls for patience back on white Christians.

Beginning in the late 1960s, a new theology of Black power emerged, drawing upon the biblical prophetic tradition. This Black theology moved away from former attempts to deemphasize race in theology to reclaiming blackness as significant and sacred. Theologians such as James Cone did this through "imparting blackness (whether physically or metaphorically) on God or Jesus as a necessary instrument of liberation."[36] For Cone and others, black images of God communicated a God who identified with the oppressed and was acquainted with their particular form of suffering. This Black theology would join with liberation theology among Latin Americans – and, later, feminist, womanist, and *mujerista* theology – to offer a critique of an Anglo-centric American Protestantism.

In an era of renewed culture wars, Black Protestants occupied a precarious place on the American religious spectrum. While most Black Protestants typically supported more liberal economic policies and constituted a reliable voting bloc for the Democratic party, they also tended to support conservative family values and traditional interpretations of human sexuality.

This allowed for limited cooperation between Black and conservative white Protestants. The later years of the twentieth century saw white Protestants repudiate their former racism to varying degrees. Some publicly repudiated this racism, as when both the SBC and the Assemblies of God issued public apologies for their roles in sustaining a racist society. Stephens notes that Christian psychologist and writer James Dobson, who had once opposed interracial marriage, later retracted his statements.[37] Such evangelicals adopted the language of colorblindness, arguing that God's plan for the family applied to all, regardless of race.

Other white evangelicals attempted to move beyond rhetoric to engage in interracial ministry pursuits. Dowland examines the manner in which the Promise Keepers movement, under the leadership of University of Colorado football coach Bill McCartney, encouraged men not only to become better fathers and husbands, but also to acknowledge and repent of racism.[38] Many white evangelicals cooperated with Black churches on matters of family values, united in opposition to such threats as same-sex marriage. Some began to speak of abortion as racial genocide and an attempt to control Black bodies. Still, white Christians such as Dobson maintained that race relations could be transformed only when hearts and minds changed, and opposed multicultural education as promoting moral relativism and the destruction of Western culture.[39] While mainline Protestants were typically more progressive on matters of race, their churches remained essentially segregated, as these churches continued to draw from white, affluent echelons of society.[40]

In subsequent years, historically Black churches struggled to retain a younger generation, even as the prosperity gospel appealed to a growing Black middle class. The popularity of television preacher T. D. Jakes illustrates this trend. Jakes' entrepreneurial, media-savvy ministry grew from 50 in 1996 to 3,000 by 2008, appealing to an interracial audience across the nation. The landscape of Black Protestantism would continue to shift into the twenty-first century, thanks to increasing immigration of Black Protestants from the global South. This new wave of immigrants has resulted in new congregations, primarily of the Pentecostal and charismatic variety; they emphasize the supernatural and tend to be less institutional and more personality-driven than historically Black churches in the United States. These shifts have brought new tensions and distinctions between these disparate strands of Black Protestantism in America.

Black Protestantism has not been the only subset of American Protestantism to undergo remarkable shifts as a result of immigration. In his *Latino Pentecostals*, Gaston Espinosa charts the growth of Latinos in the Assemblies of God and Church of God denominations. These Latino Pentecostals differ from their white counterparts in their participation in progressive politics and protest movements. Today, Latinos constitute the largest ethnic minority in the United States, and that percentage is only projected to grow. Approximately 93 percent of Latinos identify as Christian, and almost 30 percent of those as Protestant. The projected growth in the numbers of Latino Protestants and others from the global South points to the ever-changing nature of American Protestantism and promises new religious realignments along lines of religion, politics, and culture in the twenty-first century.[41]

CONCLUSION

The terrorist attacks of September 11, 2001, did not have as much of a specific, direct impact on American Protestantism as the cultural upheavals of the Vietnam era did. Following a brief uptick in church attendance across the religious spectrum, long-standing membership trends continued. White, mainline congregations aged and shrank while younger evangelical and Pentecostal congregations grew. Despite increased suspicion of foreigners and stricter border controls, immigration continued to swell and diversify American Protestantism. The militant masculinity dominant in white evangelicalism, which had softened slightly at the end of the Cold War, flexed its muscles again as the long-running War on Terror began. The enhanced masculinization of white evangelicalism contrasted with the egalitarian gender ideology and renewed anti-war mood of the mainline, although women constituted no more than 25 percent of the clergy in any mainline denomination. Unexpected and largely unnoticed at the time, rising religious disaffiliation would soon become a major challenge for American Protestantism. The denominational competition that characterized the 1960s and the political fracture of the subsequent decades receded, while a new category, the religious "nones," emerged.

In sum, over the roughly four decades between Vietnam and 9/11, the white mainline declined in numbers and power, while evangelicalism grew politically potent. Pentecostalism was the most racially diverse of the main Protestant traditions, and it boasted the biggest churches and biggest celebrities. Neither the mainline's progressive politics nor evangelical attempts at racial reconciliation built many bridges to historically Black churches, which continued pressing for racial justice after the end of the civil rights movement. Immigrants and other racial minorities boosted the membership rolls of some Protestant churches, especially

Pentecostal churches, but people of color were generally not well represented in the leadership ranks. Arguments about race, sexuality, and war shifted over time but never went away. In that one sense, the end of this historical period was not so different from its beginning.

NOTES

1 Tom Brokaw, "Foreword: Change Was in the Air," in *LIFE in the 1960s: The Decade When Everything Changed* (New York: LIFE Books, 2016), 6.
2 Scholars generally consider mainline Protestantism to include the United Methodist Church (UMC), Presbyterian Church (USA), Episcopal Church (USA), Evangelical Lutheran Church in America, American Baptist Churches, Disciples of Christ, and the United Churches of Christ. These denominations boasted distinct heritages but also claimed a set of common characteristics including modernism, ecumenism, formal worship, activism, and theological liberalism.
3 William R. Hutchison, ed., *Between the Times: The Travail of the Protestant Establishment in America, 1900–1960* (Cambridge: Cambridge University Press, 1989).
4 Elesha J. Coffman, *The Christian Century and the Rise of the Protestant Mainline* (New York: Oxford University Press, 2013).
5 Jill K. Gill, *Embattled Ecumenism: The National Council of Churches, the Vietnam War, and the Trials of the Protestant Left* (DeKalb, IL: NIU Press, 2011).
6 R. Marie Griffith, *Moral Combat: How Sex Divided American Christians and Fractured American Politics* (New York: Basic Books, 2017).
7 Daniel K. Williams, *Defenders of the Unborn: The Pro-Life Movement before Roe v. Wade* (New York: Oxford University Press, 2016).
8 Heather Rachelle White, *Reforming Sodom: Protestants and the Rise of Gay Rights*, 1st ed. (Chapel Hill: University of North Carolina Press, 2015).
9 David A. Hollinger, *After Cloven Tongues of Fire: Protestant Liberalism in Modern American History* (Princeton, NJ: Princeton University Press, 2013), 18.
10 James David Hudnut-Beumler, ed., *The Future of Mainline Protestantism in America*, The Future of Religion in America (New York: Columbia University Press, 2018).
11 Hollinger, *After Cloven Tongues of Fire*, 45.
12 Robert Wuthnow, *The Restructuring of American Religion: Society and Faith since World War II* (Princeton, NJ: Princeton University Press, 1989).
13 Darren Dochuk, *From Bible Belt to Sunbelt: Plain-Folk Religion, Grassroots Politics, and the Rise of Evangelical Conservatism* (New York: W. W. Norton, 2011).
14 Dochuk, *From Bible Belt to Sunbelt*, xvii.

15 Kevin Michael Kruse, *One Nation Under God: How Corporate America Invented Christian America* (New York: Basic Books, 2015).

16 Matthew Avery Sutton, *American Apocalypse: A History of Modern Evangelicalism* (Cambridge, MA: Belknap Press of Harvard University Press, 2014).

17 Sutton, *American Apocalypse*, 327–331.

18 Sutton, *American Apocalypse*, 345–366.

19 Daniel K. Williams, *God's Own Party: The Making of the Christian Right* (New York: Oxford University Press, 2010), 2.

20 Williams, *God's Own Party*, 6.

21 Williams, *God's Own Party*, 2.

22 Barry Hankins, *Francis Schaeffer and The Shaping of Evangelical America*, Library of Religious Biography (Grand Rapids, MI: Eerdmans 2008).

23 Williams, *Defenders of the Unborn*.

24 Kristin Kobes du Mez, *Jesus and John Wayne: How White Evangelicals Corrupted a Faith and Fractured a Nation* (New York: Liveright, 2020).

25 Seth Dowland, *Family Values and the Rise of the Christian Right* (Philadelphia: University of Pennsylvania Press, 2015).

26 Hilde Løvdal Stephens, *Family Matters: James Dobson and Focus on the Family's Crusade for the Christian Home* (Tuscaloosa:University of Alabama Press, 2019).

27 Barry Hankins, *Uneasy in Babylon: Southern Baptist Conservatives and American Culture* (Tuscaloosa: University of Alabama Press, 2002).

28 David R. Swartz, *Moral Minority: The Evangelical Left in an Age of Conservatism* (Philadelphia: University of Pennsylvania Press, 2012); Brantley W. Gasaway, *Progressive Evangelicals and the Pursuit of Social Justice* (Chapel Hill: University of North Carolina Press, 2014).

29 Amy Collier Artman, *The Miracle Lady: Kathryn Kuhlman and the Transformation of Charismatic Christianity* (Grand Rapids, MI: Eerdmans Publishing Co., 2019).

30 John Wigger, *PTL: The Rise and Fall of Jim and Tammy Faye Bakker's Evangelical Empire* (New York: Oxford University Press, 2017).

31 Kate Bowler, *Blessed: A History of the American Prosperity Gospel* (New York: Oxford University Press, 2013).

32 R. Marie Griffith, *God's Daughters: Evangelical Women and the Power of Submission* (Berkeley: University of California Press, 1997),

33 Kate Bowler, *The Preacher's Wife: The Precarious Power of Evangelical Women Celebrities* (Princeton, NJ: Princeton University Press, 2019).

34 Paul Harvey, *Through the Storm, Through the Night: A History of African American Christianity* (Lanham, MD: Rowman & Littlefield Publishers, 2011).

35 Carolyn Renée Dupont, *Mississippi Praying: Southern White Evangelicals and the Civil Rights Movement, 1945–1975* (New York: New York University Press, 2013).

36 Harvey, *Through the Storm, Through the Night*, 123–124.
37 Stephens, *Family Matters*, 150–153.
38 Dowland, *Family Values and the Rise of the Christian Right*, 215–223.
39 Stephens, *Family Matters*, 137–139.
40 Hudnut-Beumler, *The Future of Mainline Protestantism in America*, 33–37.
41 Gastón Espinosa, *Latino Pentecostals in America: Faith and Politics in Action* (Cambridge, MA; London: Harvard University Press, 2014).

Part II

The Religious Culture of American Protestantism

5 Bible, Doctrine, and Theology

JASON E. VICKERS

American Protestantism is a complex form of Christian religion. In many towns and cities across America, it is not uncommon to see half a dozen different Protestant churches within a few blocks of one another. Sometimes American Protestant churches occupy three or even four corners of a busy intersection. For the uninitiated, this can be rather confusing. It is natural to wonder whether these churches have anything in common.

The majority of American Protestant denominations and churches exist because of theological disagreements among descendants of European Reformation churches. In European countries where Protestantism took hold, the Reformation resulted in national or state churches. For example, in England, the Reformation led to the establishment of the Church of England. This did not put an end to theological disagreement. It simply meant that those who disagreed with the official teachings or doctrines of the "established church" came to be classified as "dissenters." In some cases, the government even tolerated dissenting churches. Even so, aligning one's self with a dissenting church could have significant social, political, and economic consequences.

From the beginning, America attracted Protestant groups who had theological disagreements with the established or state-sponsored churches in their countries of origin. Members of these groups were often ambivalent about the official confessional statements of the great European Reformation churches, let alone older creedal materials associated with Roman Catholicism. In the end, many Protestant churches in America opted to retain some of these materials (including, eventually, the Westminster Catechism, the Book of Concord, and the Anglican Thirty-Nine Articles of Religion), but always with the provision that their authority ultimately depended upon their alignment with the clear teachings of the Bible. No creed or confession was to be viewed as a rival to Scripture for establishing what should be believed, taught, and confessed. Moreover, the Bible could be called upon to critique, modify, or even reject doctrines contained in creeds and confessions, regardless of how old confessional materials were or what status they enjoyed in Roman Catholic or European Protestant churches.

For the vast majority of American Protestants, then and now, the Bible alone (*sola Scriptura*) is authoritative for doctrine and theology. This does not mean that American Protestants agree on what the Bible says or how it should be interpreted. As Joseph T. Lienhard once quipped, "To say that the Bible is authoritative is to begin a discussion, not to end it."[1] With this in mind, one way to begin making sense out of American Protestantism is as a centuries-long argument about what the Bible teaches (the word "doctrine," from the Latin *doctrina*, simply means "teaching"). Indeed, it is not too much to say that a "restorationist" impulse permeates all of American Protestantism. To be sure, all American Protestant churches and denominations do not self-identify as Restorationist.[2] But the idea that, over time, doctrine and theology are prone to corruption and therefore in need of constant monitoring and correction is one that it is widely shared and deeply, if sometimes only implicitly, held. In this way, American Protestantism embodies the dictum, *Ecclesia semper reformanda est* (the church is always reforming).[3]

As already noted, *sola Scriptura* does not mean that American Protestant churches refuse to acknowledge the ancient or classical creeds of Christianity (e.g., the Apostles' Creed and the Nicene-Constantinopolitan Creed), let alone the confessional statements of their European Protestant ancestors. Many American Protestant denominations recognize and endorse such doctrinal materials. But recognition and endorsement are provisional. Should it turn out that some aspect of those materials does not align with the Bible, the doctrines contained in creeds and confessions can be revised or even discarded. When pressed, American Protestants of diverse denominational affiliations, as well as opposing social and political sensibilities, embody (even if they do not explicitly or officially embrace) the dictum, "We have no creed but the Bible." Few American Protestants would see any creed or confessional statement as a court of final appeal. Appeals to creeds and confessions matter only insofar as they can be shown to align with or derive from the Bible. This is as true of so-called liberal Protestants as it is of conservative or evangelical Protestants in America. As will be evident in what follows, the difference between liberal and evangelical Protestants is not over *whether* the Bible is authoritative, but how to read and interpret the Bible.

Because American Protestants have often been ambivalent about the teachings contained in creeds and confessions, American Protestantism has from time to time been something of a hothouse for the growth of quasi-Christian movements, including Deism, Unitarianism, panentheism, and other forms of "rational" and "natural" religion.[4] While this might sound counterintuitive at first, it is an altogether predictable development. The same can be said for the various forms of liberal and progressive Christianity that have flourished within American Protestantism. The difference between those who embrace the doctrinal content enshrined in the ancient creeds and European Protestant confessions and those who modify or reject some or even all of that content often comes down to how these different groups read and interpret the Bible.[5]

With this in mind, the remainder of this chapter will introduce readers to American Protestant views of the Bible, doctrine, and theology. Initially, it will discuss the commitment to biblical authority in American Protestantism, including the ongoing debate over how to read and interpret the Bible. Next, it will discuss the doctrines most common to American Protestant churches and denominations, including doctrines about God, creation, human nature and sin, the atoning work of Christ on the cross, the work of the Holy Spirit, salvation, the church and sacraments, and the future of the world. In each case, the chapter will identify the most basic affirmations or teachings across official doctrinal statements of American Protestant churches and denominations.[6] It will also identify areas of development, paying special attention to the ways in which the Bible is often the source of disagreement and debate.

Official American Protestant doctrinal statements tend to be brief or modest in what they affirm, remaining silent on many directly and indirectly related matters. For example, many American Protestant churches and denominations affirm that God created the world. Some go so far as to say that God created the world *ex nihilo* (out of nothing), contrasting God's eternal and independent nature with the temporal and dependent nature of creation. But most remain silent with respect to *when* God created the world or whether God is continually creating the world. The latter issues, which often remain unaddressed at the level of official doctrine, tend to be the ones hotly debated by American Protestants today. In this and other areas of doctrine and theology, American Protestants can vigorously disagree with one another while embracing the doctrinal statements of their respective churches and denominations. In other words, official doctrine does not preclude theological disagreement any more than the Bible does; if anything, it generates it.

BIBLICAL AUTHORITY

Nothing is more emblematic of the way in which a widely held belief in American Protestantism can become the basis of intense argument and disagreement than the belief that the Bible is the Word of God or that the Bible is authoritative. On the one hand, virtually all American Protestant churches and denominations claim to have a "high view" of Scripture, though what precisely is meant by that phrase can vary.[7] Minimally, a "high view" of Scripture involves a belief that the Bible contains special divine revelation not available through other means, most notably knowledge of the identity, nature, and purposes of God. By extension, most American Protestants believe that the Bible is therefore the primary source or basis for doctrine and theology, as well as for Christian spirituality and ethics.

On the other hand, while the official doctrinal statements of most American Protestant churches and denominations affirm that the Bible contains special divine revelation and is therefore authoritative for doctrine, theology, and the Christian life, there is deep disagreement across the theological landscape as to how these affirmations should be understood. For starters, there are long-standing disagreements about *where* divine revelation takes place in connection with the Bible. Classically speaking, conservative or evangelical American Protestants locate divine revelation in the words of Scripture themselves. In one way or another, God communicated the words of Scripture to the biblical authors, ensuring the truth and reliability of the propositional contents of the Bible. Even here, a range of views exist, including word-for-word or direct dictation to a more general form of inspiration. By contrast, liberal Protestants in America tend to locate divine revelation in the religious experiences of the biblical authors and their respective religious communities.[8]

The foregoing description barely scratches the surface of the debate, though.[9] For example, there are additional debates about the nature of language in connection with the Bible. Some insist that the Bible's language is straightforward and primarily descriptive of historical events. Others acknowledge that the Bible contains different kinds of language, ranging from simple descriptive language, the aim of which is clearly to depict events or states of affairs in the world, to poetic and imaginative language, to performative language such as the language of worship, prayer, and petition contained in the book of Psalms.

Perhaps the most intense debate among American Protestants has to do with the scope and purpose of the Bible's revelatory content. A good way to see what is at stake here is to notice the different ways that American Protestants use the word "inerrant" to describe the Bible.[10] For some, the Bible is completely or totally inerrant without qualification. Others claim that the Bible is inerrant in all that it affirms, leaving room for believers to hold beliefs about all sorts of things that the Bible does not speak about. Yet another option is the view that the Bible is inerrant in all things pertaining to salvation, or what is sometimes known as soteriological inerrancy. Embedded in this view is a belief or claim that the purpose of the Bible is to help human beings know God and ultimately to attain salvation. More comprehensive or expansive views of the Bible's inerrancy often coincide with the notion that, in addition to saving knowledge, the Bible contains historical, moral, and even scientific knowledge. These differing views of the scope and purpose of divine revelation in Scripture are often the source of some of the deepest disagreements among American Protestants – including disagreements over the age of Earth, evolution, and a host of moral issues such as slavery, violence and war, polygamy, and homosexuality.

Finally, as already mentioned, American Protestants also hold a range of views concerning the relationship between the Bible and Christian doctrine and theology, including the doctrines contained in the classical Christian creeds, as well as the doctrines affirmed in Protestant confessions of faith and other doctrinal statements. At one end of the spectrum, some hold that doctrines found anywhere other than Scripture are historical curiosities at best. They have no authority for theology or the Christian life. This view is summed up in the popular expression "No creed but the Bible" and tends to flourish among "restorationist" traditions, which is to say, American Protestant churches and denominations that prioritize the apostolic period of church history (the time when the original apostles and biblical authors were still alive). At the opposite end of the spectrum are churches and denominations that recognize the authority of the classical creeds, most notable the Apostles' Creed and the Nicene Creed, as well as other confessional materials such as the Westminster Catechism or the Anglican (and, later, Methodist) Articles of Religion. Among those who regard creeds and other doctrinal statements as authoritative, there are differing views concerning the relationship between those materials and the Bible. Most imagine the relationship to be one of clear derivation, insisting that the

doctrines contained in the classical creeds and other confessional materials have obvious biblical roots. At times, this clear derivation view has
led some to question or challenge specific doctrines, most notably the
doctrine of the Trinity as expressed in the Nicene Creed, on the grounds
that the terminology or vocabulary central to the Creed is not itself
biblical. In response to this objection, other American Protestant theologians have suggested that the doctrines contained in the classical creeds,
especially the doctrine of the Trinity, express the logic or "grammar" of
Scripture and are therefore consistent with the Bible, even if they use
non-biblical terminology.[11]

GOD: THE HOLY TRINITY AND THE DIVINE ATTRIBUTES

While a few American Protestant groups reject Trinitarian formulas in
the name of *sola Scriptura*, the majority of American Protestants identify
and worship God the Father, Son, and Holy Spirit, which is to say, the
divine and blessed Trinity. The vast majority of official American
Protestant doctrinal statements and related confessional and catechetical materials explicitly affirm the doctrine of the Trinity. In addition,
American Protestant hymnody and liturgical practices, most notably
baptismal initiation rites, affirm God's triune nature and identity.
Nearly all denominations and churches in American Protestantism baptize people in the name of God the Father, Son, and Holy Spirit.

In addition to identifying and worshipping God as the blessed and
Holy Trinity, most American Protestants view God's nature in terms of
the qualities designated by the so-called classical divine attributes –
including omniscience, omnipotence, goodness, simplicity, timeless-
ness, immutability, and impassibility – and affirm them in official doctrinal and catechetical materials. They are also routinely affirmed in
American Protestant worship, with countless hymns and songs celebrating God's goodness, and praising God as eternal, unchanging, all-
knowing, and the like.

Yet tensions or challenges have surfaced from time to time. In recent
years, for instance, many American Protestant feminist and womanist
theologians have challenged the doctrine of the Trinity on the grounds
that it deifies maleness and thereby contributes to patriarchy and gender
discrimination in society.[12] Other American Protestant theologians
have challenged or even rejected some classical divine attributes, most
notably immutability and impassibility. Process theologians and open
theists have argued that classical theism – which is to say, the view of
God associated with the classical attributes – is based on an outdated and

ultimately non-biblical metaphysics.[13] From an entirely different direction, theologians influenced by Karl Barth, the twentieth-century Swiss Reformed theologian, have questioned whether the classical attributes ultimately identify a different God than the Triune God revealed in the Bible. Perhaps the best example of this can be seen in the work of Robert Jenson, an American Lutheran theologian, who is known for his insistence that God's identity should be understood strictly in terms of the saving events narrated in Scripture, namely, the deliverance of Israel and the resurrection of Jesus from the dead.[14] More recently, Katherine Sonderegger, an American Episcopal theologian, has argued that, contrary to the idea that they derive primarily from Greek philosophy, the classical attributes of deity have strong biblical credentials.[15]

Finally, with respect to the doctrine of God, different American Protestant traditions emphasize some divine attributes more than others. For example, Reformed or Calvinist churches and denominations tend to put special emphasis on divine sovereignty.[16] By contrast, Wesleyan and Methodist churches and denominations tend to emphasize divine grace and love, while many Pentecostal and Charismatic churches stress God's healing power.[17] Historically speaking, arguments between members of these and other traditions concerning the doctrine of God often turn on whether a particular view does justice to all that the Bible says about God. For example, while Wesleyans do not deny the sovereignty of God, they are prone to maintain that, in order to be fully biblical, the Reformed emphasis on sovereignty needs to be balanced by an emphasis on divine grace and love.

CREATION, HUMAN NATURE, AND SIN

For at least a century, and especially since the famous Scopes trial in 1925, the doctrine of creation has been a flashpoint for theological controversy in American Protestantism.[18] In many ways, the controversy is as much about how one reads and understands the Bible as it is about the doctrine of creation itself. On the one hand, many theological conservatives insist that the creation story in the Book of Genesis is to be understood in a literal way as a description of events that took place in history. Adam and Eve are to be understood as real individual human beings, and the six days of creation are to be understood as six 24-hour days. Animating the concern for a literal interpretation of Genesis in some conservative quarters is a fierce opposition to popular scientific accounts of creation, most notably the theory of evolution and the Big Bang.[19]

On the other hand, classical liberal Protestants and contemporary theological progressives tend to read the creation account as an imaginative or symbolic story that makes important theological claims about God's relationship to creation and God's purposes or intentions for human beings and other creatures. American Protestants on this end of the theological spectrum are indifferent toward or even opposed to the notion that Adam and Eve should be taken as literal, historical people. Similarly, they tend to oppose the notion that God created the world in six 24-hour days, preferring an account of creation in which God's creative activity is ongoing or continual.

An equally, if not more, significant theological disagreement related to creation in American Protestantism has to do with the aforementioned doctrine of creation *ex nihilo*. According to this doctrine, God created and/ or creates the world "out of nothing." The point or purpose of the doctrine ultimately has to do with the contingent and dependent character of creation. Unlike God, creation does not exist independently and eternally. Within American Protestantism, one can discern three views of God's relationship to creation. First, there is the classical view in which God creates the world out of nothing and then sustains the world in its being. Jonathan Edwards, arguably American Protestantism's greatest theologian, famously taught that God thinks the world "out of nothing in every moment."[20] A second view, frequently associated with Deism, holds that God created the world out of nothing, endowed it with natural laws that govern it from day to day, and then left the world to run according to said laws. On this view, God is not actively involved in sustaining and guiding creation. Once created, the world is self-sufficient. Third, some American Protestants reject the doctrine of creation *ex nihilo* in favor of what is sometimes called *panentheism*. On this view, God and creation should not be thought of apart from one another. In some sense, the world, like God, is eternal.

Despite these disagreements, most American Protestants affirm the revelatory significance of creation or what is sometimes called natural revelation. The basic idea is that creation mirrors or reflects the divine attributes and therefore occasions the praise and glory of God. American Calvinist or Reformed theologians like Jonathan Edwards have been especially prone to view creation, in John Calvin's apt expression, as the "dazzling theater" of God's glory.[21] And no part of creation reflects the divine attributes more than human beings. Unlike inert objects or "lower animals," human beings have extraordinary capacities, including the capacity to think, to assign value, to create, to act, and above all to love. In these and many other ways, human beings mirror or reflect their creator. This is what American Protestants mean when they say that human beings are made in the image of God (*imago Dei*). At the same time, depending on whether one affirms the doctrine of creation *ex nihilo* and all that it signifies, there are also at least two crucial ways in which human beings are unlike God: in their contingency and in their freedom in relation to goodness and love.

American Protestants also affirm the fundamental goodness of creation. In its very existence, creation bears witness to the sheer goodness and love of God. Rightly understood, God neither depends on nor otherwise needs creation. Thus, whatever exists does so as a matter of divine gratuity and generosity. On a more pedestrian level, creation is good in the sense that it consists of all that human beings need to survive and flourish, including bare sustenance and extraordinary beauty. In turn, human beings are charged by God to steward creation. They are to receive and care for creation as a gift of inestimable worth and value, both as a means of physical and spiritual sustenance in itself, and as a means by which human beings can discern God's nature, experience the presence of God, and glorify God.

Finally, American Protestants affirm the vulnerability and volatility of creation. Unlike God, human beings are free in their relationship to goodness and love, which includes the intrinsic and instrumental goodness of creation. In short, they are free to acknowledge and steward creation as a gift from God that occasions both trust in the goodness of God and the glorification of God as the giver of all life, but they are also free to relate to creation in ways that are destructive of both creation and themselves. And while there is some debate about whether and how Adam and Eve's fall into sin depicted in the book of Genesis extends to all human beings, in the end, American Protestants believe and teach that all human beings exercise their freedom in destructive ways. The debate and disagreement here are an obvious extension of the debate and disagreement over how to read the Bible and especially the book of Genesis. American Protestants who read the creation account in Genesis in a historical or literal way tend to believe that Adam and Eve's sin is somehow transmitted to their offspring and ultimately, through them, to all human beings. On this account, sin is like a genetic feature passed along from the first humans to all subsequent human beings. By contrast, those who read Genesis in a more symbolic way will tend to see Adam and Eve as a story about what happens to every human being. Both camps affirm the universality of human sinfulness.[22] Rather than trusting in God's goodness and love (witnessed to by the very existence of creation), all human beings relate to creation as a commodity to be consumed, possessed, and hoarded, and to each another as rivals for creation's resources. Across space and time, human history becomes a relentless and often violent competition for control and ownership of the Earth, including control and ownership of human beings through slavery. The destruction and violence are the moral consequences of humanity's collective failure to trust God. But the situation is even worse than that. Sin also has epistemic consequences. Indeed, the worst part about the human predicament is that human beings do not realize that there is a problem. In traditional theological terms, they are totally depraved. Apart from God's help, they simply cannot think rightly about God, creation, or even themselves. They cannot conceive of creation as a gift to be freely and joyously received from God and freely and joyously shared with one another.

THE GOSPEL OF JESUS CHRIST: SALVATION FROM SIN AND THE RENEWAL OF ALL THINGS

Nothing is more central to American Protestant theology than the concept of the gospel. As commonly used, the term "gospel" simply means "good news." This raises the question: what is the good news? In the New Testament, the Apostle Paul puts it this way: "But God proves his love for us in that, while we were still sinners, Christ died for us" (Romans 5:8, NRSV).

Just as creation is the free gift of God, so too is salvation. In both cases, human beings are not in a position to make demands of God. They do not have a right to salvation any more than they have a right to creation. They can only receive it as a gift. Similarly, they cannot earn or deserve salvation any more than they can earn or deserve creation. It is, strictly speaking, a matter of divine mercy and love. It is something that God does "while we were still sinners." On this point, American Protestants speak with a unified voice.

In addition to being a matter of sheer gratuity or divine grace, American Protestants also affirm that salvation is something that God accomplishes for human beings through the suffering and death of Jesus Christ. If no concept is more central to American Protestantism than the gospel, then no symbol is more central than the cross. God does not save human beings by waving a magic wand or by simple proclamation. Rather, God saves human beings through Jesus' death on the cross. To see the significance of this, it is imperative to recall that, for American Protestants, Jesus of Nazareth is not simply a human being who died a gruesome and violent death. He is the eternally begotten Son of God. He is God incarnate in human flesh. And this means that the salvation of human beings is costly to God. The one who dies to save human beings from their sins is fully human, but he is also fully divine.

While American Protestants are unified in their emphasis on the gospel and the saving significance of Jesus' death on the cross, there are at least four vigorous and long-standing debates around these emphases. First, there is a debate about the scope of the salvation accomplished through the suffering and death of Jesus Christ. Some in the Reformed or Calvinist tradition maintain that Christ's saving work on the cross applies only to a group of people known as "the elect," which is to say, those human beings who are eternally predestined by God for salvation. All remaining human beings are predestined to eternal damnation. At first glance, this may seem harsh or unfair. However, it is also consistent with other doctrines held by Reformed Christians, most notably the universality of sin and the mercy and justice of God. On the one hand, the universality of sin means that no one deserves to be saved. If God gave human beings what they deserved, then all people would be eternally damned. On the other hand, the fact that some people are elect to salvation reflects the mercy of God, whereas the justice of God is reflected in the election of some people to damnation. Others, especially those in Wesleyan and Arminian traditions, insist that Christ's atoning sacrifice on the cross is for all people, a doctrine known as the unlimited atonement. Wesleyan and Arminian groups go on to insist that all people *can* therefore be saved, but they stop short of universalism, a doctrine that holds that all people *will* be saved. In recent years, a few prominent American Protestant pastors and theologians have made controversial remarks in favor of universalism.[23] However, no major American Protestant denominations give official support to the doctrine.

Second, American Protestants sometimes differ with one another over the manner in which Christ's suffering and death procures salvation. It is one thing to say *that* it does so; it is another thing to say *how* it does so. To take up the question of how, precisely, Christ's suffering and death on the cross is of saving significance is to venture into the territory of the doctrine of the atonement. Suffice it to say, American Protestants hold a range of views here: Christ as a satisfaction offering for human sin, as a substitute who accepts the punishment that humans deserve for their sin, as making a ransom payment that frees human beings from captivity to the Devil, as a new Adam, and as a moral example to be emulated.[24] All of these ways of understanding how Christ's suffering and death brings about salvation can be seen in American Protestant theology and hymnody. It is common, for example, to hear American Protestants singing praises and expressing their gratitude to Christ for paying their debts or taking their place on the cross. At the same time, it is important to note that most official doctrinal or confessional statements stop short of endorsing any particular view of the atonement.

Third, in recent decades, many American Protestant theologians have been raising questions about whether salvation should be thought of exclusively in connection with Christ's suffering and death on the cross. These theologians are not denying the importance of the cross. Rather, they are asking whether the incarnation and resurrection of Christ are also of saving significance, and whether the total work of Christ (and not just his suffering and death) gestures toward an even grander and more comprehensive vision of redemption. The main idea here is that the incarnation and bodily resurrection of Jesus suggest that God's redemptive work encompasses the whole of creation, and not just human beings or human souls.[25]

Fourth, American Protestants often disagree over whether God's salvation is available in other world religions. Sometimes, this debate takes the form of the question: Are devout adherents of other religions "anonymous Christians?" The deep theological issue here is whether the same God who saves human beings through Christ's suffering and death on the cross is somehow at work, say, in Buddhism or Islam. More specifically, theologians ask: Is the suffering and dying Christ somehow present, though unrecognized, in other religions. On balance, the majority of American Protestant churches and denominations across time have tended to reject this notion. However, there has always been a minority group more open to the idea that God might somehow be present and at work in other religions in ways that are of saving significance.

It should be noted that each of these four areas of disagreement and debate occurs within American Protestantism because of differences over how to read and interpret the Bible. For example, all of the major views of the atonement mentioned above find support in Scripture. Similarly, Calvinists and Wesleyans both point to Scripture in their ongoing debate over the scope of the atonement. Lienhard's aphorism bears repeating: appealing to the authority of the Bible is a good way to begin a debate, not to end it.

Finally, whatever else American Protestants believe about salvation, their emphasis on the Gospel and the cross of Christ reflects a deep conviction that salvation is primarily God's work. It is something that God does. But is it exclusively a matter of divine action, or do human beings have a role to play in their salvation and perhaps even in the redemption of creation itself?

PARTICIPATING IN GOD'S SALVATION: SPIRIT, CHURCH
AND SACRAMENTS, AND THE FUTURE OF THE WORLD

For American Protestants who embrace either the doctrine of eternal
double predestination or the doctrine of universalism, the question of
whether human beings have a role to play in their salvation would seem
to lack significant purchase. In the first case, insofar as salvation has to
do with any particular human being's ultimate destiny, it is strictly
a matter of eternal divine decree. There is absolutely nothing that
anyone can do to change his or her eternal destiny. Similarly, those
who embrace universalism would seem to have little motivation for
thinking about whether human beings must do something in order to be
saved. All people will ultimately be saved, regardless of how they live.
By contrast, American Protestants who reject eternal double predestination and universalism are often preoccupied with the question of what
human beings must do to be saved. Furthermore, many of them can be
equally concerned with the question of whether there is anything that
human beings can do to lose or forfeit their salvation.

With respect to whether human beings must do something in order
to be saved, the most common answer is that salvation is by faith alone.
Good works do not procure salvation. Human beings cannot earn their
salvation by doing good things, helping other people, advocating for
social justice, and so on. Having said this, when American Protestants
affirm that salvation is by faith alone, they do not mean believing in
things for which there is no evidence. Faith, rightly understood, means
putting one's trust in Jesus' suffering and death on the cross. But it is
precisely here that a question arises. Can human beings do even this?
Are they capable of trusting Jesus for their salvation, especially if trust
is an act of the free will? The most common answer is no, they cannot,
at least not without the help of the Holy Spirit. The epistemic consequences of sin, as mentioned previously, prevent human beings from
discerning the truth about Jesus' identity and the significance of his
saving work. If people cannot discern who Jesus really is, then they
cannot make a meaningful decision as to whether to trust Jesus for their
salvation.

For many American Protestants, especially those in Wesleyan and
Arminian traditions, this is where the work of the Holy Spirit comes into
play. First and foremost, the Spirit illumines human minds concerning
the identity of Jesus Christ and their need for his saving work. This
aspect of the Spirit's work is often called awakening. So illumined or
awakened, human beings are still not in a position to put their trust in

Jesus. The reason for this is simple. If it were enough simply to know the truth about God, then human beings would never have sinned in the first place. Thus, after awakening people to the truth, the Holy Spirit must work within their minds and hearts, enabling them to put their trust in Jesus. In other words, faith, rightly conceived, is not an act of the unaided human will. Rather, it is itself a divine gift. By themselves, human beings are unable to put their trust in Jesus. They are utterly dependent on the help of the Holy Spirit.

This gives rise to an additional question: Can human beings resist or reject the work of the Holy Spirit in bringing them to faith? And it is at precisely this point that debate among American Protestants can become quite heated. For many, especially Calvinists, divine grace is irresistible. Sooner or later, those whom God has elected to salvation will respond to the work of the Holy Spirit. For others, it is possible to resist and even reject divine grace, including the gift of faith. To summarize, while all are agreed that salvation comes through faith alone, there is considerable disagreement concerning whether human beings, having been made aware of the truth about the person and work of Christ, can refuse to put their trust in him.

A second area of emphasis and debate where the work of the Holy Spirit is concerned has to do with what salvation by faith involves or entails. For some, salvation by faith is primarily a matter of one's legal standing before God. In other words, it involves a change in status that ultimately plays out in the afterlife. Those who, with the Spirit's help, put their trust in Jesus will be with God in eternity. They are justified or made righteous in the eyes of God. By contrast, those who reject the Spirit's work will suffer eternal damnation.

For others, especially Wesleyans and Pentecostals, putting one's trust in Jesus and thereby being justified is only the beginning of salvation; indeed, the Holy Spirit is just getting started. Having enabled people to see the truth about Jesus and their dependence upon him for salvation, the Holy Spirit begins to renew people from within, enabling them to love God and neighbor, to keep God's commandments, and so on. These aspects of salvation are known as regeneration and sanctification. Over time, the Holy Spirit transforms people intellectually, spiritually, and morally, so that, far from simply believing in or trusting in Jesus, they also obey him and resemble him in all that they think, say, and do. In short, the Holy Spirit works to make believers Christlike.

At this stage, it is natural to ask – where and how does the Holy Spirit do these things? Two answers are prominent in American

Protestantism. On the one hand, the Pietist impulse in American Protestantism manifests itself in the emphasis on the human heart. Those influenced by Pietism insist that, from awakening all the way through to sanctification, salvation is primarily a matter of the Holy Spirit's work within. In short, the human heart is the primary location of the Spirit's work.[26]

On the other hand, some American Protestants envision the work of the Holy Spirit in close connection with the church and sacraments or, more broadly, the means of grace. On this account, the Holy Spirit works to transform human lives in and through the sacramental life of the church, which is to say, through preaching, baptism and the Lord's Supper (or Holy Communion), immersion in Holy Scripture, and other practices like corporate worship, prayer, and fasting. In other words, the work of the Holy Spirit within human minds and hearts does not happen in a vacuum, and it is not exclusively internal; it is mediated through creaturely means.[27]

Yet another area of debate has to do with the point or purpose of the Spirit's transforming work. Regardless of the degree of emphasis on active participation in the sacramental life of the church as the means by which the Spirit transforms human lives, a lingering question remains: to what end? Historically speaking, many American Protestants have viewed the primary purpose or goal of the Spirit's sanctifying work as preparing people for heaven, which is to say, for a strictly future reality that human beings will enter after they die.[28] Many others have related the work of the Spirit in the church and in the lives of believers to the Kingdom of God, a matter about which there has been strong debate across the centuries. For example, some American Protestants have insisted that the Kingdom of God will take place on Earth at the second coming of Jesus Christ. Among people who hold this view, some maintain that Christians should be preparing the world morally and politically for Christ's second coming. In fact, some go so far as to teach that Christ will not come until the world is adequately prepared, an idea which has served as motivation for Christian social and political activism.[29] Still others believe that Christ's second coming will ultimately culminate with the destruction of the world as we know it, a view that can significantly undermine any motivation to work for the social, moral, and political transformation of human society. In extreme cases, the latter view has even contributed to the formation of cults which have withdrawn from society in the name of maintaining purity while awaiting a cataclysmic "end times" event.[30]

Today, American Protestant views of the world's future and the relationship of Christians to it are undergoing significant changes. These changes are due in part to a sidelining of the doctrine of Christ's second coming. The imminent return of Christ is simply not at the forefront of American Protestant theology and preaching the way that it has been in the past. On a more positive note, the heightened focus on the doctrines of the incarnation and the bodily resurrection of Christ described above has led many American Protestant theologians to think about salvation in more dynamic and embodied ways. And because it is difficult to imagine human embodiment, either now or in the future, apart from a material or physical world in which human bodies make sense – a world that can be touched with human hands, walked upon with human feet, and savored with human mouths – there is a growing emphasis within some quarters of American Protestantism on the need for Christians to be stewards of creation.[31] As with other doctrines, the extent to which American Protestants will heed the call to practice "creation care" or to embrace an environmental ethic will turn largely on the ability of theologians and preachers to make a convincing case from Scripture for their views.[32]

CONCLUSION

The one thing that unites American Protestant churches and denominations is the insistence that the Bible is the ultimate authority for matters pertaining to doctrine, theology, and the Christian life. But how American Protestants read and interpret the Bible has varied widely across space and time, leading to deep disagreements over the identity and nature of God, God's relationship to creation, the manner and meaning of salvation, and the future of the world. American Protestants are united in their belief in the authority of the Bible, but that belief has not led to doctrinal and theological unity.

From one vantage point, the lack of doctrinal and theological unity among American Protestants might be a cause for skepticism concerning the intelligibility and cohesiveness of the Bible. Then again, theological and doctrinal differences can also be seen as reflecting the sheer fecundity of the Christian Scriptures. Far from a monolithic and monotone book, the Bible was written, edited, and compiled over many centuries. It represents multiple perspectives on a fundamentally mysterious subject matter. Indeed, one way to think about the Bible is to envision it as containing a robust and vigorous theological conversation about God's nature and purposes for human beings and for creation.

After all, there are two accounts of creation, two accounts of God's deliverance of Israel from captivity, and four accounts of Jesus' life and ministry.[33] Moreover, there are different kinds of literature, ranging from history to poetry, letters, gospels, and apocalyptic material. Given such diversity of time, perspective, and genre, it should hardly come as a surprise that the Bible has yielded significant doctrinal and theological debate in American Protestantism.

On this latter way of thinking about Scripture, it is conceivable that opposing sides in American Protestant theological disagreements each have biblical support for their views. And this raises an important question, namely, is there a limit to the range of views that can be attributed to the Bible on any given doctrinal or theological topic? For example, what, if anything, prevents American Protestants from reading Scripture in an anti-Trinitarian way? Or to put the matter positively, what, if anything, requires American Protestants to read and interpret Scripture in a Trinitarian way? In both Roman Catholicism and Eastern Orthodoxy, Scripture is read and interpreted in the light of the ancient or classical creeds, most notably the Nicene Creed. The creeds and ecumenical councils function as guardrails that set limits to what can be believed, taught, and confessed about God, the person of Jesus, and the like. By contrast, among American Protestant groups, there are no widely agreed upon guardrails for reading and interpreting the Bible. To be sure, American Protestant churches and denominations have official doctrinal or confessional materials, but as noted above, these materials are always to be read in the light of Scripture and not the other way around. In principle, they are always subject to revision or even rejection.

Finally, in addition to the classical creeds, Roman Catholics have a living source of authority in the form of the Magisterium. This is especially crucial when one recognizes that, just as there can be debates over the meaning of Scripture, there can also be debates over how to interpret and appropriate the classical creeds and other doctrinal materials. In stark contrast, American Protestant churches and denominations do not recognize a common living authority for settling doctrinal, theological, and political disputes amongst themselves. Rather, each church or denomination has its own mechanisms for dealing with internal disagreements, an arrangement which more or less ensures that doctrinal disunity will be a hallmark of American Protestantism for the foreseeable future. The only question that remains is whether persistent dissent and disagreement is salutary for the knowledge of God.

NOTES

1 Joseph T. Lienhard, *The Bible, the Church, and Authority* (Collegeville, MN: Liturgical Press, 1995), 78, as quoted by Douglas M. Koskela, "The Authority of Scripture in Its Ecclesial Context," in *Canonical Theism: A Proposal for Theology & the Church*, ed. William J. Abraham, Natalie B. Van Kirk, and Jason E. Vickers (Grand Rapids, MI: Eerdmans, 2008), 210.

2 See Chapter 22 by Mark E. Powell, this volume.

3 For a recent example of this impulse in American Protestant theology, see *Always Reforming: Explorations in Systematic Theology*, ed. A. T. B. McGowan (Downers Grove, IL: IVP, 2007); also see Roger E. Olson, *Reformed and Always Reforming: The Postconservative Approach to Evangelical Theology* (Grand Rapids, MI: Baker Academic, 2007).

4 See especially E. Brooks Holifield, *Theology in America: Christian Thought from the Age of the Puritans to the Civil War* (New Haven, CT: Yale University Press, 2003).

5 For liberal and progressive forms of American Protestant theology, see Gary Dorrien, *The Making of American Liberal Theology*, 3 vols. (Louisville, KY: Westminster John Knox Press, 2001–2006).

6 Examples of these confessional statements include the United Methodist Church's *Articles of Religion* and *Confession of Faith*, and the Evangelical Lutheran Church of America's Book of Concord (which includes both the *Augsburg Confession* and Martin Luther's *Shorter Catechism*). For readers interested in what specific American Protestant churches and denominations teach about any particular doctrine, official doctrinal statements are in most cases a quick internet search away; also, see *Creeds and Confessions of Faith in the Christian Tradition*, ed. Jaroslav Pelikan and Valerie Hotchkiss, 4 vols. (New Haven, CT: Yale University Press, 2003).

7 Craig D. Allert, *A High View of Scripture? The Authority of the Bible and the Formation of the New Testament Canon* (Grand Rapids, MI: Baker Academic, 2007).

8 See George Lindbeck, *The Nature of Doctrine: Religion and Theology in a Postliberal Age*, 25th anniversary edition (Louisville, KY: Westminster John Knox Press, 2009).

9 For a range of views, see David Kelsey, *The Use of Scripture in Recent Theology* (London: SCM Press, 1976).

10 See *Five Views on Biblical Inerrancy*, ed. J. Merrick and Stephen M. Garrett (Grand Rapids, MI: Zondervan, 2013).

11 David Yeago, "The New Testament and the Nicene Dogma: A Contribution to the Recovery of Theological Exegesis," *Pro Ecclesia* vol. 3, no. 2 (May, 1994), 152–164.

12 Marjorie Procter-Smith, *In Her Own Rite: Constructing Feminist Liturgical Tradition* (Ashland City, TN: OSL Publications, 2013).

13 Bruce G. Epperly, *Process Theology: A Guide for the Perplexed* (London: T&T Clark, 2011). See also Gregory A. Boyd, *God of the Possible: A Biblical Introduction to the Open View of God* (Grand Rapids, MI: Baker Academic, 2000).

14 Robert W. Jenson, *Systematic Theology*, 2 vols. (Oxford: Oxford University Press, 2001). For an introduction to Jenson's work, see Chris E. W. Green, *The End Is Music: A Companion to Robert Jenson's Theology* (Eugene, OR: Cascade Books, 2018).

15 Katherine Sonderegger, *Systematic Theology: The Doctrine of God* (Minneapolis: Fortress Press, 2015).

16 For more on the Reformed tradition, see Chapter 18 by Edwin Woodruff Tait, this volume.

17 For more on Wesleyan and Pentecostal traditions, see Chapter 23 by Douglas M. Strong and Chapter 24 by Chris E. W. Green, this volume.

18 For more on this, see Chapter 3 by Andrea L. Turpin, this volume.

19 See *Three Views on Christianity and Science*, ed. Paul Copan and Christopher L. Reese (Grand Rapids, MI: Zondervan, 2021).

20 *The Works of Jonathan Edwards*, ed. Wallace Anderson (New Haven, CT: Yale University Press, 1980), vol. VI, 241.

21 John Calvin, *Institutes of the Christian Religion*, ed. John T. McNeill (Louisville, KY: Westminster John Knox Press, 1960), 1.5.8.

22 See Thomas H. McCall, *Against God and Nature: The Doctrine of Sin* (New York: Crossway, 2019).

23 Rob Bell, *Love Wins: A Book about Heaven, Hell, and the Fate of Every Person Who Ever Lived* (New York: HarperOne, 2012); also William H. Willimon, *Who Will Be Saved?* (Nashville: Abingdon Press, 2004).

24 For different views of the doctrine of the atonement, see Joshua M. McNall, *The Mosaic of Atonement: An Integrated Approach to Christ's Work* (Grand Rapids, MI: Zondervan, 2019).

25 Beth Felker Jones, *Marks of His Wounds: Gender Politics and Bodily Resurrection* (New York: Oxford University Press, 2007).

26 See Roger E. Olson and Christian T. Collins Winn, *Reclaiming Pietism: Retrieving an Evangelical Tradition* (Grand Rapids, MI: Eerdmans, 2015).

27 See Chris E. W. Green, *Toward a Pentecostal Theology of the Lord's Supper*: Cleveland, TN: CPT Press, 2012; Jason E. Vickers, "Holiness and Mediation: Pneumatology in Pietist Perspective, *International Journal of Systematic Theology* vol. 16, no. 2 (April 2014), 192–206.

28 For more on heaven and hell, see Jerry L. Walls, *Heaven, Hell, and Purgatory: Rethinking the Things That Matter Most* (Grand Rapids, MI: Brazos Press, 2015).

29 See Douglas M. Strong, *Perfectionist Politics: Abolitionism and the Religious Tensions of American Democracy* (Syracuse, NY: Syracuse University Press, 2002).

30 For example, see David Chidester, *Salvation and Suicide: An Interpretation of Jim Jones, the Peoples Temple, and Jonestown*, rev. ed. (Bloomington: Indiana University Press, 2003).

31 See Norman Wirzba, *From Nature to Creation: A Christian Vision for Understanding and Loving Our World* (Grand Rapids, MI: Baker Academic, 2015).

32 See Ellen Davis, *Scripture, Culture, and Agriculture: An Agrarian Reading of the Bible* (Cambridge: Cambridge University Press, 2008).

33 For more on this, see Thomas B. Dozeman, *Holiness and Ministry: A Biblical Theology of Ordination* (Oxford: Oxford University Press, 2008), ch. 1.

6　Worship and Preaching

JONATHAN A. POWERS

INTRODUCTION

Ever since the first Pilgrims set foot in the New World, religion in America has been characterized by diversity of belief and practice. America is not unique in this sense. Protestants have never reached consensus regarding essentials of the Christian faith, nor have they agreed on what is necessary for proper worship of God. No singular doctrine or liturgical rubric defines Protestantism. It is not a monolithic entity but rather a pluralistic phenomenon, continually changing, adapting, and evolving. Consequentially, each movement within Protestantism is unique with its own distinct convictions and customs.

It is precisely the varied nature of Protestantism that makes it a difficult subject to examine. Any study of the phenomenon risks reductionist treatment. Nonetheless, there is much to be gained from careful inspection of particularities found within Protestantism since oftentimes the particularities are indicative of larger realities. The treatment of American Protestant worship presented here is thus narrow, incomplete, and by no means exhaustive. Many important liturgical movements and developments have been omitted in favor of concentrating on one particular segment of American Protestantism, namely evangelical revivalism. There are four primary reasons for this limited focus: (1) Evangelical revivalism was the first purely American worship tradition; (2) Evangelicalism has been the single largest Protestant movement in America since the 1700s; (3) Liturgical practices that developed during the early American evangelical revival period have affected the worship piety of nearly every American Protestant tradition and movement since; (4) The revivalist worship piety of evangelicalism has by and large remained consistent and prevalent in American Protestantism to the current day.

Given the prominence of the evangelical worship tradition and its impact on American Protestantism, a general overview of the movement is helpful to distinguish specific characteristics of American Christianity. The following material thus provides a broad survey of the worship customs and mindsets that developed in America over the past 300 years through the agency of the evangelical revival movement. Likewise, it identifies significant factors that influenced American evangelical worship practice and piety.

THE INFLUENCE OF MODERNITY

The religious landscape of the early 1700s was fashioned by a number of significant cultural and philosophical antecedents. In particular, American Protestantism developed during the era of the Enlightenment, a period also referred to as the Age of Reason or the Modern Era. Central to the Enlightenment was the rise of a new rationalism in philosophy and science where human cognition reigned supreme. The movement challenged all forms of authority and elevated individual judgment in favor of the personal pursuit of knowledge and virtue. Modern thinkers believed they possessed new knowledge that gave them a privileged position to judge the errors of the past and allowed them to advance into an improved, more excellent future. These thinkers questioned previously presumed ideologies regarding philosophy, religion, politics, science, technology, and social structures. As a result, many traditional, long-held beliefs were dismissed as primitive and outdated. The natural world was privileged in place of the supernatural, progress in place of tradition, and the secular in place of the sacred.

The church did not escape this philosophical shift. Many in the church felt under attack by the rationalistic approach of modernity while others sought to utilize reason to a greater degree in relation to the faith. Various Christian traditions reacted differently to Enlightenment sensibilities, which effected practices in worship. For example, in 1793 the philosopher Immanuel Kant published *Religion within the Limits of Reason Alone* where he stated there are three kinds of "illusory" faith: the faith in miracles; the faith in mysteries; the faith in the means of grace.[1] Within this writing Kant specifically addressed sacramental practice, claiming that the sacraments of baptism and communion have no real efficacy and are void of any true divine power. Instead, Kant proposed that the sacraments are meritorious only inasmuch as they produce virtue. To view them as a means of divine grace is "a religious illusion which can do naught but work counter to the spirit of religion."[2] Thus, for Kant, the only quality worth emphasizing in sacramental acts is the way they aid in inspiring a person toward honesty and upright living. This was a challenge to the traditional sacramental view that God acts in self-giving love through tangible means. Moreover, the efficacy of the sacraments was based in human activity rather than divine. Kant's assertions resulted in a view that the sacraments are mere memorials rather than effective signs of grace. This sacramental mindset eventually became widespread amongst Protestant traditions in the West.

Kant's promotion of a rational religion over and against an illusory one was a dramatic shift from the faith of his predecessors. While Kant's views on traditional authority and supernatural absence were not fully embraced by the church at large, many of his ideas (as well as teachings similar to his) still impacted the Protestant church in both Europe and America. By and large, Enlightenment philosophers deemed belief in God as futile. Human reason was the only thing necessary to understand the universe and to proceed into a better, more virtuous future. Thus, God's work in the Scriptures, especially through Jesus Christ, were acts to be remembered and valued as good moral instruction. These skeptical shifts were detrimental to the orthodox faith of the church. Despite the erroneous optimism of the modern era, Christianity found itself in the thick of a cynical and corrosive society. The peril of an exclusive focus on rationality and logic meant the rejection of all authoritative claims of revelation, faith, and tradition, especially since all were external, untrustworthy influences. The modern mentality called into question the credibility of biblical witness, historic testimony, and religious authority.

Consequentially, another challenge modernity posed to Christian orthodoxy was skepticism toward the venerable institutions and traditions of the past. As a general rule, modernity encouraged suspicion of any traditional truth claim regardless of the source of the claim. Truth was not validated simply because something was traditionally or institutionally held to be true. Rather, for modernists, tradition had to be put under scrutiny and sometimes rejected in favor of cultural succession and more rational approaches to knowledge. What this meant for the modern church was that it could no longer rely on traditional doctrines of the faith but instead had to reinterpret the faith for a new age. By elevating individual judgment and interpretation over and against the historical witness of the church, Christianity dismissed many long-held beliefs and practices. Nothing was too sacred to be safeguarded from scrutiny, alteration, and dismissal.

The Enlightenment philosophy of naturalism also posed a challenge to Christian orthodoxy. Naturalism asserted that natural rather than spiritual laws ruled and governed the universe. Likewise, it insisted that nothing existed beyond the natural elements, principles, and relationships found in the world. Similar to Kant's promulgation of an illusory faith, naturalism called into question the supernatural aspects of the Bible, the sacraments, and God's activity in the world. Because they believed science held all the proof for how the world functions and works, many modernists concluded the spiritual world was artificial. There was no place in the natural world for a reigning and ruling God. At best, God was a distant and uninterested deity who set the cosmos in motion but then stepped back to let the world work out on its own. The result of naturalism was a disenchanted people who allowed the natural order to dictate the rules and laws that governed life. Ontological truth was found in the world, not outside of it.

In light of the challenges posed by the Enlightenment, Protestant thinkers in the modern era had to find new ways to articulate the Christian faith and lead people in the worship of God. There were three primary responses. The first was to accept modern naturalism, deny supernatural activity, and consider the teachings of Christianity as myth. This response was known as "theological liberalism" or "liberal theology." Many modern religious scholars were unable to reconcile the contradictions they saw between science and Scripture, reason and the Bible, and historical evidence and the Christian faith. They therefore decided the proper route to discover the true core of the Christian faith was to "demythologize" Christianity, i.e., deny any supernatural elements such as miracles or the resurrection in search of only reasonable, historic fact. Traditional doctrines were claimed to be non-informative and non-discursive symbols of inner feelings, attitudes, and biases. Liberal theology ultimately landed on virtue (or sometimes love) as the main purpose of the Christian faith, with Jesus Christ as its central character and model since Jesus was *the* human model of love and virtue. The supernatural aspects of his life were held to be nothing more than narrative fabrication used to help ancient, unlearned people accept his teaching. Liberal theologians believed they could strip these narrative aspects away, however, and focus solely on Jesus' moral qualities. As a result, they turned worship into an opportunity to hear about Jesus' moral and ethical example, which Christians were to imitate. Preaching was the most prominent means for promoting good moral character and inspiring virtuous living. Liturgical acts such as confession, singing, and prayer served as reminders of the human need for growth in virtue.

The second response to modernity came from those in the church who were unwilling to relinquish the foundational creedal beliefs of Christianity. In their response to both modern philosophy and liberal theology, this group of "conservative" theologians utilized what is called "evidential apologetics," i.e., a proof-oriented defense of Christianity that attempted to rationalize the faith. Although their goal was to fight against aspects of modernity corrosive to the historic Christian faith, these conservatives bought into modernity's emphasis on reason and objective truth. Their hope was to build structures of certainty for faith-based claims; these structures were founded upon critical defenses of biblical texts, the doctrine of inerrancy, discoveries in archaeology, and other analytical proof of what they claimed to be biblical Christianity. Eventually, what resulted from conservatives' efforts was a purely rational and propositional approach to Christian faith. Worship was a safe space where Christians could gather, focus on, and affirm these truths. The sermon was a key feature of the worship service, and preaching seen as a useful tool for accenting the fundamental beliefs of the Christian faith. Other traditional liturgical acts of worship became suspect, however, since conservatives decided traditional liturgical practices should be accepted solely on the basis of biblical sanction.

Conservatives had two disparate approaches for discerning what constituted biblical worship. The first approach was to permit only worship explicitly affirmed in Scripture. Any and all other practices were seen as human inventions and thus prohibited. As a result, many churches eschewed artwork, the recitation of the creeds, prayers of confession, and even musical instruments in the worship service. The second approach to biblical worship was to allow any practice not explicitly prohibited in Scripture, so long as it was agreeable to the peace and unity of the church. While this approach was much more accepting of traditional liturgical practices, the reading of the Bible and the sermon were still elevated as the most essential components of the service. All other acts of worship were negotiable.

Whereas the church's first two responses to modernity highly favored the intellect over the emotions, a third response in many ways ran counterculturally to Enlightenment rationalism. This response stressed the importance of experiential religion and emphasized the necessity of a personal experience of God's salvation by asserting that true worship takes place in the heart. The governing mindset undergirding experiential religion was that Christian faith is not dependent upon acceptance of propositional truth but is based on an individual relationship and commitment of one's whole being to God. Worship ensued through the immediate and spontaneous movement of God, who was manifest in powerful, emotional responses. All formalized liturgical forms of worship were dismissed as unnecessary since they limited the spontaneous activity of God. Preaching was done to "revive" the hearts of those who needed to be awakened to a saving faith. Services often climaxed in a call to conversion or deeper repentance. Above all, pastors wanted worshippers to know that, contrary to the claims of modernity, God was not dead nor distant but could be known in a deeply personal way.

Despite the Protestant church's varied responses to the Enlightenment, a common characteristic was present in each, namely the glorification of the individual. Modernity perpetuated a culture of autonomous authority through its concentration on individual reason and knowledge. The dual focus on rationalism and experience within the church during the modern era likewise placed the individual at the center of the Christian faith and established a worship piety directed by human education and/or personal intimacy with God. This heightened attention to human edification was not done to position the human individual above God, but rather out of a human desire for a personal, authentic experience of God. The church refused to allow modernity to destroy God; thus, it felt an urgency for people to understand objective matters of the Christian faith and to know God in a personal way. This passion within the church for a vigorous inward, heartfelt religion paved the way for the American evangelical revival tradition that would extend throughout the eighteenth, nineteenth, and twentieth centuries.[3]

THE ANTECEDENTS OF AMERICAN EVANGELICAL REVIVALISM

The American evangelical revival tradition emerged in the 1700s out of a spiritual movement taking place in Europe's state churches.[4] The movement began in the middle of Europe, quickly spread to the British Isles and Britain's North American colonies, and soon impressed the entire West with the spiritual power of the new birth.[5] Prior to the evangelical movement, Protestant churches in Europe were divided by a variety of cultural and ethnic boundaries. There was much infighting regarding issues of biblical interpretation, religious piety, doctrinal confessions, and governmental politics.[6] In the midst of such Protestant infighting, two groups emerged that would pave the way for revival in the Americas – British Puritanism and Continental Pietism.

The British Puritan movement arose in the late 1500s. It was based in dissatisfaction felt by many in England concerning high-church Anglicanism. Convinced that salvation is possible only through God's Word and by the Holy Spirit – rather than through external forms and rubrics of religion – the Puritan goal was to strip away anything that might stand in the way of a sinner's reception and understanding of the Bible. The Puritans therefore opposed any Roman Catholic element that appeared in Anglican worship, such as the wearing of vestments by clergy, making the sign of the cross in the rite of baptism, the presence of artwork in the worship space, and the use of anything in worship that was not explicitly commanded in Scripture. The Puritans argued that worship instead should first and foremost be rooted in the preaching of God's Word. Likewise, the Puritans emphasized authentic, saving faith as an affair of the heart, which requires an inward transformation and personal encounter with Jesus Christ.

By the late 1620s, it became apparent to the Puritans that they would not succeed in their quest to "purify" the Church of England of its outward religion. Therefore, a group of as many as 20,000 English Puritans led by John Winthrop set sail in 1630 for the New World, arriving at the Massachusetts Bay colony with the purpose of establishing a holy commonwealth that would be a "city on a hill" and a beacon of pure, godly religion to the rest of the world.[7] The successful establishment of the New England colonies was of the utmost importance in the development of Congregationalism, the term preferred by the American Puritans and gradually adopted by their counterparts in Britain. By the latter half of the seventeenth century, however, the Puritan experiment in the American colonies had failed. To this point, Randall Balmer observes, "The community had fallen short of the standards of godliness set by the first generation. The rise of the merchant class had undermined the original Puritan vision, and there was evidence aplenty of God's displeasure: drought, fires in Boston, and King Philip's War."[8] Thus, by the early decades of the nineteenth century, pastors in New England had ceased trying to establish an unsullied society and instead focused on preaching a message of repentance.

In addition to British Puritanism, Continental Pietism was a significant influence on American evangelicalism. Originating in seventeenth-century Germany (as the country is now known), Pietism accentuated personal transformation through spiritual rebirth, personal renewal, individual devotion – often through reflection on sermons and the singing of hymns – and intimate piety. Likewise, Pietism contributed to religious practice by promoting commitment to evangelism, social action on behalf of the poor, a biblical foundation for theology and ethics, and experience as the basis of religion.[9]

Many Pietists believed and often asserted that their movement was a second phase of the Reformation. In contrast to the dry and overly intellectual scholasticism that they alleged developed in the generations following the Protestant Reformation, Pietists claimed true religion was based in a heartfelt faith. The copious doctrinal divisions between Protestant movements were proof to the Pietists that Protestant Christianity had focused too much on rational concerns. Therefore, Pietist leaders placed less emphasis on doctrinal divisions and instead focused on religious experience and the affections. Theological conflict should be engaged only when useful for changing people's hearts, the Pietists claimed. Moreover, worship, especially the sermon, should serve primarily to edify the congregation.

THE BIRTH OF AMERICAN EVANGELICAL REVIVALISM

The two traditions of Puritanism and Pietism were brought together in American Protestantism in the 1730s and 1740s through a series of revivals known as the First Great Awakening.[10] Seeds had already been planted for the Great Awakening through the Puritan experiment in the colonies and its newfound focus on repentance. However, it was through the influence of Pietism that the desire for religious renewal and personal assurance of salvation was instigated amidst the uproar of revival. Consequentially, a growing emphasis in American religion was placed on the "inner life" of the believer.

This inward-focused Pietistic sensibility had a great effect on American religious institutional life and practice. In the early eighteenth century, the religious landscape of the American colonies was quite diverse. The Congregational Church was the primary established church in New England while the Quakers, Dutch Reformed, Anglican, Presbyterian, Lutheran, Congregational, and Baptist churches all contended with each other in the more religiously lenient Middle colonies.[11] Furthermore, although the Anglican church was the official established church in the Southern colonies, a significant number of Baptists, Quakers, and Presbyterians were also present.[12] Despite the varieties of denominations extant through the American colonies, church involvement was quite low among the colonists. Only about 5 percent of the population were church members. In addition to the failure to engage and keep up with the continual population growth occurring in the colonies, the influence of Enlightenment rationalism led many of the colonists to turn to atheism, Deism, Unitarianism, and Universalism.[13] Moreover, beliefs that African slaves and Native Americans were "less-than human" and not eligible for salvation led to their exclusion from church participation.[14] The sacraments (most notably baptism) were withheld from such persons, giving the impression that they were unfit for God's salvation.[15]

In response to the lack of church membership in the colonies, and in light of the growing focus on inward religious life, ministers influenced by New England Puritanism and European Pietism began to call for revival. Specifically, these ministers believed that the American colonies needed to be "awakened" to the experience of inward religion and personal piety. Therefore, they blended together elements of Puritanism and Pietism to cultivate a sentiment in the American colonies based on vibrant worship through seasons of revival, outpourings of the Holy Spirit, and converted sinners experiencing God's love in a personal way. This evangelistic sentiment was the seedbed for the revival worship tradition that would later flourish in America.

By the 1740s, revivals had become a regular occurrence in America, particularly in New England. One of the most influential evangelical revivals occurred in 1734–1735 in Northampton under the leadership of the Congregationalist minister Jonathan Edwards. Utilizing a master's thesis he developed at Yale University, in the fall of 1734 Edwards preached a sermon series on justification by faith alone – a major doctrine of the evangelical revivals and also a doctrine characteristic of the Protestant Reformation.[16] The response to Edwards's preaching was incredible as revival broke out in Northampton and hundreds of individuals experienced conversion. The revival ultimately spread to twenty-five communities in western Massachusetts and central Connecticut until it finally began to decline by the spring of 1735.[17]

By and large, the Great Awakening had a unifying quality that dismantled institutional, confessional, and ethnic boundaries. Douglas Sweeney observes:

> In a work of amazing grace and by the power of the Holy Spirit, untold numbers of Protestant leaders began to join hands across [ecclesial] boundaries and to collaborate in the work of gospel ministry. They did not establish a new church. Rather, they labored ecumenically – *inter*denominationally and *pan*-geographically – cosponsoring revivals, concerts of prayer, and common fasts. They traded pulpits with one another and promoted itinerate gospel preaching, thereby undermining zoning systems that had long divided their churches.[18]

Seeking to avoid the routine of religion and preferring a vibrant and experiential spiritual life, preachers offered the evangelical message of salvation to any regardless of gender, race, or status. To this point,

Randall Balmer remarks that evangelicalism, like Puritanism and Pietism, "insisted on a warmhearted piety as the basis for salvation and the sign of regeneration."[19] Likewise, Sydney Ahlstrom observes how "a bond of fellowship" was created among evangelicals through a primary focus on conversion and regeneration as the mark of true religion:

> [The Great Awakening's unitive effects] were felt in two ways. Paramount was the way in which the renewed emphasis on Christian experience and the religious affections led to the recovery of an old aspect of Puritanism: an inclination to regard conversion and regeneration as a bond of fellowship that transcended disagreements on finer points of doctrine and polity ... Almost equally important was the geographical corollary to this discovery. Fellowship became not only interdenominational but intercolonial ... As for the social and political consequences of the Awakening, they are so important and so widely ramified that they can be discussed only in the context of the country's ongoing experience.[20]

Though the revivals had a unifying effect on American culture, the First Great Awakening also incited a division between the evangelical revivalists and traditional Protestants in America. Similar to their Puritan and Pietist predecessors who influenced the American evangelical revival culture, the revivalists of the First Great Awakening brought to the American colonies a detachment from religious rituals, ceremonies, sacramentality, and hierarchy. Consequentially, the evangelical movement made the experience of Christianity intensely subjective to the average person by fostering deep introspection, emotional conviction, and a commitment to a new standard of morality. It brought a message to American Protestantism that emphasized personal experience and the need for salvation by faith in Jesus Christ. As a result, the evangelical revivalism manifest in the First Great Awakening bred a worship culture that was full of zeal for the conversion of sinners but had little interest in the liturgical traditions of the church.

THE EXPANSION OF AMERICAN EVANGELICAL REVIVALISM

The intense spiritual fervor of eighteenth-century revivalism laid a foundation for the evangelical revival tradition that would later unfold as the singular most prominent religious movement in America.[21] In particular, a second series of revivals known as the Second Great Awakening surfaced during the first four decades of the nineteenth century. These revivals originated at camp meetings in Kentucky and Tennessee in the 1790s and early 1800s, and later swept across New England and the American frontier. Extraordinary numbers of people converted to Christianity at these revivals due to the enthusiastic preaching and congregational participation that occurred in the meetings.

One of the primary ways the revivals of the Second Great Awakening transformed the religious climate of America was through a new worship practice known as the altar call. The altar call was a public invitation given directly after the sermon which encouraged unrepentant sinners to come forward to a chancel rail, mercy seat, or anxious bench to make a personal commitment to God. The primary purpose of the altar call was to summon the unconverted to an experience of salvation; however, for those already converted, it was also used to implore believers toward growth in sanctification. While the altar call originated in revival meetings, it quickly found its way into the regular worshipping life of the church. Notably, some Protestant denominations rejected the practice, claiming it depended too much on a contrived emotional experience and was thus manipulative. Nevertheless, the altar call became a common feature of worship in the fastest-growing American Protestant movements of the nineteenth century, especially in denominations such as the evangelical Methodists and Baptists. The inclusion of this new practice by American Protestant evangelicals marked a major alteration in the order and conduct of worship. It pivoted worship into an appeal to the unconverted, increasingly blurring the distinction between worship and evangelism. Preaching maintained a central role in the service, but it was used as a means of stimulating the affections due to its usefulness in attracting large numbers of converts to the Christian faith. Thus, as evangelicalism grew in prominence in America throughout the 1800s, a distinct "revivalist" form of worship became prevalent in the church.

The Second Great Awakening also marked a significant theological shift in the religious climate of American Protestantism, a shift best seen through a comparison of the respective representative figureheads of each revival movement, Jonathan Edwards and Charles Finney. Primarily, Jonathan Edwards regarded the First Great Awakening to be an unprompted and unmerited "gracious visitation of the divine" whereby God demonstrated his mercy for all to see.[22] He believed revival was the work of God, not a human effort. As a Calvinist, Edwards accepted that God alone chose when and where to move and determined who was and was not saved. Although he never refrained from proclaiming the message of salvation to anyone who would hear, he believed it was God who made revival happen by arousing the hearts of the elect.

On the other hand, Charles Finney declared in his lectures on *Revivals of Religion* that revival was "the work of man" rather than God, stating, "revival is not a miracle" but "the result of the right use of the appropriate means."[23] Likewise, Finney suggested that salvation was open to all human beings; thus, he stressed that individuals could assert their own free will in choosing to be saved. To a great extent, Finney's religious convictions were suitable to early nineteenth-century America because his theology fit the temper of the times. As a newly independent nation, America had seized control of its political destiny. Finney assured the American people they could be in control of their religious destiny as well. To this point, Randall Balmer observes, "Finney's formula had obvious appeal in the new nation, especially among a people inebriated with self-determinism. And to this day we Americans cherish the notion of rugged individualism and control of our own destinies."[24]

Between the heightened individualism perpetuated by modernity and the American idealization of the self-made person, Finney's optimistic view of human potential found a convenient home in the nineteenth century. To be fair, Finney acknowledged that neither revival nor conversion could occur without the aid of the Holy Spirit; however, he also insisted that human effort was also necessary if either revival or conversion were to transpire. He claimed that God does not coerce the spiritually lost or complacent; rather, God gives useful means for the church to use to persuade sinners of their need for him. Moreover, God does not elect certain people for salvation but instead enables sinners by his grace to pick themselves up by their bootstraps and determine their own spiritual destination. It is thus the responsibility of each person to make his or her own individual and immediate decision for salvation.

A significant feature of Finney's approach to revival was his sanctioning of "liturgical pragmatism," a result-oriented approach to worship that seeks to do worship in order to accomplish a goal, typically the conversion of sinners. Because Finney believed human sin could only be countered by "religious excitements," he argued that worship must be done in a way to arouse spiritual fervor within the gathered people.[25] In contrast to certain contemporaries who prescribed liturgical practices solely based on commands from biblical texts, Finney argued that God established no set worship rubric or particular liturgical measures in the Scriptures. Instead, pastors are to "use the faculties [God] has given" to discern what means of worship are appropriate for each age and to weed out practices that are no longer effective.[26] Finney thus developed several "new measures" that he believed were conducive to revival, namely mass advertising, prolonged services, and the inclusion of the "anxious bench," a pew placed at the front of the congregation where sinners sat for prayer during the meeting. The essential test of meaningful worship for Finney was a pragmatic one, as James White observes.[27] Does a practice of worship work to move the people? If so, it should be kept. If not, it should be rejected.

Finney's pragmatic views ultimately generated an attitude in the American evangelical church that religious traditions should be disregarded if they do not prove to be as effective as newer methods in producing converts to the faith. The bottom line of worship was to achieve results qualifiable through the emotional reaction of the people and quantifiable by the number of attendees and/or converts in the service. Consequentially, the substance of nineteenth-century evangelical revivalist worship was unbridled evangelism dependent upon gripping preaching and a stimulated personal experience of God's saving work.

THE EVOLUTION OF AMERICAN EVANGELICAL REVIVALISM

The American evangelical revival tradition continued to flourish over the nineteenth and twentieth centuries, birthing numerous new movements such as Pentecostalism – which emphasized the spontaneous manifestation of Spirit-filled gifts in worship through speaking in tongues, divine healing, and exuberant physical expression – and the praise and worship movement – which had a concern for the immediacy of the Spirit, a desire for intimacy, and a conviction that music and informality presented the best way to connect with people of a post-Christian culture.[28] As new groups emerged, despite their differences in doctrine and praxis, they held firm to the worship model fashioned by evangelical revivalism. Even long-standing denominations such as Lutherans, Methodists, Presbyterians, and Quakers slowly began adopting pragmatic approaches and techniques of evangelical revivalism in their worship. Sunday services were typically done in three parts: (1) a time of singing preliminary to the sermon; (2) the sermon; (3) a time of response or ministry time. While the sermon still dominated the service, music occupied a more prominent role, encouraging active lay participation through enthusiastic congregational singing. Music was a powerful emotional stimulant in summoning the congregation to spiritual reflection. A prolonged time of music prior to the sermon set the stage for the preaching. A final hymn or song of invitation set the mood for people to respond. Musical texts were often introspective and personal rather than liturgical in nature, a characteristic evident in the American gospel hymns and Black spirituals written during the nineteenth and twentieth centuries.[29] Additionally, the use of familiar, indigenous musical styles made singing accessible, effective, and pleasing – all components highly valued in evangelical revivalist worship piety.

The expansion of the role of women and African Americans in worship was another significant development in American Protestantism during the nineteenth and twentieth centuries.[30] Though not all groups would accept leadership from women and/or Blacks, by the mid-nineteenth century it was not uncommon to see women and Blacks leading in prayer, conducting singing, sharing testimonies, and preaching, especially in camp meetings and revival services. The Black community greatly contributed to the evangelical revival tradition through its already established culture of vigorous singing and exuberant vocal response to preaching, prayer, and testimony. Conversely, revivalism provided the Black church a model for worship and an evangelical piety that still endures today.

One of the greatest shifts that occurred in the evolution of American evangelical revivalism over the late nineteenth and twentieth centuries concerned sacramental practice and meaning. The Second Great Awakening began as what Mark Galli calls "a Communion retreat" in Cane Ridge, Kentucky in August 1801.[31] Churches around the region gathered together to worship for a weekend, preparing themselves for and then partaking in the Eucharist on Sunday morning. There was an excitement, seriousness, and eagerness among the people for the sacrament. By the late nineteenth century, however, the Eucharist was no longer considered an essential element of worship. Evangelical pragmatism and Enlightenment rationalism combined to devalue the sacraments. Many traditions began to treat communion and baptism as ordinances – i.e., commands of Jesus to be followed – rather than sacraments – i.e., means of receiving God's grace and self-giving love. When celebrated, the Eucharist was seen more as a memorial of Christ's death and a chance to reflect on individual remorse. As James White observes:

> [T]he prevalent attitude to the Eucharist that survives even today in many Protestant churches is a Garden of Gethsemane piety: Christ died for you, so cannot you at least do a bit better? The message of the Lord's Supper tends to be simply "Be good." This moralizing fits in

very well with the pragmatic approach to worship. Sacraments really do nothing more than reinforce preaching with visual aids.[32]

Like the Eucharist, the practice of baptism was also impacted by evangelical revivalism and Enlightenment rationalism. In particular, baptism became a means of identifying the converted. Believer's baptism became the preferred practice in many Protestant churches. The ecclesial commitments of baptism all but disappeared in favor of acknowledging an individual convert's decision to follow Christ. Consequentially, for over two centuries American Protestantism has primarily emphasized human understanding and personal intention over and against the self-giving love of God in sacramental practice.

On the whole, preaching has prevailed as the chief part of worship in American Protestantism. Whether done for evangelistic or educational purposes, preaching stands at the center of evangelical worship piety. This emphasis is not only evident in the conduct of American Protestant worship, (i.e., the time given to the sermon) but seen also in the concerns of American Protestant Christians. For instance, in August 2016 the Pew Research Center released the results of a poll conducted amongst American Protestant adults that asked what they look for when choosing a church or place of worship.[33] The study revealed that US adults look first and foremost for a place where they like the preaching. In fact, 83 percent of those polled said preaching was the primary influence on their choice of where to worship.

Undoubtedly, preaching has held and continues to hold the primary position in American Protestant worship. Above all, for American Protestants, when it comes to worship, preaching reigns supreme. Although this elevated view of preaching is a typical feature of American Protestantism, the content of preaching greatly varies. In the 1700s and early 1800s, almost all revivalist preaching focused on the conversion of sinners. While many evangelical churches continue to emphasize conversion (either initial or renewed) in their preaching, topical sermons related to spiritual self-improvement have also become common. Alternatively, Black churches often treat preaching as a testimony to the power of the proclaimed Word of God, which brings freedom to reshape lives. Charismatic sermons attend to God's radical healing power at work in a person's life. Other Protestant factions have used preaching to promote a Social Gospel, emphasizing social concerns, personal morality, and Christian activism in the world. However, regardless of the content, American Protestants still believe there is power in preaching to bring real change in people's lives.

NOTES

1 Immanuel Kant, *Religion within the Limits of Reason Alone*, trans. Theodore M. Greene and Hoyt H. Hudson (New York: Harper & Row, 1960) 182.
2 Kant, *Religion within the Limits of Reason Alone*, 188.
3 For further reading on modernity and its effects on Christian worship, see Thomas Oden, *After Modernity ... What? Agenda for Theology* (Grand Rapids, MI: Zondervan, 1990); Robert Webber, *Ancient-Future Worship: Proclaiming and Enacting God's Narrative* (Grand Rapids, MI: Baker Books, 2008); James White, *A Brief History of Christian Worship* (Nashville: Abingdon, 1993); James White, *Protestant Worship: Traditions in Transition* (Louisville, KY: Westminster John Knox Press, 1989).
4 Evangelicalism is a complex subject of study with many historical, theological, and social connotations. For the sake of this chapter, the term "evangelicalism" refers to a historic movement, not a church, denomination, or social/political group.
5 See Douglas Sweeney, *The American Evangelical Story* (Grand Rapids, MI: Baker Academic, 2005), 27. Also, for more on the evangelical movement in America, see Sydney Ahlstrom, *A Religious History of the American People* (New Haven, CT: Yale University Press, 1972); Frances Fitzgerald, *The Evangelicals: The Struggle to Shape America* (New York: Simon & Schuster, 2017); Barry Hankins, *American Evangelicals: A Contemporary History of a Mainstream Religious Movement* (New York: Rowman & Littlefield Publishers, 2008); Mark Noll, *American Evangelical Christianity* (Malden, MA: Blackwell, 2001).
6 Sweeney, *The American Evangelical Story*, 27–29.
7 See Abram C. Van Engen, *City on a Hill: A History of American Exceptionalism* (New Haven, CT: Yale University Press, 2020), 130–148, 169–182.
8 Randall Balmer, *Blessed Assurance: A History of Evangelicalism in America* (Boston: Beacon Press, 1999), 15.
9 For more on Pietism, see Hartmut Lehmann, James Van Horn Melton, and Jonathan Strom, eds., *Pietism in Germany and North America 1680–1820* (New York: Routledge, 2019); Hughes Oliphant Old, *Moderatism, Pietism, and Awakening*, vol. V of *The Reading and Preaching of the Scriptures in the Worship of the Christian Church* (Grand Rapids, MI: Eerdmans, 2005); F. Ernest Stoeffler, ed., *Continental Pietism and Early American Christianity* (Eugene, OR: Wipf & Stock, 2007).
10 For more on the First Great Awakening, see Thomas S. Kidd, *The Great Awakening: The Roots of Evangelical Christianity in Colonial America* (New Haven, CT: Yale University Press, 2007); Mark A. Noll, *The Rise of Evangelicalism: The Age of Edwards, Whitefield and the Wesleys* (Downers Grove, IL: Intervarsity Press, 2003); and Howard John Smith, *The First Great Awakening: Redefining Religion in British America, 1725–1775* (Vancouver:

Fairleigh Dickinson University Press, 2015); Sweeney, *The American Evangelical Story.*

11 Smith, *The First Great Awakening,* 1.

12 Smith, *The First Great Awakening,* 1.

13 Smith, *The First Great Awakening,* 2.

14 Rebecca Anne Goetz, *The Baptism of Early Virginia: How Christianity Created Race* (Baltimore: John Hopkins University Press, 2015), 110.

15 Goetz, *The Baptism of Early Virginia,* 110–111.

16 Sweeney, *The American Evangelical Story,* 47.

17 Noll, *The Rise of Evangelicalism,* 78.

18 Sweeney, *The American Evangelical Story,* 29.

19 Balmer, *Blessed Assurance,* 30.

20 Ahlstrom, *Religious History,* 293–294.

21 For more on the Second Great Awakening, see Mark A. Noll, *A History of Christianity in the United States and Canada* (Grand Rapids, MI: Eerdmans, 1992); Sweeney, *The American Evangelical Story;* Robert Webber, *Worship Old & New: Revised Edition* (Grand Rapids, MI: Zondervan, 1994); White, *A Brief History of Christian Worship;* White, *Protestant Worship.*

22 Jonathan Edwards, *A Faithful Narrative of the Surprising Work of God in the Conversion of Many Hundred Souls in Northampton, Massachussettes, A.D. 1735* (New York: Dunning & Spalding, 1832).

23 Charles G. Finney, *Lectures on Revivals of Religion* (New Tappan, NJ: Revell, n.d.), 15.

24 See Balmer, *The Making of Evangelicalism,* 19–22.

25 Finney, *Lectures on Revivals of Religion,* 1–2.

26 Finney, *Lectures on Revivals of Religion,* 251.

27 White, *Protestant Worship,* 177.

28 Webber, *Worship Old & New,* 128. For more on late nineteenth- and twentieth-century developments of worship, see Lester Ruth and Swee Hong Lim, *Lovin' on Jesus: A Concise History of Contemporary Worship* (Nashville: Abingdon, 2017); Robert Webber, ed., *Twenty Centuries of Christian Worship,* vol. II of *The Complete Library of Christian Worship* (Nashville: StarSong Publishing, 1994); White, *A Brief History of Christian Worship;* White, *Protestant Worship.*

29 Of course, gospel hymns and spirituals were not solely introspective and personal. For example, Black spirituals also had a sociopolitical function, such as in the underground railroad and the Civil Rights movement. For more on the role and function of Black music, see Samuel A. Floyd, Jr., Melanie L. Zeck, and Guthrie P. Ramsey, Jr., *The Transformation of Black Music: The Rhythms, the Songs, and the Ships of the African Diaspora* (Oxford: Oxford University Press, 2017).

30 For more on the development of worship within the American Black church, see Melva Wilson Costen, *African American Christian Worship* (Nashville: Abingdon, 1993); Albert J. Raboteau, *Canaan Land: A Religious History of*

African Americans (Oxford: Oxford University Press, 2001); Milton
C. Sernett, ed., *African American Religious History: A Documentary
Witness*, 2nd ed. (Durham, NC: Duke University Press, 1999).

31 Mark Galli, "Whatever Happened to Communion and Baptism?"
Christianity Today, July 10, 2019, www.christianitytoday.com/ct/2019/july-
web-only/whatever-happened-to-communion-baptism.html.

32 James White, *Protestant Worship*, 181.

33 "Choosing a New Church or House of Worship: Americans Look for Good
Sermons, Warm Welcome," Pew Research Center, August 23, 2016, www
.pewforum.org/2016/08/23/choosing-a-new-church-or-house-of-worship/.

7 Education

STEVEN HOSKINS

At least since the days of the "Old Deluder, Satan" act of 1647, which enforced the public teaching of literacy so as to allow American children to read the Bible for themselves, American Protestants have forcefully employed education in their efforts to Christianize America.[1] Those efforts eventually included not only the forming of publicly provided schools as the 1647 law demanded – a primary level school for every town with 50 citizens and a university preparatory school for towns with a population of at least 100 – but a vast and impressive array of educational platforms, institutions, purveyors, and popularizers that have had a wide-ranging effect on American history and culture. The narrative of those efforts, now over 400 years in the making, argues for a nuanced and complex reading of the subject of American Protestant education.

EDUCATION CENTRAL TO AMERICAN PROTESTANTISM

Arguing for "a broader definition of education and a different notion of historical relevance" in his landmark book *Education in the Formation of American Society*, Harvard's Bernard Bailyn noted that in American history, education must be considered "not only as formal pedagogy but as the entire process by which a culture transmits itself across generations; ... education in its elaborate, intricate involvements with the rest of society, and ... its shifting functions, meanings, and purposes."[2] So it is with the history of education in American Protestantism.

This chapter is a concatenation of multiple representations of one thing – education – depicting within a web of existence its various realities, both as idea and as the experience of how that idea was practiced, dependent on the relevance of occasion or place in that history. The details – language, actions, symbols, and ideas – within that history have the capacity for imagining the whole, the ability to understand how American Protestant education happened and how it molded experience, stirred imaginations, linked Protestants in America to their Reformation roots, and helped to keep the goal of a Christianized America in front of them.

Many historians, Bailyn included, maintain not only that Protestantism has been the guiding force in American history, but that the history of America and American Protestantism are so integral and intertwined with its educational endeavors that they provide the broadest spectrum possible within which to interpret it.[3] Beginning with Robert Baird's *Religion in America*, published in 1844, the claim has been clear: America is "a great Protestant empire" and education has been one of the foremost, if not the single most pervasive, among its driving forces.[4] Baird's claim was cemented in history books throughout the nineteenth century and, as late as 1970, Sydney Ahlstrom's magisterial *A Religious History of the American People* argued the point, explicitly and tacitly.[5]

Since 1970, historians have continued the theme, at times with a less than enthusiastic nod to Protestant consensus, and added to it the fruits of "new" social and statistical historical methodologies. Virtually every historian of American religion in Martin Marty's historiographical catalogue of "The American Religious Protestant Canon" argues the point of Protestant ubiquity in American history as well.[6] The idea that America is or has been a "Protestant Empire" of sorts is pervasive, so pervasive in fact that the list of those who do not affirm Protestantism as the guiding force in American history among religious historians is short but meaningful. Among them, Amanda Porterfield argues that Protestantism was an evangelical oppressive force that arose only against the majority Enlightenment philosophy of the deists and Jon Butler, and, observing the variety of religious expressions actually present in any form, calls early America a "spiritual hothouse."[7] Given the consensus of historians and historiographical considerations on the subject, even if American Protestantism was, at times, oppressive and was a "spiritual hothouse," it was a hothouse planted in the soil of Protestant efforts and grown by Protestant values and energy.

Such a reading of the subject of education presents its challenges. Reading that history as a river with many tributaries, rather than a monolithic "city on a hill," calls for examining the broader questions and historical manifestations through which it was implemented to be considered alongside of and within the choices, desires, and interactive expressions of the people who lived it. It acknowledges the difficulty of conceptualizing the topic given that American Protestantism is divided into three sub-species: fundamentalists concerned with particular Protestant orthodoxies on the one hand, modernists working to incorporate new definitions and educational practices into the Protestant fabric on the other, and Evangelicals in between, balancing the necessity of instruction in the language of the Bible with the tolerant, enlightened values of faith in human goodness and righteousness in the burgeoning and developing "Religion of the Republic," as Sydney Meade branded it.[8] Each one of these has their own interesting history of education, and the interchange between them often drives any narrative presentation of American Protestant education. There is also present throughout the story the conviction that many, if not most, Protestants held fast as they educated: they believed that conversion and doctrinal obedience would necessarily follow their efforts.

Three historiographical considerations guide the discussion. First, alongside the many and varied works devoted to the considerable efforts and expressions of American Protestant education, many wider histories of American education argue the point for a Protestant consensus in the field and need to be consulted as valuable resources. Lawrence Cremin's three-volume comprehensive work on the history of American education weighing in at over 1,700 pages, the second volume of which won the Pulitzer Prize for History, takes the history of American education as a Protestant effort writ large across the canvas of its vast four centuries noting its successes and failures.[9] Cremin's understanding of Protestantism is inclusive enough to include churches, families, New England towns, schools, and newspapers; he widens the consideration of instructional methods to go beyond textbooks and bulletin boards and include church windows, television shows, and computer games, all of which contribute to a broadened consideration of Protestant education and the many directions it has taken. In addition, Cremin broadens Bailyn's cultural definition of education to include "the deliberate, systematic, and sustained effort to transmit, evoke, or acquire knowledge, attitudes, values, skills, and sensibilities, and any learning that results from the effort, direct or indirect, intended or unintended."[10] Such a reading of Protestant education, then, demands that it be understood as a part of the wider American story written into the fabric of the *longue durée* or extensive past of America.

Second, the scholarship of American Protestant education, considered in its entirety, has produced a well-nuanced presentation of the formally and informally negotiated landscape over time. Some scholars like Glenn Miller employ the convenience of chronology as the means to presentation. His sweeping three-volume work on formal theological education covering 1,700 pages and almost four centuries divides the subject of formal theological schooling into historical eras that reflect

Protestant schooling during the periods of Protestant dominance, negotiation, and pluralism.[11] Other scholars have told the story through the
intentions Protestants employed as they educated.

Six comprehensive themes emerge in those narratives and should
always be considered in interpreting Protestant education: (1) literacy so
as to read the Scriptures well, including the idea of academic achievement; (2) orthodoxy and the preservation of Protestant theological purity; (3) evangelism; (4) the establishment of morality as the negotiation
between Protestantism with values of the Enlightenment understood as
the basis of a civil society; (5) nurture over/against educating for conversion; and (6) the place of Protestant thought in the intellectual development of America, especially as Protestants conformed to changing roles
in America over time and dealt with the demands of government and
secular accrediting bodies. Alongside the dates and themes that overlap
in history and often exist together in contested environments, some
scholars have noted geography made a difference in the agency, practice,
and idealism of Protestants as they educated. In the northeast Puritanism
provided the guiding light for education; in the South education created
an aristocracy and later a platform of revivals for the masses; in the
Midwest missionary educational efforts from the Eastern seaboard provided means, teachers, and literature for the movement; those Protestant
missionaries intruded into established religions in the West; and all the
while American Protestant education borrowed from its Transatlantic
Reformation roots in both thought and organizational structure.

Still other approaches have used Protestantism as a dominant mentality around which a multi-versed history can be told. Some have articulated the story through the missionary spirit that formed institutions
across the land like the Sunday School and the Christian college, and
some by telling the stories of specific culturally negotiated forms of
Protestantism that emphasize human agency and the negotiation
between religions and cultures.[12] Many methodologies, uses, and intentions contribute to the story of Protestant education and intellectual life
in America.

Third, the idea of a post-Protestant America or at least a less-
Protestant dominated history has emerged since 1970, and new historical
questions and methodologies have arisen in its wake, reshaping the
narrative of education. An impressive range of works by historians of
the last fifty years weaves a narrative that includes people and ideals
often left out or silenced by the consensus histories (the stories of
women, African Americans, Native Americans, Protestant interaction
with Catholicism and other religions), constructing competing versions

of Protestantism and the education that accompanies it. David Hall's amended version of Ahlstrom's *Religious History of the American People* capitalizes on Ahlstrom's observation in 1970 that America may be in a post-Protestant era, with a new introduction and additional chapter written over three decades after Ahlstrom's death, noting many additions from "new" histories and historians to the narrative.[13] The many essays in the anthology *American Christianities*, edited by Catherine Brekus and W. Clark Gilpin, while challenging a "Protestant consensus," broaden the narrative to read "Christian" or "religious," but also use some form of the word "Protestant" over 200 times in the Table of Contents and Introduction alone.[14] The inclusion of these stories, negotiating issues ranging from politics to sexuality to science, is necessary for a more complete and sympathetic presentation of the force of Protestant education in America over time.

Such a reading of the history of American Protestant education argues that history is ill-served by dichotomizing the forces and participants in the story and that reductionist readings of "sacred versus secular," "church versus society," or "big history versus micro-history" have limited value. Triumphalist claims in regards to American Protestantism or monolithic readings of the development of education in that history are certainly restricted. A more complete recounting of educational history sees the narrative as a testimony to the continuity of American Protestant education and a more expansive range of forces and approaches to writing that history. It also considers the validity and potency of traditions within that continuity, accounting for the engagement of wills among the efforts and ideologies of the players who have graced the stage.

The vigor with which historians have taken to narrating education in the history of American Protestantism is impressive. The subject has produced vast numbers of books, monographs, speeches, laws, and other apparatuses recounting the general idea and its particular expressions. Heather Day's *Protestant Theological Education in America: A Bibliography*, a Lilly Endowment-sponsored project, includes over 5,200 entries on the subject.[15] Another single-volume annotated select bibliography on religious schools in America stretches over 350 pages.[16] The most complete and ongoing timeline on the history of education in America maintained online with helpful hypertexts and lessons plans for teachers includes over 500 entries: many relate to the efforts of American Protestants and their opponents, with over 100 listings since 2000, and the last update in March 2020 covering the closing of schools and cessation of in-person classes across America due to the COVID-19 pandemic includes religious schools and Christian colleges.[17]

What follows in this chapter is a short chronology of American Protestant education since the early 1600s. The goal herein is to give a basic account of that history and illustrate various expressions of Protestant education within American society and culture as they occurred within the changing demands of circumstance. Seen as links to broader histories and stories, the intention is that readers, historians, and interested parties will find a variety of ways to think about American Protestant Education and be able to compare the values and histories they articulate.

EDUCATION IN THE COLONIES

When the first Protestant colonists arrived in America, they brought their religion and its commitment to education with them. Dependent upon their European Protestant Reformation roots, they found that the instructions and ideology of both Luther and Calvin and their many followers informed their educational labors. Luther's valuing of education as the second highest purpose of the church following worship and his Sermon on "On the Duty of Sending Children to School" (1530) and Calvin's virtually egalitarian, at least for Protestants, organization of the educational system of Geneva for men and women, regardless of their age or vocation, were strong influences throughout the colonies as they created schools alongside and within houses of worship.[18] Literacy for Bible reading was the goal of education and the creation of a Protestant Christian culture in the "New World" the grander ambition.

The educational ideals of the Reformers proved to be at work almost immediately with the arrival of the colonists. The home was the site of education for many Protestants and a school to evangelize Native Americans was begun in Virginia as early as 1620. In 1635, the Syms School, a "free school" to teach literacy leading to scriptural understanding and formation, was started in Virginia. In that year, the first Latin Grammar School was established in Boston for the sons of the upper class who were expected to lead the Protestant efforts in church, business, and the legal professions. "Dame Schools" for girls were soon created alongside them. Harvard College, the first Protestant institution of higher education, was founded in 1636 and the Harvard Press, the first of many publishing houses devoted to the proliferation of Protestant ideals and printing Bibles and books, was launched two years later. Virtually all schools of higher education in America founded over the next 150 years were Protestant, as well.[19]

Throughout the next few decades, Protestant efforts at education multiplied throughout the colonies. Schools fueled by different churches and a variety of Protestant theological viewpoints thrived. The colony of Massachusetts passed laws between 1642 and 1648 designed to ensure that their students were not only literate but imbued with the doctrines of the faith and the laws of the commonwealth. *Virginia's Cure* (1661), written to the Bishop of London, merged the values of Protestantism with nationalism by arguing that education was needed to create citizens who were fit for employment in both church or state – and to convert the "Heathen" by teaching them alongside the children of the English colonists.[20] In 1690, the first *New England Primer* which included both the *Westminster Catechism* and John Cotton's *Spiritual Milk* – a sixty-four question catechism based on both Testaments – was printed.[21] Replacing the *Horn Book* (an English primer) as the main conduit to literacy, the publication proved popular with Puritans and Lutherans in the colonies and became the premier educational publication in early America with sales rivaling those of the Bible.

The eighteenth century saw evangelists, pastors, missionaries, Mennonites, Presbyterians, and Lutherans, among others, following the pathway of education throughout the colonies. The Presbyterians, who founded no colony, established Princeton in 1746 under the leadership of John Winthrop. Winthrop infused Protestant education with the enlightenment values of a reasonable religion that harmonized Scripture with the principles of reason, revelation, and nature. Henry Muhlenberg established one of the first parish schools in America in New York's St. Matthew's church in 1752, educating students with the Bible and Luther's *Small Catechism* as the main textbooks. The Mennonite Christopher Dock's *Schul-Ordnung* or *School Management Guide*, published in 1770, was the first book about teaching printed in America and included instructions for teachers and hymns.[22] In mid-century, itinerant evangelist George Whitefield, an Anglican clergyman who visited America seven times and was known as the "Divine Dramatist," used newspapers as platforms for developing spirituality and literacy in reading his sermons and the Scriptures. In the decades of the 1740s–1760s, Samuel Davies, a Presbyterian clergyman, received permission to travel the backwoods of Virginia where he taught rural immigrants, mostly Germans and Scots-Irish, to read along with enslaved African Americans. Throughout the century and into the next two, Protestants used education as a tool to evangelize Native Americans. They established schools among the Cherokee, Choctaw, and Seminole tribes, incorporated the published language books and newspapers of the

Cherokee in their missional efforts, and trained some Native Americans to be missionaries.[23]

EDUCATION IN POST-REVOLUTIONARY AMERICA

After the American Revolution in 1776, Protestants adapted to the changes of the establishment clause of religion in the Constitution and the growing control of schools by state legislatures. A diverse number of denominations launched elementary schools, academies, and college-preparatory institutions and Protestants continued to build colleges like Mount Holyoke (1836) for women and the first coeducational Protestant school at Oberlin College (1837). The establishment clause and the concern to provide education for all citizens by the states became a long public and legal debate for Protestants involving nationalism, school control, finance, educational curriculum, and instruction as states formed their own educational systems.

With the creation of the first public secondary school in Boston in 1821 and a law passed in 1827 that required public schools be open to all children, the state of Massachusetts and its Secretary of Education, Horace Mann, led the century-long struggle to establish public controlled, non-sectarian schools across America that would replace church and religious-controlled institutions. Armed with McGuffey Readers, first published in 1836 and selling over 1 million copies by 1900 – teaching the basics of literacy in a developmental fashion alongside stories which reinforced William McGuffey's Calvinist values, adherence to the commandments of Scripture, and allegiance to "our best friend Jesus" who "died on the cross for us" – public schooling replaced Protestant-sponsored schools while teaching the values and lessons that had been the staple and property of Protestant education.[24] Several efforts to obtain public funding for Protestant schools were waged in court battles from New York to Illinois to Wisconsin, but ultimately failed.[25] With the founding of the National Teachers Association (today's National Education Association) in 1857, a national public school teachers' union, and the United States Department of Education after the Civil War in 1867, eventually the ideal of officially Protestant-led public education in America became a memory.

In response to the transition of state and nationally mandated schooling across the United States and the demands of the national economy on the working class, the first American Protestant Sunday Schools began to appear in the mid-1780s. Borrowing the Protestant "Day School" idea and the Sunday School movement of Robert Raikes from Protestants in England, Sunday Schools quickly dotted the skyline of the new nation. In Philadelphia, William Elliott began the wave of Sunday Schools, which were usually held in churches, and a year later the Methodist Bishop Francis Asbury established a Sunday School in Virginia which included enslaved people among its students.

At first, the Sunday School was seen as complementary to the common or public schools of the new states – teaching American enlightened values of honesty, decency, efficiency, and citizenship through the Bible. As the century progressed, Sunday School became a nationwide remedy for the lack of Protestant doctrinal instruction in public schools and an evangelistic tonic for human sinfulness. The Philadelphia Sunday and Adult School Union organized in 1817. Using Bibles provided by the American Bible Society (founded in the previous year), it mustered together the educational efforts of the Sunday Schools in Pennsylvania and expanded to become the National Sunday School Union in 1824. The Union, whose archives hold over 500,000 pages of material produced between 1817 and 1915, held its first national conference in 1830.[26] With a universal curriculum for all Sunday Schools, it followed the nation's westward expansion with a mission to "concentrate the efforts of Sabbath school societies in different regions of our country ... to disseminate useful information, circulate moral and religious publications ... and so endeavor to plant a Sunday School wherever there is a population."[27]

The popularity of the Sunday School Union saw additional benefit. The Vacation Bible School movement eventually arose out of the Sunday School. As Protestants added new educational techniques and nurture to their arsenal of theological aims at mid-century, theologians like Horace Bushnell wrote extensively on the subject, calling for development of the whole person and challenging conversion as the sole aim of Protestant education. His first works were published as Sunday School literature.[28]

While the Sunday School provided Protestants their most extensive educational platform, that platform was complemented by the rise of the Second Great Awakening at the turn of the nineteenth century and the revivals and camp meetings it spawned throughout the period. While Sunday Schools reached primarily cities and towns with burgeoning populations, the gatherings of camp meetings reached rural populations, as well, and became an educational forum in their own right. "Schools of the Prophets" and "Schools of Prayer" gave religious and literacy instruction, and as the century moved on they provided platforms for clergy, evangelism, missionary, and musical training, and an abundance of reading material that included books, pamphlets, and monthly and weekly newspapers such as Methodist Phoebe Palmer's *Guide to Holiness*. The movement produced its own educational guidelines, as evidenced by Charles Finney's *Lectures on the Revivals of Religion* published in 1835.[29] Eventually the camp meeting movement became an institution and with that power created its own schools and colleges like Asbury University, founded by the evangelist Henry Clay Morrison in 1890, and Anderson University (founded 1918), which still holds a yearly camp meeting on its campus.

Protestant education in the late nineteenth century continued to adapt to the circumstances of the nation. In 1899, the same year that Jane Adams started the settlement house movement using democratic rather than religious instruction to reinforce values and ethics for immigrants in Chicago, the Gideons organization began passing out free copies of the King James Bible to students in public and private schools and to hotel visitors. Some camp meetings sought a middle ground by becoming Chautauquas, with a more expansive curriculum designed to provide wholesome entertainment and cultural edification alongside Christian instruction.

By the end of the century, Protestant denominations had mostly abandoned the idea of their own day schools, with a few notable exceptions like the Missouri Synod Lutheran Church. Most Protestant children attended public school. The landmark United Stated Supreme Court decision of 1893 *Pierce v. Society of Sisters*, often called the "magna carta" of private schools and ironically brought by a Catholic school, maintained the right of parents to "direct the upbringing and education" of their children. The decision was to prove most influential in the educational efforts of Protestants in the next hundred years.

EDUCATION IN THE TWENTIETH CENTURY

The history of American Protestant education in the twentieth century proved a battleground. Protestant infighting took up questions of biblical criticism, the debate between science and religion, and the role of Protestants and their educational efforts in American public life.[30] Protestants struggled to maintain not only their doctrinal views, but also their place and legitimacy within American education. Wide-ranging academic voices debated theology, often taking sides and sometimes forming new schools aimed at maintaining orthodoxy as they developed professional standards and institutions of their own, designed to measure up to the "secular" educational systems of the nation.

The fundamentalist–modernist controversy, with its roots in the 1890s at Princeton, dominated the century and led to the dissembling and fragmentation of many denominations and their educational efforts. The debates intensified in force at the turn of the twentieth century. The progressive Religious Education Association (REA) professionalized the ranks in 1903 and brought the discipline into the modern world, inviting John Dewey to be the speaker at their first national conference in 1906. George Allen Coe became the de facto leader of the REA from its beginning and remained its guiding light until his death in 1952. His monumental efforts in forming its twin goals of making religious education a force in general education curricula and bringing progressive educational ideas like child-centered learning with the teacher as guide rather than the dispenser of knowledge earned him the title, "Father of Religious Education."

Parallel and competing efforts in professionalizing the field followed. Soon the conservative National Union of Christian Schools formed in 1920 (today's Christian Schools International, a coalition of mainly conservative Protestant schools); it aimed at restoring the "Christian America" ideal of the earliest American Protestants and providing standards of curriculum and teaching. The formation of these competing professional organizations signaled the beginning of the divide between conservative and liberal Protestants that shaped the history of education in the century.

With the Scopes Monkey Trial in Dayton, Tennessee in 1925, the debate between Protestants deepened. Bryan College, with a mission to provide college education with a "Christian worldview," was started just days after the court case ended. The teaching of evolution versus "intelligent design" in regards to human creation created a minefield for Protestants and an orthodoxy test; it prompted new schools like Bryan College, served as fuel for Protestant and public school textbooks, and produced legal cases over the subject in American courtrooms into the twenty-first century.[31]

As the twentieth century unfolded, the fundamentalist–modernist debate both strengthened and divided Protestant higher education. Some Protestant colleges, and even seminaries, separated from their historical denominational moorings and became non-denominational, and a few became secular. Some affirmed their doctrinal commitments and created confessional statements. Many remained in the middle, evangelically Protestant but neither confessionally fundamentalist nor avowedly modernist. Most sought accreditation from the regional secular associations in the region where they are located. Some Protestant schools created their own associations like the Council for Christian Colleges and Universities, which began in the 1970s; it provided professional development for faculties, student programs, and legal advocacy. Many denominations and churches that sponsored their own schools also established presence and often property on secular campuses for the purposes of evangelism and formation. Some denominations established campus ministries and some independent Protestant groups formed ministries to reach secular college students such as InterVarsity (1941) and Campus Crusade for Christ (1951). These followed after the manner of voluntary educational associations that included the YMCA, the YWCA, and the Student Volunteer Movement of the previous century. The Association of Theological Schools, founded in 1918, became the accrediting body for mainline Protestant seminaries and over the last century was expanded to include Protestant evangelical, Roman Catholic, Orthodox, and Jewish seminaries. It is recognized by the United States Department of Education as the accrediting body in the field.[32]

The story among day and private Protestant schools was no different. The civil rights movement and enforced desegregation after the *Brown v. Board of Education, Topeka* decision of 1955 changed and segregated Protestants and their schools. Losses in legal challenges to practices of public prayer, including the recitation of the Lord's Prayer and Bible reading in public schools in the 1960s, pushed Protestants and Protestant educational methods, many favored by White Protestant churches, further and further out of the public school system and the mainstream of American culture. It also strengthened efforts at providing alternative Protestant scholastic offerings.

While most Protestants in America attended public schools, Sunday Schools and youth groups (both church-based and non-denominational) organized around the leadership of Youth Specialties, a Protestant youth ministry organization, in the 1980s and began offering some educational programming. Enrollment in Protestant denomination and local church-based kindergarten through grade 12 schools rose significantly in the last half of the twentieth century. Conservative and liberal denominations from Quakers to Episcopalians to Southern Baptists all saw increased numbers as approximately 10,000 Protestant day schools were established between 1960 and 1990. As of the year 2000, enrollment in those schools exceeded 1 million students.[33]

The end of the century also saw an interesting return to the ideas and practices of previous centuries. Many Protestants have opted to return to the Puritan ideal of the earliest days of America. The Protestant home school movement picked up steam in the 1980s, serving as many as 100,000 students in 2000, and offered yet another Protestant avenue of education.[34] The Milwaukee Parental Choice program (1990) provided the option of public funding for private schools, including Protestants. School voucher programs in a number of states have provided Protestants with yet another educational option in America. The McGuffey Reader of the eighteenth-century public school is being republished for twenty-first-century Protestant use.[35] These forms of education continue to grow and have given rise to established and accredited curriculums from a variety of publishing houses: Protestant textbooks, teaching manuals, video lessons, and even computer role-playing games and Vacation Bible School curricula, with characters from the Bible and American history and culture supplementing the effort.[36]

"The Protestant effort to make American civilization Christian has had a long, complicated history with many fascinating chapters ... At their best, they looked and worked toward the future, and they struggled to translate their dreams into reality. From the successes and failures there is much to learn."[37] So begins the last paragraph of Robert Handy's *A Christian America*, providing a fitting framework through which to view the narrative of American Protestant education. That 400-year narrative is indeed a winding river with many tributaries, ideologies, and goals. The struggle and failure to maintain power and presence and to train Protestants in America underscores the reality that narrating the story of American Protestant education must be done through a variety of voices and with an eye to platform and purpose. *Educationem semper Reformandem* (education is always reforming) is the story.

Protestants in America have practiced their faith educationally at home, in schools, and through professional associations and confessional ministries that, taken together, tell the story of persistent, generous, engaging, and inclusive Protestantism in America. Some have seen their mission as being to teach orthodox beliefs, some to nurture each person to their full humanity, and many to evangelize and convert souls. Many Protestant efforts in education have cultivated literacy even for beginning learners and some have encouraged the highest levels of academic excellence and achievement, maintaining Protestantism's viability as a competitive force within the intellectual development of America. Protestant morality and values and the cultivation of a society based on them have been instilled, rehearsed, and argued by teachers, students, ministers, and advocates in many ways and places. To read, and to read the Bible written into the fabric of the nation – its people and its culture and its values – has been the unifying aim of the educational labors of American Protestants.

NOTES

1   *Records of the Governor and Colony of Massachusetts Bay*, 1647, accessed
     May 1, 2020, www.mass.gov/files/documents/2016/08/ob/deludersatan.pdf.
2   Bernard Bailyn, *Education in the Forming of American Society* (Chapel Hill:
     University of North Carolina Press, 1960), 14.
3   Bernard Bailyn, "Remarks by Dr. Bernard Bailyn," The White House Evening
     Millennium Lecture Series, February 11, 1998. The Clinton White House
     Archives, accessed May 1, 2020, https://clintonwhitehouse4.archives.gov/te
     xtonly/Initiatives/Millennium/bbailyn.html.
4   Robert Baird, *Religion in America* (New York: Harper and Brothers 1844), 15.
5   For a late nineteenth-century example, see Daniel Dorchester, *Christianity in
     the United States* (New York: Hunt and Eaton, 1888); also see
     Sydney Ahlstrom, *A Religious History of the American People* (New Haven,
     CT: Yale University Press, 1970).
6   Martin Marty, "The American Religious History Canon," *Social Research*
     vol. 53, no. 3 (Autumn 1986), 513–528.
7   Amanda Porterfield, *The Transformation of American Religion* (New York:
     Oxford University Press, 2001), 26–27; Jon Butler, Grant Wacker, and
     Randall Balmer, *Religion in American Life* (New York: Oxford University
     Press, 2011).
8   Robert Lynn, "The Uses of History: An Inquiry into the History of American
     Religious Education," *Religious Education* vol. 67, no. 2 (1978), 84;
     Sidney Meade, *The Nation with the Soul of a Church* (New York: Harper and
     Row, 1975), 94.
9   Lawrence Cremin, *American Education: The Colonial Experience*
     (New York: Harper and Row, 1970), *American Education: The National
     Experience, 1783–1876* (New York: Harper and Row, 1980), and *American
     Education: The Metropolitan Experience, 1876–1980* (New York: Harper and
     Row, 1990).
10 Cremin, *American Education: The Metropolitan Experience: 1876–1980*,
     ix–x.
11 Glenn Miller, *Piety and Intellect: The Aims and Purposes of Ante-Bellum
     Theological Education* (Atlanta: Scholars Press, 1990), *Piety and Profession:
     American Theological Education: 1870–1970* (Grand Rapids, MI: Eerdmans,
     2007), and *Piety and Plurality: Theological Education since 1960* (Leonia, NJ:
     Cascade Books, 2014).
12 Anne Boylan, *Sunday School: The Formation of an American Institution,
     1790–1880* (New Haven, CT: Yale University Press, 1988); William Ringenberg
     with Mark Noll, *The Christian College: A History of Protestant Higher
     Education in America*, 2nd ed. (Grand Rapids, MI:Baker Academic, 2006).
13 Sydney Ahlstrom, *A Religious History of the American People*, 2nd ed. with
     a foreword and concluding chapter by David Hall (New Haven, CT: Yale
     University Press, 2004).

14 Catherine Brekus and W. Clark Gilpin, eds., *American Christianities: A History of Dominance and Diversity* (Chapel Hill: University of North Carolina Press, 2011). See also Brekus. "Contested Words: History, America, Religion," *The William and Mary Quarterly* vol. 75, no. 1 (January 2018), 2–36.

15 Heather Day, *Protestant Theological Education in America: A Bibliography* (Metuchen, NJ: Scarecrow Press, 1985).

16 Thomas C. Hunt, James C. Carper, and Charles R. Kniker, *Religious Schools in America* (New York: Taylor and Francis, 1986).

17 *American Educational History: A Hypertext Timeline*, accessed May 1, 2020, www.eds-resources.com/educationhistorytimeline.html.

18 Martin Luther, "A Sermon on Keeping Children in School" (1530), accessed May 1, 2020, www.angelfire.com/ny4/djw/lutherantheology .lutherchildreninschool.html; James L. Codling, *Calvin: Ethics, Eschatology, and Education* (New York: Cambridge Scholars Publishing, 2010).

19 Donald Tewksbury, *The Founding of American Colleges and Universities before the Civil War* (New York: Ayer Co., 1969), 9.

20 *Virginia's Cure, To His Grace, the Lord Bishop of London by R.G.*, The Library of Congress, accessed May 1, 2020, http://nationalhumanitiescenter .org/pds/amerbegin/permanence/text2/VirginiaCure.pdf.

21 *New England Primer* (facsimile of the 1777 reprint edition), Internet Sacred Text Archive, accessed May 1, 2020, www.sacred-texts.com/chr/nep/1777/.

22 Samuel Pennypacker, "Christopher Dock," in *Historical and Biographical Sketches* (Philadelphia: Robert A. Tripple, 1883), 89–153.

23 Edward E. Andrews, *Native Apostles: Black and Indian Missionaries in the British Atlantic World* (Cambridge, MA: Harvard University Press, 2013).

24 William McGuffey, *The Eclectic Reader, Levels 1–6* (Cincinnati: Truman and Smith, 1836–1839). See John Westerhoff, *William McGuffey and His Readers: Piety, Morality, and Education in Nineteenth Century America* (Nashville: Abingdon, 1978).

25 Stephen J. Denig, "Public Support for Religious Education in the Nineteenth Century," *Journal of Christian Education* vol. 13, no. 1 (Spring 2004), 81–95.

26 Barbara Skolosky, *Guide to the American Sunday School Union Papers: 1817–1915, Microfilm Edition* (Sanford, NC: Microfilming Corporation of America, 1980).

27 Philadelphia Sunday and Adult School Union, "Constitution and Minutes," *Sunday School Union Papers, Microfilm Edition*, May 13–July 1, 1817.

28 Horace Bushnell, *Discourses on Christian Nurture*, Massachusetts Sabbath School Society (Boston: Sabbath School Society, 1847).

29 Palmer served as the editor of *The Guide to Holiness* from 1864 to 1874 after she purchased the journals *The Guide to Christian Perfection* and *Beauty of Holiness* and combined them into The Guide to Holiness; see William Kostlevy, *Historical Dictionary of the Holiness Movement*, 2nd ed.

(Lanham, MD: Scarecrow Press, 2009), 196–198; Charles Finney, *Lectures on Revivals of Religion* (New York: Leavitt, Lord, and Co., 1835).

30 George Marsden, *Fundamentalism and American Culture* (New York: Oxford University Press, 2006).

31 Edward Larson, *Summer for the Gods: The Scopes Trial and America's Continuing Debate over Science and Religion* (New York: Basic Books, 2006).

32 Glenn T. Miller, *A Community of Conversation: A Retrospective of The Association of Theological Schools and Ninety Years of North American Theological Education* (Pittsburgh: Association of Theological Schools, 2008).

33 James Carper, "Protestant School Systems," Encyclopedia.com, accessed May 1, 2020, www.encyclopedia.com/education/encyclopedias-almanacs-transcripts-and-maps/protestant-school-systems.

34 Gretchen Whilhelm and Michael Firmin, "Historical and Contemporary Developments in Home School Education," *Journal of Research on Christian Education* vol. 18 (2009), 303–315.

35 Johann Neem, "The Strange Afterlife of William McGuffey and His Readers," *The Hedgehog Review* vol. 20, no. 2 (Summer 2018), 114–123.

36 See Michael Anthony and Warren Benson, *Exploring the History and Philosophy of Christian Education: Principles for the 21st Century* (Grand Rapids, MI: Kregel, 2003).

37 Robert Handy, *A Christian America: Protestant Hopes and Historical Realities* (New York: Oxford University Press, 1971), 225.

8 Work and Vocation

JOSHUA R. SWEEDEN

Work and vocation represent distinct subjects with their own history, development, and embodiments. Each warrant individual treatment beyond what can be accomplished in this chapter. American Protestantism does offer a prime example of how calling, labor, employment, social status, wealth, personhood, and community are theologically interwoven. Indeed, work and vocation in American Protestantism reflect the collision of social, political, economic, and ecclesial realities of the changing contexts in North America from the seventeenth through the twentieth centuries. And those collisions did not occur in a vacuum, as if separate from a set of overarching resources and dispositions from which American Protestants constructed worldviews and practices. In this regard, American Protestants have drawn from the embedded theological assumptions of their Protestant predecessors in Europe, though not uniformly and not without adaptation to the unique American landscape.

In this chapter, I frame the historical and theological development of American Protestant understandings of work and vocation to highlight its unique contributions and contemporary challenges. From this exploration, three themes emerge that deserve consideration beyond the limits of the chapter. First, American Protestant theologies of work and vocation reflect an ongoing tension between the spiritual and temporal planes. In this regard, understandings of work and vocation remain subject to the ebbs and flows of American Protestant eschatology and its extreme variations – from, for example, premillennial dispensationalism on the one hand to postmillennialism on the other.

Second, American Protestant practices and articulations of work and vocation are interwoven with prevailing American Protestant theologies. Eschatology may be a prime example, but understandings of work and vocation are also deeply intertwined, even if indistinguishably and unknowingly, with doctrines of God, anthropology, and soteriology. Protological (doctrine of the first things) positions are commonly employed, which inevitably encompass and require interdependence with an eschatological position (doctrine of last things).

Yet, despite this clear (and necessary) interlacing of work and vocation with doctrinal positions, American Protestant understandings of work and vocation frequently exhibit theological inconsistency. Arguably, this is because work and vocation are so central to human existence. In their concrete expressions, they cannot function in theological abstraction but constantly reflect the historical, social, political, and economic contexts that also demand their allegiance.

Finally, a third theme prompting consideration is the heightened and somewhat unique context of consumerism that shapes American Protestant understandings of work and vocation. Consumerism presents an especially potent challenge for contemporary American Protestants who must resist the subtle co-opting of theologically informed understandings of work and vocation by the "consumerist machine."

Work and vocation are analyzed separately below with their interconnections highlighted to demonstrate their interlacing in the American Protestant landscape. In many ways this interlacing, coupled with various theological impulses, makes for a potent case study of how seemingly ordinary and mundane aspects of human life can become a conduit of so much promise and peril. It is an understatement to say that work and vocation are meaningful, formative, and central to human existence. Still, both subjects defy definition and common experience; they are never experienced or understood univocally. Each person, context, and situation can so shape work and vocation that their commonality from one person to another is stripped down to the basic reality of their unavoidableness. When overlaid with theological perspectives, work and vocation can take form as variegated as human experience itself – only now charged with divine significance.

WORK: DIVERSELY (MIS)UNDERSTOOD

Within its relatively short history, American Protestantism has condemned and condoned work, lauded and cursed it, desired and dispelled it. Work's varied understandings may indicate one inherent condition: it can easily be used as a tool to support prevailing ideologies. And while this is true, work is not without agency to cultivate and nurture life, community, and worldview. Work has power, and in American Protestantism we see both its power to subjugate and its power to subvert.

Work's varied understandings and engagement stem from its ambiguity. As David Jensen notes, "Attempting to define work is as elusive as defining the human person. Most of us have a rather gut-level reaction to work: we know it when we see it."[1] To this we might add Mark Twain's analysis, "and I do not like work, even when another person does it."[2] Apparently, most us *know* work and prefer to avoid it. Work has largely been construed as drudgery or toil within Christian history. This undoubtedly stems from Christian interpretations of Genesis 3:14–19, the so-called "curse of toil" that follows Adam and Eve's banishment from the Garden of Eden. Interpreters of the passage highlight the presence of pain, toil, and sweat in work as if to suggest each are a newfound result of sin. Some readers of Genesis 3 even assume work itself is the curse; a new requirement for human survival outside the garden. But this neglects the significance of alienation in the passage, which highlights the *increase* of hardships in the daily processes of production and consumption. Work itself is not the curse. Indeed, God worked (Gen. 2:2–3), declared everything good (Gen. 1:31), and commanded the 'adam to "till and keep" the garden (Gen. 2:15). The alienation correlative with sin is the subject of Genesis 3:14–19; it offers a portrait of an unholy creation disconnected from God. Alienation is both the consequence of sin and emblematic of it. Beginning with alienation from God, illustrated in Genesis 3 by human fear and hiding, alienation proliferates in relation to all creation like spokes on a wheel or ripples in a pond. The "curse" in Genesis 3 is in many ways a description of the effects of alienation at various levels: alienation from God, from self, from other living things (animate and non-animate), from the land, from time, and even from things produced (e.g., bread).

Emphasizing work as a curse – as though the problem is the thing itself – only further enables work to be used as an agent of alienation. In this regard, work has generally been viewed as instrumental; a necessary means or tool to accomplish some other purpose or end. The work itself has little value and is therefore not celebrated as joy or gift. It is drudgery and to be avoided. Thomas Aquinas's distinction between the contemplative life and the active life represents this long-standing sentiment in the Christian tradition. For Aquinas, "the contemplative life is more excellent than the active." He cites Luke 10:24 and how Mary, rather than Martha who busies herself, has "chosen the best part."[3] The active life has purpose, but only in that it "conduces to the contemplative by quelling the interior passions which give rise to phantasms whereby contemplation is hindered."[4] Early desert monastics represent this distinction as well: their contemplative life and ascetic ideal demanded freedom from the

distractions of society and pressures of daily life. This narrow instrumen-
talism of work shifted dramatically in communal monasticism and the
Benedictine tradition. Though work remained a means of providing neces-
sities and countering idleness (which Benedict referred to as the "enemy of
the soul"), it found intrinsic value and integration into the rhythms of the
Benedictine life. Benedict understood labor to be a fundamental part of the
monastic life, not just a means to ensure opportunities for contemplation.
In *Benedict's Rule*, manual labor complements a contemplative and pray-
erful life.[5] This does not mean that work is no longer instrumental or
functional. Indeed, labor sustained monasteries. Benedict even acknowledges, "[the monastery] will really be in the best monastic tradition if the
community is supported by the works of its own hands. It is just what our
predecessors did, and the apostles themselves."[6] Yet Benedict does combine work's instrumental and intrinsic value. As Joan Chittister notes,

> Benedictines were to "earn their bread by the labor of their hands," and
> no devotion was to take the place of the demands of life ... At the same
> time, work is not what defines the Benedictine ... The monastic does
> not exist for work. Creative and productive work are simply meant to
> enhance the Garden and sustain us while we grow into God ... Work
> periods, in fact, are specified just as prayer periods are. Work and prayer
> are opposite sides of the great coin of life that is both holy and useful,
> immersed in God and dedicated to the transcendent in the human.[7]

Benedict stated that "all the community must be occupied at definite
times in manual labor and at other times in *lectio divina*."[8] This established the rhythm of work and prayer in Benedictine life. As the tradition
developed, manual work was not only valued by Benedictines but in
some cases considered holy.[9]

Work can be engaged for pleasure or curiosity; it can be a type of
play. But even in such cases, work remains functional. Play has purpose. Yet, when work is understood as only instrumental then what we
do and how we do it has little meaning or value. American Protestant
views of work reflect these tensions within Christian history. At times
American Protestants give work teleological value, though more generally work capitulates to the prevailing social and economic ideologies of the day.

WORK IN THE CONTEXT OF AMERICAN PROTESTANTISM

The unique attributes of American Protestant understandings of work
are highly reflective of the social, political, economic, and religious

impulses of the early American landscape. Puritanism and Pietism carried their unique emphases across the Atlantic and shared a pragmatic and semi-ascetic disposition toward worldly things. For work, this translated to the valuing of simplicity, thrift, quality, self-denial, and stewardship for the common good. The influences of sixteenth-century reformer John Calvin, seventeenth-century English Puritan Richard Baxter, and eighteenth-century Methodist John Wesley highlight this lineage and provide a common thread across the different Protestant streams they represent. In his *Institutes of Christian Religion*, for example, Calvin notes the Christian duty of "seeking to benefit one's neighbor," which cannot be accomplished "unless you give up all thought of self and ... get out of yourself."[10] Denying oneself and living in moderation coincides with his emphasis on stewarding God's resources, which includes the gifts of work and industry:

> Whatever benefits we obtain from the Lord have been entrusted to us on this condition: that they be applied to the common good of the church ... So, too, whatever a godly man can do he ought to be able to do for his brothers, providing for himself in no way other than to have his mind intent upon the common building of the church. Let this, therefore, be our rule for generosity and beneficence: We are stewards of everything God has conferred on us by which we are able to help our neighbor, and are required to render account of our stewardship.[11]

Reiterating the importance of stewardship, Calvin later states that all things are "so given to us by the kindness of God, and so destined for our benefit, that they are, as it were, entrusted to us, and we must one day render account of them."[12] The individual's moral responsibility to properly use God-given gifts/talents is a frequent theme in Protestantism and highlights a teleological approach to work. Work can be a means of testifying to and participating in the in-breaking kingdom of God. Christians are to be stewards, not only of the things their work produces, but also with their abilities and skills. Beyond meeting basic needs, one's work is to benefit the neighbor, which all Christians will have to account for at the day of judgment.

Baxter offers a stronger Puritan vision of the Christian duty to work diligently and on behalf of the poor. Here we see an ethic that emphasizes "the public welfare or the good of many is to be valued above our own," and that every person is "bound to do all the good he can for others."[13] Baxter even states that "he that has the most wages from God should do him most work," meaning those who have been given more or can do more, must do more. A person "must labor for the good of the society which he belongs to."[14]

In many places Wesley echoes Calvin and Baxter. In his sermon, "The Use of Money," for example, Wesley considers the maxim of gain, save, and give all you can. Wesley suggests "we are to gain all we can without hurting our neighbor"; we cannot "hurt anyone in his substance." By this Wesley meant Christians are not to "devour" a neighbor's lands or houses or take unreasonable interest. We cannot, Wesley said, "consistent with brotherly love, sell our goods below the market price. We cannot study the ruin of our neighbor's trade in order to advance our own ... none can gain by swallowing up his neighbor's substance, without gaining the damnation of hell."[15] Gain should come by "honest industry" and use of "all possible diligence."[16] Work and the talents and industriousness a person possessed are gifts for one's neighbor in service to God. A person is a steward of those gifts and God is proprietor. Just as Calvin wrote that we "are required to render account of our stewardship," Wesley asserted that we will "give account of our stewardship" when we are "no longer stewards" (i.e., upon death).[17] Wesley largely addressed the manner in which money, "the most comprehensive talent," was employed, but he understood work, too, as a talent of which God was ultimately proprietor.[18]

The shared emphases of Calvin, Baxter, and Wesley on work – diligence, stewardship, self-denial, responsibility to neighbor – continue to find resonance in American Protestantism today. But the theologies of these influential forebearers did not go unscathed by the rise of capitalism and industrialism in the nineteenth and early twentieth centuries. The so-called "spirit of capitalism" was especially potent in the American landscape. Sociologist Max Weber credited Protestantism, particularly Calvinism and Puritanism, for imbuing capitalism with religious values to support larger capitalist ideologies. Published in the 1905, *The Protestant Ethic and the Spirit of Capitalism* remains an influential but contested thesis. His argument that religious values were employed to support the capitalist position has been largely sustained, though debate continues as to whether Protestantism is any more liable here than Catholicism, Judaism, or pseudo-theologies like humanism.

Two of Weber's findings are worth noting as indicative of the intertwining of early capitalism and Protestantism. First, under the spirit of capitalism "economic activity is an end to itself" only "now invested with moral value."[19] Protestantism supports or at least complements an ideal of profit and moneymaking as a kind of *telos* – a goal worth pursuing. Weber argues it does this even though it "runs counter to the moral feeling of entire [previous] eras" in which money was a means for supporting one's livelihood or the common good.[20] Secondly, Weber identifies how the religiously infused spirit of capitalism prioritized the "work over the worker." Since the purpose of work is to support economic activity, the product becomes valued over the producer. Workers and their labors become increasingly evaluated for their productivity and effectiveness, encouraging an employer to use strategies and devices to "get the maximum performance out of 'his' workers, and to increase the 'work rate,' of piecework."[21] The shift ultimately increased assessment and calculation of workers in terms of use value with the worth of a worker being quantifiable as a unit of exchange, i.e., money. Weber insightfully notes capitalism's dependence upon cheap labor, a fact only further evidenced since the publication of *The Protestant Ethic and the Spirit of Capitalism*: "Certainly, capitalism demands for its growth the presence of a surplus population that it can hire cheaply on the 'labor market.'"[22]

The early twentieth century solidified Weber's analysis. Frederick Winslow Taylor's "time-and-motion studies" and his published four principles from *The Principles of Scientific Management* became symbolic of a new wave of management.[23] In "Taylorism," employee labor is specialized, controlled, and analyzed for output. The manager becomes a type of skilled mental technician who assesses and adjusts systems to maximize productivity. Michael Budde describes Taylorist forms of labor control as "'scientific management,' technology utilized to enhance worker output, docility, and surveillance; polarization between skilled mental workers and unskilled workers; and increasing mechanization, leading to rapidly rising productivity and a higher ratio of capital goods per worker."[24] The influence of Taylorism is readily seen in Henry Ford's assembly line. Here, Taylor's principles are applied to manufacturing design and factory systems. As Richard Sennett argues, "Fordism takes the division of labor to an extreme: each worker does one task, measured as precisely as possible by time-and-motion studies; output is measured in terms of targets that are, again, entirely quantitative."[25] Fordism continued through the industrial period, including post-World War II production, and then began to diminish in the 1970s. This gave way to post-Fordism in which traditional assembly lines decreased but worker specialization increased in order to meet new patterns of small volume, flexible production. Jytte Klausen states that postindustrialist theory "paints a picture of the disappearing, so-called Fordist, manual worker in work clothes smeared with grease, who has been displaced by a post-Fordist employee in casual clothes using tools directed by computers. The change in working conditions is presumed to have been accompanied by a change in consciousness from that of a 'worker' to that of a 'technician.'"[26] These patterns are driven by information technologies which enable manufacturers to better quantify demand.

Taylorism and Fordism have left a lasting mark on American Protestant understandings of work. The social and economic context that supported the widespread adoption of Taylorism and Fordism was shared by a Protestantism deeply conjoined with the capitalist spirit. American Protestantism retained some of the moral sensitivities of its Protestant predecessors – e.g., Calvin, Baxter, Wesley – but otherwise appears to have been captivated by an individualist and consumerist worldview. Wealth became a worthy if not noble pursuit, relegating work to an instrumental status.

The influence of Adam Smith and the theological and anthropological undertones of his economic theory are at least partly responsible. Smith believed that increased economic exchanges could benefit both persons and society, creating stability and spurring societal development. The division of labor, he contended, would allow each person to exchange "that surplus part of the produce of his own labour, which is over and above his own consumption." This would allow every person to become "in some measure a merchant," which would grow a commercial society and increase prosperity.[27] Smith presupposed that it was natural for humans to want to exchange. Smith states, "This division of labour, from which so many advantages are derived, is not originally the effect of any human wisdom . . . It is the necessary, though very slow and gradual, consequence of a certain propensity in human nature which has in view no such extensive utility; the propensity to truck, barter, and exchange one thing for another."[28] More specifically, Smith understood self-interest and personal gain to be propensities of (depraved) humanity; exchange was simply what was required to achieve wealth. His economic proposal sought to take into account human inclinations for the greater good of society. Max Lerner wrote of him: "First, Smith assumes that the prime psychological drive in man as an economic being is the drive of self-interest. Secondly, he assumes the existence of a natural order in the universe which makes all the individual strivings for self-interest add up to social good. Finally, from these postulates, he concludes that the best program is to leave the economic process severely alone – what has come to be known as laissez-faire, economic liberalism, or non-interventionism. "[29] Invariably, then, work became viewed as a means to wealth and happiness. It was a tool, something to be ordered and manipulated. The division of labor illustrated work's suppleness but also reified the dominant modern perspective of work as toil and drudgery, something to be cursed, avoided, and engaged only as a means to some other end.

Interestingly, Karl Marx offered an alternative economic theory that was similarly based on universal theological and anthropological claims. For Marx, the human propensity was not self-interest and personal gain, but the desire to be a "universal producer."[30] Humans are predisposed to relationship and mutuality. Work is a form of cooperation that cultivates the creative impulses of humans, who through participation with the world, edify both themselves and society. Marx was concerned that the division of labor and unrestrained economic motivation for productivity reduced work to "use value" and increased the alienation of workers from both community and the products they produced. This led, Marx argued, to the objectification of labor and treatment of work as "exchange value." Work is valued for the generation of capital, but "the worker contributes labour as use value to be exchanged against capital ... it [labor] only has exchange value for the worker; tangible exchange value."[31]

In other words, Marx feared work became a commodity under capitalism and the worker's labors – skills, capacities, creativity – became tools or instruments to be employed in exchange for participation in the economy. Marx believed work should be "a mode of human expression by which humans recognize their own nature and creative capacities." Douglas Meeks summarizes Marx's position stating, "According to Marx we express our humanity through artistic, theoretical, and technological work. Work is the revelation of one's hidden, inner self ... Only because Marx's estimation of work is so high does he so radically criticize work as it exists in the modern world. People will not recognize their alienation through work until they have been asked to take their work seriously as their self-creation."[32] If work was instrumental, it was instrumental in its ability to enhance human life and improve society. The economic measurement of work should be replaced by a social measurement of work which valued its capacities as art and creativity. Work as exchange value, Marx feared, meant "that the worker cannot enrich himself as a result of this exchange, since (like Esau, who exchanged his birthright for a mess of pottage) he gives up his creative power for the ability to work, as an already existing quantity."[33] Marx's view of work is predicated by anthropological assumptions that, as Shlomo Avineri suggests, gives humanity a "world shaping function." Marx believes labor is "man's process of self-becoming because it is man's specific attribute."[34] The theological overtones are anything but subtle.

The juxtaposition of Smith and Marx highlights another tension between work's instrumental and intrinsic value that was transferred to the American landscape. As economic theories collided and the rise of industrialism and modern work patterns replaced traditional workshops and guilds, American Protestant understandings of work became intertwined with an emerging set of economic ideologies. These ideologies were less reflective of the admonitions of early Protestants but were no less theological in scope. This enabled capitalism and American Protestantism to become unique bedfellows in the twentieth century.

VOCATION AND THE PROTESTANT CONTRIBUTION

Under the influence of Martin Luther, Christian understandings of vocation took an explicit turn from a narrow conceptualization as religious work to an inclusive designation for the priesthood of all believers. Protestant theologies of vocation readily reflect Luther's development of calling beyond the clerical paradigm. The emphases continued into American Protestant understandings of vocation which, like understandings of work, leaned on Protestant predecessors: Luther, Calvin, Baxter, Wesley.

Luther's theology of vocation reflects his emphasis on *sola fide* and rejection of salvation through works. Since faith alone was grounds for salvation, clericalism could not signal a superior service or ensure salvation. Luther believed, as William Placher notes, that "no one should feel compelled to enter a monastery or convent and become some sort of super-Christian in order to contribute to one's salvation through works. Rather, we should stick to where God has put us and serve God there."[35] Luther's critique of clergy structures in the Roman Catholic Church undoubtedly fed his theological development. Gary Badcock notes that Luther, coinciding with his stress on the priesthood of all believers, sought to make "no distinction between religious and secular works, as if God was more pleased with one than with the other."[36] Works are acceptable to God only by faith, which is an expression of the gospel available to all people.

As vocation was extended beyond religious work and clerical roles, "calling" took on new meaning. All Christians now had at least two callings, a spiritual calling (common to all Christians and the Christian life) and an external calling (to a specific station or office in the world). These distinctions have remained but are more commonly called "general" and "special" or "particular" calling. The beauty of Luther's reformulation of vocation is its valuing of the breadth of human work and service. All work now functions (or has the potential to function) as part of the ministry and witness of God's reign. God's work in the world is not limited to the clergy or the walls of the church. For Luther and later Protestants this coincided with a pre-Constantinian vision of the church in the world. The challenge of Luther's reformulation came with its embedded social stratification through determination and status. For Luther, "One's 'external calling', therefore, was wherever one was – whether blacksmith, serf, or clergyperson."[37] Persons were assigned a status and standing in the world and were called to faithfully exercise their abilities in that station. Social mobility was not part of his equation, and vocation could, if abused, become as much a tool of oppression as a tool of freedom. Placher notes, "Luther's conviction that each person has a calling and should stick to it was an enemy of social mobility. The simple shepherd who wanted to work his way up to be a merchant found no support in Luther's theology."[38]

Though a contemporary of Luther and sometimes considered part of the "second generation" of the Reformation, Calvin's theology of vocation was largely developed independent from Luther. Even still, Calvin offered similar emphases. Christian duty and stewardship play a prominent role in Calvin's understanding of calling and vocation, as it had in his understanding of work. He employs language of general and special calling, though, as Placher notes, "in a different way – the 'general calling' was the word that anyone could hear in preaching, inviting them to faith; a 'special calling' worked only in the hearts of the elect, to bring them to faith."[39] Also, while Calvin extends vocation beyond religious work he similarly ties vocation to social status and station:

> [God] has appointed duties for every man in his particular way of life. And that no one may thoughtlessly transgress his limits, he has named these various kinds of "callings." Therefore each individual has his own kind of living assigned to him by the Lord as a sort of sentry post so that he may not heedlessly wander about through life ... Accordingly, your life will then be best ordered when it is directed to this goal. For no one, impelled by his own rashness, will attempt more than his calling will permit, because he will know that it is not lawful to exceed its bounds. A man of obscure station will lead a private life ungrudgingly so as not to leave the rank in which he has been placed by God.[40]

Vocation and calling for Calvin were teleological in orientation. Though they assigned one's social station and specific contribution to society, that contribution reflected God's order. To live into one's vocation was to participate in God's purposes and intents. Positively, this offered the potential for persons to see their calling and station as expressions of divine gifts being properly directed through a faithful servant. Calvin offers this threefold rule on vocation, work, and one's station in the world:

> Let this be our main principle: that the use of God's gifts is not wrongly directed when it is referred to that end to which the Author himself created and destined them for us, since he created them for our good, not for our ruin ... The second rule will be: they who have slender and narrow resources should know how to go without things patiently, lest they be troubled by an immoderate desire for them. If they keep this rule of moderation, they will make considerable progress in the Lord's school ... Scripture has a third rule with which to regulate the use of earthly things ... It decrees that all those things were so given to us by the kindness of God, and so destined for our benefit, that they are, as it were, entrusted to us, and we must one day render account of them.[41]

Baxter and Wesley reflect this Protestant lineage with small variations. Vocation extends beyond religious work and calling is understood as both general and particular, including the place or position of one's labor. The themes of stewardship, duty, and contribution to the good of society are evident. There is also emphasis on diligence and the avoidance of idleness. Baxter's vision of calling is integrated with God's design and intent for the good of society. It is less static and socially immobile than Luther and Calvin, though it is specific: "A calling is a stated, ordinary course of labor ... [one in which] a man is best skilled ... therefore he doth it better than he could do another work, and so wrongs not others, but attains more the ends of his labor."[42] Vocation is what one does best, not simply where one is placed. At the same time, Baxter did assume a social hierarchy. Certain callings were more useful and necessary for the good of society: "the magistrates, the pastors, and teachers of the church, schoolmasters, physicians, lawyers, husbandmen (ploughmen, graziers, and shepherds), and next to them are the mariners, clothiers, booksellers, tailors, and such others that are employed about things most necessary to mankind."[43] Wesley, attentive to the plight of the poor, was more apt to provide opportunity for social mobility. His ministry largely focused on the general calling of Christians as he sought renewal in the church. He echoes emphases of his predecessors, providing at times clear instructions regarding proper stewardship of gifts and talents. Wesley's most widely recognized writing on vocation comes from a prayer in his *Directions for Renewing Our Covenant with God.* The prayer was not an attempt to offer a vocational theology, but its popularity and influence have extended well beyond its original intent. Placed in the context of the eighteenth century, with Luther, Calvin, and Baxter in the backdrop, the prayer captures many themes and emphases of Protestant understandings of vocation:

> I am no longer my own, but yours. Put me to what you will, rank me with whom you will; put me to doing, put me to suffering; let me be employed for you, or laid aside for you, exalted for you, or brought low for you; let me be full, let me be empty; let me have all things, let me have nothing; I freely and heartily yield all things to your pleasure and disposal. And now, glorious and blessed God, Father, Son and Holy Spirit, you are mine, and I am yours. So be it. And the Covenant which I have made on earth, let it be ratified in heaven.[44]

EMERGING VOCATIONAL THEOLOGIES

Protestantism imbued work with meaning when it moved vocation beyond its clerical captivity and assigned it to labor and occupation. To whatever degree that played a role in how Americans align self-worth and identity with their work, Protestantism certainly created a fertile seedbed for what Derek Thompson called a religion of "workism."[45] If, as he suggests, Americans believe work "is not only necessary to economic production, but also the centerpiece of one's identity and life's purpose," then it would be especially true among American Protestants, who were "reared from their teenage years to make their passion their career and, if they don't have a calling, told not to yield until they found one."[46] Assigning calling to work invariably raises the stakes of employment beyond mere instrumental or exchange value. Deep within American Protestantism lies the conviction that one's work has divine significance. By the mid-twentieth century, pressure to find or discover one's calling replaced historic emphases of simply accepting or affirming one's calling (i.e., taking satisfaction in one's station). The shift coincided with greater levels of educational attainment and increased occupational opportunities in the American context. As a result, vocational theologies became more attentive to the inward and outward dimensions of calling. This is readily seen, for example, through recent writings of Parker

Palmer and Frederick Buechner, whose statement, "The place God calls you to is the place where your deep gladness and the world's deep hunger meet" has become a common adage.[47]

General and particular calling remain the dominant categories to discuss calling in American Protestantism, though theologians like Doug Koskela include the category of "missional calling." If general calling refers to the vocation of all Christians to live faithfully in love of God and neighbor, and particular calling refers to the call to a specific task, occupation, or assignment, then missional calling breaks the duality by referring to something more specific than general calling but less direct than particular calling. Koskela describes missional calling as calling that aligns with a person's gifts and "involves something you are passionate about and which gives you joy." It is about "the main contributions your life makes to God's kingdom ... the 'mission statement' of your life."[48] Vocation here is not tied to a particular occupation, industry, or technical skill, but instead the various expressions a person's passions and gifts take throughout their life.

As North America undergoes post-Christendom shifts, the category of missional calling may offer a stopgap for sustaining ministerial identity in American Protestantism. Alongside declines in religious affiliation and church attendance, professional clergy are decreasing. Additionally, the occupational permanence and social immobility assumed in early Protestantism neither reflect the transitional and transient nature of work today nor are shared by contemporary Christians. Even those disaffected and disenfranchised with the church can find solace in their missional calling and the hope that they can use their God-given passions and gifts for the benefit of others.

THE FUTURE OF WORK AND VOCATION: WHO/WHAT WILL SHAPE THE THEOLOGICAL IMAGINATION?

The deep theological wells of American Protestantism provide a critical resource for future of work and vocation. Theologies of work and vocation are dynamically constructed through an inevitable correlation of context and tradition. The examples in this chapter offer a simple reminder of how American Protestant understandings of work and vocation, like all Christian thought and practice, do not exist in a vacuum. The future of work and vocation will depend greatly on the social, political, and economic realities shaping the American landscape. But to avoid being a mere reflection of prevailing ideologies and pressures, American Protestants will need to increasingly draw from the resources of their tradition. This involves both recovering appropriate emphases and weighing current understandings of work and vocation against a rich storehouse of wisdom.

Critical engagement with understandings of work and vocation demands identification and evaluation of influential narratives and liturgies functioning in the broader society. In some cases, the narratives and liturgies rival theologically rooted perspectives, in other cases they challenge and inspire new and more theologically robust articulations of work and vocation.

Consumerist narratives and liturgies dominate the current landscape of American Protestantism. In fact, consumerism is so prevalent and infused with all aspects of American life that it may be impossible to distinguish where one "ism" (Protestantism) begins and the other (consumerism) ends. Consumerism has taken "work as exchange value" to its logical extreme: we now work to consume. The notion that we work for the weekend, suffer from 9-to-5 in order to play later, and thank God when it's Friday all reflect a perspective of work as a mere tool or instrument to be endured in order to satisfy our primary identity as consumers. The danger is that these sentiments toward work become self-fulfilling prophecies. Similarly, vocation is a powerful tool in the hands of consumerism. Contemporary theologies of vocation provide an important corrective to short-sighted and overstated emphases on social station as direct calling, but American Protestants now face the challenge of maintaining emphases of obedience and stewardship in a context where personal preference and individual freedom to attach/detach from any community, task, or thing is prioritized. Fortunately, American Protestantism is not without resources, but it must continually endeavor to sustain a tradition that found intrinsic value in what we do and why we do it.

NOTES

1 David Jensen, *Responsive Labor: A Theology of Work* (Louisville, KY: Westminster John Knox Press, 2006), 2.

2 Mark Twain, "The Lost Napoleon," in *Europe and Elsewhere* (New York: The Mark Twain Company, 1923), 172.

3 Thomas Aquinas, *Summa Theologica*, Q. 182.1, in *Callings: Twenty Centuries of Christian Wisdom on Vocation*, ed. William Placher (Grand Rapids, MI: Eerdmans, 2005), 157.

4 Aquinas, *Summa Theologica*, Q. 182.2, 159.

5 Joan Chittister, *The Rule of Benedict: Insights for the Ages* (New York: Crossroad, 1992), 132.

6 Benedict, *Saint Benedict's Rule*, trans. Ampleforth Abbey (Mahwah, NJ: HiddenSpring, 2004), 117.

7 Chittister, *The Rule of Benedict*, 134, 132

8 Benedict, *Saint Benedict's Rule*, 117.

9 For more on how the monastic tradition reflects the tension within Christianity between work's instrumental and teleological value, see Joshua Sweeden. *The Church and Work: The Ecclesiological Grounding of Good Work*. (Eugene, OR: Pickwick Publications, 2014), 34–37.

10 John Calvin, *Institutes of the Christian Religion*, vol. I, Book 3, ed. John T. McNeill and Forest Lewis Battles (Philadelphia: Westminster John Knox Press, 1960), 695.

11 Calvin, *Institutes of the Christian Religion*, vol. I, Book 3, 695.

12 Calvin, *Institutes of the Christian Religion*, vol. I, Book 3, 720.

13 Richard Baxter, *The Practical Works of the Rev. Richard Baxter*, in *Callings*, ed. Placher, 280.

14 Baxter, *The Practical Works of the Rev. Richard Baxter*, 280.

15 John Wesley, "The Use of Money" (1760), in *John Wesley's Sermons: An Anthology*, ed. Albert C. Outler and Richard P. Heitzenrater (Nashville: Abingdon Press, 1991), 351.

16 Wesley, "The Use of Money," 352.

17 John Wesley, "The Good Steward" (1768), in *John Wesley's Sermons*, ed. Outler and Heitzenrater, 426.

18 Wesley, "The Good Steward," 428.

19 Peter Baehr, Introduction to Max Weber, *The Protestant Ethic and the Spirit of Capitalism and Other Writings* (New York: Penguin, 2002), xvii.

20 Max Weber, *The Protestant Ethic and the Spirit of Capitalism and Other Writings* (New York: Penguin, 2002), 25.

21 Weber, *The Protestant Ethic and the Spirit of Capitalism*, 15.

22 Weber, *The Protestant Ethic and the Spirit of Capitalism*, 17.

23 Frederick Taylor, *The Principles of Scientific Management* (New York: Harper Bros., 1911).

24 Michael Budde, *The (Magic) Kingdom of God: Christianity and Global Culture Industries* (Boulder, CO: Westview, 1997), 22.

25 Richard Sennett, *The Craftsman* (New Haven, CT: Yale University Press, 2008), 47.

26 Jytte Klausen, "The Declining Significance of Male Workers: Trade Union Responses to Changing Markets," in *Continuity and Change in Contemporary Capitalism*, ed. Herbert Kitschelt, Peter Lange, Gary Marks, and John D. Stephens (Cambridge: Cambridge University Press, 1999), 263.

27 Adam Smith, *An Inquiry into the Nature and Causes of the Wealth of Nations*, ed. Edwin Cannan (New York: Random House, 1937), 22.

28 Smith, *The Wealth of Nations*, 13.

29 Max Lerner, "Introduction," in Smith, *The Wealth of Nations*, viii.

30 See Shlomo Avineri, *The Social and Political Thought of Karl Marx* (London: Cambridge University Press, 1968), 122.

31 Karl Marx, *The Grundrisse* (New York: Harper and Row, 1971), 80.

32 Douglas Meeks, *God the Economist: The Doctrine of God and Political Economy* (Minneapolis: Fortress Press, 1989), 144.

33 Marx, *The Grundrisse*, 81. He further states that work's exchange value is "predetermined by a past process" of exchange. Work, therefore, is objectified before it even begins.

34 Avineri, *The Social and Political Thought of Karl Marx*, 85.

35 *Callings*, ed. Placher, 205.

36 Gary Badcock, *The Way of Life* (Grand Rapids, MI: Eerdmans, 1998), 35.

37 See Gustaf Wingren, *Luther on Vocation*, trans. Carl C. Rasmussen (Eugene, OR: Wipf and Stock, 2004).

38 *Callings*, ed. Placher, 207.

39 *Callings*, ed. Placher, 232.

40 Calvin, *Institutes of the Christian Religion*, vol. I, Book 3, 724.

41 Calvin, *Institutes of Christian Religion*, vol. I, Book 3, 720.

42 Baxter, *The Practical Works of the Rev. Richard Baxter*, 281.

43 Baxter, *The Practical Works of the Rev. Richard Baxter*, 283.

44 John Wesley, "A Service for Such as Would Make or Renew Their Covenant with God," [a modern adaptation], in *John and Charles Wesley: Selected Writings and Hymns*, ed. Frank Whaling (Minneapolis: Paulist Press, 1981), 387.

45 Derek Thompson, "Workism Is Making Americans Miserable," *The Atlantic*, February 24, 2019, www.theatlantic.com/ideas/archive/2019/02/religion-workism-making-americans-miserable/583441/.

46 Thompson, "Workism Is Making Americans Miserable."

47 Frederick Buechner, *Wishful Thinking: A Seeker's ABC* (New York: HarperCollins, 1993), 119. See also Parker Palmer, *Let Your Life Speak: Listening for the Voice of Vocation* (San Francisco: Jossey-Bass, 2009).

48 Doug Koskela, *Calling and Clarity: Discovering What God Wants for Your Life* (Grand Rapids, MI: Eerdmans, 2015), 2.

9 Politics and Government

DANIEL K. WILLIAMS

Protestants have had more influence than any other religious group on American politics. Indeed, their influence has been so great that the history of American politics cannot be separated from the history of American Protestantism. All but two of the thirty-nine signers of the US Constitution were Protestant. For the first half-century after the signing of the Constitution, all Supreme Court justices and members of presidential cabinets were Protestants. Before the twenty-first century, all but one of the American presidents were Protestants either by family heritage or personal practice, and all but a handful of major-party presidential nominees were as well. Protestants have played a role in shaping the political ideology of every major party in the United States and in formulating nearly every major public policy. This sweeping Protestant control of American government is perhaps not surprising, because until the beginning of the twenty-first century, a majority of the American population was Protestant.

American Protestants vary widely in their view of government, and at various extremes on the Protestant spectrum, one can find Protestants who believe that Christians should abstain from all political activity, including voting (the view of some – though not all – Amish); Protestants who believe that the United States should be a Christian nation directly governed by biblical law (the position of one Christian Right faction known as "theonomists" or "Christian Reconstructionists"); and Protestants who believe that the state should be completely secular, with an absolute separation of church and state (the view of a few liberal mainline Protestants, including the Protestant leaders of Americans United for the Separation of Church and State).[1] Most American Protestants, though, have held positions somewhere between these extremes. Most Protestant denominations have encouraged their members to vote and to do so with Christian convictions in mind. And though political views vary widely among Protestants, most American

Protestants outside of the extremes mentioned above have generally subscribed to the following beliefs about politics:

1. In keeping with the denominational view of Christianity (that is, the view that no single denomination has a monopoly on religious truth, and that the universal church of Jesus Christ is composed of members of multiple denominations), most American Protestants from the late eighteenth century to the present have supported the separation of church and state and both the "establishment" and "free exercise" clauses of the First Amendment. They have generally supported the right for individuals to worship (or not worship) at the religious establishment of their choice, and they have believed that the US government should not create a religious establishment or endorse one religious denomination or sect to the exclusion of others.

2. In keeping with the spirit of Protestant individualism, rationality, the Reformation principle of "sola scriptura," and the view that every individual has the right to interpret the Bible for himself or herself, American Protestants have generally been suspicious of any religious organization's attempt to control the minds or votes of its followers and impose its religious principles on others through public law. This, in practice, meant that – despite their professed religious toleration – Protestants of all types have often been hostile to non-Protestant religious political influence. Large numbers of eighteenth- and nineteenth-century American Protestants were fearful of Catholic political influence and, after 1830, the political influence of the Church of Jesus Christ of Latter-Day Saints – partly because they believed (perhaps erroneously) that both of these religious groups did not subscribe to the American principle of church–state separation and would attempt to create a non-Protestant theocratic political order. In the twenty-first century, some evangelical Protestants made similar charges against Islam. And in the late twentieth and early twenty-first centuries, many liberal Protestants expressed anxiety about the alleged theocratic leanings of the Christian Right.

3. While subscribing to the principle of church–state separation, American Protestants have also generally seen political activity as a moral enterprise, governed by broadly shared (Protestant-inspired) norms. Because of the historic Protestant emphasis on religiously guided ethical living, Protestants across the theological spectrum have been guided by their religious tradition in campaigning for moral regulation. In the nineteenth century, Protestants campaigned for the

regulation of slavery and alcohol. In the twentieth century, many liberal Protestants invoked Scripture in supporting civil rights and campaigning against the Vietnam War, while a number of conservative Protestants took their religious views into the public square by campaigning against abortion and gay rights.

These Protestant-inspired tenets of political behavior are so deeply engrained in the nation's consciousness that their appeal has extended well beyond Protestant circles. But as uncontroversial as most of these tenets might seem to Americans today, their development was a contested part of the nation's Protestant history. The English Protestants who initially settled the American colonies in the seventeenth century did not necessarily share all of these views, and their adoption was a product of competition and tension between opposing groups of factionalized Protestants. Today most of these tenets might meet with considerably less controversy, but the ongoing conflicts between competing groups of Protestants continue to shape American political debates and will likely do so for the foreseeable future.

FROM PROTESTANT ESTABLISHMENT TO PROTESTANT MORAL CAMPAIGNS

The first Protestants to settle in North America were seventeenth-century Anglicans and English Puritans who believed in a church establishment. At the time, England, like most of Europe, was influenced by the 1,000-year-long heritage of Christendom. This model for Christian civilization featured a close relationship between church and state and gave the government responsibility for protecting true religion and cultivating moral virtue and piety in its citizens. English common law, which included stiff penalties (sometimes including execution) for blasphemy and adultery, was loosely based on biblical precepts. Both Anglican Virginia and Puritan Massachusetts adopted a similar legal code and, like England, both required citizens to attend services of the established church. But the Puritan emphasis on individual conversion and a church community composed only of regenerate people who could give a testimony of divine grace operating in their hearts was an uneasy fit for the model of Christendom. Less than a decade after the establishment of the Massachusetts Bay Colony in 1629, dissenting Puritans in the colony, including Anne Hutchinson and Roger Williams, challenged both the theology and politics of the Puritan church establishment. Williams became a Baptist, with a strong view of church–state separation. The colony of Rhode Island that he established became the first colony in North America to renounce the idea of church establishment and offer full religious toleration to all worshippers of God, including Jews. In the late seventeenth century, the Quaker colony of Pennsylvania did the same. The Quakers embraced religious toleration because they rejected established social hierarchies, as well as violence and other conventional forms of coercion, and because they believed that the inner light of the Holy Spirit was equally accessible to every person. Williams and his fellow Baptists did so because they believed that true religion was a matter of the converted heart and could therefore never be enforced by a political authority. State interference in religion would only corrupt the church, so the best political protection the church could ask for would come not from a zealous magistrate who sought to promote "true religion" but rather from a religiously tolerant state that allowed churches the freedom to worship God as they saw fit without favoring any single version of religion.[2]

In the late eighteenth century, Enlightenment rationalist Protestants (some of whom were deists, Unitarians, or part of a group of theologically liberal Anglicans called "latitudinarians") and evangelical Baptists and Methodists worked together to dismantle church establishments and enshrine the protection of religious liberty in state constitutions. By the early nineteenth century, only two states (the Puritan strongholds of Connecticut and Massachusetts) still had established churches; even in those states, church establishment ended by the 1830s. At the federal level, the US Constitution prohibited religious tests for office, and the First Amendment prohibited Congress from making a law "respecting an establishment of religion, or prohibiting the free exercise thereof." Evangelical Protestants – such as Baptists, Methodists, and members of the newly created Disciples of Christ – were especially strong advocates of the new democratic message of liberty. But in the minds of most American Protestant Christians – including the evangelical Baptists who had been vocal advocates of church–state separation – this did not mean the end of Protestant Christian influence in state or national law; it meant only that the state could not elevate the privileges of one particular church or denomination above all others. Most American Protestants believed that state and national law should reflect broadly agreed-upon moral norms that they assumed were based on religious precepts. In keeping with this view, blasphemy laws penalized those who spoke profanely or disparagingly about Jesus Christ. Many Northern Congregationalist and Presbyterian ministers of the early nineteenth century wanted to go further and protect the Christian Sabbath by prohibiting commerce on

Sunday. But when the post office and canal boat companies insisted in the 1820s that they would do business on all seven days of the week, these Protestant ministers lost their campaign.[3]

Protestant campaigns to regulate alcohol sales and prohibit slavery proved more enduring. Before the 1820s, neither alcohol nor slavery had been a major concern for most white American Protestants. Although the transatlantic slave trade had disturbed many white Americans (including even some enslavers) in the late eighteenth century, only a minority of white Christians – notably, the Quakers, Methodists, and a handful of Northern Reformed Protestant ministers – had spoken out against slavery per se. But the Second Great Awakening, which promoted a born-again conversion experience and a life of socially engaged holy living as identifying marks of the authentic Christian experience, led to new Protestant-inspired moral reform campaigns which, for at least a few Northern evangelicals, included anti-slavery.

While some Northern white evangelicals and Unitarians became increasingly concerned about slavery in the 1830s–1850s, African American Protestants, who had almost invariably experienced slavery themselves or witnessed its effects among family members, went further and made anti-slavery activism the center of their political theology. Like other African-American Protestants, members of the African Methodist Episcopal Church (AME) – the nation's first African-American Protestant denomination – adopted a theology of liberation centered on the Exodus narrative and believed that enslaved people who liberated themselves were doing the Lord's work. Leading Southern white theologians disagreed. Adopting a pro-slavery theology of patriarchal hierarchy, they argued that the Bible condoned slaveholding, and that those who argued that slavery was immoral were unbiblical. On the eve of the Civil War, the majority of American Christians of all races were Bible-believing evangelical Protestants who held to a similar theology of personal conversion and biblical authority, but they held radically opposing views on the question of slavery. The white Methodist, Baptist, and Presbyterian denominations – the nation's largest Protestant religious bodies – divided over slavery during the generation preceding the Civil War, with none of these groups reuniting until well into the twentieth century.[4]

Alcohol regulation was a less divisive cause, but still controversial. Prior to the 1820s, hardly any Christian group had proscribed all alcohol consumption – though, in keeping with Scripture, drunkenness was generally condemned. But in the 1820s – and, to an increasing extent, in the 1830s and 1840s – some evangelical Protestants, especially in the

North, began mobilizing against liquor because of their concern about the nation's extraordinarily high alcohol consumption rate, which was approximately four times as high as it would be at the beginning of the twenty-first century. For the first few years of the temperance movement, as it was called, Protestant temperance advocates did not call for a ban on all alcohol but focused their efforts on voluntary pledges to abstain from hard liquor (while still, in some cases, allowing the moderate use of wine). By the mid-1830s, many temperance advocates shifted toward a complete opposition to all alcohol, and at the beginning of the 1850s, they began enacting state prohibition laws. Eleven states, beginning with Maine, adopted prohibition laws during the 1850s, a decade of unusually high rates of Irish Catholic and German immigration. Because many Protestants associated working-class European Catholic immigrants with high rates of alcohol abuse, the temperance campaign often drew on anti-Catholic sentiment and sometimes coexisted with political efforts to enact more restrictive immigration policies – though many temperance advocates also embraced progressive social justice causes, such as opposition to slavery.

The nation's pre-Civil War state prohibition laws did not survive the Civil War, but after the 1860s, temperance advocates renewed their campaign – and this time, women took the lead. The Women's Christian Temperance Union (WCTU), which was founded in Ohio in 1874 and which Frances Willard (a Methodist) led for much of the late nineteenth century, was the largest American women's social or political organization during the Gilded Age. Although its primary goal was always the enactment of a national prohibition law, the WCTU also advocated for a more comprehensive social justice platform that included women's voting rights and protective labor laws. In the late nineteenth and early twentieth centuries, the temperance campaign probably attracted more support from American Protestants across the theological spectrum than any other political cause. Although Episcopalians, German Lutherans, and a few other Protestant groups generally opposed the temperance movement, ministers and active lay members from most other Protestant denominations – ranging from evangelical Southern Baptists and Methodists to Northern Congregationalists and Presbyterians – supported it. At a time when American evangelical Protestantism was experiencing growing (and often acrimonious) divisions between fundamentalists and liberal "modernists," Prohibition, which finally became a political reality with the passage of the Eighteenth Amendment in 1919, was perhaps the only major political cause that both groups endorsed. Liberal Protestants envisioned Prohibition as a way to reduce poverty and promote social reform, and fundamentalists saw it as a way to curb sin. Despite initial Protestant unity on the issue, liberal Protestants quickly abandoned the cause after the perceived failure of Prohibition. Many conservative Protestants (especially Southern Baptists) continued to promote restrictions on the sale of alcohol, at least at the local level, for several more decades, but by the end of the twentieth century, alcohol restrictions were no longer a significant political priority for any Protestant group.[5]

On most other political issues, fundamentalists and modernists of the early twentieth century took diametrically opposing stances. Many liberal or mainline Protestants (as the modernists were eventually called) embraced the Social Gospel, a theology of social justice pioneered by New York Baptist pastor Walter Rauschenbusch and Ohio Congregationalist pastor Washington Gladden at the end of the nineteenth century and also shaped by African-American Protestant theology. The Social Gospel, which held that Christians could do the work of the kingdom of God by engaging in societal reform, was in some ways a continuation of early nineteenth-century evangelical political campaigns against slavery and other social evils, but also marked a departure from evangelical individualistic views of sin and salvation.[6]

In 1908, many of the nation's leading Protestant denominations – including, among others, Methodists, Presbyterians, Disciples of Christ, and the Northern Baptist Convention (although not the Southern Baptist Convention) – joined forces to form the largest ecumenical Christian association the nation had yet seen: the Federal Council of Churches (FCC). Guided by the principles of the Social Gospel, the FCC issued the "Social Creed of the Churches" (1908), which called for workers' rights, a living wage, the abolition of child labor, and the "abatement of poverty."[7] Race relations, which were not yet a major concern for most white Social Gospel advocates, were not included in the Social Creed, but as African-American Protestant denominations, such as the AME and the National Baptist Convention, joined the FCC, the FCC created new committees on race relations and added racial justice to its mission. Interracial cooperation and the rights of African Americans were particular concerns for two of the leading liberal Protestant ecumenical organizations of the early twentieth century: the Young Men's Christian Association (YMCA) and the Young Women's Christian Association (YWCA).[8]

Fundamentalists, by contrast, rejected the Social Gospel's emphasis on societal uplift through church activism. Many fundamentalists subscribed to an end-times theology shaped by premillennial dispensationalism, which held that the kingdom of God could not be ushered in by human action; instead, the world would continue to become more evil before the imminent second coming of Christ. Nearly all fundamentalists believed that the church should prioritize preaching the gospel and making individual Christian converts over political activity – priorities that they thought modernist Protestants had reversed. This did not mean, however, that fundamentalists rejected politics entirely. On the contrary, they embarked on a series of political campaigns to oppose the secularization of American society, because they believed that the nation's survival depended on its adherence to Christian morality.

Led by three-time Democratic presidential candidate and former secretary of state William Jennings Bryan, fundamentalists campaigned for legislation restricting the teaching of evolution in public schools – a campaign that succeeded in banning evolutionary teaching in several Southern states, including, most famously, Tennessee, the site of the notorious Scopes Trial of 1925. Liberal Protestants, who accepted evolution, viewed these fundamentalist campaigns as an anti-intellectual embarrassment to the cause of Christianity, but fundamentalists believed that prohibitions on evolutionary teaching in public high schools were necessary to protect young people from the influences of religious infidelity and amoral philosophy, as well as preserve the Christian identity of the nation and the authority of parents.

Fundamentalists also engaged in political campaigns to limit the influence of Catholics whom they viewed as a threat to the republic, just as many of their nineteenth-century Protestant forebears had. In 1928, many Methodist and Baptist ministers in the South broke with their region's long-standing support for the Democratic Party to campaign against Democratic presidential candidate Al Smith, a New York Catholic who opposed Prohibition. Some conservative Protestants of the 1920s supported the Ku Klux Klan's campaign for a Protestant America, believing that Jewish and Catholic immigrants were a threat to the nation's Protestant values. In the 1930s, virulent anti-Semitism played a central role in the right-wing fundamentalist Protestant political movements of Gerald Winrod and Gerald L. K. Smith. Most fundamentalists did not embrace such overt anti-Semitism, but their suspicion of large centralized state programs (which they identified both with their liberal Protestant opponents and with biblical prophecies of the anti-Christ) prompted some, especially in the North, to oppose the New Deal. President Franklin D. Roosevelt's social welfare programs received strong support among evangelical Baptists and Pentecostals in the impoverished South, but in the North, fundamentalist magazines warned against New Deal programs.[9]

For much of the mid-twentieth century, mainline Protestants exercised more political influence than fundamentalists (or, as some of them were called after the 1940s, evangelicals). With the exception of John F. Kennedy (a Catholic), nearly every US president of the twentieth century was a mainline Protestant, with even the few Southern Baptists (Harry Truman, Jimmy Carter, and Bill Clinton) often attending mainline Protestant services. Mainline Protestant clergy of the mid-twentieth century generally supported the liberal consensus of the early postwar era, which combined support for the nation's fight against international Communism with advocacy of anti-poverty initiatives and an expanded social welfare state.

During the 1920s and 1930s, many mainline Protestant churches supported the peace movement, but in the 1950s, they were more likely to embrace theologian Reinhold Niebuhr's "Christian realism," which provided a justification for the Cold War by suggesting that in a sinful world the state had a duty to use force to combat evil. Although there were a few dissenting voices (including Niebuhr's), most white Protestants of the 1950s supported the American civil religion of the era, which linked American democracy and the nation's fight against Communism with a religious purpose. A majority of Protestants supported classroom prayer in public schools, the addition of the phrase "under God" to the Pledge of Allegiance, and the adoption of "In God we trust" as a national motto during the 1950s. Mainline Protestant clergy, like their evangelical counterparts, warned in the 1950s about the dangers of "secularism." As most American Protestants had done for the past 150 years, they supported church–state separation even while arguing for the increased influence of religion in public life. By the 1950s, though, many mainline Protestant ministers no longer saw religion in exclusively Protestant terms. Because of their belief in equality and religious tolerance, they increasingly advocated for acceptance of Jews and Catholics as co-equal members of a "tri-faith" America. Many evangelicals of the era – especially Billy Graham – also supported the Cold War and the civil religion of the Eisenhower presidency, but usually without mainline Protestants' religious ecumenism.[10]

LIBERAL PROTESTANT POLITICS IN THE 1960S AND BEYOND

Before the 1960s, American Protestant politics was dominated by the institutions and beliefs of the white mainline Protestant establishment. The civil rights movement and anti-war protests of the 1960s brought new voices into the national political conversation, severed mainline Protestants' close relationship with the political establishment, and fractured Protestants along ideological lines.

The civil rights movement was so closely connected to the Black Protestant church that historian David Chappell called it a "religious revival."[11] It was the product of decades of Black Christian faith that God would one day deliver his people from oppression, just as he had delivered the children of Israel from Egyptian slavery. Throughout the late nineteenth and early twentieth centuries, Black pastors and theologians such as Georgia AME bishop Henry McNeal Turner, New York City Baptist minister Adam Clayton Powell, Jr., and religion professor Howard Thurman preached a message of civil rights and social justice. Powell served for more than two decades as a Democratic representative in Congress, where he made civil rights legislation his major priority. Thurman wrote one of the most influential books of African-American political theology: *Jesus and the Disinherited* (1949), which argues that following Jesus means identifying with the oppressed.[12]

Martin Luther King, Jr., and other African-American ministers of the civil rights movement, such as Baptists Ralph Abernathy and Fred Shuttlesworth and United Church of Christ minister Andrew Young, formed the Southern Christian Leadership Conference to promote nonviolent civil rights activism – an activism grounded in the neo-orthodox view of societal sin that Reinhold Niebuhr posited, the ethic of nonviolent resistance that Mohandas Gandhi modeled, and the Social Gospel that had deep roots in both Black and white liberal Protestant churches. King was raised in a Black evangelical Baptist faith but educated in a white Northern liberal Protestant seminary and graduate program in religion, and his message was a synthesis of Black Christian Exodus-based theology and twentieth-century liberal Protestant views that were rooted in the Social Gospel and personalist theology. Many other African-American Protestants active in the civil rights movement, such as Fannie Lou Hamer, retained a traditional biblical literalism that motivated them to work for racial justice while identifying themselves with the oppressed people of God in the Old and New Testaments.[13]

For a half-century after the civil rights movement, Black Protestant politics continued to be shaped by a commitment to racial justice and relief for the poor, as well as a critical stance toward American institutions of power. Jesse Jackson, a younger ally of King, attempted to continue King's vision in the late twentieth century through civil rights organizations that combined the cause of racial justice with equal rights for women and gays and lesbians. With the strong support of Black voters (especially in the South), Jackson won a substantial number of delegates when he ran on a liberal platform in his race for the Democratic presidential nomination in 1984 and 1988. After the 1980s, Black Protestant churches continued to play a central role in every Democratic presidential contest. All Democratic presidents of the late twentieth and early twenty-first centuries – including Jimmy Carter, Bill Clinton, Barack Obama, and Joe Biden – owed their victories partly to the overwhelming support they received from Black Protestants, and they developed close relationships with Black ministers and other Black Protestant supporters. Obama, who for years was a member of a Black United Church of Christ congregation in Chicago, had an especially close relationship with the Black church, a relationship that subsequent Democratic presidential candidates Hillary Clinton and Joe Biden also tried to cultivate. But Black Protestants of the early twenty-first century did more than merely support Democratic presidential candidates; they also pushed the Democratic Party to make racial justice and poverty relief higher priorities. Liberal Black ministers such as William Barber, who organized "Moral Mondays" to advocate for a religiously inspired social justice in his home state of North Carolina, preached a politics of the left that was shaped by the experience of racial oppression and the biblical promise of liberation and justice.[14]

African Americans' civil rights activism also reshaped white liberal Protestant politics. Although white liberal Protestants had made racial equality a priority before the 1960s, the African-American civil rights movement pushed them to do more to challenge the white power structure, including the use of nonviolent civil disobedience. Many young white liberal Protestant ministers participated in civil rights demonstrations in Selma, Alabama, and elsewhere, and some went to jail for their actions.

A number of white liberal Protestant ministers, such as Yale University chaplain William Sloan Coffin, Jr., also mobilized against the Vietnam War (as did Martin Luther King, Jr., and several other African-American civil rights leaders). Their willingness to protest against the American military effort in Vietnam weakened the historically close relationship between mainline white Protestantism and the US government and led a new generation of liberal Protestant ministers to embrace the politics of prophetic protest.[15]

Equality of all human beings, justice to correct ongoing oppression, and peace to replace American militarism became the guiding political principles of many liberal Protestants for the rest of the twentieth century and beyond. Like Coffin, they embraced the cause of gay rights, with some of the most liberal Protestant denominations, such as the United Church of Christ and later the Episcopal Church, leading the fight for gay rights legislation and the legal recognition of same-sex marriage. As liberal Protestant denominations began ordaining women and promoting them to senior positions of leadership and professorships in theological education, a new generation of Christian feminists became vocal advocates of women's rights, commonly taking pro-choice positions on abortion and strongly supporting the Equal Rights Amendment, sexual harassment legislation, and LGBTQ rights. Anti-war activism and the promotion of nonviolence remained important causes for liberal Protestants, with liberal Protestant clergy joining with like-minded advocates from other faith traditions to oppose nuclear arms buildup in the 1980s, the Gulf War in the 1990s, the Iraq War in the early twenty-first century, and the proliferation of handguns and assault rifles in recent years.[16]

As the politics of mainline Protestant ministers moved leftward, their visible public influence diminished. Membership numbers in mainline Protestant denominations began falling in the 1960s and continued to drop for the next half-century. While the causes of this decline are complex and continue to be debated, one factor is the unusually low retention rates for young people raised in mainline Protestant churches; many who leave their childhood faith become religious "nones," but the values of social justice and equality that they acquired from their childhood religious experiences remain with them in secularized form. While white Democrats today are less religious than Americans as a whole, their values and political priorities closely correspond to the statements of liberal Protestant agencies such as the National Council of Churches and the *Christian Century*. Thus, even though many Americans currently view the Democratic Party as the more secular party, its secular adherents hold values that closely parallel – and are, in some cases, shaped by – the values of liberal Protestantism, and many of its religious adherents are deeply rooted in the Black church or the Social Gospel tradition.[17]

EVANGELICALS AND THE CHRISTIAN RIGHT

As mainline Protestant's long-standing overt influence on politics began to diminish or become more diffuse, conservative white evangelicals' political influence increased. By the late 1970s, the nation's largest

Protestant denomination (the Southern Baptist Convention) was a predominantly white evangelical church, and its membership numbers were rapidly increasing. Nearly all of the nation's largest Protestant congregations (multi-thousand-member megachurches) were also evangelical. The majority of the nation's most popular televangelists and Christian radio broadcasters were evangelicals. Evangelicals, who for much of the mid-twentieth century were poorer and less educated than mainline Protestants, now had the resources to exercise political power. And, for most white evangelical Protestants, their political priorities were diametrically opposed to those of the Black church or white liberal Protestantism.[18]

A majority of white evangelicals had supported Republican presidential candidates in most elections since the mid-twentieth century (if not before), but their alliance with the Republican Party became significantly stronger after the creation of the Christian Right in the late 1970s. The Christian Right was a grassroots political movement associated with organizations such as Baptist pastor Jerry Falwell's Moral Majority (and, in the 1990s, Pat Robertson and Ralph Reed's Christian Coalition); it intended to use political lobbying and voter registration drives to mobilize conservative Christians to vote *en masse* for candidates who were pledged to support the movement's anti-secular and Christian nationalist views. In the view of many white evangelicals, the United States had once been a Christian nation, but the cultural liberalism of the 1960s and 1970s had compromised the nation's Christian identity. Supreme Court decisions in the early 1960s against classroom prayer and devotional Bible reading in public schools were one example of this secularization. Other unwanted changes included second-wave feminism, the gay rights movement, the proliferation of pornography, and *Roe v. Wade* (the 1973 Supreme Court case that legalized abortion nationwide). In the view of Christian Right advocates, all of these changes threatened both the two-parent nuclear family and the nation's Christian identity. Hoping to restore the civil religious consciousness that had characterized American public life in the 1950s, they advocated a strong military defense against Communism, a more overt recognition of God in public life, and opposition to the sexual revolution in the name of "pro-family" politics. In the 1980s, the Christian Right gave strong support to President Ronald Reagan, and it continued to endorse Republicans in every presidential election thereafter.[19]

On almost every issue, liberal Protestants and Black Protestants opposed the Christian Right. Liberal Protestants especially objected to the Christian Right's support for military buildup and foreign wars and its lack of interest in anti-poverty programs – stances that liberal Protestants believed were incompatible with the teachings of Jesus. But conservative evangelicals believed that poverty relief was a task for the church and Christian individuals, not the government. And on military issues, conservative evangelicals (who, unlike many liberal Protestants, had generally supported the Vietnam War) believed that the United States had a duty to oppose "godless" Communism and, later, Islamic terrorism.[20]

By the end of the 1980s, abortion and gay rights were the Christian Right's main concerns. Though the anti-abortion campaign began among Catholics, conservative evangelicals joined the cause in the 1970s and gave it increased priority in the 1980s. For most Christian Right advocates, abortion was a political litmus test; they refused to support any candidate who endorsed abortion rights, which meant, by the end of the twentieth century, that very few Democrats could win their support. Homosexuality, many conservative evangelicals believed, was a threat to the family and the institution of marriage.

On abortion, Christian Right advocates succeeded in securing numerous restrictions even if, by the end of the second decade of the twenty-first century, they still had not secured their primary objective of overturning *Roe v. Wade*. On gay rights, by contrast, they rapidly lost ground. When the Supreme Court declared in *Obergefell v. Hodges* (2015) that marriage equality was a constitutionally protected right, many Christian Right advocates feared that their own religious freedom to refuse to endorse same-sex marriage might be in danger. They redoubled their efforts to shift the Supreme Court to the right – efforts that increased their commitment to the Republican Party. Republican presidents George W. Bush and Donald Trump received stronger support from white evangelicals than from almost any other religious or demographic group, and this support was critical to their election victories.[21]

Conservative white evangelicals' campaigns against abortion and same-sex marriage brought them into close alliance with Catholics, ending a long-standing American anti-Catholicism that had existed since the Puritans. Although liberal Catholics remained loyal to the Democratic Party and opposed the Christian Right, conservative evangelicals found champions for their cause among many Catholic Republican politicians and conservative intellectual leaders.

A minority of perhaps 20 to 25 percent of white evangelical voters opposed the Christian Right and supported the Democratic Party most of the time because of their concerns about poverty and the rights of racial minorities. Identified with Jim Wallis, Ronald Sider, *Sojourners* magazine, and a younger generation of "Red Letter Christians," this progressive evangelicalism emphasized the statements of Jesus about concern for the poor and strongly protested against restrictive immigration policies and American military power. Unlike conservative white evangelicals, progressive evangelicals resisted Christian nationalism; drawing on Anabaptist theology, they saw Christians as citizens of a heavenly kingdom who should not identify the cause of Christ with any earthly political power.

On most political issues, progressive evangelicals identified more closely with liberal Protestants than with other evangelicals, but on abortion and homosexuality, they frequently took moderately conservative stances – sometimes by describing themselves as "consistently pro-life" because of their simultaneous opposition to abortion, war, and the death penalty. While many leaders of progressive evangelicalism are white, the movement has also attracted some Blacks, Asians, and Hispanics. Hispanic evangelicals, in particular, tend to be very conservative on abortion, but also strongly opposed to conservative white evangelicals' support for restrictive immigration policies. And the minority of Black Protestants who affiliate with white evangelical churches have frequently criticized the Christian Right's stances on race and poverty, even if they agree with other aspects of white evangelical theology.[22]

Today American politics continues to be shaped by competing Protestant political concerns. The quest for racial and social equality and the rights of the poor and marginalized – a quest not uniquely Protestant, but one which has characterized liberal Protestantism, Black Protestantism, and progressive evangelicalism – continues to influence the Democratic Party, whether the influence comes through religious or secular channels. The concern for the nation's Christian identity and protection of the two-parent family, which has characterized the Christian nationalism of many conservative white evangelicals, has shaped the Republican Party's agenda. As the nation's partisan polarization has increased, the rift between the politics of the Religious Left and the Religious Right has also become more pronounced, and Protestants on both sides of the divide have made alliances with like-minded non-Protestants. A contemporary liberal Protestant might have far more in common politically with a secular Jew who champions racial, social, and gender equality than with a conservative evangelical Protestant who votes Republican, while a conservative evangelical Protestant probably has more in common politically with a conservative Catholic who supports the Christian Right agenda on abortion and same-sex marriage than with a pro-choice liberal Protestant who endorses LGBTQ rights.

But underneath these often acrimonious political debates, a few points of shared Protestant political heritage shape the views of nearly all American Protestants today. Whether conservative or liberal, they believe in individual religious freedom and religious pluralism; they do not want the state to aid one particular denomination or religious group to the exclusion of others. And nearly all practicing Protestant Christians, whether conservative or liberal, view politics as a moral endeavor and want state policy to reflect moral priorities. They may disagree on which moral priorities are most urgent and which strategies or policies are most likely to achieve their moral objectives, but they are united by a common conviction that moral imperatives – which both sides believe are grounded in their Christian faith – should be translated into political mandates. As the percentage of Americans who are Protestant continues to decline, Protestants' direct influence on politics may ultimately become more diffuse, but the sizable number of American Protestants who believe in a religiously inspired moral vision for the nation will no doubt continue to bring their concerns into the political sphere.

NOTES

1 For overviews of religious influence on American politics, see Kenneth
  D. Wald and Allison Calhoun-Brown, *Religion and American Politics*, 8th ed.
  (Lanham, MD: Rowman & Littlefield, 2018); and Mark A. Noll and Luke
  E. Harlow, eds., *Religion and American Politics: From Colonial Times to the
  Present*, 2nd ed. (New York: Oxford University Press, 2007). For a history of
  Christian Reconstructionist ideas, see Michael J. McVicar, *Christian
  Reconstruction: R. J. Rushdoony and American Religious Conservatism*
  (Chapel Hill: University of North Carolina Press, 2015).

2 Edmund S. Morgan, *Roger Williams: The Church and the State*, 2nd ed.
  (New York: W. W. Norton, 2006); Frank Lambert, *The Founding Fathers and
  the Place of Religion in America* (Princeton, NJ: Princeton University Press,
  2003), 21–206.

3 Steven K. Green, *The Second Disestablishment: Church and State in
  Nineteenth-Century America* (New York: Oxford University Press, 2010);
  Nathan O. Hatch, *The Democratization of American Christianity* (New
  Haven, CT: Yale University Press, 1989); David Sehat, *The Myth of American
  Religious Freedom* (New York: Oxford University Press, 2011), 1–72; Robert
  H. Abzug, *Cosmos Crumbling: American Reform and the Religious
  Imagination* (New York: Oxford University Press, 1994), 105–124.

4 Albert J. Raboteau, *Canaan Land: A Religious History of African Americans* (New York: Oxford University Press, 1999); Bertram Wyatt-Brown, *Lewis Tappan and the Evangelical War against Slavery* (Cleveland, OH: Case Western Reserve University Press, 1969); Molly Oshatz, *Slavery and Sin: The Fight against Slavery and the Rise of Liberal Protestantism* (New York: Oxford University Press, 2012); Mitchell Snay, *Gospel of Disunion: Religion and Separatism in the Antebellum South* (New York: Cambridge University Press, 1993); Mark A. Noll, *America's God: From Jonathan Edwards to Abraham Lincoln* (New York: Oxford University Press, 2002), 386–421; E. Brooks Holifield, *Theology in America: Christian Thought from the Age of the Puritans to the Civil War* (New Haven, CT: Yale University Press, 2003), 494–504.

5 Ruth Bordin, *Frances Willard: A Biography* (Chapel Hill: University of North Carolina Press, 1986); W. J. Rorabaugh, *Prohibition: A Concise History* (New York: Oxford University Press, 2018); Gaines M. Foster, *Moral Reconstruction: Christian Lobbyists and the Federal Regulation of Morality, 1865–1920* (Chapel Hill: University of North Carolina Press, 2002), 163–220.

6 Christian H. Evans, *The Social Gospel in American Religion: A History* (New York: New York University Press, 2017).

7 Federal Council of Churches, Social Creed of the Churches, December 4, 1908, https://nationalcouncilofchurches.us/common-witness/1908/social-creed.php.

8 Nancy Marie Robertson, *Christian Sisterhood, Race Relations, and the YWCA, 1906–46* (Urbana: University of Illinois Press, 2007).

9 Matthew Avery Sutton, *American Apocalypse: A History of Modern Evangelicalism* (Cambridge, MA: Harvard University Press, 2014); George M. Marsden, *Fundamentalism and American Culture*, 2nd ed. (New York: Oxford University Press, 2006), 206–211; Michael Kazin, *A Godly Hero: The Life of William Jennings Bryan* (New York: Alfred A. Knopf, 2006); Edward J. Larson, *Summer for the Gods: The Scopes Trial and America's Continuing Debate over Science and Religion* (New York: Basic Books, 1997); Leo P. Ribuffo, *The Old Christian Right: The Protestant Far Right from the Great Depression to the Cold War* (Philadelphia: Temple University Press, 1983); Wayne Flynt, "Religion for the Blues: Evangelicalism, Poor Whites, and the Great Depression," *Journal of Southern History* vol. 71 (2005), 3–38.

10 Kevin M. Kruse, *One Nation under God: How Corporate America Invented Christian America* (New York: Basic Books, 2015); Stephen J. Whitfield, *The Culture of the Cold War*, 2nd ed. (Baltimore: Johns Hopkins University Press, 1996), 77–100; William Inboden, *Religion and American Foreign Policy, 1945–1960: The Soul of Containment* (New York: Cambridge University Press, 2008); Kevin M. Schultz, *Tri-Faith America: How Catholics and Jews Held Postwar America to Its Protestant Promise* (New York: Oxford University Press, 2011); Grant Wacker, *America's Pastor: Billy Graham and the Shaping of a Nation* (Cambridge, MA: Harvard University Press, 2014).

11 David L. Chappell, "Religious Revivalism in the Civil Rights Movement," *African American Review* vol. 36 (2002), 581–595. For religion in the civil rights movement, see also Charles Marsh, *God's Long Summer: Stories of Faith and Civil Rights* (Princeton, NJ: Princeton University Press, 1997).

12 Paul Harvey, *Through the Storm, through the Night: A History of African American Christianity* (Lanham, MD: Rowman & Littlefield, 2011), 79–82, 107, 111; Howard Thurman, *Jesus and the Disinherited* (Nashville: Abingdon Press, 1949).

13 David J. Garrow, *Bearing the Cross: Martin Luther King, Jr., and the Southern Christian Leadership Conference* (New York: William Morrow, 1986); Kay Mills, *This Little Light of Mine: The Life of Fannie Lou Hamer* (New York: Dutton, 1993).

14 For Barber's politics, see William J. Barber II with Jonathan Wilson-Hartgrove, *The Third Reconstruction: How a Moral Movement Is Overcoming the Politics of Division and Fear* (Boston: Beacon Press, 2016).

15 Michael B. Friedland, *Lift Up Your Voice Like a Trumpet: White Clergy and the Civil Rights and Antiwar Movements, 1954–1973* (Chapel Hill: University of North Carolina Press, 1998).

16 For a history of liberal Protestant ministers' support for gay rights, see Heather R. White, *Reforming Sodom: Protestants and the Rise of Gay Rights* (Chapel Hill: University of North Carolina Press, 2015). For an overview of feminist religious consciousness in the 1970s, see Lilian Calles Barger, "'Pray to God, She Will Hear Us': Women Reimagining Religion and Politics in the 1970s," in *The Religious Left in Modern America: Doorkeepers of a Radical Faith*, ed. Leilah Danielson, Marian Mollin, and Doug Rossinow (New York: Palgrave Macmillan, 2018), 211–232.

17 For a case study of liberal Protestant influence on the Democratic Party, see Mark A. Lempke, *My Brother's Keeper: George McGovern and Progressive Christianity* (Amherst: University of Massachusetts Press, 2017).

18 For the growth of evangelicalism in the 1970s, see Steven P. Miller, *The Age of Evangelicalism: America's Born-Again Years* (New York: Oxford University Press, 2014).

19 Daniel K. Williams, *God's Own Party: The Making of the Christian Right* (New York: Oxford University Press, 2010); Seth Dowland, *Family Values and the Rise of the Christian Right* (Philadelphia: University of Pennsylvania Press, 2015).

20 For the clash between these competing ideologies, see James Davison Hunter, *Culture Wars: The Struggle to Define America* (New York: Basic Books, 1991). For religious debates over war and foreign policy in the late twentieth and early twenty-first centuries, see Andrew Preston, *Sword of the Spirit, Shield of Faith: Religion in American War and Diplomacy* (New York: Alfred A. Knopf, 2012), 501–613.

21 For the historical origins of evangelical support for Trump, see John Fea,
    Believe Me: The Evangelical Road to Donald Trump (Grand Rapids, MI:
    Eerdmans, 2018).

22 Brantley W. Gasaway, *Progressive Evangelicals and the Pursuit of Social
    Justice* (Chapel Hill: University of North Carolina Press, 2014); David
    R. Swartz, *Moral Minority: The Evangelical Left in an Age of Conservatism*
    (Philadelphia: University of Pennsylvania Press, 2012); Brian Steensland and
    Philip Goff, eds., *The New Evangelical Social Engagement* (New York:
    Oxford University Press, 2014).

10 Temperance

JENNIFER WOODRUFF TAIT

It was October, 1874; 35-year-old Frances Willard (1839–1898) stepped to a podium in Chicago and delivered for the first time a speech called "Everybody's War," which she would repeat many times over the next decades as she campaigned against the use and sale of alcohol.[1] "We are taught to pray: 'Thy kingdom come, Thy will be done,'" she told her listeners. "Where? 'On earth.' We sing the sacred hymn: '[B]ring forth the Royal diadem and crown Him Lord of all.' We as a people believe what this good book says when it plainly again and again declares that Christ is again going to rule on earth. How is he going to rule until we get all the rum shops out of the way?"[2]

Willard, previously the Dean of Women at Northwestern University, was now devoting herself full-time to temperance work. Only a month after "Everybody's War" she would attend the founding convention of the Woman's Christian Temperance Union (WCTU), and by 1879 she would become the organization's president.[3] Years later, some historians would stereotype Willard, the WCTU, and indeed the entire temperance movement as hopeless backwards fundamentalists. In 1920 self-identified progressive Charles Beard (1874–1948), one of the founders of the New School of Social Research, described those in favor of national Prohibition as full of "Philistinism, Harsh restraint, Beauty-hating, Stout-faced fanaticism, Supreme hypocrisy, Canting, Demonology, Enmity to True art, Intellectual Tyranny, Grape juice, Grisley sermons, Religious persecution, Sullenness, Ill-Temper, Stinginess, Bigotry, Conceit, Bombast."[4] And in the 1960s, famed sociologist Joseph Gusfield linked them with the reactionaries of his own day who protested against "fluoridation, domestic Communism, school curricula, and the United Nations."[5]

But in the heyday of the temperance reform, temperance – like women's suffrage and abolitionism – stood in the foreground of the progressive reform agenda, and temperance reformers believed themselves to be basing their actions on the latest scientific research and on up-to-date sound philosophical arguments.

WHAT IS TEMPERANCE?

Before "temperance" became the acknowledged name of a reform move-ment, it was the common English name of a virtue historically valued in Greco-Roman culture and in the early church. Drawing on Plato, who identified an ideal city as being filled with people who were "wise, brave, sober and just," early Christian thinkers referred to these as the *cardinal* virtues (naming them prudence, justice, temperance, and fortitude) and added to them the three *theological* virtues of faith, hope, and love.[6] As part of these sets of virtues, temperance was commonly described as being an exercise of moderation, restraint, and self-control. The modern Catholic Catechism still defines it as "the moral virtue that moderates the attraction of pleasures and provides balance in the use of created goods. It ensures the will's mastery over instincts and keeps desires within the limits of what is honorable."[7]

In the colonies and the early days of the new nation, if Americans applied the word "temperance" to alcohol consumption at all, they would have used it to denote moderate, restrained consumption. However, there actually *wasn't* a lot of moderate, restrained consump-tion of alcohol in the early republic:

> Heavy drinking ... characterized American social life from the time the colonies were first settled. Political campaigns, liturgical occa-sions, and everyday labor all furnished occasions for generous con-sumption of alcohol. Taverns were plentiful and, in many cases, pleasant centers of eighteenth-century social and political gathering. Popular drinks included beer, hard cider, and rum; the upper classes enjoyed European wines. Between 1710 and 1835, the average American of drinking age consumed between 5.1 and 7.1 gallons of absolute alcohol per year.[8]

In one famous but not entirely unusual example, George Washington (1732–1799) ran up a bar bill in 1787 of over $17,000, adjusted for infla-tion, for his farewell party shortly before the signing of the Constitution: 55 attendees drank 54 bottles of Madeira wine, 60 bottles of claret, 8 bottles of whiskey, 22 bottles of porter, 8 bottles of cider, 12 bottles of beer, and 7 bowls of punch; an additional 16 musicians and waiters put away 16 bottles of claret (one bottle per musician!), 5 of Madeira, and 7 bowls of punch. The group also ate relishes and olives to go with the river of alcohol, and broke a few glasses.[9]

In the first few decades of the nineteenth century, trends of con-sumption and employment made this river of booze overflow traditional social bounds. Whiskey (often of poor quality and high alcoholic content) overtook rum as the national drink after blockades during the Revolution made rum scarcer. Cities began to grow, and factories to increase and to mechanize. Young men moved to cities to work there and became attracted to the "sporting" culture marked by easy access to alcohol and prostitutes. Impersonal hotels replaced village taverns.[10] People grew concerned. They began to work for the prohibition, first of hard liquor, and eventually of beer and wine as well; they often applied the word "teetotal" to their efforts for total prohibition of all alcohol, but more often than not Americans also seized on that old word for the virtue of moderation and self-control: *temperance*. (British anti-alcohol crusaders generally kept using the word "teetotalism.") Only now, they defined it as total abstinence from alcohol and related vices. As the Methodist *Discipline* (the denomination's book of church order) put it:

> Temperance, in its broader meaning, is distinctively a Christian virtue, enjoined in the Holy Scriptures. It implies a subordination of all the emotions, passions and appetites to the control of reason and conscience, Dietetically, it means a wise use of suitable articles of food and drink, *with entire abstinence from such as are known to be hurtful.*[11]

Temperance advocates believed that "the word of God, the teachings of science, and the lessons of experience all combine[d] in declaring total abstinence from intoxicating beverages to be the duty of every individual."[12] And their work had results. Those seven gallons a year of absolute alcohol drunk per person in 1835 were the peak. After that, consumption declined, to 3.1 gallons in 1840, 2.6 in 1910, 1.2 just after Prohibition, and "even after every moral loosening the 20th century wrought, from flappers to the counterculture movement, by the year 2000, the average American drank less than a gallon of absolute alcohol ... more than *six gallons* less a year than their ancestors had about 200 years before."[13]

But many advocates did not realize they had been so successful, at least not for a while.[14] As a result, they changed American culture – not only in ways they intended, but in ways they did not.

SCIENTIFIC TEMPERANCE

Critics of temperance work argued that alcohol was not always spoken of negatively in the Bible. Reformers responded by using modern scientific discoveries to aid in their biblical interpretation. In this, they were not alone; despite some later caricatures of Christians being at war with new scientific discoveries, the nineteenth century actually featured considerable religious trust in science.[15] One of the first uses of science to argue the temperance cause was the use made of a famous pamphlet by Presbyterian physician Benjamin Rush (1746–1813), *An Inquiry Into the Effects of Ardent Spirits upon the Human Body and Mind* (1785), soon republished as *An Inquiry into the Effects of Spirituous Liquors on the Human Body: To Which Is Added, a Moral And Physical Thermometer* (1790). Rush may be better known today for being a member of the Continental Congress, but his pamphlet was widely reprinted and his example widely cited. It contained an image of a thermometer attributing healthful effects to wine and beer in moderation, but describing a variety of gruesome effects caused by ardent spirits: "Idleness, Peevishness, Quarrelling, Fighting, Lying, Swearing, Obscenity, Swindling, Perjury, Burglary, Murder, Suicide ... Sickness, Puking ... Tremors of the Hands in the Morning, Bloatedness, Inflamed Eyes, Red Nose and Face, Sore and swelled Legs, Jaundice, Pain in the Limbs," leading to "Dropsy, Epilepsy, Melancholy, Madness, Palsy, Apoplexy," and finally "DEATH."[16]

Soon other doctors began to discover that beer and wine (perceived as healthy drinks in the early nineteenth century) could affect the body in similar ways. The most famous experiments were those done on Alexis St. Martin, a Canadian voyageur, by William Beaumont (1785–1853), a doctor attending St. Martin after he was injured by a musket. The injury left an open wound in St. Martin's side, and Beaumont took the opportunity to give him food and drink – everything from beer to mustard – and observe the results. He wrote, "Condiments ... affect [the stomach] as alcohol or other stimulants do – the present relief afforded is at the expense of future suffering ... Simple water is, perhaps, the only fluid that is called for by the wants of the oeconomy [sic]."[17] The experiment soon came to the attention of Methodist layman and physician Thomas Sewall (1786–1845) of Washington, DC. Sewall publicized Beaumont's work and published his own pamphlet with drawings of how stomachs deteriorated from consuming alcohol; they were supposedly from his own dissections, although controversy arose about whether teetotal stomachs were as undisturbed as he drew them.[18]

It is difficult to underestimate the approval Protestant temperance advocates gave to these and similar experiments. Tract-writers told the story of these scientific experiments and produced tracts on alcohol's lack of nutrition, danger as a medicine (no small point in an era when doctors regularly prescribed it for illness and pain), and poisonous qualities.[19] Sewall's own popular tract *The Effects of Intemperance* described how alcohol roused the human system "to a state of feverish excitement" causing drunkards to ignore "the Sabbath and the house of worship."[20] The WCTU even supported a course of Scientific Temperance Instruction (STI) developed by Connecticut Congregationalist Mary Hunt (1830–1906) in 1879. Almost a decade later, the Methodist General Conference noted in a report that STI was now "providing for scientific temperance instruction in the public schools of thirty-four States and territories, under which six and half million children and youth are being taught the evils of alcoholic beverages."[21]

BIBLICAL ARGUMENTS

But such approval landed activists in an interpretive quandary. Whiskey and other spirits are not mentioned in the Bible. Beer and wine, however, are – and not every mention of them is negative. The conclusion many activists came to was that God's works should serve as the key to God's word: modern science should be used as an interpretive key to the Bible.[22] Because science had determined the negative effects of wine and beer, the positive mentions of them in the Scriptures must refer to non-alcoholic drinks. This position was commonly called the "two-wine theory," and those who held it often felt it to be necessary in order to maintain a high view of scriptural inspiration. A review of *Lectures on Temperance* (1847) by Presbyterian minister Eliphalet Nott (1773–1866) summarized the argument:

> Whenever wine is spoken of approvingly, as a blessing, and as an emblem of the mercy of God in Christ, the pure, original, unfermented, unintoxicating juice of the grape is intended ... to attach any other meaning to the sacred text involves not only a high reflection on the wisdom and benignity of the Deity, but the word of inspiration in most palpable contradictions and inconsistencies.[23]

This exegetical argument was popularized in 1849 in *Scriptural View of the Wine Question* by Congregationalist professor Moses Stuart (1780–1852); he argued that terms for both fermented and unfermented wine appeared in the biblical text, with commendations of wine referring to the unfermented version and condemnations to the fermented kind:

> Why may I not take it for granted, that when [the Biblical writers] ranked wine with corn and oil, they expected to be understood, as

speaking of a wine that might truly be ranked with them, as a lawful and useful beverage? And why not understand them as prohibiting and denouncing only such wine, as every body [*sic*] knew would produce intoxication?[24]

The argument soon predominated among most American temperance advocates, and even spread to Britain, where Anglican orator Frederic Lees (1815–1897) and Baptist minister Dawson Burns (1828–1909) combined to produce the *Temperance Bible Commentary* (1868). This book sold prominently on both sides of the Atlantic, and its careful examination of every biblical text referring to wine (and many verses referring to God's "pure" drink, water, as well) influenced a generation of clergy and activists.

For example, one text temperance writers needed to wrestle with was the wedding at Cana (John 2:1–11) where Jesus turned water into wine. Lees and Burns wrote that he did there only more quickly what, as God, he did all the time in nature, transforming the fluid inside grapes "into a luscious juice, food for the healthy and medicine to the sick."[25] Methodist minister Leon Field wrote in his own temperance New Testament commentary, *Oinos* (1883), that at Cana Christ must have made grape juice because "no other is made, all else is manufactured. Nothing less than omnipotence could make one drop of the pure juice of the grape. The art of man can manufacture any amount of alcoholic wine."[26] Methodist minister and secretary of the National Temperance Society D. C. Babcock (1835–1917) asserted, based on readings like these, "The word and works of God [are] not in conflict, and ... we do not condemn the use of such wine as Jesus made."[27]

COMMON-SENSE REALISM AND REFORM

These biblical and scientific arguments took place in a larger philosophical and cultural context – and it is one which sheds light not only on temperance but on other nineteenth-century reforms. Protestant thinkers in this era were broadly committed to the philosophy of empiricism, the idea "that sense experience is the ultimate source of all our concepts and knowledge."[28] More particularly, they were steeped in the version of this idea that derived from Francis Bacon (1561–1626) via the epistemological framework of Scottish Enlightenment philosopher Thomas Reid (1710–1796):

Bacon advocated the doctrine of the "two books" – God's truths were taught equally in both Scripture and nature, with the created world guiding proper Biblical interpretation. Many nineteenth-century American thinkers united Bacon's ideas with Protestantism so closely that Protestant theology was considered Baconian by default.[29]

Reid placed Bacon's pursuit of truth in both natural and scriptural realms within a framework Reid called "common-sense realism": any person of common sense whose mind is operating *within normal parameters and under the correct conditions* will naturally believe certain things about himself or herself, the world, and the nature of existence.[30] Charles Hodge (1797–1878), one of the chief American proponents of this view, put it this way in his *Systematic Theology:*

> The man of science comes to the study of nature with certain assumptions. 1. He assumes the trustworthiness of his sense perceptions. Unless he can rely upon the well-authenticated testimony of his senses, he is deprived of all means of prosecuting his investigations. The facts of nature reveal themselves to our faculties of sense, and can be known in no other way. 2. He must also assume the trustworthiness of his mental operations. He must take for granted that he can perceive, compare, combine, remember, and infer; and that he can safely rely upon these mental faculties in their legitimate exercise.[31]

Two things are particularly important about the nineteenth-century dedication to common-sense realism. First of all, most Protestant thinkers applied these ideas broadly – not just to the study of science and the interpretation of the Bible. Secondly, for them the normal parameters and correct conditions under which data could be taken in from the outside world *automatically excluded* any use of stimulants to mind or body.

Viewed from this angle, the unity behind *many* nineteenth-century lifestyle reforms, not just temperance, comes into sharper focus. Whether reformers were protesting against tobacco use, dancing, the eating of rich food, gambling, the theater, sexual immorality, or alcohol – and whether they strove to replace those activities with Christian worship, drinking water, eating plain food, scientific education, outdoor exercise, wholesome family reading, or the singing of Christian and temperance hymns – the motive was the same: "The practices encouraged ... were precisely those practices that would preserve the ability to perceive reality accurately and thus make appropriate moral decisions. The practices they rejected all had in common their interference with this process."[32] In other words, as modern computer programmers often say: garbage in, garbage out.[33] This hymn about water by John Marsh (1788–1868), Congregationalist minister, corresponding secretary of the American Temperance Union, and author of a famous temperance hymnal, shows starkly the contrasts they made:

> Tell me not of the sparkling bowl,
> That glows with red'ning fire;
> Oh tell not of the joy of soul
> The wine-cup can inspire.
> A brighter glass – a purer joy –
> A healthier draught I sing;
> Nature's own cup without alloy –
> Pleasure that reason can enjoy –
> Health from the bubbling spring.[34]

And a children's temperance songbook of decades later warned:

> Touch not the cup when the wine glistens bright . . .
> Though like the ruby it shines in the light;
> Touch not the cup, touch it not.
> The fangs of the serpent are hid in the bowl,
> Deeply the poison will enter thy soul,
> *Soon it will plunge thee beyond thy control;*
> Touch not the cup, touch it not.[35]

Language regarding the intellectual deception wrought by improper amusements of all sorts ran through every genre of Protestant reform writing in the nineteenth century, from catechisms to songbooks to scientific textbooks to cookbooks to novels to apologetic works to biblical commentary. Scientific temperance educator Julia Colman (1828–1909) wrote in her textbook *Alcohol and Hygiene*: "You have only to watch the drinking man to see how completely he is deceived. He does not judge correctly of anything. Full of silly conceits, he fancies himself rich when he has not a cent in his pocket; he lifts his foot high in the air to step over a stick, and if he falls, he fancies it was the sidewalk flew up in his face."[36] A tract called "Beware of Bad Books" warned against books of "fiction, romance, infidelity, war, piracy, and murder" as " 'poison' . . . as much to be shunned as the drunkard's cup."[37] Similar complaints troubled Methodist minister James Buckley (1836–1920) in his *Christians and the Theater*, written the same year as Colman's book; he warned against excitement "caused by the surrender of the judgment to the illusion . . . the matter received [from plays] is not such as to improve the character, but to loosen the springs of virtue and purity; and . . . the sympathies are very often, if not generally, drawn out by and to improper objects."[38]

ECONOMIC QUESTIONS

Temperance advocates didn't just worry about the kind of thinking improper amusements produced; they were concerned about the effect of these amusements on the American work ethic. From the 1920s (when Charles Beard was writing) up through the 1970s (shortly after Gusfield wrote *Symbolic Crusade*), it was common among many historians of reform in America to attribute the temperance movement solely to economic factors.[39] Although that was clearly not the case, economic concerns did play a role.

Temperance advocates had two particular concerns here. The first was a concern for the effect of alcohol and other stimulating behaviors on the workforce: as more and more people lived close together in cities and were employed in industrial pursuits, behavior which might previously have been tolerated in small rural settlements became a greater problem. Reformers focused particularly on young men who were thronging to urban areas away from families and previously established social roles. These young men

> were supposed to be following a clear ideal. They were to work hard at their jobs and gradually learn the business so they could advance. They were to board in a respectable boarding house, take their leisure in the parlors of middle-class houses, go to lectures, read for self-culture, join associations of fellowship and improvement, and attend church on Sunday.[40]

Instead, they found themselves tempted by saloons, gambling, theaters, and prostitution (which had a closer association to the theater in the nineteenth century than in the twenty-first). Although reformers wanted to prevent women becoming addicted to alcohol as well, most examples given in temperance literature involved the temptation, and the eventual salvation or damnation, of boys and young men who wanted to get ahead in life and in business but were derailed – or, if they chose wisely, not derailed – by alcohol abuse and other bad habits.[41] Advocates even argued that these considerations should be applied to rural life in tracts such as the popular "The Well-Conducted Farm" from the American Tract Society; it argued that ceasing to give strong drink to farm workers, a common practice at the time, would make them happier, healthier, and more devout.[42]

The second economic concern motivating reformers was the effect of "stimulating" behaviors on the nation's economy. Arguments for temperance, whether in catechisms, textbooks, tracts, or even biblical commentaries, often featured very precise estimates of how much money was being wasted each year by the manufacture and sale of alcohol. From John Marsh in the 1830s estimating $100 million a year, to Methodist ministers Jonathan Crane (1819–1880; he was also an abolitionist and the father of author Stephen Crane) and Charles Fowler (1837–1908) in the 1870s with estimates respectively of $680 million and $863 million a year, the actual numbers varied, but the attempt to measure this waste by precise calculations did not.[43] Even though the money was fueling a large and profitable American industry, activists argued that it was all illicit profit with a destructive end. Crane contended:

> If the fact that so many people derive their support from the manufacture and sale is proof that the traffic is a valuable public interest, what shall we say of picking pockets? Do not thieves and gamblers keep money in circulation? ... What is added to the common good by the grand army of some 200,000 men whose sole business is to mix drink? What is added to the public well-being by the 56,663 men who are employed, directly or indirectly, in supplying the American people with beer?[44]

And Julia Colman taught the same lesson in one of her catechisms for pre-teen children: "If the people that now spend their time in rum-selling and rum-drinking should go to raising food and making clothing and other good things, these would be cheaper for everybody."[45]

ALCOHOL, IMMIGRATION, AND EUGENICS

Temperance activists were also concerned about the role lifestyle reforms would play in keeping America white, Anglo-Saxon, and Protestant. They criticized all whom they considered to be of a lower class both socioeconomically and morally – basically, anyone whose ancestry did not descend from bourgeois Protestant English stock. These concerns could be seen even early on, in the ire directed at the boisterous lower-class temperance group called the Washingtonians.[46] But when a new wave of immigration – some of it from new parts of the world – began in the 1850s, fears increased.

Daniel Dorchester (1827–1907), a Methodist minister and prolific author, wrote in a temperance history in the 1880s that new immigrants had come to the country "grossly addicted" to intemperance.[47] As so often was the case in temperance apologetics, he cited precise statistics to back up his argument: in 1876 Philadelphia, there were 8,034 stores or taverns selling liquor: of these, only 205 were run by "Americans."[48] Those defined as non-Americans included, in his terms, Chinese, Italians, Spaniards, Welsh, Africans, French, Scotch, English, Germans, and Irish; over 3,700 of the vendors were connected to prostitution, according to the survey Dorchester cited, and about 5,200 had previously been criminals.[49]

Activists feared the perceived immorality of immigrants; they also feared immigrant Catholicism. Nearly all Irish immigrants were Catholic, and most German ones were either Catholic or Lutheran. Reformers feared two things about the Catholic attitude toward alcohol, and indeed religion in general: "the naturally emotional Catholic temperament and the superstitions encouraged by Catholic theology."[50] Both presented a problem for a common-sense approach. Excess emotion directed to the wrong objects had proved a perennial problem for temperance writers, and the combination of such excess with a worldview supposedly based on inherited tradition and not rational argument seemed to them a deadly combination.[51] This was seen in countless depictions of Catholics in popular media and in the ambivalent attitude toward Catholic temperance reformers such as Father Theobald Mathew (1790–1856); Mathew was criticized both for his overly emotional temperance revivalism and the supposedly superstitious hero-worship of his followers, and praised for his inability to chant properly and his love of Protestant brass bands. Some claimed he had even renounced Catholicism before he died.[52]

Fears about immigration and Catholics even made it into cookbooks. Temperance cookbooks (which eliminated all alcohol from recipes) formed a genre all their own, but regular cookbooks and household manuals carried forth the same agenda. Catharine Beecher (1800–1878), one of nineteenth-century America's foremost domestic advisers (as well as the sister of Harriet Beecher Stowe and daughter of Lyman Beecher) made this explicit in her famous *Treatise on Domestic Economy* – first released in 1841 and still going strong in revisions and reprints up to 1868. There she advised Victorian matrons to avoid condiments, spices, "luxurious" foods, and, in fact – she claimed based on a scientific study she had consulted – anything that an Italian Catholic might have given up for Lent. Her ideal diet, betraying its English (and tacitly Protestant) bias, was "plain and well-cooked animal food, not too recently killed, and eaten in moderate quantity, with bread, rice, or roasted potatoes."[53]

But reformers did not only fear problems brought into the country by immigrant outsiders. They feared "outsiders" already present. This statement from the Methodist General Conference (the denomination's lawmaking body) in 1868 about the need for national alcohol prohibition shows just how much they feared them:

> Our rescued people of the South greatly need its protection, so that the liberties they have just received may not prove an occasion of their ruin. Our foreign population require it to deliver them from the vices which their old-world habits have wrought in them, and to build them up in virtue. Our Indian tribes need it to transform themselves from savages to men, as the white man's whiskey now transforms them from savages to demons.[54]

In fact, concerns about all American "bad habits" had a eugenic tinge throughout the nineteenth century: activists were concerned that the continual practice of such habits would weaken white Protestantism. They feared that drunkards and those trapped by other habits would pass degeneracy on to children who might be "feeble-minded" or experience, as Crane put it,

> paroxysms of morbid restlessness and indefinable longing, when no employment contents them, no pleasures already known to them attract, no healthy food or drink satisfies, but ... the first casual taste of the intoxicant thrills them with insane rapture, and marks them for a mad career and a doom from which all human tenderness and pity toil in vain to save them.[55]

Some – including medical doctors – even went so far as to recommend that American Protestants needed to rethink their entire system of hospitals, medical advances, and missions of compassion, because these had allowed an entire class of "constitutionally diseased" people to arise; one doctor protested in the American Medical Association's journal of record that such undesirables were "permitted and enabled to form marriage unions resulting in progeny, defective, dependent, and to be cared for as themselves."[56] The doctor, William Schrock, recommended regulating marriages to ensure race survival.

PROHIBITION AND THE TWENTIETH CENTURY

Most immediately, temperance reformers succeeded beyond their wildest dreams with the ratification of the Eighteenth Amendment in 1919 and the passage of the Volstead Act that same year which provided for federal enforcement of the amendment. Effects to write prohibition into state and federal law dated all the way back to the Maine Law of 1851, the first of more than a dozen state prohibition laws that legislatures and courts battled over for the next seven decades.[57]

But the Eighteenth Amendment, even though it cut American liquor consumption in the short term, turned out to be a tremendous flop in the long run. Liquor-making and liquor-selling went underground, prompting a rise in organized crime.[58] Public opinion turned against legal strictures on liquor sale and consumption, and in 1933 the Twenty-First Amendment repealed the Eighteenth, throwing the matter back to the states – some states maintained some form of prohibitory laws until the 1960s, and some municipalities still do.

Parallel to these legal developments came equally important social and cultural ones. Common-sense realism, once dominant among Protestant cultural elites, was by the 1920s replaced in most Protestant halls of power by philosophical (and, in the Christian context, exegetical) outlooks "characterized by the development of historical consciousness and a commitment to science and theology as progressive, dynamic, and developmental."[59] These outlooks had precedent in nineteenth-century theology in the works of thinkers such as Amos Bronson Alcott (1799–1888), Horace Bushnell (1802–1876), Ralph Waldo Emerson (1803–1882), and Henry David Thoreau (1817–1862); but now they came into the ascendancy. Common-sense realism continued to motivate the scientific and philosophical arguments of the burgeoning fundamentalist movement – as it does even down to the twenty-first century – but it was abandoned as a serous method of thought by mainline Protestants by the mid-1920s.[60]

At the same time, there was an impulse from the 1920s onward to normalize the very "minor vices" temperance and lifestyle activists had fought against – and in fact to channel these minor vices into rebellion against the bourgeoise.[61] Again, this was an impulse that had simmered in the background during the nineteenth century, from *Huckleberry Finn* to the aesthetic movement, but it now gained the societal upper hand.

Within several generations, temperance and its associated lifestyle reforms – once a central pillar motivating the Protestant mainstream – became seen as the province of fundamentalists and viewed as arbitrary rules from a hidebound past. Even for those who maintained allegiance to these reforms, their progressive origins were now murky: "Giving up drinking or smoking or wearing jewelry or going to movies remained as boundary markers of evangelical identity in settings where their connection with ministry to the poor and marginalized had long disappeared."[62]

Many Protestants still hoped Christ would come to rule on earth, and that necessary precursors included clearing away sinful, or at least historically oppressive, habits of thought and behavior. But they no longer believed, as Willard had hoped, that the rum shops were included on that list.

NOTES

1 Portions of this chapter are adapted from Jennifer Woodruff Tait, "Christ Versus the Rum Shops," *Christian History* no. 138 (2021), 19–21, and are used by permission of Christian History Institute.

2 Chad Beckman et al., "Frances Willard and the Woman's Christian Temperance Union, 1874–1898," Center for Women's History and Leadership, Learning Resource Guide, Frances Willard House Museum and Archives, accessed November 19, 2020, https://franceswillardhouse.org/wp-content/uploads/HST391-2-wctu1.pdf.

3 Carol Mattingly, *Well-Tempered Women: Nineteenth-Century Temperance Rhetoric* (Carbondale: Southern Illinois University, 1998), 58.

4 John Burnham, *Bad Habits: Drinking, Smoking, Taking Drugs, Gambling, Sexual Misbehavior, and Swearing in American History* (New York: New York University Press, 1993), 40.

5 Joseph Gusfield, *Symbolic Crusade: Status Politics and the American Temperance Movement* (Urbana: University of Illinois Press, 1963), 10–11.

6 Plato, *Republic* IV.427, from *Plato in Twelve Volumes*, vols. V and VI, trans. Paul Shorey (Cambridge, MA, Harvard University Press), 1969, www.perseus .tufts.edu/hopper/text?doc=Perseus%3Atext%3A1999.01.0168%3Abook%3 D4%3Asection%3D427e. See Ambrose, "On the Duties of the Clergy," 1.24, 1.27, accessed March 6, 2021, www.ccel.org/ccel/schaff/npnf210/npnf210.iv .i.ii.xxiv.html and https://ccel.org/ccel/schaff/npnf210/npnf210.iv.i.ii.xxvii .html.

7 Catholic Church, "The Virtues," *Catechism of the Catholic Church*, 2nd ed. (Vatican: Libreria Editrice Vaticana, 2012), paragraph 1809, www.vatican.va/ archive/ccc_css/archive/catechism/p3s1c1a7.htm.

8 Jennifer Woodruff Tait, *The Poisoned Chalice: Eucharistic Grape Juice and Common-Sense Realism in Victorian Methodism* (Tuscaloosa: University of Alabama Press, 2011), 9.

9 "Entertainment of George Washington at City Tavern, Philadelphia, September 1787," Teaching American History, accessed November 21, 2020, https://teachingamericanhistory.org/resources/convention/citytavern/.

10 See W. J. Rorabaugh, *The Alcoholic Republic* (New York: Oxford University Press, 1979); Mark Lender and James Martin, *Drinking in America: A History* (New York: The Free Press, 1982), 30–35, 48–51; John J. Rumbarger, *Profits, Power, and Prohibition: Alcohol Reform and the Industrializing of America,*

1800–1930 (Albany: State University of New York Press, 1989); David
Conroy, *In Public Houses: Drink and the Revolution of Authority in Colonial
Massachusetts* (Chapel Hill: University of North Carolina Press, 1995); Helen
Lefkowitz Horowitz, *Rereading Sex: Battles over Sexual Knowledge and
Suppression in Nineteenth-Century America* (Knopf: New York, 2002); and
A. K. Sandoval-Strausz, *Hotel: An American History* (Cambridge, MA: Yale
University Press, 2007).

11 *Doctrines and Discipline of the MEC, 1880* (New York: Phillips and Hunt,
1880), 36, emphasis mine.

12 *Journal of the General Conference of the Methodist Episcopal Church, 1892*
(New York: Hunt and Eaton, 1892), 492.

13 Jennifer Woodruff Tait, "This Is What a Progressive Looks Like," *Christianity
Today* (June 2014), 44, www.christianitytoday.com/ct/2014/june/teetotalers-
i-never-knew-alcohol.html. Some good histories of the temperance move-
ment include Norman Clark's *Deliver Us from Evil: An Interpretation of
American Prohibition* (New York: Norton, 1976); Ian R. Tyrell, *Sobering Up:
From Temperance to Prohibition in Antebellum America, 1800–1860*
(Westport, CT: Greenwood Press, 1979); Jack Blocker, *Give to the Winds Thy
Fears: The Women's Temperance Crusade, 1873–1874* (Westport, CT;
Greenwood Press, 1985) and *American Temperance Movements: Cycles of
Reform* (Boston: Twayne, 1989); and Joe Coker, *Liquor in the Land of the Lost
Cause* (Lexington: University Press of Kentucky, 2007).

14 See Daniel Dorchester, *The Liquor Problem in All Ages* (New York: Phillips
and Hunt, 1884), for many statistics on nineteenth-century alcohol consumption, implying that at least some temperance advocates realized the
decline by the late nineteenth century.

15 David Lindberg and Ronald Numbers, eds., *God and Nature: Historical
Essays on the Encounter between Christianity and Science* (Berkeley:
University of California Press, 1986); and *When Science & Christianity Meet*
(Chicago: University of Chicago Press, 2003); and James C. Ungureanu,
*Science, Religion, and the Protestant Tradition: Retracing the Origins of
Conflict* (Pittsburgh: University of Pittsburgh Press, 2019).

16 Woodruff Tait, *The Poisoned Chalice*, 21.

17 William Beaumont, *Experiments and Observations on the Gastric Juice, and
the Physiology of Digestion* (Plattsburgh, NY: F. P. Allen, 1833), cited in
Eliphalet Nott, *Lectures on Biblical Temperance*, 2nd ed. with notes by F. R.
Lees (London: Trubner, 1866), 80–82.

18 Thomas Sewall and Edward Delavan, *The Pathology of Drunkenness, Or the
Physical Effects of Alcoholic Drinks: With Drawings of the Drunkard's
Stomach; A Letter Addressed to Edward C. Delavan, Esq.* (Albany, NY: C.
Van Benthuysen, 1841; repr. New York: NTSPH, 1884); Emil C. Vigilante,
"The Temperance Reform in New York State 1829–1851" (Ph.D. diss., New
York University, 1964), 217–222.

19 Woodruff Tait, *The Poisoned Chalice*, 23.

20 Thomas Sewall, "The Effects of Intemperance," in *Select Temperance Tracts* (New York: American Temperance Society, c. 1830s), 3, www.gutenberg.org/files/27146/27146-h/27146-h.htm#INTEMPERANCE.

21 *Journal of the General Conference of the MEC, 1888* (New York: Phillips and Hunt, 1888), 457. See also Jonathan Zimmerman, "'When Doctors Disagree': Scientific Temperance and Scientific Authority, 1891–1906," *Journal of the History of Medicine* vol. 48, no. 2 (1993), 171–197; and *Distilling Democracy: Alcohol Education in America's Public Schools, 1880–1925* (Lawrence: University Press of Kansas, 1999).

22 Woodruff Tait, *The Poisoned Chalice*, 4–5.

23 P., "Nott's Lectures on Temperance," *Methodist Quarterly Review* (October 1847), 543, 545.

24 Moses Stuart, *Scriptural View of the Wine Question, In a Letter to the Rev. Dr. Nott, President of Union College* (New York: Leavitt, Trow, and Co., 1849), 51.

25 Frederic Richard Lees and Dawson Burns, *The Temperance Bible-Commentary* (New York: Sheldon, 1870), 278.

26 *Oinos: A Discussion of the Bible Wine Question* (New York: Phillips and Hunt, 1883), 61.

27 D. C. Babcock, *The Temperance Movement versus the Liquor System*, Home College Series no. 66 (New York: Phillips and Hunt, c. 1880s), 8.

28 Peter Markie, "Rationalism vs. Empiricism," in *The Stanford Encyclopedia of Philosophy*, ed. Edward N. Zalta, July 6, 2017, https://plato.stanford.edu/archives/fall2017/entries/rationalism-empiricism/.

29 Woodruff Tait, *The Poisoned Chalice*, 4.

30 Woodruff Tait, *The Poisoned Chalice*, 4; see also Sydney Ahlstrom, "The Scottish Philosophy and American Theology," *Church History*, no. 24 (1955), 252–272; George Marsden, "Everyone One's Own Interpreter: The Bible, Science, and Authority in Mid-Nineteenth-Century America," in *The Bible in America: Essays in Cultural History*, ed. Nathan Hatch and Mark Noll (Oxford: Oxford University Press, 1982), 79–100; Grant Wacker, "The Demise of Biblical Civilization," in *The Bible in America*, ed. Hatch and Noll, 121–138, and *Augustus H. Strong and the Dilemma of Historical Consciousness* (Macon, GA: Mercer University Press, 1985), 9–19. For more on common-sense realism applied to science and biblical interpretation, see George Marsden, *Fundamentalism and American Culture*, 2nd ed. (Oxford: Oxford University Press, 2006), and Mark Noll, *America's God: From Jonathan Edwards to Abraham Lincoln* (Oxford: Oxford University Press, 2002).

31 Charles Hodge, *Systematic Theology* (New York: Scribner, 1871–1873), vol. I, 9.

32 Woodruff Tait, *The Poisoned Chalice*, 5.

33 "Work with New Electronic 'Brains' Opens Field for Army Math Experts," *The Hammond Times* (November 10, 1957), 65.

34 John Marsh, *Temperance Hymn Book and Minstrel, A Collection of Hymns, Songs, and Odes for Temperance Meetings and Festivals* (New York: American Temperance Union, 1847), 74.

35 *Cold-Water Army Song Book* (Charleston, IL: A. H. Davis, c. 1890), 1, emphasis mine.

36 Julia Colman, *Alcohol and Hygiene: An Elementary Lesson-Book for Schools* (New York: NTSPH, 1883), 117.

37 "Beware of Bad Books," repr. in *Popular American Literature of the Nineteenth Century*, ed. Paul Gutjahr (New York: Oxford University Press, 2001), 59.

38 James Buckley, *Christians and the Theater* (New York: Phillips and Hunt, 1883), 65.

39 In addition to Gusfield, *Symbolic Crusade*, Rorabaugh, *The Alcoholic Republic*, and Rumbarger, *Profits, Power, and Prohibition*, see James Timberlake, *Prohibition and the Progressive Movement, 1900–1920* (Cambridge, MA: Harvard University Press, 1963); Marianna Adler, "From Symbolic Exchange to Commodity Consumption: Anthropological Notes on Drinking as a Symbolic Practice," in *Drinking: Behavior and Belief in Modern History*, ed. Susanna Barrows and Robin Room (Berkeley: University of California Press, 1991), 376–398; and Robert Fuller, *Religion and Wine: A Cultural History of Wine Drinking in the United States* (Knoxville: University of Tennessee Press, 1996).

40 Horowitz, *Rereading Sex*, 142. See also Howard Chudacoff, *The Age of the Bachelor: Creating an American Subculture* (Princeton: Princeton University Press, 1999).

41 Woodruff Tait, *The Poisoned Chalice*, 67–73, 75, 80.

42 "The Well-Conducted Farm," in *Select Temperance Tracts*, accessed February 13, 2021, www.gutenberg.org/files/27146/27146-h/27146-h.htm# WELL-CONDUCTED_FARM.

43 Woodruff Tait, *The Poisoned Chalice*, 64.

44 Jonathan Crane, *Arts of Intoxication: The Aim, and the Results* (New York: Phillips and Hunt, 1870), 237.

45 Julia Colman, *Catechism on Alcohol with Responsive Exercises on Temperance* (New York: NTSPH, 1874), 22.

46 Woodruff Tait, *The Poisoned Chalice*, 47–48. See Jed Dannenbaum, *Drink and Disorder: Temperance Reform in Cincinnati from the Washingtonian Revival to the WCTU* (Urbana: University of Illinois Press, 1984).

47 Dorchester, *The Liquor Problem in All Ages*, 399.

48 Dorchester, *The Liquor Problem in All Ages*, 401.

49 Dorchester, *The Liquor Problem in All Ages*, 401. For more on the connection between taverns, crime, and prostitution, see Horowitz, *Rereading Sex*, and Steven Paul DeVillo, *The Bowery: The Strange History of New York's Oldest Street* (New York City: Skyhorse, 2019).

50 Woodruff Tait, *The Poisoned Chalice*, 78.
51 See Woodruff Tait, *The Poisoned Chalice*, 37–61, for more on temperance and emotion, as well as *American Cool: Constructing a Twentieth-Century Emotional Style* (New York: New York University Press, 1994) and John Corrigan, *Business of the Heart: Religion and Emotion in the Nineteenth Century* (Berkeley: University of California Press, 2002).
52 Woodruff Tait, *The Poisoned Chalice*, 78–79. See William Shea, *The Lion and the Lamb: Evangelicals and Catholics in America* (Oxford: Oxford University Press, 2004), 56–57.
53 Catharine Beecher, *A Treatise on Domestic Economy* (New York: Marsh et al., 1841), 83–84.
54 *Journal of the General Conference of the MEC, 1868* (New York: Carlton and Lanahan, 1868), 626.
55 Crane, *Arts of Intoxication*, 185.
56 William Schrock, "Man According to Nature," *Journal of the American Medical Association* vol. 1, no. 7 (August 25, 1883), 208–209. For the persistence of these ideas into the twentieth century, see Amy Laura Hall, *Conceiving Parenthood: American Protestantism and the Spirit of Reproduction* (Grand Rapids, MI: Eerdmans, 2007).
57 Woodruff Tait, *The Poisoned Chalice*, 71. For more on statutory prohibition, see Clark, *Deliver Us from Evil*; Ian Tyrell, *Sobering Up: From Temperance to Prohibition in Antebellum America, 1800–1860* (Westport, CT: Greenwood Press, 1979); Thomas Pegram, *Battling Demon Rum: The Struggle for a Dry America, 1800–1933* (Chicago: Dee, 1998); and Kyle Volk, *Moral Minorities and the Making of American Democracy* (Oxford: Oxford University Press, 2014). Horowitz, *Rereading Sex*, discusses parallel efforts to regulate American sexual behavior.
58 FBI.gov, "The FBI and the American Gangster," accessed February 27, 2021, www.fbi.gov/history/brief-history/the-fbi-and-the-american-gangster.
59 Woodruff Tait, *The Poisoned Chalice*, 122. For more, see Marsden, *Fundamentalism and American Culture*, and William Hutchinson, *The Modernist Impulse in American Protestantism* (Cambridge, MA: Harvard University Press, 1976).
60 See Marsden, *Fundamentalism and American Culture*; Joel Carpenter, *Revive Us Again: The Reawakening of American Fundamentalism* (New York: Oxford University Press, 1997); Edward J. Larson. *Summer for the Gods: The Scopes Trial and America's Continuing Debate over Science and Religion* (New York: Basic Books, 1997); and Mark Noll, *America's God: From Jonathan Edwards to Abraham Lincoln* (Oxford: Oxford University Press, 2002), especially 367–438.

61 See Burnham, *Bad Habits*, and Christian Smith, ed., *The Secular Revolution: Power, Interests, and Conflict in the Secularization of American Public Life* (Berkeley: University of California Press, 2003).

62 Woodruff Tait, "This Is What a Progressive Looks Like," 45. See also Donald Dayton with Douglas Strong, *Rediscovering an Evangelical Heritage: A Tradition and Trajectory of Integrating Piety and Justice* (Grand Rapids, MI: Baker, 2014).

11 Gender, Sexuality, and Marriage

ELIZABETH H. FLOWERS AND KAREN K. SEAT

Baptist Women in Ministry (BWIM) has long defied the conservative trajectory of its denomination of origin, the Southern Baptist Convention (SBC), America's largest Protestant denomination. In 2008, when BWIM celebrated the twenty-fifth anniversary of its founding to support women seeking ordination, the group branded T-shirts with the logo "This Is What a Preacher Looks Like." The T-shirts were a surprise hit, selling out immediately. The buzz around the T-shirts led to a hashtag, weekly blog, related social media sites, and book of sermons. "This Is What a Preacher Looks Like" social media posts highlighted women undertaking traditional ecclesial tasks in their local churches, such as preaching, baptizing, or conducting weddings. Others displayed the "Preacher" tag while in more domestic and familial settings, baking or gardening, sometimes with their husbands and children in tow. On BWIM's Facebook page, one mother-daughter ministerial duo even posted a snapshot of themselves in their "Preacher" T-shirts at Southern Baptist Theological Seminary, an institution acclaimed by conservative evangelicals for its patriarchal theology. "Give them hell," read one of the Facebook comments. "Oh the irony!" observed another.[1]

Overall, the T-shirts and hashtag succeeded because they disrupted historical gender norms in Southern Baptist life. According to these standards, women were not to be found in the pulpit nor were preachers expected to be in the kitchen with a husband and children. Moreover, while white women were predominant in the early photographs, eventually African-American, Asian-American, and Latina women appeared with the BWIM slogan, adding to the irony, as the Southern Baptist Convention not only advocated for women's submission in marriage and ministry but was also established in support of slavery and had later promoted racial segregation. The gender tensions raised and reflected in "This Is What a Preacher Looks Like" were inseparable from histories of race and ethnicity as well.

There are many ways to tell the history of gender, sexuality, and marriage in American Protestantism. We open with this story because American Protestantism's long, and often troubled, association with patriarchy is as much a part of its story today as it was at the country's founding. The women in the T-shirts clearly upset patriarchal notions of divine order and power and the connected regulation of sexuality and marital relations. In this story, Southern Baptists are representative of Protestants who, throughout their history, have been deeply invested in and conflicted by these gender constructions and norms.

Gender is a term with multiple and sometimes contradictory meanings. Here, we are using gender primarily in reference to cultural constructions of womanhood and manhood, which Protestants employed both to regulate particular roles and behaviors and to resist them. It is important to note that some gender theorists have also collapsed the constructed nature of gender and gendered identities with that of sex, thereby questioning the male–female binary. While we likewise reject gender essentialism, we still hold that perceived bodily differences led to certain collective experiences, as well as marginalizations, in Protestant life. Thus, we use the language of sex (how Protestants distinguished women and men) in relation to gender (their constructions, expressions, and performances of womanhood and manhood). All the while, though, we examine the instability of the discourse, and the ways sexuality further complicated these categories. We are aware, too, that some scholars in American religion have argued for sexuality as its own analytical category, discrete from gender. Still, Protestants most often debated sexuality in the context of gender. The ways Protestants constructed notions of womanhood and manhood were integral to the ways they understood, conformed to, and disputed certain sexual identities and expressions; thus we treat them as connected.[2]

As we narrate this particular history, several interrelated themes emerge. First, it is not a tale of either lineal progress or decline. Overall, two competing impulses around gender came to characterize Protestant life: one that insisted on a particular God-ordained gender order, often starting with the home and moving outward to church and society, and another that downplayed or sometimes altogether dismissed gender injunctions and hierarchies as contrary to divine intention. As the historian Ann Braude notes, religion baptized gender roles with transcendent values,[3] and the medium for Protestants in that process was the Bible. But biblical interpretation has been varied and contested among Protestants, often reflecting their own cultural investments.

Thus, a second theme is that Protestantism's "modernist–fundamentalist" divide, usually seen as a far-reaching dispute over how to read the Bible, was closely connected to and driven by wider cultural debates regarding gender. New ways of interpreting the Bible eventually led to the proliferation of feminist theologies and other theologies of liberation in the twentieth and twenty-first centuries. Spurning these transformations, the rejection of feminism – and later, LGBTQ+ equality – became a central feature of conservative evangelicals' identity and their prevailing hermeneutic of biblical inerrancy.

There were, of course, multiple distinctions within these impulses. Even within a particular camp, scriptural interpretations were fluid and changing. But as unstable as these interpretations might have been, a third and overarching theme is that gender has functioned as one of the most active organizing forces in Protestant life. Protestants drew on gender to control behaviors and regulate boundaries as well as to question and challenge them.

The sectarian nature of Protestantism, observed historians Susan Juster and Lisa MacFarlane, "has been a persistent source of conflict but it has also been a vital source of political innovation and cultural regeneration."[4] Nowhere are the contending functions of conflict and creativity better exemplified than in Protestants' grappling with gender, which shaped Protestant theologies, rearranged their alliances, and splintered their institutions. By the twenty-first century, gender had usurped denominational loyalties, along with the theological movements and social forces that had formed them, as a primary marker of identity and belonging. Thus, careful attention to gender, especially as it includes marriage and sexuality, broadens, refines, and sometimes alters our understanding of Protestantism.

PURITAN PATRIARCHS, REVIVALIST SHE-PREACHERS, AND THE EMERGENCE OF TRUE WOMANHOOD

Protestants in colonial British America ranged from Church of England loyalists to a diversity of dissenting groups. At times, women in the more radical non-conformist traditions attempted a measure of religious autonomy. But for those who established tax-supported dominance, namely Puritans/Congregationalists in the New England colonies and Anglicans to their south, patriarchy was central to the ways they ordered their "new world." White women were consigned to submission in marriage and denied ministerial status in the church; enslaved people, whose conversions white Protestants debated, were denied legal marriage as a sign of their inferiority. Thus, as slavery advanced, ideologies of race developed alongside those concerning gender.

Marriage was expected of the most privileged members of society, and with it, the British common law of coverture, in which a woman's social, legal, and economic identity was subsumed by her husband's. This legal arrangement resonated with the prevailing Protestant hermeneutic, which took the order of creation in Genesis 2 (Eve was created second, from Adam's rib, before the two became one flesh) as well as the story of the fall in Genesis 3:16 (in which the man would rule over the woman) as binding biblical mandates for the marital relationship. Indeed, until the Great Awakening revivals, most Protestants accepted a one-sex model of gender, insisting that the woman was an inferior version of the man.

During the seventeenth and eighteenth centuries in colonial British America, a well-ordered Protestant household was the measure of a pious and prosperous society. The home was a microcosm of the church, and thriving households rested on an observance of the hierarchy instructed by male ministers and civil magistrates. As their statures rose, households also incorporated indentured servants and enslaved persons, eventually creating the plantations of the South. Strict hierarchies, with husbands at the head, followed by wives, children, and indentured and enslaved individuals, with women usually following men, were understood to reflect the household codes prescribed in New Testament texts that admonished wives to submit to their husbands and slaves to obey their earthly masters. When the Puritan midwife Ann Hutchinson began holding Bible studies in her house after the weekly Sunday meeting, critiquing the sermon and teaching men as well as women, she was excommunicated and banished from Massachusetts Bay Colony, with one of the ministers at her church trial declaring: "You have stept out of your place, you have rather bine a Husband than a Wife and a preacher than a Hearer; and a Magistrate than a Subject."[5] And for being "wholly guided by his wife," Hutchinson's husband, William, was characterized by the colony's governor, John Winthrop, as "a man of a very mild temper and weak parts."[6]

The stirrings of evangelical Protestantism initially disrupted prevailing social hierarchies. The anti-authoritarian revivalism of the First Great Awakening, which fomented revolutionary fervor in eighteenth-century America as it spread the independent spirit of evangelicalism, rose again in the Second Great Awakening of the antebellum period. Not only were the majority of its participants women, but the revivals frequently violated the gender and racial codes that ordered ecclesial life. Many "old-school" Protestants (Puritan Congregationalists and Presbyterians as well as Anglicans), for example, recoiled in horror at the revivals' display of emotions, which they associated with women. They were dismayed over the excessive weeping and wailing of "effeminate" revival preachers and horrified that Baptists and Methodists permitted women, or "she-preachers," to enter the pulpit. Historians later described this period as one of the feminization of American religion.[7]

Enslaved persons as well as freedmen and freedwomen also converted and preached during the Great Awakenings. While white Baptist and Methodist congregations did allow them membership, they consigned Black members to church balconies, and ultimately many Black Protestants left to form their own denominations. Many white congregations in the antebellum South still debated the rights of enslaved men and women to marry and, even more, to remarry, particularly in light of the growing controversy over slavery and the internal slave trade. Withholding the option of legal marriage and family relations for enslaved persons continued as a way to reinforce their racial subordination.

Despite some fluidity of gender roles during revivals, the Great Awakenings stopped short of advocating for equality. Stepping outside of gender and racial norms in revival settings could be better tolerated if viewed as the working of the spirit rather than as an intentional challenge to established social hierarchies. Women such as famed Baptist revivalist Martha Stearns Marshall, for instance, or evangelist Harriet Livermore, both of them white, were seen as moved or even possessed by the Holy Spirit in ways that enabled them to transcend their gender. The Black Methodist itinerant Jarena Lee had to battle racism as well, underscoring the greatness of "the Lord" in claiming that "by the instrumentality of a poor colored woman," who was Lee herself, he "poured forth his spirit among the people."[8]

Overall, as Baptist and Methodist churches came to dominate the religious landscape in the United States, they tamed their more radical impulses, refusing women ordination and referencing their public speaking as "exhorting" or "testifying" rather than preaching. Many also modulated revivalism's emotional excesses. This renewal of hierarchical gender roles was connected to the emerging white middle class in a variety of denominations. These Protestants, however, did not simply reinscribe colonial gender roles as previously understood and practiced. By the nineteenth century, a two-sex model of gender, in which women were seen less often as "inferior men" (the one-sex model) and rather as a separate sex altogether, with unique virtues, prompted what historians have described as the "cult of true womanhood."[9]

The historian Barbara Welter famously illuminated the ways ante-bellum popular culture fixated on the ideal of domesticated women functioning in a separate sphere from that of politics and the expanding wage economy, these being the realms of men. Seen as more naturally pious and morally superior to men, women were expected to uphold Protestant virtue in the absence of an established church. In an 1808 sermon, the Presbyterian minister Samuel Miller proclaimed that the wife's duty was to serve as "the counsellor and friend of the husband." Miller admonished the wife to make "it her daily study to lighten his cares, to soothe his sorrows, and to augment his joys" so that she would be to her husband "like a guardian angel" who "watches over his interests, warns him against dangers, comforts him under trials; and by her pious, assiduous, and attractive deportment, constantly endeavors to render him more virtuous, more useful, more honourable, and more happy."[10] As long as women and men remained in their designated roles, marriage held the potential of a companionable relationship, with the home becoming as religiously significant in moral instruction as the church.

Of course, true womanhood was a construct available to very few beyond the upper elite and aspiring middle class. Industrialism produced a new working class, whose women and children labored long hours in factories and mills. The South remained largely rural, with women and children farming alongside men. Ideals and experiences of gender, sexuality, and marriage continued to be profoundly shaped by race and ethnicity. But true womanhood remained an ideal in nineteenth-century American Protantism, shaping both progressive and conservative movements.

REFORM, SUFFRAGE, AND THE NEW WOMAN

Early American Protestants who pushed the boundaries of prescribed gender roles, particularly boundaries regarding women, were usually driven by religious fervor rather than any desire for egalitarianism. As a nascent feminist movement developed in the nineteenth century, however, Protestantism reflected a broad range of responses to hierarchical social arrangements and gender norms. Protestants attended the Seneca Falls Convention in 1848, which launched first-wave feminism and a movement for women's rights, including suffrage. It is no coincidence that many early and noted Protestant feminists, pious activists such as Sarah and Angelina Grimke and Lucretia Mott, were first part of the more radical wing of abolitionism. They took from it the language of freedom, rights, and equality, which they then applied to women, and they tied these liberative impulses to their understanding of the gospel stories. Those connected to suffrage and women's rights were also often prominent among those advocating for women's ordination, the two movements overlapping. Antoinette Brown, for instance, who was ordained by her Congregationalist church in 1853 on the basis of a "feminism of equality," was active in the National American Woman's Suffrage Association. Anna Howard Shaw, the first ordained Methodist woman, served as the organization's president.[11]

Protestant women in the nineteenth-century suffrage movement believed Christianity was on their side. They made the case that, interpreted properly, the Bible promoted equality. Elizabeth Cady Stanton, the editor of the *Woman's Bible* who was largely denounced for her condemnation of historical Christianity, commended the inclusivity of Jesus in the gospels. Former enslaved Sojourner Truth also reminded her audience at an 1851 women's rights gathering that Jesus "never spurned woman from him."[12] Still, Protestants who advocated for egalitarianism within the church as well as in the home and larger society remained a minority and often came from denominations outside the mainstream, such as the Methodist Protestant Church (a populist offshoot of the Methodist Episcopal Church), the Society of Friends (Quakers), the American Unitarian Association, and other more congregational-based traditions. Far greater in number were those who used the tenets of true womanhood to organize social reforming ministries, only later joining forces with twentieth-century suffragists.

During the nineteenth century, the abolition of slavery, rapid urbanization and industrialization, and mass immigration transformed American society and culture at an unprecedented pace, creating what Protestants decried as a multitude of social problems. Embracing true womanhood's vision of the inherent piety and caretaking abilities of the "female sex," many Protestant women felt it their Christian duty to extend their moral influence beyond the home to "homes without walls."[13] They founded orphanages, schools for freedmen and freedwomen and poor children, and settlement houses for newly arrived immigrants. They also began to push into the political realm, eventually advocating for compulsory education, child labor laws, temperance, and an end to prostitution. And yet when it came to women's suffrage or their running for office, most Protestants agreed with the popular Congregationalist minister Horace Bushnell, who called such an act the "re-sexing of their sex." As he noted, "in giving the ballot [to women] we shall give stones for bread."[14]

Ultimately, the greatest challenge to women's disenfranchisement came from a surprising source: the Woman's Christian Temperance Union (WCTU), founded in 1873. By the twentieth century, it had become not only the largest Protestant women's interdenominational organization of the Progressive Era but the most robust network connecting Protestant women's social reform to the women's suffrage movement. Treading cautiously, the WCTU's leaders recognized the power of the vote to achieve their aims and sought to harmonize women's activism with the rhetoric of true womanhood. Its long-time president, well-known Methodist Frances Willard, often spoke of the power of women's "mother-love" and insisted that "mother-hearted women are the salvation of the race." If women, the moral guardians of home and society, were given the vote, they could "lift humanity out of its sins."[15] Men, she noted, could achieve the moral purity of women, but only if they too assumed (and voted for) women's social causes.[16]

The WCTU was one of the few white-led Protestant organizations of its time permitting Black women membership; nevertheless, chapters were racially segregated. Overall, the politics of race meant that the social reforming activities of Black and white women ran parallel to one another.[17] While many goals overlapped, including women's suffrage (even as Black men continued to be disenfranchised), Black women's reforming efforts focused more heavily on combatting the violence of racism.[18] African Americans who sought to change and reform the United States faced heightened dangers. The anti-lynching campaign of Ida B. Wells, for instance, led to threats of her own lynching. Moreover, unlike white women, Black Protestant women reformers, overwhelmingly middle class, struggled not as much against the tenets of true womanhood as against the prevailing assumption that Black women were, by nature, inferior to the ideal, thus compelling them to navigate a "politics of respectability" in their public activism.[19]

Protestant women frequently saw their efforts at reform as promoting middle-class American ideals of gender and marriage, which to their minds were biblical. Nowhere was this more apparent than in missions. While the sending of missionaries was initially perceived as a manly enterprise, the religious equivalent of manifest destiny, women again deployed the language of domesticity and true womanhood to proclaim "the world their household."[20] Women's denominational mission boards, separate from men's, trained and funded women missionaries both abroad and domestically. Male missionaries, who were married,

"Christianized" through evangelism and preaching; women missionaries, usually unmarried, "civilized" by working alongside "heathen" women and purportedly, if not ironically, instructed them on the ways to become "proper wives and mothers." Because Protestants closely associated what they perceived as illegitimate practices of gender and sexuality to illegitimate religion, conversions to Christianity were authenticated by an embrace of American Protestant ideals of gender, marriage, and sexuality. Owing to the value they placed on gender and marriage in the Christianization of nations, Protestants overwhelmingly encouraged and supported women's missionary work. By the end of the nineteenth century, women outnumbered men on the mission field, with a few, such as the Southern Baptist missionary to China, Lottie Moon, achieving celebrity status back home.

While Protestant women promoted true womanhood in both their social reforming and missions activities, they also stretched it to its limits, as these movements helped to normalize women's career, political, and even ecclesiastical ambitions. As Braude notes, "while the temperance movement thrust women into unprecedented leadership in local and occasionally state government and public institutions, the women's missionary movement transformed women's roles within the churches." The "mammoth accomplishments" of women in missions certainly forced congregations and denominations to "question the legitimacy of women's exclusion from lay rights" in their churches, especially after women received the right to vote in US elections.[21]

The fundamentalist–modernist controversy was likewise driven by anxieties over changing gender roles within Protestantism and American society at large.[22] By 1900, most states had overturned a number of laws rooted in coverture. A majority allowed women to control their income, and the number of women working for wages was steadily increasing. In 1920, the Nineteenth Amendment granting women the vote ushered in the era of the "new woman," who, characterized by autonomy and independence rather than domesticity and submission, directly threatened true womanhood. Fundamentalists were brought together, in part, by their resistance to the new woman; they clung to an idealized past, denying the ways true womanhood had been negotiated rather than embodied. They declared suffrage as evidence that reform-minded and modernist-thinking Protestants were on the wrong track. The growth of religious diversity through immigration and US expansion, as well as a growing public acceptance of modern science, only added to their anxieties. Premillennialists, they warned that America was headed for Armageddon and that the new woman would actually precipitate its collision course with Satan's army. Popular fundamentalist preacher John R. Rice warned followers to beware of "bobbed hair, bossy wives, and woman preachers," whom he also compared to fallen and rebellious angels. Men tempted to marry the new or modern woman, he cautioned, would discover her as one who "obeys nobody."[23]

Rice also attacked effeminate men. Citing Paul's letter to the Corinthians, he preached that "among the adulterers and fornicators and drunkards and thieves and covetous and extortioners, God put the effeminate. To be effeminate is a horrible sin in God's sight." And then, having blamed women for the fall, he also asserted the "first sin with which God chided Adam, after the fall, was this: Because thou hast hearkened unto the voice of thy wife."[24] Fundamentalists like Rice promoted a more entrenched and belligerent form of masculinity in the wake of the new women and clothed their understandings of gender and eventually sexuality in the language of inerrancy. There were, of course, many issues associated with the rise of fundamentalism, but gender anxiety was certainly one of the most potent, and by combining it with upset over racial upheavals, fundamentalists found the South fertile ground in which to take root, wait, and grow.

WOMEN'S RIGHTS, CIVIL RIGHTS, AND THE CHRISTIAN RIGHT

Protestant conflicts around gender and sexuality escalated throughout the twentieth century, ultimately driving the American culture wars of the 1980s and 1990s.[25] As inheritors of Protestant fundamentalism, late-twentieth-century conservative evangelicals sought to safeguard many tenets of patriarchy and domesticity. Partnering with like-minded Catholics and Mormons, they formed the Christian Right. Progressives who promoted change were primarily from the mainline denominations but also included a notable minority within evangelicalism. These more liberal Protestants, inspired by the second-wave feminist movement of the 1960s and 1970s, developed their own movements for women's rights and gender equality, challenging conservative Christian understandings. As the conflict became more and more polarizing – invoking sexuality, family structures, and marital arrangements – each side questioned the authenticity of the other's Christianity. Denominations fragmented and split, most notably the SBC. A growing number of conservative evangelicals abandoned denominations altogether, opting for independent, non-denominational Bible churches and parachurch organizations.

To be sure, while progressive movements ultimately emerged from mainline Protestantism, these denominations did not readily or immediately embrace change. In fact, mainline Protestants had been central to the 1950s "Happy Days" ideal of the two-parent nuclear family and with it, traditional gender roles in a new consumer-driven domesticity that became central to postwar middle-class identity, especially in predominately white suburbs. As more and more Americans attained middle-class security, the average marital age dropped and fertility rates rose. Not only did church attendance in the country's major denominations reach record highs, so too did their monetary offerings, making the 1950s family a bedrock of Protestant institutional building. Most Protestant clergy proclaimed the nuclear family as a bulwark of American society and culture.

And yet, while some women enjoyed the trappings of this new domesticity, others felt limited by its tenets; and many, especially Black Americans and other racial and ethnic minorities, were largely shut out of it altogether. Overall, new domesticity was integral to the development of a postwar white culture, which, in turn, began to falter in the late 1950s. Once again, the fight for women's rights was inspired by the struggle for racial justice led by Black Protestants. The civil rights movement demonstrated again that issues of gender were entangled with those of race. The "I Am a Man" placards held by the striking Memphis sanitation workers as they marched with Martin Luther King, Jr., on the day of his death, for instance, decried the ways white America had deployed gender as well as race as a weapon to deny Black Americans their full human dignity. Black women – if outside the white kitchen, and thus white control – were depicted as conniving Eves and modern-day Jezebels.[26] With miscegenation laws firmly in place, Jim Crow and systemic racism conspired to fix ideals of manhood and womanhood as essentially white.

The civil rights movement awakened many Protestants to the need for wholescale changes that soon extended to gender. In addition to efforts toward confronting and combatting racism, as early as 1956, both the Presbyterian Church (USA) and the Methodist Church permitted the ordination of women. While Baptist denominations usually operated congregationally, the Black Progressive National Baptist Convention promoted the ordination of women upon its founding in 1961, and white Southern Baptists ordained their first woman in 1964. But with only a handful of women pursuing ordination and seminary education – and little support or prospects for placement – men still preached from the pulpit, while women mostly populated the pews.

The advent of second-wave feminism and its legislative efforts, however, did lead to unprecedented improvements for women more broadly in education and in historically male-dominated jobs, changing perceptions of wage-earning career women. Those supportive of feminism, including a rising number of professional women, resolved to abandon Protestant churches unless they reconfigured gendered divisions of labor. The steady march of change was evident in Philadelphia in 1974, when three retired Episcopal bishops controversially ordained eleven women as priests, with nearly 2,000 gathered in support, two years prior to the Episcopal Church's formal approval.

The ordination of women, observed Barbara Brown Zikmund, necessitated a "letting go" of male sacramental agency in the Episcopal and Lutheran traditions and of biblical literalism among evangelicals.[27] Feminist theologians provided paths forward. Catholic feminist theologians initially influenced high-church Protestants to reject an exclusively male priesthood while Protestant scholars like Phyllis Trible and Letty Russell brought a rigorous feminist lens to the Bible and enlivened the field of biblical studies with a new focus on women's experience. Letha Scanzoni and Nancy Hardesty helped launch the evangelical feminist movement with their widely read *All We're Meant to Be* (1974), in which they maintained that the gospel's broader impulses of liberation and transformation proclaimed an end to long-standing hierarchies and divisions.[28]

Protestants influenced by feminist theology created liturgies and hymns with inclusive language and imagery, called for the retrieval of the lost maternal character of God, and urged more women to empty the pews and claim a place at the pulpit. By the early 1990s, an estimated 10 percent of Protestant clergy were women.[29] (Even into the twenty-first century, that number would not change substantially, with the exception of some smaller mainline and progressive denominations, such as the United Church of Christ, which saw about a quarter to a third of clergy positions filled by women.) If that number was still far from achieving any gender equity, it was one that alarmed conservative evangelicals.

Both women and men were at the forefront of the antifeminist movement that escalated the culture wars in the final decades of the twentieth century. During the 1970s, Catholic lawyer, activist, and mother of six Phyllis Schlafly formed STOP ERA, a coalition that connected traditional Catholic women like herself to conservative Protestant and Mormon women in a bid to defeat the Equal Rights Amendment. Gender, it seemed, had the power to transgress long-standing religious boundaries. To achieve her goal, Schlafly portrayed feminism as a secular movement determined to destroy the nuclear family, and with it, traditional Christian understandings of gender, especially those regarding women's place in the home. Moreover, she highlighted abortion and homosexuality as central to the feminist agenda, along with the passage of the amendment.[30] In fact, the popular conservative mantra "God Created Adam and Eve, Not Adam and Steve" had its origins as a protest sign at one of Schlafly's STOP ERA rallies.

While some evangelical women such as Beverly LaHaye and Anita Bryant followed Schlafly's example and became prominent antifeminist figures, many questioned the propriety of such public politicking, where women appeared to sidestep male authority. Instead, they resisted feminism by writing books for other women, developing women's programming in their local churches, and eventually hosting parachurch women's conferences. Together, they shaped a concept of "biblical womanhood," which applied submission to every aspect of women's lives, from marriage and homemaking to lovemaking and child-rearing. Describing the home as a "microcosm" of the "hierarchy of the cosmos itself," bestselling writer Elisabeth Elliot explained that "a woman is never a man's life in the same sense that a man is a woman's life, and this is the way it was meant to be – woman was made for man, not man for woman."[31] Once again, Genesis 2 and 3:16 were seen as templates for marriage, with Eve often presented as the first feminist, her sin being that of disobedience to her husband, who represented God's authority. In the wake of feminism, these women gravitated to the stricter New Testament passages on submission, often referring to themselves as "Titus 2" women, and their literature demonstrated a particular proclivity for the "gentle and quiet" submission of 1 Peter 3:1–6. As one popular author put it, "none of the verses say 'Be submissive if your husband is right, if he is a Christian, or if you can understand the outcome.' No, God supplies no such exceptions to your obedience to your husband."[32]

According to historian Seth Dowland, "the centrality of gender" and "the importance of authority" together "animated the concept of family values."[33] During the 1980s, conservative political organizations such as the Moral Majority and the machinations of its evangelical leadership – particularly Jerry Falwell, who served as the face of the early Christian Right – convinced countless preachers along with their congregations to join their fight for the preservation of the American family. As one megachurch pastor declared: "FEMINIST THINKERS ARE OUT TO SUBVERT YOUR WOMEN AND TO BRING IN THEIR HEATHEN HEAVEN to do this through a HUMANIST/FEMINIST/SOCIALIST [agenda]. STAND UP AND BE

COUNTED BEFORE THE TIME RUNS OUT FOR AMERICA."[34] Overall, the Christian Right was a patriarchal movement that mobilized and then unleashed the belligerent masculinity of earlier fundamentalism.[35] As with fundamentalism, it was also predominately white and closely connected to the "southern strategy" of the Republican Party.[36]

While the Christian Right waged its war in the political realm, churches and denominations feuded as well. Conservative evangelicals linked biblical inerrancy, which once had been most closely associated with the battle against evolution, to a mandated hierarchy of male authority and female submission. As conservatives in this camp assumed control of the SBC, for example, one of their first measures was the passage of a resolution in 1984 excluding women from pastoral leadership and ordination "to preserve a submission God requires because the man was first in creation and the woman was first in the Edenic fall."[37] This interpretation had a long history and stronghold in Protestant life; nevertheless, it now occurred in a postfeminist context, and conservatives were faced with an unprecedented public outcry, with many voices coming from within the evangelical camp.

The impulses that informed each position contained shifting currents. It is telling that when conservative evangelicals established the Council on Biblical Manhood and Womanhood in 1987, the organization's founding "Danvers Statement" explicitly rejected the hermeneutic linking women's submission to Eve's fall. During the late 1980s and 1990s, conservative evangelicals downplayed the more strident language of patriarchy and submission, although not rejecting its underlying premise, and coined the new term "complementarianism." As articulated in the Danvers Statement, complementarianism proclaimed that men and women were "equal before God as persons" while "distinct in their manhood and womanhood." A majority moved from advocating a three-point patriarchy (in marriage, church and society) to a two-point patriarchy (in marriage and church only), which explained why conservative evangelicals would later endorse Sarah Palin for US vice president while barring women from the pastorate.[38] Within the growing Pentecostal movement, which was increasingly Hispanic, and in Black churches, women frequently served as co-pastors with men, though technically under the man's spiritual coverage. Finally, some men countered the aggressive masculinity that defined much of the Christian Right, and instead sought to be "soft patriarchs."[39] With its refrain of "servant leadership," the men's parachurch organization Promise Keepers filled the Washington Mall in 1997 with hundreds of thousands of men pledging "moral, ethical and sexual purity" and the commitment to "build strong marriages and families through love, protection and biblical values."[40]

There were changes among progressive Protestants too. Increasingly attentive to theologies developed by women of color, they sought to align their churches with intersectional social justice causes.[41] Katie G. Cannon, Delores S. Williams, and Emilie Townes, for example, were among the first womanist scholars to draw on the experiences of Black women to critique the ways racism and classism, along with sexism, formed systems of oppression.[42] Womanists turned to the Genesis account of the slave woman Hagar, whom God had sustained in the wilderness, as an allegory of survival and hope. Other theologians eventually applied intersectional analyses to Protestantism from Asian American, Latino/a, and Native American perspectives.[43] Progressive Protestants continued to read the stories of Jesus as maps for building inclusive forms of community. Over time, that community included varying expressions of gender and sexuality.

SAME-SEX ORDINATION AND MARRIAGE EQUALITY

With the advent of the birth control pill in 1960, Protestants, like other Americans, began to more openly embrace the pleasures of sex. Separating sex from reproduction eventually led to new questions about the nature and purpose of gender and marriage. Most Protestants welcomed the US Supreme Court's 1965 *Griswold v. Connecticut* ruling, which fully legalized contraceptives for married couples, as they believed this did not undermine moral sexuality. The popular Christian literature of the 1970s was replete with sex-positive messages for married Christians, with progressives and conservatives alike proclaiming the "joys of sex."[44] But as first-trimester abortion was legalized with the 1973 *Roe v. Wade* Supreme Court decision, and as homosexuality found growing acceptance among Americans over the years, the fissures that had divided Protestants only deepened.[45]

Conflict over the issue of homosexuality had been brewing since the 1960s, and by the twenty-first century differences around acceptable forms of sexuality had become one of the most divisive wedges for Protestants in the new millennium. Many second-wave feminists had embraced the gay and lesbian rights movements, though early on most Protestant advocates of women's rights were not comfortable with the connection. Those denominations that advocated for the full inclusion of gay and lesbian Christians, such as the United Church of Christ (which had issued a statement of support as early as 1969) were seen as outliers, even to the mainline tradition. In 1986, the Evangelical and Ecumenical Women's Caucus controversially issued a statement "in favor of civil rights for homosexual persons," splintering the organization, which had formed in the early 1970s to support women's ordination. When in 1992 the Metropolitan Community Church, founded during the 1960s as a refuge for gay Christians, attempted to join the National Council of Churches, its efforts were spurned. It was not until the twenty-first century that the more prominent mainline denominations began to seriously rethink and grapple openly with the matter of same-sex relations.

In 2003, the Episcopal Church made headlines by consecrating Gene Robinson as its first openly gay bishop. Wearing a bullet-proof vest to the ceremony, Robinson became bishop in front of an audience of more than 3,000, which included his long-time partner.[46] Other mainline churches followed. In 2009, the Evangelical Lutheran Church in America (ELCA) adopted a statement that permitted its congregations "to open the ministry of the church to gay and lesbian pastors and other professional workers living in committed relationships."[47] In 2011, after decades of advocacy by More Light Presbyterians, the Presbyterian Church (USA) became a part of this progressive sea change too. Soon, these mainline denominations also included broader expressions of gender and sexuality, as represented by the acronym LGBTQ+ (as it most commonly reads). While the issue of marriage was often more contentious than the ordination of gay or lesbian ministers, those denominations that favored the ordination of LGBTQ+ persons supported the 2015 *Obergefell v. Hodges* decision, in which the Supreme Court ruled that the Fourteenth Amendment required states to recognize same-sex marriage.[48] The PC(USA) website, for example, posted an approving news article stating, "The Presbyterian Church (U.S.A.) is celebrating the U.S. Supreme Court ruling that same-gender couples have a constitutional right to marry nationwide, striking down bans in 14 states. Church leaders believe today's ruling is a step in the right direction as society's views have continued to change in recent years."[49]

Such developments came with pushback both from within and outside the mainline denominations. Both the ELCA and the Presbyterian Church (USA) reported losing significant membership, and soon after the Episcopal Church consecrated Robinson, several dioceses splintered to create their own Anglican communions. The United Methodist Church, the largest of the mainline denominations, struggled bitterly over whether to accept the ordination of LGBTQ+ members and same-sex marriage, and in 2020 its bishops proposed a plan to split the denomination due to the ongoing impasse, to the heartache of many.[50] "It hurts to be estranged from [Methodists on the other side of the issue]," wrote one seminary professor, "Some of these relationships are likely unrecoverable except by a miracle of God."[51]

The most vocal critique of expanding LGBTQ+ rights came from conservative evangelicals. Having long been bitterly opposed to the ordination of anyone other than heterosexual men, these evangelical critics viewed the struggles of mainline progressive traditions as a predictable result of denominations straying from biblical truth. In their view, the departure had begun with the rise of modern biblical criticism in the nineteenth century, which led liberals to harmonize their theology with modern science, the ordination of women, and ultimately LGBTQ+ ordination and marriage. Wayne Grudem, one of the theologians most associated with complementarianism, argued that "abandoning biblical inerrancy" and "saying that Genesis is wrong" had ultimately led to the "final step" of the liberal slide: the "approval of homosexuality."[52]

Conservative evangelicals were deeply disturbed when the Supreme Court legalized same-sex marriage; indeed, some lamented the 2015 *Obergefell* decision as a death knell, claiming that they now lived in a "post-Christian nation."[53] The following year, an astounding 81 percent of white evangelicals participating in the US presidential election voted for Donald Trump, overlooking his marital infidelities and other sexual indiscretions for his promise to move the country's courts in more conservative directions, especially regarding marriage and abortion.[54] In 2017, the Council on Biblical Manhood and Womanhood drafted the Nashville Statement to express widespread evangelical discontent with the state of sexuality in the twenty-first century. The statement declared "that God designed marriage to be a covenantal, sexual, procreative, lifelong union of one man and one woman" and denied that it was possible for "faithful Christians" to approve of "homosexual immorality or transgenderism."[55] By 2020, the statement had over 24,000 signers, including evangelicalism's most prominent names.

The homepage of the Council on Biblical Manhood and Womanhood website presented the 2017 Nashville Statement alongside the 1987 Danvers Statement as twin documents representing their side of the Protestant divide on gender, marriage, and sexuality.[56] The celebratory language of progressives around *Obergefell* and ever-growing support of broad gender and sexual identities represented the other pole of a deeply divided American Protestantism. This twenty-first century rift, however, was not new. American Protestants have always wrestled with how to harmonize social and spiritual hierarchies with their faith's commitment to individualism and their country's celebration of democracy and equality.

NOTES

1 Baptist Women in Ministry Facebook page, July 2, 2019, www.facebook.com /BaptistWomen/photos/a.176218253638/10156331248423639/?type=3.

2 For recent essays that provide a helpful overview of the scholarship and theories here and also influenced and challenged our understanding, see Ann Braude, "Women, Gender and Religion in the United States," in *The Oxford Handbook of American Women's and Gender History*, ed. Ellen Hartigan-O'Connor and Lisa G. Materson (New York: Oxford University Press, 2018), 391–414; Gillian Frank, Bethany Moreton, and Heather R. White, "Introduction: More than Missionary: Doing the Histories of Religion and Sexuality Together," in *Devotions and Desires: Histories of Sexuality and Religion in the Twentieth-Century United States*, ed. Frank, Moreton, and White (Chapel Hill: University of North Carolina Press, 2018); Sarah E. Johnson, "Gender," in *The Blackwell Companion to Religion in America*, ed. Philip Goff (Oxford: Wiley-Blackwell, 2010), 147–162; and Anthony Michael Petro, "Religion, Gender, and Sexuality," in *The Columbia Guide to Religion in American History*, ed. Paul Harvey and Edward Blum (New York: Columbia University Press, 2012), 188–212. See too these earlier works: Ann Braude, "Women's History Is American Religious History," in *Retelling U.S. Religious History*, ed. Thomas A. Tweed (Berkeley: University of California Press, 1997), 87–107; Catherine A. Brekus, "Introduction: Searching for Women in Narratives of American Religious History," in *The Religious History of American Women: Reimagining the Past*, ed. Catherine A. Brekus (Chapel Hill: University of North Carolina Press, 2007), 1–50; Susan Juster and Linda MacFarlane, "Introduction: 'A Sperit in de Body,'" in *A Mighty Baptism: Race, Gender, and the Creation of American Protestantism*, ed. Susan Juster (Ithaca, NY: Cornell University Press, 1996), 1–15; and Judith Weisenfeld, "On Women and Gender in the Study of African American Religious History," *Journal of Africana Religions* vol. 1, no. 1 (2013), 133–149.

3 Braude, "Women, Gender, and Religion in the United States," 391.

4 Juster and MacFarlane, "Introduction: 'A Sperit in de Body,'" 5.

5 "A Report of the Trial of Mrs. Anne Hutchinson before the Church in Boston," in *The Antinomian Controversy: 1636–1638: A Documentary History*, ed. David D. Hall (Middleton, CN: Wesleyan University Press, 1968), 382–383; quoted in Susan Hill Lindley, *"You Have Stept Out of Your Place": A History of Women and Religion in America* (Louisville, KY: Westminster John Knox Press, 1996), 5.

6 The description, which is often quoted, can be found in *The Journal of John Winthrop, 1630–1649*, ed. Richard S. Dunn, James Savage, and Laetitia Yeandle (Cambridge, MA: Harvard University Press, 2009), 290.

7 See Ann Douglas, *The Feminization of American Culture* (New York: Knopf, 1977).

8 Jarena Lee, "The Life and Religious Experiences of Jarena Lee," in *Sisters of the Spirit*, ed. William L. Andrews (Bloomington: Indiana University Press, 1986), 45–46. On female preaching during the Great Awakening revivals, see Catherine A. Brekus, *Strangers and Pilgrims: Female Preaching in America, 1740–1845* (Chapel Hill: University of North Carolina Press, 1998).

9 For a brief explanation of this shift, see Brekus, *Strangers and Pilgrims*, 14–15, 149.

10 As quoted in Barbara Welter, "The Cult of True Womanhood: 1820–1860," *American Quarterly* vol. 18, no. 2, part 1 (Summer 1966), 170. For a critique of true womanhood and the ways historians initially used the term, see Linda Kerber, "Separate Sphere, Female World, Woman's Place: The Rhetoric of Women's History," *Journal of American History* vol. 75, no. 1 (June 1988), 9–39; and Amy Kaplan, "Manifest Domesticity," *American Literature* vol. 70, no. 3 (1998), 581–606.

11 Mark Chaves, *Ordaining Women: Culture and Conflict in Religious Organizations* (Cambridge, MA: Harvard University Press, 1997), 79. On interpretations of women's ordination, see especially chapters 2 and 4 of Chaves.

12 For details on Sojourner Truth's famous speech, see Nell Irvin Painter, *Sojourner Truth: A Life, a Symbol* (New York: W. W. Norton, 1996); and The Sojourner Truth Project, accessed October 17, 2020, www.thesojournertruthproject.com.

13 Carol Crawford Holcomb, *Home without Walls: Southern Baptist Women and Social Reform in the Progressive Era* (Tuscaloosa: University of Alabama Press, 2020). While her focus is on Southern Baptist women, Holcomb explores them in the broader context of Protestant women's social reforming efforts.

14 Horace Bushnell, *Women's Suffrage: The Reform against Nature* (New York: Charles Scribner and Company, 1869), 89. See too the Bushnell reference in Ann Braude, *Sisters and Saints: Women and American Religion* (New York: Oxford University Press, 2001), 80.

15 Braude, *Sisters and Saints*, 80.

16 On suffrage, see Ellen Carol Dubois, *Suffrage: Women's Long Battle for the Vote* (New York: Simon and Schuster, 2020). On the WCTU and women's temperance, see Ruth Bordin, *Woman and Temperance: The Quest for Power and Liberty, 1873–1900* (New Brunswick, NJ: Rutgers University Press, 1990).

17 For an overview of Black women's social and political movements in the United States, see Martha S. Jones, *Vanguard: How Black Women Broke*

Barriers, Won the Vote, and Insisted on Equality for All (New York: Basic Books, 2020).

18 Carolyn DeSwarte Gifford, "Nineteenth- and Twentieth-Century Protestant Social Reform Movements in the United States," in *Encyclopedia of Women and Religion in North America*, ed. Marie Cantlon, Rosemary Radford Ruether, and Rosemary Skinner Keller (Bloomington: Indiana University Press, 2006), 1031.

19 Evelyn Brooks Higginbotham first used the term "politics of respectability" in her work on Black Baptist women. See Higginbotham, *Righteous Discontent: The Women's Movement in the Black Baptist Church: 1880–1920* (Cambridge, MA: Harvard University Press, 1993). On Black women's social reform, and the ways reformers invoked respectability, see Judith Weisenfeld, *African American Women and Christian Activism: New York's Black YWCA, 1905–1945* (Cambridge, MA: Harvard University Press, 1997). In considering women in the more theologically conservative and Pentecostal Church of God in Christ, Anthea Butler further complicates the notions of respectability and reform, *Women in the Church of God in Christ: Making a Sanctified World* (Chapel Hill: University of North Carolina Press, 2012).

20 See Patricia Hill, *The World Their Household: The American Woman's Foreign Mission Movement and Cultural Transformation, 1870–1920* (Ann Arbor: University of Michigan Press, 1985). See too Dana Robert, *American Women in Mission: A Social History of Their Thought and Practice* (Macon, GA: Mercier University Press, 1997).

21 Braude, *Sisters and Saints*, 86.

22 See Margaret Bendroth, *Fundamentalism and Gender, 1875 to the Present* (New Haven, CT: Yale University Press, 1993); and Betty A. DeBerg, *Ungodly Women: Gender and the First Wave of Fundamentalism* (Minneapolis: Fortress Press, 1990).

23 John R. Rice, "Bobbed Hair, Bossy Wives, and Women Preachers!" accessed July 5, 2020, www.jesus-is-savior.com/Books,%20Tracts%20&%20Preachi ng/Printed%20Sermons/Dr%20John%20Rice/bobbed_hair_and_bossy_ wives.htm. Rice also expanded the sermon as a book with the same title.

24 Rice, "Bobbed Hair, Bossy Wives, and Women Preachers!"

25 See R. Marie Griffith, *Moral Combat: How Sex Divided American Christians and Fractured American Politics* (New York: Basic Books, 2017), xi–xii.

26 For more on the Jezebel trope in North American history and culture, see Tamura A. Lomax, *Jezebel Unhinged: Loosing the Black Female Body in Religion and Culture* (Durham, NC: Duke University Press, 2018).

27 Barbara Brown Zikmund, "The Protestant Women's Ordination Movement," in *Encyclopedia of Women and Religion*, ed. Cantlon et al., 949–950. See too Chaves, *Ordaining Women*, 84–129.

28 See Braude, *Sisters and Saints*, 100–108; J. Shannon Clarkson and Letty M. Russell, "North American Women Interpret Scripture," *Encyclopedia of*

Women and Religion, ed. Cantlon et al., 33–45; and Elizabeth H. Flowers, *Into the Pulpit: Southern Baptist Women and Power since World War II* (Chapel Hill: University of North Carolina Press, 2012), 152–154.

29 Barbara Brown Zikmund, Adair T. Lumis, and Patricia Mei Yin Chang, *Clergy Women: An Uphill Calling* (Louisville, KY: Westminster John Knox Press, 1998), 6.

30 See Seth Dowland, *Family Values and the Rise of the Christian Right* (Philadelphia: University of Pennsylvania Press, 2015).

31 Elisabeth Elliot, *Let Me Be a Woman* (Wheaton, IL: Tyndale House Publishers, 1976), 132–133, 114.

32 Darien Cooper, *You Can Be the Wife of a Happy Husband* (Wheaton, IL: Victor Books, 1974), 82–83.

33 Dowland, *Family Values*, 12.

34 Flowers, *Into the Pulpit*, 86.

35 On evangelicals and masculinity, see Kristin Kobes de Mez, *Jesus and John Wayne: How White Evangelicals Corrupted a Faith and Fractured a Nation* (New York: W. W. Norton, 2020).

36 On gender and the Christian Right, see Dowland, *Family Values*; and Daniel K. Williams, *God's Own Party: The Making of the Christian Right* (New York: Oxford University Press, 2010).

37 "Resolution on Ordination and the Role of Women in Ministry" (resolution, Southern Baptist Convention, Kansas City, MO, June 12–14, 1984), www.sbc.net/resource-library/resolutions/resolution-on-ordination-and-the -role-of-women-in-ministry.

38 See Karen K. Seat, "From Molly Marshall to Sarah Palin: Southern Baptist Gender Battles and the Politics of Complementarianism," in *A Marginal Majority: Women, Gender, and a Reimagining of Southern Baptists*, ed. Elizabeth H. Flowers and Karen K. Seat (Knoxville: University of Tennessee Press, 2020), 199–224.

39 See, for example, W. Bradford Wilcox, *Soft Patriarchs, New Men: How Christianity Shapes Fathers and Husbands* (Chicago: University of Chicago Press, 2004).

40 Ellen Gamerman, "Promise Keepers Looks to Make History: Christian Men's Rally Could Rival Attendance of Million Man March," *Baltimore Sun*, October 4, 1997, www.baltimoresun.com/news/bs-xpm-1997-10-04-199727 7070-story.html.

41 By the 2020s, the term "BIPOC" (an acronym for Black, Indigenous, and people of color) increasingly replaced the phrase "people of color" in English language discourses about race and ethnicity in the United States. For more on the use of the term, see Sandra E. Garcia, "Where Did BIPOC Come From?" *New York Times*, June 17, 2020, www.nytimes.com/article/what-is- bipoc.html.

42 See Emilie M. Townes, "Womanist Theology," in *Encyclopedia of Women and Religion*, ed. Cantlon et al.

43 See, for example, Clara Sue Kidwell, Homer Noley, and George E. "Tink" Tinker, eds., *A Native American Theology* (Maryknoll, NY: Orbis Books, 2001); Rita Nakashima Brock, Jung Ha Kim, Kwok Pui-lan, and Seung Ai Yang, eds., *Off the Menu: Asian and Asian North American Women's Religion and Theology* (Louisville, KY: Westminster John Knox, 2007); Stacey M. Floyd-Thomas and Anthony B. Pinn, eds., *Liberation Theologies in the United States: An Introduction* (New York: New York University Press, 2010); and Loida I. Martell-Otero, Zaida Maldonado Pérez, and Elizabeth Conde-Frazier, eds., *Latina Evangélicas: A Theological Survey from the Margins* (Eugene, OR: Cascade Books, 2013).

44 See, for example, Amy DeRogatis, *Saving Sex: Sexuality and Salvation in American Evangelicalism* (New York: Oxford University Press, 2014).

45 On Protestants and the LGBTQ+ movement, especially as it pertains to ordination and marriage equality, see Griffith, *Moral Combat*, 273–310; and Heather R. White, *Reforming Sodom: Protestants and the Rise of Gay Rights* (Chapel Hill: University of North Carolina Press, 2015).

46 Elizabeth Adams, *Going to Heaven: The Life and Election of Bishop Gene Robinson* (Brooklyn, NY: Soft Skull, 2006), 188.

47 "Human Sexuality: Gift and Trust," Evangelical Lutheran Church in America, August 19, 2009, www.elca.org/Faith/Faith-and-Society/Social-Statements/Human-Sexuality.

48 For a history of same-sex marriage that includes *Obergefell*, see Nathaniel Frank, *How Gays and Lesbians Brought Marriage Equality to America* (Cambridge, MA: Harvard University Press, 2017).

49 Rick Jones, "PC(USA) Advocates Celebrate Supreme Court Decision on Same-Gender Marriage," Presbyterian Church (USA), June 26, 2015, www.pcusa.org/news/2015/6/26/pcusa-celebrates-supreme-court-decision-same-gende/.

50 Campbell Robertson and Elizabeth Dias, "United Methodist Church Announces Plan to Split over Same-Sex Marriage," *New York Times*, January 3, 2020, https://nyti.ms/36qy3Ze; "Ask the UMC: What is the Church's Position on Homosexuality?" The United Methodist Church, accessed August 2, 2020, www.umc.org/en/content/ask-the-umc-what-is-the-churchs-position-on-homosexuality.

51 Sam Hodges and Kathy L. Gilbert, "Reaction to GC2019 remains strong," UM News, March 5, 2019, www.umnews.org/en/news/reaction-to-gc2019-remains-strong.

52 Wayne Grudem, *Evangelical Feminism: A New Path to Liberalism?* (Wheaton, IL: Crossway Books, 2006), 28, 35, 249.

53 See Rod Dreher, "Orthodox Christians Must Now Learn to Live as Exiles in Our Own Country," *TIME*, June 26, 2015, https://time.com/3938050/orthodox-christians-must-now-learn-to-live-as-exiles-in-our-own-country/; and James Dobson, "Life in Post-Christian America," *Dr. James Dobson's August 2015 Newsletter*, Dr. James Dobson's Family Talk,

www.drjamesdobson.org/news/commentaries/archives/2015-newsletters/august-newsletter-2015.

54 "An Examination of the 2016 Electorate, Based on Validated Voters," Pew Research Center, August 9, 2018, www.pewresearch.org/politics/2018/08/09/an-examination-of-the-2016-electorate-based-on-validated-voters/. For more on conservative evangelicals' motivations for voting for Donald Trump in 2016, see John Fea, *Believe Me: The Evangelical Road to Donald Trump* (Grand Rapids, MI: Eerdmans, 2018). It is important to note that the majority of white Protestants voting in the 2016 presidential election also favored Trump.

55 "Nashville Statement," https://cbmw.org/nashville-statement/.

56 The Council on Biblical Manhood and Womanhood, accessed August 2, 2020, https://cbmw.org.

12 From Slavery to Black Lives Matter: American Protestants and Race

DENNIS C. DICKERSON

Protestantism's diverse beginnings in Europe during the sixteenth century intersected with the European discovery of the Americas. Populating the New World with capitalists in both commerce and agriculture required a workforce starting in the seventeenth century of unfree persons, including a largely white corps of time-limited indentured servants and a permanent caste of African enslaved people condemned to lifetime servitude. This system of dehumanization through the transatlantic slave trade and chattel slavery drew upon racism as its economic and religious rationale. Amid these transoceanic developments Protestants, who predominated among the earliest white settlers in European North America, within this century-old movement developed their theology and social ethics in a concretized context of Black subjugation.

The majority of the 10 million kidnapped African enslaved people who survived the "Middle Passage" were shipped as human cargo across the Atlantic between the sixteenth and nineteenth centuries. They were overwhelmingly enslaved in the Catholic colonies of Portugal, Spain, and France throughout the Caribbean and Central and South America. Those who blended their indigenous African religions with Catholicism outnumbered their African counterparts in North America and in most parts of the West Indies where Black enslaved people were predominantly exposed to Protestantism.[1]

Planters, mainly in a region stretching from the Chesapeake to Charleston, and Protestant preachers espoused uncomplicated Christian tenets that lent scriptural support to the racialized dehumanization inherent in African chattel slavery. They avoided such scriptures as John 8:36 (KJV) which declared that "if the Son therefore shall make you free, you will be free indeed." This passage, when expansively interpreted, mandated manumission from slavery and strongly signified spiritual equality among believers in Jesus Christ, whether white or Black. Planters had to confront whether conversion to Christianity required manumission from slavery. Though the answer was an unambiguous "No," some enslavers who espoused Christianity still were troubled by tenets in John 8:36 and other verses like it. Though some freed their slaves, the vast majority left their chattel unexposed to Christian missionaries. While such sects as the Quakers understood Christianity's "inner light" as requiring a denunciation of human bondage and admonished their members to free enslaved people, most Christian groups mimicked the Society for the Propagation of the Gospel in Foreign Parts (SPG), an Anglican missionary group, founded in 1701. To circumvent the opposition of enslavers and reassure them about their intentions, the SPG, who never prioritized plantation missions, muted their disdain of Black servitude in order to persuade enslavers that their aim lay in a lackluster catechesis and not in the temporal equality between whites and Blacks.[2]

Some Africans encountered Christianity in Africa and came to the Americas already familiar with the beliefs and rituals of a religion that had been present on the continent for centuries. Enslaved people from among the Kongo, for example, adopted Christianity from the Portuguese in the fifteenth century. The vast majority of enslaved persons, exposed to Protestantism in British North America, whether they rejected it or grafted its rituals and precepts onto their tribal beliefs, never abandoned sensibilities derived from their African religious background. Whether the retention of burial practices, belief in a pantheon of gods reminiscent of sundry divine beings in Christianity, or ecstatic worship practices grounded in spirit possession, Africans absorbed Protestant evangelism within these African religious frameworks. Several scholars have discussed how the trajectories of African religious practices influenced the content of Afro-Protestantism. Charles H. Long, for example, suggested that whatever was specifically remembered or forgotten, a palpable African religiosity persisted among African Americans. Long identified "Africa as a historical reality and religious image" as salient features in Afro-Protestant formation and development. The significance of the African historical beginnings of Black enslaved people and their separation from their ancestral lands constituted both a longing and a connection to the sacred significance of their indigenous origins.[3]

Long added that this theme merged into a heightened Black consciousness about the slaves' "involuntary presence" in North America and how this realization informed how they reconstructed their religion through Afro-Protestantism. God, the Supreme Being, affirmed in African traditional tribal religions and in Christianity, was experienced by African Americans in light of their memory of Africa and through their involuntary experience in America. God, whether in traditional or trinitarian conceptions, spoke to Blacks through Protestantism on matters of their freedom, humanity, and as a powerful arbiter of their future possibilities.[4]

As Long demonstrated, the African-American embrace of Protestantism was informed by a capacious African spirituality that ranged from conjure to other beliefs that Blacks viewed as ancient and authentic and that whites arrogantly perceived as heathen and blasphemous. Blacks, while separated from their ancestral land and the regular rituals of their foundational faiths, poured the memory of these practices into their encounters with Protestantism. Out from these syncretic events, African Americans constructed a faith consciousness full of queries about theodicy and in quests for spiritual and scriptural resources to sustain their humanity.

Protestant populations encountered Africans and attributed to them mysterious spiritualities that could either harm or heal. Puritans in the late seventeenth and early eighteenth centuries often ascribed witchcraft to women and their male kin. Salem Village in Massachusetts in 1692, a site notorious for witchcraft trials, hurled this charge against three women, one of whom, a slave, Tituba, reputedly came from Barbados, a major destination in the transatlantic slave trade. Though the other two defendants pled innocent, the Black woman confessed and described their involvement in some occult practices. A smallpox epidemic in Boston in 1721 brought a Puritan minister, Cotton Mather, and a physician to a slave, Onesimus, who came either from the Caribbean or directly from Africa. His advice about inoculation techniques proved credible and effective. A century later in Charleston, Gullah Jack, though a member in the African Methodist Episcopal congregation, had the reputation for sorcery and was feared because of his skills in conjuring. All three reflected the presence of Africanisms within African-American religious communities like those in the Seas Islands of Georgia and South Carolina.[5]

Black Protestant congregations, while Christian in doctrine and practice, coexisted with religious influences that drew from African indigenous and Muslim backgrounds. At the First African Baptist Church in Savannah, founded in 1773, for example, African Arabic calligraphy was inscribed on some of the pews. Moreover, prayer symbols, probably derived from the BaKongo people, were depicted in holes on the sanctuary floor. Until 1808, when the transatlantic slave trade ended, Africans replenished the African-American population with religious practices indigenous to the "mother" continent. Perhaps this factor explains what Daniel A. Payne noticed and denounced among African Methodist Episcopal Church members in Baltimore in the 1840s. He targeted "bad customs of worship" that he viewed as being performed "in the most extravagant form." These ecclesial irregularities energized Payne, a Lutheran seminary alumnus, into a vigorous determination to remove any African traces from African-American Christianity.[6]

Though some scholars dispute the extent of African religious influence upon African Americans, most agree that the period after the Great Awakening, notwithstanding the stubborn remnants of African spirituality interspersed with Muslim religious memory, became a benchmark in Black religion. Great Awakening revivals both in churches and in the informal settings of "open air" preaching exposed Blacks to Protestantism. Winthrop Hudson asserted that little was known about the African religious heritage prior to 1750; he is surely correct that most Blacks, after the mid-eighteenth century, became Baptists and Methodists after the marginal impact of the Great Awakening of the 1740s.[7]

Hudson stressed that slaves, with geography and the passage of time distancing them from their African religious past, voluntarily selected what they would adopt among available Protestant sects. Despite their presence among Anglicans, Presbyterians, Congregationalists, and some few Dutch Reformed churches, African Americans overwhelmingly chose to be Baptists and Methodists. African Americans readily responded to the special efforts, despite roadblocks to mingling with slaves, that clergy in these sects directed toward them. Baptist and Methodist reputations as anti-slavery proponents, their rhythmic and extemporaneous preaching, their singing tones, and their receptivity to ecstatic worship resonated with Blacks. Within Baptist and Methodist meetings and classes, Blacks functioned in spiritual equality within these ecclesial assemblies and were commonly referred to as "brother" and "sister." Some Blacks held office and were authorized to preach and at times allowed to form their own separate congregations.[8]

Flowing out from these developments was the launch of independent Black churches whose founding drew from the readiness of Baptists and Methodists to license Black preachers. In Williamsburg, Virginia, Moses (whose surname is unknown) and Gowan Pamphlet became, as a result of Great Awakening evangelism, founders of a Black congregation likely in 1776.

Pamphlet, the pastor, ministered to 330 members; that number reached 500 in the following decade. In 1793 the congregation was accepted into the white-led Dover Baptist Association. Pamphlet and the Williamsburg Baptists typified several other Black Baptist congregations served by these late eighteenth-century Black preachers in South Carolina, Georgia, and Virginia.[9]

Pamphlet's Black Methodist contemporaries included Harry Hosier, born a slave in North Carolina in around 1750, and later manumitted. In 1780 he and white Methodist minister Francis Asbury (elected a bishop in 1784) partnered in preaching and alternated in delivering sermons to receptive audiences. Upon hearing Hosier preach, Benjamin Franklin declared him, in spite of his lack of literacy, "the greatest orator in America." Black Harry, as he was called, along with Richard Allen, another former slave and Methodist convert, attended the "Christmas" Conference in 1784 which formally established the Methodist Episcopal Church in America. Hence, Hosier and Allen could rightly claim to be among the formal founders in the United States of the first Methodist denomination. Unlike Pamphlet, Hosier did not serve a congregation but decided to remain as an evangelist. Both clergy showed what possibilities lay ahead for Black clergy as linchpins for the institutional development of autonomous Black Protestant congregations across a broad denominational spectrum.[10]

The impressive array of Black churches mainly established in the Northeast and Midwest between 1780 and 1840, though principally Baptist and Methodist, also included significant Presbyterian, Congregational, and Episcopal parishes. Three ecclesial assemblies of Black Methodists emerged as interstate denominations formed in 1813, 1816, and 1821. The African Methodist Episcopal Church (AME), though its denominational structure was formalized in 1816, had origins in 1787 when its parent group, the Free African Society (FAS) started in Philadelphia. FAS founder Richard Allen and his partner Absalom Jones deployed their mutual aid society for ecclesial purposes when a raw racist incident was hurled against them and others in their party at St. George Methodist Episcopal Church. They walked out and two congregations emerged from the FAS. They were St. Thomas Episcopal Church and Bethel African Methodist Episcopal Church, both dedicated in 1794. Allen, who was committed to Methodism, declined St. Thomas's invitation to become its rector and afterwards Jones was chosen in his place.[11]

Allen stayed focused on protecting Bethel Church from white Methodist incursions against the congregation's autonomy. Similar departures from segregated settings and treatment in other white Wesleyan congregations in the Middle Atlantic drew them together with Allen and Daniel Coker, the leader of a Baltimore group, to form the AME denomination. Coker, elected the body's first bishop, resigned in favor of Allen, who served until his death in 1831. Black Methodists based in Wilmington, Delaware, led by Peter Spencer, started the Union Church of Africans in 1813. Their counterparts in New York City in 1821 founded the African Methodist Episcopal Zion Church (AMEZ). Each organization, like the AME, attracted congregations from neighboring states to form these respective religious bodies. African-American congregations that remained organically connected to white denominations were similarly significant within various free Northern Black communities. Just as St. Thomas became a major Black congregation in Philadelphia with members like the wealthy sail maker James Forten as a parishioner, so did St. Philip's Episcopal Church, founded in 1818, develop as one of New York City's largest and most influential Black parishes. Founded in 1827, St. James Episcopal Church in Baltimore was opened for worship for Blacks who were both free and slave.[12]

Will Gravely explains several factors that spurred the rise of independent Black churches in the late eighteenth and early nineteenth centuries. Whether Baptist or Methodist or Presbyterian or Episcopal, this Black Protestant ecclesia rose out from common circumstances. Despite uneven success in Black evangelization across several sects, Gravely noted that racially "prescriptive practices by whites" stirred the resentment of Black parishioners. Blacks in New York City in what became the AMEZ faced restrictions in their ministerial and membership rights in John Street Methodist Episcopal Church. They withdrew in 1796 and formed their own Church of the African Society a few years later. Moreover, the retreat of white churches from earlier anti-slavery principles mixed with strong support for Black church development from influential sponsors like Benjamin Rush, a Philadelphia physician and signer of the Declaration of Independence. Rush was a benefactor to both Allen and Jones.[13]

Additionally, according to Gravely, in Philadelphia, Boston, and Newport, Rhode Island, there were preexisting quasi-religious organizations that easily morphed into churches. Both the emerging congregations and the parent community-based groups became resilient institutions because of a Black populace large enough to sustain such assemblies. Moreover, the growing presence of Black preachers presented these large free Black populations with ministerial leadership. Also, key to the permanent establishment of Black churches lay in their successful suits in the courts against white denominational efforts to claim both land and buildings purchased and built by Black preachers and parishioners.[14]

These Northern churches connected themselves to the slave population. In a retrospective about the antebellum period, AME minister

Theophilus G. Steward declared that those in slavery are "our brethren in affliction." He added "that very affliction has served to bind us together by the two-fold cord-sympathy, for the oppressed, and love for man." He asserted that

> our fathers have passed through the fiery furnace of slavery and escaped to the North, where a nominal or partial freedom reigns; they have taught us in infancy to remember those in bonds as being bound with them; and from our churches, our firesides and our closets have gone up the petition: "O Lord, remember those that are bound down under hard task masters, our brethren in affliction."

He climaxed his sermon by saying "break every yoke, snap in sunder every chain, and let the oppressed go free!"[15]

Steward's statements typified the attitudes and actions of Northern Black churches as venues for abolitionist meetings, stations on the Underground Railroad, and pulpits from which activist African-American clergy inveighed against slavery. Some pastors, including a disproportionate number of Black Presbyterian and Congregational ministers, were conspicuous in their partnership with white co-religionists in the anti-slavery cause. Theodore Dwight Weld, a white abolitionist, represented evangelicals based at Cincinnati's Lane Theological Seminary who articulated abolitionism as core to their Christian authenticity. While Weld, a member of the American Anti-Slavery Society, pursued the tactic of moral suasion, Henry Highland Garnet, a slave escapee and a Black Presbyterian pastor, pushed abolitionism beyond the sphere of nonviolence toward the possibility of armed rebellion. At the 1843 National Convention of Colored Citizens meeting in Buffalo, Garnet declared to slaves: "Let your motto be resistance! resistance! resistance! No oppressed people have ever secured their liberty without resistance. What kind of resistance you had better make, you must decide by the circumstances that surround you, and according to the suggestion of expediency." The clear implication was that the spilling of blood resulting from Black liberatory efforts was a real possibility.[16]

Similarly crucial to the broader welfare of African Americans was opposition to colonization. Protestant whites pursued anti-slavery through the resettlement of Blacks, both free and slave, in Africa either in Liberia or Sierra Leone. The American Colonization Society, founded in 1817, drew support from such Black church leaders as Daniel Coker among the AMEs and Lott Carey among the Baptists.

White Presbyterians in 1854 established Ashmun Institute in Chester County, Pennsylvania to educate Blacks as the carriers of Christian civilization to heathen Africans – misnamed because of pervasive ignorance about the continent's ancient religious heritage. AMEs worried that colonization was a scheme to rid the United States of the free Black population and to remove them as active advocates involved in undermining slavery. The denomination's 1851 New York Annual Conference declared that colonization sought "to destroy the fixedness of our people in their native country." This objective intended "to remove a large increasing and improving free population, that they may hold our Brethren the more quietly and securely in bondage." Any AME preacher "guilty of knowingly suffering, allowing, or permitting any Colonization preacher or lecturer to officiate" in any of their church venues should be "suspended from all official standing" for a year.[17]

An alignment between abolitionist and anti-colonization Black and white Protestants solidified an anti-slavery religious phalanx in the antebellum North. Protestants joined both William Lloyd Garrison's American Anti-Slavery Society and Lewis Tappan's American and Foreign Anti-Slavery Society, while white evangelicals constituted a distinct constituency who were sometimes unaffiliated. Black abolitionists also joined either the Garrisonians or Tappanites. Frederick Douglass, the escaped slave and AMEZ exhorter, was recruited by Garrison while the AME minister and later bishop Daniel A. Payne was offered a full-time lectureship by the Tappanites. Whether the tactic of immediatism or political abolition was espoused, anti-slavery discourse reached such intensity that it facilitated splits in the largest of predominantly white-led Protestant denominations. The fissure of the Methodists in 1844 focused on whether a Southern bishop should retain the slaves that his wife brought into their marriage. This domestic matter matured into an ecclesial dispute resulting in the Methodist Episcopal Church (MEC) yielding to the creation of a separate Southern sect, the Methodist Episcopal Church, South (MECS). Northern blacks in the MEC remained in their own congregations, while the MECS maintained a mission in slave evangelization that involved free Blacks in the South, like South Carolina's Henry M. Turner, later an AME bishop. He, like others, were licensed as MECS exhorters and deployed to preach to their slave brethren in chapels set aside for them on plantation premises.[18]

In these same Southern venues, diametrically different espousals of Protestantism existed between Black and whites. Nat Turner, a Virginia slave, led a slave revolt involving a few dozen followers in 1831 that resulted in the killing of sixty whites. Turner's sense of being a chosen vessel for an apocalyptic judgment upon slavery drew directly from his own interpretation of the Hebrew Bible. Moreover, Turner's understanding of Scripture presaged the same Protestant sensibilities that led John Brown to execute a raid in 1859 against the federal arsenal at Harper's Ferry, Virginia. There he would unsuccessfully seize arms for a widespread rebellion of slaves. Like Turner, Brown, according to one scholar, did not believe that government, already corrupted by the "slave power," possessed a "monopoly on violence." Rather, Turner and Brown, seeing the sin of slavery, drew upon "a higher law" to justify the deployment of violence to wash away from the American republic the stain and stench of slavery. Most slaves, however, imbibed the lyrics of spirituals that serve as guideposts to escape. "Steal Away" and "Go Down, Moses" expressed both a longing for freedom and provided the metaphorical maps to achieve this objective. Egalitarian biblical themes that slaves heard in sermons, whether directly asserted by Black preachers or inadvertently and unintentionally mentioned by white sympathizers to Black bondage, emphasized spiritual equality among believers, humankind's common condition as sinners needing salvation, and the urgent necessity of "getting right with God." Surely a slave who was "saved" occupied a superior status within these salvific spheres than an enslaver who did not know Jesus Christ in the pardon of his or her sins.[19]

Nonetheless, those enslavers who claimed salvation saw no conflict between the enslavement of human beings and an espousal of Christianity. Their zeal for their Protestantism still allowed for scriptural interpretations that buttressed their belief in Black bondage and admonished their chattel to heed Paul's instruction in Ephesians 6:5 (KJV): "Servants, be obedient to them that are your masters according to the flesh, with fear and trembling, in singleness of your heart, as unto Christ, doing the will of God from the heart." This Pauline passage was an anathema to the slave grandmother of seminal religious thinker Howard Thurman. He recalled reading the Bible to her except for the Pauline scriptures. She remembered, long after slavery had ended, that the minister whom her slave master sent to preach to her and others in bondage periodically cited the Ephesians text about slaves obeying their masters and emphasizing that it was God's will that Blacks should be slaves. If they were good, the preacher said, then they would receive the Lord's blessings. Once emancipated, Thurman's grandmother refused to listen to any thing coming from Paul. These scriptural admonitions were reinforced by numerous examples of slavery in the Bible and the absence of any condemnation against human bondage. A white Baptist minister in Virginia, Thornton Stringfellow, asserted that "the Old Testament and the New sanction slavery, but under no circumstances enjoin its abolition, even among saints." He added "if pure religion, therefore, did not require its abolition under the law of Moses, nor in the church of Christ – we may safely infer, that our political, moral and social relations do not require it in a State."[20]

For Black Protestants, free and slave, the Civil War and Reconstruction era became periods of jubilee in which divine intervention accomplished their freedom. While white Southerners in the Confederacy believed that their quest for political independence included the unambiguous right to hold slaves, President Abraham Lincoln belatedly asserted a different interpretation of the nation's founding documents that required a recognition of Black citizenship. In his Second Inaugural Address in 1865, Lincoln declared that the Civil War showed "all the wealth piled by the bondman's two hundred and fifty years of unrequited toil shall be sunk, and until every drop of blood drawn with the lash shall be paid by another drawn with the sword, as was said three thousand years ago, so still it must be said 'the judgments of the Lord are true and righteous altogether.'" Blacks, far from being bystanders in bringing about their emancipation, fled farms and plantations whenever federal soldiers were near, volunteered for the army when Lincoln opened enlistments to them, and welcomed fourteen Black ministers who applied for chaplaincies in various regiments in the US Colored Troops.[21]

Black and white denominations, based in the North and South, viewed the release of 4 million African Americans from slavery as an unparalleled evangelistic opportunity. Southern white religious bodies believed that the establishment of separate Black organizations presented the best method for African-American membership recruitment. The MECS – wishing to prevent AME, AMEZ, and ME bodies from absorbing their Black members – organized the remnant of its Black communicants in 1870 as the Colored Methodist Episcopal Church (CME). The Cumberland Presbyterian Church in 1874 launched the Colored Cumberland Presbyterian Church. Northern white bodies, namely the Baptists, Congregationalists, Methodists, and Presbyterians, started missionary organizations that planted churches, often with adjacent parochial schools. African-American bodies outdistanced their white counterparts in their appeal to ex-slaves. All were active in establishing colleges. The Congregational-affiliated American Missionary Association, for example, started Fisk in Nashville, Straight in New Orleans, and Atlanta University. The AMEs launched schools in every Southern state, though not all of them survived. Their major educational ventures included Allen in South Carolina, Morris Brown in Georgia, and Edward Waters in Florida.[22] The example of antebellum Black ministers who were influential abolitionists provided a paradigm for numerous Black clergy who drew upon the votes of newly enfranchised ex-slaves to attain local, state, and federal offices. Richard H. Cain, South Carolina state senator and US Representative, pursued a "gospel of freedom" as pastor of Charleston's Emanuel AME and an influential politician. Cain's counterparts in Florida also were immersed in ministry and politics. One of them, Josiah H. Armstrong, a Pennsylvania native, served in the Union Army and mustered out of the military in Florida. He entered the AME ministry and was elected to the state legislature and served from 1871 to 1875. Later, Cain, like Armstrong, was elected to the AME episcopacy, in 1880 and 1896 respectively.[23]

Between the end of Reconstruction and the start of World War I, Protestantism encountered the impact of accelerated industrialization in American society. Such Protestant thinkers as Washington Gladden, a Congregationalist, believed that churches should critique how exploitative industrial capitalism spurred and sustained systemic poverty, labor exploitation, and slums. A Social Gospel movement drew from these religious sensibilities. Progressive white Protestants, both clergy and laity, especially in urban areas, became Social Gospel advocates; some Black ministers did as well. In Chicago Reverdy C. Ransom relinquished his pastorate of Bethel AME to open, in 1900, the Institutional Church and Social Settlement. The AME funded the purchase of an impressive edifice and physical plant where Ransom and his wife, Emma, organized a broad range of social services including a kindergarten, employment bureau, and a forum for the discussion of contemporary issues. In a report to the 1904 AME General Conference, Ransom said that the Institutional Church "was established to meet and serve the moral, social and industrial need of our people." He added that "our Gymnasium is open twice a week to Women and twice a week to Boys." He noted that the employment bureau "furnishes cooks, maids, second girls, laundresses, waiters, porters, butlers, stenographers, type-writers and all forms of day labor to those in need of such help, and assist those seeking employment to get work." From 1903 through April 1904, for example, 238 job vacancies had been filled. This new model of ministry in white and Black churches paralleled socialist advocates who protested the role of capitalism in exalting private property over the interests of the collective welfare of workers and the poor. Ransom and fellow AME George W. Slater and Baptist George W. Woodbey promulgated these perspectives.[24]

At the other end of the ecclesiastical spectrum was the expansion of missionary movements to African and Asian areas that European imperialists had colonized. African-American denominations and Blacks within white Methodist and Presbyterian bodies participated in robust overseas ministries. The AME and AMEZ denominations, for example, planted churches in West and South Africa and in the Caribbean. Women's missionary societies among Black Baptist and Methodist bodies undertook a large share of the funding of congregational and educational projects. The Women's Parent Mite Missionary Society (WPMMS) of the AME, for example, educated Charlotte Manye of South Africa at Wilberforce University in Ohio, the denomination's flagship school. She returned to her country's Transvaal region to maintain a school for African boys and girls, notwithstanding male tribal opposition to women's education. "With me it goes pretty hard to see children on the mud floor," said Manye to AME missionaries meeting in their 1903 quadrennial convention in Pittsburgh. She added that "a few pounds will buy the wood and I can get someone to make the benches so please tell my mothers about this." That Manye used familial language in describing her sponsors as "mothers" suggests that the usual assertion of civilizational hierarchy did not characterize the transatlantic relationship between Manye in Africa and her "mothers" in America. WPMMS officers, buoyed with Manye's ministry, wanted to replicate their initiative with Adelaide Tansti, "a native African student at Wilberforce." They hoped that Tansti also "may be thoroughly equipped to go back to her native land to bear the glad tidings of salvation."[25]

Holiness and Pentecostal movements in the nineteenth century ascended to a spiritual climax in 1906 in Los Angeles. A Black clergyman, William J. Seymour, born in Texas and schooled by a holiness minister, Charles Parham, in Topeka, Kansas, preached the doctrine of glossolalia, the spiritual gift of speaking in tongues. Innumerable pilgrims, Black and white, flocked to the Azusa Street revivals to hear Seymour and receive palpable evidence from the Holy Ghost that they were both "saved and sanctified" through this audible spiritual gift. From these marathon revivals emerged several denominations including the Black Church of God in Christ, whose founder and Azusa Street participant, Charles Harrison Mason, consecrated the white preachers who established the similarly populous Assemblies of God.[26]

Few Protestants, except for some Pentecostals, raised objections to World War I, but blessed military personnel and certified chaplains to serve in the armed forces. The unprecedented carnage of the war, mainly because of modernized and more deadly techniques of warfare, gave rise to transatlantic pacifism through such groups as the Fellowship of Reconciliation (FOR) and the American Friends Service Committee (AFSC). Though Blacks populated the military and the chaplaincy, pacifist perspectives scarcely affected their attitudes toward war because it was an ironic source for economic and vocational opportunities. World War I also generated an unprecedented Black migration that initiated a demographic shift from the agricultural South to the industrial North. As Blacks flocked by the multiple thousands to major Northern urban and industrial centers to work in steel, auto, electrical manufacturing, and rubber industries, churches grew exponentially and expanded the Black religious landscape to include traditional denominations; newer sects that were spiritualist and Holiness; and others that were Black nationalist, Jewish, and Islamic. Moreover, growing Black churches married Social Gospel initiatives begun earlier in the twentieth century with expanded community outreach, sometimes in cooperation with corporately funded welfare capitalism. These churches, like those in the antebellum period, provided platforms for pastors to align the church and civic interests of their parishioners.[27]

Adam Clayton Powell, father and son, at Abyssinian Baptist Church in New York City, and Archibald J. Carey, also father and son, as bishop and pastors to a succession of AME congregations in Chicago, blended ecclesial and public office roles. The younger Powell served a Harlem district in Congress and the junior Carey was elected to the city council in the Windy City and appointed to federal offices in the Eisenhower presidential administration. During the Depression of the 1930s and World War II in the early 1940s, Black Protestant pastors and parishioners shifted from the Republican Party to Franklin D. Roosevelt's Democratic Party. Reverend Marshall L. Shepard, the pastor of Mt. Olivet Tabernacle Baptist Church in Philadelphia, represented his congregation and community in the 1930s and 1940s as a member of the Pennsylvania legislature. Black churches encouraged parishioners to take advantage of New Deal programs and join the Congress of Industrial Organizations that brought Black workers in mass production industries into unions. As in previous wars, a pervasive presence of Black Protestants again populated the military chaplaincy during World War II.[28]

The pacifism that drew from revulsion at the widespread mortality of World War I mobilized Protestants to pursue peace objectives and to connect with the growing global influence of Mahatma Gandhi and his nonviolent insurgency against British imperialism in India.

Ransom, now the editor of the *AME Church Review*, likened Gandhi to Jesus: both brown-skinned and apostles of love and reconciliation. E. Stanley Jones, a long-time MEC minister and missionary in India, echoed Ransom's description of Gandhi's resemblance to Jesus. A. J. Muste, successively a Dutch Reformed and Congregational minister and Quaker adherent, became head of the FOR. This discursive terrain coincided with a generation of Black religious intellectuals who imbibed the tenets of liberal Protestantism and its impulse to reconstruct American society in the direction of economic equity and religiously based movements against anti-Black discrimination and segregation. They studied at seminaries such as Union, Chicago, and Yale, where the scholarship of Protestant professors such as Shirley Jackson Case advanced an understanding of the historical Jesus as a model for social insurgency. Mordecai W. Johnson, Benjamin E. Mays, Howard Thurman, and William Stuart Nelson, all Black Baptists, congregated at Howard University and its School of Religion. At this educational venue and at other Black institutions, they taught and inspired a subsequent gener-ation of seminary-trained activists who would strongly influence and shape the 1950s and 1960s civil rights movement. They included national leaders, both Baptists and Methodists; Martin Luther King, Jr., of the Southern Christian Leadership Conference (SCLC) and James Farmer of the Congress of Racial Equality (CORE), and local leaders Kelly Miller Smith and Andrew White in Nashville and Frederick C. James in Sumter, South Carolina. Their mentors, Mays, Thurman, and Nelson, interacted in India with Gandhi and adopted and diffused the tenets on nonviolence.[29]

These strands of liberal Protestantism, pacifism, and nonviolence converged in the ministry of Black Methodist minister James M. Lawson, Jr. The son of an AMEZ pastor who later shifted to the Methodist Episcopal Church's segregated Central Jurisdiction, Lawson was reared in Massillon, Ohio. Besides his education at Baldwin-Wallace College, he was molded by the Methodist Church's youth camps whose ethos urged participants to become Jesus Followers who would oppose injustice and war; he was also influenced by A. J. Muste and FOR. These formative ideas moved Lawson to denounce the Korean War and spend thirteen months in federal incarceration for refusing induction into the military. His release was based on Methodist sponsorship of a teaching and coach-ing stint in India at Hislop College. There, in the context of an in-depth study of Gandhian nonviolence, Lawson read in Indian newspapers about King's successful leadership in the Montgomery bus boycott in 1955–1956. When Lawson enrolled at the School of Theology at Oberlin

College, King, a visiting lecturer, convinced Lawson to come South to apply his singular credentials as a theoretician and tactician of nonviolence. Now, as FOR's Southern secretary, in cooperation with the Nashville Christian Leadership Conference (an affiliate of King's SCLC), he operated nonviolent workshops for students from Nashville's four Black institutions of higher education. These trainees became a vanguard spurring successful sit-ins in early 1960 against downtown retailers. Lawson also worked with SCLC and schooled the newly organized Student Nonviolent Coordinating Committee (SNCC) on the philosophy and praxis of nonviolence, and became involved in Memphis with the sanitation workers' strike in 1968 along with the soon to be martyred King. The SCLC leader credited Lawson for infusing nonviolence into the civil rights movement.[30] While the nonviolence of King and Lawson became a defining feature of the civil rights movement and Black churches were a major support for the NAACP, National Urban League, and other Black justice organizations, their integrationist and racial reconciliation objectives did not convince all African Americans that these goals were unambiguously desirable. The ideology of Black Power, with its emphasis on historic Black self-determination, armed defense of African Americans, and African-based cultural pride, challenged the King/Lawson allegiance to Christian tenets. While civil rights leaders were, in their own right, radical and insurgent in their emulation of Jesus, Black Power advocates wrongly viewed them as too accommodating to goals of interracial comity. In 1966, however, the National Committee of Negro Churchmen acknowledged, as Black Power advocates asserted, that white racism permeated American society, that Black anger expressed in urban rebellions should be channeled into "metropolitan development for equal opportunity," and that Black empowerment and justice remained urgent priorities. The organization released in the *New York Times* a position statement in support of Black Power. James H. Cone, a theologian of AME background who later taught at Union Theological Seminary in New York City, published *Black Theology and Black Power* in 1969. The classic study legitimated the right of Blacks to assert their humanity against ruthless and systemic white oppression and to protect it with every ethical tool whether nonviolence or armed self-defense. "If the system is evil," Cone declared, "then revolutionary violence is both justified and necessary." The Black Protestant clergy across the spectrum of the historic African-American denominations and their counterparts in the white ecclesia acquiesced to the confrontational and unmanageable rhetoric of Black Power. James Forman pressed Black and white Protestants even further in a demand for reparations delivered in a 1969 worship service that he disrupted at Riverside Church in New York City. Because white churches colluded with slave and segregated systems of Black oppression, the Caucasian church owed millions to Blacks to be deposited in a Black Economic Development Conference (BEDC). Some white denominations complied, but only partially, never fully embracing the reparations concept.[31]

In 1984 the United Methodist Church outdistanced the historic Wesleyan Black bodies in the election of an African-American woman, Leontine T. C. Kelly, to the episcopacy. Several others followed Kelly into the bishopric. Similarly, the Episcopal Church ordained Barbara Harris in 1988 as a suffragan bishop. Six other Black women including Paula E. Clark, elected as Bishop of the Chicago Diocese in 2020, emulated Harris's episcopal ascent. The AME, while behind in electing a female bishop, had Jarena Lee who Richard Allen licensed in 1817 after an initial rebuff as a pioneer woman preacher. Bishop Henry M. Turner ordained Sarah Ann Hughes as an itinerant deacon in the North Carolina Annual Conference in 1885, but his successor, Bishop Jabaz P. Campbell, rescinded the ordination and his colleagues sustained his action at the 1888 General Conference. Largely because of the marathon efforts of Martha Jayne Keys, AMEs authorized the ordination of women in 1948 as local deacons, in 1956 as local elders, and in 1960 as itinerant deacons and elders. Carrie T. Hooper sought the episcopacy at the 1964 General Conference, but it was not until 2000 that Vashti Murphy McKenzie became the first female bishop in the AME. The AMEZ followed in 2008 with the episcopal election of Mildred Bonnie Hines and the CME did the same in 2010 with Teresa Snorton. Bishop McKenzie was joined in the AME episcopacy in 2004 with Carolyn Tyler Guidry and Sarah F. Davis, and in 2016 with E. Anne Henning Byfield.[32]

Black Power themes persisted through the remainder of the twentieth century and spilled over into the beginning two decades of the twenty-first century. The scourge of Black mass incarceration that a series of federal and state laws and the war on drugs caused and facilitated was highlighted in the 2010 publication of Michele Alexander's *The New Jim Crow: Mass Incarceration in the Age of Colorblindness*. Parallel to this development was the increased visibility of police violence directed at Black youth and the callous aloofness of the justice system toward these deaths. The murder of Trayvon Martin in 2012 in Florida and the acquittal of his murderer, George Zimmerman, galvanized three Black female activists to found Black Lives Matter (BLM) in 2013. Subsequent police killings of Michael Brown in Ferguson, Missouri in 2014 (no charge was pursued against the police), and George Floyd in

Minneapolis, asphyxiated in 2020 by a policeman's knee on his neck, propelled BLM protests as an influential movement that decentered Protestants, both Black and white, as primary defenders of Black humanity.[33]

Though hardly on the frontline, Black churches, as with the Black Power movement, increasingly identified with issues that BLM spot-lighted. Bishop Adam J. Richardson of the AME penned a litany in 2014, in the aftermath of the Michael Brown murder. The litany leader was scripted to say: "Today we're wearing black – a reminder of our common roots designed and lifted by the Creator from the soil of Africa, a Genesis from which all humanity evolved. Thus we affirm the value, worth and dignity of all human beings and locally declare that Black lives matter!" Later, Bishop Richardson listed the tragically long roster of young Blacks killed by the police and like "Rachel weeping for her children," he concluded by repeating that "Black lives matter!" On December 13, 2020, pro-Donald Trump demonstrators who denied his loss in the recent presidential election saw BLACK LIVES MATTER signs at two venerable Black congregations in Washington, DC. The BLM signs, standing in front of Asbury United Methodist Church and Metropolitan African Methodist Episcopal Church, were torn down and torched.[34]

Though following rather than leading, Black Protestants identified with Black Lives Matter and stood in stark contrast with white seminary presi-dents in the Southern Baptist Convention (SBC). The SBC had, in various resolutions beginning in 1995, acknowledged complicity with slavery and identification with a racial status quo that maintained Black subordination. Hence, apologies were extended to African Americans, some of whose congregations affiliated with the denomination. In 2012 a Black pastor, Fred Luter, Jr., of Franklin Avenue Baptist Church in New Orleans, was elected the first Black SBC president. Nonetheless, six SBC seminary heads disallowed any teaching of critical race theory and pronounced it in conflict with the Baptist Faith and Message. Critical race theory posits that racism pervades sacred and secular structures and systems in American society and must be integrated into any analysis of these institutions. Protestant poles with advocacy for Black Lives Matter at one end and opposition to critical race theory at the other end typify the yawning divide on matters of Black and white in American Protestantism.[35]

NOTES

1 Albert J. Raboteau, *Canaan Land: A Religious History of African Americans* (New York: Oxford University Press, 1999), 7–11.

2 See Herbert Aptheker, "The Quakers and Negro Slavery," *Journal of Negro History* vol. 25, no. 3 (July 1940), 331–362; Winthrop S. Hudson, "The American Context as an Area for Research in Black Church Studies," *Church History* vol. 52, no. 2 (June 1983), 160.

3 Raboteau, *Canaan Land*, 12–14; Charles H. Long, "Perspectives for a Study of Afro-American Religion in the United States," in *Significations: Signs, Symbols, and Images in the Interpretation of Religion* (Philadelphia: Fortress Press, 1986), 177–179.

4 Long, "Perspectives for a Study of Afro-American Religion," 179–180.

5 Jon Butler, Grant Wacker, and Randall Balmer, *Religion in American Life: A Short History*, 2nd ed. (New York: Oxford University Press, 2011), 60; Erin Blakemore, "How an Enslaved Man in Boston Helped Save Generations from Smallpox," History.com, April 8, 2021, www.history.com/news/smallpox-vaccine-onesimus-slave-cotton-mather; Cotton Mather, "Cotton Mather, a Boston Minister, Proselytizes for Smallpox Inoculation, 1722," in *Major Problems in the History of American Medicine and Public Health*, ed. John Harley Warner and Janet A. Tighe (Boston: Houghton Mifflin Company, 2001), 30–33; Denmark Vesey, *The Trial Record of Denmark Vesey*, intro by John Oliver Killens (Boston: Beacon Press, 1970), 76–79.

6 First African Baptist Church, accessed April 24, 2021, https://firstafricanbc.com; Daniel A. Payne, *Recollections of Seventy Years* (New York: Arno Press and *The New York Times*, 1969), 81.

7 Hudson, "The American Context as an Area of Research in Black Church Studies," 158–159; Richard J. Boles, *Dividing the Faith: The Rise of Segregated Churches in the Early American North* (New York: New York University Press, 2020), 16–17.

8 Hudson, "The American Context as an Area of Research in Black Church Studies," 160–167.

9 Thad W. Tate, *The Negro in Eighteenth-Century Williamsburg* (Williamsburg, VA: The Colonial Williamsburg Foundation, 1965), 88–90.

10 Warren Thomas Smith, *Harry Hosier: Circuit Rider* (Nashville: The Upper Room, 1981), 21–22, 25, 30.

11 Dennis C. Dickerson, *The African Methodist Episcopal Church: A History* (New York: Cambridge University Press, 2020), 31–34.

12 Dickerson, *The African Methodist Episcopal Church*, 39–43; Harold T. Lewis, *Yet with a Steady Beat: The African American Struggle for Recognition in the Episcopal Church* (Valley Forge, PA: Trinity Press International, 1996), 28–32.

13 Will B. Gravely, "The Rise of African Churches in America (1786–1822): Re-examining the Contexts," in *African American Religion: Interpretive Essays in History and Culture*, ed. Timothy E. Fulop and Albert J. Raboteau (New York, Routledge: 1979), 137; William J. Walls, *The African Methodist Episcopal Zion Church: Reality of the Black Church* (Charlotte: AME Zion Publishing House, 1974), 43–44, 56.

14 Gravely, "The Rise of African Churches in America," 139–142.

15 Theophilus G. Steward, *Fifty Years in The Gospel Ministry, from 1864–1914* (Philadelphia: AME Book Concern, c. 1921), 44.

16 Henry Highland Garnet, "An Address to the Slaves of the United States" (1843), taken from Garnet, *A Memorial Discourse* (Philadelphia: J. M. Wilson, 1865), 44–51; BlackPast, www.blackpast.org/african-american-history/1843-henry-highland-garnet-address-slaves-united-states/; see also David E. Swift, *Black Prophets of Justice: Activist Clergy Before the Civil War* (Baton Rouge: Louisiana University Press, 1989).

17 "Minutes of the Annual Conference of the New York District of the African Methodist Episcopal Church," held in Bethel Church, Second Street, New York (1851), 15–16.

18 Dickerson, *The African Methodist Episcopal Church*, 4–6; Donald G. Mathews, *Slavery and Methodism: A Chapter in American Morality, 1780–1845* (Princeton, NJ: Princeton University Press, 1965), 246–282; Stephen Ward Angell, *Bishop Henry McNeal Turner and African American Religion in the South* (Knoxville: University of Tennessee Press, 1992), 12, 15–30.

19 Raboteau, *Canaan Land*, 47–50, 58; Milton C. Sernett, *African American Religious History: A Documentary Witness* (Durham, NC: Duke University Press, 1999), 89–101; Ted A. Smith, *Weird John Brown: Divine Violence and the Limits of Ethics* (Stanford: Stanford University Press, 2015), 26.

20 Howard Thurman, *Jesus and the Disinherited* (Nashville: Abingdon Press, 1949), 30–31; "Thornton Stringfellow Argues that the Bible Is Proslavery, 1860," in *Major Problems in American Religious History*, ed. Patrick Allitt (Boston: Wadsworth Cengage Learning, 2013), 184.

21 "Abraham Lincoln's Second Inaugural Address, 1865," in *Major Problems*, ed. Allitt, 213; see Edwin S. Redkey, "Black Chaplains in the Union Army," *Civil War History* vol. 33, no. 4 (December 1987), 331–350.

22 Raboteau, *Canaan Land*, 63–69.

23 Reginald F. Hildebrand, *The Times Were Strange and Stirring: Methodist Preachers and the Crisis of Emancipation* (Durham, NC: Duke University Press, 1995), 50–72; Larry Eugene Rivers and Canter Brown, Jr., *Laborers in the Vineyard of the Lord: The Beginnings of the AME Church in Florida, 1865–1895* (Gainesville: University Press of Florida, 2002), 61.

24 Reverdy C. Ransom, *First Quadrennial Report of the Pastor and Warden of the Institutional Church and Social Settlement to the Twenty-Second Session of the General Conference and to the Connectional Trustees of the African Methodist Episcopal Church, Convened at Quinn Chapel, Chicago, Illinois* (May 1904), 4, 6–13; see Philip S. Foner, ed., *Black Socialist Preacher: The Teachings of Reverend George Washington Woodbey and His Disciple Reverend George W. Slater, Jr.* (San Francisco: Synthesis Publications, 1983).

25 *Journal of Proceedings of the Third Quadrennial Convention of the Women's Parent Mite Missionary Society of the African Methodist Episcopal Church*

Held in Wylie Avenue AME Church, Pittsburg(h), PA., From Thursday,
November 5th to 9th, 1903 (Philadelphia: AME Publishing House, circa 1903),
18–19, 90–91.

26 Calvin White, Jr., *The Rise to Respectability: Race, Religion, and the Church*
of God in Christ (Fayetteville: University of Arkansas Press, 2012), 32–39.

27 White, Jr., *The Rise to Respectability*, 59; Leilah Danielson, *American*
Gandhi: A. J. Muste and the History of Radicalism in the Twentieth Century
(Philadelphia: University of Pennsylvania Press, 2014), 53–57; Raboteau,
Canaan Land, 82–86; see also Dennis C. Dickerson, "The Black Church in
Industrializing Western Pennsylvania, 1870–1950," *Western Pennsylvania*
Historical Magazine vol. 64, no. 4 (October 1981), 329–344.

28 Dennis C. Dickerson, *African American Preachers and Politics: The Careys*
of Chicago (Jackson: University Press of Mississippi, 2010), 64–65, 80,
100–113; "Rev. M.L. Shepard, Councilman, Is Dead," *The Philadelphia*
Inquirer February 22, 1967, 36.

29 Sudarshan Kapur, *Raising Up A Prophet: The African American Encounter*
with Gandhi (Boston: Beacon Press, 1992), 28–29, 80; Randal Maurice Jelks,
Benjamin Elijah Mays, Schoolmaster of The Movement: A Biography (Chapel
Hill: University of North Carolina Press, 2012), 88–90; see also Dennis
C. Dickerson, "African American Religious Intellectuals and the Theological
Foundations of the Civil Rights Movement, 1930–1955," *Church History* vol.
74, no. 2 (June 2005), 217–235.

30 Dennis C. Dickerson, "James M. Lawson, Jr.: Methodism, Nonviolence and
the Civil Rights Movement, *Methodist History* vol. 52, no. 3 (April 2014),
168–186.

31 "Black Power: Statement by National Committee of Negro Churchmen,"
New York Times, July 31, 1966, E5, https://episcopalarchives.org/church-
awakens/items/show/183; James H. Cone, *Black Theology and Black Power*
(Maryknoll, NY: Orbis Books, 1969), 143; see also Robert S. Lecky and
H. Elliott Wright, eds., *Black Manifesto: Religion, Race, and Reparations*
(New York: Sheed and Ward), 1969.

32 Dickerson, *The African Methodist Episcopal Church*, 229–231, 519–521.

33 Michele Alexander, *The New Jim Crow: Mass Incarceration in the Age of*
Colorblindness (New York: The New Press, 2010).

34 The Christian Recorder News Break, "Black Life Matters Litany for Black Life
Matters Sunday – December 14, 2014," December 11, 2014,
www.facebook.com/TheChristianRecorder/posts/814123015313763;
Leah Asmelash and Melissa Tapia, "Protesters Ripped and Set Fire to BLM
Signs at Two DC Churches," CNN.com, December 14, 2020, www.cnn.com
/2020/12/14/us/protest-dc-blm-asbury-metropolitan-ame-trnd/index.html.

35 "Southern Baptist Seminary Presidents Nix Critical Race Theory," Religion
News Service, December 1, 2020, https://religionnews.com/2020/12/01/sou
thern-baptist-seminary-presidents-nix-critical-race-theory/.

13 Faith Healing and Modern Medicine

CANDY GUNTHER BROWN

American Protestants have expressed diverse views of how "faith" and "medicine" relate to health. Certain Protestants consider God the source of both illness and healing, while others attribute sickness to demons and wholeness to God. Some rely exclusively on either faith or medicine for healing, while others combine them. Over time, perceived tensions between faith and medicine have diminished, but not disappeared.

FROM THE BIBLE TO THE PROTESTANT REFORMATION

Healing is a prominent theme in the Bible. Exodus identifies God as "the Lord who heals you" (Ex. 15:26, NRSV). Protestant interpreters have debated the relative value of faith versus medicine in healing in part because the Bible seems to encompass contrasting views. For example, 2 Chronicles denounces King Asa because "even in his disease he did not seek the Lord, but sought help from physicians" (2 Chr. 16:12, NRSV). In the gospel accounts, Jesus healed many sick people, often crediting their "faith." For instance, Jesus healed a woman from chronic bleeding who had "endured much under many physicians" but "was no better, but rather grew worse." Having exhausted medical resources, the woman came to Jesus, reasoning that "If I but touch his clothes, I will be made well." When the woman experienced healing, Jesus reassured her that "your faith has made you well" (Mark 5:25–26, 28, 34, NRSV). The epistle of James encourages the church that "the prayer of faith will save the sick" (James 5:15, NRSV) – also commonly translated as "heal the sick" (CEB) or "make the sick person well" (NIV). Various translations of James 5:15 have generated much controversy and confusion. The Greek *sōzō* encompasses a range of meanings, including salvation from destruction, healing from disease, and deliverance from judgment. Jerome's influential Vulgate (c. 342–420) translated *sōzō* in James 5:15 with the Latin *salvo* (English "save"); this decision facilitated interpreting the passage as referring to spiritual salvation rather than physical healing. Modern translators continue to debate whether "save" or "heal" is more appropriate in this context; these decisions influence expectations about the effects of praying for the sick.[1] Yet physicians are present in the New Testament: the epistle to the Colossians not only acknowledges that the gospel writer Luke was a doctor but esteems him as "the beloved physician" (Col 4:14, KJV).

The Roman Catholic Church has, since early in its history, called upon physicians to evaluate whether remarkable healings could have resulted from medical treatment or natural recoveries, or whether they should be attributed to God's miraculous intervention in response to the prayer of faith.[2] During the Reformation, Catholics challenged Protestants to demonstrate God's approval by means of miraculous healings. German reformer Martin Luther (1483–1546) demurred that "no new and special revelation or miracle is necessary," since the Bible had already revealed God's Word.[3] Luther nevertheless did reputedly pray for healing – and considered the deathbed recovery of his friend Melancthon, for whom he himself prayed, a "direct answer to prayer."[4] Luther perceived no conflict between prayer and medicine. When the bubonic plague was raging through Europe, Luther responded:

> I shall ask God mercifully to protect us. Then I shall fumigate, help purify the air, administer medicine and take it. I shall avoid places and persons where my presence is not needed in order not to become contaminated and thus perchance ... pollute others and so cause their death as a result of my negligence ... If my neighbor needs me, however, I shall not avoid place or person but will do freely as stated above. See this is such a God-fearing faith because it is neither brash nor foolhardy and does not tempt God.[5]

Luther took the position that God can heal through prayer or medicine and that faith rejects neither.

CHASTENING THE BODY TO SANCTIFY THE SOUL

The French reformer John Calvin (1509–1564) went further than Luther in discouraging expectation of miraculous healing. Calvin's lack of experience with healing in response to prayer – despite his personal suffering from multiple, painful physical afflictions – led him to develop the doctrine of "cessationism" to argue that "the gift of healing ... has long ago ceased" because it is no longer needed to confirm the gospel.[6] Calvin reasoned that since God is sovereign and good, when people experience physical suffering it is because God is chastening them ("for whom the Lord loveth he chasteneth" [Heb 12:6, KJV]) – punishing their bodies to sanctify their souls. Calvin taught people to pray that those whom God chastens with "sickness ... or any other misery of the body" would "understand Your fatherly affection, which chastens them for their correction, that they may turn to You with their whole heart, and having turned, may receive full consolation and deliverance from every ill."[7] In this view, God sends both sickness and healing, the latter often through medical means.

During the Boston smallpox epidemic of 1721, the Puritan minister Cotton Mather (1663–1728) advocated for inoculation by a physician. Although interpreting the epidemic as divine punishment, Mather rejected the corollary that using medical treatment to resist disease was tantamount to opposing God's will.[8] Indeed, up through the nineteenth century Calvinist ministers admonished parishioners to resign themselves both to physical suffering from disease or injury and to painful therapies (some of them dangerous, such as bleeding and purging with mercury) prescribed by physicians.[9]

SANCTIFYING SOUL AND BODY

Moderating the Calvinist emphasis on sin's intractability – thus the need for regular chastening – Dutch theologian Jacob Arminius (1559–1609) expressed greater optimism that God endowed humans with ability to choose to allow the Holy Spirit to free them from sin. British Methodist founder John Wesley (1703–1791) built on Arminian ideas to develop his doctrine of "entire sanctification." Wesley reasoned that God's "perfect love" was sufficient to free Christians from committing intentionally sinful acts.[10] Rather than privileging bodily suffering as a means of spiritual sanctification, Wesley envisioned forgiveness from sin and healing of the body as complementary.

Wesley saw God less as a chastiser and more as a healer who has "more than one method of healing either the soul or the body."[11] Wesley encouraged parishioners in acute medical need to seek a "physician who fears God." Wesley himself opened medical dispensaries where he gave free consultations, and he wrote a medical textbook: *Primitive Physick; Or, An Easy and Natural Method of Curing Most Diseases* (1747). Alongside prescribing medical and folk remedies, Wesley urged readers to, "above all, add to the rest (for it is not labour lost) that old, unfashionable medicine, prayer."[12] Wesley expressed skepticism that all who "imagined themselves to be endued with a power of working miracles, of healing the sick by a word or a touch" actually had been endowed by the Holy Spirit with the gifts of healings and miracles identified in 1 Corinthians 12.[13] Nevertheless, Wesley often "joined in prayer" for others and for himself, and he attested to God's healing in response to these prayers. On one such occasion, upon praying for a traveling companion, the man recovered "before we had done" praying. Wesley perceived a causal connection: "Now, he that will account for this by natural causes has my free leave: But I choose to say, 'This is the power of God.'"[14]

Wesley believed that he himself had been "preternaturally restored more than ten times."[15] Once, "my horse was exceeding lame; and my head ached much. I thought, cannot God heal man or beast by means or without? Immediately my weariness and headache ceased, and my horse's lameness in the same instant. But what does all this prove? I believe God now hears and answers prayer, even beyond the ordinary course of nature."[16] Thus, Wesley distinguished natural, including medical, means from supernatural intervention in nature, and affirmed that God uses both to heal.

Wesley also practiced and taught practical care for the sick, as did his followers. During the Philadelphia yellow fever epidemic of 1793, Richard Allen, founder of the African Methodist Episcopal Church, and Absalom Jones, the first African-American Episcopal priest, mobilized the Free African Society in responding to pleas by white doctors (whose medical theory, inaccurately, predicted that Blacks would be immune) to tend to sick white inhabitants.[17]

Wesley envisioned sickness as a consequence of sin and credited God with both forgiving sins and healing diseases. Some of Wesley's mid-nineteenth-century American followers took this doctrine an additional step – reasoning that if sickness is a consequence of sin, and if humans can be entirely sanctified from sin, then it ought to be possible to experience freedom from all the consequences of sin, including sickness.[18] American Methodist layman Ethan O. Allen (1813–1903) has been called the "Father of Divine Healing" for promoting the idea that as God redeems Christians from the spiritual consequences of sin through entire sanctification, sanctified Christians are also redeemed from the physical consequences of sin through divine healing. In 1846, Allen persuaded a group of Methodist class leaders to pray for him – and attested to experiencing both sanctification and healing from consumption (tuberculosis) simultaneously. By contrast to the Calvinist view that God sends sickness as chastisement for sin, Allen interpreted sickness as demonic in origin and cast out evil spirits while praying for healing.[19]

Unlike Wesley, Allen rejected use of medical means as indicating lack of faith in God to heal. Among those reputedly healed through Allen's prayers was Sarah Ann Freeman Mix (1832–1884), a free Black woman and member of the African Methodist Episcopal Church. After experiencing remission of consumption, Mix spent the next seven years (until she died from a recurrence) as the first-known African American and first full-time female healing evangelist. Like Allen, Mix advised against using medical means, reasoning that trust in medicine might inhibit faith in God.[20] Similar to other leaders in the emergent "Faith Cure" movement, Mix based her prayer practices on instructions in James 5: "Is any sick among you? let him call for the elders of the church; and let them pray over him, anointing him with oil in the name of the Lord . . . Confess your faults one to another, and pray one for another, that ye may be healed" (James 5:14–16, KJV).

Mix also prayed at a distance for those who mailed their requests. In this manner, Mix prayed for Carrie Judd Montgomery (1858–1946), who had been bedridden for nearly three years after a fall in 1876. At the time Mix specified for her and Montgomery to join their prayers, as an act of faith Judd got out of bed and walked unassisted. Although she did not immediately experience relief from all her symptoms, Judd recovered her health over a period of several months. Montgomery began to pray for others, opening a "healing home" in Buffalo, New York in 1882 that became a model for similar residential prayer retreats. Judd (who married George Montgomery in 1890) continued her healing ministry, joining the Pentecostal movement in the 1900s, until her death in 1946.[21]

Judd Montgomery's "acting faith" approach to healing built on the "altar theology" of Methodist laywoman Phoebe Palmer (1807–1874). Frustrated by waiting eleven years for an emotional experience of entire sanctification, Palmer avowedly discovered a "shorter way" to holiness. Palmer concluded that one need only decide "I will be holy now," consecrating oneself to Christ by figuratively laying one's "all upon the altar." One then receives entire sanctification by "naked faith" in a "naked promise" of the Bible. The final step is to testify publicly to one's sanctification – lest one risk losing the blessing by disobeying a command in the Bible.[22] Practitioners of acting faith for healing, like Judd, did not wait to experience a cessation of symptoms before acting faith and testifying to their healing. Indeed, they worried that failure to testify might cause them to lose their healing.[23] At the extreme end of anti-medical teachings, John

Alexander Dowie (1847–1907) provocatively published a sermon entitled *Doctors, Drugs and Devils: Or, the Foes of Christ the Healer;* Dowie prohibited doctors and medicines from entering the city he founded: Zion, Illinois.[24]

Although many early Faith Cure leaders considered reliance on medicine the opposite of faith, not every leader condemned medical treatment. Charles Cullis (1833–1892), a homeopathic physician and Episcopal layman, argued influentially that Jesus's atoning death – as prophesied in Isaiah 53 – provides both forgiveness of sin and healing from physical infirmities, since "with his stripes we are healed" (Isa. 53:5, KJV). Cullis would "by no means disparage the use of medicines" and insisted that "there can be no condemnation to the one using medicine; you can certainly ask God's blessing upon the means used." Yet, in Cullis's view, the "better way" was to "take the Great Physician himself to be your healer, without medicine," since it is communion with Christ "that brings blessing and healing upon body and soul."[25]

By contrast, other nineteenth-century Protestant leaders advocated for medical treatment as an act of Christian charity, while opposing the divine-healing movement. James Monroe Buckley, editor of the influential *Methodist Christian Advocate* from 1880–1912, cited Wesley's support of free medical dispensaries in his own efforts to raise funds for Methodist hospitals. A Methodist Episcopal General Hospital was founded in Brooklyn, New York in 1881. During the next fifty years, Methodists built fifty-nine US hospitals as well as dozens of overseas missionary hospitals, and provided many services free of charge to the poor.[26] Unlike Wesley, Buckley opposed any reliance on prayer for healing. He considered "faith healing" an "excrescence on Christianity, a kind of quackery of faith" that degraded "the holy faith to the level of the superstitions of Paganism." Buckley characterized Bible-based arguments for healing as "a very superficial and unwarranted interpretation of Scripture." A key problem, in Buckley's view, was that advocates of healing through prayer diminished the "influence of Christianity by subjecting it to a test which it cannot endure." If people did not recover after prayer – which Buckley considered inevitable – then Christianity would have seemed to have failed a test of its validity. Rather, any who beheld the "moral and spiritual transformation" produced by Christianity would not "need any other proof that it is of God."[27]

Some nineteenth-century Protestants, especially those influenced by the German Higher Criticism, questioned literal interpretations of the Bible's miracle stories. In reaction against this and other expressions of the growing modernist movement in American Protestantism, theologians at Princeton Theological Seminary published a twelve-volume series, *The Fundamentals* (1910–1915). Fundamentalists insisted upon the historicity of biblical miracles – although they took a cessationist stance toward modern miracles.[28]

The divine-healing movement was infused with fresh energy by the Pentecostal revivals of the early twentieth century. Even more than reports that people were speaking in languages they had not studied (glossolalia), testimonies of healing drew participants to Azusa Street, Los Angeles, California, from 1906 to 1909.[29] Pentecostals who prayed for healing, like their nineteenth-century predecessors, tended to view healing through faith and healing through medicine as opposites.

Pentecostal John G. Lake (1870–1935) blamed doctors and cessationist theologians for the deaths of eight of his fifteen siblings. Even before becoming involved in the Pentecostal movement, Lake (influenced by Dowie) renounced all medical treatment to trust God alone for healing, after which Lake, his wife, and three of his siblings all recovered from illnesses following prayer. Lake styled himself a "doctor" (though he lacked a medical degree) and directed "Divine Healing Rooms" in Spokane, Washington from 1914 to 1920. Lake challenged doctors to use their medical equipment for a "test of the truth of the message" and avowedly orchestrated a series of experiments involving x-ray and microscopic examinations before, during, and after prayer. During the Spanish Influenza pandemic of 1918, rather than closing, Lake's Healing Rooms reputedly added extra hours, as well as disseminating public health information and supplies – and claimed that, as a result, Spokane was the "healthiest city in America."[30]

Whereas Lake sought medical validation of the efficacy of prayer, other Protestants with a healing focus insisted that God's Word is a sufficient basis for faith. Kenneth Hagin (1917–2003) testified to being healed from a life-threatening heart condition at age fifteen by a revelation of "faith in God's Word" that "whosoever shall say unto this mountain, be thou removed and be thou cast into the sea, and shall not doubt in his heart, but shall believe that those things which he saith shall come to pass, he shall have whatsoever he saith" (Mark 11:23–24, KJV). Followers of Hagin's "Word of Faith" movement, like practitioners of the nineteenth-century Faith Cure, encouraged people to claim healing by faith regardless of symptoms, and discouraged repeated prayer for the same condition as indicating lack of faith.[31] Hagin referred to the Bible as "God's Medicine" and denied that he personally ever needed a human physician.[32]

RAPPROCHEMENT OF FAITH AND MEDICINE

The Charismatic revivals of the 1960s brought a rapprochement between the prayer of faith and modern medicine. Oklahoma native Oral Roberts (1918–2009) experienced healing from tuberculosis through prayer at age seventeen. The following year, 1936, he was ordained in the Pentecostal Holiness Church and began a healing ministry. Re-ordained in the United Methodist Church in 1968, Roberts played a singular role in making a Pentecostal emphasis on gifts of the Holy Spirit accessible to mainline Protestants. As Roberts's audiences shifted toward the middle class (and his growing television ministry increased expenses), his message also shifted toward an emphasis on financial prosperity through "seed faith" giving. In 1981, Roberts opened the City of Faith Medical and Research Center in Tulsa, Oklahoma, symbolizing how the "healing streams of prayer and medicine must merge." Although the hospital closed after only eight years due to debt, it gave many Christian medical professionals a vision for how to care for patients holistically, by integrating spiritual and medical treatments. Like many Pentecostals and Charismatics who prayed for healing, Roberts rejected the term "faith healing" in favor of "divine healing" because "God heals – I don't."[33]

Although emphasizing that it is God, not human faith, that heals, mid-twentieth-century healing evangelists – Roberts among them – did sometimes explain failures by pointing toward a lack of faith or holiness in the person seeking prayer. This propensity disturbed Kathryn Kuhlman (1907–1976), the daughter of a Baptist and a Methodist, who began itinerant evangelism at age seventeen. In 1947, people began reporting healings while Kuhlman was preaching on the person of the Holy Spirit – without Kuhlman ever praying for healing. Kuhlman denied that "faith" is something one can "work up in oneself" and worried that those who try to manufacture faith will inevitably fail because they are "unwittingly looking at themselves, rather than to God." Kuhlman – who conducted "miracle services" for overflow crowds of tens of thousands representing every denomination of Protestants as well as Catholics – insisted that the personal presence of the Holy Spirit is the key to healing. Kuhlman taught that one receives both salvation and healing from God the Father through faith in the atoning work of Jesus by the resurrection power of the Holy Spirit. Because "faith" is a "gift" of God, she wrote, rather than "pray for faith; you seek the Lord, and faith will come," and, through faith, other gifts, including healing.[34]

Unlike evangelists who urged the sick to claim healing by faith, regardless of physical symptoms, or who discouraged the sick from seeking medical attention, Kuhlman spoke well of modern medicine and urged those who believed themselves healed in her services to return to their doctors for confirmation. Indeed, she insisted that medical evidence back every healing testimony she endorsed. Kuhlman invited medical doctors to attend her miracle services and called upon them to evaluate healing claims.[35]

Emulating the Roman Catholic Medical Bureau at the Shrine of Lourdes (which had been established in 1883), Kuhlman published only those cases that met four criteria, each of which was informed by medical standards. First, the disease or injury had been medically diagnosed as resulting from an organic or structural problem, involving more than the unexplained failure of a body part to function. Second, the healing had to have occurred rapidly, involving changes that could not easily be explained as psychosomatic. Third, the patient's primary physician had to verify the healing. Fourth, the healing had to have occurred long enough in the past that it could not readily be diagnosed as remission.[36] Kuhlman's book trilogy, *I Believe in Miracles* (1962), *God Can Do It Again* (1969), and *Nothing Is Impossible with God* (1974), consists of sixty healing testimonials, each of which was supported by before-and-after medical documentation. Kuhlman saw no difficulty in conceding that God works through doctors and medicine to heal, but she used medical evidence "to offer proof of the power of God" to "heal instantly without the material tools of scientific medicine."[37]

The Third Wave Charismatic movement of the 1980s continued to complicate views of "faith" and to emphasize the complementarity of faith and medicine. Former jazz musician John Wimber (1934–1997) founded the Vineyard Christian Fellowship of Anaheim, California in 1977 and led the emergent Vineyard movement. Like Kuhlman, Wimber challenged simplistic associations of healing with faith and holiness. Wimber noted that, in his own ministry, more people were healed some days than others, though he did not discern a difference in levels of faith or holiness, either in himself or in the people for whom he prayed. Wimber's "kingdom" theology emphasized that the kingdom of heaven is "already" but "not yet." Thus, failures to experience healing can be attributed to a clash between the kingdoms of God and the devil, rather than deficient faith.[38]

Wimber's model of "power healing" envisioned divine healing as proof of the power of God. Wimber encouraged not only petitionary prayer, but also prayers of command – speaking directly to diseases and demons causing sickness, commanding healing in Jesus's name and authority. By contrast to the Word of Faith movement, Wimber discouraged those receiving prayer from testifying to healing unless they experienced significant improvement in physical symptoms or had medical confirmation. Even more than Kuhlman, Wimber emphasized that any lay Christian, not just the specially gifted healing evangelist, can learn to pray effectively for healing (what he called "doing the stuff"). At the same time, Wimber encouraged use of medical means when available. Wimber himself suffered from heart attacks, stroke, and cancer during the last decade of his life, for which he sought both medical treatment and prayer.[39]

In 1994, St. Louis Vineyard pastor Randy Clark visited Toronto to preach; an apparent outpouring of gifts of the Holy Spirit, including healing, launched the "Toronto Blessing" revivals that continue to exert an influence, across the United States and globally, as of 2021. Clark founded the Apostolic Network of Global Awakening, which hosts "Schools of Healing and Impartation" and a "Christian Healing Certification Program" that is intended to equip both laity and medical professionals to pray for healing. Clark's goal is for hospitals to authorize certified healing prayer practitioners just as many hospitals already authorize practitioners of integrative therapies such as Reiki and Therapeutic Touch. Like Wimber, Clark emphasized God's love and power, above human faith, in making healing available. Clark encourages prayer recipients to testify to healing if they experience an 80 percent improvement in physical symptoms or confirmation from medical testing.[40]

Among the US churches influenced by the Toronto Blessing is Bethel Church in Redding, California, pastored by Bill Johnson, a fifth-generation Pentecostal Assemblies of God pastor.[41] In 1999, Bethel Church board member Cal Pierce "re-opened" the John G. Lake Healing Rooms in Spokane, Washington and formed the International Association of Healing Rooms (IAHR). Unlike Lake, modern Healing Rooms prayer minsters encourage doctor visits and advise those who believe themselves healed through prayer to "receive a Doctor's approval" prior to discontinuing any prescribed medication.[42] During periods of the 2020–2021 COVID-19 pandemic, many churches and healing ministries, including Bethel and IAHR-affiliated healing rooms, discontinued in-person meetings, instead offering prayer via the Internet and encouraging prayer and fasting for an end to the disease.[43] As the pandemic progressed, however, Bethel reopened, and senior leaders vocally opposed vaccine and mask mandates, fearing a conspiracy of government and conventional medical science (possibly inspired by the Antichrist) to quash religious freedom.[44]

RESIDUAL TENSIONS BETWEEN FAITH AND MEDICINE

By the third quarter of the twentieth century, relatively few American Protestants denied the germ-theory of disease or opposed modern medicine, whether or not they practiced divine healing. A notorious exception was the Pentecostal Faith Assembly Church, headquartered in Elkhart, Indiana, with affiliates spanning several states. Between the church's founding in 1973 by Hobart Freeman and his death in 1984, more than ninety church members – many of them children, as well as Freeman himself – had died after refusing medical treatment.[45]

The largest and best-known anti-medical church is Christian Science. Mary Baker Eddy (1821–1910), author of *Science and Health* (1875) and founder of the First Church of Christ, Scientist, headquartered in Boston, Massachusetts since 1894, taught that disease is a mental error rather than a physical disorder. In Eddy's view, the material world, including disease, is an illusion, and the purpose of prayer is to correct the beliefs responsible for people suffering from effects of this illusion. Eddy advised against recourse to doctors or medicine, though she herself did at times resort to both. At its heyday in 1961, the number of Christian Science branch churches globally had climbed to 3,273; by 2018, two-thirds of these churches had closed and the number of "practitioners," or faith healers, had dropped to just 1,126.[46]

The Jehovah's Witnesses, which grew out of a Bible study group founded by Charles Taze Russell in 1870, accept most modern medicine. However, in 1945, Witness leaders determined that blood transfusions violate the Bible's injunctions against consuming blood. Witnesses – who claimed 8.7 million active members worldwide in 2018 – do allow the use of non-blood alternatives. Witnesses do not endorse "faith healing" but instead hold the cessationist view that gifts of healings ceased in the post-biblical era.[47]

By the early twenty-first century, the vast majority of Americans availed themselves of modern medicine, although many continued to complement medical treatment with prayer for healing. In 2003, 72 percent of Americans polled agreed that "praying to God can cure someone – even if science says the person doesn't stand a chance."[48] A 2007 survey found that 23 percent of Americans believe that they personally have "witnessed a miraculous, physical healing."[49] A 2004 poll reported that 73 percent of US medical doctors believe that miraculous healing occurs today.[50] Counterintuitively, studies suggest that terminal cancer patients who express faith that God will heal them miraculously are more likely to pursue aggressive, non-curative, life-prolonging medical therapies as an act of faith – taking every opportunity to allow God to heal with or without medicine.[51]

Twenty-first-century Protestants regularly combine prayer for healing with modern medical treatment – as well as complementary and alternative therapies such as chiropractic, acupuncture, yoga, or meditation, although many such therapies are grounded in religious and spiritual traditions other than Christianity.[52] Testimonies of divine healing continue to abound. Those who denote healings as "divine" generally have in mind improvements that occurred unusually rapidly or in circumstances in which recovery is unexpected through merely medical means or natural healing processes. Yet, despite Kuhlman's pioneering efforts at medical documentation of miraculous healing, such documentation efforts are relatively uncommon in the twenty-first century.

Many modern pentecostals (an umbrella term that encompasses classical Pentecostals and participants in the more recent, more ecumenical Charismatic movements) exhibit reluctance to subject healing testimonials to medical scrutiny. An oft-expressed concern is that people with faith do not need medical evidence to believe that God heals, whereas skeptics who demand proof will, regardless of the quantity or quality of evidence produced, think of some excuse to discount it. In this vein, one 61-year-old retired police officer testified to having been divinely healed of metastasized stomach cancer six years before, after prayer at an IAHR Healing Room. He refused medical confirmation: "I don't want or need a MRI – I live on faith ... I don't need to test God" and "every lab test would be seen as misdiagnosis to skeptics."[53]

Certain Protestants interpret empirical tests of the efficacy of prayer as tantamount to testing God – contrary to the Bible's injunction: "Do not put the Lord your God to the test" (Deut. 6:16 and Matt. 4:7, NRSV). Others – dependent on modern medicine, yet disillusioned by its limits – express a postmodern ambivalence toward medical truth claims coupled with a heightened esteem for personal experience.[54] Postmodern pentecostals might discount the value of medical documentation and yet seek to "prove" that God heals by pointing toward the "evidence" of diminished pain, increased mobility, or sensations such as heat and tingling during prayer for healing.

TESTING FAITH WITH MEDICINE

In an age of evidence-based medicine, most medical professionals and many ordinary people rely on medical tests to determine the presence or absence of disease. Where there is a conflict between a medical evaluation and a religious claim, many Americans trust the medical verdict. Since the nineteenth century, skeptical scientists have called for medical studies of the health effects of prayer. In the "Prayer Gauge Debate" of 1872, British physicist John Tyndall challenged Christians to compare outcomes of patients who did and did not receive prayer; church leaders recoiled at the idea of measuring prayer as if it were an impersonal, natural force.[55] Since the 1980s, there have been a few randomized, controlled trials of the efficacy of prayer for healing. Several studies reported better outcomes for prayer recipients.[56] Yet, one widely publicized study found no benefits and discovered that patients who knew they had been selected for prayer actually fared worse;[57] in this latter study, all Protestant intercessors belonged to Silent Unity – a New Thought group which teaches that "prayers of supplication or petition" are "useless," as there is no personal deity outside the self.[58] A systematic review of prayer research notes that "limitations in trial design and reporting are enough to hide a real beneficial effect" and that "the evidence presented so far is interesting enough to support further study," though the review authors consider other treatments better "suited to investigation in a randomized trial."[59]

Few American Protestants since Kuhlman have been involved in medical evaluations of prayer. The Palestinian-Canadian-American Benny Hinn (b. 1952) claims to have been inspired by Kuhlman to publish a volume of ten medically documented healing narratives, *Lord, I Need a Miracle* (1993), for which a physician, Donald Colbert, MD, wrote a foreword.[60] In his book, *Only Love Can Make a Miracle* (1990), the Indian-Kenyan-American Mahesh Chavda published the death certificate of a six-year-old boy purportedly raised from the dead.[61] Similarly, the German Reinhard Bonnke (1940–2019), who spent most of his evangelistic career in Africa before moving to the United States, included in the 2003 documentary film *Raised from the Dead* a death certificate for a man avowedly resurrected through his ministry.[62] The US-based Global Medical Research Institute (GMRI), founded in 2012, has the stated mission of "applying the rigorous methods of evidence-based medicine to study Christian Spiritual Healing practices."[63] GMRI has, as of 2021, published two peer-reviewed case reports in medical journals and commenced randomized-controlled trials, using medical methodologies to examine apparent healings through prayer.[64]

AMERICAN PROTESTANTISM IN GLOBAL PERSPECTIVE

By comparison to the United States, prayer for healing is relatively more common in the global South, since the Bible is read more literally and

modern medical treatment is less available.[65] Survey researchers estimate that pentecostals make up more than a quarter of the world's
2 billion Christians, and that most classical Pentecostals and many
Charismatics report personal experiences of divine healing.[66] Surveys
suggest that pentecostals regularly combine prayer with whatever medical or folk remedies are available – and rarely reject medicine as antagonistic to faith.[67]

As globalizing processes have accelerated, both the threat and the fear
of disease have increased, thereby fuelling the growth of religious movements such as pentecostalism for which healing is a central concern.
Contrary to the prognostications of secularization theorists, modern and
postmodern peoples have continued to pray for healing even when they can
readily access the most sophisticated medical resources.[68] By the twenty-
first century, global South Christians were undertaking "reverse missions"
to the North, encouraging supernaturalist interpretations of the Bible and
renewed emphasis on divine healing and other gifts of the Holy Spirit.[69]

CONCLUSION

The relationship between faith healing and modern medicine in American
Protestantism is complex. There are numerous examples of Protestants
praying in faith for healing and trusting God to heal through medical
means. American Protestants have sometimes conflated rejection of
medicine with "faith" and acceptance of medicine with "unbelief" –
rather than following a line of logic that one may reject medicine and
still lack faith, or accept medicine without wavering in faith.[70] By this line
of reasoning, either rejecting medical treatment as contrary to faith or
pursuing life-prolonging therapies to buy time for a miracle exhibits more
faith in medicine than in God. As the world grows ever more intercon-
nected, twenty-first-century American Protestants may increasingly combine the prayer of faith with modern medicine in their quests for healing
amidst unprecedented threats to health.

NOTES

1 Francis MacNutt, *The Healing Reawakening: Reclaiming Our Lost Inheritance* (Grand Rapids, MI: Chosen, 2005), 125.
2 Jacalyn Duffin, *Medical Miracles: Doctors, Saints, and Healing in the Modern World* (New York: Oxford University Press, 2008), 8.
3 Martin Luther, *Sermons on the Gospel of St. John, Chapters 14–16*, in *Luther's Works*, vol. 24 (St. Louis, MO: Concordia, 1986), 367.

4 Martin Luther, quoted in George Cheever, *Religious and Moral Anecdotes: Carefully Selected and Classified* (London: Griffin, 1849), 270.

5 Martin Luther, "Whether One Should Flee from a Deadly Plague – To Rev. Dr. John Hess," in *Luther's Works*, vol. 43 (St. Louis, MO: Concordia, 1968), 132.

6 John Calvin, "James 5:14," in *Commentaries on the Catholic Epistles*, ed. John Owen (Grand Rapids: MI: Christian Classics Ethereal Library), www.ccel.org; John Wilkinson, "The Medical History of John Calvin," *Proceedings of the Royal College of Physicians of Edinburgh* vol. 22 (1992), 368.

7 John Calvin, *Writings on Pastoral Piety*, ed. Elsie Anne McKee (New York: Paulist, 2001), 128.

8 Matthew Niederhuber, "The Fight over Inoculation during the 1721 Boston Smallpox Epidemic," *Science in the News* (Cambridge, MA: Harvard University Graduate School of Arts and Sciences, 2014), http://sitn.hms.harvard.edu/flash/special-edition-on-infectious-disease/2014/the-fight-over-inoculation-during-the-1721-boston-smallpox-epidemic/.

9 Heather Curtis, *Faith in the Great Physician: Suffering and Divine Healing in American Culture, 1860–1900* (Baltimore: Johns Hopkins University Press, 2007), 28–29.

10 Rustin E. Brian, *Jacob Arminius: The Man from Oudewater* (Eugene, Ore.: Cascade, 2015), 89; E. Brooks Holifield, *Health and Medicine in the Methodist Tradition: Toward a Journey of Wholeness* (Eugene, OR: Wipf & Stock, 1986), 114.

11 John Wesley, quoted in Robert Southey, *The Life of Wesley; And the Rise and Progress of Methodism* (London: Longman, 1820), 243.

12 John Wesley, *Primitive Physick; Or, An Easy and Natural Method of Curing Most Diseases* (London: Hall, 1747), vii.

13 John Wesley, "The Nature of Enthusiasm" (1755), in *The Works of the Reverend John Wesley, A.M.*, ed. John Emory, 5th. ed, vol. I (New York: Emory & Waugh, for the Methodist Episcopal Church, 1831), 332.

14 John Wesley, quoted in Southey, *Life of Wesley*, 277.

15 John Wesley, "Letter to Charles Wesley," September 28, 1760, in *The Works of the Reverend John Wesley*, ed. John Emory (New York: Methodist Episcopal Church, 1831), 662.

16 John Wesley, quoted in Southey, *Life of Wesley*, 277.

17 Samuel A. Gum, "Philadelphia Under Siege: The Yellow Fever of 1793," *Center for the Book* (Summer 2010), www.pabook.libraries.psu.edu/literary-cultural-heritage-map-pa/feature-articles/philadelphia-under-siege-yellow-fever-1793.

18 Paul G. Chappell, "Origins of the Divine Healing Movement in America," *Spiritus: ORU Journal of Theology* vol. 1, no. 1 (1985), 10.

19 Rosemary D. Gooden, "Introduction," in Mrs. Edward Mix, *Faith Cures & Answers to Prayer* (Syracuse, NY: Syracuse University Press, 2002), xxii, xxxii.

20 Mix, *Faith Cures*, 22.

21 Jennifer A. Miskov, *Life on Wings: The Forgotten Life and Theology of Carrie Judd Montgomery (1858–1946)* (Cleveland, TN: CPT, 2012), 21.

22 Phoebe Palmer, *The Way of Holiness: With Notes by the Way; Being a Narrative of Religious Experience Resulting from a Determination to be a Bible Christian* (New York: Palmer & Hughes, 1867), 43, 60, 105.

23 Miskov, *Life on Wings*, 207.

24 John Alexander Dowie, *Doctors, Drugs and Devils: Or, the Foes of Christ the Healer* (Zion, IL: Zion Printing and Publishing House, 1901).

25 Charles Cullis, *The Seventeenth Report of the Consumptives' Home: And Other Institutions Connected with a Work of Faith, to September 30, 1881* (Boston: Willard Tract Repository, 1881), 28.

26 Holifield, *Health and Medicine*, 53–55.

27 James Monroe Buckley, *An Address on Supposed Miracles Delivered Monday, September 20, 1875, before the New York Ministers' Meeting of the M. E. Church* (New York: Hurd & Houghton, 1875), 23, 26, 45; Buckley, *Faith-Healing, Christian Science, and Kindred Phenomena* (New York: Century Company, 1892), 46.

28 George M. Marsden, *Fundamentalism and American Culture* (New York: Oxford University Press, 2006), 17, 118.

29 Cecil M. Robeck, Jr., *The Azusa Street Mission and Revival: The Birth of the Global Pentecostal Movement* (Nashville: Nelson, 2006), 142.

30 Kemp Pendleton Burpeau, *God's Showman: A Historical Study of John G. Lake and South African/American Pentecostalism* (Oslo: Refleks, 2004), 155–156.

31 Kate Bowler, *Blessed: A History of the American Prosperity Gospel* (New York: Oxford University Press, 2013), 19, 44.

32 Kenneth E. Hagin, *God's Medicine* (Tulsa, OK: RHEMA, 1977), 26–27.

33 David Edwin Harrell, *Oral Roberts: An American Life* (San Francisco: Harper & Row, 1985), 91, 102, 125, 183–86, 212, 262, 299, 333, 386; Harrell, *All Things Are Possible: The Healing and Charismatic Revivals in Modern America* (Bloomington: Indiana University Press, 1975), 90.

34 Kathryn Kuhlman, *I Believe in Miracles: Streams of Healing from the Heart of a Woman of Faith*, rev. ed. (Gainesville, FL: Bridge-Logos, 1962; 1992), 224, 228–229.

35 Kuhlman, *I Believe in Miracles*, 1–2.

36 Duffin, *Medical Miracles*, 7–8.

37 Kathryn Kuhlman, *God Can Do It Again: Amazing Testimonies Wrought by God's Extraordinary Servant*, rev. ed. (Gainesville, FL: Bridge-Logos, 1969; 1993); Kathryn Kuhlman, *Nothing Is Impossible with God: Modern-Day Miracles in the Ministry of a Daughter of Destiny*, rev. ed. (Gainesville, FL:

Bridge-Logos, 1974; 1999), 73–100; Amy Collier Artman, *The Miracle Lady: Kathryn Kuhlman and the Transformation of Charismatic Christianity* (Grand Rapids, MI: Eerdmans, 2019), 62.

38 Carol Wimber, *John Wimber: The Way It Was*, 2nd ed. (London: Vineyard Churches UK, 2019), 110.

39 John Wimber and Kevin Springer, *Power Healing* (San Francisco: Harper & Row, 1987); Wimber, *John Wimber*, 167, 195.

40 Randy Clark, *Lighting Fires* (Nashville: Thomas Nelson, 2011); Global Awakening, https://globalawakening.com/, accessed April 3, 2020.

41 Bill Johnson, *When Heaven Invades Earth: A Practical Guide to a Life of Miracles*, rev. ed. (Shippensburg, PA.: Destiny Image, 2003), 21.

42 Cal Pierce, *Preparing the Way: The Reopening of the John G. Lake Healing Rooms in Spokane, Washington* (Hagerstown, MD: McDougal, 2001), 15, 105; Healing Rooms Ministries, "Disclaimer," https://healingrooms.com/index .php?src=johnglake&document=69, accessed April 3, 2020.

43 Bethel Church, Redding, www.facebook.com/bethel.church.redding/, accessed April 3, 2020; Healing Rooms Ministries, www.facebook.com/hea lingrooms/, accessed April 3, 2020.

44 Annelise Pierce, "Bethel Church's Bill Johnson Compares COVID Vaccines to 'Mark of the Beast,'" *ShastaScout*, October 15, 2021, http://shastascout.org /bethel-churchs-bill-johnson-compares-covid-vaccines-to-mark-of-the-beast /, accessed December 1, 2021; R. V. Scheide, "Bethel Church Joins Shasta County Anti-Vaccination Crusade," *Food for Thought*, October 13, 2021, http://anewscafe.com/2021/10/13/redding/bethel-church-joins-shasta-countys-anti-vaccination-crusade/, accessed December 1, 2021.

45 Michael Gryboski, "New Documentary 'Children of Faith Assembly' Takes on Controversial Faith-Healing Church Connected to 91 Deaths," *The Christian Post*, April 16, 2015, www.christianpost.com/news/new-documentary-children-of-faith-assembly-takes-on-controversial-faith-healing-church-connected-to-91-deaths.html.

46 Gill Gillian, *Mary Baker Eddy* (Cambridge, MA: Perseus Books, 1999), 655, 667; Rodney Stark, "The Rise and Fall of Christian Science," *Journal of Contemporary Religion* vol. 13, no. 2 (1998), 190–191; Donald Prothero and Timothy D. Callahan, *UFOs, Chemtrails, and Aliens: What Science Says* (Bloomington: Indiana University Press, 2017), 165; Caroline Fraser, *God's Perfect Child: Living and Dying in the Christian Science Church*, 2nd ed. (New York: Picador, 2019), 518.

47 N. Kiran Chand, H. Bala Subramanya, and G. Venkateswara Rao, "Management of Patients Who Refuse Blood Transfusion," *Indian Journal of Anaesthesia* vol. 58, no. 5 (2014), 658–664; Jehovah's Witnesses, "2019 Grand Totals," www.jw.org/en/library/books/2019-service-year-report/201 9-grand-totals/, accessed April 3, 2020; Jehovah's Witnesses, "Our Readers Ask . . . Do Jehovah's Witnesses Practice Faith Healing?" *Watchtower*

Online Library, https://wol.jw.org/en/wol/d/r1/lp-e/2010729#h=2, accessed April 3, 2020.

48 Claudia Kalb et al., "Faith and Healing," *Newsweek*, November 10, 2003, 44–56.

49 Rodney Stark, *What Americans Really Believe: New Findings from the Baylor Surveys of Religion* (Waco, TX: Baylor University Press, 2008), 57.

50 Robert D. Orr, "Responding to Patient Beliefs in Miracles," *Southern Medical Journal* vol. 100 (December 2007), 1263.

51 Michael J. Balboni and Tracy A. Balboni, *Hostility to Hospitality: Spirituality and Professional Socialization within Medicine* (New York: Oxford University Press, 2020), 42.

52 Candy Gunther Brown, *The Healing Gods: Complementary and Alternative Medicine in Christian America* (New York: Oxford University Press, 2013), 16.

53 Interview by author, telephone, January 15, 2008.

54 Eric Patterson and Edmund J. Rybarczyk, eds., *The Future of Pentecostalism in the United States* (Lanham, MD: Rowman & Littlefield, 2007), 3.

55 John Oliver Means, ed., *The Prayer-Gauge Debate* (Boston: Congregational Publishing Society, 1876), https://quod.lib.umich.edu/cgi/t/text/text-idx?c=moa&cc=moa&sid=95e3f6e828e116b80d4cccd93c806bc1&view=text&rgn=main&idno=AGA3363.0001.001.

56 Randolph C. Byrd, "Positive Therapeutic Effects of Intercessory Prayer in a Coronary Care Unit Population," *Southern Medical Journal* vol. 81 (1988), 826–829; William S. Harris et al., "A Randomized, Controlled Trial of the Effects of Remote, Intercessory Prayer on Outcomes in Patients Admitted to the Coronary Care Unit," *Archives of Internal Medicine* vol. 159 (1999), 2273–2278; Dale A. Matthews, Sally M. Marlowe, and Francis MacNutt, "Effects of Intercessory Prayer on Patients with Rheumatoid Arthritis," *Southern Medical Journal* vol. 93 (December 2000), 1177–1186; Candy Gunther Brown, Stephen C. Mory, Rebecca Williams, and Michael J. McClymond, "Study of the Therapeutic Effects of Proximal Intercessory Prayer (STEPP) on Auditory and Visual Impairments in Rural Mozambique," *Southern Medical Journal* vol. 103, no. 9 (2010), 864–869.

57 Herbert Benson et al., "Study of the Therapeutic Effects of Intercessory Prayer (STEP) in Cardiac Bypass Patients: A Multicenter Randomized Trial of Uncertainty and Certainty of Receiving Intercessory Prayer," *American Heart Journal* vol. 151 (2006), 934–942.

58 Neal Vahle, *The Unity Movement: Its Evolution and Spiritual Teachings* (Philadelphia: Templeton Foundation Press, 2002), 246–247.

59 Leanne Roberts, Irshad Ahmed, and Andrew Davison "Intercessory Prayer for the Alleviation of Ill Health," *Cochrane Database of Systematic Reviews* 2 (2009), art no. CD000368, doi:10.1002/14651858.CD000368.pub3: 15.

60 Benny Hinn, *Lord, I Need a Miracle* (Nashville: Thomas Nelson, 1993).

61 Mahesh Chavda, *Only Love Can Make a Miracle* (Charlotte, NC: Mahesh Chavda Ministries, 2002), 80–81.

62 Daniel Ekechukwu and Reinhard Bonnke, *Raised from the Dead: A 21st-Century Miracle Resurrection Story!* DVD (Orlando: Christ for All Nations, 2003).

63 Global Medical Research Institute, www.globalmri.org/, accessed April 3, 2020.

64 Clarissa Romez, David Zaritzsky, and Joshua W. Brown, "Case Report of Gastroparesis Healing: 16 Years of a Chronic Syndrome Resolved after Proximal Intercessory Prayer," *Complementary Therapies in Medicine* vol. 43 (2019), 289–294; Clarissa Romez, Kenn Freedman, David Zaritsky, and Joshua W. Brown, "Case Report of Instantaneous Resolution of Juvenile Macular Degeneration Blindness after Proximal Intercessory Prayer," *Explore* (2020), 1–5.

65 Philip Jenkins, *The New Faces of Christianity: Believing the Bible in the Global South* (New York: Oxford University Press, 2006); M. V. Gumede, *Traditional Healers: A Medical Practitioner's Perspective* (Braamfontein: Skotville, 1990), 38, 203.

66 Pew Forum on Religion and Public Life, *Spirit and Power – A 10-Country Survey of Pentecostals* (Washington, DC: Pew Forum, October 5, 2006), www.pewforum.org/2006/10/05/spirit-and-power/.

67 Candy Gunther Brown, *Testing Prayer: Science and Healing* (Cambridge, MA: Harvard University Press, 2012), 190–192.

68 Harvey Cox, *Fire from Heaven: The Rise of Pentecostal Spirituality and the Reshaping of Religion in the Twenty-First Century* (Reading, MA: Addison-Wesley, 1995), xv.

69 Candy Gunther Brown, ed., *Global Pentecostal and Charismatic Healing* (New York: Oxford University Press, 2011), 21.

70 Kimberly Alexander, *Pentecostal Healing: Models in Theology* (Blandford Forum: Deo, 2006), 102.

14 Mental Illness

HEATHER HARTUNG VACEK

In 2016, Michael Emlet, a family doctor turned biblical counselor, urged fellow caregivers to be neither too suspicious of, nor too ready to affirm, medical diagnostic labels in their work. Writing to other Protestants, the theologically trained physician affirmed the value of the Bible to treat mental illness, supplemented by psychiatric insight. Christians "can't afford to keep our heads in the sand with a dismissive and isolationist posture," he proclaimed. "Nor can we afford simply to accept the entire psychiatric diagnostic enterprise at face value. We need a balanced, biblically (and scientifically!) informed approach."[1]

Like many before and after him, Emlet integrated scientific and spiritual counsel in response to suffering. Three centuries earlier, the New England clergyman Cotton Mather had also combined medical knowledge, theological wisdom, and practical advice in hopes of ushering in healing for mental ailments.[2] To be sure, much changed between when Mather and Emlet dispensed counsel, but both attributed ultimate healing to God. Though believers across time drew different conclusions based on their contexts, they endeavored to tend to mental illness faithfully, effectively, and with attentiveness to religious and secular knowledge.

This chapter traces developments in American Protestant responses to mental illness from Mather's world to Emlet's. The professionalization of medicine, shifting theological emphases, and cultural forces shaped reactions that ranged from benign neglect by many to impassioned advocacy by a few. Christians enter the narrative in various roles: ministers, physicians, sufferers, family members, advocates, seminary professors, and a variety of mental health professionals. The identities of some spanned those categories. Across time, churchgoers and religious leaders deployed terms for distress that included distraction, possession, madness, melancholy, insanity, mental illness, and later, diagnostic terms such as depression, bipolar disorder, post-traumatic stress disorder, and schizophrenia. Regardless of labels, as individuals and groups of believers thought about mental illness, sought meaning, and responded amid distress, their context-specific claims of what seemed awry shaped assessments of how best to deploy available resources.

MENTAL ILLNESS IN THE COLONIAL ERA

In the colonial era, physical and mental suffering prompted believers to turn toward God. Before the rise of scientific medicine, clergy served as authoritative guides in navigating distress as families and communities provided care for sufferers. Rather than stigmatizing ailments, Protestants understood illness as part of creation, an expected part of life, and a condition that warranted response from those nearby. Many colonial European-Americans worshipped in churches molded by a Reformed Calvinist theology, a theological system that foregrounded a sovereign God in covenant relationship with humans. In that context, right relationship with God formed the aim of the life of faith and fashioned responses to suffering, including mental illness.

As broadly educated public intellectuals, ministers like the Puritan leader Cotton Mather (1663–1728) spoke authoritatively not only about religion but also about health and healing. In 1724, Mather completed *The Angel of Bethesda*, the only comprehensive medical volume in the North American colonies. Drawing from centuries of medical wisdom, the text offered spiritual counsel and pragmatic advice. The clergyman viewed the experience of illness as wasted if not used for spiritual benefit and argued sickness should prompt believers to search their souls and turn to God for healing.[3] Chapters on "Madness" and "Melancholy" described symptoms of mental illness, speculated about causes, and suggested treatments. Mather offered advice alongside a primitive medical establishment he both trusted and challenged. The minister deployed his intellectual authority to adjudicate helpful and harmful medical care. He recommended medical assistance for ailing family members but also bemoaned the "Uncertainties of the PHYSICIANS" and sparred with the nascent medical community about the safety of vaccinations, which he supported more strongly than many doctors.[4]

Mather understood sin – whether personal or original – as being at the root of illness, but no more so for mental than physical ailments. The cause of much sickness and mental distress remained a mystery, but Mather speculated that sins against God (e.g., "willful repudiations" of God's covenants and critiques of clergy) could cause madness.[5] He also assumed the devil's work to thwart God's will in the world might bring mental illness. Many, including Mather's father Increase, understood a role for the devil in provoking believers to suicide. In later centuries, the impulse to end one's life would be understood as the result of deep depression and diagnosed as illness, but Increase Mather proclaimed "self murder" as evidence of disbelief and sin.[6] Similarly, spiritual leader Sarah Osborn (1714–1796) blamed sin and demonic enticement for her suicidal temptations.[7] The senior Mather preached about suicide in hopes of preventing its occurrence; Osborn shared her experience to help others avoid similar distress. Both displayed awareness of sin as a possible cause of life-threatening illness and centered their reflections on right relationship with God.

Despite presumptions that sin or supernatural forces lay behind mental maladies, little actual stigma surrounded sufferers. Cotton Mather's discussion of madness and melancholy avoided direct blame for those distressed. In contrast, he offered contempt for individuals afflicted with venereal diseases, refusing even to present remedies for those ailments. Wide acceptance of mentally ill clergy also demonstrated that the stigma that would later thwart Christian responses to mental illness had not yet emerged. The experiences of clergymen like the Revs. Joseph Moody and Samuel Checkly, whose ministries continued despite their odd behavior, displayed public provision for authority figures that experienced mental distress.[8] Moody proved unable to appear in public without a handkerchief over his face and preached with his back to his congregation. After personal losses, Checkley lost the ability to speak without weeping and delivered sermons in gibberish.

Mather assumed Christian discipleship required caring for all neighbors with "patience, generosity, and humor," including those with mental illnesses.[9] With little social infrastructure, and before the rise of formal or systematized medical treatments, care of mentally ill citizens fell to colonial families and local communities. Public almshouses and legal guardianship provisions enabled communities to provide care when the burden proved too great for families.

Mather prescribed spiritual and material responses to mental maladies, foremost among them prayer. The medicinal recommendations he compiled included topical, ingested, and behavioral remedies that ranged from the astute to the absurd, including careful attention to diet, encouragement for outdoor exercise, herbal remedies, leeches for bloodletting, and "Living Swallows, cut in two, and laid reeking hot unto the shaved Head."[10] Along with providing relief, Mather's prescriptions served primarily to prompt believers to forge a faithful relationship with God, the giver of life and source of salvation.[11] Given Mather's broad religious and societal authority, many colonial sufferers and those who cared for them heeded his counsel.

MENTAL ILLNESS IN THE REVOLUTIONARY ERA

By the Revolutionary era, the rise of secular healing vocations began to supplement the Protestant quest for right relationship with God. The work of physician and patriot Benjamin Rush (1746–1813) exemplified that shift. While Colonial Protestants identified the dilemma presented by mental illness as distancing believers from God, after a dose of Enlightenment empiricism later churchgoers pivoted to see suffering *itself* as the problem. Simultaneously, epistemological shifts ushered in an optimism that human intellect would uncover solutions to all problems, including mental illness.

Rush combined childhood lessons from the Presbyterian church about an active faith with the hope he later found in Universalist teachings of universal salvation. This pairing of religious convictions – combined with a focus on biological causes for illness – shaped Rush's understanding of human suffering. Because God equipped humans to find solutions to suffering and made salvation available to all, disease proved a reality of embodied existence in need of healing – rather than evidence of sin or even simply a prompt to turn toward God.

In 1812 the doctor published *Medical Inquiries and Observation upon the Diseases of the Mind*, which systematized observations about the symptoms, causes, and treatments for mental maladies. Rush assumed naturalistic and biological rather than supernatural causes for mental disorders and named malfunctions in the vascular system as the cause of physical and mental illnesses. As a result, Rush recommended treatments to balance disrupted physical processes that included bloodletting, purges, and dietary changes. He identified predispositions to suffering that included falls, isolation, great pain, intense study, extravagant joy, grief, singleness, poverty, and creative professions.[12] In addition, Rush and others suspected that excessive religious enthusiasm could prompt mental illness.[13]

Rush's categorized observations began the country's formal transition to a medicalized understanding of mental illness. Scientific systematization also challenged sin as the sole source of mental illness. Rush acknowledged this when he contended that many "anti-social" behaviors some considered sinful, including "suicide, impulse to murder, habitual lying, drunkenness, and compulsive stealing," might instead have biological roots.[14] Even in the case of suicide, Rush refused to declare that those who took their lives had committed an unpardonable sin.

Like Mather, little stigma surrounded mental illness in Rush's accounts. He affirmed that the afflicted came from all corners of society. He recorded illness in women, men, leaders, laborers, investors, servants, and clergy and noted that mental illness sometimes emerged in "persons of exemplary piety and purity of character" with a randomness he likened to other natural phenomena such as earthquakes. Friends and family appeared in Rush's accounts, including his son, John, who spent decades institutionalized with a "deep melancholy" after killing a friend in a duel. Though Rush's writing avoided condemnation of sufferers, the Rush family never made John's condition public, indicating shame or stigma might lurk in some settings.[15]

Rush provided direct assistance to the mentally ill and advocated for worthy institutional care. A commitment to Christian charity fueled his public support for the creation of entities like the Philadelphia Humane Society (1780) and efforts by Quakers to establish the Pennsylvania Hospital (1751), the first in the colonies. When he joined that hospital's staff a quarter century later, he directed the ward for "maniacal patients," hoping to improve treatments that were sometimes neglectful or violent.[16]

As the new nation formed, the professionalization of medicine meant that doctors unseated clergy as the foremost intellectuals in matters of health and healing. Ministers continued to provide care for distressed congregants, but at times they also affirmed the superior authority of medical colleagues in matters of physical and mental illness. The Rev. Samuel Phillips, for example, urged parishioners to seek medical attention at "the first sign of distraction" and declared that perceptions that mental distress had nothing to do with biology were wrongheaded.[17] As the nineteenth century began, Christians sought the amelioration of mental illness, but their mode of participation had shifted and was poised to change again.

MENTAL ILLNESS IN NINETEENTH-CENTURY PROTESTANTISM

Nineteenth-century Protestant engagement centered on shaping institutionally based care for mental illness. For Protestants who were willing to work alongside the rapidly professionalizing medical establishment, advocacy for institution building opened vocational pathways unavailable to believers lacking training as clergy or physicians, or those barred from such careers by gender or social standing. Dorothea Dix's (1802–1887) pursuit of humane care for sufferers pioneered Christian advocacy on behalf of mentally ill Americans during the new nation's first century. By embodying a contagious moral authority rooted in Protestant faith, and fueled by scientific and political optimism, Dix operated with a new sort of public religious authority and helped launch and expand thirty American hospitals for the insane. As Dix worked, a combination of Enlightenment hopefulness, giddiness over the successful new nation, and confidence in the power of religion to bring change made a cure for all ills – medical or social – seem possible. Concurrently, a democratic spirit paired with energy from the religious revivals of the Second Great Awakening emboldened Protestants to take individual responsibility for matters of faith and social change. The American Protestant land-scape diversified significantly beyond broadly Calvinist theological roots during the nineteenth century, but believers of all stripes rallied around social issues including abolishing slavery, curbing intemperate drinking, and providing medical care.

Early in the century, Christians launched institutional responses to mental illness. In 1817 Quakers in Philadelphia opened the Friends Asylum for the Relief of Persons Deprived of the Use of Their Reason, the first dedicated institution for the insane in the United States. Private institutions like the Friends Asylum that initially offered care only to Quakers, however, failed to meet growing demand for specialized treat-ment. Dix laid claim to expanding care in institutions many hoped would cure mental illness, and helped launch public alternatives.

Dix, like Mather and Rush, felt a divine call to harness scientific advances to serve God's purposes in the world. The daughter of a Methodist itinerant minister in rural New England, she later moved to Boston and adopted what she saw as the more socially engaged faith of Congregationalism and its offshoot, Unitarianism. Dix taught school for many years, but not until her fifth decade did she find what seemed a God-given vocation. Teaching Sunday School in a city jail exposed Dix to the horrible conditions endured by inmates, many who lived with mental ailments. Alarmed by their distress, she set out to report on the conditions of sufferers around the country. As she visited alms-houses and other facilities where mentally ill citizens languished, Dix met non-institutionalized members of the social elite, clergy, phys-icians, and lawmakers. Those contacts formed an eager audience for her discoveries and enabled action. Dix learned of institutional needs from asylum physicians and pressed lawmakers and private citizens to commit financial resources to improve care. Her work to improve institutional conditions tapped into the optimistic Protestant sense of moral responsibility and, in a time of significant public infrastructure building, expanded the provision of care for mentally ill Americans.

The quality of medical treatments remained uneven during the nineteenth century, but scientific advances prompted professional specialization. By 1841, sixteen public and private mental hospitals operated in the United States and new institutions opened in the following years.[18] The first superintendents of those facilities formed a tight-knit group of physicians who formalized the practice of asylum medicine. Dix befriended the majority of the early "alienists" as she traveled. Most, like Dix, were Protestants who found divine purpose in their mission to help less-fortunate Americans.

Despite the formation of a medical guild devoted to the care of mentally ill citizens, treatment protocols lacked standardization until late in the century. Rush's 1812 treatise proved outdated long before the next general psychiatric text by an American appeared in 1883, and the classification of disorders remained relatively unchanged from the prior centuries; mania, monomania, melancholia, dementia, and idiocy formed the common diagnostic categories. Eventually, most alienists shifted from seeing inflammation of the blood vessels as the cause of mental illness to a conviction that irritation of the nervous system was at fault. As a result, doctors abandoned harsh bloodletting and purging treatments and sought gentler medicinal and psychological remedies. Asylum doctors assumed physical causes, but treatments often focused on presumed behavioral deviations that were easier to identify and treat, including "intemperance, masturbation . . . faulty education . . . excessive religious enthusiasm, jealousy, and pride."[19] Precise etiologies remained mysterious, but alienists proved optimistic about the healing power of the sequestered asylum care they curated.

Notwithstanding Dix's advocacy and the commitment of other Christians, optimism about the curative potential of asylum care proved unrealistic. By the late nineteenth century, demand for specialized care far exceeded capacity; squalid, crowded institutions and an increasing number of chronic patients ignited suspicion about those suffering with mental illness. Americans increasingly deemed one another valuable members of society based on economic productivity; those unable or unwilling to work, including the poor and the mentally ill, emerged as problematic citizens. In addition, cures for physical ailments appeared more readily than remedies for mental illness, deepening wariness that those who experienced mental distress might be complicit in their affliction. Because persons confined to asylums were detached from dreams of

American progress and prosperity, stigma became firmly affixed to the nation's mentally ill and the presumed economic drain they represented. Eventually this stigma would inhibit Protestant engagement with sufferers, but Dix's example of public advocacy as a "sacred cause" and her assertion that all were worthy of care opened avenues for lay Protestants to work alongside clergy and medical professionals.[20]

MENTAL ILLNESS IN THE TWENTIETH CENTURY

During the twentieth century, providing quality care for the afflicted and reflecting on the meaning of suffering formed the foci of Protestant clergy, physicians, and laypersons. Anton Boisen (1876–1965), a Presbyterian clergyman with firsthand experience of mental illness, held a unique vantage point. In 1920, during the first of five hospitalizations for psychosis, Boisen encountered the theological and medical systems of prior centuries and found neither brought adequate healing. The future seminary professor viewed some mental illnesses as biological disorders to be treated by physicians but believed other forms of mental distress had spiritual causes and were best attended to by clergy and medical professionals properly informed about religion. In response, he worked to reconnect the spheres of medicine and religion that had cleaved in the prior century. Boisen pioneered clinical pastoral education for seminarians, established mental health chaplaincy, and paved the way for pastoral theology as a formal academic discipline. Seminary curricula changed in response and ministers sought continuing education in psychological methods to supplement their caregiving.

Medicine continued to serve as a vocational avenue for Protestants, including the psychiatrist Karl Menninger (1893–1990). The lifelong Presbyterian's medical practice combined scientific knowledge, a Calvinist sense of vocation, and a dose of Christian realism. Like Dix, Menninger invoked sin not as the cause of distress, but as the failure to respond to those in need. Within a decade of entering medical practice in Kansas, Menninger formalized his long-standing interest in mentally ill patients by opening a residential psychiatric hospital, the Menninger Sanitarium. Founded in the 1925, the later-renamed Menninger Clinic treated patients, trained psychiatrists, and attracted ministers for continuing education. For Menninger, science and religion formed part of the same whole, responding faithfully in the face of suffering; he saw little need to keep psychiatry and religion at a distance, even while adamant that primary authority in diagnosis and treatment rested with physicians.

Despite a century of dedicated medical attention to mental illness, underlying causes remained elusive. As professionals weighed biological and psychological origins, the arsenal of treatment options mushroomed, as did debate about best approaches. Psychiatrists deployed new drugs to calm agitated patients and advocated new remedies including malarial fever therapy, shock therapy, and prefrontal lobotomy.[21] Sigmund Freud's psychoanalytic techniques appeared and drew both discipleship and skepticism. Menninger deployed a combination of psychodynamic, developmental, biological, and adaptive explanations, and rejected supernatural causes, moral failures, and heredity at the root of mental illness. Treatment innovations, however, proved difficult to deploy in overpopulated hospitals, and new medical technologies brought some comfort but few cures.

Alongside individual vocational pursuits, groups of Protestants pursued collective advocacy. Asylums including the Dutch Reformed Pine Rest Christian Hospital joined earlier Quaker institutions in providing alternatives to state-run facilities.[22] American Mennonites, motivated by the deplorable conditions they discovered serving as conscientious objectors in public mental hospitals during World War II, opened seven mental health centers under the auspices of the Mennonite Mental Health Services. Collective advocacy extended beyond institutions. In 1947, the ecumenical Chicago Church Federation urged the state to remedy institutional care and encouraged churchgoers to become knowledgeable advocates. In 1959, the Greater Minneapolis Council of Church Women partnered with state health and welfare agencies to promote the well-being of discharged patients.[23] In such work, mental hygiene efforts aimed at improving the respectability of American citizens often motivated Christian engagement. Widespread religious advocacy on behalf of mentally ill citizens peaked mid-century and dwindled by the century's end. Stigma deepened, and massive deinstitutionalization of public mental health facilities in the 1960s prompted a need for alternate care so sizable that collective Protestant efforts failed to provide solutions. Believers turned their attention to other social issues including impoverished foreign children, prayer in schools, and abortion.

Stigma deterred action and kept Protestants from admitting maladies. Portrayals of mental illness in film and print that aimed to remedy appalling institutional conditions instead influenced perceptions of sufferers as morally suspect and beyond help.[24] Menninger acknowledged this reality and lamented that the attitudes of "uninformed" Americans led to "cruel stigma ... in the minds of too many good people."[25] Because of stigma, Protestants frequently disguised the identities of sufferers. In

1968, an ordained Presbyterian elder wrote pseudonymously to divulge his experiences after his wife's bouts of severe depression.[26] Three decades later, an evangelical scholar declared, "Of all the forbidden subjects in the church, mental illness may be the surest conversation stopper, even though evidence suggests that it may be as pervasive in the church as it is in the broader society."[27] Despite widespread suffering, Protestants failed to integrate conversation about mental illness comfortably into their collective life, and the bulk of Protestant reaction did little to alleviate suffering or mitigate a sense of despair on the part of those directly affected.

MENTAL ILLNESS IN THE TWENTY-FIRST CENTURY

In the twenty-first century, the failure of medical science to guarantee cures and some easing of stigma has enabled lay and ordained believers to claim a reshaped authority to speak about mental illness.[28] Churchgoers hoped transparent conversation – theological and practical – would bring comfort, if not healing.

Greater understanding of illness has helped reduce stigma, which has led to new kinds of public conversations. Believers have described suffering in detail. They have named suicidal thoughts, hallucinations, fear, and deep darkness and wondered how the church contributed to mental health.[29] Writers have confessed experience with anxiety,[30] depression,[31] bipolar disorder,[32] schizophrenia,[33] and suicide.[34] Greater public awareness of mental illness and the input of notable Christians have helped open discussion. Following their son's suicide, Kay Warren and her husband, well-known evangelical pastor Rick Warren, spoke frequently about the need for churches to respond more quickly and faithfully.[35] Similarly, writer Amy Simpson's book about growing up with a mentally ill mother inspired others to speak.[36] Popular publications profiled diverse sufferers: men, women, children, professors, artists, writers, and the unemployed. A notable change from the prior century was the appearance of clergy as those afflicted.[37] Episcopal priest Kathryn Greene-McCreight discussed depression in popular periodicals and her book *Darkness Is My Only Companion*.[38] Scholar and African Methodist Episcopal minister Monica Coleman's *Bipolar Faith* profiled decades of struggle with illness.[39] Clerical accounts of mental illness included both practical and theological counsel.

Though more frequent conversation eased some discomfort with mental illness, stigma continued to shape Protestant experience.[40] Presbyterian pastor and future seminary president Craig Barnes, for example, relayed surprise in discovering that a congregant whom he had known for seven years had a son living with schizophrenia. Not until the crisis of the son's arrest did his mother share his illness and name her own need for care.[41] Questions posed to sufferers by fellow believers implied personal culpability: "'Are you secretly gay?' 'Do you have some unconfessed sin?' 'Are you possessed by a demon?'"[42] Stigma kept some clergy quiet about their own distress. Psychologist Matthew Stanford's research identified a "double stigmatization" of mental illness for clergy.[43]

In addition to testimony by laity and clergy, Christian scholars weighed in. Reformed theologian John Swinton's work proved influential among American Protestants and offered theological reflection on suffering and disability that pointed believers toward faithful action.[44] Fuller Seminary-trained clinical psychologist Marcia Webb explored how believers understood mental disorder in *Toward a Theology of Psychological Disorder*.[45] Focused theological work was supplemented by theologically trained health professionals who dispensed prescriptions for faithful navigation of mental health care.[46] Twentieth-century theological accounts foregrounded human flourishing, demonstrating a broader post-Enlightenment anthropological turn in theological reflection. John Swinton's definition of mental health centered human experience: "Mental health problems are unique experiences that occur in the lives of irreplaceable individuals who have their own unique stories, histories, dreams, and desires; people who are deeply loved by God, and whom God desires God's church to love without boundaries."[47]

Alongside ongoing debate about the origins of mental illness, believers offered reasons that suffering might be advantageous. In 1976, a Yale professor had linked the heightened self-awareness brought about by mental illnesses to greater sensitivity to the self and greater possibilities for "high spiritual accomplishments."[48] A similar sense that God and humans could bring good out of suffering and that "suffering is soul-making" continued in twenty-first century conversation.[49] After the suicide of her son, for example, Christine Scheller shared, "I trust that for me the crucible will forge a better person, and lead to peace."[50] Twenty-first century Protestants professed the reality of mental illness and, as churchgoers had for centuries, tried to understand their distress through the eyes of faith.

Believers turned to a combination of secular and sacred cures. Though rarely discussed in earlier popular publications, the use of drugs to treat mental illnesses appeared frequently and largely unquestioned in twenty-first-century accounts. "Thank God for pharmaceuticals," proclaimed clergyman Matt Gaventa in response to his father's clinical depression.[51] When surveyed, many clergy voiced little concern about relief via psychiatric pharmaceuticals, believing medication should be used, either in moderation or any time it could ease symptoms.[52] At times, however, reservations appeared. Anglican scholar Joel Scandrett named his use of antidepressants but noted the limits of drugs, especially as they might mute "emotions that are essential components of spiritual maturity."[53] Protestants also named relief and comfort in mental illness that came from religious practice. Evangelical personality Joni Eareckson Tada testified that prayers lifted her husband's depression.[54] Amy Simpson revealed that a spiritual experience had brought her assurance of God's presence amid her mother's illness.[55] Professional counseling also remained part of the mix of treatments. Debate about the most faithful relationship between Christian counseling and psychology occupied seminary professors but proved missing from conversations by laity and clergy.[56] Few sufferers, their family members, or ministers publicly questioned counseling methodologies – marking a dramatic change from the prior century when debate about psychology and psychiatry filled the pages of Protestant periodicals.[57]

Most discussion included a plea for Christians to take action. Churchgoers were called to educate themselves, offer support, and turn to God for healing.[58] Collective advocacy diversified as twenty-first century Protestants gathered for conferences to discuss mental health and new advocacy organizations emerged.[59] Believers attended events focused on responding well to mental illness, support groups like the Mental Health Faith Alliance and Fresh Hope offered companionship, and resources proliferated as denominations launched mental health initiatives.[60] Most frequently, Protestants called for accompaniment of those in distress, and named a Christian responsibility not to abandon the families of those who committed suicide or other sufferers.[61]

Finally, in the twenty-first century, the mental well-being of Protestants became an object of study. Social scientists explored whether religious beliefs and practices contributed to or detracted from mental illness. Sociologists investigated whether deviating from religious norms shaped mental health.[62] Public health professionals wondered how belief in biblical inerrancy shaped mental well-being.[63] Biblical counselors explored connections between seeking psychological help and the spiritual health of pastors.[64] Studies paid increasing attention to ways in which demographics – including gender, race and ethnicity – shaped perceptions of suffering and ecclesial responses.[65] Results differed about whether religious affiliation and practice contributed to mental health, but the relationship between faith and medicine proved intriguing for believers and scientists alike.

Suffering caused by mental maladies appeared consistently from the colonial era through the twenty-first century. Amid that distress and across more than three centuries, American Protestants sought to bring healing, make meaning, find treatments, and assess Christian responsibility in the face of mental illness. The public intellectual Rev. Cotton Mather, the biblical counselor Dr. Michael Emlet, and many believers in between deployed a mix of sacred and secular resources, as they thought best. The impulse to respond faithfully to suffering spanned both time and the diversity of Protestant belief and practice, but shifting medical protocols and changes in surrounding culture resulted in a variety of theological, intellectual, and practical reactions.

NOTES

1   Michael R. Emlet, "What's in a Name? Understanding Psychiatric Diagnoses," *Journal of Biblical Counseling* vol. 30, no. 1 (2016), 68.

2   Discussion of Cotton Mather, Benjamin Rush, Dorothea Dix, and Anton Boisen draws from chapter-length treatments of each in Heather H. Vacek, *Madness: American Protestant Responses to Mental Illness* (Waco, TX: Baylor University Press, 2015). Used with permission.

3   Cotton Mather, *The Angel of Bethesda*, ed. Gordon W. Jones (Barre, MA: American Antiquarian Society: Barre Publishers, 1972), 8–9.

4   Mather, *The Angel of Bethesda*, 186–191.

5   Vacek, *Madness*, 18.

6   Increase Mather, "A Call to the Tempted: A Sermon on the Horrid Crime of Self-Murder" (The Ethics of Suicide Digital Archive), accessed October 15, 2019, https://ethicsofsuicide.lib.utah.edu/selections/increase-mather/; Catherine A. Brekus, *Sarah Osborn's World: The Rise of Evangelical Christianity in Early America* (New Haven, CT: Yale University Press, 2013), 361.

7   Brekus, *Sarah Osborn's World*, 65–70.

8   Vacek, *Madness*, 22.

9   Vacek, *Madness*, 23. See also Brekus, *Sarah Osborn's World*, 218.

10   Vacek, *Madness*, 24.

11   See also Brekus, *Sarah Osborn's World*, 91.

12   Vacek, *Madness*, 41.

13   For more on the connections drawn between religious enthusiasm and mental illness, see Loren A. Broc, "Religion and Insanity in America from Colonial Times to 1900" (Ph.D. diss., University of Rochester, 2013).

14 Vacek, *Madness*, 40.

15 Vacek, *Madness*, 39–40, 45.

16 Vacek, *Madness*, 34, 51.

17 Vacek, *Madness*, 43.

18 Vacek, *Madness*, 75.

19 Vacek, *Madness*, 77; Gerald N. Grob, *The Mad Among Us: A History of the Care of America's Mentally Ill* (New York: Free Press, 1994), 59–60.

20 Vacek, *Madness*, 80.

21 Vacek, *Madness*, 131.

22 Vacek, *Madness*, 133.

23 Vacek, *Madness*, 140.

24 See Albert Q. Maisel, "Bedlam 1946: Most U.S. Mental Hospitals Are a Shame and a Disgrace," *Life*, May 6, 1946; Albert Deutsch, *The Shame of the States* (New York: Harcourt, Brace and Company, 1948); and Mary Jane Ward, *The Snake Pit* (New York: Random House, 1946).

25 Karl A. Menninger, *The Vital Balance: The Life Process in Mental Health and Illness* (New York: Viking Press, 1964), 408.

26 Jim Bryan, "Life's Hard Questions: How Should the Church Handle Mental Illness?" *Presbyterian Life*, September 1, 1968, 4–5.

27 Don E. Eberly, "Prayer, Prozac, and the Healing of America," *Christianity Today*, October 7, 1996, 59–61.

28 For discussion of the limitations of psychiatry, see Anne Harrington, *Mind Fixers: Psychiatry's Troubled Search for the Biology of Mental Illness* (New York: W. W. Norton & Company, 2019).

29 Michael R. Lyles, "Is Your Church Healthy for People with Mental Illness?" *Christianity Today*, October 2017, www.christianitytoday.com/pastors/201 7/october-web-exclusives/is-your-church-healthy-for-people-with-mental-illness.html.

30 Laura Turner, "The Gift of Fear," *Christianity Today*, July/August 2016, 76–78.

31 Dan G. Blazer, "The Depression Epidemic," *Christianity Today*, March 2009, 22–31; Frederick Niedner, "Barely Enough: Manna in the Wilderness of Depression," *Christian Century*, January 25, 2012, 11; Matt Gaventa, "What Love Can't Fix: My Dad's Descent into Depression," *Christian Century*, February 4, 2015, 10–11.

32 Jeff Gundy, "Darkness and Light: Jane Kenyon's Spiritual Struggle," *Christian Century*, January 24, 2006, 27; David Weiss, "God of the Schizophrenic: Rediscovering My Faith amid the Ravages of Mental Illness," *Christianity Today*, April 2011, 46.

33 Craig Barnes, "Demoniacs Have Names: A Challenge for Ministry," *Christian Century*, November 17, 2009, 11; Weiss, "God of the Schizophrenic," 43.

34 Sarah Pulliam Bailey, "Son of Obama Faith Adviser Dies in Apparent Suicide," *Christian Century*, January 8, 2014, 16; Gordon Marino, "Review of

Stay: A History of Suicide and the Philosophies against It," Christian
Century, April 30, 2014, 45–46. Some, including theologian John Swinton,
warned against the church's adoption of medical labels; see John Swinton,
"Time, Hospitality, and Belonging: Towards a Practical Theology of Mental
Health," *Word & World* vol. 35, no. 2 (2015), 172.

35 Ed Stetzer, "Suicide, Mental Illness, and the Church: An Interview with Kay
Warren," *Christianity Today*, October 2017, www.christianitytoday.com/e
dstetzer/2017/october/suicide-mental-illness-and-church-interview-with-
kay-warren.html.

36 Amy Simpson, *Troubled Minds: Mental Illness and the Church's Mission*
(Downers Grove, IL: InterVarsity Press, 2013).

37 Katelyn Beaty, "Staying Alive in a Suicidal World," *Christianity Today*, July/
August 2014, 28; William H. Hudnut, Jr., "Are Ministers Cracking Up?"
Christian Century, November 7, 1956, 1288.

38 Kathryn Greene-McCreight, "In God's Hands: Mental Illness and the Soul,"
Christian Century, May 2, 2006, 28–30; and *Darkness Is My Only
Companion: A Christian Response to Mental Illness* (Grand Rapids, MI:
Brazos Press, 2006).

39 Monica A. Coleman, *Bipolar Faith: A Black Woman's Journey in Depression
and Faith* (Minneapolis: Fortress Press, 2016). See also coverage of Evangelical
pastors Perry Noble and John Mark Comer in Beaty, "Staying Alive in
a Suicidal World," 28.

40 "10 Ways Mental Illness Is Stigmatized in the Church," 2013, http://amy
simpson.com/2013/06/10-ways-mental-illness-is-stigmatized-in-the-church
/; Robyn Henderson-Espinoza, "The Silent Stigma of Mental Illness in the
Church," *Soujourners*, May 10, 2017, https://sojo.net/articles/silent-stigma-
mental-illness-church.

41 Barnes, "Demoniacs Have Names," 11.

42 Weiss, "God of the Schizophrenic," 45.

43 Greg Warner, "When Depression Leads Pastors to Suicide," *Christian
Century*, December 1, 2009, 15.

44 John Swinton, *Resurrecting the Person: Friendship and the Care of People with
Mental Health Problems* (Nashville: Abingdon Press, 2000) and *From Bedlam
to Shalom: Towards a Practical Theology of Human Nature, Interpersonal
Relationships, and Mental Health Care* (New York: P. Lang, 2000).

45 Marcia Webb, *Toward a Theology of Psychological Disorder* (Eugene, OR:
Cascade Books, 2017), 5.

46 Michael R. Emlet, *Descriptions and Prescriptions: A Biblical Perspective on
Psychiatric Diagnoses and Medications* (Greensboro, NC: New Growth
Press, 2017). Matthew S. Stanford, *Grace for the Afflicted: A Clinical and
Biblical Perspective on Mental Illness* (Downers Grove, IL: Intervarsity Press,
2008).

47 Swinton, "Time, Hospitality, and Belonging," 173.

48 Louis K. Dupré, "Wounded Self: The Religious Meaning of Mental Suffering," *Christian Century*, April 7, 1976, 328–331.

49 Marino, "Review of *Stay: A History of Suicide and the Philosophies against It*," 46.

50 Christine A. Scheller, "In the Valley of the Shadow of Suicide: A Mother Catches Glimmers of Hope after Losing a Son," *Christianity Today*, April 24, 2009, 41.

51 Gaventa, "What Love Can't Fix," 11. See also: Weiss, "God of the Schizophrenic," 42, 44; Norman B. Bendroth, "Brainstorm: Finding Hope with William Styron," *Christian Century*, May 1, 2007, 9.

52 Ed Stetzer, "The Church and Mental Illness Part 2: Medicine and Therapy," *Christianity Today*, December 9, 2014, www.christianitytoday.com/edstet zer/2014/december/church-and-mental-illness-part-2-.html.

53 Joel Scandrett, "My Life with Antidepressants: They Helped, At Least in the Beginning," *Christianity Today*, March 4, 2009, 26.

54 Sarah Pulliam Bailey, "Suffering Servants: Chronic Pain and Depression Taught Joni Eareckson and Ken Tada to Put Each Other's Needs First," *Christianity Today*, April 2013, 69.

55 Amy Simpson, "The Shadow of Schizophrenia: Where God Was Amid My Mom's Mental Illness," *Christianity Today*, July/August 2013, 55.

56 See Eric L. Johnson, ed., *Psychology & Christianity: Five Views*, second ed. (Downers Grove, IL: IVP Academic, 2010) and Stephen P. Greggo and Timothy A. Sisemore, eds., *Counseling and Christianity: Five Approaches*, 1st ed. (Downers Grove, IL: IVP Academic, 2012).

57 Stetzer, "The Church and Mental Illness Part 2: Medicine and Therapy;" "Faith or Therapy First," *Christianity Today*, January/February 2015, 16. Evangelicals proved more suspicious of the secular medical and social scientific methods, placing more credence on scriptural wisdom and other religious sources of authority.

58 Amy Simpson, "My Top 5 Books on Mental Illness," *Christianity Today*, January/February 2013, 76.

59 Harold G. Koenig, *Faith and Mental Health: Religious Resources for Healing* (Philadelphia: Templeton Foundation Press, 2005).

60 See Grace Alliance, http://mentalhealthgracealliance.org/; Fresh Hope, http://freshhope.us/; *Comfort My People: A Policy Statement on Serious Mental Illness with Study Guide* (Presbyterian Church [USA] Advisory Committee on Social Witness Policy, 2008), http://oga.pcusa.org/publica tions/serious-mental-illness2008.pdf; the United Church of Christ Mental Health Network, http://mhn-ucc.blogspot.com/p/about.html; and the United Methodist Ministries in Mental Illness, www.umc.org/what-we-believe/ministries-in-mental-illness.

61 Bendroth, "Brainstorm," 10; Greene-McCreight, "In God's Hands: Mental Illness and the Soul," 29; Blazer, "The Depression Epidemic," 30.

62 A. H. Mannheimer and T. D. Hill, "Deviating from Religious Norms and the Mental Health of Conservative Protestants," *Journal of Religion and Health* vol. 54, no. 5 (2015).

63 Neal Krause and Kenneth I. Pargament, "Biblical Inerrancy and Depressive Symptoms," *Pastoral Psychology* vol. 67, no. 3 (2018).

64 E. D. Salwen, L. A. Underwood, G. S. Dy-Liacco, and K. R. Arveson, "Self-Disclosure and Spiritual Well-Being in Pastors Seeking Professional Psychological Help," *Pastoral Psychology* vol. 66, no. 4 (2017).

65 Tonya D. Armstrong, "African-American Congregational Care and Counseling: Transcending Universal and Culturally Specific Barriers," *Journal of Pastoral Care and Counseling* vol. 70, no. 2 (2016); Rosalyn Denise Campbell and Tenesha Littleton, "Mental Health Counselling in the Black American Church: Reflections and Recommendations from Counsellors Serving in a Counseling Ministry," *Mental Health, Religion & Culture* vol. 21, no. 4 (2018); and M. A. Robinson, S. Jones-Eversley, S. E. Moore, J. Ravenell, and A. Christson Adedoyin, "Black Male Mental Health and the Black Church: Advancing a Collaborative Partnership and Research Agenda," *Journal of Religion and Health* vol. 57, no. 3 (2018).

15 Protestant-Catholic Ecumenism and the Meanings of American Freedom

MAURA JANE FARRELLY

On February 27, 2010, the liberal columnist Nicholas Kristof published a piece in the *New York Times* in which he praised the work that evangelical, Catholic, and mainline Protestant relief groups had been doing in India, Africa, and especially Haiti, where an earthquake had killed more than 100,000 people a little more than a month earlier. Pointing specifically to an organization called "World Vision," an evangelical group that boasts of its partnerships with "all Trinitarian churches" and provides aid to people of all faiths in nearly 100 countries, Kristof wrote of the work he had witnessed while on assignment for the *Times* – including that of priests and nuns, whom he said he had seen in Africa "heroically caring for AIDS patients, even quietly handing out condoms." Kristof praised the efforts of religiously guided and ecumenically minded humanitarian groups like World Vision, calling them the "new internationalists." He then chastised his fellow liberals for believing that money from the United States government should not be channeled through faith-based organizations because such groups could not be trusted not to use the money for proselytizing.[1]

The same day Kristof published his column, the magazine *First Things* published an interview with the Catholic intellectual George Weigel. Weigel spoke specifically about the work he had done with *First Things'* founder, Richard John Neuhaus, a Roman Catholic priest who had died the year before. Neuhaus was a convert to Catholicism. Born in 1936, he was ordained originally by the Missouri Synod of the Lutheran Church – a conservative denomination that would suffer a schism fourteen years later, in 1974. Neuhaus followed the more progressive wing of the Missouri Synod, affiliating himself with what eventually became known as the Association of Evangelical Lutheran Churches. He maintained strong connections, however, with his former colleagues in the Missouri Synod.[2]

Those former colleagues – friendly, though they may have been – almost certainly did not approve of Richard John Neuhaus's conversion to Catholicism in 1991. Ten years after this cradle Lutheran became a Catholic, the Missouri Synod suspended a high-ranking pastor who had participated in a massive inter-faith service held in Yankee Stadium to honor the victims of the September 11 attacks. When explaining its decision, the Synod called the Catholic, Jewish, Muslim, and Hindu participants in the service "pagan clerics" and lamented that the Reverend David Benke had sent a "crystal clear signal" to people attending the service (or watching it on television) that "while there may be differences to how people worship and pray, in the end, all religions pray to the same God."[3]

It was a shocking statement. By 2001, the antagonistic posture toward ecumenism exhibited by the Missouri Synod had become fairly arcane in mainstream Christian circles, especially when it came to Protestant-Catholic relations. In fact, when asked which of *First Things'* contributions to the public discourse he was most proud of, George Weigel pointed specifically to the rapprochement that had come to characterize evangelical and Catholic interactions in the United States. *First Things* had given, in his words, "a platform to the new ecumenism embodied in 'Evangelicals and Catholics Together.'"[4]

ECT, as it is more commonly called, is a joint statement, written and released in 1994 by Fr. Richard John Neuhaus and Chuck Colson, a convert to evangelical Christianity who founded Prison Fellowship Ministries in 1976, after serving time in a federal penitentiary for his involvement in the Watergate scandal. ECT – along with its follow-up statement a year later, ECT II – was eventually signed by more than thirty scholars and religious leaders, including Mark Noll, the esteemed Notre Dame historian who was named one of the "25 Most Influential Evangelicals in America" by *Time* magazine in 2005; Pat Robertson, who vied for the Republican Party presidential nomination in 1988 and founded the Christian Broadcasting Network, which has been producing radio and television news programming from an overtly Evangelical perspective since 1961; and Fr. Avery Dulles, a Jesuit who, like Richard John Neuhaus, was a convert to Catholicism and had been teaching theology at Fordham University in 1994 when he signed ECT. Dulles would eventually be elevated to the College of Cardinals by Pope John Paul II in 2001.[5]

The evangelical and Catholic ecumenism embodied in ECT is very different from the ecumenism found at World Vision. Let us not forget that those priests and nuns Nicholas Kristof claimed to have seen handing out condoms were technically going against their church's teachings on birth control when they did so. Four years after Kristof published his column, World Vision was forced to back away from an announcement that it would start hiring people who were in same-sex marriages, in part because some Catholic donors to the organization balked at the idea.[6] Marriage is a sacrament in Catholicism – and is defined doctrinally, therefore, as a union between one man and one woman. World Vision's ecumenism has occasionally stumbled when trying to reconcile itself with Catholic beliefs that have social implications.

The ecumenism embodied in ECT has not been stymied by such disagreements, however, because social issues like birth control and gay marriage are precisely the foundation upon which the ecumenism of ECT is based. The Christian unity promoted in the document is political, rather than theological. ECT calls upon Christians of all stripes to put their theological differences aside so that they can work together to combat a host of legal and cultural influences at work in American society: abortion – which the statement calls "the leading edge of an encroaching culture of death"; multiculturalism – which the statement insists means "affirming all cultures but our own"; and secularism – which the signers of ECT believe has forced religion out of the public square; encouraged the government to replace families, churches, and voluntary associations in people's lives; promoted pornography, infidelity, and promiscuity in American culture; and led to a publicly funded education system that espouses "moral equivalence between the normative and the deviant."[7]

Regardless of why or how well Catholics and evangelical Protestants have been "coming together" in recent years, the phenomenon is remarkable because it is a radical departure from the trajectory that Catholics and Protestants were on for most of the last 400 years of America's history. Long before the United States was even the "United States" – back when it was still a collection of British colonies in North America – Protestants viewed Catholicism as a threat to national identity, individual liberty, personal salvation, and the stability of free government. Their fears continued up through the presidential campaign of John F. Kennedy, who famously met with the Greater Houston Ministerial Association in 1960 so that he could try to convince nervous Protestant voters that "I believe in an America where the separation between Church and State is absolute" and "no public official either requests or accepts instructions on public policy from the pope."[8]

Understanding why Protestants viewed Catholicism (if not necessarily Catholics themselves) with so much fear and loathing is important, because it reveals much about the evolution of American understandings of freedom, which for decades were forged unabashedly in opposition to the Catholic Church and its understanding of what freedom was and how people could attain it. To be sure, social issues like birth control and gay marriage have helped to create the "new ecumenism" that George Weigel spoke of in 2010 when recalling his work with Richard John Neuhaus. Just as important, however, have been the inequities that were caused by the advent of modern, industrial capitalism in the late nineteenth century. Those inequities forced American Protestants in the mid-twentieth century to stop using the Catholic Church as a foil when defining freedom and the conditions that sustain it.

When they accepted the premise of the New Deal programs put forward by Franklin Roosevelt, an Episcopalian, in the 1930s, and the Great Society programs put forward by Lyndon Johnson, a follower of the Disciples of Christ, three decades later, American Protestants accepted that the individualistic and "hands-off" approach to freedom that had been shaped by their theology was not enough to sustain freedom in the modern era. In an age of massive, multinational corporate conglomerates and the wealth polarization that such conglomerates made possible, America's Protestants understood that individual rights alone could not help people access the freedom that was available to them as human beings. Freedom needed more support than what the mere exercise of individual rights was able to provide. This new, more communally oriented understanding of freedom was compatible in some important ways with the understanding of freedom the Catholic Church had been putting forward for centuries.[9]

At the same time, the Vatican was challenged by forces in the twentieth century to adopt an understanding of freedom that *it* had vehemently rejected for centuries. Prior to the Second Vatican Council (1962–1965), the church–state separation enshrined in America's Bill of Rights was anathema to the Catholic Church. "Error has no rights" was the phrase that animated the Vatican's relations with secular authorities, and as the only earthly institution that contained the fullness of divine truth, the Catholic Church was believed to be the only proper partner for any state.[10]

But in the midst of the Cold War, Pope John XXIII worried that the world was being threatened by "a temporal order which some have wished to reorganize excluding God." Under such circumstances, any belief in God became preferable to Communism. The Pope convened the Second Vatican Council, therefore, to consider several modern questions, including the questions of religious liberty and ecumenism. The result was *Dignitatis humanae*, which recognizes religious freedom as a "social and civil right," grounded in "the dignity of the human person as this dignity is known through the revealed word of God and by reason itself." This understanding gave real weight to the power and obligation of individual conscience, and in so doing, it recognized as legitimate one of the pillars upon which the Protestant Reformation had been based.[11]

THE EARLY HISTORY OF AMERICAN ANTI-CATHOLICISM

Fears of Catholicism – or what many English-speaking Protestants in the early modern period called "Popery" – fueled the colonization of New England in the seventeenth century.[12] These fears also played an important role in tipping the cultural scales toward independence from Great Britain in the eighteenth century. Choosing to break from one's country, after all, is no easy endeavor – not just economically and militarily, but also psychologically. In the mid-1770s, an irrational but nevertheless *real* belief that King George III of England planned on "establishing" the Roman Catholic Church in America took root in the colonies. This belief helped many colonists who had been reluctant to see their king as hopelessly corrupt to finally get on board with the independence program.

The Quebec Act of 1774 did nothing more than tolerate the free practice of Catholicism in an overwhelmingly Catholic colony that England had acquired from France eleven years earlier, after winning the French and Indian War. In the lower thirteen colonies, however, the act was an interpreted as a clear sign that every English man and woman in North America would soon be subjected to what South Carolina's Judge William Henry Drayton called a "most cruel tyranny in Church and State ... fed with blood by the Roman Catholic doctrines." John Adams worried that "the barriers against popery, erected by our ancestors" would be "suffered and destroyed" by the Quebec Act, "to the hazard even of the Protestant religion." Alexander Hamilton told his fellow New Yorkers to fear the act. "Does not your blood run cold," he asked them, "to think an English Parliament should pass an Act for the establishment of Popery and arbitrary power?"[13]

By the time King George III approved the Quebec Act, Catholicism had been a bogeyman in British colonial America for quite some time. Indeed, nearly a century and a half earlier, John Winthrop had leveraged what were – already in 1630 – long-standing British fears of Catholicism to convince people they needed to move from England to Massachusetts. Journeys across the Atlantic Ocean were extraordinarily dangerous in the seventeenth century, and many of the people who subscribed to

Winthrop's Calvinist theology did not believe, at first, that such a journey was necessary. They shared his disdain for the Church of England, believing that church's ministers failed to provide the leadership God demanded. They were not convinced, however, that the Church of England's problems were so bad that true followers of Christ needed to leave.

To convince them, Winthrop reminded his co-religionists that French priests were working actively in North America to convert the native population to Catholicism. Under such circumstances, migration to the New World would be a "service to the church of great consequence," as the Puritans would be able to "raise a bulwark against the kingdom of Antichrist, which the Jesuits labor to rear up in those parts." As far as English society and the condition of the Church of England were concerned, Calvinists needed to understand just how bad things really were. "The fountains of learning and religion are so corrupted," the future governor of Massachusetts maintained, that "most children (even the best wits and fairest hopes) are perverted, corrupted, and utterly overthrown by the multitude of evil examples of the licentious government of those seminaries."[14]

The problem with England's schools and seminaries was that the leader of the Church of England, King Charles I, had publicly expressed his admiration for some of the key elements of Catholic theology. He had also taken a full-blown Catholic as his wife and tolerated all sorts of "popish ceremonies" within England's nominally Protestant church.[15] All good Puritans understood why this was a problem; John Winthrop wanted them to understand that it was not a problem that could be fixed by staying in England. To reform Christianity in their country, the "purifiers" needed to leave. They needed to go someplace new where they would be able to build a model society for the people back home to witness, learn from, and eventually replicate.

The relics of Catholicism that remained in the Church of England (also known as the "Anglican Communion") consisted primarily of the church's hierarchical structure – its deacons, who answered to priests, who answered to bishops – along with some of the church's prayer books and liturgical practices, which Puritans thought got in the way of an individual's ability to commune with God. People who subscribed to the theology of John Calvin believed every man, woman, and child was obliged to personally confront the reality of his or her sinfulness and accept the opportunity for salvation made available to humanity through the sacrifice of Christ. Rituals, sacraments, and the false authority of priests were thought to get in the way of that confrontation. The only authority any Christian needed was the authority of Scripture.

"Every man must give an account of himself to God," the Baptist minister John Leland wrote from his home in Massachusetts in 1791. The Bible was not "so intricate and high, that none but the letter learned ... can read it." The idea that "the ignorant part of the community are not capacitated to judge for themselves supports the Popish hierarchy." To truly realize his obligation to God, Leland believed, "every man ought to be at Liberty to serve God in that way that he can best reconcile it to his conscience."[16]

"Liberty," to use Leland's word, was extremely important to Calvinists in the seventeenth and eighteenth centuries – especially to Baptists like John Leland, who had a more individualistically oriented understanding of salvation than even the Congregationalists and Presbyterians with whom they shared a Calvinist theology. This emphasis on liberty is the reason New England's Puritans are still said to have come to North America in the name of "religious liberty," even though they hanged Quakers, banished many of their fellow Calvinists, railed against Catholics, and removed Indian children from their tribes in an effort to convert them to Christianity.[17] Many English Calvinists pointed to liberty as essential to the realization of God's wishes for humanity, even as they were also quite unwilling to tolerate "false religion" in the name of securing that liberty for everyone. Liberty was central to the way English Calvinists on both sides of the Atlantic understood themselves in the mid-seventeenth century, not just as people of God, but as people of England, as well. It was the reason the Puritans were so strongly opposed to the Catholic Church. Not only did that church thwart liberty by standing between the individual and God, it was also foreign. The leader of the Catholic Church did not live in London; he lived in Rome.

Gradually, this association between Christianity and liberty, liberty and Protestantism, and Protestantism and English identity became more diffuse in the Anglo-American world, spreading beyond the Calvinists who had emphasized the association early on and into the greater Anglican community, culminating in the Glorious Revolution in 1689. When they ousted their Catholic king, James II, and ignored the traditional line of monarchical succession so that they would not have to place his Catholic son on the throne, the predominantly Anglican members of England's Parliament set themselves up as global defenders of what they called "the Protestant Interest."[18] The purpose of government, they insisted, was to protect human freedom – and because "freedom," as they understood it, was defined in thoroughly Protestant terms, a Catholic like James II could never be the leader of a free state.

It was not that there was no freedom within Catholicism. It was that the Catholic understanding of freedom was radically different from the Protestant one – and unacceptable, therefore, to the Members of Parliament. For Protestants, freedom was the absence of mediation or outside restraint. It was the "power of acting as one thinks fit," in the words of the eighteenth-century English jurist William Blackstone, whose legal and philosophical commentaries were consulted by members of the First and Second Continental Congresses and the US Constitutional Convention. Blackstone understood that membership in a society meant that people couldn't *always* act as they thought fit; for the sake of peace, people came together and agreed to laws that restrained their behavior in some way. Such restraints, however, should extend "no farther than is necessary and expedient for the general advantage of the publick," according to Blackstone. Proper societies were ones that defined freedom as the absence of outside restraint, even as they accepted the necessity of certain restraints. Proper societies also understood that some freedoms – the freedom to own property, for instance, or to assemble openly with one's peers – were "a right inherent in us by birth." Such rights could not, therefore, ever be restrained, modified, or forfeited, regardless of what anyone perceived to be necessary.[19]

In contrast, the Catholic Church taught that freedom was the fulfillment of God's wishes for humanity – and this fulfillment could not be accomplished by any human being on his own. In this sense, John Leland's assessment of Catholicism was correct. For a Catholic – and particularly a Catholic who lived and worshipped before the Second Vatican Council brought changes to Catholicism in the 1960s – freedom was something to be sought and realized only through the body of the church.[20] Only when a man or woman finally understood and realized the will of God could true freedom be attained, and regardless of what Martin Luther had said in the sixteenth century about the importance of *sola scriptura*," Catholic leaders insisted that Scripture and human reason, on their own, were not enough to understand the will of God. People needed the guidance of bishops and theologians who had pondered the mysteries of Christianity for decades and consulted the writings of those who had pondered these same mysteries before them.

"How can it appear unto me that I may be assured that this Book is the word of God," one young Catholic convert asked his Protestant father in 1623. "I have ever found Protestants to be extremely puzzled in this point." *Sola scriptura* did not "carry credit sufficient whereupon to build and infallible Faith," the convert explained, because Scripture had been translated countless times over the centuries, and "Luther himself differeth in about 30 places ... in several translations of St. Matthew's Gospel." The Scriptures were not as "easy and plain" as Protestants like John Leland believed they were. "The Trinity, Unity in God, the Incarnation, Resurrection and Ascension of Christ, our most B[lessed] Savior ... do involve great and hidden mysteries and profound difficulties," the young man told his father. Only with the help of the "great Clerks and Holy Fathers" of the Catholic Church could the fullness of the Word of God be understood – and "freedom," in the Catholic understanding of the word, attained.[21]

For a Catholic, freedom was not something a person was born with, as people like John Leland and William Blackstone insisted; it was, rather, something a person *achieved*. The reason "many [people] imagine that the Church is hostile to human liberty," Pope Leo XIII explained, was that human beings tended to "pervert the very idea of freedom, or they extend it at their pleasure to many things in respect of which man cannot rightly be regarded as free."[22]

The ability to act "as one thinks fit" did not, in and of itself, constitute freedom, according to Leo. "Man is, indeed, free to obey his reason [and] to seek moral good," the pope observed. "Yet he is free also to turn aside to all other things; and in pursing the empty semblance of good, to disturb the rightful order and to fall headlong into the destruction which he has voluntarily chosen." Human beings had the power to think it "fit" to act in ways that were sinful – and the "possibility of sinning," Leo insisted, "is not freedom, but slavery." When a man sinned, he became a slave to the passions that fueled that sin – and people chose to sin because they were incapable, on their own, of understanding the will of God. "The condition of human liberty," therefore, "necessarily stands in need of light and strength to direct its actions to good and to restrain them from evil. Without this, the freedom of our will would be our ruin."[23]

Proper societies, the Catholic Church taught, were not societies that placed the fewest and least confining restraints on human behavior; they were, rather, societies where leaders and citizens alike were guided by the light and strength of the Catholic Church.[24] This pre-Vatican II understanding of church–state relations brought an unavoidable sense of urgency to beliefs like the one Sam Adams expressed in 1772, when he insisted that Catholics, by "recognizing the pope in so absolute a manner" had introduced into government "that solecism in politicks, Imperium in imperio, leading directly to the worst anarchy and confusion, civil discord, war and bloodshed."[25]

Imperium in imperio – a state within a state. When the Revolutionary War was over and the colonies had achieved their independence from Great Britain, would American Catholics accept that the new states would not be guided by the "wisdom" of the Catholic Church, since those states' residents overwhelmingly subscribed to a Protestant understanding of freedom? Could Catholics be trusted not to allow their clerical leaders to become a state within a state – one that would stand in opposition to the foundation of individual freedom upon which America was to be built?

These anxieties fueled much of the anti-Catholic rhetoric that permeated the independence movement. The questions were primarily rhetorical, however. Inflammatory words about the Quebec Act had made great copy in the campaign for independence, but the fact of the matter was that very few Catholics lived in the "thirteen original colonies" when the Treaty of Paris that ended the Revolutionary War was signed in 1783 – no more than 30,000, according to one estimate, out of a population of nearly 3.9 million.[26]

In half a century, however, that would begin to change. By 1850, Roman Catholicism was the largest single denomination in the United States – a distinction it continues to hold today. Not only that, but the vast majority of this increase was in the form of immigration from Ireland. Between 1845 and 1850, more than 838,000 immigrants arrived in the United States just from that country, making nearly a quarter of the inhabitants in Boston, New York, Philadelphia, and Baltimore immigrant and Irish.[27]

Irish Catholicism in the nineteenth century was different from the kind of Catholicism found in continental Europe, where most Catholics lived under Catholic regimes that did not oppress them. Irish Catholics tended to be very deferential to their priests, taking instruction from them on a host of issues, both sacred and secular. This was because the Catholic Church in Ireland was one of the few institutions that opposed the oppressive policies of the English government and worked to make the lives of Irish peasants better. Educational leaders in Massachusetts seemed to recognize that England was partly responsible for how "priest-ridden" Ireland's Catholics were. In 1848, they blamed the "systemic oppression of bad rulers at home" for the "ignorance and degradation" that characterized the Irish immigrant community in Boston. Regardless of the cause, however, the blind faith Irish immigrants seemed to place in their priests terrified Massachusetts' Protestant leaders. Given that these immigrants were able to vote, the situation seemed destined to create the *imperium in imperio* that people like Sam Adams had warned about.[28]

PROTESTANTS AND CATHOLICS IN THE NINETEENTH CENTURY

At various points in the second half of the nineteenth century, Protestant leaders tried to prevent Catholics from becoming the *imperium in imperio* they feared. These efforts fell into two primary categories: first, Protestants tried to block Catholics from participating in American democracy, since it was Catholics' participation, in conjunction with their priestly deference, that seemed to pose the greatest threat to American freedom; and secondly, Protestants tried to make Catholics less "Catholic." The nation's public schools became the epicenter of this second effort – with the ironic result being that the Bible was slowly removed from curricula it had dominated for more than two centuries, and Catholics created a "parochial" school system that dominated the Catholic experience in America for generations and hindered the development of Protestant-Catholic cooperation.

The effort to block Catholic participation in American democracy was embodied most overtly in the efforts of some Protestant lawmakers to extend the amount of time it would take before an immigrant could be qualified to vote. To this day, there is no requirement in the US Constitution that people voting in federal elections be American citizens. Every *state* now has that requirement, but the provision did not become universal in the states' constitutions until the early twentieth century. There is also a congressional law that requires voters in federal elections to be US citizens, but that law was not passed until 1996 – and of course a statute law does not have nearly the enduring power that a constitutional mandate has.[29]

In the nineteenth century, most Irish immigrants were eligible to vote as soon as they got off the boat – provided they were male and over the age of twenty-one. Members of the Native American or "Know Nothing" Party wanted to change that. While the Know Nothings were never a powerful national party the way the Democrats and Republicans are today, they did manage to capture nearly 20 percent of the seats in Congress in 1854. The also captured a majority of the seats in the state legislatures of Massachusetts and Pennsylvania in 1854 and 1855, along with the mayors' offices in Philadelphia, Boston, Washington, DC, and San Francisco.[30]

Know Nothing lawmakers tried to enact legislation on the federal and state levels that would have required immigrants to live in the country for twenty-one years before they were allowed the vote. The rationale these lawmakers gave for the change was that native-born American men had to wait for twenty-one years before they were allowed to vote; immigrants to the United States, therefore, should have to wait that long, too.[31] Really, though, what the lawmakers hoped to accomplish was a change that would keep priest-ridden Catholics from voting as a block.

Their efforts failed – but they testify to how frightening the immigrant/Catholic presence in the United States was to some Protestant leaders in the mid-nineteenth century. "The monarchists and statesmen of Europe well know the fruitlessness of any attempt to destroy our republic by open invasion," one Lutheran pastor remarked to his seminarians in 1838. "The only mode of reaching us is indirect action." That indirect action included sending ignorant European Catholics to live in the United States, according to the pastor, Simon Schmucker. Once there, these Catholics would vote for tyrannical leaders who would, in turn, implement the directives of tyrannical monarchs. "We are met by the objection that papists, when interrogated, deny every intention hostile to our liberties," Schmucker told his audience. "We answer ... the secret has not been confided to them. They have only been taught implicitly to obey the priest and pope and councils, at the hazard of eternal ruin, and thus, in due time, as common soldiers, to obey their commanders."[32]

Most Protestant leaders were not as paranoid as Simon Schmucker. They worried about the impact that immigration would have on the political landscape in the United States, but they did not believe there needed to be an actual plan in order for the Catholic Church to destroy American democracy. Catholic voters would ruin things simply by failing to think for themselves as they cast their votes; they would ruin things simply by failing to be free.

To that end, Protestant educational reformers in the mid-nineteenth century worked to build public school systems and implement curricula that they believed would cultivate independent thinking. Most did not see themselves as working to make Catholic schoolchildren a little bit "Protestant." In fact, when he removed the New England primer from Massachusetts' schools because it was full of references to Calvinist theology, Horace Mann, a Unitarian who directed the state's board of education, actually saw himself as ridding the public schools of distracting "sectarianism."[33] As far as the differences that separated one Protestant denomination from another were concerned, Mann was probably right to see his efforts in this way. But when he embraced an "American" understanding of freedom as part of his effort to reform the public schools, Mann and other reformers like him also implicitly endorsed a "Protestant" understanding of freedom. Many Catholic parents (and certainly the priests advising them) saw this effort for what it was – and they refused to participate.

Nowhere was the obtuseness of Protestant educational reformers more clearly manifest than in their insistence on the use of the King James Bible in the public schools. This English translation of Hebrew, Aramaic, and Greek versions of the Old and New Testaments was a perfect example of the dueling understandings of freedom found along the Protestant–Catholic divide. Accepted by most English-speaking Protestant denominations, the King James Bible had been commissioned by James I in 1604 and completed in 1611. Following James's orders, the translators did not include any pictures or marginal notes with their translations, as such additions were seen by the Church of England's Archbishop of Canterbury as "instructional" – and therefore dangerously "papist."[34]

The Vatican did not endorse or sanction the King James Bible. The only bible that English-speaking Catholics were supposed to read was the Douay-Rheims Bible, which was a sixteenth-century English translation of a fourth-century Latin translation that St. Jerome had completed, drawing upon Hebrew, Aramaic, Greek, and Latin sources. The Douay-Rheims Bible was extensively annotated, with a preface that provided insight into the translation process and marginal notes that provided theological and historical context.[35] It was, in many respects, an embodiment of the Catholic understanding of Scripture as something far too complex for any one person to fully access entirely on his or her own.

The issue of which Bible was an appropriate one for America's future citizens to be reading became an increasingly contentious issue in the nineteenth century. During one summer, Catholics and Protestants even rioted over the debate. At least fourteen people died in Philadelphia between May and July of 1844, and the property damage was estimated at about $150,000 – the equivalent today of more than $4 million (putting the riots over racial injustice that occurred in some cities in the summer of 2020 in useful perspective).[36]

Gradually, instead of rioting, Catholics responded by removing their children from the public schools. Bishops raised money in Europe to create a Catholic school system in the United States, ultimately decreeing that "no parish is complete till it has schools adequate to the needs of its children." As these schools were built – and nuns were found to staff them – priests across the country instructed Catholic parents to send their children to Catholic schools "whenever practicable" and to avoid any situation where "Protestants, Jews, and Infidels meet promiscu-ously." "Watchful Catholic parents," the bishop of Rochester, New York, warned in 1893, "would never allow their children to associ-ate with such [people] ... justly fearing contamination."[37]

The result was the "ghetto mentality" that historian Garry Wills has said dominated American Catholicism in the first half of the twentieth century. From the late nineteenth century until the end of the World War II – if not the post-Vatican II era of the 1960s and 1970s – American Catholics worked in the same industries, settled in the same urban enclaves, frequently consumed the same entertainment, and sent their children exclusively to Catholic schools. Under such circumstances, Protestant-Catholic partnerships were difficult, if not impossible to accomplish.[38]

Some Protestants saw what was happening and tried to prevent it. When education officials in Cincinnati, Ohio, contemplated banning "all religious books, including the Holy Bible" from the city's public schools in the 1870s, it was because nearly half of Cincinnati's school children were enrolled in Catholic schools. Henry Ward Beecher – whose father, Lyman, had been a bit of an anti-Catholic firebrand forty years earlier – pushed to have the Bible removed, because he hoped that doing so would convince Catholic parents to send their children to Cincinnati's public schools. To soften the blow to Christian sensibil-ities, the younger Beecher presented his proposal as a thoroughly "American" initiative. "Compulsory Bible [instruction] in schools is not in accordance with [the] American doctrine of liberty of conscience," he insisted. The effort worked, and by 1875, the Bible was gone from Cincinnati's public classrooms. Schools in San Francisco and Chicago soon followed that lead. But Catholic schoolchildren did not return.[39]

TRI-FAITH AMERICA

The Protestant–Catholic ecumenism we are seeing in the United States today – whether the variety manifest in the international humanitarian efforts of groups like World Vision, or the variety manifest in efforts to transform the legal and cultural landscape in the United States, like those of ECT and the many political action committees it has spawned – probably had its beginnings in the efforts of the National Council of Christians and Jews (NCCJ) to create what one historian has called a "Tri-Faith America" in the 1930s and 1940s.[40] In response to rising anti-Semitism in Europe and rising anti-Catholicism in the United

States, the NCCJ put together what were known as "Tolerance Trios" and sent the groups out on speaking tours throughout the United States.

These trios consisted – always – of a Protestant, a Catholic, and a Jew. Usually – and preferably – the representatives of each faith group were also clergymen who could speak with real authority about the beliefs and practices that characterized their denominations. The lectures were organized through local churches, synagogues, and schools. The unabashed goal of the Trios was to cultivate religious tolerance by allowing audiences to ask any questions that came to mind – with the backdrop of fascism in Europe giving added weight to Trios' answers.

Religious tolerance was not technically a Catholic value when these Trios were zig-zagging across the country, however. Vatican II had not happened yet, and error still had no rights, as far as Rome was concerned. That required the priests participating in the Tolerance Trios to "fudge" their answers sometimes, in the same way, perhaps, that those priests and nuns Nicholas Kristof observed in Africa "fudged" when they were asked how best to prevent the spread of HIV – and answered by handing out condoms. During the very first Tolerance Trio lecture hosted by the NCCJ, held at Columbia University in October of 1929, a woman in the audience asked Father J. Elliott Ross whether he believed she would be going to hell, since she was a Methodist. At the time, Catholic teaching made it clear that there was no salvation outside the Roman Catholic Church, and so the answer Father Ross should have given was "yes."

Instead, he deflected, replying at first, "That's up to you!" by way of generating some laughter and putting his audience at ease. He then "fudged" and told the woman that "in Catholic theology, God in his infinite wisdom allows freedom of conscience." He admitted that his preference would be to have everyone in the audience embrace Catholicism, but "as long as your reason and conscience truly lead you to do otherwise, you have as good a chance to get to heaven as any Catholic."[41]

It was an answer that would have displeased Pope Pius XI greatly, had he been privy to it. But somewhere up in Heaven, John Leland was probably smiling.

NOTES

1 Nicholas Kristof, "Learning from the Sin of Sodom," *New York Times*, February 27, 2010, www.nytimes.com/2010/02/28/opinion/28kristof.html; Church Resource Team, "8 Distinctives of World Vision's Christian Engagement," June 17, 2016, World Vision, https://church.worldvision.org/bl og/_bloq_blog_articles/8-distinctives-of-world-visions-christian-engagement.

292 The Religious Culture of American Protestantism

2 Editorial Board, "On the Square: An Interview with George Weigel," *First Things Online,* February 27, 2010, www.firstthings.com/web-exclusives/20 10/02/interview-with-george-weigel; Joseph Bottom, "Introduction," in Richard John Neuhaus, *The Best of "The Public Square",* Book Three (Grand Rapids, MI: Eerdmans, 2007), ix.

3 "Senior Lutheran Suspended for Going to 'Pagan' Service," *Irish Times,* July 8, 2002, www.irishtimes.com/news/senior-lutheran-suspended-for-going-to-pagan-service-1.1087816; Associated Press, "Lutheran Panel Reinstates Pastor after Post-9/11 Interfaith Service," *New York Times,* May 13, 2003, www.nytimes.com/2003/05/13/nyregion/lutheran-panel-reinstates-pastor-after-post-9-11-interfaith-service.html.

4 "On the Square"; Daniel J. Wakin, "Seeing Heresy in a Service for Sept. 11; Pastor Is Under Fire for Interfaith Prayers," *New York Times,* February 8, 2002, www.nytimes.com/2002/02/08/nyregion/seeing-heresy-service-for-sept-11-pastor-under-fire-for-interfaith-prayers.html.

5 Timothy George and Thomas G. Guarino, eds., *Evangelicals and Catholics Together at Twenty* (Grand Rapids, MI: Brazos Press, 2015), 174; "The 25 Most Influential Evangelicals in America: Rick Santorum," *Time,* February 7, 2005, http://content.time.com/time/specials/packages/article/0,28804,1993235_1993243_1993316,00.html; Tara Isabella Burton, "Understanding the Christian Broadcasting Network, the Force Behind the Latest Pro-Trump TV Newscast," *Vox,* August 5, 2017; Robert D. McFadden, "Cardinal Avery Dulles, Theologian, Is Dead at 90," *New York Times,* December 12, 2008.

6 Sarah Pulliam Bailey, "World Vision Reverses Course on Same-Sex Marriage Policy," *National Catholic Reporter,* March 24, 2014.

7 Richard John Neuhaus and Charles Wendell Colson, "Evangelicals and Catholics Together: The Christian Mission in the Third Millennium," in *Evangelicals and Catholics Together at Twenty,* ed. George and Guarino, 16, 18, 17.

8 John F. Kennedy, "Speech of Senator John F. Kennedy, Greater Houston Ministerial Association." Rice Hotel, Houston, TX. September 12, 1960, available at "Transcript: JFK's Speech on His Religion," December 5, 2007, National Public Radio, www.npr.org/templates/story/story.php?storyId=16920600.

9 Maura Jane Farrelly, *Anti-Catholicism in America, 1620–1860* (New York: Cambridge, 2017), 192–193.

10 Pius IX, "The Syllabus of Errors Condemned by Pius IX," December 8, 1864, *Papal Encyclicals Online,* www.papalencyclicals.net/Pius09/p9syll.htm.

11 John XXIII, *Humanae salutis* (Convocation of the Second Vatican Council), December 25, 1961, in Ann Michele Nolan, *A Privileged Moment: Dialogue in the Second Vatican Council, 1962–1965* (New York: Peter Lang, 2006), 65; Paul VI, *Dignitatis humanae* (Declaration of Religious Freedom), December 7, 1965, Archives of the Holy See, www.vatican.va/archive/hist_

councils/ii_vatican_council/documents/vat-ii_decl_19651207_dignitatis-humanae_en.html; Farrelly, *Anti-Catholicism*, 193–194.

12 Evan Haefeli, ed., *Against Popery: Britain, Empire, and Anti-Catholicism* (Charlottesville: University of Virginia Press, 2020).

13 William Henry Drayton, "Charge of William Henry Drayton" in *American Archives, Fourth Series*, ed. Peter Force (Washington, DC, 1837), vol. VI, 959; C. H. Van Tyne, "The Influence of the Clergy, and of Religious and Sectarian Forces on the American Revolution," *American Historical Review* vol. 19 (1914), 59–62; John Adams, *The Works of John Adams, Second President of the United States*, ed. Charles Francis Adams (Boston: Little, Brown, 1850), vol. II, 252; Ezra Stiles, *The Literary Diary of Ezra Stiles*, ed. Franklin Bowditch Dexter (New York: Scribner, 1901), vol. I, 455; Alexander Hamilton, *A Full Vindication of Matters of Congress from Calumnies of their Enemies* (1774), cited in *The American Catholic Historical Researches* vol. 6, no. 4 (1889), 160.

14 John Winthrop, "Reasons to Be Considered for Justifying the Undertakers of the Intended Plantation in New England and for Encouraging Such as Whose Hearts God Shall Move to Join with Them in It," in *The Puritans in America: A Narrative Anthology*, ed. Alan Heimert and Andrew Delbanco (Cambridge, MA: Harvard University Press, 1985), 71–72.

15 John Tracy Ellis, *American Catholicism* (Chicago: University of Chicago Press, 1969), 25; Mark A. Noll, *A History of Christianity in the United States* (Grand Rapids, MI: Eerdmans, 1992), 35; Arnold Oskar Meyer, "Charles I and Rome," *American Historical Review* vol. 19 (1912), 13–26.

16 John Leland, "The Rights of Conscience Inalienable," in *The Writings of the Late Elder John Leland*, ed. L. F. Greene (New York: G. W. Wood, 1845), 181, 185.

17 Farrelly, *Anti-Catholicism in America*, 20.

18 Thomas S. Kidd, *The Protestant Interest: New England After Puritanism* (New Haven, CT: Yale University Press, 2004).

19 William Blackstone, *Blackstone's Commentaries for the Use of Students at Law and the General Reader*, ed. Marshall D. Ewell (Boston: Soule and Bugbee, 1882), 21.

20 For more on the debate about whether Vatican II "changed" the Roman Catholic Church, see Pope Benedict XVI, "A Proper Hermeneutic for the Second Vatican Council," and Avery Cardinal Dulles, "Nature, Mission, and Structure of the Church," in *Vatican II: Renewal within Tradition*, ed. Matthew L. Lamb and Matthew Levering (New York: Oxford, 2008), ix–xv and 25–36; and John W. O'Malley, "The Style of Vatican II," *America*, February 24, 2003.

21 N.N. *An Epistles of a Catholicke young gentleman, (being for his religion imprisoned.) To his Father a Protestant* (London, 1623), 12–13, 19.

22 Leo XIII, "Libertas: On the Nature of Human Liberty," June 20, 1888, *Papal Documents Online*, http://w2.vatican.va/content/leo-xiii/en/encyclicals/documents/hf_l-xiii_enc_20061888_libertas.html.

23 Leo XIII, "Libertas."

24 Samuel Moyn, "Religious Freedom between Truth and Tactic," in *Politics of Religious Freedom*, ed. Winnifred Fallers Sullivan, Elizabeth Shakman Hurd, Saba Mahmood, and Peter G. Danchin (Chicago: University of Chicago Press, 2015), 135–141; Avery Dulles, "Dignitatis Humanae and the Development of Catholic Doctrine," in *Catholicism and Religious Freedom* (Lanham, MD: Rowman and Littlefield, 2006), 43–66.

25 Samuel Adams, "The Rights of the Colonists," November 20, 1772, in *The Writings of Samuel Adams*, ed. Harry Alonzo Cushing (New York: Putnam, 1904), vol. VIII, 359.

26 J. F. Regis Canevin, "Loss and Gain in the Catholic Church in the United States, 1800–1916," *Catholic Historical Review* vol. 2 (January 1917), 380–381; "1790 Fast Facts," US Census Bureau, accessed on January 21, 2021, www.census.gov/history/www/through_the_decades/fast_facts/1790_fas t_facts.html.

27 Gerald Shaughnessy, *Has the Immigrant Kept the Faith? A Study of Immigration and Catholic Growth in the United States, 1790–1920* (New York: Macmillan, 1925), 134, 145; John Gilmary Shea, "Catholic Losses in America," *United States Catholic Historical Magazine* vol. 4 (1891–1892), 80; Roger Finke and Rodney Stark, *The Churching of America, 1776–2005: Winners and Losers in Our Religious Economy* (New Brunswick, NJ: Rutgers University Press, 2006), 119; D. A. E. Harkness, "Irish Emigration," in *Interpretations*, vol. II of *International Migrations*, ed. Walter F. Willcox (New York: National Bureau of Economic Research, 1931), 265; Kevin Kenny, "New Directions in Irish-American History," in *New Directions in Irish-American History*, ed. Kenny (Madison: University of Wisconsin Press, 2003), 5; D. A. E. Harkness, "Irish Emigration," in *Interpretations*, 265.

28 John Jordan, "Irish Catholicism," *The Crane Bag* vol. 7, no. 2 (1983), 106–116; Harriet Martineau, *Society in America* (New York: Saunders and Otley, 1837), vol. II, 323; "Extract from an 1848 Report by the Massachusetts State Senate," in Stephen A. Brighton, *Historical Archaeology of the Irish Diaspora: A Transnational Approach* (Knoxville: University of Tennessee Press, 2009), 73.

29 Stanley A. Renshon, *Allowing Non-Citizens to Vote in the United States: Why Not?* (Washington, DC: Center for Immigration Studies, 2008), 7; Jamin B. Raskin, "Legal Aliens, Local Citizens: The Historical, Constitutional, and Theoretical Meaning of Alien Suffrage," *University of Pennsylvania Law Review* 141 (April, 1993), 1391–1470; Gerald M. Rosberg, "Aliens and Equal Protection: Why Not the Right to Vote?," *Michigan Law Review* vol. 75, no. 5 (April–May, 1977), 1092–1093; Stanley L. Engerman and Kenneth L. Sockoloff, "The Evolution of Suffrage Institutions in the New World," *Journal of Economic History* vol. 65, no. 4 (December, 2005), 898.

30 Michael F. Holt, "The Politics of Impatience: The Origins of Know Nothingism," *Journal of American History* vol. 60, no. 2 (1973), 309–331; Ray Allen Billington, *The Protestant Crusade, 1800–1860: A Study in the Origins of American Nativism* (New York: Macmillan, 1938), 408–409, 412; "Diary and Memoranda of William L. Macy," *American Historical Review* vol. 3 (1919), 643; J. Michael Gallman, *Receiving Erin's Children: Philadelphia, Liverpool, and the Irish Famine Migration, 1845–1855* (Chapel Hill: University of North Carolina Press, 2000), 158; Darcy G. Richardson, *Others: Third-Party Politics from the Nation's Founding to the Rise and Fall of the Greenback-Labor Movement* (New York: IUniverse, 2004), 206.

31 Billington, *The Protestant Crusade*, 203.

32 S. S. Schmucker, *Discourse in Commemoration of the Glorious Reformation of the Sixteenth Century* (Philadelphia: Henry Perkins, 1838), 123–125.

33 Gabriel Compayré, *Horace Mann and the Public Schools in the United States*, trans. Mary D. Frost (New York: Thomas Y. Crowell, 1907), 49.

34 David Daniell, *The Bible in English: Its History and Influence* (New Haven, CT: Yale University Press, 2003), 431, 439, 458, 488.

35 Daniell, *The Bible in English*, 283.

36 Elizabeth M. Geffen, "Industrial Development and Social Crisis, 1841–1854," in *Philadelphia: A 300-Year History*, ed. Russell F. Weigley (New York: Norton, 1982), 357; John Back McMaster, *A History of the People of the United States from the Revolution to the Civil War*, 8 vols. (New York: Appleton, 1915), vol. VII, 376–377; Katie Oxx, *The Nativist Movement in America: Religious Conflict in the Nineteenth Century* (New York: Routledge, 2013), 57–58; "Consumer Price Index Estimate (1800–)," Federal Reserve Bank of Minneapolis, accessed May 28, 2016, www.minneapolisfed.org/community/teaching-aids/cpi-calculator-information/consumer-price-index-1800.

37 "Pastoral Letter of the Archbishops and Bishops of the United States, Assembled in the Third Plenary Council of Baltimore," in *Memorial Volume: A History of the Third Plenary Council of Baltimore* (Baltimore: Baltimore Publishing Co., 1884), 17; "Editorial Notes – The German Catholic Benevolent Union," in *The Catholic Record: A Miscellany of Catholic Knowledge and General Literature* (Philadelphia: Hardy and Mahoney, 1875), 124; Bishop Bernard McQuaid to Pope Leo XIII, January 16, 1893, in Frederick J. Zwierlein, "Bishop McQuaid of Rochester," *Catholic Historical Review* vol. 5 (1920), 340–341.

38 Garry Wills, *Bare Ruined Choirs: Doubt, Prophecy, and Radical Religion* (Garden City, NY: Doubleday, 1971), 15; Mark S. Massa, *Catholics and American Culture: Fulton Sheen, Dorothy Day, and the Notre Dame Football Team* (New York: Crossroads, 1999), 1–20.

39 Steven K. Green, *The Second Disestablishment: Church and State in Nineteenth Century America* (New York: Oxford University Press, 2010),

276, 278; Ray Allen Billington, "The Burning of the Charlestown Convent," *New England Quarterly* vol. 10, no. 1 (1937), 18–19; Nancy R. Hamant, "Religion in the Cincinnati Schools, 1830-1900," *Historical and Philosophical Society of Ohio, Bulletin*, 21 (1963), 239–251; Ward M. McAfee, *Religion, Race, and Reconstruction: The Public School in the Politics of the 1870s* (Albany: State University of New York Press, 1998), 38–39.

40   Kevin M. Schultz, *Tri-Faith America: How Catholics and Jews Held Postwar America to Its Protestant Promise* (New York: Oxford, 2011), especially 15–96.

41   Schultz, *Tri-Faith America*, 38; James E. Pitt, *Adventures in Brotherhood* (New York: Farrar, Straus & Co., 1955), 28–29.

16 Missions

MELODY MAXWELL

"Ye are the light of the world. A city that is set on an hill cannot be hid."
Biblical verses such as this one, from Matthew 5:14 (KJV), have inspired
American Protestants from their beginnings to serve as exemplars of the
Christian faith to the world around them. Overall, American Protestants
have demonstrated a strong commitment to global missions and missionary work throughout their history, urging the importance of converting others to Protestant Christianity. This emphasis began during the
early days of American settlement by Europeans, with missions efforts
among native Americans, those of African descent, and eventually overseas groups.

American Protestant missions efforts peaked during the modern
missionary movement of the nineteenth century, with thousands of
missionaries – including women and students – serving around the
world with strong support from churches and mission boards. During
the twentieth century, support for missions among mainline Protestants
declined due to secularism and religious pluralism, while evangelical
Protestants undertook innovative new forms of missions. Throughout
the centuries, a commitment to missions has both reflected and shaped
American Protestant self-understanding.

BEGINNINGS

From their beginnings in the sixteenth-century Reformation, Protestants
sought to be faithful to New Testament ideals of Christianity. They
rejected many of the traditions of the Catholic Church in order to return
to "Scripture alone" as their authority. Protestants believed that their
form of faith was more biblical – and thus more correct – than those of
adherents of the Catholic or Orthodox traditions. This idea, embedded in
Protestant self-understanding, eventually led many Protestants to seek
to spread their form of Christianity to others, even those of other
Christian traditions.

European Protestants began to migrate to North America in the seventeenth century. Puritans settled in New England with the vision of demonstrating their faith to the world around them, seeking to glorify God and to exemplify a society devoted to God. Even the charter of the colony of Massachusetts, established by the Anglican Charles I, stated the goal that the colonists might "win and incite the natives of the country to the knowledge of the only true God and Saviour of mankind and the Christian faith."[1] While colonists' primary goal was for their own survival, they also expressed concern for the Native Americans around them, whom they believed were destined for eternal punishment unless they embraced the truth of the Christian gospel.

Puritan John Eliot made special efforts to convert the Algonquin people and exemplified the missionary zeal of some Puritans during this period.[2] He translated the Bible into the Algonquin language and gathered converts into "praying towns," removing them from their indigenous contexts. In his view, Indians needed to not only embrace Christianity but "civilization" in order to follow Christ. However, this extractionistic strategy failed when war broke out between colonists and Native Americans and many "praying towns" were destroyed. In the middle colonies, Moravian missionaries, led by David Zeisberger, adapted their message and methods more to the culture and language of indigenous peoples, emphasizing piety and love over doctrine. However, their efforts did not yield many converts.[3] These early missionary efforts were exceptional, but they demonstrated that converting others to Christianity (and often Christian culture) was a goal of early American Protestantism.

Attempts at effecting conversions grew rapidly with the introduction of the First Great Awakening in the American colonies beginning in the 1730s, reflecting the changing self-understanding of American Protestants.[4] Under the leadership of men such as Jonathan Edwards and George Whitefield, thousands of colonists experienced religious awakenings at outdoor revival meetings as well as in churches. The idea of a dramatic conversion experience and personal faith spread across the colonies and beyond. As a result of revival stirrings, missionary David Brainerd ministered among Native Americans in various regions of the Northern colonies, receiving acclaim for his efforts with Jonathan Edwards' publication of his diary.[5] The Second Great Awakening of the opening years of the nineteenth century brought similar religious impulses. While they did not consider themselves missionaries, circuit-riding Methodist preachers and entrepreneurial Baptist preachers established numerous converts and congregations across western frontier regions of the United States.[6] As a result of these awakenings,

American Protestants prioritized a personal conversion experience for anyone seeking to join the faith.

During these years, persons of African descent, many of whom were enslaved, were exposed to the Protestant faith prevalent in the United States, including among slave masters. Although few white Protestants served as missionaries to African Americans, many African Americans converted to Christianity, especially during the Great Awakenings. They often embraced the Bible's themes of freedom and justice rather than the idea of submission emphasized by their masters. George Liele, freed by his master in 1778, moved from South Carolina to Jamaica five years later, both to escape re-enslavement and because he had British sympathies. Liele, a Baptist, preached to enslaved persons in Jamaica, converting thousands and establishing numerous churches.[7] He was not officially recognized as a missionary at the time because of his race and his lack of connection to a formal missions-sending structure. However, in hindsight it is clear that Liele was the first American missionary to go to another country. His efforts demonstrated that conversionary sentiments had spread among diverse segments of American Protestants.

By the early 1800s, American Protestant denominations gradually began to engage in more formal missions work. In 1803, the Presbyterian General Assembly formed a Standing Committee on Missions. Other groups established small missionary societies.[8] The American foreign missions movement is often considered to have begun with efforts stemming from the Haystack Prayer Meeting of 1806. In that year, five students from Williams College were caught in a rainstorm and prayed from beneath a haystack, committing themselves to missionary work. They went on to study at Andover Seminary, where Adoniram Judson joined the group. In 1810, the young men approached Congregationalist leaders about forming a mission board to support them so that they might serve overseas. The American Board of Commissioners for Foreign Missions resulted – the first foreign mission board in the United States. Judson and his wife, Ann, went out with this board but became Baptists on their way to Asia in 1812. The Judsons famously engaged in missions work in Burma, inspiring generations of Americans.[9] The era of formal American Protestant missions work had begun.

THE "GREAT CENTURY"

Historian Kenneth Latourette famously referred to the nineteenth century as the "Great Century" of Christian expansion.[10] In retrospect, historians and missiologists may question whether Protestant efforts to spread "civilization" as well as Christianity during this period were "great" in quality. However, there is no debating that American Protestant missions efforts during this period were great in quantity. During the nineteenth century, enthusiasm for and participation in missions work among American Protestants reached its peak. This increase in missions shaped American Protestant self-understanding as church members and leaders of various denominations embraced the priority of missions work and of converting others to their faith. American Protestants came to view themselves as a people with an important message and a global mission. The modern missionary movement had arrived.

Multiple factors contributed to the growth of American Protestant missions during this period. This was an era of global exploration and advances in travel, when western powers founded colonies and the popular press reported on the journeys of explorers in regions hitherto unknown to Westerners. With this exploration came a sense of progress and optimism, especially among those in the newly created United States of America. The United States, many of its citizens felt, had a "manifest destiny" to spread across the North American continent. This spirit of progress likely contributed to Americans' zeal for foreign expansion as well.[11] The growth of colonialism also provided new territories in which Westerners might evangelize. Numerous American Protestant missionaries moved to colonies managed by European powers, especially England, and found there a haven for their evangelization. During the nineteenth century, many new regions of the world were opened to Americans literally through their travels and figuratively in their imaginations.

Although England sent more missionaries than the United States during this period, American missions efforts grew rapidly. The entrepreneurial spirit and activism of the new republic were well suited to the development of new mission societies. Most Protestant denominations created their own foreign missionary societies during the nineteenth century, as the Congregationalists had pioneered in 1810.[12] Baptists formed the General Missionary Convention of the Baptist Denomination in the United States of America for Foreign Missions, or Triennial Convention, to support missionaries like the Judsons in 1814; the Methodists organized the Missionary Society of the Methodist Episcopal Church in 1819.[13] African-American missionaries, who were sometimes not accepted by white Protestant denominations, formed their own denominational mission boards. They focused on Africa, including regions colonized by formerly enslaved persons. The Lott Carey Foreign Mission Convention was one example.[14] In addition, interdenominational mission organizations also developed, focusing on specific regions or tasks, such as the Africa Interior Mission. One mission board, the Christian and Missionary Alliance, even developed into a denomination. Such boards provided formal structures to further the cause of Christian missions. They allowed missions advocates from churches across the country to join forces to strengthen their efforts and promoted awareness of and involvement in missions among clergy and laypeople alike.

Supported by such boards, American missionaries ventured out to Africa, Asia, and Latin America, among other regions. Missions work generally began in coastal areas and later spread to interior regions. Missionaries used strategies such as education, healthcare, and evangelism to spread their faith among indigenous peoples whom they encountered on the mission field. Many missionaries founded schools for children in which they taught the English language and western customs along with Christianity, believing that educating the next generation was key to "Christianizing" their societies. Some missionaries later established secondary schools and Bible colleges for their converts; graduates of these institutes proved to be some of the most successful indigenous evangelists.

Another strategy popular among both missionaries and indigenous peoples was healthcare. Mission boards founded hospitals and clinics in locations around the world, most of which did not have adequate medical care by western standards. Doctors and nurses sought to share their faith in word and deed as they assisted patients in their facilities and on trips to remote locations. Despite the presence of medical professionals on many mission fields, a number of missionaries in this era succumbed to diseases to which they were not accustomed. In fact, Africa became known as the "white man's grave." Some missionaries left America with their possessions in coffins, anticipating early deaths on the mission field. As their health allowed, missionaries embarked upon direct evangelistic efforts, taking preaching tours through remote villages and witnessing on the streets of major cities. Through such efforts they attracted many curious onlookers, most of whom learned about Christianity – and met an American – for the first time. All of these endeavors were met with modest success; most missionaries saw relatively small numbers of converts. Indigenous Christians who worked alongside the missionaries proved some of the most able evangelists among their own peoples. Still, many were hesitant to convert because of the association of Christianity with western styles of living.

Indeed, western Christians of the time thought that converting to Christianity involved adopting western culture, which they believed could not be separated from the Christian faith. American Protestant missionaries (among others) imported western hymns, church buildings, and customs to lands thousands of miles away from the United States. To varying levels, converts adopted a new culture along with Christianity. Along with cultural changes came a frequent association with colonialism, as missionaries were often seen as agents of western powers. Historians debate the influence and relationship of colonial powers to missions work. In some instances, missionaries allied themselves closely with colonial rulers. In others, missionaries stood up for indigenous peoples and opposed colonization. Regardless, colonialism opened to missionaries many lands that would have otherwise remained closed. However, it also associated Christianity with western imperialism in the minds of many who lived in these areas.[15]

American Protestant missions efforts not only influenced recipients of missions work but also had a reflexive influence on American Protestants themselves.[16] A knowledge of missions broadened American Protestants' understanding of the world and its cultures and religions, which they typically regarded as both exotic and pagan. Learning about missions work and reading letters from missionaries also convinced American Protestants of what they believed was their vital role in promoting "Christian civilization" worldwide. Because of Protestants' dominance in American culture at the time, even secular publications promoted missionary efforts. The modern missionary movement captured the attention of the American public in ways not seen before or since. During this movement, the establishment of missionary societies, conferences, training schools, and publications provided meaningful leadership experiences for many Americans, including women and students, who were not serving in ordained clergy positions. These two groups played significant roles in the American Protestant missions movement of this era.

In fact, the majority of American Protestant missionaries in the nineteenth century were women. In the second half of the century, a woman's missionary movement arose among Protestant women in the United States (and other parts of the English-speaking world), as women gained more leisure time and empowerment and began to form societies to support a variety of causes. As part of the woman's missionary movement, women of multiple Protestant denominations, both Black and white, formed their own missionary societies in rapid succession. In many denominations, women's mission boards were independent of larger denominational boards; in others, they served as auxiliaries. The Woman's Foreign Missionary Society of the Methodist Episcopal Church was an example of the former; the Woman's Auxiliary of the Domestic and Foreign Missionary Society of the Protestant Episcopal Church of the latter.[17]

The motivation of such boards was to send female missionaries, often single women, to reach women overseas whom they believed male missionaries could not evangelize because of customs related to gender roles. For the first time, thousands of American women went overseas as missionaries in their own right. They worked predominantly among women and children and did not serve as ordained ministers in churches. Southern Baptist missionary Lottie Moon, for example, was famous for her evangelistic work among Chinese women (and occasionally men), and she mobilized American women for missions support through her frequent correspondence from the mission field. Reports from missionaries like Moon convinced most American Protestant women of the necessity of women's missions work.

Students also played a significant role in Protestant missions efforts toward the end of the nineteenth century. Recalling the Haystack Prayer Meeting, the Student Volunteer Movement for Foreign Missions was established in 1888. This organization built on the momentum begun two years earlier, when 100 students attending a conference led by D. L. Moody at Mt. Hermon, Massachusetts, had committed to becoming missionaries. The slogan of the Student Volunteer Movement was "the evangelization of the world in this generation"; adherents signed a pledge stating their intention to become foreign missionaries. Under the leadership of John Mott, the movement spread to college campuses across the United States and involved more than 40,000 students, many of whom did eventually become missionaries.[18] This movement not only contributed to American Protestant missions but also affected the views and vocations of many American students, providing them with what they considered an essential role in the task of world evangelization.

As the nineteenth century ended, the reach of American Protestant missionaries was noteworthy. Through the modern missionary movement, Christianity had rapidly spread to every inhabited continent, with significant involvement from American Protestants. Adherents of Christianity rose from 23 percent of the world's population in 1800 to 35 percent of the world's population in 1914, thanks in large part to the modern missionary movement.[19] Those American Protestants who did not serve as missionaries overwhelmingly supported the missions movement and believed that part of their duty as Christians was to evangelize and civilize non-Christians around the world. American optimism combined with Protestant fervor to make the nineteenth century the heyday of American Protestant missions.

TWENTIETH-CENTURY CHANGES

The widespread support that Protestant missions efforts enjoyed among nineteenth-century Americans waned in the following century as American self-understanding changed. The advent of two world wars not only occupied young men who might otherwise have been missionaries but also ended the optimism that had been prevalent in American society in previous years. Hopes of encircling the world with the message of Christ were replaced with fear of enemies, pessimism about human nature, and at times a questioning of Christian values. Some wondered how nations that called themselves Christian could have been involved in such brutal wars. Pioneer mission fields had seen enough success that some Americans doubted whether western missionaries were still needed there. In addition, the onset of the Great Depression meant that funds available for missions were often scarce. Protestant missions efforts no longer enjoyed the broad acceptance in the United States that they had in the previous century.

American Protestants also found themselves fractured in their response to developments in scientific and biblical knowledge. The rise of evolution and higher criticism, among other topics, provoked varying reactions. Modernists embraced the new theories and sought to incorporate them into their faith; fundamentalists eschewed these developments as anti-Christian and retrenched their conservative position. Multiple white American Protestant denominations divided as these two factions strengthened. This debate drew attention away from missions work and, in the case of modernists, resulted in questions regarding the necessity of cross-cultural evangelism.[20] African-American Protestants, however, did not experience this same divide, as they generally emphasized social ministry alongside conservative theology as part of the holistic freedom that they believed Christ offered. International mission work was not a significant emphasis of most African-American Protestants during the twentieth century, as issues of justice in the United States often demanded their attention.[21]

Most white American Protestant denominations eventually settled on the side of the modernists, becoming known as "mainline," with evangelical and fundamentalist groups breaking away to form their own organizations. Mainline missions leaders, influenced by the Social

Gospel movement as well as theological liberalism, emphasized ministry to human needs as they became increasingly uncertain about the
necessity of converting others. They focused more on alleviating poverty, healing the sick, and improving society than on preaching the
exclusiveness of Christ. One historian refers to "liberals' steadily lessen-
ing sense of the danger and iniquity in non-Christian religious systems"
during this time.[22] A major goal of historic Protestant missions work –
that of converting individuals around the world to Christianity – was
called into question. Mainline thinkers began to explore the possibility
of finding God in other religious systems. The idea of religious pluralism,
though controversial, began to gain acceptance among Protestant
thinkers as well as within American society at large.

During the 1930s, American Protestants debated such ideas in public
forums. In 1932, the report of the Laymen's Foreign Missions Inquiry,
entitled *Re-Thinking Missions* and financed by John D. Rockefeller, was
published. This report was written by an interdenominational team of
American Protestants, led by W. E. Hocking, who visited mission fields
to investigate the work taking place there. Its conclusions challenged
traditional understandings of missions work and called for adherents of
world religions to work together. "We believe that the time has come to
set the educational and other philanthropic aspects of missions work free
from organized responsibility to the work of conscious and direct evangelism," the report opined.[23] It also exhorted missionaries not to speak
against non-Christian religions and discussed the need for missionaries
to transfer leadership to nationals on established mission fields, suggesting that smaller numbers of American missionaries were needed in the
future.

The Hocking report, as it was frequently called, was met with significant controversy. Leaders of several Protestant denominations dis-
tanced themselves from the report, although in the years that followed
many mainline Protestant mission boards followed its recommendations. Regardless of denominational views on the report, it was evident
that Protestant missions leaders no longer agreed on the goals and necessity of their work; missionaries and their role had become a subject for
public debate and the reshaping of American Protestant self-
understanding. Indeed, a few weeks after the Hocking report was published, acclaimed Presbyterian missionary Pearl Buck spoke to a crowd of
2,000 in New York City on the question, "Is there a case for foreign
missions?"[24] That such a question would be debated publicly would
have been almost unthinkable to American Protestants fifty years
prior. In addition to conversations among Protestant leaders, secular

American magazines during this time published hundreds of articles debating missions work.[25] Many Americans were no longer convinced that converting non-Christian peoples was an essential part of Christians' task.

While overall national sentiment regarding missions work had changed, evangelical and fundamentalist Protestants renewed their focus on evangelistic missions efforts, perhaps even bolstered by mainline opposition to this type of work. Evangelicals viewed ideas such as those of Hocking and Buck with alarm and sought to return their churches and American culture to what they believed were more biblical sentiments. Their countercultural stance, they believed, represented traditional Christianity, from which mainline Protestants had strayed. Evangelicals claimed to be the true heirs of historic conversionary American missions efforts, although those from mainline denominations disagreed. The self-understandings of the two groups diverged over their definition of missions work, among other issues.

The years following World War II saw a significant increase in missions efforts by evangelical American Protestants. Multiple missions organizations were founded by servicemen who had observed what they considered to be spiritual and physical needs while stationed overseas and, characteristic of the activist American disposition, sought to remedy these conditions. Other organizations were created because of conservatives' displeasure with mainline Protestant mission boards' emphasis on social ministry rather than evangelism. True to the entrepreneurial spirit of American evangelicalism, evangelicals from multiple denominations joined together to advance specialized missions work through new interdenominational missions agencies. They formed organizations focused on Bible translation, missions aviation, broadcasting, compassionate ministries, and ministry with specific people groups, among other emphases. These included Wycliffe Bible Translators, Missionary Aviation Fellowship, Far Eastern Broadcasting Company, World Vision, New Tribes Mission, and many others.[26]

The success of such missions organizations among evangelicals only furthered their priority of missions as integral to their identity. This work was supported in many quarters by a premillennial emphasis on hastening Christ's return through converting people of all nations (Matthew 24:14).[27] Along with evangelical zeal, improvements in communication and transportation in the mid-twentieth century helped these ministries succeed. Even the widely publicized killing of five evangelical missionaries in Ecuador in 1956 furthered the missionary cause among evangelicals, who admired the commitment of these men and their families.[28] During this period, the United States surpassed England as the leading missionary-sending country. American evangelicals rather than mainline Protestants had taken up the missions cause.

In the second half of the twentieth century, evangelical missions efforts grew further, while mainline Protestant missions work continued to decline. Ideologies such as multiculturalism, religious pluralism, secularism, and postmodernism were prevalent in American culture and often adopted by mainline adherents, shaping their self-understanding. No longer was the prototypical American assumed to be a conversionary Protestant; instead, those of all cultural and faith backgrounds (including no faith) were celebrated. Religion grew less important in a prosperous consumer society; exclusive truth claims were disparaged and replaced with affirmations of individual preferences. In addition, the role of Americans in foreign nations was questioned. Many Americans believed that missionaries interfered with indigenous cultures and religions, and should cease their efforts. Among American Protestants only evangelicals, with their self-consciously countercultural approach, remained committed to conversionary missions work.

In addition, the era of western colonialism drew to a close during these years, with the rapid founding of independent nations replacing colonies around the world. Almost all of Africa, for example, was decolonized between 1950 and 1970. Residents and leaders of former colonies asserted a nationalism that often manifested itself in a dislike of Westerners, whom they associated with colonial power. Some countries, such as China, expelled western missionaries.[29] At times missionaries faced violence and even death in newly independent states, whose people often resented their presence. In 1971, John Gatu, a Presbyterian leader in East Africa, called for a moratorium on western missionaries. In his words, "the churches of the Third World must be allowed to find their own identity, and the continuation of the present missionary movement is a hindrance to this selfhood of the church."[30] Gatu and his supporters believed that western missions kept the African church in a perpetual state of subordination. Even if they did not call for a complete suspension of missions efforts, indigenous Christians on many mission fields urged missionaries to transfer leadership responsibilities to the national church. American Protestant mission boards undertook this devolution with various levels of speed and enthusiasm. Mainline Protestants proved the most open to handing over leadership to national Christians, in part because support of missions work had waned among their constituency, and also because of their sensitivity to diversity. Evangelical mission boards undertook such transitions at various levels, often shifting their missions force to more unreached groups of people rather than withdrawing personnel from overseas. Western missionary work continued to be an important part of evangelical Protestants' self-understanding.

In addition to the engagement of unreached people groups by evangelicals, both evangelical and mainline Protestants began in this period to recognize the importance of contextualizing their missions efforts to the cultures of the peoples among whom they worked.[31] No longer did missionaries seek to impart both Christianity and western civilization; the events of previous years, as well as advances in missionary anthropology, demonstrated that this strategy was unwise. Instead, to varying levels missionaries sought to adapt the forms of their faith to indigenous cultures without changing their core message. They were aided in these efforts by indigenous Christians and the growing influence of world Christianity. By the end of the twentieth century, more Christians lived in non-Western than Western countries. The new shape of world Christianity forced American Protestants to reconsider their identity, although some did this more readily than others. American Protestants were no longer the dominant force in global Christianity, although they maintained a significant influence due to their resources and history.[32]

In the early twenty-first century, mainline American Protestants continued to deemphasize evangelistic missionary work while maintaining global humanitarian efforts at a lesser level than in previous years, and often in partnership with non-Western Christians. Evangelical American Protestants also forged new partnerships with global Christian leaders, churches, and organizations, and their work continued to thrive, with much higher numbers of evangelical than mainline missionaries serving internationally. Evangelicals maintained their priority on conversion while also conducting humanitarian efforts – usually accompanied by the verbal proclamation of the gospel. Evangelical missions work experienced rapid growth during this period, with large numbers of evangelicals – especially young people – participating in short-term mission trips. These trips, often between one and two weeks long, typically engaged groups of American evangelicals in international service projects and evangelism in locations marked by material poverty.[33] Made possible by advances in wealth, technology, and travel, short-term mission trips alternately created reciprocal relationships and exploited non-Western Christians. They reshaped many American evangelical Protestants' understanding of their identity as part of the global church, although without necessarily changing their behavior. As of 2020, the predominance of short-term missions shows no sign of declining in the near future.

CONCLUSION

Overall, missions work – from international missionary service to missions support at home – has been a significant element of American Protestantism from its beginnings to the present day. Thousands of American Protestants, both liberal and conservative, have traveled internationally (and cross-culturally in the United States) in efforts to share the good news of Christ with others in word and deed. Mainline American Protestants have been significantly influenced by the modern missionary movement, although today they may identify more closely with the backlash against missions that emerged in the twentieth century. Similarly, evangelical Protestants' contemporary missions efforts build on those of previous centuries while incorporating new motivations and tools in an attempt to convert all people groups. It is impossible to understand American Protestants without examining their commitment to global missions and missionary work throughout their history.

NOTES

1 Stephen Neill, *A History of Christian Missions* vol. II (New York: Penguin, 1986), 191–192.
2 See John B. Carpenter, "New England Puritans: The Grandparents of Modern Protestant Missions," *Missiology: An International Review* vol. 30, no. 4 (2002), 519–532.
3 Jon Butler, Grant Wacker, and Randall Balmer, *Religion in American Life: A Short History* (New York: Oxford University Press, 2008), 97–98. See also Karl-Wilhelm Westmeier, "Becoming All Things to All People: Early Moravian Missions to Native North Americans," *International Bulletin of Missionary Research* vol. 21, no. 4 (1997), 172–176.
4 See Thomas S. Kidd, *The Great Awakening: The Roots of Evangelical Christianity in Colonial America* (New Haven, CT: Yale University Press, 2009).
5 David Brainerd and Jonathan Edwards, *The Life of David Brainerd, Missionary to the Indians: Chiefly Taken from His Own Diary and Other Private Writings* (London: T. Nelson, 1749).
6 See Robert L. Gallagher and John Mark Terry, *Encountering the History of Missions: From the Early Church to Today* (Grand Rapids, MI: Baker Academic, 2017), 238–240.

7 Alan Neely, "Liele, George," in *Biographical Dictionary of Christian Missions*, ed. Gerald H. Anderson (New York: Macmillan Reference USA, 1998), 400–401. See also David T. Shannon, Julia Frazier. White, and Deborah Bingham Van Broekhoven, *George Liele's Life and Legacy: An Unsung Hero* (Macon, GA: Mercer University Press, 2013).

8 Paul Pierson, *The Dynamics of Christian Mission: History through a Missiological Perspective* (Pasadena, CA: William Carey International University Press, 2009), 215.

9 Ann soon died; Adoniram married two other times. See Rosalie Hall Hunt, *Bless God and Take Courage: The Judson History and Legacy* (Valley Forge, PA: Judson Press, 2005).

10 Kenneth Scott Latourette, *The Great Century, A.D. 1800–1914* vol. IV of *A History of the Expansion of Christianity* (London: Eyre and Spottiswoode, 1941).

11 For an exploration of similar themes related to Southern Baptist missions, see Robert Nash, "The Influence of American Myth on Southern Baptist Foreign Missions, 1845–1945" (Ph.D. dissertation, Southern Baptist Theological Seminary, 1990).

12 Many denominations also formed home missionary societies, sometimes employing returned foreign missionaries for such work. At other times, home missionaries went on to serve in foreign missions.

13 See Carol Crawford Holcomb, "Baptist Missions and the Turn toward National Denominational Organizations: The Baptist Missionary Society and the Triennial Convention: 1792/1812," in *Turning Points in Baptist History: A Festschrift in Honor of Harry Leon McBeth* ed. Michael E. Williams, Sr. and Walter B. Shurden (Macon, GA: Mercer University Press, 2011), 114–127; and J. M. Reid, *Missions and Missionary Society of the Methodist Episcopal Church*, 2 vols. (New York: Phillips, 1880).

14 For more on African-American missions history, see Vaughn Walston and Robert Stevens, *African-American Experience in World Mission: A Call Beyond Community* (Pasadena, CA: William Carey Library, 2002), 25–76.

15 See Norman Etherington, ed., *Missions and Empire* (Oxford: Oxford University Press, 2008); and Carlos F. Cardoza-Orlandi and Justo L. González, *To All Nations from All Nations: A History of the Christian Missionary Movement* (Nashville: Abingdon Press, 2013).

16 See Daniel H. Bays and Grant Wacker, eds., *The Foreign Missionary Enterprise at Home: Explorations in North American Cultural History* (Tuscaloosa: University of Alabama Press, 2003). For more on the influence of American missions on world Christianity and vice versa, see Mark A. Noll, *The New Shape of World Christianity: How American Experience Reflects Global Faith* (Downers Grove, IL: IVP Academic, 2013); and Jay Riley Case, *An Unpredictable Gospel: American Evangelicals and World Christianity, 1812–1920* (New York: Oxford University Press, 2012).

17 See R. Pierce Beaver, *American Protestant Women in World Mission: A History of the First Feminist Movement in North America* (Grand Rapids, MI: Eerdmans, 1980); and Dana L. Robert, *American Women in Mission: A Social History of Their Thought and Practice*, ed. Wilbert R. Shenk (Macon, GA: Mercer University Press, 1996).

18 Gallagher and Terry, *Encountering the History of Missions*, 270. See also Michael Parker, *The Kingdom of Character: The Student Volunteer Movement for Foreign Missions (1886–1926)* (Lanham, MD: American Society of Missiology, 1998).

19 Noll, *The New Shape of World Christianity*, 41, citing David Barrett's *World Christian Encyclopedia* (New York: Oxford University Press, 1982).

20 See James Alan Patterson, "The Loss of a Protestant Missionary Consensus: Foreign Missions and the Fundamentalist-Modernist Conflict," in *Earthen Vessels: American Evangelicals and Foreign Missions, 1880–1980*, ed. Joel A. Carpenter and Wilbert R. Shenk (Grand Rapids, MI: Eerdmans, 1990), 73–91; and George M. Marsden, *Fundamentalism and American Culture: The Shaping of Twentieth-Century Evangelicalism, 1870–1925* (New York: Oxford University Press, 1980).

21 See Mary Beth Mathews, *Doctrine and Race: African American Evangelicals and Fundamentalism between the Wars* (Tuscaloosa: University of Alabama Press, 2018).

22 William R. Hutchison, *Errand to the World: American Protestant Thought and Foreign Missions* (Chicago: University of Chicago Press, 1987), 105. See also Grant Wacker, "Second Thoughts on the Great Commission: Liberal Protestants and Foreign Missions, 1890–1940," in *Earthen Vessels*, ed. Carpenter and Shenk, 281–300.

23 Laymen's Foreign Missions Inquiry and William Ernest Hocking, *Re-Thinking Missions: A Laymen's Inquiry after One Hundred Years* (New York: Harper & Bros., 1932), 326.

24 Grant Wacker, "The Waning of the Missionary Enterprise: The Case of Pearl Buck," in *The Foreign Missionary Enterprise at Home*, ed. Bays and Wacker, 191–205. See also Soojin Chung, "The Missiology of Pearl Sydenstricker Buck," *International Bulletin of Mission Research* vol. 41, no. 2 (2017), 134–141.

25 Hutchison, *Errand to the World*, 156. See also Sarah E. Ruble, *The Gospel of Freedom and Power: Protestant Missionaries in American Culture after World War II* (Chapel Hill: University of North Carolina Press, 2014).

26 See Gallagher and Terry, *Encountering the History of Missions*, 314–331.

27 An emphasis on converting people groups rather than nations emerged beginning in the 1970s.

28 See Kathryn T. Long, "In the Modern World, But Not of It: The 'Auca Martyrs,' Evangelicalism, and Postwar American Culture," in *The Foreign Missionary Enterprise at Home*, ed. Bays and Wacker, 224–236.

29 See Neill, *A History of Christian Missions*, 423.

30 John G. Gatu, "Missionary, Go Home," *International Documentation* vol. 63 (July 1974), 70.

31 For the genesis of the idea of unreached people groups among evangelical Protestants, see Ralph Winter, "The Highest Priority: Cross-Cultural Evangelism," Lausanne Congress on World Evangelization, Lausanne, Switzerland, July 20, 1974, www.lausanne.org/content/the-highest-priority-cross-cultural-evangelism. For the history of the missiological idea of contextualization, see David Jacobus Bosch, "Mission as Contextualization," in *Transforming Mission: Paradigm Shifts in Theology of Mission* (Maryknoll, NY: Orbis Books, 1991), 420–432.

32 For more on world Christianity, see Jenkins, Philip, *The Next Christendom: The Coming of Global Christianity* (New York: Oxford University Press, 2002); Douglas G. Jacobsen, *The World's Christians: Who They Are, Where They Are, and How They Got There* (Malden, MA: Wiley-Blackwell, 2011); and Scott W. Sunquist, *The Unexpected Christian Century: The Reversal and Transformation of Global Christianity, 1900–2000* (Grand Rapids, MI: Baker Academic, 2015).

33 See Brian M. Howell, *Short-Term Mission: An Ethnography of Christian Travel Narrative and Experience* (Downers Grove, IL: IVP Academic, 2012); and Robert J. Priest, *Effective Engagement in Short-Term Missions* (Pasadena, CA: William Carey Library, 2008).

Part III
Theological Traditions

17 Anglicanism

ROBERT W. PRICHARD

The Episcopal Church (or, to use its legal name, The Protestant Episcopal Church in the United States of America) is the direct descendant of the Church of England in colonial North America and the primary claimant to represent the Anglican tradition in the United States. It is a member of the Anglican Communion.[1]

THE ANGLICAN COMMUNION

The Anglican (from the Latin word for English) Communion is a term that has been used since the middle of the nineteenth century to refer to the international family of churches that descend from the Church of England. Worldwide, churches in the Anglican Communion are strongest in numbers in former British colonies, especially in Africa, but they are found in many other nations of the world as well. Churches in the Anglican Communion follow one of three conventions for naming; they use "Anglican" in their title, as in the Anglican Church of Canada; "Episcopal" (i.e., having bishops), as in the Episcopal Church of Scotland; or a national identifier, such as the Church of Nigeria. Some churches employ two or all three of these identifiers, such as the Anglican Episcopal Church of Brazil (Igreja Episcopal Anglicana do Brasil).

As of 2021, there were forty-one member churches (also called provinces) in the communion. There are four member churches in the United Kingdom: England, Wales, Scotland, and Ireland (which includes both the Republic of Ireland and Northern Ireland). The majority of the other members have boundaries that coincide with that of a single nation, though some incorporate several nations (Central Africa, Southeast Asia, the West Indies, etc.). The Episcopal Church includes the fifty states and eleven dioceses (subunits with a bishop of which three are required to constitute a member church) that are extra-national: Colombia, Cuba, the Dominican Republic, Ecuador, Europe, Haiti, Honduras, Puerto Rico,

Taiwan, Venezuela, and the Virgin Islands. Four of the forty-one member churches (Bangladesh, South India, North India, and Pakistan) are ecumenical bodies that are also recognized by other denominations. There are also five national or local churches (Bermuda, the Falkland Islands, Portugal, Spain, and Sri Lanka) that lack the three dioceses needed to constitute a member church; they participate in the communion under the supervision of the Archbishop of Canterbury.

The member churches are autonomous but cooperate with one another through four "instruments of communion": recognition of the Archbishop of Canterbury (the senior bishop in the Church of England, with a see that dates back to 597) as the first among equal primates (chief bishops of member churches) and spiritual leader of the communion; the sending of bishops to the Lambeth Conference (since 1867 in roughly ten-year intervals), representation (in rotation) at the Anglican Consultative Council (since 1971 at approximately three-year intervals), and representation at the "Primates' Meeting" (held occasionally since 1979). The three member churches on the North American continent recognized by the Anglican Communion are the Episcopal Church, the Anglican Church of Canada, and the Anglican Church of Mexico (La Iglesia Anglicana de México).

The Anglican Church in North America, or ACNA (formed in 2009), is a coalition of church bodies, some of whom departed from the Episcopal Church as early as 1873 (with the formation of the Reformed Episcopal Church); it presents itself as a defender of a Bible-based Anglican orthodoxy, from which it suggests that the Episcopal Church and the Anglican Church of Canada have departed. It is not at this time a participant in the four instruments of communion but is represented at the Global Anglican Future Conference's Council of Primates, which was created in 2008 as an alternative to the Primates' Meeting.

HISTORY OF THE EPISCOPAL CHURCH

After a failed attempt to settle on Roanoke Island (1685–1687) in what is now North Carolina, the British were able to begin a permanent colony at Jamestown in Virginia (1607). The colonists brought the Church of England with them; until the 1620 arrival of the Pilgrims in Plymouth, Massachusetts, the Church of England was arguably the only denomination in British colonial North America.

The Church in Virginia would not be a carbon copy of the Church in England, however. Indeed, the character of the church in England was in flux, and the Virginia church took on characteristics that distinguished it from its English counterpart. For example, by the middle of the seventeenth century Virginia vestries were selecting their own clergy, a right exercised by patrons in England. The colonial church would also have no bishops for the entire colonial era. In the late seventeenth century, the Bishop of London began to appoint commissaries (priests with a commission to represent the bishop) as a partial remedy. They spoke on behalf of the church and attempted to impose discipline on errant clergy. Initially, the Bishop of London appointed commissaries for Virginia and Maryland but later extended the system to the Carolinas, New York, Pennsylvania, and Massachusetts. The system lacked authorizing Parliamentary legislation, however, and would be scaled back as a result in the second half of the eighteenth century.

Of the colonies that would eventually form the United States, only Virginia had an organized Church of England before the 1680s, with the remaining colonies then in existence either aligned with other denominations (Massachusetts, Connecticut, and New Hampshire with the Congregational Church; Rhode Island with Baptists; Pennsylvania with the Friends; and Maryland with Roman Catholics) or pursuing a more laissez-faire policy. From the time of their arrival in Massachusetts Bay in 1630, the Congregationalist Church would be the largest American denomination. For the remainder of the colonial period, the Church of England and the Presbyterians vied for second place. Congregationalists lost their distinction of being the largest single denominations to the Methodists in the early nineteenth century; the Methodists in turn would be passed up in numbers by Roman Catholics and Baptists by the early twentieth century (though the number of Protestants as a whole continues to this day to be greater than the number of Roman Catholics).

Membership of the Church of England plummeted at the American Revolution due to popular opposition to things English, the loss of aid and direction from the United Kingdom, the departure of many clergy and lay members for territories that remained loyal to Britain, and the conversion of parishioners to Methodist and Baptist churches. By the nineteenth century Episcopalians had fallen into sixth place in terms of numbers. Nevertheless, the church retained importance after American independence due to the prominence of its parishioners in public life and to its leadership in ecumenism, education, and social ministry. The leadership of the United States in world affairs since World War II has also given the Episcopal Church an outsized – and at times problematic – role in the Anglican Communion.

THE CHURCH PRIOR TO 1688

The London Company (1606–1624) and the governors it appointed directed the life of the Virginia colony, including its religious practice. It limited potential colonists to Protestants, selected clergy for parishes, and directed use of the Book of Common Prayer, the official liturgy of the Church of England. In 1624, the English monarch took direct control of the colony; supporters of the action cited the high death rate from disease and attack by Native Americans. Charles I, who followed James I to the throne in 1625, showed relatively little interest in the colony, however, beyond the possibility that it might be used for purposes of taxation. It was during his reign and during the English Civil War (1642–1651) that ended his rule that Virginia vestries were able to consolidate the claim to select their rectors (the rector was the chief clergyperson in a parish).

The English Parliament, which prevailed over Charles I, called an assembly of theologians at Westminster and supported their remaking of the Church of England along Presbyterian lines. Oliver Cromwell, the head of the Parliament's New Model Army, was Puritan in sentiment but favored independent (i.e., congregational) rather than presbyterian ecclesiology. As a result, he was more interested in enforcing the negative half of the Presbyterian program (eliminating bishops, prayer books, and the Articles of Religion of the Church of England) than the positive half (formation of presbyteries, adoption of the Westminster Confession of Faith, and use of the *Directory for Worship*). He sent a fleet to Virginia to secure allegiance to his rule; the colonial legislature agreed to halt use of the Book of Common Prayer after one year, but it is unclear whether the colonists complied with that direction after the departure of the fleet.

Virginia's legislature (the General Assembly, established in 1619) created counties and parishes as the colonists expanded from their early settlements. It designated land for the support of the church (the glebes) and gave the vestries the right to tax the populace both for support of the church and for public welfare matters, such as the care of widows, orphans, the poor, and the sick. Each parish had a principal church building (often located at the midpoint between the larger plantations in the area) and in most cases one or more "chapels of ease" to serve outlying areas. The clergyman was assisted by lay readers, who presided at worship when the clergyperson was elsewhere in the parish, and by a sexton, who had responsibility for keeping the church building in good order. Of these three positions, the only one ever occupied by women during the colonial era was that of sexton.

In comparison to New England, the Virginia church followed a moderate policy regarding perceived misconduct or heresy. There were none of the executions for witchcraft or heresy that took place in seventeenth-century New England, though some Quakers were exiled. Communities of non-Anglican Protestants who immigrated were allowed to form congregations of their own (so long as there was already a Church of England parish in existence in the county) and were in some cases excused for a period from paying the church tax.

While a few clergy (such as Morgan Godwyn in Virginia, the author of *The Negro's and Indians Advocate* in 1680) questioned the creation of a legal system of racial slavery for persons of African heritage in the middle and latter half of the seventeenth century (something that had been lacking in English law prior to that time), most did not. Opposition was made problematic by the participation of Kings Charles II (1660–1685) and James II (1685–1688) in the Royal African Company, to which the Parliament gave a monopoly for the transportation of enslaved persons to British colonies, and by colonial governmental decisions denying that baptism had any effect on one's enslaved status (an argument that enslaved persons were making in court) and penalizing clergy presiding at interracial marriages. There would be stronger opposition to the enslaving of Native Americans, something that would be banned in most colonies in the early part of the following century.

FROM THE GLORIOUS REVOLUTION (1688) TO THE AMERICAN REVOLUTION

The position of the Church of England in North America improved significantly after William III (1689–1702) and Mary II (1689–1694) replaced James II on the British throne following the Glorious Revolution. Mary and her sister Anne (queen, 1702–1714), who followed William to the throne, showed particular interest in the Church of England. Henry Compton (Bishop of London, 1675–1713), who had been entrusted with Mary and Anne's education during their youth, encouraged and supported their efforts. He appointed the first colonial commissaries for Virginia (1689), Maryland (1695), and the Carolinas (1707). Commissary James Blair, who served in Virginia from 1689 to 1743, founded the College of William and Mary (1693) in Williamsburg with the hope that it might educate future clergy and Native Americans. Thomas Bray (1656 or 1658–1730), the first Maryland commissary, spent little time in the colony but formed three missionary societies that would be of great help to the colonial church: the Society for Promoting Christian Knowledge (SPCK,

1698), which provided for colonial libraries; the Society for the Propagation of the Gospel in Foreign Parts (SPGFP, 1701), which supported missionaries; and Dr. Bray's Associates (1730), which supported ministry to and education of African Americans. Queen Anne introduced legislation (Queen Anne's Bounty) to redirect certain church funds – which had had been seized by the Crown during the nationalization of the Church of England under Henry VIII – to improve clergy salaries, build new church buildings, and cover the costs of travel for those clergy who volunteered for service in the British colonies. Anne also made gifts of land and communion silver to individual colonial parishes. She supported legislation for the introduction of bishops in the colonies but died before action could be taken in Parliament.

The royal patronage and the missionary societies expanded the colonial Anglican church beyond Virginia. The Church of England was established roughly following the Virginia model in Maryland (1702), South Carolina (1706), Georgia (1758), Nova Scotia (1758), and North Carolina (1765). New York adopted an establishment of the "Protestant religion" in six counties in 1693, an ambiguous provision that made it unclear which Protestant denomination was to benefit. Queen Anne's grant of 215 acres of land in Manhattan (1705), however, provided the first Church of England parish in New York (Trinity Church, Wall Street, 1697) with a valuable resource from which the parish continues to benefit to this day.

Many of the theological tendencies that current-day Episcopalians now routinely attribute to the English Reformation date from this period of time: a rational approach to the exposition of religion (advocated by such authors as Archbishop John Tillotson and John Locke as an alternative to the religious-fueled violence of the English Civil War), acceptance of natural science (something evidenced by the science books in the SPCK libraries), and toleration of religious dissent (William and Mary's Act of Toleration of 1689). Bishop Gilbert Burnet's *Exposition of the Thirty-Nine Articles* (1699), which would become required reading for nineteenth-century Episcopalians preparing for ordination, suggested that the formularies of the Church of England allowed for either an Arminian or Dortian understanding of predestination, a position that would partially shield members of the Church of England from arguments that divided many Christians of the Reformed tradition.

When Bishop of London Edmund Gibson conducted a survey of colonial parishes in 1724, he found 161 parishes located in nine colonies, with the greatest number in Virginia, Maryland, New York, and South Carolina. Clergy reported full churches in times of fair weather, ministry to African Americans, and a rate of receiving holy communion greater than that in England. (Prior to 1970, rubrics in the Book of Common Prayer limited communion to those confirmed by a bishop or "ready and desirous to be confirmed." Colonial members of the Church of England, who would have no resident bishops until 1785, took advantage of the later provision and received communion after instruction in the faith by their parish clergy.)

In the years before the American Revolution, colonial members of the Church of England would be influenced by two theological trends that were also important in the United Kingdom: the high-church movement and the Great Awakening. The high-church movement was a response to greater toleration of dissent and theological diversity following the Glorious Revolution. Supporters of the movement accepted the right of other Protestants to practice religion but questioned the theological legitimacy of any church that lacked bishops. They stressed their differences with other Protestants. The *Catechetical Lectures* of Thomas Bray, for example, presented a high-church form of covenant theology that suggested that God was not "under any promise, or engagement to hear the prayers" of clergy with non-episcopal ordination.[2] The argument was used by SPG missionaries, particularly in New England, where missionary George Pigot persuaded seven faculty members and recent graduates of Congregationalist Yale College to sign a 1722 petition expressing their doubts about non-episcopal ordination. Four of the group, including Timothy Cutler (1683 or 1684–1765) and Samuel Johnson (1696–1772), were reordained in the Church of England. Such converts would provide an aggressive leadership for a growing Church of England in New England and New York.

The Great Awakening was the colonial version of the evangelical revival that swept Protestant areas of Europe, beginning in the seventeenth century with the Pietist movement among German Lutherans. Supporters of the movement paired the classic Protestant doctrine of justification by grace through faith with a sentimentalist psychology and small group meetings. Preachers described the experience of new birth or regeneration that a justified person should feel, and members of groups held one another responsible for living in ways that accorded with justification. Church of England clergy George Whitefield (1714–1770) and John (1703–1791) and Charles Wesley (1707–1788) were among the chief preachers of the movement in England. Whitefield visited the American colonies on seven occasions, engaging in preaching tours beginning in 1740 in which he popularized the ideas of the Awakening. The Wesleys' single stay in the colonies was not particularly successful, but they had the organizational ability that Whitefield lacked and were able to dispatch sympathetic clergy and lay preachers to America to provide the leadership for a network of Methodist societies with ties to the colonial Church of England. Those societies became a separate Methodist Episcopal Church in December 1784. Whitefield's habits of insulting the leading Anglican theologians of William and Mary's reign, characterizing the failure of Church of England clergy to give him unlimited access to their pulpits as persecution, and collaborating with clergy of non-episcopal churches were off-putting to many clergy of the Church of England in the colonies – particularly those of high-church sentiment. A number of individual clergy in the Middle and Southern colonies ordained after 1760 did become supporters of the Awakening, however. They taught about new birth and either supported Methodist societies or formed "Whitfilian" small groups of their own. They generally did not choose sides in the debate between Whitefield's Dortian approach to Predestination and the Wesleys' Arminian approach.

High-church clergy consistently opposed the Awakening, presenting the Church of England as an ark to which reasonable Christians could flee to avoid sentimental worship. They were also the primary force behind a series of conventions in the middle colonies and New York (1760–1767) that brought together clergy from multiple colonies in order to shape a common response to the Awakening and to appeal to England for colonial bishops whom they presumed would support their opposition. By the early nineteenth century, however, many of the innovations of the Awakening – use of hymns of modern composition in worship; more lively forms of preaching; church designs with prominent pulpits located in the center of the chancel; and creation of small groups for prayer, education, and fellowship – would become standard throughout the Episcopal Church.

FROM THE AMERICAN REVOLUTION TO 1873

The Church of England in the thirteen colonies found itself at a distinct disadvantage because of the American Revolution. Their clergy had all taken oaths of allegiance to the king, and many laypersons also saw obedience to the monarch as basic to their faith. The church's fixed forms for public worship (in the English Book of Common Prayer of 1662) included prayers for the king and royal family. The highest clerical authority in England – Archbishop of Canterbury Frederick Cornwallis – was the uncle of an important general in the British army. The Revolution also cut American members of the Church of England off from their only source of ordination (bishops in England) and from important financial resources (church taxes in the colonies that had established the Church of England and contributions from British missionary societies – both of which were suspended with the onset of the Revolution). The Church of England's most successful ministry to Native Americans prior to the war had been to the Iroquois Federation in western New York; Mohawk leader Thayendanegea or Joseph Brant (1743–1807), who had been supportive of that ministry, organized a loyalist military unit in the Revolution and led the way in resettlement in Canada at the war's conclusion. With the exception of the few efforts in the middle colonies mentioned above, members of the church in various colonies lacked any structure to hold them together as a denomination; they were to that point a series of churches in individual colonies that had been connected to missionary societies in England and (in some cases) to the Bishop of London but lacking any formal connection with one another.

At least three separate efforts to remedy the organizational problems were in play by 1784. First, there was an effort led by William Smith (a Scottish immigrant who had become provost of the College of Philadelphia) and his former pupil William White (rector of the United Churches of Philadelphia) to organize as a denomination around a series of lay and clergy conventions. Smith, who had relocated to Maryland, led the clergy in that state to take initial organizational steps. White wrote a pamphlet (*The Case of the Episcopal Churches Considered*, 1782) urging other states to follow suit, leading to a preliminary meeting in Philadelphia in May of 1784. Though later Episcopal historians have not generally emphasized the fact, the proposals made in White's pamphlet borrowed heavily from the organizational pattern of the (Presbyterian) Church of Scotland; indeed, it can be argued that the proposals would be more closely reflected in the Presbyterian Church constitution of 1789 than in the revised constitution adopted by Episcopalians in the same year. Secondly, clergy of the Church of England in Connecticut, upset by the efforts of White and Smith, met in a clergy convocation (to which no laypersons were invited) and elected two senior priests as candidates for the episcopate. The younger of the two – Samuel Seabury (1729–1796) – accepted the election and traveled to England for ordination. He was unable to secure consecration for a variety of reasons: the existence of an established Congregational Church in Connecticut, the lack of published minutes or lay representatives in the electing convocation, and the lack of Parliamentary legislation allowing ordinations for clergy outside of the United Kingdom. Parliament would act in two steps to remedy the last of these obstacles, adopting legislation allowing the ordination of deacons and priests (1784) and legislation allowing the ordination of bishops (1786). Seabury was undeterred by the delay and went to Scotland where he was ordained a bishop in November 1784 in Aberdeen by three bishops of the Episcopal Church of Scotland (which was not at that time officially recognized by the Church of England because of its continuing allegiance to the descendants of James II, who had been replaced in the Glorious Revolution of 1688). Finally, there was an organizational effort by the leaders of the Methodist societies, who attempted to take advantage of the confused ecclesiological situation following the Revolution to secure the consecration of bishops to preside over their societies, which to that point had functioned as a reform movement within the Church of England. Charles Wesley held a preliminary conversation with Samuel Seabury about the possibility that he might ordain Methodist preachers as clergy. John Wesley, however, had other ideas; he designated Thomas Coke (an ordained Church of England clergyman who supported the Methodist movement) and Francis Asbury (the Methodist lay preacher who remained most active in America during the Revolution) as superintendents (an alternate translation of the Greek New Testament word for bishop), and asked them to organize a Methodist Episcopal Church in America. They did so through a conference that began on Christmas Eve of 1784. Parallel efforts would not be completed in England until after the death of John Wesley in 1791.

There would be several organizational and liturgical differences between the two resultant denominations – known at the time as the Protestant Episcopal Church and the Methodist Episcopal Church. Methodists would, for example, give their superintendents organizational powers similar to Church of English bishops, but a smaller liturgical role. Episcopal bishops had an important liturgical role but had more limited organizational power than their English counterparts. Both made revisions to the English Book of Common Prayer, but Episcopalians understood the book to be mandatory, while Methodist regarded John Wesley's revision of the prayer book (*The Sunday Service of the Methodists in North America*, 1784) as optional.

After pursuing separate efforts for five years, the White and Seabury groups united in the two sessions of the General Convention in 1789, with the convention idea modified to allow a bicameral form with a House of Deputies for laity and clergy (understood prior to 1982 to mean presbyters and since 1982 to mean deacons or presbyters), and a separate House of Bishops. The same body adopted an American revision of the Book of Common Prayer that dropped references to the English monarchy, added a prayer for the President of the United States, and substituted the Scottish prayer of Eucharistic consecration (a revision of that in the first English prayer book of 1549) for the English prayer of consecration (in English prayer books from 1552). Despite later efforts by Methodist Superintendent Thomas Coke (1747–1814) and first Episcopal Bishop of Virginia James Madison (1749–1812), Methodists and Episcopalians were unable to establish any formal ties. (An attempt by Episcopalians and Northern Methodists to enter into an ecumenical union in 1939 would also fail, as Methodists concentrated on reuniting internal divisions created by the Civil War. In the early twenty-first century, however, Methodist and Episcopalians signed a series of accords; the outcome of those efforts has been complicated by discussions in 2019–2020 of division of the United Methodist Church over disagreements about human sexuality and holiness of life.)

During the years following the 1789 General Convention, Episcopalians concentrated on regaining the ground that they had lost in the thirteen colonies at the time of the American Revolution. It would not be until 1817 that North Carolina would be represented at General Convention, and until 1844 that New Hampshire was fully organized with a bishop of its own. Virginia, which had had the oldest and largest colonial Church of England on the eve of the Revolution, had a set of particular problems of its own, with the legislature seizing the buildings and property of vacant parishes up until this was halted by a decision of the US Supreme Court (*Terrett v. Taylor*, 1815).

In the meantime, Episcopalians were less attentive to the needs of those Americans who were moving to the west. While individual clergy and laity were able to organize dioceses and elect bishops in Ohio (1819) and Kentucky (1832), the General Convention was not able to come up with a consistent plan for western missions until 1835, when it agreed on funding missionary bishops for unincorporated areas.

Despite the depressed numbers in the denomination in the early nineteenth century, Episcopal laity continued to play important roles in national life. Half of the first fourteen US presidents were affiliated with the Episcopal Church – George Washington, James Madison, James Monroe, William Henry Harrison, John Tyler, Zachery Taylor, and Franklin Pierce – and Thomas Jefferson had been reared in the tradition. A number of popular authors were also connected with the church, including Mason Locke Weems (1759–1825), creator of popular historical sketches of American leaders; novelists Susanna Haswell Rowson (1762–1824), author of *Charlotte Temple* (1791), Sally Sayward Wood (1759–1855), and

James Fennimore Cooper (1798–1851); and poet Sarah Wentworth Apthorp Morton (1759–1846).

Later church historians would point to the War of 1812 (when an Episcopalian was president and no members of the denomination sided with the British) or to the 1811 consecration to the episcopate of John Henry Hobart of New York and Alexander Viets Griswold of Rhode Island (the first bishops born in the second half of the eighteenth century) as the moment in which the denomination began to grow in numbers, though statistical indicators suggest an uptick in membership later in the decade.

New York and Bishop Hobart led the way in this new growth of the church, with the number of Episcopal clergy in the State of New York increasing fivefold from 1811 to 1831 and the number of congregations listed in the diocesan journal increasing more than sevenfold in the same years. As both the rector of Trinity Church, Wall Street in New York City and the bishop, Hobart was able to direct parish funds to the founding of chapels in the city and to a diocesan missionary society that would create a string of new congregations in the western part of the state. He recruited clergy who agreed with his high-church principles of non-cooperation with other Protestants and non-involvement in the political order. Nine years after Hobart's death in 1839, Episcopalians in the western part of the state became numerous enough to form a separate Diocese of Western New York, making New York the first state with more than one Episcopal diocese.

Hobart's focus on a high-church vision in New York and his habit of suggesting that clergy who did not accept his principles might do better elsewhere contributed to the formation of a counterbalancing evangelical party in Virginia and the District of Columbia led by William Holland Wilmer, president of the General Convention's House of Deputies (1820–1826), and William Meade (1789–1862), the third bishop of Virginia. Evangelicals emphasized similarity to other Protestants and cooperated with them in ecumenical endeavors such as the American Bible Society and the American Sunday School Union. They focused on lively preaching and the importance of adult faith, and they were more likely to support moral campaigns such as the temperance movement than their high-church co-religionists.

Episcopalians in Virginia, and other dioceses in which their church had previously been established by law, adopted a new mission strategy. Rather than seeking to locate congregations so as to be accessible to the entire population – a strategy that often led to locating church buildings in rural areas roughly equidistant between population centers – they began to focus on ministry in the growing number of towns and cities. By 1860 the percentage of clergy in Southern towns and cities who were Episcopalian (16%) was equal to that of Baptists and exceeded only by the number of Methodists (30%). With most of the nation rural at that point, however, the percentage of Americans who were communicants in the Episcopal Church would never rise above 1% nationwide in the nineteenth century.

Both evangelical and high-church Episcopalians founded seminaries to train sympathetic clergy. The General Theological Seminary in New York and the Protestant Episcopal Theological Seminary in Virginia (more commonly called Virginia Theological Seminary) in Alexandria were the first. Both groups supported publications (the *Churchman* in New York and the *Washington Theological Repertory* and the *Southern Churchman* in Virginia), and both sought allies in other parts of the country.

Prior to the 1840s, the theological differences between the two church parties were of emphasis. Both subscribed to a two-foci theology according to which regeneration (which generally took place sacramentally in infant baptism) and renewal (adult ownership of the faith of baptism) were seen as necessary for salvation. Episcopalians supported the idea by appealing to Titus 3:4–5, which refers to both "the washing of *regeneration*," and the "*renewing* of the Holy Ghost" as means of salvation. The evangelicals emphasized adult renewal and high-church Episcopalians emphasized baptism as the source of regeneration (a term that most other Protestants used of adult conversion).

Theological emphases in the church shifted in the 1840s as a result of the influence of the English Oxford Movement. The movement in England had initially focused on high-church opposition to Parliamentary legislation to reform the church, something that the supporters of the Oxford Movement argued could only be undertaken by bishops. The movement would, however, later involve a renewed appreciation of the theological and liturgical character of the western church during the late classical and medieval periods, when bishops often opposed secular political leaders. It was this later emphasis on theological and liturgical heritage that attracted the attention of high-church Episcopalians in America, some of whom began to identify themselves as Anglo-Catholics (rather than Protestants), to adopt styles of worship that approximated that of the Roman Catholic Church, and to argue that conversion experience was illusory.

Evangelical Episcopalians attempted to suppress the high-church movement in the early 1840s and again in the years immediately following the Civil War. Some early supporters of Oxford ideas, including Bishop Levi S. Ives of North Carolina (Bishop Hobart's son-in-law), responded to criticism by converting to the Roman Catholic Church. By the 1870s, however, tables had turned, and bishops with Oxford Movement sympathies in such places as Chicago and New York began to take action against evangelical Episcopalians for amending the baptismal liturgy (by dropping the reference to baptism as regeneration) and engaging in ecumenical worship with other Protestants.

The earliest woman to seek ordination to the priesthood in the Episcopal Church may have been a parishioner from Pennsylvania who wrote to Bishop William White (the senior or presiding bishop from 1795 to 1835) in 1811 to inquire about the possibility. Her name was omitted in the published version of the letter that appeared in a White biography in the nineteenth century. General Convention would not adopt canonical changes allowing ordination of women to the presbyterate and episcopate until 1976, but women would make some inroads into positions of leadership in the mid-nineteenth century. Beginning in the 1850s Episcopal women began to form sisterhoods. The term was initially ambiguous, used either of efforts to follow the example of Lutherans in Kaiserswerth, Germany who had revived the diaconate for women (1835) or of Roman Catholic monastic orders for women, which were growing rapidly in the nineteenth century. Anne Ayres (1816–1896) was arguably the inspiration for both efforts. In 1845 she committed herself to be a sister working with rector William A. Muhlenberg (1797–1877) in the Church of the Holy Communion in New York, a pattern similar to that of the early Lutheran deaconesses in Germany. In 1852 she organized the Sisterhood of the Holy Communion, an order devoted to nursing that did not involve life vows; in 1863 three members of the sisterhood left the order to found the Community of St. Mary, which had lifelong vows and an increased emphasis on devotional activity. During the nineteenth century, women's altar guilds began to assume the responsibility for preparing church buildings for worship; Josephine Smith Wood would later produce a *Manual for Altar Guilds* (1892) that laid out the responsibilities of such groups.

The General Convention of the Episcopal Church, its highest legislative authority, did not speak against slavery before the Civil War. This was in part a product of the party structure of the church. High-church Episcopalians (who recalled the negative consequences of support of the British in the Revolution) opposed making any statements on what they regarded as political matters. Much of the strength of the evangelical party in the Episcopal Church was south of the Mason–Dixon line;

evangelical Episcopalians cooperated with Presbyterians and others (an ecumenical collaboration rejected by high-church Episcopalians) in supporting the American Colonization Society that encouraged slaveholders to free enslaved persons and settle them in Liberia, but very few Southern Episcopalians spoke publicly in support of mandatory abolition. African-American clergy in the few congregations of free persons in the North generally favored immediate emancipation over the colonization approach, as in the case of Absalom Jones (1746–1818), the first African-American clergyperson in a hierarchical denomination. He was a leader in a protest against the Colonization Society in 1817. Advocacy of immediate abolition in the North often came at a cost. When, for example, Peter Williams, Jr. (1786–1840) joined the Board of the American Anti-Slavery Society, a mob set fire to St. Philip's Church, Harlem (1834), at which he served. Some white Northern evangelical Episcopalians, particularly among the laity, also supported abolition. John Jay (1745–1829), for example, was the first president of the New York Manumission Society (1785).

The Episcopal Church divided after the start of the Civil War, with the formation of a separate Protestant Episcopal Church in the Confederate States of America. The two groups reunited in 1865, when the General Convention agreed to seat the two Southern bishops who had been least enthusiastic about secession (Thomas Atkinson of North Carolina and Henry Lay of Arkansas).

Ministry to African Americans in the South prior to the war had been primarily conducted through special chapels located on large plantations; this ministry collapsed with the end to slavery. The church responded to the shift by creating the Protestant Episcopal Freedman's Commission (1865–1878) that focused on education and evangelism. The church established a series of academies and colleges for African Americans and a theological seminary. At the same time, the church attempted to recapture the momentum in ministry to Native Americans that had been lost with the ending of British missionary support at Revolution. This ministry was most active in Minnesota, where Emmegabowh became the first Ottawa deacon (1859) and priest (1867), and in South Dakota, where representatives of Native American congregations created the Niobrara Convocation (1870) to coordinate their work.

In 1872 the bishops of the Episcopal Church attempted to end the fight between high-church Episcopalians who were influenced by the Oxford Movement and evangelical Episcopalians over the term regeneration by adopting a resolution declaring that the use of the term in the

Book of Common Prayer's baptismal service did not mean that "a moral change in the subject of baptism is wrought in the Sacrament."[3] The compromise, which did not explicitly say that a moral change of life was expected of adults, was insufficient for some evangelical Episcopalians. In the following year Charles E. Cheney (1836–1916) of Chicago and Bishop George D. Cummins (1822–1876) of Kentucky led the way in the formation of a separate Reformed Episcopal Church, which adopted a revised edition of the Book of Common Prayer that removed the word regeneration from the baptismal service. Although the strength of the new denomination was primarily in the North, some African-American congregations in the South joined the denomination as well because of the more egalitarian treatment given them.

FROM 1873 TO 2020

The Episcopal Church enjoyed a steady, though moderate, growth in numbers – both in absolute terms and percentage of the US population – during the end of the nineteenth and the first two-thirds of the twentieth century, reaching a high point of 3.647 million baptized members in 1966. During that time, however, there were shifts in membership patterns; a rapid growth in the number of congregations prior to 1920 was followed by a period of consolidation (made possible in part by the invention of the automobile) with fewer, though larger congregations and – particularly following World War II – an expansion in the growing suburban areas. After 1966, the denomination began to decline in numbers, a trend followed by many other mainline Protestant churches.

World War I brought a US alliance with the United Kingdom and an increased appreciation for things British, converting what once had seemed a negative connection to England into something more positive. During the war, the Episcopal Theological School in Cambridge, Massachusetts, devoted itself to training chaplains. After the war St. Thomas Church on 5th Avenue in New York City founded an English-style boys' choir school (1919). Episcopal clergyman W. A. R. Goodwin led the way in transforming Williamsburg, which had been the capital of colonial Virginia in the eighteenth century, into a major historical tourist site (1927). Parishes and dioceses adopted heraldic insignia and began to use English terminology for parts of their church buildings.

The aesthetic preference for things British was accompanied by an organizational attempt to emulate large businesses. In the first quarter of the twentieth century, the General Convention adopted standard financial reporting methods for congregations and dioceses, replaced a seniority leadership system with an elected presiding bishop, effectively replaced the antiquated system of pew rents with a system of annual pledges, conducted a "National Wide [giving] Campaign," adopted mandatory retirement ages and a pension system for clergy, reshaped the church canons into a more organized system, and united the various voluntary overseas missionary societies into a centralized program.

In the modernist–fundamentalist debates of the 1920s, Episcopalians generally took a nuanced modernist stance, allowing non-literal reading of debated biblical passages but insisting on the truth of the traditional creeds and liturgy of the church. The House of Bishops issued a pastoral letter in 1923 that distinguished *belief in* the creeds (which was expected of all clergy) from statement of the facts *that we believe* (about which there was some leeway for interpretation). William Montgomery Brown (1855–1937), the Bishop of Arkansas, did not accept the distinction, claiming that no one actually believed in the creeds. He became the only bishop in the denomination to be removed from office for heresy (1924).

Episcopalians generally supported modern medicine over faith healing; laywoman Helen Flanders Dunbar (1902–1959) would, for example, become the first director of the Council for the Clinical Training of Theological Students, which began in 1930 as a way to organize internships for theological students in hospitals. George Atwood, a clergyman from Ohio, wrote an Episcopal tract popular in the first two-thirds of the twentieth century that presented the Episcopal Church in a conversation between a rector and three laymen of whom "the Doctor" was the most vocal. The tract explained that "the Episcopal Church teaches the Bible truth, but it demands the use of reason and of spiritual appreciation in gathering the central truths from the Bible."[4]

The ministry of the Episcopal Church from 1880 to the 1920s was characterized by a series of special ministries and organizations that were intended to meet the needs and to evangelize targeted language, economic, medical, and ethnic groups. Much of the work in such groups was undertaken by female volunteers and professionals, to whom the church was giving increasing recognition. The General Convention of 1871 approved the formation of the Women's Auxiliary to the Board of Missions, of which Mary Abbot Emery Twing (1843–1901) became the first General Secretary in the following year. Subsequent conventions adopted national canons on Deaconesses (1889) and monastic orders

(1913), putting ministries that had been supported on local levels on a more formal national basis. The representatives of many of the special ministry groups participated in the Episcopal Church Congress (1874–1934), a church think tank for social action and modernist ideas.

In some cases, dioceses organized archdeaconries led by priests or bishops suffragan (assisting bishops without the right of succession) to focus on these special ministries. It was in this later role as bishops suffragan that the first two African-American bishops were chosen in 1918 to serve in the Episcopal Church in the United States: Henry Delany (1858–1958) in North Carolina and Edward Demby (1859–1957) in Arkansas.

This strategy of special ministries was a generally successful evangelical approach; it also could also become the means to impose racial segregation. Many Southern dioceses defined their "Archdeaconries for Colored Work" as including all persons of color, which had the effect of suggesting that they could not be members of congregations not included in the archdeaconries. Some congregations elsewhere in the nation followed a similar policy, though without official canonical change. By the 1930s some in the church began to speak out about the inequalities involved in this approach, however. The House of Bishops, for example, refused to accept the election of a bishop in Arkansas (1932) because whites and Blacks had been required to assemble separately for the voting, and the supporters of the winner of the diocesan election had used racial slurs in campaigning. In the 1940s all Episcopal dioceses (except for South Carolina) abandoned their separate Archdeaconries for Colored Work, and the General Convention accepted a report critical of treatment of racial minorities. Presiding bishop Henry Knox Sherrill (1890–1980) served on President Truman's Committee on Civil Rights (1946–1948), which recommended the end to voting restriction, school segregation, and separation of military units based on race.

The desegregation of Episcopal colleges and seminaries in the South took place in the 1950s, and that of Episcopal private secondary schools in the 1960s. The number of Latino members of the denomination increased after 1960, with Cuban American clergy providing important leadership both in the United States and in missionary dioceses elsewhere in Latin America. Some, such as Max Salvador (1929–2004), founder of La Iglesia de Todos los Santos in Miami, the first self-supporting Episcopal Cuban-American congregation in the United States, were clergy before emigrating. Others such as Onell Soto (1932–2015) – who later became in succession Bishop of Venezuela, Assistant Bishop of Alabama, and Assistant Bishop of Atlanta – entered the ordained ministry in the United States. The denomination remained largely European American in composition, however, with origins in the British Isles and Germany most common.

General Convention accepted women as deaconesses in the nineteenth century and some individual dioceses allowed women to serve in their diocesan conventions in the early twentieth century, but women did not gain full access to leadership until the 1970s. The 1970 General Convention seated women as deputies and erased the distinction between female deaconesses and male deacons. The Convention of 1976, prodded by two sets of irregular ordinations of women to the priesthood, opened the presbyterate and episcopate to women. By the end of the twentieth century, women slightly outnumbered men as students in theological seminaries of the Episcopal Church; because of their higher average age at entrance, however, women remain a minority of active clergy. In 1989 Barbara Harris (1930–2020) was elected Bishop Suffragan of Massachusetts, becoming the first woman to become a bishop in the Anglican Communion. Other elections followed, including that of Katharine Jefferts Schori (b. 1954), who served in succession as the Bishop of Nevada (2001–2006) and the Presiding Bishop (2006–2015). Female leadership was also evident in the House of Deputies in the late twentieth and early twenty-first century with three women (Pamela Chinnis, Bonnie Anderson, and Gay Jennings) among the four people who served as presidents of that body between 1994 and 2024.

In the 1990s and the following decade, much of the attention of the Episcopal Church was focused on that status of gay and lesbian persons. Membership was not in question; the General Convention had affirmed in 1976 "that homosexual persons are children of God who have a full and equal claim with all other persons upon the love, acceptance, and pastoral concern and care of the Church."[5] The debate in the 1990s was over whether or not bishops would follow a 1979 General Convention statement excluding gay and lesbian person from consideration for ordination. The pro-ordination side prevailed in 2003, when the convention approved the election of openly gay V. Gene Robinson (b. 1947) as Bishop Coadjutor (bishop with right of succession) of New Hampshire. In the following decade, the debate moved to the question of marriage with General Convention approving a same-sex marriage rite in 2015, shortly after the US Supreme Court affirmed the right to same-sex marriage.

The debate over same-sex marriage and the election of a female presiding bishop contributed to the withdrawal of more than 100,000 Episcopalians. Individual parishes and five dioceses – Fort Worth, Pittsburgh, Quincy in Illinois, San Joaquin in California, and South

334 Theological Traditions

Carolina – attempted to retain church property while leaving the Episcopal Church, triggering a decade of expensive litigation, with results that were not entirely satisfactory to either side. In 2009 many of the departing members formed the Anglican Church in North America (ACNA), which affirmed ties with the generally more trad- itional Anglican churches of the global South, stressed the importance of biblical literacy and evangelism, opposed same-sex marriage, and allowed individual dioceses to determine whether or not to ordain women.

The 2015 General Convention elected Michael Bruce Curry (b. 1953), who had been Bishop of North Carolina, as the successor to Presiding Bishop Jefferts Schori. Curry was the first African American to occupy the position. He moved into that position of leadership at a point in which the percentage of African Americans in the Episcopal Church was declining, in part a result of the church division that created ACNA. A 2014 Pew Research Study indicated that the percentage of African Americans in the Episcopal Church (4%) was one-third of that in ACNA (12%).

Four Episcopalians occupied the White House in the twentieth century – the two Roosevelts, Gerald Ford, and George H. W. Bush. A fifth president, Lyndon Johnson, was married to an Episcopalian, and a sixth, George W. Bush, was raised in the Episcopal Church but con- verted as an adult to Methodism. Most other presidents made occa- sional visits to St. John's Church, Lafayette Square (across from the White House) or the National Cathedral in Washington. This connec- tion to presidency did not always equate with support for presidential policies, something that was made clear by Cotesworth P. Lewis's 1967 anti-war sermon at Bruton Parish, Williamsburg, Virginia to a congregation that included Lyndon Johnson, as well as Bishop Mariann Edgar Budde of Washington's 2020 criticism of Donald Trump's use of military and police to move demonstrators for the Black Lives Matter movement away from St. John's Church so that he could pose before it holding a Bible.

By the close of the twentieth century, Episcopalians were gradually losing some of their over-sized role in American political life. In 1991 the number of Episcopalians in the House of Representatives, which had averaged over 50 from 1965 to 1983, dropped below 40; it remained in the 30s until 2019, when the number dropped to 22. Something similar is true of the judiciary. From 1789 to 2020, 29% of Supreme Court justices (33 of 114) were associated with the Episcopal Church, including 35% of the chief justices (6 of 17). In 2020 only 1 member of the court had connections with the Episcopal Church; 5 of the other 8 were Roman Catholic and three were Jewish.

ETHICS

Historian Frank Sugeno argued in 1984 that the most consistent value informing Episcopal social ethics was an "establishmentarian ideal," the belief that the church has a responsibility not only for its members but for the population and institutions of the nation in which it is located.[6] He traced the idea back to the Church of England's role as an established church. One can point to some exceptions, such as the high-church Episcopal refusal to participate in American political life from the early federal period to the 1860s, which was a reaction to negative results of high-church support for the British during the American Revolution. In the main, however, Episcopalians have held to this establishmentarian ideal.

Although church membership is predominantly European American (90% according to a 2014 Pew Research study) and financially secure (the highest average income among Christian denominations also according to a 2014 Pew study), lay and ordained leaders often support social policies aimed primarily at improving the status of lower income persons and ethnic minorities. The denomination was among the earliest supporters of Social Gospel ideas of the late nineteenth century, supporting settlement houses and advocating the rights of workers. Lay member Frances Perkins (1880–1965), Franklin Roosevelt's Secretary of Labor (1933–1945) and the first woman to serve on the cabinet, helped to translate many Social Gospel ideals into practice. Clergyman Samuel Shoemaker (1893–1963) played a key role in developing the spiritual goals of the Alcoholics Anonymous movement. Presiding Bishop (1965–1974) John E. Hines called the church to respond to the plight of the urban poor and championed the creation of a General Convention Special Program (1967–1973) to provide resources for the empowerment of disadvantaged groups.

In terms of personal ethics, Episcopalians were perhaps the slowest mainline Protestant denomination to accept divorce and remarriage. It would not be until 1973 that the church revised its canons to make remarriage in the church generally available, a move that made the church a popular denomination of second resort for divorced Roman Catholics. The denomination wrestled in the 1990s and the first decade of the twenty-first century with finding an appropriate response to same-sex behavior – with a resultant schism and the formation of the more socially conservative ACNA – before approving same-sex marriage in 2015.

STRUCTURE

The Episcopal Church was reorganized after the American Revolution as a combination of a traditional hierarchical denomination and an American democratic structure. The highest authority in the church is the General Convention, a bicameral body with a House of Bishops and a House of Deputies composted of an equal number of clergy and lay deputies elected by diocesan conventions, which are composed of all resident clergy and lay representatives elected by vestries (parish councils) of congregations. Vestries of self-supporting congregations elect their own rectors (with either consent or absence of objection by the bishop); diocesan conventions elect bishops (with the consent of a majority of bishops and dioceses). At the time of organization, the House of Deputies could override the decisions of the House of Bishops with a 4/5 vote; that provision was dropped in 1808. Since that time, all legislation needs the majority approval of both houses. Among issues that may be decided by the Convention are the denomination's national budget, changes in liturgical texts and practices, qualifications for ordination, and ecumenical agreements.

The House of Deputies has an elected president, initially an ordained person but since the 1960s alternating between clergy and laypersons. Initially, the bishop who was most senior by date of consecration presided over the House of Bishops; following World War I, however, the position was made elective and the Presiding Bishop's role expanded from presidency of meetings of bishops to include an executive role in the leadership of the denomination as a whole. Since the 1940s the position has been full-time. The rules and responsibilities of church members and organizations are laid out in the *Constitution and Canons*, which is constantly revised. Among significant changes in the past century were the decisions to admit women as deputies (1970), deacons (1970), priests (1976), and bishops (1976); and the signing of ecumenical accords with other churches beginning with the Evangelical Lutheran Church (1999–2000). Individual dioceses have their own constitutions and canons.

LITURGY

Episcopalians have a written liturgy, which is contained in the Book of Common Prayer, often simply called the prayer book. There have been four American editions (1789, 1892, 1928, 1979). The book is not copyrighted, and portions of it are occasionally used by Christians of other denominations. Since 1871 the church has also approved a separate hymnal; prior to that time, selected hymns were printed with the prayer book. The current edition of the hymnal was approved in 1982.

The primary Sunday service is the Holy Eucharist, for which the prayer book provides two forms, one contemporary (Rite 2) and the other in the Elizabethan language in which the earliest English prayer books (1549, 1552) were composed (Rite 1). In contrast to the Methodist Church, which bases its Eucharistic prayer on the English prayer book of 1552, the Episcopal Church's traditional Eucharistic prayer is drawn from the prayer book of 1549 – a result of the influence of the Episcopal Church of Scotland, which follows that tradition. The prayer book also contains services for daily prayer, Baptism and Confirmation, pastoral services such as marriage and burial, and a liturgical psalter. The services in the book are translations and revisions of the late medieval Latin liturgy of the Roman Catholic Church, to which significant changes have been made. The prayer book of 1979, for example, aligned the liturgy with the principles of the Liturgical Movement, an ecumenical effort to create a more participatory and celebratory worship with less emphasis on penitence and clerical leadership. Unlike some other Protestant denominations, the Episcopal Church understands use of the prayer book as mandatory for public worship (rather than its being simply encouraged or made available).

Since the second decade of the twentieth century, the denomination has also authorized a series of supplemental texts, the use of which is dependent largely upon the choice of parish clergy. The first of these supplemental liturgies was the *Book of Offices: Services for Occasions Not Provided for in the Book of Common Prayer* (1917), approved by the House of Bishops. Three other editions, which were approved by both houses of General Convention, followed. The book was revised and renamed the *Book of Occasional Services* in 1979, with frequent revision thereafter. General Convention also approved a calendar of saints (*Lesser Feasts and Fasts*) in 1963; later General Conventions approved multiple expansions and revisions that attempted to balance the largely white, clerical male list of figures in the initial edition with more laypersons, women. and persons of color. Beginning in 1987 the General Convention also approved a series of supplemental inclusive language texts, which would eventually be named the *Enriching Our Worship* series. The Standing Commission on Liturgy and Music, to which General Convention entrusts supervision of the liturgy, asked the General Convention of 2018 for funds to begin work on a new edition of the

Book of Common Prayer but suggested that work would take at least a decade.

THEOLOGY

Churches of the Anglican Communion accept the sixteenth-century Thirty-Nine Articles of Religion, which is included as an appendix to American editions of the Book of Common Prayer, as a common statement of faith. Prior to the twentieth century, the writing of commentaries on the Thirty-Nine Articles was the major form of theological discourse in the communion. Episcopal seminaries in the United States used commentaries written by British authors during most of the nineteenth century, especially Gilbert Burnet's *Exposition of the Thirty-Nine Articles* (1699) and Edward Harold Browne's *Commentary on the Thirty-Nine Articles* (1854).

In the early twentieth century, Episcopalians began to nuance their relationship with the Thirty-Nine Articles, which include polemical language about what were regarded as Roman Catholic errors. The General Convention, for example, voted to omit the Thirty-Nine Articles from the 1928 edition of the Book of Common Prayer but reversed that decision three years later. The General Convention followed the opposite strategy with the 1979 prayer book, retaining the Articles but putting them in an expanded historical document section that also included the statement on the two natures of Christ from Chalcedon (451), the Athanasian Creed (included in English prayers books but absent from earlier American editions), the Preface from the first Book of Common Prayer (1549), and the Chicago-Lambeth Quadrilateral (1886, 1888).

Since the early twentieth century, Episcopal theologians have been attracted to presentations of the faith that balance an appreciation for traditional ideas of the faith with modern textual and scientific advances. One common strategy has been to claim that the church has no theology except that of the early church, and then to interpret the teaching of the early church in ways compatible with contemporary concerns. Another approach has been to treat the Chicago-Lambeth Quadrilateral as the successor to the Thirty-Nine Articles. The quadrilateral was a later nineteenth-century statement about ecclesiology and ecumenism that identifies four elements as "essential to the restoration of unity among the divided branches of Christendom": the Old and New Testaments, the Nicene Creed, the sacraments of Baptism and the Lord Supper, and the historic episcopate.[7]

Among American authors that twentieth-century Episcopal theologians found attractive were the neo-orthodox theologians of mid-century (particularly at Union Theological Seminary in New York where a number of Episcopal seminary professors did their doctoral work) and the "Yale School" narrative theologians of the 1970s and 1980s, whose number included Episcopalian Hans Frei (1922–1988). One theologian of the Episcopal Church currently at work on a systematic theology is Katherine Sonderegger at Virginia Theological Seminary. Volume I of her projected multivolume *Systematic Theology* appeared in 2015.

In a broad sense it is possible to talk about an Anglican-Methodist-Pentecostal direction in theology that can be distinguished from Reformed or Roman Catholic traditions, both of which have more focused views of authority. The tradition posits a broad set of authorities, enumerated by twentieth- and twenty-first-century Episcopalians and Methodists as either three (Scripture, Tradition, and Reason) or four (by adding experience). This allows a greater place for claims to inspiration by the Holy Spirit, a possibility developed in the Pentecostal churches formed in the early twentieth century and in the charismatic movement within mainline denominations in the 1960s and 1970s.

NOTES

1 For further study, consult the following: *Anglican and Episcopal History* (a quarterly journal published by the Historical Society of the Episcopal Church); Sheryl A. Kujawa-Holbrook, *Freedom Is a Dream: A Documentary History of Women in the Episcopal Church* (New York: Church Publishing, 2002); David Hein and Gardiner H. Shattuck, Jr., *The Episcopalians* (Westport, CT: Praeger Publishers, 2004); Robert W. Prichard, *A History of the Episcopal Church*, 3rd rev. ed. (New York: Morehouse Publishing, 2014); Anthony Milton, Jeremy Gregory, Rowan Strong, Jeremy Morris, and William L. Sachs, eds., *The Oxford History of Anglicanism*, 6 vols. (Oxford: Oxford University Press, 2017–2018).

2 Thomas Bray, *Catechetical Lectures*, fifth lecture in Robert W. Prichard, *Readings from the History of the Episcopal Church* (Wilton, CT: Morehouse-Barlow, 1986), 27.

3 *Journal of the ....General Convention ... 1871* (Hartford, CT: The Church Press, 1872), 183.

4 George Parkin Atwater, *The Episcopal Church: Its Message for Men of Today* (Akron, OH: Parish Publishers, 1917), 160.

5 General Convention, *Journal of the General Convention of ... The Episcopal Church, Minneapolis 1976* (New York: General Convention, 1977), C–109.

6 Frank E. Sugeno, "The Establishmentarian Ideal and the Mission of the Episcopal Church," *Historical Magazine of the Protestant Episcopal Church* vol. 53 (December 1984), 285–292.

7 "The Chicago-Lambeth Quadrilateral 1886, 1888," Book of Common Prayer (1979), 876–879.

18 The Reformed Tradition

EDWIN WOODRUFF TAIT

When the Reformed tradition came to North America it already had a century of history behind it.[1] The Reformed had no founding figure of similar stature to Martin Luther, though later John Calvin (1509–1564) was anachronistically given that role. The early Reformed were Swiss and South German theologians with a strong grounding in Renaissance humanism, who, like their north German counterparts, sought approval of civil authorities for reforms they wished to introduce. They disagreed with Luther on certain key points, primarily the nature of Christ's Presence in the Lord's Supper.

The Reformed tradition, from the beginning, systematically refashioned medieval Catholicism according to what it believed to be the pattern laid out in the Bible and the early church. Reformed Christians saw Scripture as a comprehensive manual for Christian faith with relevance for political and social issues as well as strictly theological ones. Compared to other Christian traditions, they gave the Old Testament more direct relevance to life in the Christian community and spoke of the entire sweep of salvation history as the story of one people of God – heirs of the same promises, subject to the same judgments. This habit powerfully influenced not only the theology of American Protestantism but Americans' sense of their identity as a nation.

COLONIAL PURITANISM

The first Reformed Christians to settle in what is now the United States were French Huguenots seeking religious liberty. Their unsuccessful attempts demonstrate the attraction North America held for those subject to European persecution and inspired by the story of Israel to seek a new Exodus and a new Promised Land. The English succeeded where the Huguenots failed, establishing the first permanent English-speaking settlement in North America at Jamestown in 1607. Jamestown settlers were citizens of the English commonwealth and thus belonged to the

Church of England, simply the English commonwealth considered under its religious aspect and still, in 1607, part of the broader Reformed community.[2]

New England Puritanism, first arriving in what is now Massachusetts in 1620 on board the *Mayflower*, was originally a movement within the Church of England seeking greater conformity with Reformed churches on the Continent. Puritanism was both a deeply rigorous intellectual tradition and a populist one, seeking to evangelize an English society Puritans believed had largely lapsed into atheism during sixteenth century religious chaos, and early on developed a pietistic emphasis on the experience of conversion as a sign of regeneration. Since the Reformed held that only those eternally chosen by God experienced regeneration, to be assured of one's regeneration was to be assured of one's eternal election and final salvation; thus complexities of scholastic theology were inextricably bound up with a deeply personal and profoundly experiential piety.

The "Pilgrims" who arrived at Plymouth Rock in 1620 were Separatists, Puritans who had concluded that the Church of England was hopelessly bound up with the Catholic "Antichrist." Several Separatist congregations emigrated to the Netherlands, one led by John Robinson (1576–1625). After about a decade, Robinson's congregation decided to emigrate to America; Robinson preached them a farewell sermon in which he exhorted them to "follow me no further than you have seen me follow the Lord Jesus Christ."[3] Both Lutherans and Calvinists, Robinson warned, had remained shackled to their favored theologians, but Robinson was "verily persuaded the Lord hath yet more truth and light to break forth from his holy word."[4] In centuries to come, the Reformed zealously followed this advice, vying with one another to create ever more radical movements following "more truth and light" they saw breaking forth from the pages of Scripture.

The large Winthrop Fleet in 1630 brought Massachusetts Bay Colony's charter and its first governor, John Winthrop (1588–1649). The new settlers represented a moderate, mainstream variety of Puritanism. One of their spiritual leaders, John Cotton (1585–1652), preached a sermon to his parishioners, "God's Promise to His Plantation"; shortly before landing, Winthrop preached a sermon of his own which has come to be known as the "City on a Hill" sermon. While Cotton's was more famous at the time, Winthrop's evocative image has become, since its nineteenth-century rediscovery, one of the most powerful symbols of America's often messianic self-consciousness.[5] Both reflect the Reformed understanding of the church as a covenant community and apply it to the new "plantation" in North America, warning the colonists that God will bless or curse them insofar as they maintain or break the terms of God's providence.[6] The polarity between Robinson's "God hath yet more light" and Cotton and Winthrop's fidelity to confessional Reformed orthodoxy defines the space in which all versions of Reformed Protestantism exist.

DISSENTERS

This tension became apparent in the early years of the Massachusetts Bay Colony. In Puritan Massachusetts, each congregation was independent, calling its own minister and managing its own affairs; yet the church was supported by the colonial government and all citizens were expected to support it and respect its authority. Minister Roger Williams (1603–1683) was too devoted a Separatist to be comfortable with this. The ability of other churches to intervene in the face of his increasingly radical teachings was highly limited; civil authorities, on the other hand, could and did step in.[7] Williams was forced to leave in 1636 and founded Rhode Island, a haven of religious liberty for dissenters, where he began the first Baptist congregation in North America. Baptists found success in the American environment, with a complex and generally adversarial relationship to the Reformed tradition from which they had, in large measure, sprung.[8] Anne Hutchinson (1591–1643) also began as a zealous proponent of Puritan theology. She claimed an immediate awareness of the indwelling Holy Spirit, which she saw as the only true sign of election, rejecting the view that good works played an important role as evidence of grace. She and her followers were labeled "antinomians" and banished from Massachusetts in 1638. If Williams was the father of the Baptist tradition and free-church American Protestantism generally, Hutchinson exemplifies a different strand of radical American religion – redoubtable women who have challenged male clergy and claimed direct spiritual authority based on their experience of the Spirit.

The Puritans have been simultaneously revered as champions of freedom and virtue and fathers of American democratic institutions, and reviled as dour tyrants who fled persecution only to become persecutors themselves.[9] Both stereotypes contain truth. Early New England, while having plenty of social inequality, was egalitarian compared to most European societies. Literacy was high and education was valued, for both men and women. People of humble status were able to participate actively in political institutions. And even the Puritans' most glaring moral failures – the infamous Salem witch trials of 1692–1693, the genocidal treatment of Native Americans, and the acceptance of slavery – found dissenters from within Puritan society who grounded their objections in their own staunch Reformed faith. Yet these failures, and the broader patterns of intolerance and authoritarianism from which they sprang, are part of the story as well.

PURITAN THEOLOGY

Among distinctly Reformed elements in New England society, we can outline four major themes.[10]

Providentialism. Reformed Christians gave belief in divine sovereignty a prominent place in their theology. This did not fundamentally differentiate them from other early modern Christians; Reformed distinctiveness was primarily a matter of emphasis. This providentialism led New England Puritans to interpret events of their lives and their society as part of a divine drama of judgment and mercy.

Covenantalism. Reformed Christians believed themselves to be the New Israel, bound to God in a covenant relationship. They understood this in light of Deuteronomy's promises of God's blessing on covenant-keeping and his curse on covenant-breaking. Both church and society were seen as covenants humans entered into under God.

Sin and Grace. Reformed Christians had inherited from the Augustinian tradition the conviction that humans came into the world with wills distorted by sin so that, unless healed by grace, they were unable to love God and their neighbors truly; only those whom God chose responded in repentance and faith. Luther added the doctrine of *sola fide* – the basis for God's acceptance of a person as righteous is solely that person's faith in the death and resurrection of Jesus. The Reformed accepted this modification and added the doctrine that only the elect ever experienced regeneration. These teachings were challenged by Jacob Arminius (1560–1609) and affirmed at the Synod of Dordt (1618–1619). Many New England theologians taught a "federal theology" which placed this drama of sin and grace in the context of a set of divine covenants: God was utterly sovereign and humans helpless to save themselves apart from

God's "effectual calling," but God had also covenanted to save people who met certain conditions.

Reverence for the Word. All saving knowledge of God was mediated by the revealed Word, identified in classic Reformed theology with the written text of Scripture. This made the study of Scripture, and study in general, a central preoccupation; Harvard University was founded in 1636 to provide a liberal arts education primarily to prospective clergy. In Reformed thought, properly understanding Scripture depended on studying the Bible's original languages and cultures and the work of theologians and biblical exegetes. They also believed Scripture only functioned salvifically when it was proclaimed and interpreted. Preaching was a major source of entertainment as well as instruction, functioning as a means of social and political criticism, and fostering qualities that put New England at the center of American intellectual and social life.

THE HALFWAY COVENANT

The "Cambridge Platform" drawn up by John Cotton and Richard Mather (1596–1669) in 1648 provided for the independence of each congregation and forbade either church or civil authorities to interfere with the other. The Platform accepted the doctrinal portions of the English Westminster Confession (1647) while dissenting from its Presbyterian approach to church polity. Along with church government, the Cambridge Platform also addressed a growing controversy over conditions for church membership. Applicants for membership were expected to recount their experience of conversion. Those who were orthodox in doctrine and upright in life but lacked such a testimony were doomed to be shut out from church membership. But what about their children? In Reformed theology, baptism was historically seen as parallel to circumcision. Just as children of Israelite parents were circumcised under the Old Covenant, so children of Christian parents should be baptized under the New. If children of unconverted persons could not be baptized, the entire covenant community threatened to fall apart. Hence, it became increasingly common to allow the unconverted "halfway" membership which allowed their children to be baptized. About four-fifths of New England churches adopted this approach by 1700; by 1708 one observer claimed halfway members outnumbered full members by four to one.

Influential pastor in Northampton Solomon Stoddard (1643–1729) believed all adults who had been baptized as infants, professed an orthodox set of Christian beliefs, and lived upright lives should be accepted as members with access to the sacraments. In 1677 he began tacitly ignoring the distinction between "halfway" and "full" members, and soon persuaded his congregation to accept this approach openly. Stoddard also advocated a more formal structure of accountability above the local church, leading to accusations of crypto-Presbyterianism.

By the early eighteenth century, New England Congregationalism was fracturing into two distinct styles of Reformed Christianity. One was centered on Boston and Harvard, committed to congregational independence. The other centered on the Connecticut Valley, with a semi-Presbyterian polity and a more open approach to church membership, using preaching and the sacraments to convert those who were already members. The line was not a sharp one; the central educational institution of the "western" variant of Congregationalism, Yale University, was founded in 1702 with the assistance of Increase Mather (1639–1723), patriarch of Boston Congregationalism. By this time Mather had been ousted from his position as President of Harvard by a group of Boston merchants associated with Brattle Street Church, which included more "liturgical" elements than other Congregational churches and no longer required applicants for membership to testify to their conversion experience.

THE GREAT AWAKENING

In the 1730s in Northampton, Stoddard's successor and grandson Jonathan Edwards (1703–1758) recognized emotional manifestations in his congregation as legitimate signs of God's work and proceeded to encourage, document, and defend them. Edwards was one of colonial America's great intellectuals, a philosopher and theologian who seemed an unlikely leader for a frontier revival movement. But in that respect he typified the entire Puritan tradition, which had long combined careful, even pedantic, scholarship with belief that a profound experience of conversion formed the heart of genuine Christianity.[11] In the 1740s, the arrival of Anglican evangelist George Whitefield (1714–1770) spurred a broader revival which Edwards recognized and applauded. By working with Whitefield, Edwards pointed toward a new ecumenism, joining with Presbyterians and even Anglicans in a broadly Reformed evangelical renewal.

Shaped by Lockean empiricism and other contemporary intellectual currents as well as classic Reformed theology, Edwards argued for the possibility of a direct human perception of divine grace as a spiritual "light."[12] The effect of this perception was an emotional response which could be distinguished from purely "natural" emotions in its nature and in its effects. Edwards repeatedly pointed to the revival's solid spiritual fruit as evidence of its supernatural origin. He defended traditional Reformed doctrines but did so using philosophical arguments drawn from contemporary Enlightenment thought and the language of psychology, making a sustained case for a perceptible psychological dimension to the spiritual life. In doing this he became the father of modern American theology.

Edwards's ministry to Northampton ended in his dismissal in 1750 after he attempted to reverse his grandfather's policy and deny communion to people he considered unconverted. He took a position in the frontier town of Stockbridge ministering to a largely Native American congregation, where he wrote three significant philosophical treatises: *An Inquiry into the Modern Prevailing Notions of the Freedom of the Will* (1754), *The Great Christian Doctrine of Original Sin Defended* (1758), and *The Nature of True Virtue* (published posthumously), in which he argued that the love of God was the source of all virtue, and identical with disinterested benevolence, but that it had been withdrawn from the human race due to the sin of Adam and Eve. In 1758 Edwards became president of Princeton University. His association with this flagship Presbyterian institution cemented his position as an ecumenical leader of revivalistic Calvinism and marked a growing rapprochement between "New Light" Congregationalism and "New Side" Presbyterianism.

COLONIAL PRESBYTERIANISM

Presbyterians established the first presbytery in America in 1706, in Philadelphia. Presbyterianism was, of the two English-speaking Puritan traditions, more obviously oriented toward confessional orthodoxy and ecclesiastical unity; indeed, its first major American debate concerned the Westminster Confession. Scottish and Northern Irish Presbyterian churches required clergy to subscribe to it; in 1727 Irish minister John Thomson proposed the Synod of Philadelphia do so too. He was opposed by Jonathan Dickinson (1688–1747), a former Congregationalist who believed such requirements violated the supreme authority of Scripture. In 1729 the Synod passed an act requiring verbal assent to the Confession as a condition of ordination – but candidates could also express their scruples.

Also in 1727, Scottish-born Irish clergyman William Tennent (1673–1746) founded the first Presbyterian educational establishment in America, the derisively labeled "Log College" in Neshaminy, Pennsylvania, for the education of clergy, including his own sons William and Gilbert (1703–1764) – a small and informal institution which did not have authority to grant diplomas. In 1737, the Synod of Philadelphia required ministers to have college diplomas or else be examined by a committee, and required itinerant clergy to receive permission before preaching in the area – moves directed against the Tennents and other advocates of revivalistic preaching. The new Presbytery of New Brunswick became the center of "New Side" Presbyterianism favoring revivalistic, evangelical piety over traditional confessional emphases. Gilbert Tennent was now minister of the church in New Brunswick and the new presbytery's natural leader. Philadelphia, on the other hand, remained the center of the "Old Side" – traditional confessional Presbyterianism emphasizing doctrinal orthodoxy and moral behavior rather than a conversion experience.

"New Side" Presbyterianism and "New Light" Congregationalism had a great deal in common. Both supported revivalism, saw religious experience as a key sign of the work of God in the soul, and valued it above traditional dividing points of doctrine and polity. Their alternatives – Old Light Congregationalism and Old Side Presbyterianism – were more committed to denominational distinctiveness. For Presbyterians, this meant the confessional orthodoxy of Westminster. But Congregationalists were committed to the independence of local congregations, to fostering a robust and participatory civic life, to rigorous intellectual investigation, and to the promotion of virtue. All these were compatible with Puritan orthodoxy but could also exist easily without adherence to traditional doctrines of original sin, predestination, and the need for conversion. Indeed, those doctrines might seem more hindrances than helps. Thus, Boston minister Charles Chauncy (1705–1787) could question traditional doctrines of sin and grace while also seeing himself as a champion of historic Congregationalist orthodoxy against the fanatical revivalism of the Great Awakening.

THE NEW DIVINITY

In 1768, Scottish minister and philosopher John Witherspoon (1723–1794) was called as president of Princeton. The only clerical signer of the Declaration of Independence, he functioned as a political, intellectual, and spiritual leader and was influenced by the Scottish philosophy of "common-sense realism," which treated the deliverances of the senses as fundamentally reliable if not interfered with.[13] It formed the foundation for a robustly historical, evidence-based defense of traditional Christian doctrine, cohered with a careful study of the literal sense of Scripture as the sufficient basis for Christian faith, and fit with a growing interest in the natural sciences.

Edwards's students continued to explore his profound reworking of Reformed theology, chief among them Joseph Bellamy (1719–1790), Samuel Hopkins (1721–1803), Jonathan Edwards, Jr. (1745–1801), and Nathanael Emmons (1745–1840). Their complex justifications for traditional Calvinist doctrines became, in the eyes of later generations, the classic form of New England Puritanism. The nineteenth-century New England cultural renaissance defined itself largely by reaction against this theology, which many saw as abstruse and cruel. And yet these "New Divinity" theologians were harbingers of new currents of thought.

While they all lacked Edwards's idealistic metaphysics, they applied his understanding of true virtue to emphasize disinterested benevolence; a truly regenerate person should be willing to be damned for the glory of God, and a true believer would seek to do good in the world without expecting reward. Their concern with theodicy led to a reworking of the doctrine of the Atonement as not an intrinsic necessity of God's nature, but rather an indispensable part of God's moral government of the universe. These changes led to criticisms from remaining "Old Light" conservatives who formed the third of Congregationalism's major factions, led by Ezra Stiles (1727–1795), president of Yale.[14] But after his death he was succeeded by Timothy Dwight (1752–1817), grandson of Edwards and an heir of the New Divinity. Remaining "moderates" joined forces with the New Divinity in the name of orthodoxy and finally, in 1825, forced a division between themselves and liberal Congregationalism, which had abandoned the doctrine of the Trinity and embraced the label Unitarian.

THE SECOND GREAT AWAKENING

The years of the American Revolution were not prosperous for any version of American Christianity. Most revolutionary leaders, nominally Anglicans or Congregationalists, sat loosely to traditional Christian orthodoxy. Thomas Jefferson (1743–1826) expressed sympathy with the Unitarians and thought they were destined to become the dominant religion in America. Early Unitarians were considerably more conservative than deists such as Jefferson; they believed in the infallibility of Scripture and the reality of miracles, and made biblical arguments in the best Reformed manner. Unitarianism looked like a progressive, reasonable, moderate compromise between traditional Christian doctrine and Deism, and Jefferson had good reasons (other than his own biases) for predicting its triumph. But that is not what happened.

In the Second Great Awakening, the new wave of revivals beginning in the 1790s, revivalistic evangelicalism established itself as the dominant religious force in the country and remained so until the Civil War. The Second Great Awakening saw the explosive growth of Methodists and Baptists and the creation of new movements rejecting important parts of the Reformed tradition.[15] Yet New England Congregationalism continued to play a key role as the intellectual and cultural heart of Protestantism. Under Timothy Dwight's leadership, Yale University became a center of evangelical piety, nurturing a generation of leaders including Lyman Beecher (1775–1863) and Nathaniel Taylor (1786–1858) who created what became known as the "New Haven theology" – developing precisely those points of the New Divinity most at odds with traditional Calvinism and paving the way for an evangelicalism that downplayed or rejected total depravity and predestination.

Meanwhile, Harvard's takeover by proto-Unitarians in 1805 prompted clergyman and geographer Jedidiah Morse (1761–1826) to rally the two "orthodox" factions of Congregationalists to establish Andover Theological Seminary in 1807 – the first true seminary in America.[16] Previously, the task of educating clergy had been carried out by universities. Students who wished to read for the ministry studied privately with a learned minister, but there was no graduate course of ministerial study. Andover was dedicated to specialized advanced study of theology, biblical languages, church history, and related disciplines. Its most famous early faculty member was Moses Stuart (1780–1852), formerly of Harvard, who wrote a famous Hebrew grammar and introduced German critical scholarship to the American intellectual scene – and was also a devout evangelical and fierce opponent of Unitarianism. Seminaries and divinity schools proliferated across America, becoming the centers of a new wave of liberalism at century's end.

Students at both Yale and Andover became interested in foreign missions and organized the first American missionary societies. They also joined with other evangelicals in creating voluntary societies to promote a host of causes, from the abolition of slavery to the regulation of alcohol to the enforcement of Sunday as a day of rest. Brothers Arthur

(1786–1865) and Lewis Tappan (1788–1873) used their successful business ventures to fund several causes and several educational institutions which played a major role in abolitionism and other movements of radical reform.

THE EARLY NINETEENTH CENTURY

On the denominational spectrum of the early nineteenth century, Presbyterians occupied a middle position. With a highly educated clergy, they had a more elite status than Methodists and Baptists, but were more successful on the frontier than Congregationalists or Unitarians and had more popular appeal than Episcopalians. Wherever they went in newly occupied western territories, they founded educational institutions, and Presbyterian churches came to function as cultural centers as well as places of worship, combining geographical range and popular appeal on the one hand with cultural and intellectual heft on the other.

Intellectual though they were, Presbyterians were also often at the heart of frontier revivalism alongside their Methodist and Baptist rivals. The Second Great Awakening's most famous revival erupted in August 1801 at Cane Ridge, Kentucky, in an ecumenical communion service hosted by local Presbyterian minister Barton Stone (1772–1844). The practice of having infrequent and solemn communion services was a staple of Scottish Presbyterianism. But in inviting Methodists and Baptists to participate, Stone was breaking with Presbyterian tradition. The meeting attracted about 10 percent of Kentucky's population and led to the development of "camp meetings" in which people intentionally camped out for a series of days or weeks to hear preaching – a movement that pulled adherents away from careful adherence to doctrinal standards and ecclesiastical structures. Presbyterians in the Appalachians influenced by revivalism formed the Cumberland Presbyterian Church, which rejected traditional Reformed doctrines of grace and affirmed free will. Stone also left Presbyterianism; he and his followers began calling themselves "Christians" and disclaiming allegiance to any specific denomination. He joined with another former Presbyterian minister, Alexander Campbell (1788–1866), to create the Disciples of Christ, a fellowship of independent congregations committed to following the New Testament and rejecting "man-made" creeds and confessions.[17]

Congregationalists were largely absent from the South and West in part by their own doing. The 1801 Plan of Union between Presbyterians and Congregationalists committed both churches not to plant congregations where the other was already established. This largely confined

Congregationalism to the Northeast, while giving the Presbyterians free rein in the rest of the country. But the evangelical, "New Light" wings of these two denominations had to a great extent become interchangeable by 1801. Lyman Beecher, for instance, began as a Congregationalist, attended Yale and studied with Dwight, pastored both Presbyterian and Congregationalist churches, and in 1832 became president of Lane Theological Seminary in Cincinnati, where he was accused (and acquitted) of heresy for his support of "new measures" in evangelism.

These "new measures" were associated with another ecumenical New Haven theologian, Charles Finney (1792–1875). Finney lacked Beecher's educational credentials; after a dramatic conversion he had read for the ministry in the old-fashioned manner. Revivals he led in upstate New York helped establish the region's fame as the "burned-over district." While a Presbyterian, Finney had little use for traditional Presbyterian confessional standards; he believed that the self-centeredness of the will could be overcome through persuasion, that the Holy Spirit worked through psychological and rhetorical means rather than in an ineffable, supernatural manner, and that through the influences of the Spirit the human will could be freed from sin. He defined Christian perfection in terms inherited ultimately from Edwards –a perfect, disinterested benevolence, conforming the human will to the will of God.[18]

Finney's optimistic, postmillennial eschatology fueled his abolitionism. In this he followed his mentor George Gale, who in 1827 founded the Oneida Institute (1789–1861) with money from the Tappan brothers, a revivalist, abolitionist school where students were required to do manual labor. One Oneida student, Theodore Weld (1803–1895), founded Lane Seminary in Cincinnati, again with Tappan money. Weld's first choice for president was Finney, who declined. Weld then invited Beecher. However, Beecher was less committed to abolitionism than Weld or Finney; eventually, Weld led a group of thirty-two abolitionist students to another new Ohio institution, Oberlin. By leveraging the Tappans' financial backing, Weld was able to persuade Oberlin to allow free discussion of abolition, to admit students without regard to race, and to call Finney as president.

ALTERNATIVES TO REVIVALISM

There were three alternatives to revivalism in antebellum American Calvinism. First was the resurgence of confessional Presbyterianism. In 1812 Presbyterians established a seminary at Princeton dominated by old-school Presbyterianism. First president Archibald Alexander (1772–1851) and his student Charles Hodge (1797–1878) made Princeton Theological Seminary a bastion of Presbyterian orthodoxy even as flames of ecumenical, quasi-Arminian revivalism were spreading all around them.[19]

The second, quite different voice was the cultured one of Horace Bushnell (1802–1876), a Yale-trained Congregationalist pastor in Connecticut who maintained good relations with Unitarians. The Bible, for Bushnell, spoke to the imagination rather than being a manual of truth for the analysis of common-sense realism. He rejected both penal substitution and the governmental theory of the atonement, championing the "moral influence" theory, and mistrusted the sudden spiritual transformations of revivals. In his influential *Christian Nurture* (1847), he argued that the ideal process of spiritual growth was a gradual nurturing beginning at birth so a child would never be aware of having been anything other than a Christian.

A third source of resistance to all-conquering revivalism was found among Reformed churches of non-British origins. The Dutch Reformed (after 1867 the Reformed Church in America, RCA) had existed in New York since 1628 but remained limited in numbers and influence until the influx of nineteenth-century immigration. They were unfavorable to both revivalism and abolitionism. The German Reformed Church in the United States, on the other hand, quickly felt the influence of Pietism and revivalism. Many German immigrants were already part of Pietist movements, and the Awakenings moved clergy to embrace the new emphasis on "heart religion." In 1767, Philip Otterbein (1726–1813) attended a revival service led by Mennonite Martin Boehm (1725–1812) and famously exclaimed, "we are brothers," leading to the formation of a German denomination with strong affinities with Methodism, the United Brethren in Christ. In the 1820s in Pennsylvania, another German Reformed minister, John Winebrenner (1797–1860), aroused controversy by fraternizing with Methodists and allowing non-ordained people to preach in his pulpit. As in Presbyterianism, a fissure was opening between those who saw revivalism as the natural expression of Reformed theology and those who saw it as a threat.

German Reformed resistance to revivalism came to center on the denominational seminary, established in Carlisle, Pennsylvania in 1825 and relocated first to Mercersburg and eventually to Lancaster. During the 1840s, it experienced brief fame from John Nevin (1803–1886) and Philip Schaff (1819–1893), whose shared theological emphases were dubbed the "Mercersburg Theology." Nevin came to the seminary (and the denomination) in 1840. Having grown up Presbyterian and studied at Princeton, he became disillusioned with what he called "Puritanic Presbyterianism." His *The Anxious Bench – A Tract for the Times* (1844) attacked Finney's "new measures" as a substitute for real repentance. *The Mystical Presence* (1846) argued for a doctrine of the spiritual Real Presence of Christ in the Eucharist, appealing to Calvin for support.

In 1843, Swiss church historian Schaff joined the faculty. Trained in Germany, Schaff's evangelical piety took new developments in German theology and scholarship seriously while also prizing a broad orthodoxy. His inaugural address at Mercersburg, "The Principle of Protestantism," created controversy leading to a heresy trial, though Schaff was acquitted. Rather than denouncing Catholicism as a false church, Schaff looked forward to an eventual synthesis in which Protestantism and Catholicism, purified from their errors, could unite in a fuller and more orthodox Christianity. Schaff's ecumenism and Nevin's sacramentalism together formed a high-church movement within the Reformed tradition. They made a permanent mark on the worship of the German Reformed Church by serving on a committee to revise the denomination's liturgy, and Schaff's multivolume history of Christianity became a classic text.[20]

ABOLITIONISM, SLAVERY, AND THE CIVIL WAR

As Mark Noll has pointed out, the Civil War was a theological crisis.[21] Because of antebellum Protestants' common-sense scriptural hermeneutic, combined with a suspicion of church tradition and a conviction of Scripture's ultimate, unique authority, abolitionists found it hard to make a case for the inherent, non-negotiable evil of slavery; Reformed Protestants, stressing biblical authority and the importance and relevance of the Old Testament for Christians, were prone to see some degree of acceptance of slavery as theologically necessary.

The debate over slavery and the war affected Presbyterians and Congregationalists differently. Congregationalists, largely centered in New England and with a tradition of championing liberty and social reform, varied from moderate emancipationists to abolitionists, with a generational trend toward the latter. Northern New School Presbyterians and "Presbygationalists" like the Beechers shared this pattern. Lyman Beecher, an advocate of gradual emancipation and colonization, did not see slavery as intrinsically sinful; his daughter Harriet Beecher Stowe (1811–1896) wrote the most famous piece of abolitionist propaganda, *Uncle Tom's Cabin* (1852). His son Henry Ward Beecher

(1813–1887), an influential New York minister, supplied rifles to fellow Congregationalist John Brown in Kansas, dubbed "Beecher's Bibles." John Fee (1816–1901), a Presbyterian student at Lane, became an abolitionist missionary in Kentucky, broke his ties with the denomination, purchased land in the western foothills of the Appalachians, and founded a church (Union Church), a town (Berea), and a college in the style of Oberlin (Berea College), all embodying his abolitionist Reformed principles.

The outbreak of war radicalized people who had hitherto been moderate. The reading of Romans 13 that had led them to be cautious about abolitionism as an attack on the established order led them to champion it when it was linked to defending the Union. The North–South division over slavery cut across the New School/Old School division within Presbyterianism, resulting in the formation of four new denominations out of one, though the war ultimately made the Old/New division seem less important, and Southern Presbyterians reunited in 1864, with Northerners following suit in 1869.

The only Presbyterian denomination to divide based on race was the Cumberland Presbyterian Church, a product of the Second Great Awakening. Southern Presbyterianism was solidly on the side of enslavers and had little appeal to enslaved people compared to Methodists and Baptists. However, there were Black Presbyterians – about 14,000 in the antebellum South. While most worshipped in white-run churches, there were a few African-American congregations, most notably First Colored Presbyterian Church in New York City. Its first four pastors were all leading abolitionists and prominent intellectuals; one, Theodore Sedgwick Wright, helped found the American Anti-Slavery Society with William Lloyd Garrison (1805–1879) and Arthur Tappan.

Abolitionism, and nineteenth-century social reform movements generally, gave women a position of more prominence than they had previously held. Antoinette Brown Blackwell (1825–1921), first woman ordained in the Reformed tradition, illustrates this intersection. Brown grew up in an environment influenced by Finney and New School abolitionists, graduating from Oberlin. She was licensed to preach by Congregationalists but ordained by Luther Lee (1800–1889), a Wesleyan minister; eventually having a crisis of faith, she left the pastorate, serving as an itinerant speaker for years before becoming a Unitarian minister.

THE GILDED AGE

In the Gilded Age, Reformed evangelistic, missionary, and social reform endeavors expanded, as did their network of educational institutions.

Elements anticipated by Bushnell and Mercersburg became more prominent; growing wealth expressed itself in large Gothic church buildings, with new pipe organs and robed choirs. Bushnell's concept of Christian nurture influenced proliferating Sunday School material. While Sunday School had begun to educate and evangelize poor children, it became primarily a way of catechizing children of church members.[22] Urban churches developed large facilities and functioned as community centers as well as places of worship.

Reformed theological schools became the center of new controversies. They had from the time of Moses Stuart on been in close connection with German theological institutions. In the late nineteenth century, however, conservatives within American Protestant denominations became concerned that this German influence was leading to a new set of departures from the faith.[23] Contrary to common belief, evolution was not the focus. While Hodge had denounced Darwin's theory as fundamentally atheistic and was unconvinced that any theory of evolution was compatible with the biblical narrative, he represented part of a complex spectrum of opinion.[24] Harvard botanist Asa Gray (1810–1888), a devout evangelical Presbyterian, was a close friend and supporter of Darwin. James McCosh (1811–1894), president of Princeton University, defended the compatibility of Darwin with Christianity.

Rather, the focus of the "fundamentalist–modernist controversy" was nineteenth-century critical biblical scholarship. Appropriately, the flashpoint was the Old Testament. Charles Briggs's (1841–1913) inaugural address as professor of biblical theology at Union on "The Authority of Scripture" (1891) laid out clearly points at issue between liberal and conservative factions of Presbyterianism. Briggs argued that concepts of the verbal inspiration and inerrancy of Scripture interfered with hearing the voice of God. He distinguished between the words of Scripture, which he saw as capable of error, and the fundamental authoritative message from God, and further aroused conservative ire by acknowledging the church and human reason as authorities alongside Scripture. Briggs saw his own position as in keeping with the historic creeds and professed adherence to the Westminster Confession, but he was charged with heresy, defrocked, excommunicated in 1893, and joined the Episcopal Church. He did not, however, leave Union Seminary. Rather, Union severed its ties with Presbyterianism rather than lose him. As a result, it entered the twentieth century as a non-denominational seminary of broadly Reformed heritage, committed to academic freedom, and the flagship institution of liberal Protestantism.

Briggs's most formidable intellectual opponents were the Princeton theologians who had inherited Hodge's mantle: his son and successor as president Archibald Alexander Hodge (1823–1886) and A. A. Hodge's successor, Benjamin Breckenridge Warfield (1851–1921). Their position, which became the classic conservative Protestant approach, was that God guided human authors of Scripture so they expressed exactly what God intended. There was room in this view for figures of speech, for approximation, and for a sensitive appreciation of culture. But error, as the Princeton theologians defined it, was impossible in books inspired by God.

DISPENSATIONALISM

As in controversies dividing Congregationalists a century earlier, there were three parties in late nineteenth-century Presbyterianism; the third saw themselves as evangelical Christians who happened to be Presbyterians. They were committed to Scripture's authority and saw "higher criticism" as a threat to evangelical faith, but their primary concern was practical piety and evangelism. Chief among them, in the tradition of mass evangelism pioneered by Whitefield and Finney, was D. L. Moody (1837–1889), a Congregationalist who founded an independent congregation in Chicago. His associate J. Wilbur Chapman (1859–1918) was a Presbyterian minister; Billy Sunday (1862–1935), a protégé of Chapman's and also a Presbyterian, was the leading popular evangelist of the early twentieth century. Another important Presbyterian evangelist, Arthur Tappan Pierson (1837–1911), prominently promoted foreign missions.

All these figures were influenced by dispensationalism, the theological and exegetical system developed by J. N. Darby (1800–1882) and promulgated by the Plymouth Brethren. Cyrus Scofield (1843–1921), author of a popular reference Bible that formed generations in dispensational theology, was a Congregationalist and a Moody protégé who joined the Southern Presbyterians. Dispensationalist evangelicals tended to be connected to the Keswick Conference in England, an interdenominational gathering of evangelicals promoting a version of holiness theology that a "deeper Christian life" was possible through total surrender of one's will to God. Like Finney, these ecumenical revivalist Presbyterians and Congregationalists articulated a perfectionism which they saw as compatible with Reformed theology. They feared modernism for reasons more visceral and experiential than those of the Princeton theologians but nonetheless deep.

However, their embrace of dispensationalism sharply broke from historic Reformed claims that the church was one continuous reality existing in Old and New Testaments. Pierson radically accepted believer's baptism in 1896, remarking wistfully that if only Presbyterianism would do so it would be "the true Catholic Church of the world."[25] Canadian Presbyterian minister A. B. Simpson (1843–1919), after ministering in Louisville and New York, resigned in 1883 to begin what became the Christian and Missionary Alliance. Just as with earlier expressions of revivalistic Calvinism, the dispensationalist evangelical wing of American Reformed Protestantism showed signs of detaching itself altogether from the Reformed tradition. This was nothing new. Neither was the alliance forming between Princetonian confessionalists and dispensationalists. The difference was the outcome.

After Briggs's expulsion there were two more heresy trials in the 1890s. In 1893 a group of eighty-seven clergy led by New York minister and poet Henry Van Dyke signed a "Plea for Peace and Work," arguing that heresy trials distracted from denominational mission. Van Dyke (1852–1933) argued that the Westminster Confession needed to be revised to affirm God's love for all humanity and the salvation of all who died in infancy; he was able to get the denomination to accept a non-binding resolution on this. His moderation and irenicism appealed to many in the New School tradition who saw evangelism as more important than doctrinal controversy.

Dispensationalist Keswick Presbyterians wanted evangelism done by people untainted by "modernism" and were less concerned about institutional control. Moderates and liberals, on the other hand, sought to maintain a complex institutional network of mission agencies to coordinate efforts. They emphasized attention to physical needs in mission efforts, against the primary dispensationalist goal of bringing individuals to Christ in preparation for the imminent Second Coming. While the dispensationalist expectation of apocalypse has often been seen as a despairing response to the challenges and complexities of the Gilded Age, for them it was a message of joyful expectation.

THE FUNDAMENTALIST–MODERNIST CONTROVERSY

In 1909, the General Assembly enacted a "Doctrinal Deliverance" identifying five doctrines as essential to Christian faith: the inspiration and inerrancy of Scripture, Jesus's virginal conception, his atoning death, his bodily resurrection, and the historicity of his miracles – drawing on the distinction its predecessor body had made in 1729 between essential and inessential aspects of the Westminster Confession. Presbyterian oil magnate Lyman Stewart (1840–1923), a dispensationalist evangelical, sponsored a series of pamphlets defending the five articles of the "Doctrinal Deliverance" as the "Fundamentals" of the Christian faith; the series was a joint production of dispensationalists and confessional conservatives of several denominations. A. T. Pierson was a primary contributor, with five essays; Warfield wrote the article on the deity of Christ.

In 1922 Harry Emerson Fosdick (1878–1969), a Baptist serving the First Presbyterian Church in New York City, published a sermon called "Shall the Fundamentalists Win?" challenging what he saw as the fundamentalist mania for declaring sincerely pious people false Christians because they failed to affirm specific doctrines. This led to conservatives attempting to oust him. General Assembly, however, had had enough of heresy trials and insisted the local presbytery had to deal with Fosdick, who resigned and moved to the non-denominational Riverside Church. Among his opponents was populist orator and activist William Jennings Bryan (1860–1925), a Presbyterian elder. Bryan was also concerned about what he saw as the nefarious consequences and dehumanizing effect of Darwin's theory; he was not what was later called a "young-earth creationist" but refused to accept the idea that human beings shared ancestry with other animals.

But opposition to these conservative attempts to impose orthodoxy were growing. At Princeton itself, theology professor Charles Erdman (1866–1960), one author of the Fundamentals, concluded that infighting was damaging the cause of the gospel and ran for moderator under the slogan "Peace, Purity, and Progress." New Testament professor J. Gresham Machen saw this as a surrender to modernists, and in *Christianity and Liberalism* (1923) described liberal theology as something fundamentally different from historic Christianity. In the same year, a group of moderate and liberal clergy issued the "Auburn Declaration" rejecting the Five Fundamentals' authority and arguing that American Presbyterianism had always allowed broad interpretive freedom to local presbyteries. The 1926 General Assembly affirmed this, closing off the possibility of conservatives using the Assembly to punish those they saw as unorthodox, and also reorganized Princeton Seminary so that it was no longer a bastion of Old School orthodoxy. In 1929, Machen left Princeton with some colleagues and founded Westminster Seminary to continue the Princetonian intellectual tradition.

The final stage in the controversy was provoked in 1932 by the interdenominational report *Rethinking Missions*, which argued that missionary efforts, too narrowly focused on conversion, should stress humanitarian efforts and interreligious cooperation; it was supported by

Presbyterian missionary and novelist Pearl Buck (1892–1973). The report was repudiated by the denomination and Buck resigned in 1933. For Machen, this was not good enough. He criticized the board for not forcing missionaries to affirm the Fundamentals and established his own mission organization which sought contributions from Presbyterian congregations; he and seven others were tried in 1936 and expelled from the denomination. He established the Orthodox Presbyterian Church (OPC), but further conflict in the new denomination led to a second split in 1938, with leader Carl McIntyre (1906–2002) founding the Bible Presbyterian Church. This mirrored fractions happening all across the conservative American Protestant spectrum; fundamentalists left large denominations to found small ones or independent churches, while cooperating in parachurch ministries. Having lost the seminaries, they built on existing missionary training colleges to create Bible schools that taught a stripped-down version of a seminary education focusing on practical preparation for ministry.[26]

MAINLINE MERGERS

The Presbyterian Church in the United States emerged from this controversy shaken but still the primary representative of American Presbyterianism, now free to engage in ecumenical dialogue and biblical scholarship without constant controversy. It cemented this position in 1958 by joining with the United Presbyterian Church of North America to create the United Presbyterian Church in the United States. However, conservatives had not left. They accepted that they no longer controlled the denomination, and if they found they needed spiritual sustenance other than what was officially offered they had a host of fundamentalist radio stations, Sunday School materials, and parachurch organizations to draw on. A similar picture, though without quite as strong an evangelical presence or as bitter a series of controversies, held good in other Reformed traditions. Mergers were the order of the day, with splits sometimes resulting from mergers. In 1931 the Congregationalists merged with the "Christian Connection," a combination of two groups from the Second Great Awakening; Conservative Congregationalists left for their own small denomination in 1945. The German Reformed united with the Evangelical Church (originally a Lutheran-Reformed union church from Prussia) in 1934 to form the Evangelical and Reformed Church (ERC), and in 1957 the ERC united with the Congregational Christian Churches of the 1931 merger to form the United Church of Christ (UCC) – which became the most liberal of the mainline denominations.

The RCA had suffered its major split in 1857, when congregations formed what became the Christian Reformed Church (CRC). In the 1880s these congregations merged with others who had left the RCA as well as with new immigrants influenced by Dutch theologian Abraham Kuyper (1837–1920), champion of a revitalized confessional Calvinism and of robust engagement with society and politics. Kuyper's doctrine of "common grace" emphasized the presence of God in the world in non-salvific ways enabling Christians to work together with unbelievers in culture and society: "There is not a square inch in the whole domain of our human existence over which Christ, who is Sovereign over all, does not cry, 'Mine!'"[27] The CRC established Calvin College and Seminary in Grand Rapids, where they taught a distinctively Dutch version of confessional Reformed theology. CRC theologian Cornelius Van Til (1895–1987) taught at Princeton, became Presbyterian, and joined Machen at Westminster. He sought to reconcile the fideistic approach of Kuyper with the evidentialist approach of Warfield, developing what he referred to as "presuppositional apologetics" – arguing that believers and unbelievers had no neutral ground to compare respective truth claims. Apologetics consisted in showing unbelievers that their understanding of reality was hopelessly incoherent, driving them to Christianity as the only intelligible account of reality.

It appeared in the 1930s as if traditional Reformed theology was destined to be a small, embattled corner of American Christianity. But the mid-twentieth century changed the picture decisively when in mainline denominations the progressive, optimistic liberalism of the early twentieth century was challenged by the rise of "neo-orthodox" theology. The most famous neo-orthodox theologian was the Swiss Karl Barth (1886–1968), but his American influence was probably less than that of brothers Reinhold (1892–1971) and H. Richard Niebuhr (1894–1962). Richard was primarily an ethicist and observer of the American religious scene, famous for *Christ and Culture* (1951). Reinhold produced a somewhat modified neo-orthodoxy for Americans, attacking what he saw as the naïve utopianism of earlier liberalism. He reaffirmed, with a social and political edge, the historic Reformed doctrine of original sin – fully on display at mid-century in a world racked by war, totalitarianism, and genocide.

Yet the post-World War II years brought prosperity to mainline Protestantism. Politicians sought the advice of theologians. Churches were well attended, and religious educational and cultural programs flourished. America's "Judeo-Christian" identity was seen as a bulwark against Communism. A Presbyterian minister even suggested adding "In

God We Trust" to the Pledge of Allegiance. Alongside the Niebuhrs, German-American theologian Paul Tillich (1886–1965) became a household name in educated circles, speaking to postwar anxieties. He saw the task of theology as "correlation" of historic doctrine with the questions being asked by each generation.

After the war many second-generation fundamentalists, having grown up in a sectarian world, began distinguishing between themselves as evangelicals and those whom they continued to call "fundamentalists," claiming they sought engagement with the broader world, while fundamentalists walled themselves off from it. In 1942, Harold Ockenga (1905–1985) and others created the National Association of Evangelicals as a counterpart to the National (formerly Federal) Council of Churches; it has functioned ever since as evangelicalism's closest thing to a unifying body. In 1947, Ockenga joined with radio evangelist Charles Fuller (1887–1968), whose son had studied with Barth, to found Fuller Theological Seminary in California to offer a deeper and broader theological formation than was available in Bible colleges. Finally, Ockenga helped Billy Graham (1918–2018) and Baptist theologian Carl Henry (1913–2003) found *Christianity Today* in 1956. Henry was a student of Gordon Clark (1902–1985) at Wheaton College, another flagship neo-evangelical institution, and developed Clark's version of presuppositionalism into a comprehensive, influential evangelical systematic theology. Evangelicalism in the second half of the twentieth century now resembled the nineteenth – a vibrant network of churches and other organizations of a generally revivalist bent, affirming God's love for humanity and the need for conversion, with a Reformed intellectual core diffusing influence through the whole network.

THE RELIGIOUS RIGHT

The cultural changes of the 1960s and 1970s affected mainline and evangelical churches equally, but differently, as mainline denominations began their long decline from their mid-century boom. Mainline Reformed clergy were more likely than evangelicals to participate in the civil rights movement and other activist movements. But ironically, the evangelical version of "correlation" proved more successful. Their well-organized youth groups and parachurch ministries spoke to young people who found mainline churches boring, and they developed an evangelical "subculture" that adopted the idioms of pop culture and incorporated them into worship.[28] This emerging Christian counterculture found an unlikely star: Francis Schaeffer (1912–1984) of the Bible Presbyterian Church. In 1948 Schaeffer and his wife Edith (1914–2003) moved to

Switzerland where they established a mission and retreat center, L'Abri, a place of pilgrimage for young American evangelicals. Schaeffer was a prolific and accessible writer who popularized the term "worldview" as a way of describing overall explanatory and imaginative frameworks for dealing with reality; he inspired evangelicals to think about Christianity in terms of an allegedly comprehensive "worldview" in contrast to alternative worldviews. Schaeffer inspired unlikely disciples, including Christian rock musician Larry Norman (1947–2003), who single-handedly created what became the contemporary Christian music industry. Schaeffer also helped inspire the Christian Right – both generally by inspiring young evangelical Christians to engage with their society instead of constructing a parallel subculture, and specifically by pointing them to abortion as a galvanizing moral issue evidencing secularism's inhumanity.

A more radical influence, conservative Presbyterian Rousas Rushdoony (1916–2001), was like Schaeffer a prolific writer operating outside conventional academic networks but revered as an intellectual by his admirers. Rushdoony advocated applying biblical law to civil society, or "theonomy," as the answer to modern western collapse; his *Institutes of Biblical Law* (1973) expressed a fusion of economic libertarianism and political decentralization with extreme social and religious conservatism. Even among conservative evangelicals who balked at his belief that adulterers and homosexuals should be executed, his approach was influential; his criticism of American public schools as systematic secularist indoctrination helped inspire the rise of home-schooling and the formation of "classical Christian schools" to educate Christian children in a conservative interpretation of western civilization. On the more moderate side, Mark Noll's *The Scandal of the Evangelical Mind* (1994) criticized what he saw as evangelicalism's shallow emotionalism. Instead of Rushdoony's total replacement of secular society, Noll (b. 1946) called for evangelical Christians to bring their faith into secular cultural and intellectual institutions, and he and other Reformed historians provided insightful works which helped evangelicals situate themselves.[29] Evangelical scholars in the late twentieth century began achieving academic positions within secular, mainline, and Catholic institutions.

YOUNG, RESTLESS, AND REFORMED

Calvin College developed a strong philosophical tradition in the late twentieth century; there Alvin Plantinga (b. 1932) emerged as the best-known of a rising generation of evangelical philosophers who used tools of analytic philosophy to defend Christian faith. Plantinga developed a position he labeled "Reformed epistemology," arguing that belief in God may be "properly basic," rational to hold in the absence of evidence – rooted in Calvin's concept of the inherent *sensus divinitatis* present to all people. His philosophical work was designed to show the rationality of a faith only possible through supernatural means, rather than to convince people to accept Christian beliefs. Like New Divinity theologians before him, Plantinga articulated Reformed convictions in ways that some thought betrayed them.

Around 2000, a desire for spiritual and intellectual depth led Millennial and Generation X evangelicals to turn to Reformed thought. While some joined confessional churches such as the OPC, others remained non-denominational or formed new networks such as the "Sovereign Grace churches" or the "Acts 29 Network." Many resembled the larger megachurch phenomenon in organization and worship style while teaching Calvinist theology, such as Mark Driscoll's Mars Hill Church in Seattle, which numbered about 14,000 in 2014. Driscoll (b. 1950) was a charismatic and polarizing figure due to his macho rhetoric and penchant for taking controversial positions. The Reformed tide was rising also among Baptists. The conservative takeover of the Southern Baptist Convention included a diverse coalition of conservatives, many who identified as Reformed, including Al Mohler (b. 1959), whose Southern Baptist Seminary in Louisville served as a center of the Reformed wing of the SBC. In the historically Arminian Baptist General Conference, John Piper (b. 1946) rose to prominence as a powerful Reformed voice pastoring Bethlehem Baptist Church in Minneapolis, as did Greg Boyd (b. 1957) of Woodland Hills Church in St. Paul. Boyd advocated openness theology, which denied not only Calvinist predestination but the more common view that God eternally knows all events, and was forced out of his position as professor of theology at the denomination's seminary.

In 1983 Northern and Southern Presbyterians finally reunited in the Presbyterian Church (USA), today with 1.25 million active members. Ten years earlier, Southern conservatives, alarmed by the prospect of this reunion, had left to form the Presbyterian Church in America (PCA), which attracted a number of Northern Presbyterians and became the largest conservative Presbyterian denomination in the country, with just under 400,000 members and a broad theological tent compared to other conservative Presbyterian denominations, from Reconstructionists and strict confessionalists to mainstream evangelicals. Another prominent moderate conservative denomination, the Evangelical Presbyterian Church, originally formed in 1981 from Northern conservatives concerned about women's ordination; it has about 145,000 members. In 2012 another wave of conservatives left the PCUSA over the blessing of same-sex unions and ordination of clergy in same-sex relationships to form the Evangelical Covenant Order, which differed from other conservative Presbyterian denominations in fully accepting women's ordination and having strong female leadership, including Laura Smit, a Calvin College professor.

Twenty-first-century debates increasingly centered on questions of gender and sexuality. In 1993, feminists from mainline denominations gathered in Minneapolis for the "Re-Imagining" conference, a celebration of women's spirituality which included invoking God as Sophia, rituals with milk and honey as a feminine counterpart to the Eucharist – seen by conservatives as idolatrous goddess worship – and criticism by Presbyterian Union professor and prominent Womanist theologian Deloris Williams (b. 1937) of the idea that Jesus's death was in any sense an atoning sacrifice. A rare Black female voice in a largely white male tradition, she rooted her criticism in the abusive way atonement had been used to make Black women submit to suffering, but her remarks were taken out of context as glib dismissal of historic Christian teaching. The backlash led to a significant drop in contributions to participating denominations, demonstrating the continuing large conservative constituency within allegedly liberal mainline denominations.

CONCLUSION

In the early twenty-first century, Reformed Christians span a remarkably wide spectrum of belief and practice. They continue to serve as an intellectual "core" of Protestantism, from UCC biblical scholar Walter Brueggeman (b. 1933) to essayist and memoirist Kathleen Norris (b. 1947) and novelist Marilynne Robinson (b. 1943), both Presbyterians; and they dominate intellectual discourse in evangelicalism, from leading conservative political commentator David French (b. 1969), a PCA member, to popular author Tim Keller (b. 1950), pastor of Redeemer Presbyterian Church in New York.

The tension between confessional loyalty and the expectation that "more light" will yet break forth from the Word has worked itself out in Reformed history in complex ways. Today, in Berea, John Fee's Union

Church remains a thriving congregation under the leadership of Kent Gilbert (b. 1966), with a liberal Congregationalism centered on inclusion and social activism. Their Black Lives Matter banner bears scars of two slashings and the slogan: "Real Christians know it; Real Christians show it." One local Southern Baptist called the congregation "not a real church." Yet they are not only a church, but a church in the Reformed tradition. On the other side of the spectrum, Doug Wilson's (b. 1953) Christ Church in Moscow, Idaho, shaped by Reconstructionism and Southern Presbyterianism, is a sacramental and liturgical congregation stressing the family as the basic unit of the church, upholding a patriarchal vision of gender relations, and strategizing to restore a "godly" order in America. No two figures could be more different than Gilbert and Wilson. Yet both have a commitment to the classic Reformed goal of shaping society according to the values of God's Kingdom – with diametrically opposed visions of what that entails. The Reformed tradition may not have the dominant role in American life it once did. But its bewildering and fractious diversity is a testimony to its ongoing central role in this endlessly changing and deeply divided country.

NOTES

1 James H. Smylie, *A Brief History of the Presbyterians* (Louisville, KY: Geneva Press, 1996).
2 See Chapter 17 by Robert W. Prichard, this volume.
3 Cotton Mather, *Magnalia Christi Americana* (Hartford, CT: Silus Andrus and Sons, 1853), 64. See Stephen Tomkins, *The Journey to the Mayflower* (New York: Pegasus Books, 2020).
4 Mather, *Magnalia Christi Americana*, 64.
5 See Abram Van Engen, *City on a Hill: A History of American Exceptionalism* (Cambridge, MA: Yale University Press, 2020).
6 John Cotton, "God's Promise to His Plantation," in *The Kingdom, the Power, & the Glory: The Millennial Impulse in Early American Literature*, ed. Reiner Smolinski (Dubuque, IA: Kendall-Hunt Publishing, 1998), 19, in *Electronic Texts in American Studies* (University of Nebraska-Lincoln, 1998), accessed June 26, 2021, https://digitalcommons.unl.edu/cgi/viewcontent.cgi?article=1022&context=etas.
7 Edmund Morgan, *The Puritan Dilemma: The Story of John Winthrop* (Boston: Little, Brown, and Co., 1958).
8 See Chapter 21 by Nicholas T. Pruitt, this volume.
9 Perry Miller, *Errand into the Wilderness* (Cambridge, MA: Belknap Press, 1956).

10 Robert C. Whittemore, *The Transformation of the New England Theology* (New York: Peter Lang, 1987); Douglas A. Sweeney and Allen Guelzo, eds., *The New England Theology: From Jonathan Edwards to Edwards Amasa Park* (Grand Rapids, MI: Baker Academic, 2006).

11 George M. Marsden, *Jonathan Edwards: A Life* (New Haven, CT: Yale University Press, 2003).

12 See especially Jonathan Edwards, *A Treatise Concerning Religious Affections* (1746), www.ccel.org/ccel/edwards/affections.pdf.

13 Sydney Ahlstrom, "The Scottish Philosophy and American Theology," *Church History* vol. 24, no. 3 (1955), 252–272. See also George Marsden, *Fundamentalism and American Culture*, 2nd ed. (Oxford: Oxford University Press, 2006), 11–21.

14 Sydney Ahlstrom, *A Religious History of the American People* (New Haven, CT: Yale, 1972), 403–404.

15 See Chapter 21 by Pruitt and Chapter 23, by Douglas M. Strong, this volume.

16 See Glenn Miller, *Piety and Intellect: The Aims and Purposes of Ante-Bellum Theological Education* (Atlanta: Scholars Press, 1990).

17 See Chapter 22 by Mark E. Powell, this volume.

18 See Charles E. Hambrick-Stowe, *Charles G. Finney and the Spirit of American Evangelicalism* (Grand Rapids, MI: Eerdmans, 1996).

19 See Paul Gutjahr, *Charles Hodge: Guardian of American Orthodoxy* (New York: Oxford University Press, 2011).

20 See James Hasting Nichols, *Romanticism in American Theology: Nevin and Schaff at Mercersburg* (Chicago: University of Chicago Press, 1961); Jack Martin Maxwell, *Worship and Reformed Theology: The Liturgical Lessons of Mercersburg* (Pittsburgh:Pickwick Press, 1976); Richard E. Wentz, *John Williamson Nevin: American Theologian* (New York: Oxford University Press, 1997); D. G. Hart, *John Williamson Nevin: High Church Calvinist* (Phillipsburg, NJ: P&R Publishing, 2005).

21 See Mark Noll, *The Civil War as a Theological Crisis* (Chapel Hill: University of North Carolina Press), 2006.

22 See Anne Boylan, *Sunday School: The Formation of an American Institution, 1790–1880* (New Haven, CT: Yale University Press, 1990).

23 See Glenn Miller, *Piety and Profession: American Protestant Theological Education, 1870–1970* (Grand Rapids, MI: Eerdmans, 2007).

24 See David Livingstone, *Darwin's Forgotten Defenders: The Encounter between Evangelical Theology and Evolutionary Thought* (Grand Rapids, MI: Eerdmans, 1987); Ronald Numbers, *Darwinism Comes to America* (Cambridge, MA:Harvard University Press, 1998).

25 Delavan Leonard Pierson, *Arthur T. Pierson: A Biography* (London: James Nisbet & Co., 1912), 259.

26 See Joel Carpenter, *Revive Us Again: The Reawakening of American Fundamentalism* (New York: Oxford University Press, 1997).

27 *Abraham Kuyper, a Centennial Reader*, ed. James D. Bratt (Grand Rapids, MI: Eerdmans, 1998), 488.

28 See Tom Bergler's illuminating account in *The Juvenilization of American Christianity* (Grand Rapids, MI: Eerdmans, 2012).

29 See Carpenter, *Revive Us Again*; George Marsden, *Fundamentalism and American Culture*; and Nathan Hatch, *The Democratization of American Christianity* (New Haven, CT: Yale University Press, 1991).

19 The Lutheran Tradition

MARK GRANQUIST

INTRODUCTION

One of the largest branches of Protestantism, Lutherans have been in
North America for more than 400 years. Lutheranism was established on
this continent initially by immigrants from the historically Lutheran
areas in Europe, notably Germany, Scandinavia, and Eastern Europe.
More recent Lutheran immigrants have come from the younger
Lutheran churches in Asia and Africa. In the United States, these immigrants formed congregations and denominations mainly based on language and ethnicity, although they were also divided by theological and
religious differences. As these immigrant communities acculturated to
the use of English and to the American religious culture, they began
a long process of denominational consolidation, as well as moving into
the mainstream of national life.

Lutheranism traces its roots to the sixteenth-century reformation
begun by Martin Luther. With Luther's formal break with papal authority
beginning in the 1520s, Luther and his followers began to form their own
churches in a number of territories in Germany, and in the Scandinavian
kingdoms. The key document for this new Protestant group was the
Augsburg Confession of 1530, which provided a common theological
and organizational rationale for the new movement. Conflict with the
Catholic Imperial officials in Germany led to war, but Lutherans were
granted legal status with the Peace of Augsburg in 1555. Internal theological disputes led to the development of new theological confessions of
faith, gathered together in the Book of Concord in 1580. Lutheranism
came to dominate areas of central and northern Germany and
Scandinavia; there the movement transformed into official, state-
supported churches. In other areas of Europe, especially Eastern Europe,
Lutherans developed minority settlements in the middle of generally
Roman Catholic areas. During the seventeenth century Lutherans consolidated their theological positions, developed rich traditions of liturgy

and hymnody, and resisted Roman Catholic encroachment, including in the Thirty Years' War (1618–1648). Later in this century Lutheranism was enriched by the reforming movement of Pietism, although this development also caused internal conflict. Pietism was the impetus for much of the initial missionary expansion of Lutheranism to North America, Africa, and Asia, and has had a significant impact on Lutherans in America. In the nineteenth century European Lutheranism was influenced by rationalism, which also occasioned a confessional reaction. Lutherans in North America began to form congregations and denominations, and by 1900 the Lutherans were the third largest denominational family in the United States.[1] Lutheran missionaries formed new churches in China, India, Indonesia, and Southern and Eastern Africa, with these churches becoming independent and self-supporting after World War II. In the twenty-first century Lutheranism has seen a major growth of churches in the global South, especially in Africa, with a slight decline among Lutheranism in North America, and a significant secularization in the Lutheran areas in Europe. The largest grouping of the Lutheran churches is in the Lutheran World Federation, while a smaller grouping of more conservative churches gathers in the International Lutheran Council. Lutherans are active through the world in relief and development efforts through Lutheran World Relief and related organizations.

LUTHERANS IN COLONIAL AMERICA

The first Lutherans in North America were a party of Danish explorers looking for the Northwest Passage to Asia, who were frozen into Hudson's Bay in 1619. Most of the crew died there, including the first Lutheran pastor in America, Rasmus Jensen, and only a few returned to Denmark. There were early Lutheran colonies developed by the Swedes along the Delaware River (1638–1655) and by the Danes in the Virgin Islands (after 1672), both of which established Lutheran congregations served by pastors sent from Europe. Some of the Danish congregations remained Lutheran, while the remaining Swedish congregations moved into the Episcopal Church after the Revolutionary War. There were a number of Lutherans in the seventeenth-century Dutch colony of New Amsterdam (New York), but because of opposition from local Dutch pastors, they were not able to form a congregation until 1649; it is now the oldest continuing Lutheran congregation in the United States. The largest number of Lutherans in colonial America came from Germany, not in organized colonies but as individuals and families seeking economic advancement. The German immigrants were attracted to good land and religious freedom in the middle colonies, especially Pennsylvania, New Jersey, and New York. They began to form scattered Lutheran congregations based on language and ethnicity, but these congregations had a difficult time attracting a supply of suitable Lutheran pastors to serve them. There were organized colonies of German Lutheran refugees from the Palatine region who settled in New York in 1708 and from the Salzburg region settling in Georgia in 1734. Other Lutherans founded scattered congregations in Maryland, Virginia, and the Carolinas, as well as Nova Scotia.

The German immigration to colonial America consisted mainly of Protestants; German-language communities were generally mixed groups of Lutherans, Reformed, Moravians, Mennonites, and radical Pietists. In these ethnic communities, there was a general lack of congregations and pastors, and at times they formed "union" congregations combining different types of German Protestantism. Forming congregations of any kind was difficult; the immigrants were poor and scattered, and they received little in the way of support from the Lutheran churches in Europe. The new, voluntary religious situation of the English colonies was confusing to immigrants familiar with the established, government-supported churches of Europe. Good pastors were hard to get, as few established Lutheran pastors from Europe wanted to brave the wilds and the poverty of North America. Some pastors who did come were those who had failed in Europe or were clerical imposters. In 1703 Justus Falckner became the first Lutheran pastor ordained in North America, but there were no schools to train potential Lutheran pastors in the colonies; they either had to be educated in Europe or to study for the ministry with established Lutheran pastors in an "apprentice" system. Without an organized Lutheran church system in North America, the validity of Lutheran ordinations on this continent was questionable. For the first 100 years of its existence, North American Lutheranism lacked an organized body to bring together the scattered congregations.[2]

One of the early Lutheran leaders in colonial America was William Berkenmeyer, who arrived in 1725 to gather together the scattered Lutheran congregations in New York and New Jersey. Of more lasting success and influence was Henry Melchior Muhlenberg, who was sent in 1742 to Pennsylvania by the Pietist institution at Halle. Though his formal position was specifically as pastor to three congregations around Philadelphia, he quickly established himself as the leader of most of American Lutheranism. Muhlenberg worked to install reputable pastors in Lutheran congregations in the middle colonies, and to defend them from the encroachment of other religious groups. In 1748 Muhlenberg and others formed the Pennsylvania Ministerium, the first formal Lutheran organization in colonial America. The Ministerium worked to regulate and connect congregations, ordain and discipline pastors, and extend Lutheran influence across the region. The Lutherans developed increasing numbers of congregations, almost of which were ethnically and linguistically German, and which provided for the religious, educational, and cultural needs of these communities. Because of the lack of state support of these congregations, their pastors had to become religious entrepreneurs. Many farmed land provided them by the congregations in order to support themselves, and they often married women from the local community. Because religious life was voluntary, lay people in the local congregations gained important new power in these organizations, and eventually the lay leaders in these congregations pushed for and obtained representation in the Pennsylvania Ministerium. This was the beginning of the synodical system, so prevalent among Lutherans in America, where Lutheran organizations, called synods, consisted of Lutheran pastors and representatives of congregations who would meet together regularly (usually yearly) to consider the business of the group.[3]

In colonial America the Lutheran presence stretched from Georgia to Nova Scotia but was concentrated in the middle colonies, from Virginia to New York. Most Lutherans were farmers, always pushing out on the frontiers, seeking new and better land, especially into western Pennsylvania and down the Shenandoah Valley into Virginia and North Carolina. This strained the resources of American Lutheranism, already quite short of pastors for even established congregations. These Lutherans interacted only in a limited way with the English-speaking population, and rarely with Native Americans; some Lutherans (and even some congregations) in the South became owners of enslaved African Americans. During the Revolutionary War some Lutherans cautiously supported the revolutionary cause, but many held back, seeing the conflict as a dispute among the "English." One of Muhlenberg's sons became an American general, and other Lutherans joined the continental army. There were also Lutherans who remained loyal to the British, and some of these loyalists, as well as some Lutherans among Hessian mercenary troops, eventually moved to Ontario, beginning another Lutheran presence in Canada. By the end of the war, there were probably about 25,000 Lutherans in the new country of the United States. Because of German immigration, there were perhaps many more nominal Lutherans who lived in German ethnic communities and had occasional contacts with the Lutheran congregations.

LUTHERANS IN THE NEW AMERICAN REPUBLIC

When the new country of the United States was formed after the Revolutionary War, the size of the new nation stretched westward to the Mississippi River. Most of the territory west of the Appalachian Mountains had not yet been settled by Europeans, for British policy had been to keep European settlement east of the mountains. Freed from this restriction after the wars, American settlers poured across the Appalachians seeking new land, and displacing the Native Americans. Lutherans joined this westward movement, and pushed into Ohio, Indiana, Kentucky, and Illinois. Established Lutheran congregations in the East were seriously depleted by the movement of members to the West. There was already a serious shortage of Lutheran pastors for established congregations, and very few pastors to serve Lutherans who had gone west. Itinerant Methodist and Baptist pastors were already working on the frontier, and Lutherans had to quickly develop means to match them. Established pastors took missionary trips to the frontier to visit scattered Lutheran populations, while barely educated catechists were authorized to serve new Lutheran congregations in these new territories.

This rapid expansion meant the need for new synods to gather in the expanding Lutheran populations. The first new organization formed was the New York Ministerium in 1786, followed by new synods in North Carolina (1803), Ohio (1818), and Maryland (1820).[4] This began the rapid expansion of synods, as dozens were formed in America before the Civil War. Most of these new synods were geographical in nature, but some synods were formed out of theological differences and came to compete with already established synods. The other major dispute during these years involved the language transition from German to English, which happened primarily during the first two decades of the nineteenth century. Increasingly, younger generations of Lutherans sought worship and preaching in English, leading to sharp disagreements with others who sought to maintain the use of German. These language battles within the congregations were sometimes very difficult, but the encroaching tide of English and the needs of the younger generations prevailed, and most of the Lutheran congregations eventually made the transition to the use of English. Because of this linguistic transition, many Lutherans were influenced by the dominant Protestant revivalism of the time, which came to shape Lutheran worship and preaching. Many American Lutherans sought to emulate the religiosity of their American Protestant neighbors.

There were soon calls for a national Lutheran organization to coordinate between the regional synods, and to provide for common institutions, most notably a new seminary for the education of pastors. Under the leadership of young pastor Samuel Simon Schmucker, such an organization, called the General Synod, was formed in 1820, but its initial years were difficult, and a number of the regional synods did not join it. Schmucker also led the formation of a new American Lutheran seminary in 1820 at Gettysburg, Pennsylvania, and served as its initial president and theological professor. Schmucker was a leading figure in American Lutheranism before the Civil War but was also a controversial figure for his vision of a Lutheranism that closely resembled the dominant reformed and revivalistic American Protestantism of his day. Ever since Lutherans had come to America, but especially when they made the language transition to English, Lutherans had struggled among themselves as to how to form a distinctly "American" version of Lutheranism.

One question involved the theological authority of the sixteenth-century Lutheran confessional documents, especially the Augsburg Confession (1530), which set the Lutherans somewhat apart from the rest of Protestantism. Some American Lutherans felt that these documents were outdated; if held too strictly they would keep them separate from other American Protestants, and they also contained vestigial elements that were too close to Roman Catholicism. Schmucker and his followers sought to loosen the authority of the Lutheran Confession and to bring American Lutherans closer to the rest of Protestantism, and in 1855 introduced an "American Edition" of the Augsburg Confession, shorn of elements they thought were obsolete or divisive. But other Lutherans sought a renewal and strengthening of Lutheran confessional identity, leading to disputes and the formation of new, more strictly confessional synods, beginning with the Tennessee Synod in 1820. Interconfessional strife was a common theme of this growing and expanding American Lutheranism.

While the descendants of colonial Lutheranism (the Muhlenberg tradition) were expanding geographically and organizationally, the period after 1840 saw a new development for American Lutheranism – the beginnings of a massive new period of immigration that eventually would bring millions of European Lutherans to the United States, a process that lasted until World War I. These new Lutherans, Germans and Scandinavians, preferred to develop their own, independent Lutheran synods based on immigrant languages; they also felt that the English-speaking "Americanized" Lutherans had lost so much of their confessional identity as to be unrecognizable as Lutherans. The new

German Lutheran immigrants formed more strictly confessional, national synods including the Ohio, Iowa, Buffalo, and Missouri Synods, the last of which grew rapidly and soon became a major national Lutheran organization. New Lutheran immigrants also arrived from Denmark, Sweden, and Norway. These immigrants formed their own synods, separated not only by language but also by religious and theological issues they brought with them from their European state churches. For all these new immigrant Lutherans, there were familiar needs as they struggled to find pastors and resources to serve the immigrant populations, and wondered how to adjust to the new religious culture in the United States.

Toward the middle of the nineteenth century, the major national issue was the question of slavery, which increasingly divided all religious groups, including the Lutherans. While many Northern Lutherans initially sought to avoid the issue, seeking internal peace, some of them broke away to form abolitionist-oriented groups, such as the Franckean Synod. Southern Lutherans responded by adopting strong defenses of slavery, and when the Civil War started in 1861, formed their own national group, the General Synod South. Many new immigrant Lutheran synods were strongly opposed to slavery, and their members fought on the Union side, while the Missouri Synod, based in one of the border states, sought a mediating position on the issue. Lutherans fought on both sides of the Civil War; a major battle took place on the grounds of the Lutheran seminary at Gettysburg, but the war was especially destructive of Lutheran institutions and congregations in Georgia and the Carolinas.

AMERICAN LUTHERANISM, 1865–1940

As the United States rebuilt after the Civil War, Southern Lutheranism remained separate, and increasingly pushed their remaining African-American members into new, racially separate congregations. A few of these congregations did survive, but many of them closed due to inadequate resources and lack of pastors. There was a short-lived African-American Lutheran synod, the Alpha Synod, formed in 1889, while Northern Lutheran synods such as the Missouri and Ohio synods began mission work among African Americans in the South. The General Synod, mainly the descendants of colonial (Muhlenberg) Lutherans, suffered the loss of Southern Lutheran synods in 1861, and then another split in 1867 when more conservative and confessional elements left to form a rival organization, the General Council. A number of the established regional Lutheran synods in the East divided into competing synods within rival national organizations. The General Council was intended to also reach out and include the newer immigrant ethnic synods, but linguistic and theological issues meant that this vision was not generally successful.

After the Civil War Lutheran immigration from Europe increased dramatically, resulting in the formation of even more ethnic synods, especially in the Midwest and Upper Midwest regions. The largest of these new groups was the German-language Missouri Synod, which had become a national organization, but it had other, smaller rivals, including the Ohio, Iowa, Buffalo, and Texas synods. Missouri attempted to draw these other groups into its orbit in a new national organization, the Synodical Conference, formed in 1872. This new organization was soon torn apart by theological disputes over the doctrine of predestination (election) during the 1880s, resulting in the departure of many of the small denominations.

Scandinavian immigration to the United States increased dramatically after 1865, resulting in the formation of additional new ethnic and linguistic Lutheran denominations among them. Since these immigrants came from countries that had established state churches, and all their people were supposed to be at least nominally Lutheran, this suggested very large Scandinavian-American Lutheran denominations. Yet like other Lutheran immigrants before them, they were able only to gather in a fraction of these ethnic immigrants. A number of factors mitigated against these new ethnic Lutheran synods. There was the usual lack of pastors and congregations to gather in the new immigrants, who scattered all over the county in search of land or work. A number of Scandinavian immigrants decided to join "American" churches, and still many others took advantage of their new religious freedom to join no churches whatsoever. The Scandinavian-American Lutheran denominations were still the largest organizations within their communities, but they struggled to enroll into membership even a fraction of the immigrants. Some immigrants employed these ethnic congregations for occasional religious services but did not become members. These Scandinavian-American religious groups and their leaders had also been greatly influenced by the pietist awakenings in nineteenth-century Scandinavia, but not all immigrants were attracted by these pietistically orientated congregations.

Swedish immigrants formed the Lutheran Augustana Synod in 1860, which became the largest religious group within this immigrant community. But theological disputes and the availability of other religious options meant the formation of other, non-Lutheran ethnic denominations: the Swedish Covenant, the Swedish Evangelical Free, the

Swedish Baptists, and the Swedish Methodists. One theological dispute within this community during the 1870s caused a renewed appreciation in the Augustana Synod of its Lutheran roots. Norwegian immigrants formed a number of different synods as well, but most of them remained Lutheran of one variety or another. Pietist Norwegians out of the Haugean revivals in Norway formed their own congregations, while those closer to the state church in Norway formed the Norwegian Synod in 1853. Between these ends of the spectrum were several other different centrist Norwegian-American Lutheran groups. The Norwegian Synod was also rocked by the Predestination controversy in the 1880s, leading to divisions within this denomination. Those who left joined together with centrist denominations in 1890 to form the United Norwegian Lutheran Church. The Danish-American immigrants had two distinct Lutheran options. One was a group organized around the concept of a national or folk church for all Danes, as espoused by Danish church leader N. F. S Grundtvig; this group was commonly referred to as the "happy" Danes. The other was based on a stricter pietist morality and religiosity, and they came to be known as the "holy" Danes.

As the nineteenth century came to a close, newer Lutheran immigrants came from other areas of Europe and formed their own ethnic denominations. Immigrants from Finland predictably divided along religious lines from their home country. The largest group was the Suomi Synod, which was closely allied with the Lutheran Church of Finland. Followers of pietist leader Frederick Hedberg formed the separate "National" Finnish denomination, which eventually joined the Missouri Synod, while the followers of Lars Levi Laestadius organized congregations in the Apostolic Lutheran tradition. Icelandic Lutherans formed their own synod in the Upper Midwest and Canada. There were also German-ethnic Lutherans from Eastern Europe and Russia who formed their own distinct congregations, or affiliated with one of the German-American Lutheran denominations. Slavic Lutherans such as the Wends and the Slovaks also developed their own congregations, as did Lutherans from Poland, Hungary, and Romania. Lutheran congregations were formed by immigrants from the Baltic region, including Estonia, Latvia, and Lithuania. The congregations that these new immigrants formed were an important element of ethnic communities, providing identity and support and easing their eventual transition into America life.

Though the older Muhlenberg Lutherans had become fully integrated into American religious life, these new immigrants, now the majority of American Lutherans, still lived in separated ethnic communities segregated by language and culture. These Lutherans still used the languages of the "old country" for their worship and theology, and maintained close ties with religious groups back home. Since new immigrants continued to arrive up to World War I (and more were expected after this), these denominations continued the use of the immigrant language and customs, even though their younger generations were impatient with this situation and sometimes broke away to form their own new, English-speaking congregations. The new immigration swelled the numbers of Lutherans, and this family of denominations became the third largest Protestant group in the United States by 1890. Though large, their influence on the national scene was muted by internal divisions and linguistic barriers.

During this time, American Lutherans also built an impressive group of institutions, mainly to serve their own communities. They opened numerous schools, colleges, and theological seminaries, as well as social service institutions such as hospitals, orphanages, and homes for the aged and those with physical and mental challenges. Although many did not survive long-term, the remaining ones served as the basis for an impressive system of educational and service institutions for which American Lutherans are still known. Though they still had many pressing needs in the United States, toward the end of the nineteenth century Lutherans also began to send missionaries overseas, often in conjunction with European missionary societies. Some of the first American Lutheran missions were located in India, Liberia, Southern Africa, and China.

Early in the twentieth century, American Lutherans began an initial wave of denominational mergers that would, by the end of the century, include most American Lutherans in one of two major denominations. The initial mergers were quite a bit more modest. The three elements of the Eastern (Muhlenberg) Lutheran tradition reunited in 1918 to form the United Lutheran Church in America. Many of the various Norwegian-American Lutheran groups merged together in 1917 to form the Norwegian Lutheran Church in 1917. And in 1930 several conservative German-American denominations in the Midwest formed the American Lutheran Church (1930–1960). These mergers were complicated, with theological and organizational differences to be overcome, not to mention the historical and even personal differences between the groups. Lutherans also disagreed among themselves as to the requirements for merger, especially the degree of theological agreement necessary to allow merger to occur.

The rate of change and acculturation for Lutherans was accelerated by the events of World War I (1914–1918), which resulted in the end of

European immigration. At this time many American Lutherans still primarily used immigrant languages; as to the war they were isolationist, had mild sympathies for the German cause, and were deeply suspicious of British and French intentions. With the entry of the United States into the war in April 1917, all this changed, and American Lutherans responded to a wave of xenophobia by rushing to demonstrate their support of the American cause. Events forced the Lutheran denominations to cooperate as they had never done before in order to support military chaplaincy and war relief; this resulted in the formation of the National Lutheran Council in 1918 for permanent and continuing cooperative work. After the war, American Lutherans took the lead in relief and assistance to suffering European Lutherans, and to the support of world Lutheran missions "orphaned" by loss of resources from Europe.

These events occasioned another round of language transition which by 1930 saw almost all American Lutheran groups using English primarily. As with the previous language transition, this one was also conflicted, but inevitable; the cessation of European immigration in the 1920s added to its speed. This transition also thrust Lutherans more into the mainstream of American religious life and occasioned new theological battles among them, especially over fundamentalism and the authority of the Bible. The number of American Lutherans grew from 3.7 million in 1920 to 4.7 million by 1935 during this time of rapid social change, which they generally viewed from the margins. Lutherans were still socially conservative; they overwhelmingly supported Prohibition but viewed other social changes during the 1920s with deep suspicion. The Depression of 1929–1941 was very difficult for Lutherans, as rapidly falling voluntary funding hit congregations and institutions very hard, and a number of the weaker ones closed. Many Lutheran pastors saw their salaries cut or deferred, leading to great hardship. As with the time before World War I, Lutherans favored American isolationism and staying out of European conflicts, and there was a discernible pacifist movement among them.

LUTHERANISM IN AMERICA, 1940–2020

With the entry of the United States into World War II in 1941, most American Lutherans became supporters of the war effort, and Lutheran congregations and institutions mobilized to become a part of the national effort. Lutherans served in the armed forces, including Lutheran pastors as chaplains. Educational institutions went on a wartime footing, and the National Lutheran Council dealt with social dislocations at home, including ministry with those in defense industries. With the end of the war, the subsequent "baby boom" (1946–1964), and demographic shifts to the suburbs and to the South and West, there was an immediate need for hundreds of new Lutheran congregations and pastors to serve them. Educational institutions were jammed with students, and social service agencies expanded as well. The postwar expansion meant that American Lutheranism peaked in the mid-1960s at about 9 million members.

The postwar period also saw American Lutherans taking a leadership role among Lutherans around the world. European Lutheranism was devastated by the war and the subsequent Communist takeover of Eastern Europe, and American Lutherans raised millions of dollars to support displaced persons and settle them in new homes, including some in North America. American Lutherans also took a lead role in supporting Lutheran missions in the global South, and to prepare these young churches for autonomy as their countries achieved independence. They also played an important part in the formation of new ecumenical organizations, including the Lutheran World Federation (1947), the World Council of Churches (1948), and the National Council of Churches (1950).

Since all American Lutheran denominations were now using English, the need for separate ethnic denominations was rapidly passing. During the 1950s a series of merger negotiations occurred among the eight members of the National Lutheran Council, with the Lutheran Church Missouri Synod (LCMS) observing from the sidelines. These negotiations were complicated by structural and theological issues, and instead of a single merger, two new Lutheran denominations were formed; the American Lutheran Church (ALC) in 1960 and the Lutheran Church in America (LCA) in 1962. These two denominations and the LCMS were all roughly about the same size (2.3–2.7 million members), and although there was disappointment that a single merger was not achieved at this time, there was great optimism that a unified American Lutheran church was inevitable. These three denominations did achieve a milestone in 1966 with the formation of the Lutheran Council in the USA, which served as a joint cooperative agency. The ALC and the LCMS also achieved pulpit and altar fellowship, which was a first for the LCMS.

As American Lutherans were now fully participating in the wider life of American Protestantism, these new Lutheran institutions began to confront the social and cultural developments that were roiling American society during the 1960s – conflicts over war, race, and gender, among others. Traditionally, Lutherans had avoided direct engagement with such issues, but now some Lutherans were calling for direct conversations on these controversial topics, partly through a series of official social statements. Lutherans began a renewed push for the inclusion of African Americans into their congregations, and, after some study, the ALC and LCA decided to begin ordaining women as pastors in 1970, although the LCMS decided not to do so.

Soon after the Lutheran mergers of the early 1960s had been accomplished, many Lutheran leaders began to consider a further merger of the three major denominations together into a single Lutheran denomination. As had been the previous pattern, one initial preparation for such an eventuality was the development of a common hymnal to be used between the three groups, a process which begun in 1969. But the social upheavals and polarization of the late 1960s had extended into the Lutheran denominations and began to divide "moderates" and "conservatives" within the LCMS. In 1969 a new conservative president took control within the LCMS and began to consolidate control over denominational organizations. This included pressure on moderates who controlled the synod's leading seminary, Concordia Seminary in St. Louis; this led in 1974 to the walkout of most of its faculty and students, who formed Christ Seminary in Exile (Seminex). To support this new seminary, in 1976 some moderate congregations and pastors withdrew from the LCMS to form a new denomination, the Association of Evangelical Lutheran Congregations (AELC).

As hopes faded for a comprehensive Lutheran merger, the ALC and LCA along with the struggling AELC began to consider another merger – but without the LCMS, as the groups were veering away from each other. Negotiations began on a further merger in 1982 and resulted in the formation of a new church in 1988, the Evangelical Lutheran Church in America (ELCA). This new denomination was faced almost immediately with unresolved theological and structural issues, and struggled to find its way. When it was formed in 1988, the ELCA had 5.2 million members, while the LCMS had 2.5 million members. The next largest Lutheran group was the conservative Wisconsin Evangelical Lutheran Synod, with 400,000 members.

As with a number of other American Protestant denominations, membership in Lutheran groups plateaued during the 1970s and 1980s, and began to decline after that. Congregations matured due to shifting social patterns, and growing American Evangelical congregations attracted some Lutherans. Lutheran denominations struggled to become more ethnically diverse, reaching out to Hispanics and African Americans, but these efforts were only modestly successful. New Lutheran immigrants from Africa and Asia formed new ethnic congregations along previous lines, and some became a part of the ELCA or LCMS. New groups of refugees were sponsored by Lutheran social service agencies in partnership with local Lutheran congregations, and some of these new arrivals also became Lutheran. Meanwhile, Lutheran social service agencies grew to become one of the largest networks of such organizations in the United States.

By the 1990s, the American Lutheran denominations continued to confront internal and external issues. In the LMCS the struggles between moderate and conservative wings continued, as the denomination also tried to rebuild its seminaries and colleges. The ELCA continued to wrestle with contentious issues such as human sexuality, the doctrine of the ministry, and ecumenical relations. A controversial decision to enter into full communion with the Episcopal Church in 1999 occasioned a schism by pastors and congregations who formed the Lutheran Congregations in Ministry for Christ in 2001. The decision in 2009 to ordain homosexual pastors led to a similar withdrawal to form the North American Lutheran Church in 2010. Because of the two schisms, over 500,000 members and 700 congregations left the ELCA. Demographic declines among American Lutherans and the "graying" of congregations also affected the ELCA, whose membership has declined to 3.3 million in 2018, while the LCMS has declined to 2 million. There are probably close to 6.5 million Lutherans in 17,000 congregations in the United States in 2018, the last year for which official statistics are available.

American Lutherans still dominate a number of regions of the United States. They are especially strong in the Upper Midwest (Minnesota, Wisconsin, and the Dakotas), and relatively strong in Pennsylvania and the Midwest, from Ohio through Nebraska. There are also pockets of Lutheran strength in the Carolinas, Texas, and in areas of the West Coast. Lutherans also maintain a quality system of educational institutions (colleges, universities, and seminaries) as well as social service agencies. American Lutherans also play a leadership role among Lutherans around the world through the Lutheran World Federation and the International Lutheran Council. Although after 400 years Lutherans have become an integral part of the larger American religious world, they still form a distinctive and important tradition within the larger world of religion in the United States.

NOTES

1 General histories of American Lutheranism include Mark Granquist, *Lutherans in America: A New History* (Minneapolis: Fortress Press, 2015); L. DeAne Lagerquist, *The Lutherans* (Westport, CT: Greenwood Press, 1999);

and E. Clifford Nelson, ed., *The Lutherans in North America* (Philadelphia: Nelson Press, 1975).

2 Of reference works that cover topics in American Lutheranism, the newest is Timothy Wengert, ed., *The Dictionary of Luther and the Lutheran Traditions* (Grand Rapids, MI: Baker Academic, 2016). Also helpful is Günther Gassmann, *Historical Dictionary of Lutheranism*, 2nd ed. (Lanham MD: Scarecrow Press, 2011). Older works that are still valuable include Julius Bodensieck, ed., *The Encyclopedia of the Lutheran Church*, 3 vols. (Minneapolis: Augsburg Publishing House, 1965) and Erwin L. Lueker, *Lutheran Cyclopedia* (St. Louis, MO: Concordia, 1975).

3 Source books and readers on American Lutheran history include Eric Lund and Mark Granquist, *A Documentary History of Lutheranism: 1750 to the Present* (Minneapolis: Fortress Press, 2017); Richard C. Wolf, ed., *Documents of Lutheran Unity in America* (Philadelphia: Fortress Press, 1966); Carl S. Meyer, ed., *Moving Frontiers: Readings in the History of the Lutheran Church – Missouri Synod* (St. Louis, MO: Concordia, 1964); August Suelflow, ed., *Heritage in Motion* (St. Louis, 1988); and Theodore G. Tappert, ed., *Lutheran Confessional Theology in America, 1840–1880* (New York: Oxford University Press, 1972). On women in American Lutheranism, see Betty DeBerg, *Women and Women's Issues in North Americans Lutheranism* (Chicago: Commission for Women of the ELCA, 1992).

4 For general information on American Lutheran synodical organizations, see Robert C. Wiederaenders, ed., *Historical Guide to Lutheran Church Bodies of North America*, 2nd ed., Lutheran Historical Conference Publication 1 (St. Louis, MO: Lutheran Historical Conference, 1998). A good overview is Susan Wilds McArver, "Lutherans," in *The Blackwell Companion to American Religion*, ed. Philip Goff (Malden, MA: Wiley-Blackwell, 2010), 614–635.

20 Brethren and Mennonite Traditions

WILLIAM KOSTLEVY

Generations of Americans have associated Brethren and Mennonites with the idyllic rural landscape of Lancaster County, Pennsylvania and have assumed that these groups were culturally and theologically homogenous. However, both are actually diverse and complex bodies with long inter-connected histories. Further studies of American Protestantism, often preoccupied with Puritan and New England antecedents, have virtually ignored Mennonites and Brethren or assumed that they are two manifest-ations of a single tradition that has had little impact on American Christianity. One exception was William Warren Sweet, father of the academic study of American church history, who argued that religious radicals, such as Mennonites and Brethren, were the essential shapers of the distinctive contours of American Christianity. German immigrant theologian Paul Tillich also argued that American Protestantism owed its dynamic moralistic character to these evangelical radicals who sought not salvation from sin but a transformed social order.[1]

HISTORICAL BACKGROUND

American Mennonites, Amish and the closely related communal Hutterites date their origins to January 21, 1525 when a group of disgrun-tled radical followers of Zurich reformer Huldrych Zwingli rejected the validity of infant baptism, insisting that the only valid Christian baptism was of consenting adults. Led by a young scholar, Conrad Grebel, these so-called Swiss Brethren also rejected Zwingli's view that church reforms required government approval. Unfortunately coinciding with the out-break of a bloody peasant uprising, their simple act of baptism, or what the Zurich authorities saw as "re-baptism," resulted in vigorous persecu-tion and mass executions of the Anabaptists-literally re-baptizers.[2]

In February 1527, a group of Anabaptist leaders met at the village of Schleitheim, near the German-Swiss border and produced the Schleitheim Confession which identified characteristics of a faithful

Christian community: adult baptism, a disciplined faith community that used the ban to exclude unfaithful members, closed communion, separation from the world, and, based on a literal reading of the words of Jesus, refusal to take part in war or swear oaths.[3]

In Central Germany Anabaptism drew on other sources, including Nurnberg reformer Hans Denk who, inspired by medieval mysticism, emphasized the inner life of the Spirit over the dead letter of Scripture. Denk never organized a church, but his insistence that "no one may truly know Christ except one follows Him in life" led many into more institutional expressions of Anabaptism. If Denk emphasized a mystical spiritual kingdom, Hans Hut, a traveling bookdealer, spread the Anabaptist message throughout central Germany, Austria and Moravia, baptizing and preaching the imminent end of the world. Unlike the Swiss Anabaptists, Hut was inspired, in part by mysticism, and he emphasized the redemptive value of Christian suffering.[4]

With many of their leaders dead and the local nobility troubled by religious dissension, approximately 200 adult followers of Hut migrated further into Moravia. Adopting communal ownership of property and living after 1533 under the leadership of Jacob Hutter, these Hutterites, as they came to be known, established one of the most successful communal societies in history. During the so-called Hutterite golden period, between 1555 and 1595, perhaps as many as 30,000 members lived in intentional communities in Moravia, Slovakia, and Hungary. Each community, or Bruderhof, had one or more preachers, and men who managed their economic affairs. The remarkable efficiency led to both considerable wealth and jealousy on the part of non-Hutterite neighbors. Beginning in the 1590s the Austrian government began a campaign of persecution culminating in the forced evacuation of all Hutterites to Slovakia during the early years of the Thirty Years' War.[5]

Anabaptist ideals were spread into the Low Countries by the South German apocalyptic preacher Melchior Hoffman. A furrier by trade, Hoffman – who insisted that he was Elijah, chosen to proclaim the Second Coming of Christ – attracted a significant number of followers who were intent on establishing a physical Kingdom of God. In 1534 a group of Hoffman's followers seized power in the North German city of Munster. The movement that had aroused the hopes of many ended in disaster with the fall of the city to imperial forces and the brutal execution of many of its key figures.[6]

In the wake of the Munster debacle, a group of about 300 supporters of the failed experiment occupied a monastery near Witsmarsum in the Netherlands. Among those killed in the fighting that ensued when imperial forces stormed the monastery was a man who may have been the brother of a local Catholic priest. That priest became the namesake of today's Mennonites, Menno Simons (1496–1564). While horrified by many of the excesses of these radicals and while rejecting violence and the establishment of a physical Kingdom of God on earth, Menno shared the radicals' desire for a faithful visible community of regenerate disciples of Jesus. Under Menno's leadership, the so-called Mennonites, experienced rapid growth with over 100,000 believers in the Low Countries by the end of the sixteenth century.[7]

A brilliant polemicist and apologist, Menno emphasized an experiential faith inaugurated by a subjective conversion followed by adult believer's baptism into a disciplined community of faith from which the disobedient could, if unrepentant, be excluded or shunned. In his classic apologetic work *The Foundation Book* (1539), Menno excoriated Catholic superstition, Protestant compromises with wealth and worldly power, and the role of the educated churchly elite in the persecution of nonviolent followers of the lowly Christ.[8] He rejected both Lutheran and Reformed Protestantism for such unscriptural practices as taking part in war, infant baptism, and the welcoming of the unregenerate to the Lord's Supper. By the mid-sixteenth century, Menno was the acknowledged leader of peaceful Anabaptists in Germany and Switzerland as well the Netherlands.

As if fulfilling the biblical aphorism that the "meek will inherit the earth," the peaceful heirs of Conrad Grebel and Menno Simons survived and even thrived in Switzerland, South Germany, and the Netherlands with the more prosperous Dutch Mennonites often providing financial and moral support for remnant communities in the South. But with prosperity came division. In 1693 a renewal movement advocating more vigorous church discipline, twice-annual communion, feet washing and greater separation from the world divided Swiss and German Mennonites. Led by Jacob Ammann and popularly known as Amish, these traditionalist Anabaptists began to migrate to America in 1727.[9]

In America, Mennonites generally lived in communities with another German immigrant group committed to adult believer's baptism, often called "Dunkers" but more formally "Brethren." If Mennonites date to the social upheaval of the immediate post-Reformation era, Brethren were products of the renewal of Protestant spiritual life known as Pietism. While many Pietists remained in Reformed and Lutheran congregations, others, often referred to as "radical" Pietists, separated from what they believed were apostate churches. In August 1708 near the village of Schwarzenau in central Germany,

Alexander Mack, a Reformed millowner, his wife and six others underwent adult baptism covenanting to establish a congregation of committed Christians who would faithfully restore the beliefs, lifestyle, and
worship practices of the early Christian church. Inspired by the historical
work of radial Pietist leader Gottfried Arnold (1666–1714), the Brethren
affirmed adult believer's baptism by triune immersion in the name of the
Father, Son, and Holy Spirit; reinstitution of the Christian love feast as
described in John 13, including a meal and feet washing, and concluding
with bread and cup communion; and the practice of church discipline
including the use of the ban.[10]

The noted Church of the Brethren historian Donald F. Durnbaugh
writes that Brethren "find their beginnings at the confluence of three
religious' streams – Reformed Protestant, radical pietist, and Evangelical
Anabaptist."[11] Early Brethren had been nurtured in the Reformed faith
and affirmed most elements of traditional Protestant Christianity. As
with Pietists in general, they desired a less institutional and more inner-
directed faith focusing on the teachings of Jesus. Although Brethren
found much to admire in Mennonite communities, as a passionate
renewal movement they saw Mennonites as deficient in evangelistic
zeal and insufficiently apostolic in worship practices such as baptism.
The aggressively proselyting Brethren sent ministers to Switzerland, the
Palatine, and the Netherlands. Widely persecuted for their religious non-
conformity and such practices as refusal to serve in the military,
Brethren did find a home among Mennonites on the lower Rhine.
Beginning as early as 1683, Mennonites, encouraged by recruiters from
William Penn's recently established colony in Pennsylvania, began
migrating to America where they helped establish a largely German
community at Germantown. From 1719 to 1740 virtually all Brethren
migrated to the New World.

THE GROWTH AND DISPERSION OF BRETHREN AND
MENNONITES IN AMERICA

The initial Mennonite migration of about 200 people arrived from North
Germany between 1683 and 1702. This was followed by a more significant migration of about 4,000 Mennonites and 500 Amish from
Switzerland and South Germany between 1707 and 1774, with a third
migration of about 3,000 Amish and Mennonites from Alsace-Lorraine
and South Germany to Ohio, Illinois, New York, and Ontario between
1815 and 1860. More culturally isolated, persecuted, and less prosperous
than North German and Dutch Mennonites, South German and Swiss

Mennonites were among the primary creators of two things: the distinctive culture of religious and ethnic pluralism that came to dominate the middle colonies, especially colonial Pennsylvania; and an enduring mystique that has romanticized the Mennonite, and especially Amish, experience in America.[12]

Historians have often marveled at the relative economic success of more communally based sectarian religious communities such as Mennonites and Brethren when compared with their less communal German immigrant neighbors from Lutheran and Reformed backgrounds. Scholars have been amazed that such economic success has failed to accelerate secularization among these plain people. Far from fleeing the market economy, prosperous Mennonite and Brethren farmers in Lancaster and Lebanon Counties in Pennsylvania were strategically located with access to the expanding agricultural markets of Philadelphia and Baltimore and the profitable Atlantic trade. In effect Mennonites and Brethren were among the most successful commercial farmers in the world.[13]

Thriving in the religious culture of colonial America, Brethren evangelistic outreach found especially fertile ground among neighboring Mennonites. Not only were both groups committed to adult believer's baptism, but they shared a common opposition to war, exercised church discipline, and (beginning in Crefield, Germany) lived in the same communities with European Brethren, following Mennonites to Germantown. The first Mennonite and Brethren meeting houses were within a mile of each other.

The Brethren–Mennonite sibling rivalry has often been intense with vigorous Brethren polemics against Mennonite baptismal and worship practices, especially Mennonite use of pouring instead of immersion. But during times of stress, such as war, Brethren and Mennonites – often joined by Quakers – have worked together, perhaps most notably in the establishment and funding of the Civilian Public Service for conscientious objectors (COs) to war during World War II. In 1775, Brethren and Mennonites jointly petitioned colonial leaders to respect their peace scruples during times of war. To this day Brethren and Mennonite congregations are often found in the same communities with extended kinship networks that cross church boundaries.[14]

With an emphasis on intense inner-directed spirituality, Pietism has often proven to be divisive. The first Brethren division was inspired by Conrad Beissel, a Brethren convert, who organized his own movement that drew its membership primarily from Brethren immigrants. The movement was centered on celibacy, communal living, and direct revelation. Beissel established his community at Ephrata in Lancaster County, Pennsylvania. It became noted for its cultural achievements in printing, music, and illuminated manuscripts. Despite the Ephrata separation, Brethren experienced steady growth throughout the eighteenth century.[15]

Literature documenting the eighteenth-century religious experiences of Brethren and Mennonites is sparse. Among the most instructive are illuminated manuscripts known as *Fractur*, often created by children. In the examples that have survived, traditional Anabaptist themes of suffering and separation are often interspersed with pietist themes: the love of Jesus, the need for personal spiritual renewal, and even witticisms that are reminiscent of Benjamin Franklin's "Poor Richard."[16]

Primarily farmers with large families, Brethren and Mennonites were intrepid immigrants, always in search of fertile but inexpensive property on the frontier. By the end of the eighteenth century, both groups had expanded into central Pennsylvania and south into Maryland, Virginia, and the Carolinas with scattered Brethren congregations as far south as North Georgia and crossing into Eastern Tennessee where significant Brethren congregations remain today. Far from isolated communities of faith, both groups were profoundly impacted by the dynamic religious culture of the Second Great Awakening. In South Carolina and Georgia, Brethren congregations embraced Universalism, and in Kentucky and Southern Indiana virtually all Brethren joined Barton Stone's Restorationist Christian Church. In spite of these defections Brethren experienced continual growth as significant communities were established in Ohio's Miami Valley, Illinois, Northern Indiana, and Iowa and, by the end of the century, in Kansas, Idaho, and California, and in the early twentieth century in Washington, Wisconsin, and North Dakota.

Mennonites, reinforced by European immigrants, experienced similar growth throughout the nineteenth century. Especially significant were the 18,000 Russian Mennonite immigrants who arrived in Western Canada, Kansas, and other Midwestern states from 1874 to 1880. While ties of family, a common history, and shared core beliefs united all Mennonites, the new Russian immigrants differed in culture and ecclesiastical organization. Frequently more prosperous than Swiss and South German immigrants and with a history of more cultural engagement, many of these groups joined with other more acculturated Mennonites in the General Conference Mennonite Church (GC) while existing Mennonites organized as the more centralized Mennonite Church (MC). These highly successful Russian

Mennonite immigrants helped transform American agriculture through the popularizing of new strains of wheat especially suited for the Great Plains.[17]

Denominational purists have often sought to marginalize outside religious influences on Mennonites and Brethren, but both groups have been active participants in the rich and diverse religious culture of the North America. Russia Mennonite immigrants had been deeply impacted by a nineteenth-century Pietist renewal movement that had resulted in the formation of the Mennonite Brethren Church (MB). With an emphasis on a personal conversion experience, deeper devotional life, and a more disciplined church life, MB members, who were less wealthy, have coexisted with GC Mennonites – often establishing rival relief, mission, and educational institutions in the same communities but continuing to cooperate during times of stress.[18]

In America, Mennonites have not only divided as a result of religious renewal movements but frequently been active leaders in such movements. The revival currents associated with the First Great Awakening of the 1730s and the Second Great Awakening of the first three decades of the nineteenth century were less foreign to Mennonite experience than is commonly assumed, since Menno Simons had emphasized the "new birth." As early as 1761, Mennonite preacher Martin Boehm received, as his son remembered, "new light" with a more dramatic and intense religious experience. Ordained a Mennonite bishop, Boehm – joined by Philip Otterbein, a Reformed Pietist minister with ties to Methodism – led many Mennonites into a new denomination, the United Brethren Church.[19]

Closely related, but retaining more elements of Mennonite heritage, were the River Brethren, now Brethren in Christ (BIC). Clearly influenced by their Dunker neighbors, River Brethren embraced baptism by triune immersion, Brethren-style love feasts, a Methodist–like intense conversion experience, nonviolence, and community-based decisions about land purchases and migration. The BIC have proven especially open to outside religious currents, embracing the Holiness movement in the early twentieth century with openings to Pentecostalism that resulted in a small holiness denomination, the Fire Baptized Holiness Church. World War II general (later US president) Dwight D. Eisenhower was raised in a BIC community in Kansas. By the end of the nineteenth century, over 40,000 Mennonites, Brethren in Christ, Hutterites, and Amish lived in twenty states with nearly a third living in Pennsylvania.[20]

The more aggressively evangelistic Brethren grew at a faster rate, often at Mennonite expense and without foreign immigration. Although they were still a plain agricultural people with distinctive dress and rites, by the 1870s Brethren unity was reinforced by an annual gathering of thousands of Brethren and the itineration of deeply respected preachers. Three of the most important nineteenth-century Brethren leaders were converts to the movement. These included Henry Kurtz, a former Lutheran minister; Peter Nead, an author known as the "English preacher"; and James Quinter a schoolteacher, apologist, and evangelist. A fourth significant leader, the Virginian John Kline was a herbalist healer and traveling preacher who was murdered in 1864 for his alleged Northern sympathies.[21]

Acculturating at a faster rate than their Mennonite neighbors, Brethren were more open to outside influences. By the 1850s Brethren were being impacted by revival meetings, the temperance movement, Sunday schools and higher education. Traditionalists, led by Peter Nead and his son-in-law Samuel Kinsey, openly clashed with the more outward-looking and centralizing leadership of Annual Meeting while so-called progressives led by Henry Holsinger increasingly placed individual conscience and interpretation of Scripture above communal discernment.

In 1881 the frustrated traditionalists left the brotherhood, organizing the Old Order German Baptist Brethren. Two years later Holsinger was expelled from the church, leading to an exodus of more progressively minded members who organized a less centralized body, the Brethren Church. In 1890, there were about 4,000 Old Order Brethren and about 8,000 in the Brethren Church. The conservatives, known as German Baptist Brethren, and, after 1908, Church of the Brethren, continued to experience rapid growth with 61,000 members in 1890.[22]

THE INSTITUTIONALIZATION OF THE BRETHREN AND MENNONITE EXPERIENCE

The differences between the German Baptist Brethren and the Old Order German Baptists were essentially missional. For the Old Orders the point of Christianity was a restored New Testament church faithfully imitating all the practices of first-century Christians. For the Church of the Brethren, it was worldwide missional outreach. The growing division among Brethren was already present by the early 1850s when James Quinter joined Henry Kurtz in the publication of the monthly *Gospel Visitor*, the first Brethren periodical. Other innovations followed, including the introduction of emotionally charged evangelistic services led by preachers like Quinter and the controversial woman preacher Sarah

Righter Major, as well as support for temperance, Sunday schools, inter-denominational prayer meetings, and higher education.

In 1876 the first permanent Brethren institution of higher learning was established at Huntington, Pennsylvania, with James Quinter as president. But even more important for the future of the church was the increasing call for organized missionary outreach. As early as 1852, and in imitation of their Protestant neighbors, Brethren affirmed the centrality of missions, but it was only with the exodus of the Old Order German Baptists that the church established a mission board. Led by Illinois grocer, world traveler, and author D. L. Miller, who established the Brethren Publishing House, the General Mission Board of the Church of the Brethren had an endowment of over 1 million dollars by the early twentieth century. In 1897, Miller deeded the Brethren Publishing House over to the church. In 1899, in part as a result of a $3,000 grant from the city, the Brethren Publishing House and the General Mission Board relocated to Elgin, Illinois.[23]

By the 1920s Church of the Brethren missions had been established in India, China, and West Africa. Although thoroughly evangelistic and closely working with ecumenical Protestant partners, humanitarian concerns were often at the forefront with hospitals and schools surrounding large and usually brick churches. These churches were a far cry from the plain meeting houses where many Brethren continued to worship in rural American communities, but, in fairness, they did resemble many of the newer churches being built by a rapidly expanding denomination that claimed 200,000 members by 1960 and increasingly understood itself not as plain simple followers of Jesus but as ecumenical Protestants.[24]

As the Church of the Brethren moved toward the mainstream, the so-called progressives in the Brethren Church shifted to the right. Expanding rapidly, especially in Southern California, the Brethren Church added more than 10,000 members from 1911 to 1920. Led by Louis Bauman, pastor of the influential Long Beach (CA) Brethren Church and Alva McClain, professor at Ashland College and the Bible Institute of Los Angeles, many of the progressives embraced classic elements of fundamentalism including premillennial eschatology and a neo-Calvinist understanding of salvation. Rejecting the traditional Brethren understanding of human free will and accusing Brethren traditionalists of legalism, the so-called Grace Brethren, now Charis Fellowship, accused Ashland Theological Seminary of fostering liberalism and works-righteousness. In 1939, Brethren fundamentalists established their own seminary and college in Winona Lake, Indiana, in effect creating a new denomination around Bauman and McClain and leading to a mass exodus from the Brethren Church. Today it has over 30,000 members in the United States and extensive worldwide missions, while the Brethren Church has fewer than 10,000 members.[25]

Similar institution-building and conflicts have dominated the Mennonite experience. The GC Mennonites established a mission board, educational institutions in Ohio and Kansas, and a seminary on the campus of the Church of the Brethren Seminary in Chicago. Committed to congregational polity, GC Mennonites were not characterized by any theological consensus: conservative members supported an independent Bible school in Omaha, Nebraska, while ordained GC evangelist Theodore Epp's syndicated radio broadcast helped to create popular evangelicalism across North America. In 1894, the MB founded a mission board and established missions in India and Africa, and by the mid-twentieth century they operated schools in Manitoba, Kansas, and California.[26]

The story of MC institutionalization also parallels the Church of the Brethren experience. The key figure was Mennonite publisher John F. Funk (1835–1930). A convert of the famed evangelist D. L. Moody, Funk was the founder of the first Mennonite publication, the *Herald of Truth*, and a key figure in the 1882 establishment of the Mennonite Board of Missions. Along with co-editor and evangelist John Coffman (1848–1899), Funk did much to turn an inwardly focused people into active participants in worldwide mission. Early twentieth-century leaders Daniel Kauffman (1865–1944) and George R. Brunk, Sr. (1871–1938) did much to redirect this focus inward. More suspicious of the world, MC Mennonites, became, in Kauffman's words, "aggressive conservatives."[27] The same could be said of John Horsch (1867–1941) whose personal crusade against the alleged inroads of liberalism among Mennonites resulted in the temporary closing of Goshen College in the 1920s. It was only the creative historiography of Horsch's son-in-law Harold Bender and increased MC and GC cooperation in service projects and the response to two world wars that refocused Mennonite identity on meeting human spiritual and physical needs.

BRETHREN AND MENNONITE HISTORIANS
AND THE DISCOVERY OF A USABLE PAST

Early twentieth-century Brethren, and some progressively oriented Mennonites, sought denominational renewal through a reconstruction of their own histories. For Brethren the central figure in this historical renaissance was educator and Pennsylvania governor Martin G. Brumbaugh

(1862–1930). A nationally known figure, Brumbaugh served as educational commissioner of Puerto Rico and superintendent of the Philadelphia public school system. Embarrassed and annoyed by what he believed was the backwardness of many of his co-religionists, Brumbaugh turned to colonial Brethren history to justify active Brethren involvement in the great humanitarian causes of Progressive-era America. In his celebrated and commercially successful *A History of the Brethren* (1899), Brumbaugh argued that the two central characteristics of the Brethren were the rejection of binding creeds and freedom of individual conscience. Colonial Brethren, Brumbaugh insisted, were religious innovators who were among the first advocates of temperance, had founded the first Sunday Schools, and were champions of religious freedom and peaceful solutions to international disputes. While later Brethren historians would dispute most of Brumbaugh's claims, the individualism inherent in his reconstruction has remained the dominant interpretive paradigm for many Brethren for well over a century.[28]

Many GC Mennonites shared Brumbaugh's historical perspective. The most important was C. Henry Smith (1875–1948), the first Mennonite to receive a doctoral degree. Smith's *Story of the Mennonites* (1941) identified the early Anabaptists with freedom of individual conscience and religious toleration. However, unlike Brethren who tended to uncritically accept Brumbaugh's interpretation, MC scholars founded an entire school of historical interpretation dedicated to disputing Smith's claims and in the process deeply impacted Brethren historiography as well.[29]

It is rare for academic addresses delivered before learned societies to impact the life of the church, but such was the case with Harold Bender's 1943 presidential address to the American Society of Church History, "The Anabaptist Vision." Bender (1897–1962), the ultimate Mennonite insider, was the son of MC Mission Board president George Bender. He had studied at Goshen College, and Princeton Theological Seminary, and had received his doctorate from the University of Heidelberg (1935). In 1927, he became editor of a new academic publication, the *Mennonite Quarterly Review*. Insisting that he was "orthodox in doctrine but progressive in method," the plain–dressing Bender sought a middle way between the so-called liberalism of Mennonite progressives, like Smith, and the premillennialism that characterized many conservative Mennonites.[30] He argued that the early Anabaptists were a peaceful people apart who universally accepted the authority of Scripture and opposed chiliastic efforts to create the physical Kingdom of God on earth. Rejecting the inherent individualism of Smith, Bender insisted that the early Anabaptists were community centered, missional, scriptural, and nonviolent. Drawing on the insight of colleague Robert Friedmann (1891–1970), Bender also provided a critique of the evangelically focused Mennonite traditions dating back to the last quarter of the nineteenth century and beyond to earlier Pietist leavening of the church. As Bender and Friedmann saw it, Pietists and later evangelicals had separated salvation from ethical behavior. Using a word not yet made famous by Dietrich Bonhoeffer, Bender identified the core of authentic Anabaptism as "discipleship."[31]

Bender's Anabaptist vision found receptive audiences far beyond MC circles. Young GC Mennonites and even many Brethren who as COs had worked with Mennonites in the post-World War II reconstruction of Europe found much to admire in a message that prioritized ethics, recognized the reality of evil, and located anti-war sentiment at the heart of the New Testament. No Church of the Brethren scholar felt the power of this vision more than Donald F. Durnbaugh (1927–2005).[32]

Moving beyond the history of his own denomination, Durnbaugh located the Brethren and Mennonite experience at the center of a neglected theological tradition, the "believers' church." Published in 1968, *The Believers' Church: The History and Character of Radical Protestantism* (1968) was widely heralded as a brilliant and sectarian-friendly reinterpretation of Christian history. Durnbaugh's work drew on a 1967 conference that he co-convened with John Howard Yoder where he defined the essence of the believers' church as a body committed to the Lordship of Christ, authority of the Word, restoration of the New Testament church, separation from the world, living for the world, forming voluntary covenant communities of regenerated believers, and belief that the Spirit of God can break through denominational boundaries.[33]

As Durnbaugh saw it, early Brethren had been Pietists who had embraced an Anabaptist understanding of the church. In promoting this view, he was joined by his Bethany Theological Seminary colleague Dale W. Brown whose widely read book *The Christian Revolutionary* (1971) remains an excellent introduction to the logic of the Anabaptist renewal among Brethren. In the book, Brown turns to the Anabaptist radicals as a model of an appropriate countercultural, disciplined, prophetic, and millennially radical or revolutionary Christianity.[34]

BRETHREN, MENNONITES, AND THE TURN TOWARD SERVICE

During the Civil War, nearly all Brethren or Mennonites who joined the army were expelled from the faith community. However, in World War

I most Brethren and many Mennonite draftees served in the military as noncombatants. Those who refused to serve under military command risked imprisonment. The tragic deaths of two Hutterite draft resisters at Fort Leavenworth, Kansas sensitized public opinion to the concerns of COs about war and united Mennonite, Brethren, and Society of Friends leaders in seeking an alternative for COs in World War II. The three groups founded and funded Civilian Public Service, a program in which not only COs from peace churches but others with ethical objections to war could perform work deemed to be in the national good such as fighting forest fires, doing conservation work, and taking part in medical experiments.

Both Brethren and Mennonites had and have long traditions of mutual aid to their co-religionists and neighbors, but the worldwide missionary movement alerted church members to broader human need. By 1920 both bodies were involved in humanitarian relief efforts in North America, India, and the Middle East. In 1922, Mennonites established the Mennonite Central Committee (MCC) to provide aid to starving Russian Mennonites.[35] MCC was the joint creation of MC, GC, MB, and other Mennonite bodies. Becoming a truly worldwide organization after World War II, and often working closely with Brethren and Quakers, MCC has become one of the most respected humanitarian aid organizations in the world.

For Brethren a key figure in international aid was farmer and church youth worker Dan West (1893–1971). Gaining experience as an aid worker during the Spanish Civil War, West became convinced that a simple solution to the malnutrition of Spanish children could be provided not by handouts but by actual dairy cows. In 1943, West and a group of Indiana farmers, mostly Mennonites and Brethren, founded Heifer Project. During the immediate postwar era, thousands of cows, chickens, goats, and other animals were distributed in war-ravaged areas.

Among other important Brethren-initiated programs are the Christian Rural Overseas Program (CROP) and the Sales Exchange for Refugee Rehabilitation Vocations (SERRV). In addition to Brethren, CROP also involved Mennonites, the Evangelical and Reformed Church, Lutherans, and Catholics. SERRV was formed in 1949 when returning service commission workers brought home handicrafts for resale in the United States to assist refugee families. It has become a multimillion-dollar fair-trade organization that markets crafts made by indigenous workers in underdeveloped regions of the world through gift shops, mail order, and, in churches and other venues throughout North America. Another notable service agency was the Brethren Voluntary Service (BVS), which became the model for the Peace Corps.

It was created in 1948 as a response to Church of the Brethren youth who called for the development of a positive social program to meet human need. Over 7,000 men and women have served in BVS. Mennonites have established similar agencies including the Mennonite Voluntary Service and following the model of SERRV: Ten Thousand Villages, and a thriving network of thrift stores that fund MCC and other related charities. While not generally acknowledged, Brethren and Mennonites are among the primary creators of the concept of fair trade.[36]

As Brethren and Mennonites have sought to navigate in the modern world, they have attempted, drawing on their heritage, to find creative solutions to immediate human need. Among the most successful examples was Doris Janzen Longacre's bestselling *More-with-Less Cookbook* (1976), which drew on her Kansas Mennonite roots, a desire to reshape North American diets in light of the global food crisis, her experience as an MCC worker in Southeast Asia, and a belief that the insights of Jesus should determine all aspects of one's life. In three decades her book sold over 800,000 copies with minimal publicity.[37] Equally impressive were Mennonite efforts to reform the criminal justice system through the concept of restorative justice. Beginning in 1978 in Elkhart County, Indiana, under the leadership of Howard Zehr, the Victim Offender Reconciliation Programs (VORP) rapidly expanded across the United States. Generally led by trained volunteers, VORP facilitated meetings where victims meet with offenders to humanize the often-impersonal criminal justice system.

By the end of World War II, Brethren and GC cultural withdrawal had largely ceased, but MC activists were beginning to discuss what a responsible Christian witness to the state would entail. Building on Harold Bender's Anabaptist Vision and his own research on the origins of Swiss Anabaptism, John Howard Yoder (1927–1997) found a way forward in the teachings of the Lukan Jesus. In his classic work, *The Politics of Jesus* (1972), Yoder rejected a subjective Pietistic reading of Scripture and insisted that the Bible was political and relevant to a generation of young activists radicalized by the war in Vietnam. With its rich biblical exegesis and affirmation of certain elements of the counterculture of the 1960s, Yoder's vision proved attractive to many outside the Mennonite and Brethren ethic ghetto. Notable converts to Yoder's vision included Christian ethicists Stanley Hauerwas and even many members of mainstream Protestant and Catholic churches. But many ethnic Brethren and Mennonites were less enthusiastic about a vision that urged radicalized Christians to create alternative messianic communities on the fringes of the social order.[38]

Brethren and Mennonites were deeply impacted by the social upheaval of the 1960s. Among the most significant Mennonite civil rights activists was the ordained African-American minister, activist, and historian Vincent Harding (1931–2014). As a speech writer for Martin Luther King, Jr., Harding was at the center of the civil rights movement and the author of the noted interpretation of African-American experience *There Is a River: The Black Struggle for Freedom in America* (1981). If the civil rights movement challenged Brethren and Mennonites to work for interracial justice, the women's movement threatened the traditional patriarchal structure of their communities and families. It also inspired women to re-evaluate their place in the church and the world. One of the most articulate leaders in this re-evaluation was novelist and popular author Katie Funk Wiebe (1924–2016) who placed the experiences of Mennonite women at the center of her writing.

CONCLUSION

In 2002, the GC and MC bodies merged to form the Mennonite Church USA. With over 100,000 members in over 900 congregations, it was roughly the size of the Church of the Brethren. As one might expect from the merger of bodies with different histories, cultures, and ecclesiology, the new denomination has been fraught with tension resulting in the 2015 withdrawal of its largest conference. Debates about human sexuality, church order, and doctrine continue. Meanwhile the Amish have grown rapidly. Figures vary but a recent reliable source indicates that there are about 600,000 Brethren, Mennonites, Brethren in Christ, Amish, and Hutterites in North America.[39] But Amish culture continues to draw visitors from around the world to scenic Lancaster County and has even inspired a body of Amish-themed romance novels.[40] In all, the heirs of Grebel, Menno, and Mack remain in, and sometimes of, the world that their ancestors sought to transform into the peaceful kingdom of God. In America, they have both been creators and products of a culture that has occasionally persecuted them but has more often romanticized and idealized their attempts to serve Christ and their neighbors.

NOTES

1 William Warren Sweet, *The American Churches: An Interpretation* (New York: Abingdon-Cokesbury, 1948), 11, 18–19; Paul Tillich, *A History of Christian Thought* (New York: Simon and Schuster, 1968), 239–242.

2 George Huntston Williams, *The Radical Reformation*, 3rd ed. (Kirksville, MO: Sixteenth Century Journal Publishers, 1992).

3 Documents and an interpretation of the confession are found in John H. Yoder, ed., *The Legacy of Michael Sattler* (Scottdale, PA: Herald Press, 1973).

4 On Denk and Hut, see Williams, *Radical Reformation*, 247–287, and Werner O. Packull, *Mysticism and the Early South German-Austrian Anabaptist Movement, 1525–1531* (Scottdale, PA: Herald Press, 1977).

5 On the Hutterittes, see Werner O. Packull, *Hutterite Beginnings: Communitarian Beginnings during the Reformation* (Baltimore: Johns Hopkins University Press, 1995) and James M. Stayer, *The German Peasants' War and the Community of Goods* (Kingston, ON: McGill-Queens University Press, 1994).

6 On Hoffman, see Williams, *Radical Reformation*, 539–547 and Klaus Deppermann, *Melchior Hoffman: Social Unrest and the Apocalyptic Visions in the Age of Reformation* (Edinburgh: T&T Clark, 1987).

7 On Menno Simons, see Williams, R*adical Reformation*, 589–602, 731–753 and the helpful essays in Gerald R. Brunk, ed., *Menno Simons: A Reappraisal* (Harrisonburg, VA: Eastern Mennonite College, 1992).

8 The standard English language edition of Menno's writings is J. C. Wenger, ed., *The Complete Writings of Menno Simons, 1496–1561* (Scottdale, PA: Herald Press, 1956). An excellent introduction to Menno's thought is found in Timothy George, *Theology of the Reformers* (Nashville: Broadman Press, 1988), 252–307.

9 On the Amish, see Steven M. Nolt, *History of the Amish*, 3rd ed. (Intercourse, PA: Good Books, 2016).

10 Donald F. Durnbaugh, *Fruit of the Vine: A History of the Brethren, 1708–1995* (Elgin, IL: Brethren Press, 1997).

11 Donald F. Durnbaugh, ed., *Church of the Brethren: Yesterday and Today* (Elgin, IL: Brethren Press, 1986), 3.

12 Royden Loewen and Steven Nolt, *Seeking Places of Peace: Global Mennonite History Series: North America* (Intercourse, PA: Good Books, 2012) and Richard K. MacMaster, *Land, Piety, Peoplehood: The Establishment of Mennonite Communities in America, 1683–1790* (Scottdale, PA: Herald Press, 1985).

13 James T. Lemon, *Best Poor Man's Country: A Geographical Study of Early Southeastern Pennsylvania* (Baltimore: Johns Hopkins University Press, 1972); on the continued prosperity of Mennonites in the nineteenth century, see Theron F. Schlabach, *Peace, Faith, Nation: Mennonites and Amish in Nineteenth Century America* (Scottdale, PA: Herald Press, 1988), 33–59.

14 On Brethren–Mennonite interaction, see Durnbaugh, *Fruit of the Vine*, 38–41, 103–107, 157–161.

15 Durnbaugh, *Fruit of the Vine*, 78–99.

16 MacMaster, *Land, Piety, Peoplehood*, 157–162.

17 On the GC Mennonite Church, see Schlabach, *Peace, Earth, Nation*, 127–139, 278–288.
18 For Mennonites the important but too critical study of Pietist impact is Robert Friedmann, *Mennonite Piety through the Centuries: Its Genius and Literature* (Scottdale, PA: Herald Press, 1949)
19 MacMaster, *Land, Piety, Peoplehood*, 211–222, and Stephen L. Longenecker, *Piety and Tolerance: Pennsylvania German Religion, 1710–1850* (Metuchen, NJ: Scarecrow Press, 1994), 117–119.
20 Longenecker, *Piety and Tolerance*, 120–123, and Carlton O. Wittlinger, *Quest for Piety and Obedience: The Story of the Brethren in Christ* (Nappanee, IN: Evangel Press, 1978). For Mennonite statistics, see H. K. Carroll, *The Religious Forces of the United States* (New York: Christian Literature Company, 1893), 206–220.
21 William Kostlevy, "A Persistent Sectarian Community: James Quinter and the Nineteenth-Century Reformulation of Brethren Identity," in *The Dilemma of Anabaptist Piety*, ed. Stephen L. Longenecker (Bridgewater, VA: Penobscot Press, 1997), 85–91, and William Kostlevy, "Peter Nead's *Theological Writings on Various Subjects*: An Introduction," *Old Order Notes*, no. 27 (Spring–Summer 2003), 86–90.
22 Durnbaugh, *Fruit of the Vine*, 291–315, and Carroll, *Religious Forces*, 129–137.
23 Durnbaugh, *Fruit of the Vine*, 332–335, 343–366.
24 For Brethren statistics, see *Brethren Encyclopedia* (Philadelphia: Brethren Encyclopedia, 1984), 1465–1478.
25 Albert T. Ronk, *History of the Brethren Church: Its Life, Thought, Mission* (Ashland, OH: Brethren Publishing Company, 1968), 313, 395, 437.
26 On GC and MB developments, see James C. Juhnke, *Vision, Doctrine, War: Mennonite Identity and Organization in America, 1890–1930* (Scottdale, PA: Herald Press, 1989), and Paul Toews, *Mennonites in American Society: Modernity and the Persistence of Religious Community* (Scottdale, PA: Herald Press, 1996).
27 Beulah Stauffer Hostetler, *American Mennonites and Protestant Movements: A Community Paradigm* (Scottdale: PA: Herald Press, 1987), 193–207.
28 Durnbaugh, *Fruit of the Vine*, 389–392.
29 C. Henry Smith, *The Story of the Mennonites* 4th ed. (Newton, KS: Mennonite Publishing House, 1957), and Perry Bush, *Peace, Progress and the Professor: The Mennonite History of C. Henry Smith* (Harrisonburg, VA: Herald Press, 2015).
30 Toews, *Mennonites in American Society*, 84–95.
31 Albert N. Keim, *Harold S. Bender, 1897–1962* (Scottdale, PA: Herald Press, 1998), 306–331.
32 On Durnbaugh, see David Eller, ed., *From Age to Age: A Festschrift for Donald F. Durnbaugh* (Richmond, IN: Brethren Journal Association, 1997).

33 William Kostlevy, *Bethany Theological Seminary: A Centennial History* (Richmond, IN: Brethren Journal Association, 2005), 138–153.

34 Dale W. Brown, *The Christian Revolutionary* (Grand Rapids, MI: Eerdmans, 1971), 80. For a discussion of Brown's significance for evangelicals, see Robert Booth Fowler, *A New Engagement: Evangelical Political Thought, 1966–1976* (Grand Rapids, MI: Eerdmans, 1982), 161–162 and Kostlevy, *Bethany Theological Seminary*, 152.

35 Juhnke, *Vision, Doctrine, War*, 249–257.

36 Durnbaugh, *Fruit of the Vine*, 497–510.

37 Loewen and Nolt, *Seeking Place of Peace*, 188–191.

38 On Yoder, see Toews, *Mennonites in American Society*, 334–346, and Mark Thiessen Nation, *John Howard Yoder: Mennonite Patience, Evangelical Witness, Catholic Convictions* (Grand Rapids, MI: Eerdmans, 2006), 109–144.

39 Loewen and Nolt, *Seeking Places of Peace*, 343.

40 Valerie Weaver-Zercher, *Thrill of the Chaste: The Allure of Amish Romance* (Baltimore: Johns Hopkins University Press, 2013).

NICHOLAS T. PRUITT

INTRODUCTION

Ever since their origins during the seventeenth century, Baptists have represented an array of theological, racial, ethnic, ideological, and political backgrounds. Outside of their shared conviction regarding adult baptism, they have traversed a number of social, theological, and ecclesiastical roads. Writing in the early twenty-first century on the topic of immigration reform, one American Baptist leader appealed to their diverse heritage, claiming that "God has woven us into a coat of many colors, and we are a reflection of the American family."[1] This reference drawn from the Old Testament account of Joseph is a fitting metaphor for the history of Baptists in the United States. Baptists have always represented myriad groups and perspectives. Consequently, no single racial or social group should dominate the historical narrative of Baptists in America. Rather, as historian Joshua Grijalva has recognized, Baptist congregations are "kaleidoscopic."[2]

HISTORICAL OVERVIEW

Baptists, as a sect of Protestantism, first organized during the early seventeenth century. This followed the tumult of the Reformation, and Baptists reflected the spectrum of Protestant theology, developing both Calvinist and Arminian wings. The first Baptists came out of the dissenting tradition that was alive and well by the start of the seventeenth century in England. Growing out of the same context that produced the Puritans, the early Baptists opposed the Church of England and called for forms of church practice and spiritual devotion that they believed were more consistent with Scripture. Beginning around 1608, an English Separatist congregation under the leadership of John Smyth and Thomas Helwys sought refuge in Amsterdam, where they called for adult baptism among their followers, going so far as to re-baptize all adult church members. Some of these early Baptists later returned to England with Helwys.[3]

Little time passed before Baptists began to go in divergent directions once they had set roots in England. Those who worshipped with Helwys stressed a person's free will to convert and that Jesus Christ's salvation was offered to all. They became known as General Baptists. Thirty years later, another branch of Baptists formed, referred to as Particular Baptists. These Baptists had imbibed the theology of John Calvin and stressed that Christ's salvation was only for the elect predestined by God to enter His kingdom. Particular Baptists also cultivated one of the defining practices of later Baptists, baptism by immersion, whereby the person being baptized is fully immersed under water. Regardless of whether one was a General or Particular Baptist at this time, persecution under an English monarchy not fond of religious dissenters was always a threat during most of the seventeenth century. Most notably, John Bunyan, author of *Pilgrim's Progress*, was imprisoned for his Baptist preaching.[4]

Not surprisingly, Baptist teachings found their way to England's new colonies in North America, where many English Separatists fled. The makeshift colony of Rhode Island provided an early home for displaced Baptists. As a colony formed by Roger Williams and other former Puritans expelled from the Massachusetts Bay Colony, it cultivated a society where Protestant misfits could find sanctuary. Thus, one of the first Baptist churches was formed in Rhode Island in 1638 by Williams and Ezekiel Holliman.[5] Baptists quickly worked to settle down in their new American context, forming independent congregations throughout the colonies. By the eighteenth century, they developed significant numbers in New England and Virginia. Baptists in Maine even went on to establish a church in Charleston, South Carolina, by 1700. While maintaining autonomous local churches, Baptists developed loosely connected associations with other like-minded congregations, the first association being formed in Philadelphia in 1707.[6]

Baptists in colonial America were closely linked to the Great Awakening. The Awakening sparked evangelistic enthusiasm that reshaped the contours of many Protestant groups in America as spirited converts took their faith throughout the colonies and stirred up trouble among the entrenched old guard. These revivals were also responsible for further division among Baptists, most notably between what became known as Regular and Separate Baptists. Regular Baptists adhered to more traditional, settled religious practice, while Separate Baptists embraced the enthusiastic revivalism and itinerancy of the Awakening.

Even after the fervor of the Great Awakening of the 1740s, Baptists continued to be at the forefront of revivalism throughout the latter half of the century.[7] These revivals aided in the proliferation of Baptist congregations throughout Britain's North American colonies. Connecticut Separate Baptist Shubal Stearns moved to North Carolina in 1755, where he established a constellation of Baptist churches under the Sandy Creek Association.[8] These revivals produced a dramatic increase in evangelical churches in such colonies as Virginia, where there were only seven Separate Baptist churches in 1769. Five years later, there were fifty-four congregations.[9]

Just as in England, Baptists in colonial America faced frequent persecution. While Rhode Island provided space for followers of any faith, the rest of America was not as amenable to religious liberty. John Clarke found this out the hard way when leaving Rhode Island to venture up into Massachusetts, where he was arrested and forced to pay a fine. Clarke would have the last word, however, when he penned *Ill Newes from New England, or a Narrative of New England's Persecutions*, published in 1652.[10] Puritan New England and Anglican Virginia continued to persecute and legally discriminate against those who did not follow the established faith. Baptist ministers who led congregations outside the established church of various colonies were seen as dissidents threatening social stability. Some of the first Baptists in Puritan Boston in 1665 encountered fierce resistance to their meeting, with their church being boarded up at times. Meanwhile, taxes that Baptists paid to their colonial, and later state, governments proved onerous.[11] Estimates suggest that by the beginning of the Revolutionary War, half of all Baptist ministers in Virginia had seen the inside of a jail cell.[12]

The persecution Baptists experienced during their early history in America helps explain their enduring support for the separation of church and state. Baptists, along with other evangelicals, inherited from the Great Awakening and the subsequent Revolutionary War the understanding that religious and political liberties were closely related, as well as a strong vehemence toward the established order.[13] At the outset of the Revolutionary War, Baptists even assured Virginia's legislators that if religious freedom was granted, Baptists would unite with other denominations to "promote the common cause of Freedom" against the British.[14]

Following the Revolutionary War, dissenters clamored for religious freedom and worked vociferously to force their new states to recognize the right to worship without state interference and oversight. Key Baptist leaders at this time included John Leland and Isaac Backus, who were vocal advocates for religious liberty during the revolutionary and early national periods. Baptists, like Leland, cultivated strategic relationships with James Madison and Thomas Jefferson. In fact, it was in a letter to Connecticut Baptists that Thomas Jefferson first used the phrase "a wall of separation between church and state." And in a note Madison later wrote as president in 1811 to a group of Baptists in North Carolina, he recognized, "Among the various religious Societies in our Country, none have been more vigilant or constant in maintain[in]g that distinction [between religion and civil government], than the Society of which you make a part."[15]

Nevertheless, this espousal of the separation of church and state does not suggest Baptists believed their personal faith had no bearing on civic responsibilities. In 1785, Baptists in Orange County, Virginia, concluded a petition with the affirmation, "God save the Commonwealth."[16] Another Virginia petition outlined the relationship between civil government and Christianity during the nation's early history. It claimed that Baptists "think [the] Legislature will have sufficiently done its part in favour of Christianity when adequate provision is made for supporting those Laws of Morality, which are necessary for private and public happiness."[17] Thus, while Baptists called on the state to stop sponsoring an established form of Christianity, they still believed that their faith had political relevance and that the state should support morality in society.

Meanwhile, revivalism continued and led to many enslaved African Americans coming to the Baptist faith. Several Black Baptist preachers were even licensed as ministers. These included George Liele, Lott Carey, and David George. The latter is credited with starting the first Black Baptist church in America just before the Revolutionary War, the Silver Bluff Baptist Church in South Carolina that ministered to enslaved people in the area. Another Black Baptist church was established following the war in 1788 in Savannah, Georgia. Black Baptist churches also began in the North at the outset of the nineteenth century in Boston, New York City, and Philadelphia. Meanwhile, the late eighteenth century found some white Baptists ambivalent about the institution of slavery, and in some pockets even opposing it.[18]

The opening of the nineteenth century proved to be a critical time for Baptists in America. Missionary expansion developed along both foreign and domestic fronts. Baptists formed foreign missionary societies, beginning with the Triennial Convention in 1814 and later the American Baptist Home Mission Society in 1832.[19] Meanwhile, they advanced home missions by planting new churches. Frontier missions also allowed Baptist women opportunities not necessarily granted to them further east. In 1846, a group of Freewill Baptists even granted a preaching license to Ruby Bixby. By the 1880s, Baptists in the North also ordained women on occasion.[20]

One front of home missions was efforts to Christianize the population of enslaved people of African descent in the South. While some Baptists in the North opposed the institution of slavery, those in the South increasingly defended the practice of slavery during the first several decades of the nineteenth century, often with the argument that they were introducing enslaved people to Christian faith. This was often evident in Baptist churches where white enslavers forced enslaved people to sit in segregated sections. White Baptists in the South embraced the culture around them as they defended slavery. During the antebellum period, this would lead to a cataclysmic rupture among white Baptists in the nation. After debating whether Baptist missionary societies could commission foreign missionaries who owned slaves, Baptists in the South convened in Georgia in 1845 and formed the separate Southern Baptist Convention, sixteen years before the rest of the nation turned to civil war.

Resisting the institution of slavery, enslaved people cultivated their own Baptist traditions beyond the watchful eyes of enslavers, often in services held in slave quarters on plantations or beyond in brush harbor churches. Sometimes this faith led them toward liberation. In the case of Nat Turner, his religious calling inspired him and a group of fellow enslaved people to lead a rebellion in Virginia in 1831. Further north, David Walker, famed abolitionist and author of *An Appeal to the Coloured Citizens of the World*, also collaborated with Baptists in Boston to denounce the sin of slavery and racism.[21] This moral and political crisis over slavery broke apart the nation by 1861. During the Civil War, white Baptists fought on both sides. Baptists ministers and home missionaries served as colporteurs and chaplains and encouraged revival among the troops and on the home front.[22]

Following the war, Baptists continued their missionary work while also regrouping. Most notably, Black Baptists began forming their own independent churches separate from white churches. In South Carolina, over 27,000 Black Baptists left Southern Baptist churches by 1874.[23] That same year, the New England Baptist Missionary Convention was formed among African-American Baptists, with Rev. William Jackson, who had previously served as a chaplain of the famous 54th Massachusetts regiment, presiding.[24] In 1895, the National Baptist Convention was established, becoming the largest African-American denomination in the nation, only a generation removed from slavery.[25] Baptist communities offered vital foundations for Black lives after emancipation. Several Black colleges were formed, including Morehouse College, Spelman College, and Shaw University, with assistance and oversight from white Baptist missionary societies in the South. White Baptist support in the South for Black education often took paternalistic forms, and Morehouse College would not inaugurate its first Black president until 1913 with John Hope.[26] During Reconstruction, several Black ministers attempted to enter the political sphere and advocate for Black rights. Jesse Freeman Boulden, a former Baptist minister in Chicago, relocated to Mississippi where he worked for voting rights and even served in the state legislature.[27] Another example is that of Matthew Gaines, a Baptist pastor in Texas. Gaines served in the Texas state senate and boldly challenged the racist social order.

By the late nineteenth century, Baptists also turned to the demands of exploding urban centers. The American Baptist Home Mission Society sponsored work among immigrant communities. Out of this work came many ethnic Baptist congregations. Various Eastern European, Italian, and Asian congregations formed. Several Baptists also took up the work of social Christianity. Having worked in Hell's Kitchen and witnessed first-hand the urban squalor of New York City, Baptist seminary professor Walter Rauschenbusch helped form the Social Gospel movement. Meanwhile, white Baptists in the North organized the Northern Baptist Convention in 1907, renamed the American Baptist Convention in 1950.[28]

Baptists by the twentieth century found that they were largely products, if not leaders, of American culture and society. They reflected what historians Thomas Kidd and Barry Hankins have recognized as a dual tension between being both "insiders" and "outsiders."[29] In their connections to culture, they reflected the challenges of modernity. This amounted to pitched theological battles, with institutional consequences, by the 1920s. Much like their Presbyterian and Methodist counterparts, Baptists imploded between fundamentalists and modernists, and many of the more influential modernists and fundamentalists on the national stage came from Baptist ranks (e.g., Shailer Mathews, Harry Emerson Fosdick, William Bell Riley, A. C. Dixon, and J. Frank Norris). In fact, the term "fundamentalists" was first coined in a Baptist periodical in 1920.[30]

Baptists continued to splinter during the twentieth century, while also maintaining local congregations and associations. Battle-hardened conservative Baptists promoted theological and cultural warfare on various issues, including biblical inerrancy, evolution, gender, sexuality, alcohol, and Christian nationalism. Meanwhile, ecumenical Baptists joined the mainline Protestant movement and reflected a more moderate, mid-century liberal orientation. Black Baptists, under the weight of a Jim Crow order that denied them dignity and equal social standing in America, provided leadership and grassroots mobilization during the civil rights movement. Most notably, out of the Baptist tradition came Martin Luther King, Jr., who pastored Baptist churches in Alabama and Georgia. King and others helped form the Progressive National Baptist Convention in 1961, when they separated from the National Baptist Convention, in part over differences over the relationship between the church and social protest.[31]

Baptist ruptures continued late into the twentieth century. In 1979, the Southern Baptist Convention experienced turmoil surrounding biblical inerrancy and gender roles, and conservative leaders claimed denominational leadership and oversight of Southern Baptist seminaries. Many of these figures would steer Southern Baptists toward the Religious Right during the 1980s.[32] By the twenty-first century, Southern Baptists continued to orient themselves toward more conservative social positions and the Republican Party. With their eye on the ongoing culture wars, Southern Baptists even invited Vice President Mike Pence to speak at their annual convention in 2018. Northern Baptists, however, have tried to maintain a more moderate course on matters of theology and social ethics, but remain significantly smaller in membership compared to Southern and National Baptists.

THEOLOGICAL AND LITURGICAL TRAITS

Baptist theology and practice represent a vibrant "coat of many colors." Following the divergence in theology surrounding Arminianism and Calvinism during the seventeenth century, Baptists continued to divide on a host of other theological issues and practices. During the nineteenth century, an explosion of splinter groups formed, in part due to a lack of institutional structures. Anti-mission Baptists, largely taking the name of Primitive or Old Regular Baptists, challenged the emphasis placed on missions during their time and followed a strict Calvinism that deemphasized evangelism.[33] On the other end of the spectrum, Freewill Baptists stressed people's overall agency in choosing salvation.

In keeping with their evangelical counterparts, Baptists make the Bible central to their practice. This places Baptists squarely within the Protestant tradition and its emphasis on *sola scriptura* that dates back to the sixteenth-century Reformation. This emphasis on the Bible has contributed to many disputes over the last two centuries among Baptists. The importance of the Bible is undisputed, but how to interpret the Bible and then recognize its authority can be a contentious issue. Whether one interprets the Bible literally or more critically has been at the center of multiple Baptist debates, including over slavery, gender, and sexuality. More modern readings draw from scholarly higher criticism and acknowledge that the Bible may contain errors and must be understood contextually. On the other side are Christians who hold to the idea that the Bible is inerrant, meaning it is without any errors in the original texts.[34]

The theological notion of the "priesthood of the believer" is another inheritance from the Protestant Reformation that Baptists value. This conviction stresses that the individual Christian is accountable to God alone for their faith. While ordained pastors and deacons are recognized as leaders within the church, ultimately individual Christians must pursue faith according to the dictates of their conscience, and congregations are encouraged to vote on church matters through democratic means. Social Gospel leader Walter Rauschenbusch put it most succinctly: "Our churches are Christian democracies." Such sentiments parallel American democratic ideals, especially when it comes to the value of an individual's freedom of conscience and responsibility to one's community.[35]

Understandably, the practice of baptism is also a defining characteristic. Since their origins in the seventeenth century, Baptists have held that only people who can publicly profess their Christian conversion can be candidates for baptism. Indeed one of the earliest Baptist confessions dating to 1611 recognized that "Baptisme or washing with Water, is the outward manifestacion off dieing vnto sinn, and walkeing in newness off life ... And therefore in no wise apperteyneth to infants."[36] In turn, Baptists have espoused what is often referred to as "adult baptism," in contradistinction to what some Baptists have historically referred to pejoratively as "pedobaptist" traditions. Through baptism conducted by full immersion (being fully submersed under water), believers are then admitted into church membership.

Various Baptist groups, however, differ on how to admit new church members previously baptized in other Christian denominations. More conservative Baptist groups, such as Primitive and Landmark Baptists, developed a doctrine surrounding "alien immersion," whereby Christians wanting to join the church must be re-baptized if they are coming from a non-Baptist Christian tradition. Landmark Baptists during the mid-nineteenth century claimed that Baptist churches were the only faithful congregations since the days of the Apostles, a faithfulness premised on membership of those fully immersed in the baptismal waters.[37] During the early years of Baptist history, baptisms were performed outdoors in local rivers or other sources of water. In later history, it became common for individual churches to maintain baptismal tanks indoors.[38]

Weekly worship is a common practice among Baptist congregations. Though not as liturgical as other Protestant denominations, Baptists do adhere to several elements in nearly all services. The minister or a church member usually reads the Scripture being preached on that day, and most Baptist church congregations have a Bible placed at the front of the sanctuary. At some point during the service, an offering, or collection of financial donations, is taken. A time for worship involving singing hymns and psalms is common, though not initially practiced among early English Baptists. And while structured responses from the congregation are often resisted, spontaneous responses during the service in some Baptist cultures are welcomed, including exhortation from church members and occasionally time for testimonies. The apex of the service is usually the sermon given by the pastor, often expositing a specific passage of Scripture. Finally, many Baptist churches practice what is often called the "invitation" following the sermon, where people in attendance are called to respond in some way, usually by declaring their desire to become a Christian, "rededicate" their life to Jesus Christ, or become church members.[39]

Churches also offer the Lord's Supper, or communion, usually on a weekly or monthly basis. Baptist traditions, however, have varied on who can take the Lord's Supper. Many Baptist churches practice open communion, whereby anyone who has had a conversion experience can partake in the practice. Other Baptist churches, however, have enforced a stricter observance, called closed communion, whereby only baptized members of that particular church can take the elements of the Lord's Supper.[40]

A central tenet of Baptist churches is the often-touted "autonomy of the local church." This conviction claims that individual church congregations are solely responsible for making their own decisions. This has often led Baptist churches to reluctantly join, or outright resist, larger denominational structures and parachurch organizations such as missionary societies. When put into practice, congregational autonomy is practiced on a spectrum, with some groups like Primitive Baptists shunning any outside affiliations and others actively participating in denominational decision-making. Even among Baptist churches with membership in larger denominational structures, final governance remains in the hands of members within local congregations.[41]

Despite their resistance to creedal identity and liturgy, Baptists have produced multiple confessions and denominational statements to steer theological orientations. Early Baptists in America often had to draw from confessions produced on the other side of the Atlantic, by both General and Particular Baptists. In 1742 Philadelphia Baptists produced the *Philadelphia Confession*, which was even published by Benjamin Franklin, and later Baptists wrote the New Hampshire Confession of Faith in 1833. Historically, confessions have largely been more popular among Reformed Baptists. More recently, Southern Baptists in 1925 drew up the *Baptist Faith and Message*, which largely followed the New Hampshire Confession. The *Baptist Faith and Message* was revised in 1963 and 2000 to reflect more inerrantist interpretations of Scripture.[42] A long history of Baptist publishing also speaks to forms of implicit liturgy in terms of common Sunday School materials and other church resources. Organizational power often rested in the hands of those Baptists who controlled publishing houses, which led to occasional disputes.[43]

As Baptists continued to experience oppression in America during the colonial period, they maintained a strong belief in the separation of the two spheres of religion and politics. Once the civil and religious spheres were united, they believed tyranny was the result. A Virginia Baptist petition written in 1786 made this clear: "New Testament Churches, we humbly conceive, are, as should be, established by the Legislature of Heaven, and not earthly powers; by the Law of God, and not the Law of the State; by the Acts of the Apostles, and not by the Acts of an Assembly."[44] Many Baptists today continue to espouse the separation of church and state as fundamental to being Baptist, though an increasing number of Baptists look with suspicion on the ideal as a concession to secularism. In the end, this belief in religious liberty never led to an otherworldly faith separate from the demands of culture.[45]

CULTURAL DISPOSITIONS

While Baptists espoused the separation of church and state during historical contexts where they were in the minority and faced persecution, they never separated themselves from the public square, a marked difference between historic Baptists and Anabaptists.[46] Rather, much like their distant Puritan relatives and their aspirations for a "city upon a hill," Baptists have throughout their history maintained an eager disposition to engage politics and social reform.[47] As they acclimated to culture and rose in social ranks, they became producers of culture, rather than bystanders and outcasts. Over the course of the last 400 years, Baptists have served in the Oval Office, led social movements, and provided constant political commentary.

Baptists as a whole represent a wide range of cultural and sociopolitical dispositions. Countless writers grew up within and continued to participate in the Baptist tradition (a notable example being Maya Angelou). Out of the Baptist tradition also came the famed contralto Marian Anderson and gospel singer Mahalia Jackson. Many hymns that have become Protestant staples have Baptist authors, such as "Shall We Gather at the River," "Nothing But the Blood of Jesus" (Robert Lowry), "I Need Thee Every Hour" (Annie Sherwood Hawks), "God of Grace and God of Glory" (Harry Emerson Fosdick), and the patriotic refrain "My Country, 'Tis of Thee" (Samuel F. Smith).[48] Multiple educational institutions also had Baptist origins, including Brown University, the University of Chicago, and a host of southern institutions formed during the nineteenth century such as Baylor University. Prominent social leaders have also come from Baptist churches. Adam Clayton Powell, Jr., of the Abyssinian Baptist Church in Harlem mobilized African Americans in New York City toward justice during the 1940s and later served as a member of Congress.[49] Black ministers such as Martin Luther King, Jr., Ralph Abernathy, and Jesse Jackson were at the forefront of the civil rights movement of the 1950s and 1960s. Other Baptists, such as Jerry Falwell, led efforts to build the Christian Right during the later years of the twentieth century. Other white Baptists, such as Billy Graham, advocated for a moral society and courted political influence, while remaining reluctant to support social reform efforts such as the civil rights movement. Finally, four US presidents have identified as Baptist, one Republican (Warren Harding), and three Democrats (Harry Truman, Jimmy Carter, and Bill Clinton).

The ethnic diversity of Baptists also speaks to a complex array of Baptist orientations to culture. Baptists with an immigrant heritage worked to retain cultural identities and formed various conferences and denominations. In Texas, the Latinx population maintained their own state convention for fifty years after forming the *Convencion Bautista Mexicana* in 1910. Hungarian, Swedish, and German Baptists established separate congregations as these groups migrated over during the nineteenth and early twentieth centuries. Asian

Baptists also have a history that began during the late nineteenth century, with one of the earliest Chinese Baptist churches being formed in 1860 in Sacramento under the auspices of a white missionary. Soon similar mission projects began in San Francisco, Oakland, and Portland on the West Coast.[50] Parallel to these ethnic Baptist traditions were efforts by majority white denominations to support Americanization and cultivate American culture among immigrant groups. Northern Baptist women, for example, formed a group in 1919 promoting Christian Americanization, later renamed Christian Friendliness.

When it comes to gender, Baptists in America have largely cultivated patriarchal structures. Nevertheless, various examples survive of women having more active roles within Baptist congregations. During the colonial era, women participated in Baptist services, and Separate Baptists in southern colonies granted women the opportunity to exhort congregations.[51] In light of congregational autonomy, even a Baptist church within the Southern Baptist Convention could still independently ordain a woman to preach, which is what Watts Street Baptist Church did in 1964 when they ordained Addie Davis. Davis, however, was not able to secure a Southern Baptist pastorate following her ordination and eventually turned to the American Baptist Convention.[52] Baptist women often formed auxiliaries where they held some autonomy. Nannie Helen Burroughs organized the Woman's Convention of the National Baptist Convention in 1900, drawing assistance from white Southern Baptist women who had earlier formed their own Woman's Missionary Union.[53] Tragically, the autonomous nature of Baptist churches has also allowed for sexual abuse to go unchecked, brought to light during the recent #MeToo movement.[54]

Baptists also have a tumultuous history of racism. Originally white Baptists were resistant, or at least reluctant, to espouse slavery during their early years in America, but by the early nineteenth century as they were wedded to American culture, particularly in the South, they openly embraced slavery and forms of white supremacy. At the same time, as enslaved African people encountered Baptist churches, they embraced a religious faith that gave them a sense of purpose and liberation. Baptist ministers were important leaders during Reconstruction and the mid-twentieth-century civil rights movement. Several Black ministers contributed a prophetic critique of American society and advocated for civil disobedience. In addition to King, Howard Thurman articulated a theology that bolstered nonviolent action during the civil rights movement, and Prathia Hall demonstrated that Baptist women could also get behind the pulpit.[55] A few examples exist of white Baptist progressives, such as the Koinonia Farm community in Georgia.[56] The voluntary integration of Wayland Baptist University in Texas in 1951 is another example, a story featured in *Ebony*.[57] But many white Baptists were also ambivalent or hostile toward integration. As historians Caroline DuPont and Charles Marsh have demonstrated, many Southern Baptists defended segregation and criticized the civil disobedience of the civil rights movement, arguing instead for what they interpreted as law and order.[58]

CONCLUSION

The history of Baptists in America is a scattered narrative consisting of various theological and social positions. No one social, racial, or political group can claim to represent all Baptists. Despite English origins, Baptists quickly became a multiracial and multiethnic branch of Protestantism. Despite years of legal discrimination and segregation, these disparate Baptist communities still shaped each other. Black scholar W. E. B. Du Bois noted, "The Methodists and Baptists of America owe much of their condition to the silent but potent influence of their millions of Negro converts."[59] Out of this diversity and oftentimes chaos and struggle has come a religious tradition that has contributed much to American culture and more fully reflects the American motto of *E pluribus unum* ("out of many, one").

NOTES

1 "ABHMS Supports Comprehensive Immigration Reform," American Baptist Churches USA, January 30, 2013, www.abc-usa.org/2013/01/abhms-supports-comprehensive-immigration-reform/.

2 Joshua Grijalva, *Ethnic Baptist History* (Miami: META, 1992), 146–147.

3 Kenneth Ross Manley, "Origins of the Baptists: The Case for Development from Puritanism-Separatism," *Baptist History and Heritage* vol. 22 (October 1987), 34–46; Bill J. Leonard, *Baptists in America* (New York: Columbia University Press, 2005), 7–9; William R. Estep, Jr., "On the Origins of English Baptists," *Baptist History and Heritage* vol. 22 (April 1987), 19–26.

4 Leonard, *Baptists in America*, 9–11.

5 Leonard, *Baptists in America*, 13–14; Leroy Fitts, *A History of Black Baptists* (Nashville: Broadman Press, 1985), 22–23.

6 Leonard, *Baptists in America*, 11–12, 14–15, 19.

7 John B. Boles, *The Great Revival: Beginnings of the Bible Belt* (Lexington: University Press of Kentucky, 1996), 7; Jewel L. Spangler, *Virginians Reborn: Anglican Monopoly, Evangelical Dissent, and the Rise of the Baptists in the Late Eighteenth Century* (Charlottesville: University of Virginia Press, 2008), 90–91; Thomas E. Buckley, SJ, *Church and State in Revolutionary Virginia, 1776–1787* (Charlottesville: University Press of Virginia, 1977), 161.

8 Thomas S. Kidd and Barry Hankins, *Baptists in America: A History* (New York: Oxford University Press, 2019), 35–38.

9 Rhys Isaac, *The Transformation of Virginia, 1740–1790* (Chapel Hill: University of North Carolina Press, 1999), 173.

10 W. R. Estep, "Clarke, John (1609–1676)," in *Dictionary of Baptists in America*, ed. Bill J. Leonard (Downers Grove, IL: InterVarsity Press, 1994), 84–85.

11 Leonard, *Baptists in America*, 14.

12 John A. Ragosta, *Wellspring of Liberty: How Virginia's Religious Dissenters Helped Win the American Revolution and Secured Religious Liberty* (New York: Oxford University Press, 2010), 5.

13 Thomas S. Kidd, *God of Liberty: A Religious History of the American Revolution* (New York: Basic Books, 2010), 11–35.

14 "Petition of Baptists of Prince William County," May 19, 1776, Legislative Petitions Digital Collection, Library of Virginia, http://digitool1.lva.lib.va.us:8881/R/2BQHMFPV2VKQRJ95RB3QBY1BL4762USKET5CVTSGPE5FI96G K8-06482?func=results-jump-full&set_entry=000001&set_numbe r=759752&base=GEN01-ARC01.

15 James Madison to Jesse Jones and Others, *The Papers of James Madison Digital Edition*, June 3, 1811, http://rotunda.upress.virginia.edu.ezproxy .baylor.edu/founders/JSMN-03-03-02-0377.

16 "Baptist Association: Remonstrance," November 17, 1785, Legislative Petitions Digital Collection, Library of Virginia, http://digitool1.lva.lib.va.us:8881/R/HAVKFHR4KNG2PCADYS6A92R8J74AX8LSD2RM7PXP353ETI5 H6L-00509?func=results-jump-full&set_entry=000001&set_numbe r=759756&base=GEN01-ARC01.

17 "Baptist Association: Petition," November 3, 1785, Legislative Petitions Digital Collection, Library of Virginia, http://digitool1.lva.lib.va.us:8881/R/ PKAXCPEK1T8Q4K5CNELCBBYL6IIDMFQ339C12BTXXI4YJCKQD8-009 00?func=results-jump-full&set_entry=000002&set_number=759757&base= GEN01-ARC01.

18 Albert J. Raboteau, *Canaan Land: A Religious History of African Americans* (New York: Oxford University Press, 2001), 16–20; Leonard, *Baptists in America*, 27; Fitts, *A History of Black Baptists*, 33–39.

19 W. M. Patterson, "Triennial Convention," in *Dictionary of Baptists in America*, ed. Leonard, 269.

20 Pamela R. Durso, "She-Preachers, Bossy Women, and Children of the Devil: Women Ministers in the Baptist Tradition, 1609–2012," *Review and Expositor* vol. 110 (Winter 2013), 36–38.

21 S. D. Martin, "David Walker (1785–1830)," in *Dictionary of Baptists in America*, ed. Leonard, 281–282.

22 For Baptists and the Civil War, see Bruce T. Gourley, *Diverging Loyalties: Baptists in Middle Georgia during the Civil War* (Macon, GA: Mercer University Press, 2011); Kidd and Hankins, *Baptists in America: A History*, 133–139; George C. Rable, *God's Almost Chosen Peoples: A Religious History of the American Civil War* (Chapel Hill: University of North Carolina Press, 2012); and Randall M. Miller, Harry S. Stout, and Charles Reagan Wilson, eds., *Religion and the American Civil War* (New York: Oxford University Press, 1998).

23 Raboteau, *Canaan Land*, 68.

24 Fitts, *A History of Black Baptists*, 72–73.

25 M. C. Bruce, "National Baptists," in *Dictionary of Baptists in America*, ed. Leonard, 199; Fitts, *A History of Black Baptists*, 79–84.

26 L. H. Williams, "Morehouse College," in *Dictionary of Baptists in America*, ed. Leonard, 194.

27 Raboteau, *Canaan Land*, 69.

28 Beverly Carlson, "Chronology of the American Baptist Churches, USA," *American Baptist Quarterly* vol. 14, no. 2 (June 1995), 106–185.

29 Kidd and Hankins, *Baptists in America*, ix–x, 247, 252.

30 Leonard, *Baptists in America*, 50–62, 86, 132–135.

31 M. C. Bruce, "National Baptists," in *Dictionary of Baptists in America*, ed. Leonard, 198–199; Fitts, *A History of Black Baptists*, 98–105.

32 Leonard, *Baptists in America*, 136–140; Barry Hankins, *Uneasy in Babylon: Southern Baptist Conservatives and American Culture* (Tuscaloosa: University of Alabama Press, 2002).

33 Leonard, *Baptists in America*, 21–23, 97–98, 103–108; J. T. Spivey, "Primitive Baptists," in *Dictionary of Baptists in America*, ed. Leonard, 226.

34 Leonard, *Baptists in America*, 65, 70–72, 132–142.

35 Leonard, *Baptists in America*, 65, 80–81; Walter B. Shurden, *The Baptist Identity: Four Fragile Freedoms* (Macon, GA: Smyth and Helwys, 2013), 23–32. Quote from Leonard, *Baptists in America*, 156. See also Lee Canipe, *A Baptist Democracy: Separating God and Caesar in the Land of the Free* (Macon, GA:Mercer University Press, 2011).

36 Quoted in H. Leon McBeth, *The Baptist Heritage* (Nashville: Broadman Press, 1987), 80.

37 Leonard, *Baptists in America*, 25–26, 144–147.

38 Leonard, *Baptists in America*, 75–77, 144–147.

39 McBeth, *The Baptist Heritage*, 91–95; Leonard, *Baptists in America*, 42–46.

40 McBeth, *The Baptist Heritage*, 81–83.

41 Leonard, *Baptists in America*, 21–22; Spivey, "Primitive Baptists," 226.

42 S. J. Grenz, "New Hampshire Confession of Faith," in *Dictionary of Baptists in America*, ed. Leonard, 202–203; McBeth, *The Baptist Heritage*, 66–69, 241–242; Leonard, *Baptists in America*, 83–88.

43 Fitts, *A History of Black Baptists*, 82–83, 90–93.

44 "Representatives of Several Baptist Associations: Petition," November 1, 1786, Legislative Petitions Digital Collection, Library of Virginia, http://digitool1.lva.lib.va.us:8881/R/4PFEI72L9JM3FMNVVNN8Y5NM2CEBDMVT4XX649L6KDXYEEF1DC-07062?func=results-jump-full&set_entry=000413&set_number=759766&base=GEN01-ARC01.

45 For more on this, see Lee Canipe, *A Baptist Democracy: Separating God and Caesar in the Land of the Free* (Macon, GA: Mercer University Press, 2011).

46 Estep, "On the Origins of English Baptists," 23.

47 John Winthrop, "A Modell of Christian Charity," in *God's New Israel: Religious Interpretations of American Destiny*, rev. and updated ed., ed. Conrad Cherry (Chapel Hill: University of North Carolina Press, 1998), 40.

48 H. T. McElrath, "Hymnody, Baptist," *Dictionary of Baptists in America*, ed. Leonard, 148–149.

49 Paul Harvey, *Through the Storm, Through the Night: A History of African American Christianity* (Lanham, MD: Rowman and Littlefield, 2011), 107.

50 McBeth, *The Baptist Heritage*, 724–749; Derek Chang, *Citizens of a Christian Nation* (Philadelphia: University of Pennsylvania Press, 2010).

51 Catherine A. Brekus, *Strangers and Pilgrims: Female Preaching in America, 1740–1845* (Chapel Hill: University of North Carolina Press, 1998), 8, 50–51, 59–61, 64–66.

52 Durso, "She-Preachers, Bossy Women, and Children of the Devil," 38–39.

53 Nicholas T. Pruitt and T. Laine Scales, "'We want to help you to help us': Southern Baptist and National Baptist Women and Race Relations during the 1930s and 1940s," *American Baptist Quarterly* vol. 38 (Fall 2019), 304–329; Evelyn Brooks Higginbotham, *Righteous Discontent: The Women's Movement in the Black Baptist Church, 1880–1920* (Cambridge, MA: Harvard University Press, 1993).

54 "Spirit of Fear," *Fort Worth Star-Telegram*, December 9, 2018, www.star-telegram.com/topics/fundamental-baptist-abuse.

55 L. H. Williams, "Howard Thurman (1900–1981)," in *Dictionary of Baptists in America*, ed. Leonard, 267–268; Paul Harvey, *Howard Thurman and the Disinherited: A Religious Biography* (Grand Rapids, MI: Wm. B. Eerdmans, 2020); Courtney Pace, *Freedom Faith: The Womanist Vision of Prathia Hall* (Athens: University of Georgia Press, 2019).

56 Ansley L. Quiros, *God with Us: Lived Theology and the Freedom Struggle in Americus, Georgia, 1942–1976* (Chapel Hill: University of North Carolina Press, 2019); David Stricklin, *A Genealogy of Dissent: The Culture of Progressive Protest in Southern Baptist Life, 1920–1995* (Lexington: University Press of Kentucky, 1999).

418 *Theological Traditions*

57 "Texas College Admits Negroes: Small Baptist Institution of Wayland Is First in Dixie to Lift Its Color Ban Voluntarily," *Ebony* vol. 7 (November 1951), 35–39.

58 Charles Marsh, *God's Long Summer: Stories of Faith and Civil Rights* (Princeton, NJ: Princeton University Press, 2008), 82–115.

59 W. E. B. Du Bois, *The Souls of Black Folk*, in Harvey, *Through the Storm, Through the Night*, 167.

22 The Stone-Campbell Movement

MARK E. POWELL

The Stone-Campbell Movement is an expression of modern Protestantism that combined the evangelical revivals of the American frontier, the Enlightenment philosophy of John Locke, Thomas Reid, and Francis Bacon, and the democratic ideals of the United States.[1] The "restoration plea" of early Stone-Campbell leaders emphasized four interrelated themes: restoration, unity, missions, and eschatology. Early leaders believed that the *restoration* of the teachings, practices, and terminology of the New Testament church would lead to visible *unity* in an increasingly divided Christianity, which in turn would aid global *missions* and usher in the *millennium*.[2] In addition, they believed restoring the New Testament church would promote both greater faithfulness to God and individual freedom of conscience, as Christians would be united around the teachings, practices, and terminology of Scripture alone, not those promoted by later teachers or found in creeds of human origin.

The movement's name is derived from its early leaders Barton W. Stone (1772–1844), Thomas Campbell (1763–1854), and Thomas's son Alexander Campbell (1788–1866).[3] The term "movement" is important as well, as it denotes the early leaders' desire to unify Christians rather than begin a new denomination. Today the movement includes three major branches: the Christian Church (Disciples of Christ), the Christian Churches/Churches of Christ, and the Churches of Christ. The first of these, the Christian Church (Disciples of Christ), is formally organized as a mainline Protestant denomination. The other two branches, however, continue to resist formal structures that interfere with congregational autonomy and the stated desire to be "Christians only," although informal structures bind each of these branches together.[4]

EARLY LEADERS

The beginning of the Stone-Campbell Movement is traced back to a worship gathering in Lexington, Kentucky on New Year's Day, 1832.

There, Reformer John Smith shook hands with Barton W. Stone, thus signaling the union of the Reformers or Disciples, led by Thomas and Alexander Campbell, and the Christians, led by Stone. The Campbells and Stone all had Presbyterian backgrounds, although the Campbells also identified as Baptists from 1815 to 1830. Many of their early followers also came from Presbyterian and Baptist backgrounds. Not everyone from the two groups joined the union, but some 12,000 Reformers and 10,000 Christians united and, by the beginning of the American Civil War, grew to an estimated 200,000 adherents.[5]

Barton W. Stone and the Christians

Barton W. Stone came from an affluent Anglican family, but his interest in religion was sparked while training to be a lawyer in an environment imbued with colonial revivalism.[6] Stone had reservations about the Westminster Confession of Faith, especially its Trinitarianism and Calvinist doctrine of election, but in 1789 he navigated the ordination process and became a Presbyterian minister. In 1801 Stone and his Presbyterian church at Cane Ridge, Kentucky hosted an ecumenical communion festival, later known as the Cane Ridge Revival, which drew some 10,000 to 20,000 attendees. This landmark event of the Second Great Awakening was characterized by intense physical and emotional responses such as falling, trance-like states, shouting, and mourning. Stone, however, was most moved by the number of conversions that occurred quickly, in contrast to months or years for faith-seekers as was common among Presbyterians. For Stone, the conversions at Cane Ridge supported his rejection of Calvinism and led him to believe that God gives faith through the preaching of the gospel rather than through a special enabling work of the Spirit.

Local Presbyterian leaders opposed Stone because of his rejection of the Calvinist doctrine of election and his embrace of an ecumenical posture that downplayed Presbyterian distinctives. In response, Stone and four fellow ministers left the Synod of Kentucky in 1803 and formed the short-lived Springfield Presbytery. Within a year, Stone and his colleagues drafted the *Last Will and Testament of the Springfield Presbytery*, which declared "We *will*, that this body die, be dissolved, and sink into union with the Body of Christ at large." Stone and his colleagues sought to be Christians only and "to preach the simple Gospel, *with the Holy Ghost sent down from heaven*, without any mixture of philosophy, vain deceit, traditions of men, or the rudiments of the world."[7]

Still, this group of non-denominational Christians had a number of issues to address regarding doctrine and practice. In 1807 Stone and other Christians adopted believer's baptism as the biblical practice and were immersed. This decision worried those who affirmed infant baptism, but Stone and the Christians agreed to acknowledge both practices and did not require immersion for membership or for receiving the Lord's Supper. In the next decade, Stone sought to clarify his views on the Trinity. He rejected the doctrine in favor of a strict monotheism because he felt that the Trinity was contrary to both Scripture and human reason. Stone maintained that the Son is subordinate to the Father and is neither eternal nor fully divine. When the Son became a human being, all the fullness of God dwelled within the man Jesus, but Jesus was not God incarnate. Stone also denied the personhood of the Spirit.[8] Stone's rejection of Trinitarian doctrine is, at least in part, related to his embrace of a moral-influence theory of the atonement.[9]

Although Stone came from a slaveholding family, he began opposing slavery in 1797 soon after he moved to Cane Ridge. In the 1820s he became a supporter of the American Colonization Society, which sought to secure a colony in Africa for emancipated slaves. Stone began publishing *The Christian Messenger* in 1826 to promote both his vision of Christian unity and the colonization movement. After the colonization movement failed, Stone, a historic premillennialist, believed slavery would persist until the return of Christ and the millennial age, which he thought was near. Stone held a pessimistic view of human governments; he rejected participation in them, including the military and police, and promoted pacifism. Stone was a restorationist, but his vision of restoration was more ethical and spiritual in orientation with a separation from the world and an emphasis on kingdom living.[10] Over a lifetime of ministry, Stone left behind the affluence of his youth and embraced a lifestyle of simplicity and humility.

Thomas Campbell, Alexander Campbell, and the Reformers

Thomas Campbell settled in western Pennsylvania in 1807 after bitter experiences of religious division, including violence between Catholics and Protestants, during his early years of ministry as an Antiburgher Seceder Presbyterian in Northern Ireland and Scotland. Campbell had completed a course of study at the University of Glasgow, where he was introduced to the thought of John Locke and the Scottish Common-Sense philosophy of Thomas Reid. He was also influenced by the evangelical missions culture in Britain, which stressed Christian unity around an evangelical gospel for the sake of global missions and the inbreaking of the millennium.[11]

Frustrated by ongoing experiences of doctrinal disputes and division on the American frontier, Thomas Campbell left his local presbytery in 1809 and founded an evangelical society in Washington, Pennsylvania. His *Declaration and Address of the Christian Association of Washington* had modest immediate impact, but it would later be regarded as the founding document of the Reformers or Disciples. In *Declaration and Address*, Thomas Campbell called for the proclamation of "simple, evangelical Christianity, free from all mixture of human opinions and inventions of men."[12] He believed that the New Testament provided a pattern and perfect constitution for the church. A restored church in which any belief or practice which was as old as the New Testament would promote Christian unity and missions. In the appendix of *Declaration and Address*, Campbell, who essentially affirmed a Trinitarian view of God, addressed the issue of Arianism and Socinianism. He believed that if one proclaimed the gospel using biblical terms, one could avoid the errors of Arians and Socinians as well as the complex metaphysical language of creeds and Trinitarian theologians.[13]

Thomas's son, Alexander, arrived in western Pennsylvania with the rest of the Campbell family in 1809.[14] A shipwreck on the way to America had led to an unexpected ten-month stay in Scotland. During this time Alexander Campbell studied Scottish Common-Sense philosophy at the University of Glasgow and was influenced by evangelical leaders seeking to reform the Church of Scotland. After reading his father's *Declaration and Address*, Alexander Campbell committed himself to his father's reform efforts and continued his studies under his father's tutelage. Alexander Campbell was ordained by his father, and both Campbells preached at the Brush Run church associated with the Christian Association of Washington.

When Alexander Campbell's first child, Jane, was born in 1812, he struggled with the decision of whether to baptize her as an infant. He concluded that believer's baptism by immersion was the biblical practice and asked a Baptist minister, Matthias Luce, to baptize him and his father, mother, wife, and some other followers, on the basis of a simple confession of faith in Jesus as the Son of God. Soon afterward, the Brush Run church affiliated with the Redstone Baptist Association from 1815 to 1830. Alexander Campbell began publishing a journal, *The Christian Baptist*, in 1823.

Alexander Campbell devoted himself to restoring the "ancient order of things" and the "ancient gospel."[15] He agreed with his father that the

New Testament, especially Acts and the epistles, provided the church with a perfect pattern and constitution. In his "Sermon on the Law," delivered in 1816, Campbell divided the Bible into three dispensations: the patriarchal (Gen. 1–Ex. 19), the Mosaic (Ex. 20–Acts 1), and the Christian (Acts 2–Rev).[16] For Campbell, only texts from the Christian dispensation could authorize ecclesial practices. Further, Campbell employed a Baconian scientific method in his reading of Scripture, gathering facts from Scripture to reach certain and precise conclusions, much like a natural scientist does with facts from nature. His efforts to restore the "ancient order" led Campbell to advocate weekly observance of the Lord's Supper and to order local congregations under elders, deacons, and evangelists.

Alexander Campbell participated in five public debates, which increased his popularity and the influence of the Reformers. In his 1823 debate with the Presbyterian William Maccalla, Campbell presented his position on believer's baptism for the forgiveness of sins. The standard Baptist position held that baptism should be administered only to those who had already received an inward assurance of salvation, but Campbell argued that obedience to Christ's command in baptism is what provides an objective assurance of salvation. Campbell's rejection of the Calvinist doctrine of election, therefore, is similar to Stone's, although Campbell added that one's baptism, not simply an inward trust after hearing the gospel, provides assurance. Further, in his 1843 debate with the Presbyterian Nathan L. Rice, Campbell denied the proposition that only a bishop or ordained presbyter could administer baptism. Campbell agreed that it was appropriate for churches to ask recognized leaders to baptize, but nothing in the New Testament limits the authority of baptizing to clergy.

Walter Scott (1796–1861), a colleague of the Campbells for over forty years and a traveling evangelist, popularized Alexander Campbell's views on the ancient gospel and greatly increased the number of Reformers. His "five-finger exercise," rooted in Acts 2:38, was particularly important for spreading Campbell's understanding of baptism. After preaching, Scott summarized the human response to the gospel with five fingers: hearers are called to (1) believe the gospel, (2) repent of sin, and (3) be baptized; and in response God gives (4) forgiveness of sins and (5) the gift of the Holy Spirit and eternal life.[17] Like Stone, Scott believed one did not have to wait for a special experience before responding to the gospel. And Scott's preaching, like Stone's, brought hope to those from Calvinist backgrounds who were told to wait and pray. After Scott's death, his five points evolved into (1) *hear* the gospel, (2) *believe* the gospel, (3) *repent* of sin, (4) *confess* that Jesus is the Son of God, and (5) *be baptized*. Unfortunately, this revised version only emphasizes the human response to the gospel and not the divine promise. These five "steps of salvation" are still regularly heard at the conclusion of evangelistic sermons in some Christian Churches/Churches of Christ and Churches of Christ.

When Alexander Campbell's baptismal theology and practice were rejected by the Beaver Baptist Association in 1830, the Reformers and Baptists parted company. He began a new journal that named his postmillennial hope, *The Millennial Harbinger*. Two years later in 1832, the Campbells' Reformers and Stone's Christians began the process of uniting the two groups. Stone was far more interested in union than was Alexander Campbell, who doubted Stone's orthodoxy on the Trinity and atonement. To address Campbell's concerns, Stone agreed to limit theological speculation and use only the words of Scripture, especially when preaching. Similarly, some Christians worried that Alexander Campbell's view on believer's baptism unnecessarily excluded those who had not been immersed. Nonetheless, those who united agreed that the great confession "Jesus is the Messiah, the Son of the living God" (from Matt. 16:16), followed by baptism, was sufficient for Christian unity.

As the movement grew, the issue of cooperation between the Stone-Campbell congregations became a pressing issue. The American Christian Missionary Society (ACMS) was formed in 1849 to unite Stone-Campbell congregations for the sake of missions. Alexander Campbell was the first president of the society and served in that role until his death in 1866. Earlier in *The Christian Baptist*, Alexander Campbell had opposed missionary societies because they interfered with congregational autonomy and tended to impose doctrinal standards. Now Campbell was presiding over the ACMS, and some of his followers resisted the establishment of this new missionary society. The conflict over cooperation and missionary societies has continued among the heirs of the Stone-Campbell Movement to the present day.

Alexander Campbell opposed slavery and supported the American Colonization Society, but his gradualism distinguished him from abolitionists. Further, in 1850 he opposed civil disobedience to the Fugitive Slave Law, which required citizens to cooperate with the return of runaway enslaved people. Campbell was concerned that the division around slavery among Baptists and Methodists would likewise frustrate his efforts toward Christian unity. Campbell was a pacifist, and as a postmillennialist he thought the coming millennium would gradually include the cessation of war. Alexander Campbell and Stone would not support either side in the American Civil War, but many of those in Stone-Campbell congregations supported the governments of their respective regions. In 1861 and 1863, the ACMS unequivocally sided with the Union in the American Civil War. Southern churches viewed these actions as another example of a parachurch organization overstepping its bounds and interfering with congregational autonomy.

The union of the Reformers and Christians led to a gradual mixture of their different beliefs and practices. For example, both Stone's practice of open communion (but not necessarily open membership) and Alexander Campbell's baptismal theology became widespread within the united movement. In a few instances, as is the case with Stone's historic premillennialism and Alexander Campbell's postmillennialism, Stone-Campbell heirs, who are predominantly amillennial today, followed neither. (The Churches of Christ in particular had a sustained, vigorous debate about millennial theories in the first half of the twentieth century. By and large, the amillennial position was adopted and dispensational premillennialism was rejected.)[18] Alexander Campbell became the dominant shaper of the movement, but Stone's beliefs and practices are crucial for understanding later developments. Ongoing tensions continued to play out among their heirs, who formally divided in the early twentieth century.

MAJOR BRANCHES

Today the Stone-Campbell Movement includes three major branches: the Christian Church (Disciples of Christ), the Christian Churches/ Churches of Christ, and the Churches of Christ. The first division formally occurred in 1906, when David Lipscomb (1831–1917), a prominent leader in Churches of Christ from Nashville, Tennessee, agreed with the US Religious Census director that the more progressive Disciples of Christ and the more conservative Churches of Christ should be listed separately. Significant tensions, however, had already existed between these groups for several decades. The decision of the ACMS to support the Union during the American Civil War led to conflict between Northern Disciples, who were more wealthy and urbane, and rural Southern Disciples, who faced life-threatening poverty after the war. When explaining his decision, Lipscomb highlighted two disagreements between the two groups: missionary societies and instrumental music in worship.

Missionary societies had been controversial in the emerging Stone-Campbell Movement since Thomas Campbell's early ministry. For

Lipscomb, the ACMS had quickly become a tool of Northern Disciples to control and exert influence on Southern churches. He also felt that missionary societies were not effective in doing mission work. Lipscomb's opposition to instrumental music in worship went back to Alexander Campbell's desire to restore the ancient order. Since instrumental music is not explicitly authorized by the New Testament and was not found in early Christian worship, Lipscomb saw it as a human innovation and a pretentious display of wealth that marginalized poor Southern Disciples. Further, he maintained that instrumental music in the assembly negatively affected congregational singing.

Lipscomb was well aware, though, that these two visible issues were symptoms of larger, underlying differences. Northern Disciples were more influenced by biblical criticism and liberal theology than were Southern Disciples, and women were active in preaching among Sorthern Disciples but not among Southern Disciples. By the late nineteenth century, many Northern Disciples had abandoned Alexander Campbell's call to restore the ancient order in favor of Stone's desire for ecumenical unity around a simple faith in Jesus. Their genteel outlook and commitment to cultural engagement, however, was more reminiscent of Alexander Campbell than Stone. Southern disciples, on the other hand, had combined a religious sectarianism, influenced by Alexander Campbell's desire to restore the ancient order and to faithfully obey the positive commands of the New Testament, with a social sectarianism, influenced by Stone's countercultural, kingdom-oriented posture. Clearly the two groups had integrated their shared inheritance in different ways and had grown distant. The Disciples of Christ branch attracted many of the Northern Disciples while the Churches of Christ primarily attracted Southern Disciples and were especially strong in Tennessee, Alabama, Arkansas, and Texas.[19] The 1906 census listed the Disciples of Christ with 923,698 adherents and the Churches of Christ with 159,123 adherents.

The progressive side of the movement experienced another major division when the more conservative Christian Churches/Churches of Christ formally separated from the Christian Church (Disciples of Christ) in the late 1960s and early 1970s – although again, this division was long in the making due to lack of formal denominational structures. The influence of biblical criticism and liberal theology in Christian Churches continued to concern conservative Disciples. (The plural *Christian Churches* was used until 1968, when the singular *Christian Church (Disciples of Christ)* was formally adopted.) Further, in 1908 Christian Churches became charter members of the ecumenical

Federal Council of Churches and later in the twentieth century they joined the National Council of Churches and the World Council of Churches. For conservative Disciples, participation in ecumenical movements was a betrayal of the Stone-Campbell vision of unity, since participation signaled both the legitimacy of denominations and the denominational status of the Disciples. Further, some Christian Churches began to accept as members those baptized as infants, not just the immersed. Although the practice of open membership can be traced back to Stone, open membership was controversial when it appeared again in the 1920s because of the influence of Alexander Campbell's baptismal theology.

In 1917 the Christian Churches met in Kansas City for the first International Convention of the Disciples of Christ to encourage more organization and cooperation among Disciples. Any legislation of the convention, however, was advisory only. Two years later, the ACMS and several other Disciples missionary societies were consolidated under the new United Christian Missionary Society. These efforts toward centralization concerned conservative, "independent" Disciples, and in 1927 these independents began an alternative convention, the North American Christian Convention (NACC). The NACC (now Spire Network Conference) differed from the International Convention in that it was never a legislative meeting, but instead was a religious gathering with presentations, workshops, exhibits, and activities for families. Further, the Christian Missionary Fellowship (now Christian Missionary Fellowship International) began to support mission efforts among conservative Disciples.

The process of division was completed in 1968 when the "Restructure" of the Christian Churches culminated in a more centralized structure and a new name, Christian Church (Disciples of Christ). For conservative Disciples, Restructure was an abandonment of the Stone-Campbell vision of unity as the Christian Church (Disciples of Christ) had indeed become another mainline Protestant denomination. In 1971, the Christian Churches/Churches of Christ were listed separately in the Yearbook of American Churches for the first time. At the time of the division in 1968, the Christian Church (Disciples of Christ) reported 1,592,609 adherents and the Christian Churches/Churches of Christ reported 996,949 adherents.[20]

Given the autonomous nature of the two conservative branches, membership figures in the Stone-Campbell Movement are notoriously difficult to trace. According to the 2010 US Religion Census, the Christian Church (Disciples of Christ) had 785,776 adherents, the

Christian Churches/Churches of Christ had 1,453,160 adherents, and the Churches of Christ had 1,584,162 adherents. The Christian Churches (Disciples of Christ) reached its highest numbers in the 1950s with approximately 1.9 million adherents, but today is the fastest-declining mainline denomination in the United States with 382,248 adherents in 2018. The Churches of Christ experienced significant growth in the twentieth century, reaching approximately 1.68 million members in the early 1990s. (Religious statistics databases regularly list 2.5 million members for Churches of Christ during the 1970s, but these numbers are exaggerated.) Churches of Christ, however, have experienced a membership decline in the twenty-first century. From 2006 to 2016, Churches of Christ decreased from 1,622,563 to 1,509,877 adherents. Reliable statistics for the Christian Churches/Churches of Christ are hard to find after 2010. Global statistics for the Stone-Campbell Movement are even harder to find, but a conservative estimate is 8 million adherents for all three branches of the movement.

Today the Christian Church (Disciples of Christ) is a mainline Protestant denomination that has been on the forefront of the ecumenical movement and contemporary social justice issues. For instance, the 1979 General Assembly passed a resolution supporting the full rights of gay and lesbians and formed the Gay, Lesbian, and Affirming Disciples (GLAD) Alliance. In 2013 the General Assembly passed a resolution encouraging LGBTQ people to participate in all aspects of church life and leadership. Resolutions of the General Assembly, however, are advisory only. Universities associated with the Christian Church (Disciples of Christ) include Texas Christian University (Fort Worth, Texas) and Chapman University (Orange, California).

As members of Churches of Christ became more affluent during the twentieth century, many gradually shed both the religious sectarianism of the early Alexander Campbell and the social sectarianism of Stone.[21] Today, the two conservative branches either tend to associate with conservative evangelicalism, broadly speaking, or are sectarian in orientation. (Max Lucado, one of the most popular evangelical authors of his generation, has a background with Churches of Christ.)[22] They also tend to avoid engagement with political issues at the congregational level, although individual members may be politically active. Like most other religious groups in the United States, the Stone-Campbell Movement reflects the pluralism and polarization of the broader American culture, especially when considering all three branches.[23]

Despite their many similarities, the two conservative branches have subtle differences. Most Churches of Christ continue to sing a cappella exclusively in their worship services, while Christian Churches/ Churches of Christ are instrumental.[24] Congregations in Churches of Christ tend to be smaller and to be led by a body of elders or shepherds, while congregations in the Christian Churches/Churches of Christ can be much larger and tend to be pastor-led. The largest congregation of the Christian Churches/Churches of Christ is Southeast Christian Church in Louisville, Kentucky, which with an average attendance of 25,917 was the fourth largest congregation in the United States in 2019. The Hills Church of Christ in Fort Worth, Texas, currently the largest congregation in Churches of Christ, had an average attendance of 4,658 in 2018.

Churches of Christ have a more robust network of liberal arts universities and colleges, including Pepperdine University (Malibu, California), Abilene Christian University (Abilene, Texas), Harding University (Searcy, Arkansas), and Lipscomb University (Nashville, Tennessee). Christian Churches/Churches of Christ, on the other hand, have a number of smaller Bible colleges for training ministers, some of which have transitioned to liberal arts colleges and universities in recent years, such as Milligan University (Elizabethton, Tennessee) and Johnson University (Knoxville, Tennessee). There have been informal efforts to promote unity between the two branches, and there are good relations between members and churches of the two branches. The lack of formal structures in both branches, however, makes formal unity efforts difficult, and conservative members of Churches of Christ see the use of instrumental music in worship as a departure from New Testament Christianity.

THEOLOGICAL COMMITMENTS AND PRACTICES

The early concerns of Stone and Alexander Campbell led to distinct theological commitments and practices in the Stone-Campbell Movement. Both rejected the Calvinism of the American frontier. The message that the Spirit typically works through the preaching of the gospel to affect conversion, and one's election is assured through faith and baptism, was good news to many. Further, Alexander Campbell's effort to restore the ancient order and the conclusions he reached are significant.

The Stone-Campbell Movement views believer's baptism by immersion, preceded by faith and repentance, as the standard initiation rite of the Christian faith. Believer's baptism in the Triune name brings forgiveness of sins and the indwelling of the Holy Spirit. This practice differs from frontier Calvinism, which is reflected in the more recent evangelical practice of praying the "Sinner's Prayer" as the saving response to the gospel. It also differs from the practice of infant baptism followed by confirmation, which is common in Catholic, Orthodox, and many mainline Protestant churches. The Christian Church (Disciples of Christ) continues Stone's practice of open membership for those baptized as infants, but the Christian Churches/Churches of Christ and Churches of Christ question the biblical support for infant baptism and typically require believer's baptism for membership.

Word and Table have always been central components of worship in the Stone-Campbell Movement. All three branches of the Stone-Campbell Movement celebrate the Lord's Supper every Sunday. All three branches practice open communion and do not bar participants from receiving the elements, although it is assumed that the Supper is an act of Christian worship and participants should not partake "in an unworthy manner" (1 Cor. 11:27–28, NRSV). All three branches practice lay presidency at the Table, where the one who presides at the Table is typically a church member, not a minister. In the Christian Church (Disciples of Christ) and in Christian Churches/Churches of Christ, an elder usually presides at the Table.

Alexander Campbell preferred the language of *ordinance* over *sacrament*, but he viewed the Table as a means of grace where participants eat in Christ's presence and experience the joy of salvation. Stone-Campbell heirs, however, soon emphasized the commemorative and declarative aspects of the Table where participants remember and proclaim Christ's saving death. In recent years, representatives from all three branches have moved from a commemorative and declarative understanding of the Lord's Supper to a richer, sacramental understanding, where worshippers meet Christ and experience their present salvation at the Table.[25]

From its beginning, the Stone-Campbell Movement tried to deal with questions about the Father, Son, and Holy Spirit, including questions about the identity of Jesus and the incarnation, by strictly adhering to biblical language. In fact, the term "Trinity" itself was avoided because it is not found in the Bible. Early Stone-Campbell leaders maintained that assent to biblical confessions such as "Jesus is the Christ, the Son of the living God" was sufficient for salvation, avoided the problems raised by metaphysical speculation, and helped promote Christian unity. Stone and some of the Christians explicitly rejected the doctrine of the Trinity, but Thomas and Alexander Campbell and the Reformers were essentially Trinitarian, although they tried to avoid classic terminology. Kelly Carter, however, has demonstrated an inconsistency in Alexander

Campbell's writings, as Campbell employed non-biblical terms like *Triune, essence,* and *persons,* especially when distancing his beliefs from Unitarianism and Arianism.[26]

By and large, Stone-Campbell heirs from all three branches have maintained an implicit and irenic Trinitarianism. Nonetheless, those in the Christian Church (Disciples of Christ) who overtly reject Trinitarian doctrine typically follow the approach of liberal theologians, and those in Christian Churches/Churches of Christ and Churches of Christ who overtly reject Trinitarian doctrine typically make an argument from Scripture and reason. Especially in the twenty-first century, there has been an explicit appropriation of Trinitarian theology by scholars in the Stone-Campbell Movement.[27]

Given Alexander Campbell's emphasis on restoring the ancient order, Stone-Campbell heirs have given considerable attention to ecclesiology, although all three branches recognize that the New Testament bears witness to some variety in the worship and organization of the early church. All three, but especially the Christian Churches/Churches of Christ and Churches of Christ, emphasize congregational autonomy, where local churches are overseen by a plurality of elders or shepherds. Many in Churches of Christ see exclusive a cappella (unaccompanied) singing in worship as part of the commitment to restore the ancient order, though the issue has become less divisive in progressive churches from this branch.

If there is an orienting concern in the Stone-Campbell Movement equivalent to *justification by faith* in the Lutheran tradition, the *sovereignty of God* in the Reformed tradition, and *holiness* in the Wesleyan tradition, then it is *discipleship.* Alexander Campbell preferred the name Disciples for his followers, and the progressive branch of the movement continues to go by the name Disciples of Christ. Renewal efforts within the movement often emphasize discipleship, and the term is prominent in its publications. Further, participation in global missions has been a historic commitment in every branch of the movement, including Churches of Christ where missionaries and parachurch organizations are supported by local congregations or through voluntary, collaborative efforts. Discipleship emphasizes the desire of the movement's leaders and heirs to be simply Christians, learners at the feet of Jesus, who are actively engaged in a life of worship, spiritual growth, and participation in God's mission. The Stone-Campbell Movement is worthy of attention because, in addition to its continued influence, it is a mature representation of the ongoing desire in American Protestantism for a Bible-based, mission-oriented, non-denominational Christianity.

NOTES

1 These various influences on the Stone-Campbell Movement have been widely explored. For the influence of evangelical missions, see James L. Gorman, *Among the Early Evangelicals: The Transatlantic Origins of the Stone-Campbell Movement* (Abilene, TX: Abilene Christian University Press, 2017). For the influence of Enlightenment philosophy, see C. Leonard Allen, *Things Unseen: Churches of Christ In (and After) the Modern Age* (Siloam Springs, AR: Leafwood, 2004), 45–98. For the influence of American democracy, see Nathan O. Hatch, *The Democratization of American Christianity* (New Haven, CT: Yale University Press, 1989).

2 These themes were also prominent in transatlantic evangelical missionary societies. See Gorman, *Among the Early Evangelicals*, 25–39.

3 The term "Stone-Campbell Movement" is relatively new and is traced back to Leroy Garrett's history of the movement. See Leroy Garrett, *The Stone-Campbell Movement* (Joplin, MO: College Press, 1981) and D. Newell Williams, Douglas A. Foster, and Paul M. Blowers, eds., *The Stone-Campbell Movement: A Global History* (St. Louis, MO: Chalice Press, 2013), 4.

4 The standard reference works on the Stone-Campbell Movement are two collaborative projects by scholars representing all three branches of the movement. See Douglas A. Foster, Paul M. Blowers, Anthony L. Dunnavant, and D. Newell Williams, eds., *The Encyclopedia of the Stone-Campbell Movement* (Grand Rapids, MI: Eerdmans, 2004) and Williams et al., eds., *The Stone-Campbell Movement*.

5 Williams et al., eds., *The Stone-Campbell Movement*, 29.

6 The best critical biography of Stone is D. Newell Williams, *Barton Stone: A Spiritual Biography* (St. Louis, MO: Chalice, 2000).

7 *The Last Will and Testament of the Springfield Presbytery* is reprinted in Barton W. Stone, *The Biography of Elder Barton W. Stone Written by Himself: with Additions and Reflections by Elder John Rogers* (Cincinnati: Published for the author by J. A. and U. P. James, 1847), 51–53.

8 For a fuller presentation of Stone's "Quasi-Arianism," see Kelly D. Carter, *The Trinity in the Stone-Campbell Movement: Restoring the Heart of the Christian Faith* (Abilene, TX: Abilene Christian University Press, 2015), 89–138. Stone's rejection of Trinitarian doctrine follows the Enlightenment critique that was pervasive in his day. See Jason E. Vickers, *Invocation and Assent: The Making of Remaking of Trinitarian Theology* (Grand Rapids, MI: Eerdmans, 2008).

9 John Mark Hicks, "What Did Christ Accomplish on the Cross? Atonement in Campbell, Stone, and Scott," *Lexington Theological Quarterly* vol. 30, no. 3 (1995), 145–170.

10 Richard T. Hughes coined the phrase "apocalyptic worldview" to describe Stone's pessimistic view of the world and emphasis on kingdom living. See

Hughes, *Reviving the Ancient Faith: The Story of Churches of Christ in America* (Grand Rapids, MI: Eerdmans, 1996), 92–94, 106–113.

11 Gorman, *Among the Early Evangelicals*, 95–124.

12 Thomas Campbell, *Declaration and Address of the Christian Association of Washington* (Washington, PA: Printed by Brown and Sample, 1809).

13 Carter, *The Trinity in the Stone-Campbell Movement*, 29–46.

14 For a recent critical biography on Alexander Campbell, see Douglas A. Foster, *A Life of Alexander Campbell*, Library of Religious Biography (Grand Rapids, MI: Eerdmans, 2020). The best primary source for Alexander Campbell's mature thought is *The Christian System*, 2nd ed. (Pittsburg: Forrester & Campbell, 1839; repr. Nashville: Gospel Advocate, 1970).

15 Campbell wrote two recurring series in his first journal, *The Christian Baptist*. The first was titled "A Restoration of the Ancient Order of Things" and included thirty articles that ran from February 7, 1825 to September 7, 1829. The second was titled "Ancient Gospel" and included ten articles that appeared from January 7 to November 3, 1828.

16 Alexander Campbell, "Sermon on the Law," *Millennial Harbinger*, 3rd ser., vol. 3, no. 9 (September 1846), 493–521.

17 Scott combined two points on the final finger to retain the pedagogical appeal of his "five finger exercise." See Mark G. Toulouse, "Scott, Walter," in *The Encyclopedia of the Stone-Campbell Movement*, ed. Foster et al., 675.

18 See Hughes, *Reviving the Ancient Faith*, 137–167. For two contemporary presentations on eschatology, see Mark G. Toulouse, *Joined in Discipleship: The Shaping of Contemporary Disciples Identity*, rev. ed. (St. Louis, MO: Chalice Press, 1997), 101–135; and Mark E. Powell, John Mark Hicks, and Greg McKinzie, *Discipleship in Community: A Theological Vision for the Future* (Abilene, TX: Abilene Christian University Press, 2020), 47–67.

19 David Edwin Harrell, Jr., has explored extensively the sectional influence in the division among the Disciples of Christ. See *Quest for a Christian America, 1800–1865*, vol. I of *A Social History of the Disciples of Christ* (Tuscaloosa: University of Alabama Press, 1966) and *Sources of Division in the Disciples of Christ, 1865–1900*, vol. II of *A Social History of the Disciples of Christ* (Tuscaloosa, University of Alabama Press, 1973).

20 These reported numbers, combined, are greater than earlier statistics before the division. According to Williams et al., eds., *The Stone-Campbell Movement*, 190, the Christian Church (Disciples of Christ) had 950,000 adherents in 1971.

21 This shift provides the basic two-part structure of Hughes's presentation of the history of Churches of Christ in *Reviving the Ancient Faith*.

22 For a discussion of the relationship between the conservation branches of the Stone-Campbell Movement and evangelicalism, see William R. Baker, ed., *Evangelicalism and the Stone-Campbell Movement* (Downers Grove, IL: InterVarsity Press, 2002) and *Evangelicalism and the Stone-Campbell Movement*, vol. II (Downers Grove, IL: InterVarsity Press, 2006).

23 For a fuller presentation of the social involvement of all three branches since the 1960s, see Williams et al., eds., *The Stone-Campbell Movement*, 204–225.

24 For a discussion of the instrumental music controversy, see Everett Ferguson, "Instrumental Music," in *The Encyclopedia of the Stone-Campbell Movement*, ed. Foster, et al., 414–417. Ferguson offers a defense of a cappella singing in *The Church of Christ: A Biblical Ecclesiology for Today* (Grand Rapids, MI: Eerdmans, 1996), 268–273.

25 For contemporary presentations on baptism and the Lord's Supper, see Toulouse, *Joined in Discipleship*, 137–162 and Powell et al., *Discipleship in Community*, 115–136.

26 Carter, *The Trinity in the Stone-Campbell Movement*, 64–65.

27 For examples of this trend in Churches of Christ, see C. Leonard Allen and Daniel Gray Swick, *Participating in God's Life: Two Crossroads for Churches of Christ* (Orange, CA: New Leaf, 2001); Ron Highfield, *Great in the Lord: Theology for the Praise of God* (Grand Rapids, MI: Eerdmans, 2008), 104–138; Mark E. Powell, *Centered in God: The Trinity and Christian Spirituality* (Abilene, TX: Abilene Christian University Press, 2014); Carter, *The Trinity in the Stone-Campbell Movement*; and Powell, Hicks, and McKinzie, *Discipleship in Community*, 25–45.

23 Wesleyan-Methodist and Holiness Traditions

DOUGLAS M. STRONG

Methodism – the Christian tradition that traces its heritage to John Wesley – became the largest religious group in the United States by the 1840s. Its rapid growth began during the early years of the American republic and extended throughout the decades of the nineteenth century. Though the Methodist Episcopal Church (the name of the original Wesleyan denomination in the United States) eventually divided into a number of separate churches due to various controversies, and though waves of immigration meant that the Roman Catholic Church took over first place as the most numerous Christian group in the United States, the Methodist tradition as a whole remained the largest expression of American Protestant Christianity from the 1840s to the 1920s. Given its predominance, it is no wonder religious historians refer to the 1800s as "the Methodist age in America."[1]

The Wesleyan family of Methodist and Holiness churches has remained the third largest religious group of denominations and the second largest Protestant tradition in America throughout the twentieth and early twenty-first centuries. Owing to the breadth of geography, ethnicity, and social class that characterizes Methodism's demographic spread, historians and sociologists often view Methodism – birthed as a denomination at almost exactly the same time as the United States – as the quintessential example of American religious identity.[2]

BEGINNINGS

Such prominence has not always been the case. In the late-1730s, the brothers John and Charles Wesley, Oxford-educated, ordained clergymen in the Church of England, both spent a brief stint in the American colonies – nine months for Charles and about two years for John – as representatives of the Society for the Propagation of the Gospel in Foreign Parts. The Wesleys' missionary assignment occurred just prior to the spiritual renewal experiences that catapulted them to their later evangelistic fame in Britain. John and Charles attempted to serve the pioneer settlers of Georgia and South Carolina by introducing a "methodistic" form of highly disciplined piety that had been effective among their Oxonian colleagues but did not sit well with displaced expatriates trying to eke out a living in the New World. Indeed, during John Wesley's time in America, he incurred the enmity of most of the settlers among whom he worked. His and Charles's brief deployment in the colonies proved to be singularly unproductive, with no long-term impact other than its influence on their ensuing ministry. The most significant of those influences occurred while they were in Charleston, where the brothers witnessed the horrors of slavery. The lasting impression of seeing people kept in bondage prompted the Wesleys to work steadfastly for the demise of that despicable institution for the rest of their lives.[3]

Soon after the Wesley brothers returned to England, they experienced their legendary 1738 conversions. John's heartwarming transformation occurred at a small group meeting held on Aldersgate Street in London. Through his subsequent preaching success and organizing genius, John Wesley helped to usher in the religious revitalization movement known as the Evangelical Revival. Wesley's colleague and friend from Oxford days, George Whitefield, encouraged him in this work, and introduced him to the advantages of "field preaching" – mass evangelism conducted outside the confines of a church building. Using such unconventional tactics, Whitefield's spiritual influence expanded in Britain and, eventually, in America. He arrived in the colonies soon after John Wesley left to return to England. Unlike Wesley's seemingly futile efforts in Georgia, Whitefield's ministry to the colonists became highly successful. Whitefield's preaching sparked the Great Awakening of the 1740s and set the stage for the meteoric rise of various types of evangelical Christianity in the early years of the American republic.[4]

This Evangelical Revival spread broadly throughout the English-speaking world in the mid-eighteenth century. John Wesley's post-1738 preaching – now vivified by his newfound experience of "vital piety" – exemplified the revivalist zeal. His sermons stressed the importance of a new birth in Christ, an affective assurance of justification through the witness of the Spirit, and the necessity of living a sanctified life as the fruit of one's spiritual regeneration. Wesley understood the task of his ministry as inspiring renewal within the Church of England. Though he did not want to form a new church, the Methodist movement nonetheless gradually took on the trappings of a separate ecclesiastical body, even during his lifetime.

Evangelically awakened Irish men and women who emigrated to the American colonies in the 1760s were the first people in the New World to promote the Methodist message fruitfully. Ironically, then, though the originators of the movement had personally visited America, Methodism as an effective evangelistic venture did not take root there until thirty years after the brothers' sojourn, when some of their converts began to spread the message of "scriptural holiness throughout the land."[5]

The new seeds of Methodism in America were small and scattered. In the late 1760s, Robert Strawbridge, a devout Irish layman who settled in New Windsor, Maryland, started a biracial class meeting in his farmhouse. (Methodist "classes" were fellowship groups for evangelism and accountable discipleship, not instructional events.) Strawbridge led other classes in addition to the earliest one, and he organized them into larger "societies" (congregations) – the first communities of Methodist worship in North America. Strawbridge also had log meeting houses built at several locations. He regularly traveled a circuit in Maryland, Pennsylvania, and Virginia, in order to provide encouragement to his far-flung flock – preaching the significance of the new birth and exhorting new believers. Strawbridge had a major influence on many young lay preachers due to his popularity. He also took it upon himself to administer the sacraments of baptism and the Lord's Supper, even though most other Methodists in America, and the Wesleys back in England, insisted that sacraments could only be received from Anglican priests – since Methodism still considered itself to be a renewal movement and not its own church body.[6]

At just about the same time as Strawbridge, another Irish Methodist immigrant, Barbara Heck, began a class meeting in her home in New York City. Heck convinced her cousin, Philip Embury, to establish other classes and to start his own lay preaching. As before, African Americans joined whites in the New York classes. Moving out from the two centers of activity in Maryland and New York, Methodist spirituality began to spread throughout the middle Atlantic seaboard of the American colonies.

Across the ocean, John Wesley received reports about Methodist growth in America, along with pleas for assistance. The Americans recognized that they lacked trained leaders and an overarching structure. Consequently, beginning in 1769, Wesley dispatched British lay preachers two-by-two[7] to go to America as a response to the expressed need. Among these appointees was one young leader who eventually outshone them all: Francis Asbury, a 26-year-old unschooled preacher who, during his forty-five subsequent years of itinerant ministry, shaped

American Methodism more than any other person before or since. While Wesley's doctrine and vision determined the theological and structural grounding of Methodism in America, it was Asbury's indomitable personality and single-minded organizing focus that strengthened and extended the fledgling movement into an unstoppable evangelistic enterprise.[8]

During the Revolutionary War, nearly all British Methodist preachers returned to their home country. (Francis Asbury and one other remained.) Relationships became strained between American Methodists and Anglicans; this connection had previously been considered necessary for Methodists if they wanted to receive the sacraments. In an environment in which Americans extolled the values of independence, most American Methodists itched to become self-governing. Strawbridge's precedent of lay preachers giving themselves the right to administer sacraments was a prerogative that fit well with the desire for freedom from English authority, whether political or ecclesiastical. John Wesley faced a conundrum: If he kept true to the protocols of his beloved Church of England, American Methodists would be left adrift. But if he assisted the Americans in creating a new denomination where they could obtain access to sacramental ministry, he would precipitate a definitive rupture with Anglicanism.

After the Treaty of Paris ended the war in 1783 and the United States emerged as a fully independent nation, Wesley saw no alternative but to form a brand-new church: "As our American brethren are now totally disentangled both from the State and from the English [Church of England] hierarchy ... we judge it best that they should stand fast in that liberty wherewith God has so strangely made them free." Based on scriptural warrant, but without Anglican permission, Wesley ordained two of his trusted British Methodist preachers as "elders," whom he then considered qualified to celebrate the sacraments. He also "set apart" an already ordained Anglican clergyman, Thomas Coke, to oversee the Methodist work in America – in conjunction with Francis Asbury, whom Wesley knew had emerged as the de facto Methodist leader in America. Coke and Asbury were to serve as "joint superintendents." (He avoided using the term "bishop," in the hope of not offending Anglicans too deeply.)[9]

Wesley deputized these newly consecrated personal emissaries and sent them to the United States to meet with Asbury and other American Methodists. He commissioned them with specific instructions: they were to connect with the American lay preachers; form a denominational structure; and ordain as many as needed for effective sacramental ministry. The British envoys met together with the American preachers in December 1784 at the "Christmas Conference," held at Lovely Lane chapel in Baltimore. Following their founder's directives, and satisfying their own yearning for self-determination, the conference members formed a new denomination, which they christened the Methodist Episcopal Church (MEC). The term "Methodist" indicated their allegiance to Wesley's brand of theology and disciplined piety, and the word "episcopal" indicated their continuing commitment to connectional governance: individual congregations and preachers could not act alone but were responsible to one another under the supervision of a network of interlocking "conferences." And yet, as if to demonstrate American liberty from British control, Asbury insisted that the preachers democratically elect him and Coke to their leadership roles. The new MEC also began to refer to Asbury and Coke as bishops, rather than Wesley's preferred designation of superintendents.[10]

Around sixty preachers attended the Christmas Conference, including two African Americans, Richard Allen and Harry Hosier, and a German Pietist, Philip William Otterbein. Though Otterbein was not a Methodist – because he and other German Americans preferred to have their own ethnically specific church bodies – he nevertheless had cordial relations with Asbury and other Methodists, who expressed a similar type of spirituality. Otterbein led a group of Christians from a German background that eventually came to be known as the Church of the United Brethren in Christ. He and another German American Pietist, Jacob Albright, the founder of the Evangelical Association (later called the Evangelical Church), both developed denominational organizations in the early nineteenth century that were parallel to the MEC, in the sense that they modeled their theology and polity after Methodism.

The Christmas Conference accomplished many organizational matters for the MEC. It ordained twelve elders and consecrated Coke and Asbury for their supervisory roles. It also established an educational institution in Abingdon, Maryland – Cokesbury College, named after the two new bishops. While this particular college did not remain open very long due to a devastating fire, it was only the first of hundreds of schools to be started by the MEC, and, later, by other Wesleyan denominations.

The conference dealt specifically with several documents that Coke brought to the United States on Wesley's behalf. One of the documents Wesley sent was a revised and abbreviated version of the Anglican *Book of Common Prayer* that he titled the "Order of Sunday Service." Wesley expected the ministers of the new church to use this liturgical framework. While the conference did, in fact, officially receive the prescribed Sunday Service, most of the preachers considered it too formal for their congregants, who preferred extemporaneous worship. As part of their worship style, American Methodists enjoyed singing, and especially cherished Charles Wesley's hymns. But in general, the MEC tended to ignore any formalized liturgy – except when ordained elders celebrated the Lord's Supper.

John Wesley also sent a document known as the Articles of Religion, an abridgement of the Thirty-Nine Articles of the Church of England. The preachers at the Christmas Conference endorsed these Articles of Religion as their rule of doctrine, along with Wesley's *Standard Sermons* and his *Explanatory Notes on the New Testament*. They adopted, as well, a book that outlined Methodism's governance structure, called the *Discipline*, based on Wesley's *Large Minutes*. The Americans adhered to both documents – the Articles and the Discipline – to a much greater degree than they did to the Sunday Service.

DISTINGUISHING FEATURES

John Wesley had attained the stature of an elderly patriarch by the time of the MEC's formation. Just two years after the Christmas Conference and five years before his death at age eighty-seven, Wesley wrote an article entitled "Thoughts upon Methodism," in which he reflected on the legacy and destiny of the movement he founded. As he pondered the future prospects of Methodism in Britain and the United States, he put forward his speculation:

> I am not afraid that the people called Methodists should ever cease to exist in either Europe or America. But I am afraid lest they should only exist as a dead sect, having the form of religion without the power. And this undoubtedly will be the case unless they hold fast both the doctrine, spirit, and discipline with which they first set out.[11]

Wesley's categories of "doctrine, spirit, and discipline" are useful summarizing terms to describe the distinguishing features of Methodist theology and worship, particularly as these features persisted in, and adapted to, the American context.

Wesley's first-mentioned category ("doctrine") may not seem to be an obvious Methodist distinctive. Indeed, some critics of the tradition, and even some misinformed Methodists today, incorrectly assume that the Methodist tradition lacks doctrinal precision and coherence. Wesley and the early American Methodists would have begged to differ. US Methodists in the late eighteenth and nineteenth centuries articulated clear theological beliefs and made compelling arguments for their doctrinal positions – so much so that they won over many prior opponents to their points of view. In fact, Methodist emphases such as free grace and sanctification became so widely accepted throughout nineteenth-century American Protestantism that Congregationalists like Charles G. Finney as well as scores of New School Presbyterians, Cumberland Presbyterians, Franckean Lutherans, and Freewill Baptists were all accused by colleagues from their own religious backgrounds of being closet Methodists because of their high regard for these theological concepts.[12]

While the Articles of Religion contains the official doctrine of the MEC, everyday American Methodists learned their theology from studying the Bible, singing Charles Wesley's hymns, and reading John Wesley's writings, especially his published sermons. In these sermons, Methodists gained an understanding of Wesley's theological views, which he developed from a combination of antecedents – Christian Scripture, his Anglican and Puritan background, the influence of Continental Pietism, and his examination of the church fathers. This variety of sources culminated in a distinctive type of Wesleyan theological synthesis.[13] Many interpreters have noted how Wesley wove together religious concepts that have often been kept poles apart by other theologians, resulting in a kind of conjunctive theology that stresses both/and rather than either/or.[14]

Examples of Wesley's theological synthesis include his balance of faith with works; the pessimism of nature with the optimism of grace; acts of piety (spiritual disciplines) with acts of mercy (activism for the poor and oppressed); and justification through the pardon of sins (the relative change that God does for us through Christ) with sanctification through the infilling of God's love (the real change that God does in us through the Holy Spirit). Wesley also had a balanced perspective on salvation, which was neither universalistic (all are saved) nor fatalistic (God capriciously decides who will be saved). American Methodists adhered to Wesley's soteriological understanding; consequently, according to a nineteenth-century commentator, they held "the middle ground between Calvinism and Universalism."[15]

Wesley insisted – in contrast to a Reformed understanding of limited atonement – that the free grace all people receive preveniently from God provides everyone with the opportunity to respond by faith to Jesus's overture of forgiveness. As stated in the lyrics of one of Charles Wesley's well-known hymns: "Let every soul be Jesus' guest; / ye need not one be left behind, / for God hath bidden all mankind."[16] This inclusive

Methodist message, that God invites every single person to repent and be made a new creature in Christ, resounded throughout the new American nation, providing spiritual hope to individuals of all ethnicities and social classes, and especially to those on the margins. The Methodists' unlimited offer of salvation resonated well in a society that, at least theoretically, embraced the democratic notion that "all men are created equal."[17]

Wesley also taught that God's grace extends beyond the forgiveness of sins, to such a degree that the Holy Spirit can change justified believers into sanctified disciples. This sanctifying grace would be evident in a person's consistent intention to love God and neighbor, a measure of God's holiness manifest in human action. By inviting all Christians to "participate in the divine nature" (2 Pet. 1:4), Wesley offered believers a directional trajectory whereby they could "expect to be made perfect in love in this life." Wesley was convinced that the lifting up of this doctrine of Christian perfection (also known as holiness or sanctification) was the Methodist movement's most important contribution to Christendom. Early American Methodists taught this holiness doctrine and were convinced that its application to the lives of Christians could transform individuals and society – thereby assisting the people of the United States in their quest to "form a more perfect union."[18]

The term "doctrine," then, referred to the first category that Wesley noted as distinctive of his movement and crucial for Methodists to maintain; the second category in his short list of distinctives was the term "spirit." The Wesleyan emphasis on spirit, similar to the emphasis on doctrine, became a distinguishing feature of American Methodism. Spirit is a rather ambiguous term. It pertains to the activity of the Holy Spirit; but the term also captures the Methodist disposition to live out an affective, enthusiastic faith in Christ. For Wesley, every person could feel an assurance of faith through the witness of the Spirit. Correct beliefs (orthodoxy) are essential, but fervent life-changing encounters with God (orthopathy) are just as necessary. American Methodists identified such emotive sensations with the new birth of conversion and the "second blessing" of sanctification.

Methodists anticipated every occasion of Christian fellowship as a time for heartfelt experiential piety. Worship among American Methodists, whether in small class meetings or larger congregational settings, exploded with intense and sometimes ecstatic holy passion. Methodist preachers encouraged congregants to exhibit spontaneous outbursts of charismatic expression, which seemed scandalous to their staid Episcopalian, Presbyterian, and Congregationalist colleagues.[19]

Opponents often interpreted the Methodist stress on sanctification as an emotional paroxysm unrelated to ethical resolve. In point of fact, however, American Methodists taught that the experience of entire sanctification provided the power necessary to persist in a consistently consecrated life of obedience to the moral law (orthopraxy). The ethical consequences of this Spirit-empowered moral earnestness had huge implications for how American Methodists lived out their commitment to sanctification. They demonstrated their reception of God's holiness in their lives by their practices of self-denying personal behaviors, charitable work among the disadvantaged, anti-slavery advocacy, missionary endeavors, educational ventures, the founding of hospitals, and social justice activism – to name just some of the more conspicuous examples.[20]

The third term Wesley used to describe Methodist distinctives was "discipline," which referred to the structure that Methodism provided for individuals and churches – and which represents yet another distinguishing feature of American Wesleyanism. Wesley believed strongly that connectional administrative organization resulted in effective discipleship. As described above, Methodists in the United States engaged in fervent informal worship – but they did so within a highly organized system. Multiple tiers of Methodist discipline started with the individual member and then spread farther and farther, until this religious discipline encompassed Methodists throughout the United States, and ultimately (via missionary work) throughout the world.

Every member, for instance, was expected to practice means of grace (personal disciplines) such as prayer, fasting, Scripture study, and acts of service – a *methodical* piety. In order to strengthen these sanctified habits, each Methodist belonged to a class meeting, an example of "social holiness" – communal encouragement and accountability – in which fellow members took it upon themselves to "advise, reprove, comfort, or exhort, as occasion may require."[21] American Methodists required class meeting attendance of all members until the Civil War period, and even as late as the 1930s in some areas of the country.

The American Methodist system of tight organization extended beyond individual members to localities, and then to regions, and then to the entire nation. Class members belonged to societies (congregations), which were organized into circuits or "charge conferences," which were supervised by Presiding Elders (later called District Superintendents) in districts or "quarterly conferences," which were then collated together into annual conferences. The term "annual conference" refers both to a specific geographic administrative region and to

the regular yearly meeting of itinerating preachers in that given area –
often a state or portion of a state. Delegates from annual conferences
meet together every four years for General Conference, a body that
makes decisions for the entire denomination. Using the Wesleyan form
of discipline, American Methodists "organized to beat the devil"
through a governance system of connected accountable gatherings.[22]
Together with Wesley's aforementioned theological distinctives, particularly the concepts of free grace and Christian perfection (doctrine),
and the stress on enlivened religious experiences and dynamic worship
(spirit), this pursuit of a meticulous and highly structured form of
Christian praxis (discipline), round out the three most distinguishing
marks of American Methodism.

THE GROWTH AND FRACTURING OF METHODISM

After the 1784 Christmas Conference, the newly constituted MEC accelerated its spectacular growth pattern, propelled by several strategic
advantages: circuit riders, class meetings, and camp meetings. Circuit
riders – traveling preachers on horseback – followed settlers' westward
expansion into all corners of the American republic. Francis Asbury and
Harry Hosier, who often preached in tandem, served as just two prominent examples of the extensive reach of Methodist itinerancy. Those who
responded to the circuit rider's entreaties to be saved and sanctified were
placed into weekly class meetings to be nurtured in their faith. Class
members also met regularly for worship with other classes in their
vicinity. And camp meetings – exuberant multi-day outdoor services of
preaching, praying, and singing – became a staple of Methodist evangelistic efforts, beginning around 1800 and then continuing throughout the
nineteenth century and beyond. Famous camp meeting communities
such as Oak Bluffs on Martha's Vineyard, Ocean Grove on the Jersey
shore, Lakeside in Ohio, and Bay View in Michigan, continue to
this day.[23]

Much of Methodism's numerical growth occurred among African
Americans. Blacks responded eagerly to the Wesleyan message of free
grace available to all people, relished fervent Methodist worship, and
appreciated early Methodism's strong opposition to slavery.[24] The MEC,
however, did not maintain its original anti-racist posture and soon
bowed to pressure from the larger culture. The denomination incremen-
tally whittled away its uncompromising anti-slavery position, and local
congregations began to discriminate against African-American members. An infamous example of this creeping racism occurred as early as

1787 at St. George's MEC in Philadelphia, when white members tried to force Blacks to sit in a segregated gallery. Richard Allen arose as a leader of the African-American members, who left the white church to form their own organization – the Free African Society – later to become the nucleus of Mother Bethel African Methodist Episcopal Church.[25]

Richard Allen revered Wesley as a theological mentor and admired Asbury, who recognized Allen's leadership by approving him to be the first ordained Black Methodist. But despite his loyalty to Methodism as a movement, Allen chafed under the racist attitudes apparent in the MEC. Allen and other African-American leaders waited until one week after Asbury's death in 1816 (probably out of respect for Asbury) to establish formally a new Black Methodist denomination – the African Methodist Episcopal Church (AME). The AME General Conference approved a *Discipline* with nearly identical doctrine and polity to the MEC, except for a firm rule against slavery. Allen became the first bishop of the new church.[26]

Parallel accounts of racial exclusion resulted in other new Black Methodist denominations. In Wilmington, Delaware, Peter Spencer became the originator of two small denominations, ultimately called the African Union Methodist Protestant Church and the Union American Methodist Episcopal Church. In New York City, repeated discrimination culminated in the formation of the African Methodist Episcopal Zion Church (AMEZ) in 1821 through the efforts of Black preachers such as James Varick, the first bishop of that denomination.

Black denominations did not constitute the only separations to occur in the MEC during the years following Asbury's death. Heated arguments soon ensued over the amount of power vested in MEC bishops and presiding elders. While the bishop's power had been mostly tolerated under Asbury, the populist spirit of the Jacksonian period created the climate for a serious split in 1830, with the formation of the Methodist Protestant Church (MPC). The MPC had no bishops and mandated that annual conferences uphold equal lay and clergy representation. Another group that also desired more democratic polity, the Congregational Methodist Church, seceded for similar reasons in 1852.

The next major division in the MEC dealt, once again, with concerns that grew out of the systemic racism rampant in American society. The Methodist schism of the 1840s is often interpreted as a two-way split; but more accurately, it was a three-way breakup. The initial separation took place under the leadership of Orange Scott, a fiery presiding elder from New England, when fervent abolitionists seceded from the MEC in 1843 to form the Wesleyan Methodist Connection (WMC), later renamed the

Wesleyan Methodist Church. WMC members considered themselves to be "true Wesleyans" because they held unwaveringly to John Wesley's anti-slavery stance. Their promotion of sanctification as the theological basis for their justice advocacy prefigured later nineteenth-century debates about the importance of that doctrine.

This separation of the WMC shocked northern Methodists, who feared that entire regional units would split off from the MEC – especially conferences in New England, upstate New York, and Ohio – if the General Conference refused to take a stronger stand against slavery. The threat of mass exodus finally prompted the previously compromising northern Methodists to put their feet down at the 1844 General Conference, where they voted to suspend a slaveholding bishop. Southern Methodists found this disciplinary action to be an affront, and seceded from the MEC, establishing the Methodist Episcopal Church, South (MECS) in 1845.[27]

Slavery became just one of several concerns for those who believed that American Methodists were undervaluing Wesley's doctrine of Christian perfection or holiness. In the years before the Civil War, Phoebe Palmer, a laywoman from New York City, popularized anew the experience of entire sanctification through her writing and speaking. Her influence spread, and soon increasing numbers of Methodists enlisted in what came to be known as the Holiness movement. (The word "Holiness" is capitalized when used to speak about the Holiness movement. When the word is in lower case, it refers to the doctrinal belief of holiness or sanctification.) Palmer's interpretation of Christian perfection/holiness/entire sanctification stretched Wesley's original understanding. She encouraged believers to anticipate entire sanctification at increasingly earlier stages of their Christian life. Christian perfection, it seemed, could be achieved almost on demand. Holiness preachers expected people to apprehend sanctification as an existential crisis, similar to one's new birth experience.[28]

B. T. Roberts, an MEC elder in western New York State, received entire sanctification after hearing Palmer speak, and soon became a fervent Holiness preacher. His holiness-inspired insistence that the MEC renounce slavery, pew rentals (which paid for expensive new church buildings), costly apparel and jewelry, organs and robed choirs, alcohol and tobacco consumption, theater attendance, membership in secret societies such as the Masons, and any other perceived worldly distraction from God, resulted in his annual conference charging him with contumacy. Then, in 1860, the General Conference stripped Roberts and several other Holiness preachers of their ordination, immediately resulting in the establishment of a new Holiness denomination, the Free Methodist Church.[29]

The Civil War soon disrupted and altered the religious landscape of the United States. Methodists were represented on both sides, as Union and Confederate politicians, military officers, chaplains, and common soldiers. One outgrowth of the war and of emancipation was the separation of formerly enslaved Black Methodists from the MECS. In 1870, they formed themselves into the Colored Methodist Episcopal Church (renamed the Christian Methodist Episcopal Church in 1954). Also significant was the 1866 establishment, largely through MEC auspices, of the Freedman's Aid Bureau, which assisted in founding many faith-based Black colleges (HBCUs, or historically Black colleges and universities) that still exist today.

The Holiness movement continued to expand its impact in the years after the Civil War. Camp meetings sprang up specifically to espouse holiness teaching. Until the 1880s, most Holiness-influenced Methodists remained within the MEC and MECS. Increasingly, though, Holiness preaching became interdenominational and even non-denominational. Many churches that had no historic ties to Wesleyanism began to stress holiness. Proponents of holiness within the MEC and MECS started to fraternize more regularly with other Holiness people of whatever denomination (especially at camp meetings), and less with organizational Methodists. Consequently, Holiness adherents formed their own "bands" – groupings of likeminded Holiness advocates. Meanwhile, MEC and MECS leaders became bothered by the perceived excesses of Holiness people and mandated that Holiness preachers stick closely to the connectional structures of their denominations.[30]

By the 1880s and 1890s, many Holiness people felt ostracized and withdrew from the MEC and MECS. The Holiness bands coalesced into small denominations. Some of those new denominations remained self-consciously Wesleyan, particularly the Pilgrim Holiness Church, led by Martin Wells Knapp; the Church of God (Anderson), led by Daniel S. Warner; and the Church of the Nazarene, led by Phineas F. Bresee. (A majority of the Pilgrim Holiness Church merged in 1968 with the WMC to form The Wesleyan Church.) Each of the Holiness denominations founded colleges during this same era. Another Wesleyan-Holiness body, the Salvation Army, started initially in Britain but then came to the United States by 1880. Even with all these folks separating from the MEC and MECS, large numbers of holiness supporters remained within the major Methodist denominations, creating a Holiness leaven that lasted well into the twentieth century.

Late nineteenth-century Holiness people intentionally defied the cultural norms of the period, which they considered to be worldly. They zealously embraced asceticism – rejecting smoking, drinking of alcohol, jewelry wearing, dancing, and card playing. Also unusual was their radical egalitarianism, which led to the elevation of women to positions of spiritual leadership. Holiness bodies were the earliest Christians in the world to ordain women – though which person should be considered the very first continues to be debated. Mary Wills, ordained by the WMC in 1861, has as strong a claim to that honor as any person.[31] Some historians claim that Antoinette Brown was the first ordained woman, in 1853 – as a Congregationalist. While that is possible, contemporary accounts stated that she was "installed" as a pastor rather than formally ordained. But even if Brown's ordination was the first, it is significant that she was trained in holiness theology at Oberlin College and that the preacher at her installation service was Luther Lee, one of the leaders of the WMC.[32] Many women leaders found their voice under the aegis of the Holiness movement. Examples include: Black preachers, Jarena Lee, and Julia Foote; missionaries Amanda Berry Smith and Isabella Thoburn; the denominational founder of the Pillar of Fire, Alma White; the head ("National Commander") of the Salvation Army, Evangeline Booth; and the founder of the Women's Christian Temperance Union, Frances Willard.[33]

Late nineteenth-century Holiness people also showed signs of their countercultural proclivity by their mode of worshipping. At the same time that some of the leaders of the major Methodist denominations (MEC, MECS, AME, AMEZ) began to encourage more formal worship services, Holiness worshippers expressed their faith in more dramatic and emotional ways. People at Holiness services and revival meetings commonly shouted, fell down in religious ecstasy, and prayed for healing from physical ailments. By the 1890s, a few Holiness preachers explored the possibility that God's gift of the Holy Spirit in sanctification could be accompanied by a visible sign in a person's life. This led some Holiness believers to embrace Pentecostalism – the conviction that glossolalia (speaking in tongues) is the initial evidence of the baptism of the Holy Spirit. Most of the early leaders of the Pentecostal movement came out of the Holiness movement and therefore had close affiliations with Methodism – though Methodist and Holiness leaders typically denied the connection.[34]

Meanwhile, the larger Methodist denominations (MEC, MECS) began to act like the broader American culture, stressing their commonality with other major denominations, and thereby developing a more mainline ethos. Methodism represented the aspiring hopes of middle-class Americans.[35] By facilitating social mobility, the MEC became "the prototype of a religious organization taking on market form."[36] Late nineteenth-century Methodism became synonymous with mainstream values in the United States. Chautauqua Institution, for example, originated as a respectable Methodist educational alternative to more fervently experiential camp meetings. In 1900, the *New York Evening Post* reported that "It used to be said in President Grant's time that there were three political parties in this country: Republicans, Democrats, and Methodists – these three, and the greatest of these is the Methodists."[37] Indeed, Ulysses S. Grant – just one in a long line of nineteenth- and twentieth-century presidents with strong ties to Methodism – understood well the key role played by the religious tradition of his middle America upbringing in the emerging upscale culture of the Gilded Age.[38]

Along with the growing ambitions of the United States as a developing global power, American Methodist missionaries spread themselves around the world, subsidized to a great degree by the funding of women's missionary societies. Methodists had long supported mission work at home and abroad. Mission work within the United States started with various Native American tribes. John Stewart, an African-American preacher, led the first home mission to Native people when he ministered to the Wyandotte tribe in Ohio, beginning in 1816. Throughout the nineteenth and twentieth centuries, Methodist home missions continued among Native Americans, Latino Americans (under the leadership of Alejo Hernandez, for example), and various immigrant groups, such as Germans, Norwegians, Italians, Chinese, and Japanese. The MEC ordained the first Japanese American, Kanichi Miyama, in 1884. American Methodist foreign missions began with the MEC venture to Liberia in 1833. During the nineteenth and twentieth centuries, every Wesleyan and Holiness denomination conducted extensive foreign mission work.[39] William Taylor in the nineteenth century and E. Stanley Jones in the twentieth century are recognized as two of the best-known peripatetic Methodist missionary evangelists.[40]

By the early twentieth century, the connections that Methodists discovered on the mission field with Christians from other denominational backgrounds led them to become involved in the nascent ecumenical movement. American Methodists played a large role in ecumenism, starting with the 1910 World Missionary Conference, organized by MEC layman John R. Mott. Methodists also pursued the Social Gospel during the Progressive Era.[41] An interesting aspect of Methodists' involvement in the Social Gospel movement is the degree to which they viewed temperance and the enactment of Prohibition as a crucial part of their social witness.[42] Some Methodists during this era also embraced theological liberalism, particularly through a variant known as Boston Personalism.[43] Meanwhile, though Methodism was not unscathed by fundamentalism, it was much less affected by that religious movement than most other Protestant denominations.

The ecumenical impetus created the milieu for several twentieth-century denominational mergers. The first was the 1939 uniting of the MEC, MECS, and MPC to form the Methodist Church. This merger became known for its nefarious decision to segregate African Americans into one "Central Jurisdiction," a structure that lasted until 1970.[44] A second merger was the 1946 union of the Church of the United Brethren in Christ and the Evangelical Church to form the Evangelical United Brethren Church. And a third merger was the 1968 uniting of the denominations created by the first two mergers – the Methodist Church and the Evangelical United Brethren Church – to form the United Methodist Church (UMC).

The last-mentioned merger took place during a time of great unrest and convulsion in US society. Many challenges confronted American culture in the second half of the twentieth century. African Americans, such as AME layperson Rosa Parks, demanded their long-denied civil rights. James Cone, also raised in the AME, developed a distinctively liberationist "Black Theology," beginning with the publication of his first major book in 1969.[45] Given widespread gender inequality, women pressed for change, too. As a result, the Methodist Church ordained women, but not until 1956 – nearly a century after its Holiness siblings. The UMC elected Marjorie Matthews, its first woman bishop, in 1980, and the AME elected its first woman bishop, Vashti McKenzie, in 2000. The Immigration and Nationality Act of 1965 addressed another social concern when it lessened discriminatory practices in immigration. The Act permitted people to move to the United States from nations all over the globe. Some of the new citizens became members of Methodist and Holiness churches, thus aiding Wesleyan denominations to become more diverse. The election of Asian American and Latino bishops for service in the UMC attested to the growing diversity. And some first-generation immigrants from Korea established branches of their home Wesleyan denominations in the United States – the Korean Methodist Church and the Korean Evangelical Holiness Church.

Another late twentieth-century controversy demonstrated the influence of the sexual revolution. On the heels of the 1969 Stonewall protest for gay rights, progressives within the UMC proposed the following new statement to be placed in the 1972 *Discipline*: "Homosexuals no less than heterosexuals are persons of sacred worth." Conservatives at the same General Conference then proposed to add the words: "though we do not condone the practice of homosexuality and consider this practice incompatible with Christian teaching."[46] Despite numerous efforts by progressives to remove the latter statement, it remained in the *Discipline*, becoming a contentious issue at every General Conference thereafter. Frustrated, some progressives defied the UMC's legislative stance through "ecclesiastical disobedience" by performing same-sex marriages and ordaining openly gay and lesbian clergy; they elected an openly lesbian bishop in 2016.[47]

According to religious journalist Richard Ostling, the 1968 merger created a "sprawling empire of bishops, bureaucrats, agencies, and schools ... immersed in liberalism."[48] In response to this perception – that liberals controlled institutional power in the UMC – several unofficial, theologically conservative caucuses, such as the Good News movement, the Institute for Religion and Democracy, the Mission Society for United Methodists, and the Confessing Movement – emerged as alternatives to the official structures of the denomination. These organizations, along with many pastors, congregations, and schools which aligned with them, appeared to be a kind of parallel universe within the larger UMC.

The new UMC denomination's attempt to reformulate doctrine also proved to be contentious. Noted theologian Albert C. Outler chaired a commission at the time of the merger that drafted a document entitled "Our Theological Task." Adopted by the UMC in 1972, the document stated that – because of the many challenges facing the church in the "new age" – it was imperative "to relate the gospel to the needs and aspirations of our contemporary world." Controversially, the statement went further in declaring that "in this task of reappraising and applying the gospel, theological pluralism should be recognized as a principle."[49]

"Our Theological Task" likewise reinterpreted John Wesley's approach to doctrinal development. It summarized Wesley's method by theorizing that the founder relied on four sources to work out his theology: scripture, tradition, reason, and experience – often reduced to a shorthand form as "the Wesleyan Quadrilateral." The document contended that, while Scripture should be considered as a "guideline for doctrine," the "point of departure" for one's theological reflection may just as often come from different criteria.[50] Some historical theologians later pointed out that Wesley never articulated his methodology in such a formulaic fourfold manner, and that he always prioritized the biblical witness over other theological sources. Outler was accused of accommodating too much to theological liberalism.

Given the dissatisfaction with "Our Theological Task," another commission (chaired by Richard P. Heitzenrater) revised the document in 1988 – this time presenting Wesley's theological method in such a way that it clearly described Scripture as "the primary source and criterion for Christian doctrine."[51]

This incident reminds us that one aspect of Wesleyan distinctiveness, described earlier, is the synthesis of seemingly opposing theological positions. Wesley and early American Methodists viewed this synthesis as consistent with a careful reading of the Bible and as the best theological foundation for effective evangelism. But in practice, and especially over a long time, mediating positions are difficult to hold. Historian Donald F. Durnbaugh interprets Methodism as the Christian tradition that hews most closely to the middle on many issues, but he cautions that "the middle ground is occupied by movements which are inherently unstable." While the Methodist and Holiness movements in the United States have certainly had their share of instability, they nevertheless can still declare that they are genuine heirs of John Wesley's vision to proclaim a vital Christian gospel to all people.[52]

METHODIST MEMBERSHIP

Determining the precise number of Americans who belong to the Methodist tradition is challenging because of indefiniteness regarding whether certain religious groups should count as being legitimately Wesleyan. There is no question, however, about the validity of well-established Wesleyan denominations; and so, for the purposes of an accurate compilation, the membership of the major churches that are unmistakably Methodist or Wesleyan-Holiness are the ones that have been tabulated.

Membership in the twenty most prominent Wesleyan, Methodist, and Holiness denominations in the United States, as of 2020, was 13,643,512. Fifty-six percent of that number (7,679,850) were United Methodists; 32 percent (4,300,601) were members of five historically Black Methodist churches (in order of size: the African Methodist Episcopal Church; the African Methodist Episcopal Church, Zion; the Christian Methodist Episcopal Church; the African Union Methodist Protestant Church; and the Union American Methodist Episcopal Church); and 12 percent (1,663,061) were members of fourteen major Holiness bodies.[53]

This overall compilation of Wesleyan, Methodist, and Holiness membership statistics can be analyzed further. We can be more specific, for example, regarding African-American Methodists. While African Americans are most prevalent in the historically Black Methodist denominations, they are also represented in other Wesleyan churches. Blacks constitute around 5 percent (approximately 400,000) of the membership of the UMC – the highest percentage of African Americans in any historically white mainline Protestant denomination.[54] African Americans also make up a sizable portion of one of the major Holiness denominations – the Church of God (Anderson); and another small Holiness group listed in this compilation, the Church of Christ, Holiness (with 12,960 members), is an historically Black denomination.

More information can also be drawn out regarding the Holiness denominations counted in these statistics. The Holiness groups numbered in this compilation are those that are of significant size and are explicitly Wesleyan in their statements of belief. The five largest Wesleyan-Holiness groups, in numerical order, are: the Church of the Nazarene (626,811); the Salvation Army (413,961); the Church of God, Anderson, Indiana (233,049); The Wesleyan Church (128,740); and the Free Methodist Church (110,000). The Wesleyan-Holiness denominations with memberships under 100,000 included in this tabulation, in order of size, are: the Missionary Church; the Church of the United Brethren in Christ; the Brethren in Christ Church ("River Brethren"); the Evangelical Church of North America; the Congregational Methodist Church; the Evangelical Congregational Church; the Church of Christ, Holiness; the Churches of Christ in Christian Union; and the Evangelical Methodist Church. One factor to consider in the compilation of data regarding Holiness churches is that the percentage of worship attendance to membership is much higher in Holiness denominations than it is in mainline Methodist denominations: in many Holiness congregations, worship attendance exceeds membership, while among mainline Methodist congregations, the opposite is generally the case.

Not included in this compilation are statistics from a wide assortment of very small split-off Holiness bodies, from which it is difficult to obtain membership data. While there are a large number of these breakoff groups, each group only has a small membership – none more than a few thousand – and thus the total number of their adherents is not sizable. Some of these smaller Holiness bodies, such as the Original Church of God (Sanctified) and the Mount Calvary Holy Church, are predominantly African American, while others are predominantly white. Many of the groups were founded in the twentieth century as schisms from larger Holiness denominations. About twenty-five of the predominantly white mini-denominations are associated with the "conservative Holiness movement"; nine of them belong to a loose fellowship known as the Interchurch Holiness Convention.

Also not included in this tabulation are a number of denominations strongly influenced by the nineteenth-century Holiness movement but not explicitly Wesleyan in their theology, such as the Christian and Missionary Alliance, the Evangelical Friends Church, the Mennonite Brethren Church, the Advent Christian Church, and the Seventh-Day Adventist Church. If the membership of those churches plus the conservative Holiness movement bodies were all added to the compilation, the full number of Wesleyan, Methodist, and Holiness adherents in the United States would increase by over 2 million, from 13.6 million members to a total of around 16 million members.

In addition, some denominations typically listed as "Pentecostal" also consider themselves to be Holiness, and therefore are (at least implicitly) Wesleyan. Specifically, these Pentecostal-Holiness denominations include the Pentecostal Holiness Church, the Church of God in Christ, the Church of God (Cleveland, Tennessee), the Church of God of Prophesy, and others. If we were to include the membership of those denominations, the total number of Wesleyans would be considerably higher. It is also important to note that most Wesleyan, Methodist, and Holiness denominations have extensive constituencies outside of America – in some cases much larger than the number of members within the United States.

METHODISTS TODAY

The variety of denominations that belong under the large umbrella of Wesleyanism in America demonstrates the religious and cultural breadth of the Methodist and Holiness traditions, a breadth that often mystifies outsiders – and sometimes insiders. In relation to American politics and society, the disposition of the Wesleyan movement has been (in the words of Methodist/Salvation Army songwriter Sidney Cox) "deep and wide."

Wesleyan wideness can be demonstrated, for instance, by examining the historically Black Methodist churches. These churches tend to align with the Democratic Party politically while espousing a range of views regarding social values. That is, Black Methodists typically champion issues of racial justice, which are regarded as liberal, but they often lean more conservative on issues of personal morality such as abortion and gay rights. Meanwhile, the Holiness bodies generally see themselves as theologically conservative or "evangelical" (though not in the Reformed sense of that term). These Holiness groups tend to align with the Republican party politically, and usually espouse traditional social values.

The comprehensiveness of the Wesleyan family of churches in the United States becomes even more bewildering when analyzing the UMC, the largest denomination in the tradition. The UMC is a "big tent, theologically" that includes the full gamut of views on social, political, and doctrinal issues.[55] Though the UMC is still one denomination (as of 2020), it contains within its ranks pastors and congregations who think of themselves as theologically liberal, conservative, and moderate. Indeed, though sociologists of religion consider the UMC to be a "mainline" denomination, a designation often correlated with theological liberalism, UMC members are certainly not uniformly liberal. A 2019 commissioned research survey of religious beliefs in the UMC discovered that 20 percent identified as progressive/liberal, 28 percent identified as moderate/centrist, and 44 percent identified as conservative/traditional. The plurality inclined toward conservative positions; and, in fact, the UMC was determined to be the most conservative leaning of the mainline denominations. Nevertheless, UMC members' overall religious persuasion manifested quite a bit of theological diversity. Such all-embracing expansiveness has been difficult to hold together within a single organization, and most observers expect the UMC to divide, with each of the resulting bodies becoming less broad theologically.[56]

If such a wide spectrum exists regarding religious beliefs within the UMC, the same is certainly true for political perspectives, which range from very liberal to very conservative, with many members placing themselves in the middle. To provide just one example of this political comprehensiveness: from 1993 to 1995, the following couples were all regular attendees of the same congregation in Washington, DC, Foundry UMC: George and Eleanor McGovern; Robert and Elizabeth Dole; and Bill and Hillary Clinton –representing liberal, center right, and center left partisan positions respectively. And for a total of sixteen years (1993–2009), two American presidents in a row – Bill Clinton and George W. Bush – attended United Methodist congregations, even though they hailed from opposite political parties.[57] Even more extreme political differences become apparent when recognizing that the UMC includes the likes of Jeff Sessions, a conservative white former Senator and Attorney General from Alabama, and Emanuel Cleaver II, a liberal African-American pastor, mayor, and Congressman from Missouri.

Similar comparisons could be made regarding the wide-ranging political views of other Methodist legislators, who constitute, in 2020, the third largest religious constituency (after Roman Catholics and Baptists) of members of Congress.

The UMC remains the most geographically dispersed of any US Protestant denomination; its churches are present in most counties nationwide. More United Methodist congregations exist than there are US post offices. And once we add the historically Black Methodist and Holiness churches, it is evident that the Wesleyan tradition represents a very broad swath of American society and a large percentage of American Protestantism. The Wesleyan family of churches, born as a renewal movement, seems intent on continuing its founder's mission to "spread scriptural holiness throughout the land."

NOTES

1 Roger Finke and Rodney Stark, *The Churching of America, 1776–2005* (New Brunswick, NJ: Rutgers University Press, 2005), 44–116, 121, 156–182; Winthrop S. Hudson, "The Methodist Age in America," *Methodist History* vol. 12 (April 1974), 3–15; C. C. Goen, "The Methodist Age in American Church History," *Religion in Life* vol. 34 (1965), 562–572.

2 Finke and Stark, *The Churching of America, 1776–2005*, 113–116; Nathan O. Hatch, "The Puzzle of American Methodism," *Church History* vol. 63, no. 2 (June 1994): 175–189; and John H. Wigger, *Taking Heaven by Storm: Methodism and the Rise of Popular Christianity in America* (New York: Oxford University Press, 1998).

3 On John Wesley's life set within its historical context, see Richard P. Heitzenrater, *John Wesley and the People Called Methodists* (Nashville: Abingdon, 1995).

4 On the life of George Whitefield, see Harry S. Stout, *Divine Dramatist: George Whitefield and the Rise of Modern Evangelicalism* (Grand Rapids, MI: Eerdmans, 1991).

5 For more comprehensive histories of American Methodism, see Russell E. Richey, Kenneth E. Rowe, and Jean Miller Schmidt, *The Methodist Experience in America: A History* (Nashville: Abingdon, 2010; and Frederick A. Norwood, *The Story of American Methodism* (Nashville: Abingdon, 1974).

6 Frederick E. Maser, *Robert Strawbridge, First American Circuit Rider* (Rutland, VT: Academy Books, 1983).

7 Luke 10:1.

8 See John H. Wigger, *American Saint: Francis Asbury and the Methodists* (New York: Oxford University Press, 2012).

9 John Telford, ed., *The Letters of the Rev. John Wesley*, vol. 7 (London: Epworth Press, 1931), 237–38.

10 Dee E. Andrews, *The Methodists and Revolutionary America, 1760–1800* (Princeton University Press, 2002).

11 John Wesley, "Thoughts upon Methodism," in *The Methodist Societies: History, Nature, and Design*, ed. Rupert E. Davies, vol. 9 of *The Bicentennial Edition of the Works of John Wesley* (Nashville: Abingdon, 1976), 527.

12 Douglas M. Strong, *Perfectionist Politics: Abolitionism and the Religious Tensions of American Democracy* (Syracuse, NY: Syracuse University Press, 1999), 33–37, 93–108.

13 Albert C. Outler, "Plundering the Egyptians," in *Theology in the Wesleyan Spirit* (Nashville: Discipleship Resources, 1994).

14 E. G. Rupp, *Principalities and Powers* (New York: Abingdon, 1952), 90; Paul Wesley Chilcote, *Recapturing the Wesleys' Vision: An Introduction to the Faith of John and Charles Wesley* (Downers Grove, IL: InterVarsity, 2004); Kenneth Collins, "The Method of John Wesley's Practical Theology Reconsidered," *Wesleyan and Methodist Studies* vol. 9, no. 2 (2017), 101–122.

15 D. A. Goodsell, "Methodism: A Flash or a Flame?" *Christian Advocate* vol. 48 (2 October 1873), 313.

16 Charles Wesley, "Come, Sinners to the Gospel Feast," (1747), in *The United Methodist Hymnal* (Nashville: The United Methodist Publishing House, 1989), 339.

17 Nathan O. Hatch, *The Democratization of American Christianity* (New Haven, CT: Yale University Press, 1991).

18 Harald Lindstrom, *Wesley and Sanctification: A Study in the Doctrine of Salvation* (Wilmore, KY: Francis Asbury Press, 1998); John L. Peters, *Christian Perfection and American Methodism* (New York: Abingdon, 1956).

19 Lester Ruth, *A Little Heaven Below: Worship at Methodist Quarterly Meetings* (Nashville: Kingswood, 2000).

20 Donald W. Dayton and Douglas M. Strong, *Rediscovering an Evangelical Heritage* (Grand Rapids, MI: Baker Academic, 2014), 119–149.

21 John Wesley, "The Nature, Design, and General Rules of the United Societies" (1743), in *Bicentennial Edition*, ed. Davies, vol. IX, 67–79.

22 See Russell E. Richey, *The Methodist Conference in America: A History* (Nashville: Kingswood, 1996); and Charles W. Ferguson, *Organizing to Beat the Devil: Methodists and the Making of America* (New York: Doubleday, 1971).

23 Dickson D. Bruce, Jr., *And They All Sang Hallelujah: Plain-Folk Camp-Meeting Religion, 1800–1845* (Knoxville: University of Tennessee Press, 1974); Russell E. Richey, "From Quarterly to Camp Meeting: A Reconsideration of Early American Methodism," *Methodist History* vol. 23, no. 1 (July 1985), 199–213.

24 Albert J. Raboteau, "The Black Experience in American Evangelicalism," in *The Evangelical Tradition in America*, ed. Leonard I. Sweet (Macon, GA: Mercer University Press, 1984), 182–186; Douglas M. Strong, "A Real Christian Is an Abolitionist: Conversion and Antislavery Activism in Early

American Methodism," in *Conversion in the Wesleyan Tradition*, ed.
Kenneth J. Collins and John H. Tyson (Nashville: Abingdon, 2001), 69–82.

25 Dennis C. Dickerson, *The African Methodist Episcopal Church: A History* (Cambridge: Cambridge University Press, 2020).

26 Carol V. R. George, *Segregated Sabbaths: Richard Allen and the Rise of Independent Black Churches, 1760–1840* (New York: Oxford University Press, 1973).

27 Donald G. Mathews, *Slavery and Methodism* (Princeton, NJ: Princeton University Press, 2016).

28 Harold E. Raser, *Phoebe Palmer: Her Life and Thought* (Lewiston, NY: Mellen, 1987).

29 Howard A. Snyder, *Populist Saints: B.T. and Ellen Roberts and the First Free Methodists* (Grand Rapids, MI: Eerdmans, 2006).

30 Melvin E. Dieter, *The Holiness Revival of the Nineteenth Century*, 2nd ed. (Metuchen, NJ: Scarecrow Press, 1996).

31 Maxine Haines and Lee Haines, *Celebrate Our Daughters: One Hundred Fifty Years of Women's Wesleyan Ministry* (Indianapolis: Wesleyan Publishing House, 2004).

32 Strong, *Perfectionist Politics*, 44–45, 55–56.

33 William L. Andrews, *Sisters of the Spirit: Three Black Women's Autobiographies of the Nineteenth Century* (Bloomington: Indiana University Press, 1986); Susie C. Stanley, *Feminist Pillar of Fire: The Life of Alma White* (Eugene, OR: Wipf and Stock, 2006); Dayton and Strong, *Rediscovering*, 135–149.

34 Donald W. Dayton, *Theological Roots of Pentecostalism* (Grand Rapids, MI: Baker Academic, 1987).

35 A. Gregory Schneider, *The Way of the Cross Leads Home: The Domestication of American Methodism* (Bloomington: Indiana University Press, 1993).

36 Hatch, "The Puzzle of American Methodism," 180, 186, 188.

37 *New York Evening Post*, cited in *Methodist Magazine and Review* vol. 52 (July–December 1900), 189, and in *Public Opinion* vol. 28, no. 23 (June 7, 1900), 708. Historians have frequently attributed this (or similar) quotes to Grant himself, but (thanks to the research of theological librarian Steve Perisho) there is no evidence of such a statement being made prior to 1900. The Biblical allusion is to 1 Corinthians 13:13.

38 See Richard Carwardine, "Methodists, Politics, and the Coming of the American Civil War," *Church History* vol. 69, no. 3 (September 2000), 578–609.

39 Dana L. Robert, *American Women in Mission* (Macon, GA: Mercer University Press, 1997); Mark R. Teasdale, *Methodist Evangelism, American Salvation: The Home Missions of the Methodist Episcopal Church, 1860–1920* (Eugene, OR: Pickwick, 2014).

40 David Bundy, "The Legacy of William Taylor," *International Bulletin of Missionary Research* vol. 18, no. 4 (October 1994): 172–176; Robert G. Tuttle, Jr., *In Our Time: The Life and Ministry of E. Stanley Jones* (2019).

41 Christopher H. Evans, *The Social Gospel in American Religion: A History* (New York: New York University Press, 2017).

42 Jennifer Woodruff Tait, *The Poisoned Chalice: Eucharistic Grape Juice and Common-Sense Realism in Victorian Methodism* (Tuscaloosa: University of Alabama Press, 2011), 8–19.

43 Douglas M. Strong, "Borden Parker Bowne and Henry Clay Morrison: Conflicting Conceptions of Twentieth Century Methodism," in Henry H. Knight III, ed. *From Aldersgate to Azusa Street: Wesleyan, Holiness, and Pentecostal Visions of the New Creation* (Eugene: Wipf and Stock, 2010), 297–306.

44 William B. McClain, *Black People in the Methodist Church* (Nashville: Abingdon, 1985).

45 James Cone, *Black Theology and Black Power* (Maryknoll, NY: Orbis, 1969).

46 *The Book of Discipline of The United Methodist Church, 1972* (Nashville: The United Methodist Publishing House, 1972), 86 (para. 72.c).

47 Zac Baker, "Methodists Declare Their Intention to Ecclesiastical Disobedience by Marrying LGBT Couples," October 17, 2011, www .reconcilingworks.org/methodists-declare-their-intention-to-ecclesiastical-disobedience-by-marrying-lgbt-couples/.

48 Richard Ostling, "Why Is the Large United Methodist Church Splitting Up?" January 12, 2020, www.patheos.com/blogs/religionqanda/2020/01/why-is-the-large-united-methodist-church-splitting-up/.

49 *Discipline of The United Methodist Church,* 1972, 68–69 (para. 70).

50 *Discipline of The United Methodist Church,* 1972, 75–79 (para. 70); Ted A. Campbell, ed., *Albert C. Outler as Historian and Interpreter of the Christian Tradition* (Anderson, IN: Bristol Books, 2003), 9–17.

51 *The Book of Discipline of The United Methodist Church: 1988* (Nashville: The United Methodist Publishing House, 1988), 81 (para. 69).

52 Donald F. Durnbaugh, *The Believer's Church: The History and Character of Radical Protestantism* (New York: Macmillan, 1968), 30–31; Hatch, "The Puzzle of American Methodism."

53 The data for this compilation is derived from a variety of sources: Roger E. Olson et al., *Handbook of Denominations in the United States,* 14th ed. (Nashville: Abingdon, 2018); "Yearbook of Churches," online at http:/ yearbookofchurches.org; Association of Religion Data Archives, online at thearda.com; World Christian Database; email correspondence and telephone conversations with denomination administrators of the African Methodist Episcopal Zion Church, the Wesleyan Church, and the Churches of Christ in Christian Union; and denominational websites.

54 Ostling, "Why Is the Large United Methodist Church Splitting Up?"

55 Sam Hodges, "What Do United Methodists Really Believe?" February 12, 2019, www.umnews.org/en/news/what-do-united-methodists-really-believe.

56 Hodges, "What Do United Methodists Really Believe?"

57 Douglas M. Strong, "Exploring Both the Middle and the Margins: Locating Methodism within American Religious History," in *Doctrines and Discipline*, ed. Dennis M. Campbell, William B. Lawrence, and Russell E. Richey (Nashville: Abingdon, 1999), 233–241.

24 Pentecostalism

CHRIS E. W. GREEN

INTRODUCTION

In 1968, the Assemblies of God (AG) published a small book by David Womack entitled *The Wellsprings of the Pentecostal Movement*. In it, Womack, then the foreign missions editor for the AG, likened the movement to a "tender, young tree," smaller than the other trees but far healthier, its roots fed by an ancient subterranean stream. As he phrases it, "the Pentecostal Movement has complicated roots, but it is the taproot plunging deeply into the New Testament Church that gives it its distinctive life."[1] Shifting metaphors, Womack argues that the fire of apostolic Christianity, which had started to flicker after the death of the apostles and flamed out altogether under the rule of Constantine, had sparked again in the preaching of the Protestant Reformers and the ministries of their successors in the revivalist movements that followed – and especially the Holiness revivals in America. In God's providence, the flame of apostolic faith had finally burst into full flower again with the rise of the modern Pentecostal renewal.[2] For Womack, as for many of his fellow Pentecostals at the time, the Pentecostal movement differs not only from "dead" Christianities but also from all previous revivalist movements, because, unlike them, it represents a full and (hopefully) lasting, rather than a partial and temporary, return to the patterns of apostolic experience, belief, and practice.[3]

In January 1916, the AG's magazine, *The Weekly Evangel*, ran the first of a series of articles by B. F. Lawrence under the ambitious and ironic title: "Apostolic Faith Restored: A History of the Present Latter Rain Outpouring of the Holy Spirit Known as the Apostolic or Pentecostal Movement." Lawrence begins that first article by celebrating the many Pentecostal revivals springing up all around the world. In little more than a decade, he says, hundreds of thousands of people have come to Christ; tens of thousands have been miraculously healed from all kinds of diseases, including lunacy and demon-possession; and hundreds if not thousands have been caught up in the same missionary zeal and charismatic power that impelled the apostles into mission after the Day of Pentecost. Lawrence also contends that the Pentecostal renewal stands out from other revivals, in both reach and impact, because it, unlike other Christians movements and traditions, owes nothing to "man-made" teachings and practices. In other words, because they have thrown off the "shackles of custom" and launched out into "ways so old that moderns call them new," Pentecostals can fulfill their last-days calling:

> The older denominations have a past which is their own in a peculiar sense; they can trace the beginnings of their church and the course of its history subsequent to its foundation. The time between the beginning and the present has been sufficient to establish precedent, create habit, formulate custom. In this way they have become possessed of a two-fold inheritance, a two-fold guide of action, a two-fold criterion of doctrine – the New Testament and the church position. The Pentecostal Movement has no such history; it leaps the intervening years crying, *"Back to Pentecost."*[4]

Womack's account, like Lawrence's, is essentially hagiographical. It both dramatically understates the complications and intricacies of the movement's history, and dramatically overstates the movement's unity and likeness to the ancient churches. It identifies only two types of Pentecostalism – one intellectual and reserved (White?); the other ecstatic and emotional (Black?). Tellingly, nothing of significance is said about the many rifts and disputes that divided the earliest Pentecostals in the United States, including the virulent racism and the ruptures along racial lines, the "new light" controversy that gave rise to the Oneness movement, or the bitter conflicts over the doctrine of sanctification. And nothing is said about the scandals that shook the movement at home and abroad over the years. As much as anything else, then, Womack's work serves as a testament to the fact that Pentecostals are tempted to read their own history, as well as the history of the apostolic communities, naively and triumphalistically. Just so, it is a reminder of the need for more comprehensive, incisive, and searchingly honest accounts of the history of the Pentecostal movement in America.[5]

NOT A TREE, A RAINFOREST

No doubt, Pentecostalism spread quickly, reaching perhaps as many as fifty nations by the end of the first decade of the twentieth century.[6] But contrary to popular accounts, it did not emerge at a single place at a certain time. And wherever it did emerge, it did not arise from nothing, but in particular cultural contexts and under certain socioeconomic, political, and philosophical conditions. Womack treats Charles Fox Parham's Bethel Bible College in Topeka, Kansas as the originating center of the global movement, and the growth of the movement as steady and seamless. He refers to the revival in Los Angeles only in passing, as one of many places to which the movement spread. In 1989, the AG published a statement celebrating the Azusa Street Mission, rather than Parham's Bible school, as the original "epicenter" of the worldwide movement. In point of fact, however, there had been many "outbreaks" prior to the events at Parham's Bible school, as many of the earliest Pentecostals knew full well. Lawrence, for example, identifies "Pentecostal" revivals in Ohio, Rhode Island, Tennessee, North Carolina, and South Dakota, among other places in the USA, as well as around the world:

> There have been numerous reports from many places regarding individuals who spoke in tongues. For instance, a woman in Nebraska a member of the Baptist Church, was attending a Methodist protracted meeting when, during the preaching, she began to shout, and wound up by speaking in other tongues. Again, one of my friends tells me that her mother heard many of the Quakers in Canada speak in tongues sixty years or more ago.[7]

And Frank Bartleman, in his eyewitness account of the Azusa Street revival, announced that Pentecostalism was "rocked in the cradle of little Wales ... 'brought up' in India and then became 'full grown' in Los Angeles."[8] Now, scholars acknowledge what he and Lawrence observed at the beginning: the global Pentecostal movement emerged in different places at more or less the same time and under wildly varying circumstances.[9] Thus, even fifty years ago, when Womack's book was first published, the name "Pentecostalism" already referred not to a single, coherent movement but to a cluster or family of movements. Not a tree, but a (tropical) forest.

And the differences, divergences, and fractures have only multiplied as the movement has grown. According to Todd Johnson of Gordon-Conwell's Center for the Study of Global Christianity (CSGC), there were just over 1 million Pentecostals worldwide in 1910. By 2010, there were more than 614 million "Renewalists," constituting more than one-quarter of the global Christian population, appearing in more than 9,000 different ethnic groups, speaking some 8,000 languages, and gathered in thousands upon thousands of denominations, networks, associations, and local communities.[10] And this diversity is not only ethnic and racial, cultural and socio-economic. There are also serious – and, in some cases, seemingly irreconcilable – differences amongst Pentecostals on doctrinal formulation, theological method, the interpretation of Scripture, ecclesial authority, institutional structure, religious ethos, devotional and liturgical practices, ethical commitments, ecumenical and interreligious engagement, political identification and participation, etc. Over time, some of these differences have widened and deepened and others have faded into relative insignificance as new problems, seemingly more insistent and menacing, have emerged.

Facing the phenomenal diversity of the movement, it has become standard for scholars to refer to three broad types of Pentecostalism: first, *Classical Pentecostalism*, which emerged from the overflow of the Azusa Street revival in Los Angeles (1906–1909) and led to the founding of denominations like the AG, the Church of God (COG), and the Church of God in Christ (COGIC); second, the *Charismatic Movement*, which arose in the early 1960s and took shape within long-established Christian traditions, both Catholic and Protestant; and third, *Neo-Pentecostalism* or the *Neo-Charismatic Movement* (sometimes labeled lower-case P *pentecostalism*), which constitutes the post-denominational and largely indigenous "Third Wave" of renewal.[11] But even these categories, and the generalizations they depend upon, can easily obscure more than they illuminate. Hence, the ongoing exponential growth and burgeoning diversity makes it increasingly difficult, if not outright impossible, to provide an adequate definition or description of global Pentecostalism. As Anderson explains,

> Because of the great diversity within Pentecostal and Charismatic churches, it is very difficult to find some common unifying features or distinctiveness by which they might be defined. It is an extremely precarious task in the first place, as it gives the one who attempts it the responsibility to see that justice is done to those who might not fit precisely into this definition. Pentecostals have defined themselves by so many paradigms that diversity itself has become a primary defining characteristic of their identity.[12]

Classical Pentecostals presently stand as a minority in the movement at large, making up less than a fifth of the total population of Pentecostals. In 2010, Johnson estimated 6 million Classical Pentecostals in the USA – a majority of whom are Black – compared with 21 million Charismatics and a staggering 48 million Neo-Pentecostals/Neo-Charismatics. Tellingly, a majority of the largest and most influential Pentecostal churches and ministries (including, for example, those of T. D. Jakes and A. R. Bernard) are independent. Over time, a number of them (including, for example, Hillsong and Bethel) have separated from their parent denomination, signaling a shift away from the concerns that grounded and oriented the Classical denominations. And a majority of denominational Pentecostals are following their lead, adapting their teachings and imitating their patterns of ministry. This is a testament to what Arlene Sánchez Walsh calls the "fractious nature" of the movement, which is radically competitive and conflictual because it is "quintessentially American." And, as Johnson explains, it is a reminder that the "Third Wave" of renewal happened only in the breaking free from denominational strictures/structures:

> Since 1945 thousands of schismatic or other independent Charismatic churches have come out of the Pentecostal and Charismatic movements; these independents now number more than the first two waves combined. They consist of evangelicals and other Christians who, unrelated or no longer related to the Pentecostal or Charismatic Renewals, have become filled with the Spirit, or empowered or energized by the Spirit, and have experienced the Spirit's supernatural and miraculous ministry (though usually without recognizing a baptism in the Spirit separate from conversion); who exercise gifts of the Spirit (with much less emphasis on tongues, as optional or even absent or unnecessary) and emphasize signs and wonders, supernatural miracles and power encounters; and who leave their mainline non-pentecostal denominations but also do not identify themselves as either Pentecostals or Charismatics. In a number of countries, they exhibit Pentecostal and Charismatic phenomena but combine this with a rejection of Pentecostal terminology.[13]

But Johnson's account, helpful as it is, does not quite do justice to the movement's dense and elaborate complexities. Thanks in large part to the effects of dramatically shifting demographics – the US population doubled from 1950 to 2010, in part because nearly 60 million immigrants entered the USA during that time, mostly from Latin America and Asia (many of whom are Pentecostals reared in forms of neo-Pentecostal spirituality and theology) – as well as to the ideological and attitudinal cross-pollination that occurs via social media, television, and online ministries, the formal doctrinal positions and conventional practices of the Classic Pentecostal denominations are no longer a reliable guide to the experiences, views, or habits of particular congregations or individual believers within their churches, if indeed they ever were.

For example, most US Pentecostal denominations continue to maintain formally the doctrine of initial evidence, but in practice the vast
majority of their members never speak in tongues and do not espouse the
doctrine as binding in anything like the traditional sense. And Amos Yong,
surveying the landscape of contemporary Pentecostal scholarship, distinguishes the Cleveland School from the Springfield School (in the USA) and
the Birmingham School (in the UK). Other scholars, following his lead,
have spoken also of the Regent School. But even among those who recognize these or similar schools of thought, there is no widespread agreement
on their defining features.[14] All of this is to say that it is virtually impossible to overstate the diversity within the family of the American
Pentecostal/Renewal movements.[15] And at the risk of overextending the
metaphor, it could be argued that in the tropical forest that is
Pentecostalism, each tree now differs in one way or another from its kind,
because all the trees have been engrafted, either naturally or artificially. As
a result, it is impossible not only to determine the exact borders of the forest
but also even to fully classify the various kinds of trees in the forest with
their unique root systems, branches, leaves, shoots, and fruits. And, as
Anderson suggests, this diversity is anything but accidental or meaningless.

WHAT MAKES PENTECOSTALISM PENTECOSTAL? IDENTIFYING ESSENCE, ESSENTIALS, AND DISTINCTIVES

Some have argued "Pentecostal" should be taken as a noun, not an adjec-
tive. But they do not agree on what constitutes authentic Pentecostalism
or what belongs to its essence –and there seems to be no way to arrive at
a consensus. Terry Cross, for example, much like Harvey Cox, argues that
experience, not theology, sets Pentecostals apart from other Christian
traditions.[16] Ken Archer, following Steven Land and John Christopher
Thomas, disagrees, calling for Pentecostals to maintain a distinctive theology and a peculiar theological method focused on the Fivefold Gospel
and the narrative of the via salutis.[17] But of course "experience" is impos-
sibly tricky. And Archer readily admits both that his proposal is prescriptive, not descriptive, and that it provides an articulation for only one of the
many possible forms of Pentecostalism. It is perhaps best, then, to think of
Pentecostalism as *almost* – but not quite – a new confessional tradition.
As Justo Gonzalez says,

> While in many ways Pentecostalism has almost become a new con-
> fessional family, its impact is seen in every other Christian

confession. Part of this impact is resulting in renewed attention to the doctrine of the Holy Spirit and to eschatology. Significantly, although many see a distance and even enmity between the Pentecostal awakening and the various theologies advocating social and political liberation, the two coincide in their emphasis on hope as central to the Christian faith. Thus, it would appear in the near future theology will be much concerned with eschatology, the doctrine of the Holy Spirit, and the relationship between the two.[18]

Speaking of the Charismatic Renewal in particular, Peter Hocken identified nine "constant characteristics," all which he believes "can be found at each stage and in all [the Renewal's] different manifestations": a focus on Jesus; a flow of praise; a thirst for the Scriptures; an expectation of God's present-day speaking and acting; an urgency in mission; an awareness of the powers of evil; the use of charismatic gifts, including tongues, healing, and prophecy; a fervent expectation of the Parousia; and a commitment to the renewal of the churches through the life-giving power of the Spirit.[19] Other Pentecostals share most if not all of these characteristics. All of this is to say that Pentecostals share an unusual devotion to the centrality and supremacy of Jesus and his story, and a belief that "tradition," including dogmatic tradition, is always answerable to "a distinctive spirituality that focuses on the presence, manifestations, and power of the Holy Spirit."[20] In other words, Pentecostal spirituality, at least in many of its most characteristic forms, is a kind of mysticism.[21] But not a mysticism of withdrawal – a mysticism of mediation and intermediation. As Daniela Augustine contends, "The Spirit uplifts the Christified human life as the visible means of invisible grace toward peacebuilding and reconciliation, economic justice, sociopolitical inclusion, and ecological renewal. Indeed, the healing of the entire cosmos starts from within hallowed, Spirit-saturated humanity."[22] This is the wisdom symbolized by the altar call, which finds its center in the fulness of God's presence, and its boundaries in "the uttermost parts of the earth."

These twin commitments to mysticism and mission hold even across irreconcilable doctrinal, liturgical, and ministerial differences. How can this be? Because Pentecostals/Renewalists find commonality in a shared openness to the Spirit and a shared admiration for Jesus – as can be seen, for example, in the likeness of Oneness and Trinitarian, as well as Black and White Pentecostal liturgical expressions and ministerial practices. In this regard, what distinguishes Pentecostals from other Christians is primarily their sense of what this openness and admiration means for the ordinary Christian life – the life to which every Christian, regardless of age or sex or education or ability, can and should aspire. They hold that each and every Christian is called to live, as Jesus did, a life of ever-deepening and ever-widening mystical communion and charismatic ministry in the Spirit. In the broadest terms, then, we can say that all Pentecostals are missionally mystical and mystically missional, devoted simultaneously to fulfilling the Great Commission and to the fulfilling experience of God in prayer and praise.[23] We can perhaps also say that Pentecostals are peculiarly convinced both that the Spirit empowers believers for these mutually determined tasks and that supernatural experiences, therefore, can and should be basic to the normal Christian life. Of course, in some sense all Christians hold these convictions in one form or another, but Pentecostals, it seems, afford them an unusual importance and centrality.

This devotion to Jesus and its elemental openness to the Spirit takes many forms. Walter Hollenweger found that Pentecostals' love for Jesus was characteristically a "'blood and wounds mysticism,' an absorption in the suffering and death of Jesus, and a looking forward to the coming marriage feast with Jesus," all of which come into focus at the Lord's Table.[24] Certainly, many Pentecostals at one time shared this agonizing love for the wounded Jesus. As Steve Land explains, they understood the call to holiness as a call to the "moral integration" that made possible "a complete yieldedness and availability to God."[25] In the words of an early Wesleyan Pentecostal (perhaps William Seymour?):

> It is sweet to have the promise of Jesus and the character of Jesus wrought out in our lives and hearts by the power of the blood and the Holy Ghost, and to have that same love and that same meekness and humility manifested in our lives for His character is love ... Dear loved ones, we must have that pure love that comes down from heaven, love that is willing to suffer loss, love that is not puffed up, not easily provoked, but gentle, meek, and humble. We are accounted as sheep for the slaughter daily. We are crucified to self, the world, the flesh, and everything, that we may bear in our body the dying of the Lord Jesus, that our joy may be full even as He is full.[26]

But even then, not all Pentecostals understood their relationship to Jesus in these terms. And eventually, many Neo-Pentecostals/Neo-Charismatics in the so-called Third Wave reacted hard against these emphases, advocating instead what might be called "signs and wonders mysticism," concerned not with Jesus's suffering and death, but with his miraculous power, and anticipating not the Parousia but the in-breaking of God's kingdom in the here and now.

For some in the Word of Faith and New Apostolic Reformation movements, the emphasis falls not so much on yieldedness and availability to God as on the rights and powers of the believer who has the Spirit of God at her or his disposal.[27] These sensibilities are evident, for example, in Bill Johnson's claims in his 2014 book, *Experience the Impossible: Simple Ways to Unleash Heaven's Power on Earth*: "Faith does not come from striving; it comes from surrender." "The presence of the Lord positions us for miracles." "It is illegal to enjoy the presence of the Lord and not conquer something." "If those who do not walk with God can do miracles, then those who walk with God are without excuse." "Worshippers are positioned by God to summon nations to their destinies." "When we submit the things of God to the mind of man, unbelief and religion are the results. When we submit the mind of man to the things of God, miracles and the renewed mind are the results."[28]

R. G. Robins, among others, argues that the extended family of American Pentecostal movements is bound together by its roots in the Holiness movement in and from which it materialized. And, as Robins describes, the Holiness movement – a kind of "heroic Christianity" inspired by variations on the themes of Wesley's optimism of grace and his doctrine of entire sanctification – spread like wildfire in the years before the Civil War through the teachings of Phoebe Palmer and Charles Finney, among others.[29] In the half-century after the war, as the nation's population exploded (from 30 million in 1865 to 100 million by 1915), and as immigrants and rural migrants flooded America's cities and towns (New York City's population grew from less than 1 million in 1865 to more than 4 million by 1915; Chicago's, from less than 500,000 to more than 2 million; and Los Angeles's ballooned from no more than 5,000 to nearly 500,000 in the same period), a renewed and defiantly enthusiastic Holiness movement emerged to meet the nation's rising needs.

This renewed movement was many-splendored, galvanized by a number of never-quite-reconciled extremes and fractional contradictions, simultaneously populist and elitist, conservative and progressive, traditional and innovative, optimistic and apocalyptic, legalistic and antinomian. Holiness folk devoted themselves to living with what Wesley had called "catholic spirit," appealing to common spiritual experiences and moral commitments as the basis for broad ecclesial coalitions, seeking a transcendent unity of all true Christians. But precisely for that reason, they, and their successors in the global Pentecostal movements, found themselves caught up in endless controversies and schisms. Their intrepid efforts toward unity, as well as the upshot of their disputes, carried enormous public consequence. They championed "old time religion." Pentecostals, following the lights of the Holiness movements, obsessed with shaking off any "tradition" that restricted their freedom to move into a brighter, freer future. Many were drawn to John Nelson Darby's dispensationalism and similar "end-times" teachings. Not only did these teachings and the interpretive methods they assumed provide a virtual experience of reconciliation through the practice of harmonizing obscure passages of Scripture, but they also afforded Pentecostals a theological framework or grammar for making sense of history and their place in it.[30]

A quintessentially American frontier-mindedness led Holiness folk and then the Pentecostals to talk and act in ways that often unsteadied – but for a number of reasons only rarely subverted or actually overturned – societal norms. Women took prominent positions alongside men in more or less every region of the country. Still, they continued to face resistance to full ordination in many associations.[31] In the same way, the most radical reaches of the Holiness movement were also the most racially integrated. But many in the Holiness movement regarded such concern for racial integration nothing more than a distraction, if not outright shameful, and a betrayal of the church's true purpose. Others appealed to the discriminatory logic of the sanctified life as proof that God requires racial hierarchy. And even those who advocated racial integration in worship did not usually support full racial equality in every aspect of public life. All to say, then, Robins is at best half right: Holiness preaching challenged *aspects* of Victorian domesticity, often forcefully, but rarely if ever at its core.

From the beginning, Pentecostalism, formed in the matrix of Holiness spirituality, shared the extreme many-sidedness. Like their parents and older siblings in the wider Holiness movement, early Pentecostals were in a number of ways "countercultural." But even while they shared this message, they disagreed fundamentally on its meaning. For example, at the beginning of the twentieth century, Charles Parham and William Seymour agreed in repudiating William Durham's "finished work" teaching, although it is not clear that they actually understood it. At the same time, Parham, an outspoken supporter of the Ku Klux Klan (KKK) and an unrepentant white supremacist, condemned the interracial character of the Azusa Street missions as evil.[32] For him, "true Pentecostalism" consisted in the sanctifying and sealing work of the Spirit to establish the racial hierarchy God had eternally purposed for the flourishing of creation in the "last days" of history. Seymour agreed with Parham against Durham that believers must be entirely sanctified, subsequent to salvation, before they could receive the baptism of the Spirit. And he also affirmed Parham's belief in the end-time outpouring of the Spirit, as well as the complete restoration of the Pentecostal experience. But he held that the true "evidence" of the Spirit was neighbor-love, not tongues-speech. Just so, he remained committed to his integralist vision to the end – even after Durham, as Parham earlier had done, tried to assume leadership of the Azusa Street Mission, not on racial but on doctrinal grounds.[33]

Womack, typically, says nothing of these conflicts, but the evidence is clear: the Pentecostal movement from its beginnings was conflicted. Indeed, the movement was always, everywhere, pluriform and in dispute. Arguably, it was that very volatile intermixture, and the conflictedness and unpredictability that resulted from it, that afforded the movement its peculiar liveliness. As Harvey Cox argued, Pentecostalism grows because it is adaptable.[34] And it is adaptable because it was formed in divergences and for adaptations. So, once again, Robins turns out to be half right: the extended family of Pentecostalism is bound together not only by its roots in the Holiness movement but also by its intentional uprooting from and reaction against that movement's defining habits and convictions.

THE POWER OF THE SPIRIT OR THE SPIRIT OF POWER-STRUGGLES: THE FUTURE OF PENTECOSTALISM IN AMERICA

In all of these ways, as well as others, American Pentecostalism, like the American Holiness movement, was and is unmistakably "American" – even in its severest "countercultural" and "otherworldly" expressions. Nimi Wariboko, Walter G. Muelder Professor of Social Ethics in Boston University's School of Theology, argues that "being Pentecostal in America means that your very rationality is a problem." The Pentecostal believer, he says, appears to others as "a throwback to a bygone world." As a result, Pentecostals as a group are held in suspicion, if not treated with derision. Ordinary Pentecostals are regularly shamed and marginalized and everyday Pentecostal theology is "summarily rejected as incoherent, unintelligible, foolish, or even poisonous."[35] But Wariboko writes as an African Pentecostal who works at a large university in a major Northeastern city. His account does not ring true for, say, White middle-class Pentecostals who live in the South or the Midwest, especially those who work in politically and theologically conservative institutions, which often have more in common with fundamentalist evangelicalism than they do with historical Pentecostalism. This can be seen, for example, in their ways of reading Scripture and their understanding of water baptism and Holy Communion, both of which depart sharply from the views of early Pentecostal movement in the USA and UK.[36] Thus, even many of the Pentecostals who would agree with Wariboko's overall sense that Pentecostals are sidelined and disrespected by their fellow Americans would reject outright his account of the "plain Pentecostal life" because it is insufficiently biblicist and inadequately "conservative."

Wariboko proposes that "the Pentecostal principle" is "the capacity to begin."[37] Thanks to grace, God's action in the world, new possibilities are always emerging, presenting themselves to those who are ready to act on them. Similarly, James K. A. Smith argues that the "social imaginary" distinction to Pentecostalism is identifiable by its "radical openness to God, and in particular openness to God doing something differently or new."[38] But, as has been true from the first, this openness to and readiness for God's surprises is shared by communities who disagree, to one degree or another, on virtually every relevant theological or ethical issue. What is more, as David Daniels reminds us, these communities are plotted along the USA's defining cultural and political fault lines. Demographic projections indicate that the number of Pentecostals in America will continue to grow. Thanks in large part to new diasporas made possible by immigration, Pentecostals by 2050 will almost certainly play a leading role in American life. But it remains to be seen whether that Pentecostalism (or, better, those Pentecostalisms) will be more than a mere reflection of already-determined American differences and rivalries.[39]

From its earliest beginnings in the USA, Pentecostalism was a movement of the poor and for the poor. And because the poor always suffer worst in public crises, a century ago, Pentecostals found themselves at the center of the Spanish flu epidemic.[40] However, now, in the midst of the current Coronavirus epidemic, many Pentecostals in North America work at a remove from the poor, both geographically and spiritually, which leaves them out of touch with the material and spiritual needs of those they are called to serve first. Also at the beginning, a significant number of early Pentecostal leaders in the USA pressed for racial integration and the full inclusion of women in ministry, as well as establishing Bible schools and outreach ministries for "the least of these," including orphanages, soup kitchens, and healing houses. For them, these social justice ministries were inseparably bound up with the call to ends-of-the-earth evangelism and the higher life of prayer.[41]

Over time, however, those commitments have by and large disinte-
grated, at least for the majority of White Pentecostals in the Classical
and Third Wave families. Now, as Pentecostalism grows and its social
influence increases, its public responsibilities loom larger and larger. If it
is to be a mature movement as well as a vital one, and if it is to be
a liberating and healing presence in American society, especially for
the most vulnerable and disadvantaged, then leaders across the movement must find a way to nurture the shared spiritual depth, theological
soundness, ministerial competence, communal health, and institutional
integrity needed to do the difficult but necessary long-term work. This is
the "mature Pentecostalism" Cheryl Bridges Johns, among others, has
called for.[42]

Considering possible futures, Daniels predicts that "the North
American pentecostal-charismatic movement will be shaped by new
diasporas, transnational denominations, multiracial organizations, an
inclusive politics of race, and post-secularity."[43] And with those shifts
in mind, he raises a number of probing questions, asking why White
Pentecostals have opted to align so totally with the Christian Right, and
what hinders them from sharing the socioeconomic and political concerns of Black Pentecostals. He also wonders whether it is possible for
Black and White Pentecostals to work with other Americans to build
a more just and peaceful society, and how such a shift in thinking and
practice might be brought about. Facing the future, American
Pentecostals need to answer questions about their past and present
commitments. Moreover, if they hope to answer them well, they need
to return to the core conviction of William Seymour, a son of slaves and
one of the first fathers of the Pentecostal movement:

> The Pentecostal power, when you sum it all up, is just more of God's
> love. If it does not bring more love, it is simply a counterfeit. Pentecost
> means to live right in the 13th chapter of First Corinthians, which is
> the standard ... Pentecost makes us love Jesus more and love our
> brothers more. It brings us all into one common family.[44]

Womack's book championed an idealistic vision of Pentecostalism as
the last, best hope in America's fight against "extreme liberalism," and
Christianity's fight against "the syncretism manifested in the
Ecumenical Movement," and "the disease of separation from apostolic
sources."[45] But if American Pentecostals hope to fulfill their responsibilities as a Spirit-empowered movement, and not to splinter along the
cultural fault lines as it seems they are already at risk of doing, then
they must body forth the wisdom of Christlike love, as Seymour

recognized so clearly. And they must do so not in order to secure their own future or to preserve a preferred way of life, but in order to bear witness to the promise of Pentecost as the coming of God not for the sake of Christians and their churches but for the sake of others – for the sake of the world.

CONCLUSION

Early Pentecostals sometimes referred to Pentecost as the "outburst of love" that drew humanity into God's fellowship with God. Bishop J. H. King, for example, argues that we can love as Jesus loves because, thanks to the Spirit, "the Father's heart is in the Son and the heart of the Son is in us." Thanks to the indwelling of the Spirit, "the unity existing in Godhead is reproduced in us, and the fellowship that is enjoyed between the Father and the Son is imparted to us." The Spirit, who proceeds "from the Father to the Son," is a divine current "made to include us": the Spirit "proceeds and flows through us, establishing the same conditions, and producing the same results."[46]

In March 1910, Charles F. Hettiaratchy, a native of Ceylon (now Sri Lanka), delivered a sermon on 1 Corinthians 13 in Chicago's Stone Church. He acknowledged the experience of "wonderful and strange manifestations" and celebrated the fact that "the Lord seems to be restoring the gifts that have been lost from the church." But he warned his hearers that "in our ecstasy, in our enthusiasm, in our zeal, we seem to forget the 'more excellent way.'" And he remarks that many in Ceylon and India pray for the white missionaries to return to their homes. "It will, no doubt, surprise you to know that many good Christian people in our country have been praying the Lord to return some of the missionaries to their home land because they are not qualified; they are a hindrance to the work of God." These missionaries are concerned with leading the missions and forcing the "heathens" to accept their point of view. But the essence of Christian ministry is not leadership but service born of love, not giftedness but patience, and the readiness to forgive.

> Don't let us say we have love if, when some little opposition comes, we get upset and lose that love. How do you get on with the upsets? How do you meet the persecutions? How did you treat men when they reviled you and said all manner of evil against you falsely? Did you love them? Did you pray for them? Did you bless them? Did you have anything in your heart against them? These things test our love and prove whether or not it is divine.

For these reasons, he insists that the Pentecostal movement is far from its fullness.

> I come from a country where we have very heavy rains, tropical rains, what we call the monsoons, when the rain comes down in torrents, but before these monsoons break out we have some local showers. These local showers are forerunners of the big monsoons. Sometimes in these local showers there is a lull, and then comes the big monsoon; it bursts out in torrents and the whole country is flooded. The blessings we have had are just the local showers, and the big monsoons are yet to come. God is just getting the people prepared for the big monsoon, for the torrents of blessing.[47]

In historical perspective, then, Hettiaratchy's sermon – and the fact that he, a non-national and a person of color, is invited to give it – is seen to have been both symbolic and prophetic. It reminds us that American Pentecostalism, like all Christian movements and traditions, needs to be called back to its own deepest convictions again and again, often by "foreign" voices. And it signals the fact that the movement's fullness, and its share in catholicity, depends on its desire for God's fullness to be shared with others, a desire witnessed in unassuming openness to the many tongues of the Spirit and all-consuming adoration for the many faces of Christ.

NOTES

1 David A. Womack, *The Wellsprings of the Pentecostal Movement* (Springfield, MO: Gospel Publishing House, 1968), 13, 15.
2 Womack, *The Wellsprings of the Pentecostal Movement*, 86.
3 Womack, *The Wellsprings of the Pentecostal Movement*, 94.
4 B. F. Lawrence, "Article I: Back to Pentecost," *The Weekly Evangel* no. 121 (January 1, 1916), 4. Emphasis original.
5 See Robby Waddell and Peter Althouse, "The Promises and Perils of the Azusa Street Myth," *Pneuma* vol. 38, no. 4 (2016), 367–371.
6 Allan H. Anderson, *To the Ends of the Earth: Pentecostalism and the Transformation of World Christianity* (Oxford: Oxford University Press, 2013), 2.
7 B. F. Lawrence, "Article V: Incidents of the Spirit's Work from 1890 to 1900," *The Weekly Evangel* no. 125 (January 29 and February 5, 1916), 4.
8 Frank Bartleman, *Azusa Street* (South Plainfield, NJ: Bridge, 1980), 19; this work was originally published in 1925 under the title *How Pentecost Came to Los Angeles*.

9 See Anderson, *To the Ends of the Earth*, 1–3. See also Joe Creech, "Visions of Glory: The Place of the Azusa Street Revival in Pentecostal History," *Church History* vol. 65, no. 3 (1996), 405–424; Gary B. McGee, "'Latter Rain' Falling in the East: Early-Twentieth-Century Pentecostalism in India and the Debate over Speaking in Tongues," *Church History* vol. 68, no.3 (1999), 648–665; and Skylar Reidy, "'Holy Ghost Tribe': The Needles Revival and the Origins of Pentecostalism," *Religion and American Culture* vol. 29, no. 3 (2019), 361–390.

10 Todd M. Johnson "The Global Demographics of the Pentecostal and Charismatic Renewal," *Society* vol. 46, no. 6 (November 2009), 479–483. See also William K. Kay and Anne E. Dyer, *European Pentecostalism*, Global Pentecostal and Charismatic Studies (Leiden: Brill, 2011), 2–3.

11 See Peter D. Hocken, "Charismatic Movement," in *The New International Dictionary of Pentecostal and Charismatic Movements*, ed. Stanley Burgess and Eduard M. Van Der Maas (Grand Rapids, MI: Zondervan, 2002), 477–519.

12 Allan Anderson, *An Introduction to Pentecostalism: Global Charismatic Christianity*, 2nd ed. (Cambridge: Cambridge University Press, 2014), 2.

13 Johnson, "The Global Demographics of the Pentecostal and Charismatic Renewal," 481.

14 See Amos Yong, "Salvation, Society, and the Spirit: Pentecostal Contextualization and Political Theology from Cleveland to Birmingham, from Springfield to Seoul," *Pax Pneuma: The Journal of Pentecostals & Charismatics for Peace & Justice* vol. 5, no. 2 (2009), 22–34. See also Kenneth J. Archer, "The Cleveland School: The Making of an Academic Pentecostal Theological Tradition," in *Spirit and Story: Pentecostal Readings of Scripture. Essays in Honor of John Christopher Thomas*, ed. Blaine Charette and Robby Waddell (Sheffield: Sheffield Phoenix Press, 2020), 184–200; Hannah R. K. Mather, *The Interpreting Spirit: Spirit, Scripture, and Interpretation in the Renewal Tradition* (Eugene, OR: Wipf & Stock, 2020); and L. William Oliverio, Jr., "Contours of a Constructive Pentecostal Philosophical-Theological Hermeneutics," *Journal of Pentecostal Theology* vol. 29, no. 1 (April 2020), 1–22.

15 See Estrelda Y. Alexander, *Black Fire: One Hundred Years of African American Pentecostalism* (Downers Grove, IL: IVP Academic, 2011; David Reed, *"In Jesus' Name": The History and Beliefs of Oneness Pentecostals* (Blandford Forum: Deo Publishing, 2008); Michael Wilkinson, *Canadian Pentecostalism: Transition and Transformation* (Montreal: McGill-Queen University Press, 2009); Calvin White, Jr., *The Rise to Respectability: Race, Religion, and the Church of God in Christ* (Fayetteville: University of Arkansas Press, 2012); Gaston Espinosa, *Latino Pentecostals in America: Faith and Politics in Action* (Cambridge, MA: Harvard University Press, 2014).

16 Terry L. Cross, "The Rich Feast of Theology: Can Pentecostals Bring the Main Course or Only the Relish?" *Journal of Pentecostal Theology* vol. 8, no. 16

(January 2000), 27–47. See also Harvey Cox, *Fire from Heaven: The Rise of Pentecostal Spirituality and the Reshaping of Religion in the Twenty-First Century* (Cambridge, MA: Da Capo Press, 2001).

17 Kenneth J. Archer, *The Gospel Revisited: Toward a Pentecostal Theology of Worship and Witness* (Eugene, OR: Pickwick, 2011), 6–7.

18 Justo Gonzalez, *A History of Christian Thought* (Nashville: Abingdon, 2014), 348.

19 Hocken, "Charismatic Movement," 514–515.

20 Wolfgang Vondey, "The Unity and Diversity of Pentecostal Theology: A Brief Account for the Ecumenical Community in the West," *Ecclesiology* vol. 10, no. 1 (May 2014), 76–100.

21 See Daniel Castelo, *Pentecostalism as a Christian Mystical Tradition* (Grand Rapids, MI: Eerdmans, 2017).

22 Daniela Augustine, *The Spirit and the Common Good: Shared Flourishing in the Image of God* (Grand Rapids, MI: Eerdmans, 2019), 45.

23 Johnson, "The Global Demographics of the Pentecostal and Charismatic Renewal," 480.

24 Walter Hollenweger, *The Pentecostals: The Charismatic Movement in the Churches* (Peabody, MA: Hendrickson, 1988), 387.

25 Steven J. Land, *Pentecostal Spirituality: A Passion for the Kingdom* (Cleveland, TN: CPT Press, 2010), 123.

26 "The Character of Love," *Apostolic Faith* vol. 1, no. 3 (November 1906), 4.

27 See C. Peter Wagner, "Third Wave," in *The New International Dictionary of Pentecostal and Charismatic Movements*, ed. Stanley Burgess and Eduard M. Van Der Maas (Grand Rapids, MI: Zondervan, 2002), 1141.

28 Bill Johnson, *Experience the Impossible: Simple Ways to Unleash Heaven's Power on Earth* (Bloomington, MN: Chosen Books, 2014), 17, 19, 28, 195, 205, 229.

29 R. G. Robins, *Pentecostalism in America* (Santa Barbara, CA: Praeger, 2010), 2–3. See also Jay R. Case, "And Ever the Twain Shall Meet: The Holiness Missionary Movement and the Birth of World Pentecostalism, 1870–1920," *Religion and American Culture* vol. 16, no. 2 (Summer 2006), 125–159; Randall J. Stephens, *The Fire Spreads: Holiness and Pentecostalism in the American South* (Cambridge, MA: Harvard University Press, 2010); and David Bundy, Geordan Hammond, and David Sang-Ehil Han, eds., *Holiness and Pentecostal Movements: Intertwined Pasts, Presents, and Futures?* (University Park: Pennsylvania State University Press, 2021).

30 Larry R. McQueen, *Toward a Pentecostal Eschatology: Discerning the Way Forward* (Blandford Forum: Deo Publishing, 2012).

31 See Cheryl J. Sanders, "History of Women in the Pentecostal Movement," *Reconciliation* vol. 1 (Summer 1998), 8–11. See also Cheryl J. Sanders, *Saints in Exile: The Holiness-Pentecostal Experience in African American Religion and Culture* (Oxford: Oxford University Press, 1999).

32 See Chris E. W. Green, "The Spirit that Makes Us (Number) One: Racism, Tongues, and the Evidences of Spirit Baptism," *Pneuma* vol. 41 (2019), 1–24.

33 See Gaston Espinosa, *William J. Seymour and the Origins of Global Pentecostalism: A Biography & Documentary History* (Durham, NC: Duke University Press, 2014). See also Cecil M. Robeck, Jr., *The Azusa Street Mission and Revival: The Birth of the Global Pentecostal Movement* (Nashville: Thomas Nelson, 2006).

34 Cox, *Fire from Heaven*, 84.

35 Nimi Wariboko, *The Pentecostal Hypothesis: Christ Talks, They Decide* (Eugene, OR: Cascade, 2020), xi.

36 See Chris E. W. Green, *Foretasting the Kingdom: Towards a Pentecostal Theology of the Lord's Supper* (Cleveland, TN: CPT Press, 2012) and Chris E. W. Green, *Sanctifying Interpretation: Vocation, Holiness, Scripture*, 2nd ed. (Cleveland, TN: CPT Press, 2020).

37 Nimi Wariboko, *The Pentecostal Principle: Ethical Methodology in New Spirit* (Grand Rapids, MI: Eerdmans, 2011), 1.

38 James K. A. Smith, *Thinking in Tongues: Pentecostal Contributions to Christian Philosophy* (Grand Rapids, MI: Eerdmans, 2010), 34.

39 David D. Daniels III, "Future of North American Pentecostalism: Contemporary Diasporas, New Denominationalism, Inclusive Racial Politics, and Post-Secular Sensibilities," *Pneuma* vol. 42 (2020), 395–414.

40 See Kimberly E. Alexander, *Pentecostal Healing: Models in Theology* (Blandford Forum: Deo Publishing, 2006).

41 See Zachary M. Tackett, "As a Prophetic Voice: Liberation as a Matrix for Interpreting American Pentecostal Thought and Praxis," *Journal of the European Pentecostal Theological Association* vol. 33, no. 1 (2013), 42–57.

42 See Cheryl Bridges Johns, "The Adolescence of Pentecostalism: In Search of a Legitimate Sectarian Identity," *Pneuma* vol. 17, no. 1 (Spring 1995), 3–17; and Cheryl Bridges Johns, "Athens, Berlin, and Azusa: A Pentecostal Reflection on Scholarship and Christian Faith," *Pneuma* vol. 27, no. 1 (Spring 2005), 136–147.

43 Daniels, "Future of North American Pentecostalism," 395.

44 *The Apostolic Faith* vol. 2, no. 13 (May 1908), 3.

45 Womack, *The Wellsprings of the Pentecostal Movement*, 83, 89. 92.

46 J. H. King, "Fellowship," *The Pentecostal Holiness Advocate* (August 23, 1917), 2–3.

47 Charles F. Hettiaratchy, "But the Greatest of These Is Love," *Latter Rain Evangel* (May 1910), 9–13.

Selected Bibliography

SURVEYS

Ahlstrom, Sydney. *A Religious History of the American People*. 2nd ed. New Haven, CT: Yale University Press, 2004.

Albanese, Catherine. *America: Religions and Religion*. 5th ed. Boston, MA: Wadsworth, 2012.

Butler, Jon. *Awash in a Sea of Faith: Christianizing the American People*. Cambridge, MA: Harvard University Press, 1990.

Butler, Jon, Grant Wacker, and Randall Balmer. *Religion in American Life: A Short History*. 2nd ed. New York: Oxford University Press, 2011.

Finke, Roger, and Rodney Stark. *The Churching of America, 1776–2005: Winners and Losers in Our Religious Economy*. New Brunswick, NJ: Rutgers University Press, 2006.

Kidd, Thomas S. *America's Religious History: Faith, Politics, and the Shaping of a Nation*. Grand Rapids, MI: Zondervan, 2019.

Noll, Mark A. *A History of Christianity in the United States and Canada*. Grand Rapids: Eerdmans, 2019.

Tweed, Thomas A., ed. *Retelling U.S. Religious History*. Berkeley: University of California Press, 1997.

ANGLICANISM

Hein, David, and Gardiner H. Shattuck, Jr. *The Episcopalians*. Westport, CT: Praeger Publishers, 2004.

Kujawa-Holbrook, Sheryl A. *Freedom Is a Dream: A Documentary History of Women in the Episcopal Church*. New York: Church Publishing, 2002.

Lewis, Harold T. *Yet with a Steady Beat: The African American Struggle for Recognition in the Episcopal Church*. Valley Forge, PA: Trinity Press International, 1996.

Milton, Anthony, Jeremy Gregory, Rowan Strong, Jeremy Morris, and William L. Sachs, eds. *The Oxford History of Anglicanism*. 6 vols. Oxford: Oxford University Press, 2017–2018.

Prichard, Robert W. *A History of the Episcopal Church*. 3rd rev. ed. New York: Morehouse Publishing, 2014.

BAPTISTS

Bebbington, David. *Baptists through the Centuries: A History of a Global People.* Waco, TX: Baylor University Press, 2010.

Brooks Higginbotham, Evelyn. *Righteous Discontent: The Women's Movement in the Black Baptist Church, 1880–1920.* Cambridge, MA: Harvard University Press, 1993.

Fitts, Leroy. *A History of Black Baptists.* Nashville: Broadman Press, 1985.

Flowers, Elizabeth H., and Karen K. Seat, eds. *A Marginal Majority: Women, Gender, and a Reimagining of Southern Baptists.* Knoxville: University of Tennessee Press, 2020.

Hankins, Barry. *Uneasy in Babylon: Southern Baptist Conservatives and American Culture.* Tuscaloosa: University of Alabama Press, 2002.

Kidd, Thomas S., and Barry Hankins. *Baptists in America: A History.* New York: Oxford University Press, 2019.

Leonard, Bill J. *Baptists in America.* New York: Columbia University Press, 2005.

Shurden, Walter B. *The Baptist Identity: Four Fragile Freedoms.* Macon, GA: Smyth and Helwys, 2013.

CATHOLIC-PROTESTANT RELATIONS

Farrelly, Maura Jane. *Anti-Catholicism in America, 1620–1860.* New York: Cambridge University Press, 2017.

George, Timothy, and Thomas G. Guarino, eds. *Evangelicals and Catholics Together at Twenty.* Grand Rapids, MI: Brazos Press, 2015.

Massa, Mark S. *Catholics and American Culture: Fulton Sheen, Dorothy Day, and the Notre Dame Football Team.* New York: Crossroads, 1999.

Shea, William. *The Lion and the Lamb: Evangelicals and Catholics in America.* Oxford: Oxford University Press, 2004.

Schultz, Kevin M. *Tri-Faith America: How Catholics and Jews Held Postwar America to Its Protestant Promise.* New York: Oxford, 2011.

CIVIL WAR

Rable, George C. *God's Almost Chosen Peoples: A Religious History of the American Civil War.* Chapel Hill: University of North Carolina Press, 2012.

Miller, Randall M., Harry S. Stout, and Charles Reagan Wilson, eds. *Religion and the American Civil War.* New York: Oxford University Press, 1998.

Noll, Mark A. *The Civil War as a Theological Crisis.* Chapel Hill: University of North Carolina Press, 2006.

Stout, Harry S. *Upon the Altar of the Nation: A Moral History of the Civil War.* New York: Viking, 2006.

EDUCATION

Bailyn, Bernard. *Education in the Forming of American Society.* Chapel Hill: University of North Carolina Press, 1960.

Boylan, Anne M. *Sunday School: The Formation of an American Institution, 1790–1880*. New Haven, CT: Yale University Press, 1988.

Cremin, Lawrence. *American Education: The Colonial Experience*. New York: Harper and Row, 1970.

American Education: The Metropolitan Experience, 1876–1980. New York: Harper and Row, 1988.

American Education: The National Experience, 1783–1876. New York: Harper and Row, 1980.

Miller, Glenn. *Piety and Intellect: The Aims and Purposes of Ante-Bellum Theological Education*. Atlanta: Scholars Press, 1990.

Piety and Pluralism: Theological Education since 1960. Leonia, NJ: Cascade, 2004.

Piety and Profession: American Theological Education: 1870–1970. Grand Rapids, MI: Eerdmans, 2007.

Ringenberg, William. *The Christian College: A History of Protestant Higher Education in America*. 2nd ed. Grand Rapids, MI: Baker Academic, 2006.

Turpin, Andrea L. *A New Moral Vision: Gender, Religion, and the Changing Purposes of American Higher Education, 1837–1917*. Ithaca, NY: Cornell University Press, 2016.

Westerhoff, John. *William McGuffey and His Readers: Piety, Morality, and Education in Nineteenth Century America*. Nashville: Abingdon, 1979.

EVANGELICALISM AND FUNDAMENTALISM

Balmer, Randall. *Blessed Assurance: A History of Evangelicalism in America*. Boston: Beacon Press, 1999.

Carpenter, Joel. *Revive Us Again: The Reawakening of American Fundamentalism*. New York: Oxford University Press, 1997.

Fitzgerald, Frances. *The Evangelicals: The Struggle to Shape America*. New York: Simon & Schuster, 2017.

Hambrick-Stowe, Charles E. *Charles G. Finney and the Spirit of American Evangelicalism*. Grand Rapids, MI: Eerdmans, 1996.

Hankins, Barry. *American Evangelicals: A Contemporary History of a Mainstream Religious Movement*. New York: Rowman & Littlefield Publishers, 2008.

Kobes du Mez, Kristin. *Jesus and John Wayne: How White Evangelicals Corrupted a Faith and Fractured a Nation*. New York: Liveright, 2020.

Leigh Heyrman, Christine. *Southern Cross: The Beginnings of the Bible Belt*. Chapel Hill: University of North Carolina Press, 1997.

Marsden, George M. *Fundamentalism and American Culture*. 2nd ed. New York: Oxford University Press, 2006.

Mathews, Mary Beth. *Doctrine and Race: African American Evangelicals and Fundamentalism between the Wars*. Tuscaloosa: University of Alabama Press, 2018.

Miller, Steven P. *The Age of Evangelicalism: America's Born-Again Years*. New York: Oxford University Press, 2014.

Stout, Harry S. *The Divine Dramatist: George Whitefield and the Rise of Modern Evangelicalism*. Grand Rapids, MI: Eerdmans, 1991.

Swartz, David R. *Moral Minority: The Evangelical Left in an Age of Conservatism.* Philadelphia: University of Pennsylvania Press, 2012.
Worthen, Molly. *Apostles of Reason: The Crisis of Authority in American Evangelicalism.* New York: Oxford University Press, 2013.

HOLINESS MOVEMENT

Dieter, Melvin E. *The Holiness Revival of the Nineteenth Century.* 2nd ed. Metuchen, NJ: Scarecrow Press, 1996.
Peters, John L. *Christian Perfection and American Methodism.* New York: Abingdon, 1956.
Raser, Harold E. *Phoebe Palmer: Her Life and Thought.* Lewiston, NY: Mellen, 1987.

LUTHERANS

Bodensieck, Julius, *The Encyclopedia of the Lutheran Church.* 3 vols. Minneapolis: Augsburg Publishing House, 1965.
DeBerg, Betty A. *Women and Women's Issues in North American Lutheranism.* Chicago: Commission for Women of the ELCA, 1992.
Gassmann, Günther. *Historical Dictionary of Lutheranism.* 2nd ed. Lanham, MD: Scarecrow Press, 2011.
Granquist, Mark. *Lutherans in America: A New History.* Minneapolis: Fortress Press, 2015.
Lagerquist, L. DeAne. *The Lutherans.* Westport, CT: Greenwood Press, 1999.
Lueker, Erwin L. *Lutheran Cyclopedia.* St. Louis, MO: Concordia, 1975.
Lund, Eric, and Mark Granquist. *A Documentary History of Lutheranism: 1750 to the Present.* Minneapolis: Fortress Press, 2017.
Meyer, Carl S. ed. *Moving Frontiers: Readings in the History of the Lutheran Church – Missouri Synod.* St. Louis, MO: Concordia, 1964.
Nelson, E. Clifford ed. *The Lutherans in North America.* Philadelphia: Fortress Press, 1975.
Suelflow, August, ed. *Heritage in Motion.* St. Louis: Concordia, 1988.
Tappert, Theodore G., ed. *Lutheran Confessional Theology in America, 1840–1880.* New York: Oxford University Press, 1972.
Wengert, Timothy, ed. *The Dictionary of Luther and the Lutheran Traditions.* Grand Rapids, MI: Baker Academic, 2016.
Wiederaenders, Robert C. ed. *Historical Guide to Lutheran Church Bodies of North America.* 2nd ed. St. Louis, MO: Lutheran Historical Conference, 1998.
Wolf, Richard C., ed. *Documents of Lutheran Unity in America.* Philadelphia: Fortress Press, 1966.

MAINLINE AND LIBERAL PROTESTANTISM

Coffman, Elesha J. *The Christian Century and the Rise of the Protestant Mainline.* New York: Oxford University Press, 2013.
Hollinger, David A. *After Cloven Tongues of Fire: Protestant Liberalism in Modern American History.* Princeton, NJ: Princeton University Press, 2013.

Hutchison, William R. *Between the Times: The Travail of the Protestant Establishment in America, 1900–1960.* Cambridge: Cambridge University Press, 1989.

Wuthnow, Robert. *The Restructuring of American Religion: Society and Faith since World War II.* Princeton, NJ: Princeton University Press, 1989.

MEDICINE AND HEALING

Curtis, Heather. *Faith in the Great Physician: Suffering and Divine Healing in American Culture, 1860–1900.* Baltimore: Johns Hopkins University Press, 2007.

Grob, Gerald N. *The Mad among Us: A History of the Care of America's Mentally Ill.* New York: Free Press, 1994.

Gunther Brown, Candy, *The Healing Gods: Complementary and Alternative Medicine in Christian America.* New York: Oxford University Press, 2013.

  ed. *Global Pentecostal and Charismatic Healing.* New York: Oxford University Press, 2011.

Harrell, David Edwin. *All Things Are Possible: The Healing and Charismatic Revivals in Modern America.* Bloomington: Indiana University Press, 1975.

Jimenez, Mary Anne. *Changing Faces of Madness: Early American Attitudes and Treatment of the Insane.* Hanover, NH: University Press of New England, 1987.

Vacek, Heather. *Madness: American Protestant Responses to Mental Illness.* Waco, TX: Baylor University Press, 2015.

MENNONITES, BRETHREN, AND AMISH

Durnbaugh, Donald F. *Fruit of the Vine: A History of the Brethren, 1708–1995.* Elgin, IL: Brethren Press, 1997.

Juhnke, James C. *Vision, Doctrine, War: Mennonite Identity and Organization in America, 1890–1930.* Scottdale, PA: Herald Press, 1989.

Longenecker, Stephen L. *Piety and Tolerance: Pennsylvania German Religion, 1710–1850.* Metuchen, NJ: Scarecrow Press, 1994.

MacMaster, Richard K. *Land, Piety, Peoplehood: The Establishment of Mennonite Communities in America, 1683–1790.* Scottdale, PA: Herald, 1985.

Nolt, Steven M. *History of the Amish.* 3rd ed. Intercourse, PA: Good Books, 2016.

Ronk, Albert T. *History of the Brethren Church: Its Life, Thought, Mission.* Ashland, OH: Brethren Publishing Company, 1968.

Schlabach Theron F. *Peace, Faith, Nation: Mennonites and Amish in Nineteenth-Century America.* Scottdale, PA: Herald Press, 1988.

Toews, Paul. *Mennonites in American Society: Modernity and the Persistence of Religious Community.* Scottdale, PA: Herald Press, 1996.

Wittlinger, Carlton O. *Quest for Piety and Obedience: The Story of the Brethren in Christ.* Nappanee, IN: Evangel Press, 1978.

METHODISM

Andrews, Dee E. *The Methodists and Revolutionary America, 1760–1800.* Princeton, NJ: Princeton University Press, 2002.

Dickerson, Dennis C. *The African Methodist Episcopal Church: A History.* Cambridge: Cambridge University Press, 2020.

Mathews, Donald G. *Slavery and Methodism: A Chapter in American Morality, 1780–1845.* Princeton, NJ: Princeton University Press, 1965.

McClain, William B. *Black People in the Methodist Church.* Nashville: Abingdon, 1985.

Richey, Russell E., Kenneth E. Rowe, and Jean Miller Schmidt, *The Methodist Experience in America: A History.* Nashville: Abingdon Press, 2010.

Norwood, Frederick A. *The Story of American Methodism.* Nashville: Abingdon, 1974.

Schneider, Gregory A. *The Way of the Cross Leads Home: The Domestication of American Methodism.* Bloomington: Indiana University Press, 1993.

Snyder, Howard A. *Populist Saints: B.T. and Ellen Roberts and the First Free Methodists.* Grand Rapids, MI: Eerdmans, 2006.

Teasdale, Mark R. *Methodist Evangelism, American Salvation: The Home Missions of the Methodist Episcopal Church, 1860–1920.* Eugene, OR: Pickwick, 2014.

Wigger, John H. *American Saint: Francis Asbury and the Methodists.* New York: Oxford University Press, 2009.

Taking Heaven by Storm: Methodism and the Rise of Popular Christianity in America. New York: Oxford University Press, 1998.

Williams, Jeffrey. *Religion and Violence in Early American Methodism: Taking the Kingdom by Force.* Bloomington: Indiana University Press, 2011.

MISSIONS

Bays, Daniel H., and Grant Wacker. *The Foreign Missionary Enterprise at Home: Explorations in North American Cultural History.* Tuscaloosa: University of Alabama Press, 2003.

Beaver, R. Pierce. *American Protestant Women in World Mission: A History of the First Feminist Movement in North America.* Grand Rapids, MI: Eerdmans, 1980.

Hill, Patricia. *The World Their Household: The American Woman's Foreign Mission Movement and Cultural Transformation, 1870–1920.* Ann Arbor: University of Michigan Press, 1985.

Riley Case, Jay. *An Unpredictable Gospel: American Evangelicals and World Christianity, 1812–1920.* New York: Oxford University Press, 2012.

Robert, Dana. *American Women in Mission: A Social History of Their Thought and Practice.* Macon, GA: Mercer University Press, 1997.

Ruble, Sarah E. *The Gospel of Freedom and Power: Protestant Missionaries in American Culture after World War II.* Chapel Hill: University of North Carolina Press, 2014.

Sunquist, Scott W. *The Unexpected Christian Century: The Reversal and Transformation of Global Christianity, 1900–2000.* Grand Rapids, MI: Baker Academic, 2015.

Walston, Vaughn and Robert Stevens. *African-American Experience in World Mission: A Call Beyond Community.* Pasadena, CA: William Carey Library, 2002.

NATIVE AMERICAN CHRISTIANITY

Fisher, Linford. *The Indian Great Awakening: Religion and the Shaping of Native Cultures in Early America*. New York: Oxford University Press, 2012.

Pointer, Richard. *Encounters of the Spirit: Native Americans and European Colonial Religion*. Bloomington: Indiana University Press, 2007.

Warren, Louis S. *God's Red Son: The Ghost Dance Religion and the Making of Modern America*. New York: Basic Books, 2017.

PENTECOSTAL AND CHARISMATIC CHRISTIANITY

Alexander, Estrelda Y. *Black Fire: One Hundred Years of African American Pentecostalism*. Downers Grove, IL: IVP Academic, 2011.

Anderson, Allan H. *An Introduction to Pentecostalism: Global Charismatic Christianity*. 2nd ed. Cambridge: Cambridge University Press, 2014.

Bowler, Kate. *Blessed: A History of the American Prosperity Gospel*. New York: Oxford University Press, 2013.

Burgess, Stanley, and Eduard M. Van Der Maas, eds. *The New International Dictionary of Pentecostal and Charismatic Movements*. Grand Rapids, MI: Zondervan, 2002.

Castelo, Daniel. *Pentecostalism as a Christian Mystical Tradition*. Grand Rapids, MI: Eerdmans, 2017.

Collier Artman, Amy. *The Miracle Lady: Kathryn Kuhlman and the Transformation of Charismatic Christianity*. Grand Rapids, MI: Eerdmans, 2019.

Cox, Harvey. *Fire from Heaven: The Rise of Pentecostal Spirituality and the Reshaping of Religion in the Twenty-First Century*. Reading, MA: Addison-Wesley, 1995.

Dayton, Donald W. *Theological Roots of Pentecostalism*. Grand Rapids, MI: Baker Academic, 1987.

Espinosa, Gastón. *Latino Pentecostals in America: Faith and Politics in Action*. Cambridge, MA: Harvard University Press, 2014.

William J. Seymour and the Origins of Global Pentecostalism: A Biography & Documentary History. Durham, NC: Duke University Press, 2014.

Hollenweger, Walter. *The Pentecostals: The Charismatic Movement in the Churches*. Peabody, MA: Hendrickson, 1988.

Land, Steven J. *Pentecostal Spirituality: A Passion for the Kingdom*. Cleveland, TN: CPT Press, 2010.

Robeck, Cecil M., Jr. *The Azusa Street Mission and Revival: The Birth of the Global Pentecostal Movement*. Nashville: Thomas Nelson, 2006.

Robins, R. G. *Pentecostalism in America*. Santa Barbara, CA: Praeger, 2010.

Stephens, Randall J. *The Fire Spreads: Holiness and Pentecostalism in the American South*. Cambridge, MA: Harvard University Press, 2010.

Synan, Vinson. *The Holiness-Pentecostal Tradition: Charismatic Movements in the Twentieth Century*. 2nd ed. Grand Rapids, MI: Eerdmans, 1997.

Wacker, Grant. *Heaven Below: Early Pentecostals and American Culture*. Cambridge, MA: Harvard University Press, 2001.

POLITICS AND RELIGIOUS LIBERTY

Bonomi, Patricia. *Under the Cope of Heaven: Society, and Politics in Colonial America*. New York: Oxford University Press, 2003.

Byrd, James P. *Sacred Scripture, Sacred War: The Bible and the American Revolution*. Oxford: Oxford University Press, 2013.

Dochuk, Darren. *From Bible Belt to Sunbelt: Plain-Folk Religion, Grassroots Politics, and the Rise of Evangelical Conservatism*. New York: W.W. Norton, 2011.

Dowland, Seth. *Family Values and the Rise of the Christian Right*. Philadelphia: University of Pennsylvania Press, 2015.

Fea, John. *Was America Founded as a Christian Nation? A Historical Introduction*, 2nd ed. Louisville, KY: Westminster John Knox Press, 2016.

Foster, Gaines M. *Moral Reconstruction: Christian Lobbyists and the Federal Legislation of Morality, 1865–1920*. Chapel Hill: University of North Carolina Press, 2002.

Green, Steven K. *The Second Disestablishment: Church and State in Nineteenth-Century America*. New York: Oxford University Press, 2010.

Kidd, Thomas S. *God of Liberty: A Religious History of the American Revolution*. New York: Basic Books, 2010.

Lambert, Frank. *The Founding Fathers and the Place of Religion in America*. Princeton, NJ: Princeton University Press, 2003.

Miller, Nicholas P. *The Religious Roots of the First Amendment: Dissenting Protestants and the Separation of Church and State*. New York: Oxford University Press, 2013.

Noll, Mark A., and Luke E. Harlow. *Religion and American Politics: From the Colonial Period to the Present*. 2nd ed. New York: Oxford University Press, 2007.

Oxx, Katie, *The Nativist Movement in America: Religious Conflict in the Nineteenth Century*. New York: Routledge, 2013.

Porterfield, Amanda. *Conceived in Doubt: Religion and Politics in the New American Nation*. Chicago: University of Chicago Press, 2012.

Preston, Andrew. *Sword of the Spirit, Shield of Faith: Religion in American War and Diplomacy*. New York: Alfred A. Knopf, 2012.

Ragosta, John A. *Wellspring of Liberty: How Virginia's Religious Dissenters Helped Win the American Revolution and Secured Religious Liberty*. New York: Oxford University Press, 2010.

Smith, Christian, ed., *The Secular Revolution: Power, Interests, and Conflict in the Secularization of American Public Life*. Berkeley: University of California Press, 2003.

Smith, Gary Scott. *Faith and the Presidency: From George Washington to George W. Bush*. New York: Oxford University Press, 2006.

Van Engen, Abram C. *City on a Hill: A History of American Exceptionalism*. New Haven, CT: Yale University Press, 2020.

Wald, Kenneth D., and Allison Calhoun-Brown. *Religion and Politics in the United States*. 8th ed. Lanham, MD: Rowman & Littlefield, 2018.

Williams, Daniel K. *God's Own Party: The Making of the Christian Right*. New York: Oxford University Press, 2010.

RACE AND SLAVERY

Boles, Richard J. *Dividing the Faith: The Rise of Segregated Churches in the Early American North.* New York: New York University Press, 2020.

Gerbner, Catherine. *Christian Slavery: Conversion and Race in the Protestant Atlantic World.* Philadelphia: University of Pennsylvania Press, 2018.

Glaude, Eddie S., Jr. *Exodus!: Religion, Race, and Nation in Early Nineteenth-Century Black America.* Chicago: University of Chicago Press, 2000.

Goetz, Rebecca Anne. *The Baptism of Early Virginia: How Christianity Created Race.* Baltimore: John Hopkins University Press, 2015.

Genovese, Eugene D. *Roll Jordan Roll: The World the Slaves Made.* New York: Vintage Books, 1976.

Harvey, Paul. *Through the Storm, Through the Night: A History of African American Christianity.* Lanham, MD: Rowman & Littlefield Publishers, 2011.

Friedland, Michael B. *Lift up Your Voice Like a Trumpet: White Clergy and the Civil Rights and Antiwar Movements, 1954–1973.* Chapel Hill: University of North Carolina Press, 1998.

Fulop, Timothy E., and Albert J. Raboteau, eds. *African American Religion: Interpretive Essays in History and Culture.* New York: Routledge: 1979.

Quiros, Ansley L. *God with Us: Lived Theology and the Freedom Struggle in Americus, Georgia, 1942–1976.* Chapel Hill: University of North Carolina Press, 2019.

Raboteau, Albert J. *Canaan Land: A Religious History of African Americans.* New York: Oxford University Press, 2001.

Sensbach, Jon F. *Rebecca's Revival: Creating Black Christianity in the Atlantic World.* Cambridge, MA: Harvard University Press, 2005.

Swift, David E. *Black Prophets of Justice: Activist Clergy before the Civil War.* Baton Rouge: Louisiana University Press, 1989.

White, Calvin, Jr. *The Rise to Respectability: Race, Religion, and the Church of God in Christ.* Fayetteville: University of Arkansas Press, 2012.

THE REFORMED TRADITION

Kidd, Thomas S. *Jonathan Edwards: A Life.* New Haven: Yale University Press, 2003.

Miller, Perry. *Errand Into the Wilderness.* Cambridge, MA: Belknap Press, 1956.
 The New England Mind: From Colony to Province. Cambridge, MA: Belknap Press, 1953, 1981.
 The Puritan Mind: The Seventeenth Century. Cambridge, MA: Belknap Press, 1939, 1982.

Hall, David D. *The Puritans: A Transatlantic History.* Princeton, NJ: Princeton University Press, 2019.
 Worlds of Wonder, Days of Judgement: Popular Religious Belief in Early New England. Cambridge, MA; Harvard University Press, 1990.

Smylie, James H. *A Brief History of the Presbyterians.* Louisville, KY: Geneva Press, 1996.

Stout, Harry S. *The New England Soul: Preaching and Religious Culture in Colonial New England.* New York: Oxford University Press, 1986.

Turner, John G. *They Knew They Were Pilgrims: Plymouth Colony and the Contest for American Liberty.* New Haven, NC: Yale University Press, 2020.

Winship, Michael P. *Godly Republicanism: Puritans, Pilgrims, and a City on a Hill.* Cambridge, MA: Harvard University Press, 2012.

REVIVALISM

Boles, John B. *The Great Revival: Beginnings of the Bible Belt.* Lexington: University Press of Kentucky, 1996.

Hatch, Nathan O. *The Democratization of American Christianity.* New Haven: Yale University Press, 1989.

Kidd, Thomas S. *The Great Awakening: The Roots of Evangelical Christianity in Colonial America.* New Haven, CT: Yale University Press, 2007.

SCIENCE

Hall, Amy Laura. *Conceiving Parenthood: American Protestantism and the Spirit of Reproduction.* Grand Rapids, MI: Eerdmans, 2007.

Larson, Edward J. *Summer for the Gods: The Scopes Trial and America's Continuing Debate over Science and Religion.* New York: Basic Books, 1997.

Lindberg, David, and Ronald Numbers, ed., *God and Nature: Historical Essays on the Encounter Between Christianity and Science.* Berkeley: University of California Press, 1986.

When Science & Christianity Meet. Chicago: University of Chicago Press, 2003.

Livingstone, David. *Darwin's Forgotten Defenders: The Encounter between Evangelical Theology and Evolutionary Thought.* Grand Rapids, MI: Eerdmans, 1987.

Numbers, Ronald. *Darwinism Comes to America.* Cambridge, MA: Harvard University Press, 1998.

Roberts, Jon H. *Darwinism and the Divine in America: Protestant Intellectuals and Organic Evolution, 1859–1900.* Madison: University of Wisconsin Press, 1988.

Ungureanu, James C. *Science, Religion, and the Protestant Tradition: Retracing the Origins of Conflict.* Pittsburgh: University of Pittsburgh Press, 2019.

SEX AND GENDER

DeRogatis, Amy. *Saving Sex: Sexuality and Salvation in American Evangelicalism.* New York: Oxford University Press, 2014.

Lefkowitz Horowitz, Helen. *Rereading Sex: Battles Over Sexual Knowledge and Suppression in Nineteenth-Century America.* Knopf: New York, 2002.

Frank, Gillian A., Bethany Moreton, and Heather R. White, eds. *Devotions and Desires: Histories of Sexuality and Religion in the Twentieth-Century United States.* Chapel Hill: University of North Carolina Press, 2018.

Griffith, R. Marie. *Moral Combat: How Sex Divided American Christians and Fractured American Politics.* New York: Basic Books, 2017.

White, Heather R. *Reforming Sodom: Protestants and the Rise of Gay Rights.* Chapel Hill: University of North Carolina Press, 2015.

SOCIAL REFORM

Abzug, Robert H. *Cosmos Crumbling: American Reform and the Religious Imagination*. New York: Oxford University Press, 1994.

Carter, Heath W. *Union Made: The Rise of Social Christianity in Chicago*. New York: Oxford University Press, 2015.

Evans, Christopher H. *The Social Gospel in American Religion: A History*. New York: New York University Press, 2017.

Gasaway, Brantley W. *Progressive Evangelicals and the Pursuit of Social Justice*. Chapel Hill: University of North Carolina Press, 2014.

Graber, Jennifer. *The Furnace of Affliction: Prisons and Religion in Antebellum America*. Chapel Hill: University of North Carolina Press, 2011.

McGerr, Michael. *A Fierce Discontent: The Rise and Fall of the Progressive Movement in America, 1870–1920*. New York: Free Press, 2003.

Smith, Timothy L. *Revivalism and Social Reform in Mid-Nineteenth Century America*. Nashville: Abingdon Press, 1957.

Strong, Douglas M. *Perfectionist Politics: Abolitionism and the Religious Tensions of American Democracy*. Syracuse, NY: Syracuse University Press, 1999.

Tyrell, Ian R. *Reforming the World: The Creation of America's Moral Empire*. Princeton, NJ: Princeton University Press, 2010.

STONE-CAMPBELL MOVEMENT

Foster, Douglas A., Paul M. Blowers, Anthony L. Dunnavant, and D. Newell Williams, eds. *The Encyclopedia of the Stone-Campbell Movement*. Grand Rapids, MI: Eerdmans, 2004.

Powell, Mark E., John Mark Hicks, and Greg McKinzie. *Discipleship in Community: A Theological Vision for the Future*. Abilene, TX: Abilene Christian University Press, 2020.

Toulouse, Mark G. *Joined in Discipleship: The Shaping of Contemporary Disciples Identity*. 2nd ed. St. Louis, MO: Chalice Press, 1997.

Webb, Henry E. *In Search of Christian Unity: A History of the Restoration Movement*, rev. ed. Abilene, TX: Abilene Christian University Press, 2003.

Williams, D. Newell, Douglas A. Foster, and Paul M. Blowers, eds. *The Stone-Campbell Movement: A Global History*. St. Louis, MO: Chalice Press, 2013.

TEMPERANCE

Blocker, Jack. *American Temperance Movements: Cycles of Reform*. Boston: Twayne, 1989.

Bordin, Ruth. *Woman and Temperance: The Quest for Power and Liberty, 1873–1900*. New Brunswick, NJ: Rutgers University Press, 1990.

Burnham, John. *Bad Habits: Drinking, Smoking, Taking Drugs, Gambling, Sexual Misbehavior, and Swearing in American History*. New York: New York University Press, 1993.

Clark, Norman. *Deliver Us from Evil: An Interpretation of American Prohibition*. New York: Norton, 1976.

Coker, Joe. *Liquor in the Land of the Lost Cause*. Lexington: University Press of Kentucky, 2007.

Mattingly, Carol. *Well-Tempered Women: Nineteenth-Century Temperance Rhetoric*. Carbondale: Southern Illinois University, 1998.

Tyrell, Ian R. *Sobering Up: From Temperance to Prohibition in Antebellum America, 1800–1860*. Westport, CT: Greenwood Press, 1979.

Woodruff Tait, Jennifer. *The Poisoned Chalice: Eucharistic Grape Juice and Common-Sense Realism in Victorian Methodism*. Tuscaloosa: University of Alabama Press, 2011.

THEOLOGY

Boyer, Paul. *When Time Shall Be No More: Prophecy Belief in Modern American Culture*. Cambridge, MA: Harvard University Press, 1992.

Dorrien, Gary. *The Making of American Liberal Theology*, 3 vols. Louisville, KY: Westminster John Knox Press, 2001–2006.

Holifield, E. Brooks. *Theology in America: Christian Thought from the Age of the Puritans to the Civil War*. New Haven, CT: Yale University Press, 2003.

Floyd-Thomas, Stacey, and Anthony B. Pinn, eds. *Liberation Theologies in the United States: An Introduction*. New York: New York University Press, 2010.

Nichols, James. *The Mercersburg Theology*. New York: Oxford University Press, 1966.

Noll, Mark A. *America's God: From Jonathan Edwards to Abraham Lincoln*. New York: Oxford University Press, 2002.

Olson, Roger E. *Reformed and Always Reforming: The Postconservative Approach to Evangelical Theology*. Grand Rapids, MI: Baker Academic, 2007.

Olson, Roger E., and Christian T. Collins Winn, *Reclaiming Pietism: Retrieving an Evangelical Tradition*. Grand Rapids, MI: Eerdmans, 2015.

Sweeney, Douglas A., and Allen Guelzo, eds. *The New England Theology: From Jonathan Edwards to Edwards Amasa Park*. Grand Rapids, MI: Baker Academic, 2006.

Toulouse, Mark G. and Duke, James O, eds. *Makers of Christian Theology in America*. Nashville: Abingdon, 1997.

WOMEN

Bendroth, Margaret. *Fundamentalism and Gender, 1875 to the Present*. New Haven, CT: Yale University Press, 1993.

Boylan, Anne M. *The Origins of Women's Activism: New York and Boston, 1797–1840*. Chapel Hill: University of North Carolina Press, 2002.

Brekus, Catherine A. *Strangers and Pilgrims: Female Preaching in America, 1740–1845*. Chapel Hill: University of North Carolina Press, 1998.

ed. *The Religious History of American Women: Reimagining the Past*. Chapel Hill, University of North Carolina Press, 2007.

Sarah Osborn's World: The Rise of Evangelical Christianity in Early America. New Haven, CT: Yale University Press, 2013.

DeBerg, Betty A. *Ungodly Women: Gender and the First Wave of Fundamentalism*. Minneapolis: Fortress Press, 1990.

Douglas, Ann. *The Feminization of American Culture*. New York: Knopf, 1977.

Griffith, R. Marie. *God's Daughters: Evangelical Women and the Power of Submission*. Berkeley: University of California Press, 1997.

Juster, Susan. *Disorderly Women: Sexual Politics and Evangelicalism in Revolutionary New England*. Ithaca, NY: Cornell University Press, 1994.

Juster, Susan, and Lisa MacFarlane, eds. *A Mighty Baptism: Race, Gender, and the Creation of American Protestantism*. Ithaca, NY: Cornell University Press, 1996.

Wiley Legath, Jenny. *Sanctified Sisters: A History of Protestant Deaconesses*. New York: New York University Press, 2019.

WORK, BUSINESS, AND ECONOMICS

Corrigan, John. *Business of the Heart: Religion and Emotion in the Nineteenth Century*. Berkeley: University of California Press, 2002.

Gloege, Timothy E. W. *Guaranteed Pure: The Moody Bible Institute, Business, and the Making of Modern Evangelicalism*. Chapel Hill: University of North Carolina Press, 2015.

Kruse, Kevin M. *One Nation under God: How Corporate America Invented Christian America*. New York: Basic Books, 2015.

Meeks, Douglas. *God the Economist: The Doctrine of God and Political Economy*. Minneapolis: Fortress Press, 1989.

Placher, William, ed. *Callings: Twenty Centuries of Christian Wisdom on Vocation*. Grand Rapids, MI: Eerdmans, 2005.

Sweeden, Joshua. *The Church and Work: The Ecclesiological Grounding of Good Work*. Eugene, OR: Pickwick Publications, 2014.

Weber, Max. *The Protestant Ethic and the Spirit of Capitalism and Other Writings*. New York: Penguin, 2002.

WORSHIP

Ruth, Lester and Swee Hong Lim. *Lovin' On Jesus: A Concise History of Contemporary Worship*. Nashville: Abingdon, 2017.

White, James. *Protestant Worship: Traditions in Transition*. Louisville, KY: Westminster John Knox Press, 1989.

Wilson Costen, Melva. *African American Christian Worship*. Nashville: Abingdon Press, 2007.

Index

Abernathy, Ralph, 169, 412
Abilene Christian University, 429
abolitionism, 37–38, 44, 50, 179, 204,
    226–228, 265, 329, 350, 351, 352,
    See also slavery, opposition to
  in the Reformed tradition, 354–355
abortion, 70, 75–76, 77, 81, 162, 171,
    172–173, 174–175, 210, 212, 214,
    268, 279, 363, 454
Abyssinian Baptist Church, 233, 412
accreditation, 130
Act of Toleration, 320
Acts 29 Network, 364
acupuncture, 252
Adam and Eve, 95, 97, 145, 201, 207,
    208, 210–211
Adam and Steve, 210
Adams, John, 31, 281
Adams, Samuel, 32, 45, 285
Addams, Jane, 54, 136
Advent Christian Church, 454
advertising, 121
aesthetic movement, 191
African-American religion. *See* Black
    church
African folk religion, 42
African-Methodist Episcopal Church
    (AME), 41, 50, 164, 225–226,
    231–232, 236, 244, 445, 452
African Methodist Episcopal Zion
    Church (AMEZ), 50, 226, 236,
    445, 452
African spirituality, 222–224
African tribal religions, 222–224
African Union Methodist Protestant
    Church, 445, 452

Afro-Protestantism, 222–224
Age of Reason. *See* Enlightenment
Ahlstrom, Sydney, 128, 131
alcohol
  consumption statistics, 181
  effects of, 182–183
  lifestyle reform and, 185–186
  Scripture and, 183–184
  statistics, 180
Alcohol and Hygiene, 186
Alcott, Amos, 191
Alexander, Archibald, 353
Algonquin, 298
alienists, 266
All We're Meant to Be, 209
Allen Coe, George, 137
Allen University, 231
Allen, Ethan O., 244
Allen, Richard, 41, 225–226, 236, 244,
    439, 445
almshouses, 265
altar call, 119
altar calls, 119
American Academy of Religion,
    1
American and Foreign Anti-Slavery
    Society, 228
American Anti-Slavery Society, 227,
    228, 329, 355
American Baptist Convention (ABC),
    50, 60, 166, 407, 413
American Bible Society, 135, 326
American Board of Commissioners for
    Foreign Missions, 299
American Christian Missionary
    Society (ACMS), 424, 425, 427

Lutherans (cont.)
German, 370, 372, 374–375, 378
homosexuality and, 213–214, 382
immigration and, 374–375,
376–378
in the colonial era, 370–372
in the early republic, 373–375
in the later nineteenth century,
375–378
in the Reformation, 369
in the Revolution, 372
in the twentieth century, 378–382
in the twenty-first century, 370
in World War II, 379
language transition, 373–374,
378, 379
missions and, 378, 380
Norwegian, 374–375, 377, 378
organization, 15, 116, 371–372,
373–375, 376, 378, 379, 380–381
Pietism and, 376
race and, 381
revivalism and, 373
Russian, 377
Scandinavian, 376–377
slavery and, 372, 375
Slavic, 377
Swedish, 370, 374–375, 376
temperance and, 165
theology, 60, 95, 342, 441
women and, 209
women's ordination, 381
World War I, 378
worship, 10, 121
lynching, 205

Maccalla, William, 423
Mack, Alexander, 387
Madison, James, 33, 325, 405
Madison, James, bishop, 325
Magisterium, 105
Maine Law, 165, 191
mainline
charismatic movement, 73, 77, 248,
339, 465
clergy, 69, 82
decline, 68, 70–73, 82, 171, 330, 362
homosexuality and, 70, 212–214

in the twentieth century, 56–58, 59,
61, 62, 68–73
missions and, 297, 304–306, 307, 308
politics and, 69–70, 168–169,
170–171
race and, 81
since the 1960s, 170–171, 208, 214
social reform, 166
theology, 63, 71, 160, 168, 191,
360–362
women and, 63, 207, 365
worship, 430
Makemie, Francis, 14
manhood, 35, 76, 82, 199, 207, 211, *See
also* patriarchy; womanhood
manifest destiny, 43, 205, 300
Mann, Horace, 134
Manye, Charlotte, 232
market revolution, 34, 36
marriage. *See also* gender; same-sex
marriage; patriarchy; women**
definitions, 214
divorce and, 335
eugenics and, 190
heterosexual, 35, 76, 198, 203,
211, 214
interracial, 80, 81, 319
missions and, 206
Scripture and, 201, 205, 210
slavery and, 200, 202
marriage equality. *See* same-sex
marriage
Mars Hill Church, 364
Marsh, John, 186
Martin, Trayvon, 236
Marx, Karl, 151–152
Mary I, queen of England, 11
Mary II, queen of England, 319
masculinity. *See* manhood
Masons, 38, 446
Massachusetts Bay Colony, 162, 201,
342, 343, 403
Massachusetts Bay Company, 16
Mather, Cotton, 21, 223, 260, 261–263,
265, 272
healing and, 243
Mather, Richard, 13, 345
Mathew, Theobald, 189

Reformed tradition (cont.)
  in the twenty-first century, 364–366
  Native Americans, 344
  Old Testament and, 341, 344,
    345, 356
  organization, 12–13, 371
  Pietism and, 353
  preaching, 345
  race and, 354–355
  Scripture and, 345, 355–357, 360
  slavery and, 164, 344, 354–355
  social reform, 354–355
  Stone-Campbell Movement and, 351
  theology, 95, 99, 341, 344–345, 346,
    357–358, 361–362, 441
  women and, 354–355
regeneration, 102, 342
Regular Baptists, 403
Reid, Thomas, 21, 184–185, 419,
  421
Reiki, 250
Re-Imagining Conference, 71, 365
religion clause. *See* Constitution
Religion in America, 128
*Religion within the Limits of Reason
  Alone*, 110
Religious Affections, 19
Religious Education Association, 137
religious left, 174
religious liberty, 23, 30, 31–33, 175
  Roman Catholicism, 288
  Roman Catholics and, 280,
    283–285
religious pluralism, 175, 305
religious right. *See* Christian Right
Renaissance, 341
reparations, 236
Republicans, 75, 76, 172, 173, 174, 211,
  287, 408, 455
  African American, 233
restorationism. *See* Stone-Campbell
  Movement
resurrection, 95, 104, 285
Re-thinking Missions (Hocking
  Report), 305, 359
revivalism, 40, 109, 114, 117–123, 201,
  373, 405, *See also* evangelicalism
Revolution, 134

Revolutionary War, 20, 30, 286, 373,
  404, 438
Rhode Island. *See* Williams, Roger
Rice, John R., 207
Rice, Nathan L., 423
Righter Major, Sarah, 392
Riis, Jacob, 51
Rittenhouse, David, 21
River Brethren. *See* Brethren in
  Christ (BIC)
Riverside Church, 80, 236, 359
Roanoke Colony, 9
Roberts, B. T., 446
Roberts, Oral, 248
Robertson, Pat, 172, 278
Robinson, Gene, 71, 213, 333
Robinson, John, 342
Robinson, Marilynne, 365
Rochester Revival, 37
Rockefeller, John D., 305
Roe v Wade, 70, 172, 173, 212
Roman Catholics, 105, 148
  abortion and, 173
  cooperation with, 64, 173, 354
  drinking habits of, 165
  ghetto mentality, 290
  in the nineteenth century, 287–290
  in the Revolution, 281–286
  Irish, 286
  opposition to, 37, 42–43, 49, 54, 62,
    89, 115, 152, 161, 165, 167, 173,
    189, 279–280, 281–286,
    287–290, 297
  parochial schools, 136, 287,
    289–290
  religious liberty and, 283–285, 288
  women and, 207, 209
Roosevelt, Theodore, 334
Ross, J. Elliot, 291
Rowlandson, Mary, 20
Royal African Company, 319
rum, 179, 180, 181, 188, 192
Rush, Benjamin, 182, 226,
  263–264, 265
Rush, John, 264
Rushdoony, Rousas, 363
Russell, Charles Taze, 251
Russell, Letty, 209